THE RESEARCH TOURS: THE IMPACTS OF ORTHOGRAPHIC DISADVANTAGE

The moral right of the author has been asserted. This book is copyright. Apart from any fair dealing for the purpose of private study, research, criticism or review, as permitted under the *Copyright Act*, no part of this book may be reproduced by any process without written permission.

Published by
Literacy Plus Australia
Mackay QLD 4740
AUSTRALIA

© Susan Galletly 2023
First published 2023

www.susangalletly.com.au

 A catalogue record for this work is available from the National Library of Australia

Title:	The Research Tours
Subtitle:	The Impacts of Orthographic Disadvantage
Series:	Aussie Reading Woes trilogy, Book 2
Author:	Galletly, Susan
ISBNs:	9780645535341 (paperback)
	9780645535310 (ebook – epub)
	9780645535327 (ebook – Kindle)
Subjects:	**EDUCATION:** Educational Policy & Reform / General
	POLITICAL SCIENCE: World / Australian & Oceanian
	LANGUAGE ARTS & DISCIPLINES: Reading Skills
	FAMILY & RELATIONSHIPS: Learning Disabilities

All reasonable efforts were taken to obtain permission to use copyright material reproduced in this book, but in some cases permissions and copyright could not be established. The author welcomes information in this regard.

Cover design by Yes Peach Creative at yespeach.com.au

Cover art by Alana Smith, Temperance Art

> The Yuwi people are the traditional custodians of the land where this book was written. The author pays her respects to elders and people past, present, and future, across Australia; and honours the traditions of the Aboriginal, Torres Strait Islander, Solomon Islander and Vanuatuan people. She acknowledges, respects and greatly regrets the major wrongs our first nations peoples have experienced, due to, and as part of, white settlement.

THE RESEARCH TOURS: THE IMPACTS OF ORTHOGRAPHIC DISADVANTAGE

Aussie Reading Woes trilogy
Book 2

Dr Susan Galletly

BSpThy, MEd, PhD

For our struggling Aussie readers –
Our Spelling Generations.
Never think you're failures:
You're victims of English orthographic complexity,
And the inadequate education we've provided.
Our education support strategies are the failures:
The ones that have failed so badly to meet your needs.

For our struggling Aussie teachers,
Working far too hard, amidst inadequate resourcing.
Thank you so much! You're world class!

And for Australia, our beloved nation.
How wonderful to live here with Aussies all,
In our beautiful land, and precious democracy,
Where one can speak openly and honestly.

With many thanks to our wonderful God,
Who guides and leads.

Australian schooling will place the highest priority on
a) identifying and addressing the needs of school students,
including barriers to learning and wellbeing; and
b) providing additional support to school students who require it.
Australian Government, 2013 *Australian Education Act*

There are no such things as reading difficulties.
There are only teaching challenges.
Jackie French (Children's Laureate 2014-15)
Acceptance speech for the award of
2015 Senior Australian of the Year

Our goal is to create educational contexts
that enhance the learning of all students.
For those students with special needs,
we must ensure that the most effective means
are used to achieve this goal.
Christa van Kraayenoord, 2006

About thirty per cent of Australian children who are leaving the school system in Australia are functionally illiterate.
Brendan Nelson, Federal Minister for Education, 2005

Some men see things as they are and say, "Why?"
I dream of things that never were and say, "Why not?"
George Bernard Shaw

It always seems impossible until it's done.
Nelson Mandela

What are we up against?
- *Wasteful, unnecessary, destructive reading and learning difficulties with their debilitating impacts on far too many Australians:*
- *School years of low achievement, discouragement and low-self-esteem.*
- *Adult years of diminished career prospects, embarrassment, and feeling 'dumb'.*
- *Reading difficulties leading to reading difficulties: parents nervous of school, and unable to confidently read with their kids and support their school learning.*
- *Education woes due to our kids and teachers' excessive workload, and time pressure created by our too slow early-literacy development and too many struggling readers.*

These challenges are worthy of our best efforts!

The Goal:
By 2035, Australian education will be
routinely, efficiently, gently and easily achieving
highly effective, rapid development of children's
word-reading, spelling, writing and early-literacy skills,
in GENTLE manner,
in every early-years classroom,
in all schools across our nation,
as efficiently as is achieved routinely
across schools in regular-orthography nations
such as Taiwan, Japan and China,
with at least 98% of Australian school children
being confident, independent readers and writers,
able to read 90% of the 10,000 most-frequent words,
by age 8.5 years, or within 18 months of starting formal word-reading instruction.

Susan Galletly, 2022 *Bunyips in the Classroom: The 10 Changes*

Foreword

I'm very pleased to be writing this forward to Dr Galletly's book, *The Research Tours: The Impacts of Orthographic Disadvantage.*

It is a worthy read.

Across nations, we need to be discussing orthographies. Their impacts on education are often overlooked. While many nations use highly transparent orthographies, English is highly complex. Orthographic impacts and crosslinguistic differences are major, with widespread ramifications.

I first met Susan in 2005, when she visited us at the University of Jyvaskyla, with Professor Bruce Knight and colleagues. We spent time discussing the findings of *our Jyvaskyla Longitudinal Study of Dyslexia* (JLD).

We also explored the cross-national, collaborative COST-A8 study that so clearly showed how easily and rapidly word-reading develops in European nations that have highly transparent orthographies, and how much more difficult it is for young English readers to develop reading skills (Seymour, Aro & Erskine, 2003).

Susan and Bruce attended one of our initial GraphoGame project meetings: collaborative work by specialists in our Education and Psychology departments, combining expertise on learning theory and empirical validation studies, with expertise on Finnish sounds and spelling, all working together to develop the GraphoGame project.

We've then been colleagues down the years, communicating by email and when Susan has visited. It is rare for researchers to have strong expertise in both research and practice.

With her decades of experience working with children with learning difficulties, Susan combines the two areas well. The questions she asks are interesting and provoke reflection, and she often has answers that aren't the usual content of academic discussions.

The Challenge of Reading Difficulties

Reading difficulties can result from insufficient or inappropriate teaching, as is the case in some poor nations where resources for teacher education are low and there is little to read outside school.

Sometimes major changes in reading instruction can be difficult to implement successfully. One example of this is the move in many African countries to now teach children to read and write their local language instead of English. Not surprisingly, many teachers have continued methods they'd used for English, but the orthographies children now learn to read are fully transparent, with all words highly regular. That means children only need to know letter sounds and how to sound out words to be able to read and write all words. They definitely do not need the complex methods used for English.

The mismatch is major. The change is sensible, but English teaching methods are no longer appropriate. Interestingly, many teachers haven't learned to read their native language, even though they now teach children to read and write it. Support with GraphoLearn computer game training has proved helpful there. We are working to expand use of GraphoLearn to all nations in Sub-Saharan Africa, where orthographies of local languages are largely transparent.

In more affluent nations, most often it is weak spoken language skills that compromise learning written language skills. This presents as difficulties with language aspects of reading comprehension and written expression, and also, particularly in Anglophone nations, as word-reading and spelling difficulties.

Mastering reading and writing requires children to build connections between spoken and written language. This is the starting point for factors underlying literacy difficulties. It is also the theoretical basis of how our GraphoLearn technology works in helping readers overcome their difficulties.

The JLD Study and Its Findings

In our Jyväskylä Longitudinal Study of Dyslexia (JLD), in Finland, we showed reading difficulties (dyslexia) to be strongly associated with brain-based difficulties in differentiating acoustically close speech sounds from earliest childhood. Sounds such as those of *l, m, n* typically require a lot more practice before they are reliably differentiated in the minds of learners, to be reliably connected to the letters representing them. This difficulty can work as a bottleneck for children when they are learning to read and write.

Foreword

Severe word-reading and spelling (decoding) difficulties have a genetic basis. They can be overcome by providing sufficient practice to overcome the auditory insensitivities children have, that compromise separation of, and recognition of, speech sounds (phonemes), which, for reading and writing, children must reliably connect to letters in reading and writing.

In the Jyväskylä Longitudinal Study we followed approximately 100 children with familial risk and 100 children without that risk from when they were born, between 1993 and 1996, until now, when they're adults. Using extensive assessments that began within a few days of birth, we studied children multiple times each year, using a wide range of measures to explore their development over time.

We assessed speech perception and other aspects in infancy, diverse aspects of receptive and expressive language skills along with morphological knowledge extensively from age 12 months, and multiple aspects of phonological awareness, Rapid Automized Naming (RAN), letter naming, and Short-Term and Working Memory from age 3.5 years. Then from start of school, we also assessed many aspects of reading, literacy, learning, and academic progress.

Our research established that children with a family history of reading difficulties were four times more likely to have literacy difficulties, and that the basis of word-reading difficulties is language skills, beginning with weak sensitivity to speech sounds.

That difficulties are genetic was clear from our earliest assessments. Testing within a few days of birth, before environmental effects could be in action, clearly differentiated those children who would have reading difficulties (dyslexia) from those who would not. This was clearly evident eight years later when the children were learning to read. Importantly, the infants with the speech-perception difficulties had familial risk, with family members who had weak literacy skills.

That the problem is also perceptual, and based in speech awareness and language skills, was also established at that time. Assessments when the infants were 3 to 5 days old, involving brain recordings, using a mismatch negativity paradigm, showed those who would have dyslexia were not able to differentiate pitch differences of sinusoidal sounds, whereas this was done effectively by the other infants.

As babies, the children at-risk of reading difficulties were not processing speech sounds precisely. Then, as children, at the time they were to learn to read, these same children could not reliably perceive differences in acoustically close sounds such as *l, m, n*. This could be observed during their learning of the connections between phonemes and letters in the logs of their GraphoGame training.

As a later part of our research, we corrected this difficulty by providing extensive practice using GraphoGame, the computer game program we developed to provide extensive, engaging practice, until children can reliably discriminate sounds, and connect them to their letters.

As our research has shown consistently, now in numerous studies, preventing the most severe problems of children at risk of dyslexia may take a very large amount of practice, i.e., drilling, to be successful. The children's difficulties with speech perception are a bottleneck that impedes learning to read and write. Our research has shown the problem can be corrected with highly intensive practice, with this given preventatively where possible, as children need strong engagement for GraphoGame learning to be effective. Our research has shown this level of engagement is much easier to achieve at the time children are entering school, when children's main expectation and learning goal is to learn to read.

We have found this in Finnish children, and in children of other nations who learn to read the world's many highly transparent orthographies (spelling systems). In transparent orthographies, with all words regular, the connections between spoken and written words behave consistently at the level of phonemes and graphemes in both directions. This means learning to read and write words builds directly from speech perception and that tiny letter-sound unit: the connection of each individual phoneme to its grapheme of one or more letters that represents it.

Letter knowledge (knowing letters' names or sounds), tested on five occasions between ages 3.5 and 6.5 years, proved a very strong predictor. Each time it clearly differentiated at-risk and control groups, and those who would and would not face problems when learning what we might term Basic Literacy skills, including word-reading and spelling. At school entry, children's letter knowledge reliably identified those children who would need preventative intervention (using GraphoGame), from those who would make healthy progress.

As our longitudinal study monitored the children's development and progress, the story steadily unfolded. At 6 months of age, once more using brain measures, comparable speech perception tasks again clearly differentiated, and thus could predict, children who would have delayed acquisition of Basic Literacy skills. They also predicted children's word-reading accuracy and fluency levels.

From age 2 to 3 years and on, children's oral language skills reliably discriminated the groups, and predicted reading and school progress, even children's likely PISA achievement levels.

The JLD goals were, firstly, to identify precursors and predictors of dyslexia, developmental paths leading to reading difficulties, and impacts of environmental factors; and to explore co-occurring problems; and then, subsequently, to develop methods of intervention using dynamic assessment which identifies those who need help and shows where help is needed. Our findings have been reported in English in many papers in scientific journals. The developmental precedents of literacy acquisition established in the JLD have then been further explored and published in hundreds of other studies.

Our research showed multiple markers that can be used to identify at-risk readers, especially those in regular-orthography nations, including neonatal speech perception, early-childhood language skills, and letter knowledge. Family history, plus weakness in letter knowledge, Rapid Automized Naming (RAN) and phonological awareness clearly identified children who would develop reading difficulties. So did phonemic awareness, which is a key requirement of children taking the first steps of learning to read transparent (fully-regular) writing. In contrast, strength in those factors gave protection, preventing difficulties from developing. While weak RAN predicted ongoing fluency difficulties, weak phonemic awareness only impacted the earliest stage of word-reading development.

Letter knowledge was the strongest predicter, and children's letter knowledge at school entry proved a timely predictor, easily identifying those likely to struggle with word-reading and spelling. Importantly, it also identified the children in both at-risk and control groups who had healthy early language skills, and weakness only in the skills directly underlying reading and spelling words, including letter knowledge.

GraphoLearn and GraphoGame

Developing preventive training to reduce and remove children's speech-perception, letter-sound, word-reading and spelling difficulties was an important next step after the JLD results were collected. That was the beginning of our GraphoLearn technology (www.grapholearn.com), which was the basis of GraphoGame, its commercial form (www.graphogame.com). While a not-for-profit enterprise developed with research funding, the project partly funds itself now its use has expanded internationally.

The game builds children's letter-sound knowledge then their word-reading skills, firstly accurate reading and then confident fluency. It monitors learning and progress on an ongoing basis, tailoring activities and the skills to be focused on, to ensure each session's activities match well to children's current skills and needs.

With weak letter knowledge at the start of school the strongest predictor of weak word-reading and spelling, GraphoGame uses dynamic assessment to identify that weakness at the start of Grade 1. Dynamic assessment is used on an ongoing basis in all sessions, with the technology quickly identifying weaknesses, and immediately moving to correct them using strategic tailoring of activities.

GraphoGame has now been used for years in all Finnish schools, where it is called Ekapeli Alku. Because it also builds fluency, it is played by practically all Grade 1 children, including those with high accuracy, to build reading speed, e.g., logs show up to a third of children using it on any given day in early Grade 1.

The Importance of Strong Motivation and Engagement

In all nations, being motivated and engaged is important. Indeed, it is pivotal in literacy development. That has been well established in our research. Particularly for at-risk children, our games succeed when precisely actioned using established recommendations for timing and session frequency.

For strongest effects for at-risk readers, children's age when they start using GraphoGame is important. Children need to be maturationally and situationally ready for the program and its learning. In the context of earliest Grade 1, of now being at school and learning to read and write, GraphoGame's effectiveness is high.

Starting later, after they have begun experiencing difficulties, is too late for many children, as they lack the level of engagement needed for effective learning. Their reading difficulties lower their interest levels, and avoidance behavior often develops. Children simply don't want to practice something they associate with negative experiences. As we commented in 2006:

> *Children define themselves as learners during the very first years at school, and the consequences of failure are far-reaching. A Finnish pupil who does not learn to decode accurately [after a month or two of] the first semester of first grade may almost unavoidably perceive him- or herself as different from others. This is because, in the Finnish schools, almost everyone progresses to highly accurate decoding skills within the first 4 months of*

reading instruction at the latest (Seymour, Aro, & Erskine, 2003). The detrimental effects of comparing oneself unfavorably to others can have a general impact on one's learning strategies (mostly toward avoidance of challenging tasks) even as early as during first grade (Poskiparta, Niemi, Lepóla, Ahtola, & Laine, 2003).

Starting too early, when brain functioning is not mature in at-risk children, will also often be less successful. It is more difficult for younger children to maintain engagement, and, if bored or distracted, they risk becoming task avoidant, then prefer not to play GraphoGame.

We prevent difficulties by making sure we start at the right time.

For typical Finnish children starting school not yet reading, progress is rapid. They mostly need less than an hour of GraphoGame training to master decoding, to sound out and read all Finnish words. To achieve this rapid progress, the game must be used preventatively, as it then keeps children highly engaged. Their rapid progress might well not be achieved, had they experienced difficulties with reading prior to starting GraphoGame.

For at-risk children, GraphoGame's delivery is highly strategic. Its effectiveness can only be guaranteed if it is started during the early days of school entry into Grade 1, when Finnish children learn to read and write.

Training until children catch up to their classmates must be for 10-20 minute sessions, 2-3 times daily, across successive days, to guarantee accumulation of memory traces. Too long intervals between sessions compromise this accumulation. Often training is done as part of daily Special Education sessions. Playing GraphoGame at home is recommended, and children tend to enjoy this.

Finnish Letter Sounds and Basic Literacy

In Finland, letter names and sounds are highly consistent, with every letter name emphasising the letter's sound, which is not the case for English. Most Finnish children attend Kindergarten, at age 6 years, and there, using play-based learning and with much exposure to words and letters, e.g., classroom walls display letters in motivating ways.

Formal letter and reading instruction is not recommended at Kindergarten as, at age 6 years, it is a time for playing. However, those children interested in playing with letters are provided with opportunities to learn letters' shapes, names and sounds, and how to write them, to the extent that each child chooses.

The extent to which children are interested in written and spoken language is also a useful predictor of later reading progress. This interest leads to, and is part of, children's building of letter knowledge.

In earliest reading and writing in Finland, including in Grade 1, only capital letters are used, with no lowercase letters. This keeps early learning simpler, and cognitive load low. The words in books children read use just capital letters, and children write all words just in capitals. Lowercase letters are then introduced quite soon, during the first school semester, when children are confident readers and writers, familiar and comfortable with reading and writing.

With strong Kindergarten exposure, and it being quite easy to learn letters, if Finnish children do not know all letters when they start Grade 1, at age 7, this is a significant indicator of being at-risk. Children who know all letters are usually proficiently accurate two months into Grade 1, while those not knowing all letters can struggle.

In consequence, when GraphoGame's dynamic assessment shows weak letter knowledge, schools start GraphoGame preventive training. Most at-risk children catch up to their peers by Grade 2, and, using GraphoGame, those with severest difficulties read and write accurately by Grade 4.

In Grades 1 and 2, Finnish schools focus on building silent reading, to improve children's fluency, with comprehension a lesser focus. Most children play GraphoGame in early Grade 1, including those with strong word-reading accuracy, to build reading fluency.

Children then have the opportunity to play ComprehensionGame to build their reading comprehension and language reasoning skills. Having been developed only quite recently, ComprehensionGame has only recently been introduced to Finnish schools. It will be offered to all teachers who would like to use it.

Readers Need Both Full and Basic Literacy

Of course, reading and writing words is but one part of the literacy picture. To be literate is to have strong capability to gain knowledge by reading and express thoughts in writing, and to do these at least as effectively as one learns and communicates when one is listening and speaking.

In addition to Basic Literacy (being able to read and write), readers need what we might term Full Literacy, skills using meaningful reading, analyzing and considering the knowledge they acquire by reading, with these skills then also used when writing.

Every nation has the goal and challenge of achieving motivated, effective readers. It is a major challenge, and a very important one.

ComprehensionGame and Building of Full Literacy

After we had established our major findings on anticipating reading-related development at school age, it was time to move from uncovering probable problems in reading acquisition, to instead focus on developing a means for helping children avoid such problems. As we studied children's needs, we did this in two steps, first developing GraphoGame, then, later, ComprehensionGame.

Developing preventive training to reduce and remove the speech-perception, letter-sound, word-reading and spelling difficulties of children who experience difficulties was a major project following on from the JLD study. The goal, from the beginning, was to develop digital, game-like training for use helping learners across the world.

We soon realized that it is not just Basic reading and writing skills children need. Even more, they need what we might term Full Literacy, skills for learning and enjoying knowledge they acquire by reading, i.e., to achieve the goal of effective meaningful reading.

Across nations, boys are not as interested in reading as girls are. In Finland, we've been concerned that our results have been steadily weaker over recent PISA cycles, and are especially weak for boys.

We have learned just how crucial extensive reading outside school is for building readiness to comprehend what's read, in the texts children read.

That includes texts for school learning and also texts in assessment contexts, including PISA tests. When children are not reading extensively, their reading comprehension for all reading can fail to build to the level that is needed.

Because of this, while Basic Literacy skills are very important for those who aren't yet accurate and fluent at reading and writing words, to reach Full Literacy, more is needed.

For learning to read effectively, one needs skills for identifying what is important in the content of the text they're reading, and to do this effectively, so working memory limits aren't exceeded before key points are integrated into and accumulated in long-term memory.

Further, in today's world where false news abounds, readers need to be critical readers who know that not all that is written is true. ComprehensionGame is a strong tool towards this end.

This required a very different training environment to the one that we used in GraphoGame. To help build Full Literacy, we have developed ComprehensionGame (www.comprehensiongame.com), and are now refining and validating it.

ComprehensionGame is computer game learning that builds skills and efficiency for understanding and analyzing what one reads, and for conveying meaning effectively when writing. It will soon be made available for worldwide use.

ComprehensionGame is needed for building the reading comprehension skills of children who are not reading sufficiently. That includes reluctant readers in many nations who do not choose to read to an appreciable level outside of school, and also children such as those in Africa who do not have interesting texts available to read outside of school.

Children who are interested in reading and like to read outside school do the work themselves, building skills for comprehending texts and thinking analytically through their extensive reading. This interest is encouraged by reading to young children before they start school. They find the world they've encountered through reading to be interesting and enticing, and this motivates them to read widely, when they have basic reading skills.

For children who are not keen readers, or who read little outside of school, support is needed. They run the risk of treating all words equally, thinking the job is simply to read a string of words until it is finished. Reading this way, they then miss many opportunities to notice and take in important information, and store it in working memory. Instead their working memory is overloaded by a stream of words that have not been read for meaning.

GraphoLearn's Expanding International Use

GraphoLearn games are useful tools to support children to build Basic then Full Literacy. GraphoGame builds word-reading accuracy and fluency, while ComprehensionGame builds reading comprehension and thinking thinking analytically while reading for meaning.

In Finland, the timing of their use is sequential. GraphoGame is used preventively with at-risk readers from the start of school, and by most Grade 1 children to build fluency, and is actioned strategically for those most at risk. Then ComprehensionGame is available for use to support school learning when children are sufficiently fluent readers.

From working memory and cognitive load perspectives, sequencing

Foreword

of GraphoGame and ComprehensionGame is powerful. It helps keep cognitive load manageable and avoids overloading working memory.

Building accuracy and fluency with GraphoGame means working memory can then be focused far more on meaning.

Then, ComprehensionGame trains readers who have mastered Basic Literacy skills to think analytically while reading. It enables them to understand even more difficult texts by identifying key items of information and storing them as a summary, without overloading working memory. Further, it helps them be critical readers who appraise what they read, making them less likely to be deceived by unworthy texts and content.

The combination of Graphogame and ComprehensionGame has already shown pleasing effectiveness with previously illiterate, rural Zambian people with no access to information from the outside world.

GraphoGame, continues to be developed, now in more and more languages. ComprehensionGame works in all languages with it usually being children's teachers who upload content into the game. This is usually relevant content that is part of current school learning.

Both games are being used more and more internationally, as researchers from different nations have approached us, and as part of our UNESCO work.

With over 30 nations now currently involved, we are keen to see the games used increasingly across nations, supporting children to master Basic Literacy skills then build Full Literacy. The games are also used with older learners, and in second-language learning.

Across the world, over 600 million people lack Basic Literacy, and many more lack Full Literacy. GraphoGame is now used by over two million children, and the GraphoGame company is keen to widen its use. Being able to build knowledge by reading is one of the world's most important targets, for children and adults everywhere. Readers thus need Basic Literacy, and then Full Literacy.

Via Niilo Mäki Institute, in Jyväskylä, Finland, we have had a strong focus in nations in Sub-Saharan Africa for many years. Illiteracy is widespread, and most adults and children need help to initially acquire basic reading and writing skills, and then to achieve broad, effective literacy. This is somewhat surprising because the local languages are written as transparently as Finnish. It reflects the importance of both access to literacy and education, and the power of self-belief, believing oneself capable of acquiring literacy. When provided with appropriate instruction, using traditional means, it takes 3-4 months to master basic literacy. With GraphoGame it is substantially faster.

Full Literacy is more rare than common in Sub-Saharan Africa. We are currently documenting the effectiveness of both GraphoLearn (the research version of GraphoGame) and ComprehensionGame in rural Zambia, for both children and previously illiterate adults, with promising results. ComprehensionGame has been used in English there, as most texts for acquiring wider knowledge are in English.

Now that the internet is reaching almost all locations and artificial intelligence can provide summarized answers to knowledge-related questions, opening up routes to knowledge is likely to happen quickly in Africa, particularly if ComprehensionGame-like training environments can be run on cheap phones, which are widely used.

Using GraphoGame with English Readers

GraphoGame now has versions for complex orthographies, including English and Chinese. Whereas transparent orthographies often have less than 60 connections to be learned, less consistent orthographies have far more connections to be mastered. Being less consistent, English has over 1,000 connections, while Chinese has over 3,500.

For English, we have included larger grainsizes, rather than just using phoneme grainsize and letter sounds, which is all that is needed for children using transparent orthographies. GraphoLearn research will be valuable in exploring how effectively the games can prevent and overcome difficulties in children learning to read English.

While the Finnish learning journey for Basic Literacy is an easy and straight-forward one, that's not the case for English.

Finnish is a highly regular orthography, so it is easy for children to learn to read and write. Almost all Finnish children have quite a short, easy journey through Basic Literacy to meaningful reading and writing, most at-risk children are confident, accurate readers in Grade 2, and those with severest weakness catch up by Grade 4, using GraphoGame in its prescribed format.

Half of our children are already reading when they start Grade 1, and all but a few are highly accurate readers and writers within a few months. They are soon highly accurate at word-reading and writing, and relatively simple instruction and engaging games that build accuracy, fluency and comprehension work well.

With English being far less regular, the English learning journey is, of course, much more complex. All Finnish words are written in a consistent way at grapheme-phoneme level, as we use just one orthographic grainsize: letter-sounds. In contrast, English is an extremely complex orthography, and many words are complicated.

Through orthographic differences in consistency of letters and sounds, word-reading and spelling development create crosslinguistic differences between nations. Children's ability to read and write both common and new words, and how quickly and easily those skills develop, create wide differences. These differences impact reading and writing development, and academic progress. They also impact the time and work required for children to become literate, and consequently, how complex teaching and learning are in schools.

When learning is complicated, additional challenges arise. For children learning to read and write English while quite young, working memory is a bottleneck. Trying to both work out words and consider meaning when reading and writing, creates needs for much working memory, which is not well developed at their young age. By supporting children to automise word-reading with GraphoLearn training, mental resources are freed for use in comprehension, and working memory can be focused more effectively on meaning.

It's not possible for most English readers to learn to read just by storing letter sounds, as transparent orthography children do, because in English, no letters represent just one single sound in all words, all sounds are written with multiple graphemes and, for earliest learning, there is low consistency of letters' names and sounds.

The five English vowel letters say many different sounds, most often their commonest sounds, but also many others, those in English's many rimes, e.g., *-aw*, *-igh*, *-all*, its many schwa spellings, e.g., *be*gin, *tig*er, *litt*le, and its many words and syllables that are irregular, e.g., *one, what, who, people, write, wrong, Monday, bluer*.

Because of this, for children learning to read and write English, it's valuable to train phoneme-grapheme connections for commonest letter sounds, plus also train connections for larger units such as rimes, and more idiosyncratic words and syllables.

For English, we have therefore developed GraphoGame as two programs that can be used separately or as an integrated program. GraphoGame Phoneme uses letter-sounds to read regular words, and GraphoGame Rime uses larger units, e.g., the *ar* in words like car, the *all* in words like ball, and the *igh* in words like *high*.

Research using Graphogame Rime, Graphogame Phoneme and ComprehensionGame has potential to build useful knowledge on how best to support early-literacy development. By exploring how best to improve reading development and teaching methods, it is to be hoped that acquisition of English reading skills will move closer to the smooth learning journey of children who read and write transparent orthographies.

At its heart, much of learning to read and write is identical for English and transparent orthographies. Children learn knowledge by reading and writing, and reading and writing develop by building connections between spoken and written language.

This is much easier in nations with transparent orthographies, and more difficult in Australia and other Anglophone nations, where the connections to be learned are often inconsistent, and written language is consequently more difficult to learn.

However, children's brains, and the statistical learning they are able to achieve, are quite remarkable. Children seek out and find consistencies, and this makes it possible to learn a complex writing system such as English.

Importantly, when we provide instruction designed to optimise that statistical learning, all children are enabled, including those who otherwise might struggle. That is our goal, in developing digital support for early literacy learners.

Integrating, Not Sequencing, GraphoGame and ComprehensionGame

It's extremely important to keep in mind that the primary purpose of reading is to mediate meaning, and that really, in the end, only what we might term Full Literacy matters.

We are currently working to optimise reading acquisition through the focus on meaning being present from earliest literacy. We are doing this, moving children forward before they enter school and learn to read and write, using digital environments, which involve stories being read to children for them to then reflect on.

We are also working to combine GraphoGame and Comprehension Game to work in integrated fashion, maximizing the effectiveness of both games. We do so, building from this logical theoretical basis:

1. Learners develop *Basic Literacy* then *Full Literacy*: they equate to the *Early Literacy* and *Sophisticated Literacy* of Galletly & Knight's Transition from Early to Sophisticated Literacy (TESL) model.
2. Basic Literacy's reading and writing skills are learned most effectively when children learn the phoneme-grapheme connections of spoken and written words.

a. GraphoGame's focus has been to build Basic Literacy: accurate then fluent reading and writing of words.
3. Full Literacy skills, using reading to learn, and acquiring and reflecting on knowledge built through reading, requires learning to search for key information while reading, and to think logically, reflectively and analytically on that information.
   a. ComprehensionGame's focus has been to build Full Literacy: effective independent reading and writing using thinking at increasingly sophisticated levels.
4. Effective readers who have Full Literacy read quickly and actively search for key points of information as they read. They have trained themselves to search effectively, so working memory copes well and is not overloaded.
   a. Full Literacy with robust reading comprehension and writing develops more effectively when searching for meaning is emphasized from earliest reading.
5. To reach Full Literacy requires extensive reading, and children who do not read extensively except at school can miss out on achieving Full Literacy.
   a. Children who do negligible reading out of school need additional reading that's tailored to heighten comprehension and thinking.
   b. There is thus value in providing computer game training that combines reading of many texts with training building skills for searching for and analyzing texts' key content.
6. With few exceptions, using appropriate methods, we can all become fully literate, with the time needed to achieve it being the factor that varies across children and nations.
7. Bottlenecks in Basic and Full Literacy can be overcome with preventive training that uses ongoing dynamic assessment to identify needs and tailor instruction to meet those needs.
   a. Engagement and motivation are key factors: to achieve effective training for children, activities need to be engaging so children are motivated and maintain strong focus and engagement.
   b. Learning can be markedly increased when ongoing dynamic assessment analyzes each child's daily responses, and tailors activities and focus areas, so the child's time is spent optimally, heightening learning in needed areas.
8. Orthographies differ, which creates differences in how easy it is to master Basic Literacy skills. This, in turn, impacts when, and how easily, readers are able to achieve Full Literacy.
9. In nations with transparent orthographies, Basic then Full Literacy can be more sequential, as most children master Basic

Literacy very early in Grade 1, however
   a. Integrating GraphoGame and ComprehensionGame is likely to empower delayed readers, who may not master Basic Literacy fully until Grade 2 or 3, and
   b. Focusing on meaning from earliest reading is likely to benefit all children.
10. In nations with complex orthographies like English and Chinese, the stages are less sequential, as building reading comprehension cannot wait until after Basic Literacy has been achieved.
   a. Nations such as China support both Basic and Full Literacy by using a transparent orthography when children first learn to read and write. That beginners' orthography builds early reading and writing skills. At the same time, it also builds reading comprehension through enhancing independent reading (in similar ways to how transparent orthographies ease second language learning).
   b. For English, with a highly complex orthography impeding both Basic and Full Literacy, the challenges to overcome are more complex. In consequence, English readers are likely to benefit considerably from ComprehensionGame, after Basic reading skills are built with GraphoGame.

The Power of Learning Together in Research

It is very positive that Susan has written *The Research Tours: The Impacts of Orthographic Disadvantage*. It is a book that will create interesting and useful discussions, and it has excellent potential to stimulate new and interesting research directions.

In all nations, we work to achieve effective mature literacy skills, and the journey to that goal differs across nations. In my role as UNESCO Chair for Inclusive Literacy Learning for All (from which I've recently retired), that has been very clear.

I am still actively working on developing new digital tools that can help learners across the world towards Full literacy. In that work, I would enjoy working with Australian researchers in the future, exploring how effectively GraphoGame Phoneme, GraphoGame Rime, and ComprehensionGame programs support children and schools, and building knowledge for improving English literacy development.

Apart from our free work in poorer nations, we usually work in cooperative research arrangements with researchers who complete Doctoral studies within the project.

The next decades will be ones of research and powerful learning internationally, as we focus on optimising learning to read and write, and being effectively literate, across nations.

We learn more when we learn together, and there is much to be gained by that research. This book, with its insights and questions, will be an effective tool fostering that learning and research.

Prof Heikki Lyytinen

Emeritus Professor of Developmental Neuropsychology
University of Jyväskylä, Finland

UNESCO Chair,
Inclusive Literacy Learning for All
2015-2023

Contents

Foreword vii
A Brief Pre-Read Glossary xxvi
Welcome 1
The 10 Changes 6
We've Swiss-Cheese Research Gaps 11
Analogy Time: Pot-Bound Tomatoes 19
A Caveat 26
The Research Tours Begin 28
Research Tour 1. Too Slow Word-Reading and Spelling Development 30
Research Tour 2. Orthography Is the Key Factor 63
Research Tour 3. Success Inoculation Vs Acquired Helplessness 92
Research Tour 4. Regular Orthographies and Intellectual Disability 108
Research Tour 5. The Power of Beginners' Orthographies 113
Research Tour 6. Our Epidemic of Language Weakness 160
Research Tour 7. Literacy Components and Quadrants............. 209
Research Tour 8. Our Too Many Low Literacy Achievers 237
Research Tour 9. Needs for Workload Research 255
Research Tour 10. A Multiple Deficits Vs Phonological Basis? .. 286
Research Tour 11. Executive-Function Skills Empower Word-Reading 304
Research Tour 12. Impeded Statistical Learning 330
Research Tour 13. Unfamiliar Words: Our Standard-English Nemesis 348

Foreword

Reflections As The Tours End 385

Research Tour 14. Our Insufficiently Effective Word-Reading Intervention 396

Let's Research Together 430

The 100 Research Questions 441

Thanks 475

Reference Resources 475

A Brief Pre-Read Glossary

Orthographies and Their Impacts

Orthographies

The spelling systems that nations use, described by regularity, transparency and *Grapheme: Phoneme Correspondences (GPCs)*: the ratio of graphemes (letters and letter groups) to phonemes (sounds). *Standard Australian English* is Australia's official orthography.

Regular-Orthography Nations

The world's many nations that have chosen to use highly-regular spelling systems, either as sole orthographies, e.g., Finland, Estonia, Greece, Italy and Spain; or beginners' orthographies to expedite early-literacy development, as Taiwan, Japan and China do.

Fully-Regular Beginners' Orthographies

Highly-regular orthographies, often with one-to-one GPCs, which nations such as Taiwan, Japan and China use to ease and speed early-literacy development, greatly reduce reading and literacy difficulties, and expedite subsequent learning of their complex orthographies. In the 1960s, Anglophone nations extensively researched an English fully-regular beginners' orthography, the *Initial Teaching Alphabet* (ITA), finding it highly effective.

Orthographic Complexity

Orthographies sit on a continuum, from fully regular (transparent) to highly irregular (opaque). Most nations' orthographies are highly regular, e.g., Finnish, Greek, Italian, Spanish, Polish, beginners' orthographies and Australian indigenous orthographies. The Standard-English orthographies of Anglophone nations are highly irregular, being among the world's most complex. The continuum is also one of ease and speed of early-literacy development: regular orthographies expedite learning to read and spell, while complex orthographies impede it.

A Brief Pre-Read Glossary

Statistical Learning

Learning by noticing patterns and regularities: it's how children learn to speak, and a key aspect of learning to read and write. It can be implicit (from exposure to patterns) or explicit (being taught). With little confusion, regular orthographies optimise statistical learning, thus learning to read and spell is easy and rapid. English orthographic complexity impedes our children's statistical learning.

Orthographic Advantage

The advantages regular-orthography nations enjoy, arising from ease of learning to read and write, including effective education being achieved far more easily and less expensively.

Orthographic Disadvantage

Struggles Australia and other complex-orthography nations experience due to children learning to read and write a highly complex orthography, without a beginners' orthography. Education struggles include very slow skill development, high cognitive load, high workload, and excessive numbers of struggling readers.

'Unfamiliar' Words

Words children have to think on, to work out, when reading and writing them. For speaking and listening, the words may be highly familiar and used often. In their orthographic (written) form, however, they're unfamiliar, in the sense of not being effortlessly read and written. Reading unfamiliar words is easy in regular-orthography nations, but a major area of difficulty for Standard-English readers.

Cognitive Load and Working Memory

Cognitive Load

The amount and complexity of thinking we must do at any one time. Regular orthographies create very low cognitive load, while English orthographic complexity creates very high cognitive load, both in (a) learning to read and write, and (b) reading and writing during subject-area learning, while early-literacy skills are immature.

Working Memory

Functional processing capacity used in thinking. Orthographic complexity creates high cognitive load for Australian children, who need healthy working memory to learn to read and write. Healthy working memory is crucial for Standard English but less so for regular orthographies, as they're so easy to learn to read and write.

Educational Aspects of Our Severe Orthographic Disadvantage

Our Early Years Factory

The first three years of Australian schooling that produces both our struggling readers and struggling education, through orthographic disadvantage and insufficient resourcing, characterised by too much, too hard learning for too young children, amidst too low resourcing and supports.

Our Learning Time Challenge

Our schools lack time to teach literacy and subject-area learning effectively to the extent regular-orthography nations achieve, because we have to spend far more time building early-literacy skills than regular-orthography nations, and have much higher workload and far more struggling readers.

Generational Disadvantage

Our children who leave school with weak literacy skills often become parents who struggle to support their children's communication and literacy development. It's common for their children, in turn, to fail to develop effective literacy skills. This results in ongoing cycles of Generational disadvantage, with strong links to low Socio-Economic Status (SES) and life disadvantages.

GENTLE and HEARTSH

My acronyms for the *Gentle, Engaging, Never-Tiring, Learning Enrichment* that regular-orthography nations are able to achieve quite easily, and the *Hugely-Exhausting, Actually-Rather-Tedious Schooling Heaviness* that's too often present in Australian schools.

Our Language Weakness Epidemic

Because of generational disadvantage and Australia's very low resourcing of speech-language-pathology supports prior to and across the school years, Australia has widespread language-skills weakness, with too many children having language weakness. This gives us appreciable teaching and learning challenges.

WYSYAIN

My acronym for *What You See, You Assume Is Normal*. We tend to accept our education difficulties, rather than considering them

A Brief Pre-Read Glossary

untenable. By cruising just the Anglosphere fishbowl, ignoring the wider education world, we do lots of WYSYAINing.

Reading, Word-Reading and Phonemic Awareness

Reading

Purposeful reading for gaining knowledge, learning and enjoyment and effective reading comprehension (understanding and thinking on what one reads). Reading comprehension is tested extensively in national and international testing.

Word-Reading

The ability to read words and word-parts, in meaningful texts and as isolated words, syllables and graphemes: a subskill of reading comprehension, and a partner skill of spelling.

Phonological and Phonemic Awareness

Phonological awareness includes awareness of, and skill with, words, syllables, rhyme and phonemes. Phonemic awareness, skill with individual sounds, is needed for learning to read and write Standard English. Developing in parallel with word-reading and spelling, and thus rapidly in regular-orthography learners, its slow development in Standard-English readers creates difficulties for weaker readers.

Language Skills for Literacy

Language skills for literacy are the cornerstone of effective reading and writing. They include vocabulary, comprehension, expressive language skills and inferential thinking. We read to access meaning, and write to transfer meaning. Weak language skills are a challenge for Anglophone nations, because so many children have weak language skills, often as part of Generational Disadvantage.

Thirds and Struggling Readers

Struggling Readers

A catch-all term for our children and adults with literacy and learning difficulties. While their difficulties usually start with word-reading, they soon also struggle with reading, spelling, writing, and learning. While it's often termed *Dyslexia*, I suggest *Language, Literacy and Learning Disorder* (LLLD) as a more useful, inclusive term, as weakness in those three Ls travels together.

Thirds

A useful way to collectively consider children and their teaching and learning needs. Upper-third readers are strong achievers, middle-third readers are average achievers, and lower-third readers are weaker and struggling readers and learners.

Schools and Year-Levels

Foundation Year

Australian children commence school at age 4.5 to 5 years, in *Foundation* year, which has different names in different states. In this book, it's *Prep*, its name in Queensland, Tasmania and Victoria.

Primary Schools and High Schools

Australian children attend *primary school* (which in other nations is termed *elementary school*), then *high school*.

Year-levels

Australia uses *year-levels* (e.g., Year 2), which internationally are often termed *grade-levels* (e.g., Grade 2). Australian education has 13 year-levels: seven in primary school (Foundation to Year 6), and six in high school (Years 7 to 12).

National and International Reading Comparisons

NAPLAN

Australia's *National Assessment Program: Literacy and Numeracy*, which annually tests the reading-comprehension, written-expression, spelling, grammar and punctuation, and maths skills of children in Years 3, 5, 7 and 9. It began in 2008.

PIRLS

The *Progress in International Reading Literacy Study (PIRLS)* program that assesses the reading-comprehension skills of children in mid-primary school (Grades 4 and 5) of involved nations, every 5 years. It began in 2001.

PISA

The *Program for International Student Assessment (PISA)* that assesses the reading-comprehension skills of high-school children, aged 15 years, of involved nations, every 3 years. It began in 2000.

Welcome

Hi there. A warm welcome to *The Research Tours: The Impacts of Orthographic Disadvantage.*

This book focuses strongly on things Australian, as educational improvement is much needed here. That said, its contents and discussion are highly relevant to readers of all nations. Thus, while in inclusive tone, you'll find lots of *we, us, our children* and *here*, referring to Australia, please do feel welcome, one and all.

Australian education is currently struggling in numerous ways. That's evidenced not least in our poorly ranked classroom climates (Organisation for Economic Co-operation and Development, OECD, 2019) and too many struggling learners (ACARA, 2021; Galletly, 2022a).

You'll see it too, by visiting schools, considering work samples, observing in classrooms, and talking with teachers and children and the families of struggling learners. It's also evidenced in the research we'll explore across this book.

Australian education is a major enterprise and investment, supporting 4,000,000 children in almost 10,000 schools. We need it to work as effectively as it possibly can, for our children, teachers, families, schools and education systems, and national economy.

Orthographies are spelling systems: they impact education hugely. Ours is Standard English: it's one of the world's most complex. We've extremely high orthographic complexity, due to our 26 letters being used for 40+ sounds, in well over 560 Grapheme: Phoneme Correspondences (GPCs or spelling patterns). The confusion it creates is damaging in many ways. It creates our flood of struggling readers, along with our *Spelling Generations* – our Australians with ongoing literacy struggles. It also makes education cumbersome and expensive, both here and in other Anglophone nations.

We start our children too young on one of the world's most complex orthographies, without the benefit of a fully-regular beginners' orthography, as Taiwan, Japan and China use. Doing so activates our children's risk factors and, amidst our epidemic of language weakness, drags our children and education down. It creates too high child and teacher workload, along with our ever present *Find the Learning Time Challenge* and *Find the Caring Time Challenge*.

Are you finding unfamiliar terms a little confusing at times, e.g., *orthographies, word-reading, beginners' orthographies*? Do visit this book's small pre-read glossary for explanations of key terms. It begins this book and is a helpful early read.

I term our first three years of schooling, our *Early Years Factory* (Galletly, 2022a, In press). Characterised by too much, too hard learning for too young children with too few supports, it produces our children's slowed, impeded early-literacy development, and excessive numbers of struggling readers, and, in consequence, our struggling teachers and schools, and struggling education generally.

It's no surprise, really, that we've not reduced our too high numbers of seriously struggling readers, both locally, in our NAPLAN annual assessment program (*National Assessment Program – Literacy and Numeracy*), and internationally, in primary-school PIRLS (*Progress in International Reading Literacy Study*) and high-school PISA (*Program for International Student Assessment*) assessments (Thomson et al., 2017, 2019).

Nor is it illogical that Australia ranked 69th out of 76 nations for classroom climate: eighth worst in the world for unruly classrooms and disrupted learning (OECD, 2019). We're a bit of a mess, really.

That said, we do have company: other Anglophone nations, such as UK, USA and New Zealand, experience largely similar difficulties. The Anglosphere is struggling: in literacy and education, plus in their diverse, far-reaching impacts (Knight et al., 2019).

In my work down the decades, as a teacher, speech language pathologist, researcher and citizen, I've deeply considered research and practice here and in other nations.

We need strategic changes, if we're to ease and improve education. I'm recommending 10 Changes, built from research and practice, to transform education. They've a strong research base.

The 10 Changes are built from my theorising, and the theorising of my colleagues in Professor Bruce Knight's CQU research team that I've so enjoyed working in (Knight & Galletly, 2017, 2020; Knight et al., 2017a, 2017b, 2019, 2020, 2021).

This book, *The Research Tours* explores pertinent research areas highlighting our challenges, and our needs for, and strong value in, Australian education engaging in 10 Changes improvement.

An academic text, though nonetheless quite an easy read, it's the second book of an *Aussie Reading Woes* trilogy. The three books are
1. *Bunyips in the Classroom: The 10 Changes.*
2. *The Research Tours: The Impacts of Orthographic Disadvantage.*
3. *The 10 Changes: The Nitty Gritty.*

Books 1 and 3, *Bunyips* and *The Nitty Gritty*, bookend this book. The three are companions: they lean into and strengthen each other. They're practical, explaining what's going wrong, and why, and how our wrongs may be effectively righted. The books aren't dependent on their partners: each is an independent read, with no set reading order.

Bunyips is a brief outline of the 10 Changes and key issues. It's a quick and useful read, outlining problems, reasons and solutions.

The Nitty Gritty provides additional useful detail on orthographic complexity and the 10 Changes, showing them to be logical, important strategic changes that are well worth pursuing.

This book provides the research evidence establishing the validity of the discussion of *Bunyips* and *The Nitty Gritty*, and the 10 Changes.

Why have I written this book, and the *Aussie Reading Woes* trilogy? I could have used the time more comfortably: it's all been unpaid work done in spare time I've created by stealing time I'd otherwise have spent with family and friends, enjoying rest and relaxation.

To me, writing the books is and has been important, as education is being severely impeded by key factors that have been insufficiently considered: including those I've listed as the 10 Changes (Galletly, 2022a, 2022b, In press).

Working one-on-one with struggling learners and their families, my private practice across the years has been chock-full of observations of the injustices they experience endlessly, due to the inadequate, ineffective, insufficient education that we provide them.

It's time for change, to ethical, effective education for children one and all (Knight & Galletly, 2017; Knight et al., 2017a). It's therefore time for interest in orthographic impacts to burgeon. We must go beyond the Anglosphere if we're to find the answers we need towards impressively improving literacy levels and education here.

I'm hoping the books will be read widely, by teachers, parents, allied-health professionals and our interested general public, in addition to researchers and academics.

Towards that end, I've written the books as a useful introduction, building practical understanding of the field for interested readers.

Bunyips in the Classroom: The 10 Changes will probably be my most read book. However, with some of the 10 Changes seeming a little out of left field, it was necessary to establish the respectable research base the 10 Changes build from. Thus, I've written Book 2, *The Research Tours: The Impact of Orthographic Disadvantage*.

In addition, and continuing that primer role, I know that many readers will want far more detail than that provided in Bunyips, which is deliberately a brief, light-read introduction. Thus, I've written *The 10 Changes: The Nitty Gritty*, to complete the trilogy.

Importantly, I also want to entice many of our wonderful, hands-on practitioners into enjoying reading and reflecting on research, and perhaps then doing research. Australia needs for many of our practitioners to also be researchers. So, let's engage in research, whether it be Masters studies, or Doctoral and further work.

Reading and conducting research can be highly engaging and rewarding. So often, people dismiss it as highly complex, boring, scary, and far too hard to understand, when, for the most part, that's not the case. Towards supporting readers to enjoy exploring research and research findings, in this book I have deliberately avoided discussion of complex research designs and statistics.

In addition, while I have included a few brief analyses of data, because of the powerful evidence they provide, in each case, I use simple, descriptive statistics and clear explanations.

In this book's role as a primer for those becoming interested in orthographic impacts, and the severe orthographic disadvantage that Australia and Anglophone nations experience, I've deliberately made reference to a large number of studies and research articles. I've done this to provide a path for those who decide they'd like to read further.

Virtually all texts and journal articles on a research area, refer to and discuss other studies and articles, in the same manner I discuss research publications in this book. Citing and discussing other studies empowers keen readers, as often the most powerful way to build knowledge on an area is to note down those discussed studies which seem of interest in the text one is reading, and then locate those publications, repeating the cycle as needed and desired.

That's how I've built most of the knowledge I've gained on orthographies and their impacts: by reading and reflecting.

Welcome

Importantly, I've always prioritised taking theory through to practice, considering the practical ramifications of research findings: how they apply in schools, and in supporting our struggling readers.

Orthographies and their impacts are a massive area, far too big for one person to adequately cover. I've thus not aimed to cover it all.

Instead, I've outlined and sketched the area for my readers, current and future, boldly highlighting areas that are key, while touching but lightly on others.

Importantly, most of the literature on orthographies and their impacts is formal academic writing, and I've avoided that. Indeed, an area where my books may be a first is their being overwhelmingly a practical exploration of the everyday impacts our children, schools and families endure.

My canvas is deliberately a sturdy, practical view, of
- Current inadequacies of Australian and Anglophone education,
- The struggles of our children, families, teachers and schools,
- The strong potential we have for massive improvement, and
- Logical, practical directions we could take towards that end.

Thank you so much for joining me on the Research Tours – I count it a great privilege to have you along for the read.

The 10 Changes

Australian education desperately needs change – 10 Changes, to be exact. Using them, Australia and other Anglophone nations have potential to achieve exponential improvement, and to achieve this without excessive effort and expense. They're very good news.

It's common for research to use a thesis statement that details the research problem and likely solutions. I'll state here the thesis statement I'm using, then the 10 Changes, our ABCs of improving education, our mantra for our improvement journey, and our practical 2035 education goal (Galletly, 2022a, In press).

The Thesis Statement

This is the thesis statement for *The Research Tours*. It outlines our difficulties, likely causes and potential solutions:

Australian education is currently insufficiently effective for most students, and grossly ineffective for our lower-third students – our at-risk and struggling readers. Causal factors include English orthographic complexity and its impacts, our beginners' very young age, many children starting school highly at risk of difficulties, insufficient school resourcing, too high child and teacher workload, and our having too many struggling readers with major difficulties.

Our struggling readers' major instructional needs add additional teacher workload to what is already extremely high workload, making it excessive. This in turn reduces effectiveness of education for all our children, because our teachers are too busy to effectively meet all children's instructional needs.

This complex struggling-education problem can be resolved, and powerful positive changes are possible at relatively low expense, if we explore and implement effective methods used in other nations. Possible changes include using a fully-regular beginners' orthography when children first learn to read and write, raising our starting age for formal reading instruction, adding in strong play-based language enrichment and allied-health intervention supports prior to formal reading instruction, reducing teacher workload, and providing ample, effective school supports.

These changes have powerful potential to expedite early-literacy development and mastering of Standard-English literacy, plus reduce early-literacy difficulties, time pressure and our significantly high child and teacher workload.

These, in turn, can make Australian education both far more effective and considerably less expensive.

The 10 Changes

These are the 10 Changes – key education changes of our education future (Galletly, 2022a, 2022b, In press):

Change 1. Understand how orthographies matter: English spelling is dragging us down.

Change 2. Own our struggling reader woes: End hypocrisy and pretence.

Change 3. Weigh workload: Our children and teachers are working far too hard.

Change 4. One-size education does not fit all: Teach to the decidedly different instructional needs of upper-third and lower-third readers.

Change 5. End our data deficiency: Build strong knowledge on word-reading levels.

Change 6. Enrich every child: Ensure effective supportive tailored education.

Change 7. Insist on easy literacy development: Reach regular-orthography nations' achievement levels.

Change 8. Investigate the potential of fully-regular beginners' orthographies: They're winners.

Change 9. Play to learn first: Start Standard-English word-reading instruction from mid-Year 2.

Change 10. Build needed research knowledge as quickly as possible: Use collaborative school-based research.

The ABCs of Improving Education

These are our improvement ABCs, key tenets that will be powerful towards and in our actioning of the 10 Changes:

A. **ACT** locally while looking globally.
B. **BOOST** the lower-third to benefit everyone.
C. **CHANGE** effectively to work less and achieve more.

Our Mantra

We're using Jackie French's wise words as our mantra. Many regular-orthography nations meet their teaching challenges very effectively. Using 10 Changes improvements, so can we:
There are no such things as reading difficulties.
There are only teaching challenges.

The 2035 Goal

This is our practical, useful, 2035 goal that we'll work towards:
By 2035, Australian education will be
routinely, efficiently, gently and easily
achieving highly effective, rapid development of children's word-reading, spelling, writing and early-literacy skills,
in GENTLE manner,
in every early-years classroom,
in all schools across our nation,
as efficiently as is achieved routinely
across schools in regular-orthography nations
such as Taiwan, Japan and China,
with at least 98% of Australian school children
being confident, independent readers and writers,
able to read 90% of the 10,000 most-frequent words,
by age 8.5 years, or within 18 months of starting formal word-reading instruction.

GENTLE, above, is the *Gentle, Engaging, Never-Tiring, Learning Enrichment* that, e.g., Finland and Estonia achieve. It contrasts strongly with HEARTSH, *Hugely-Exhausting, Actually-Rather-Tedious Schooling Heaviness*, that's overly common here.

While Australian education is far bigger than the issues I'm raising, the 10 Changes have strong potential to enhance broad aspects of education here. Most apply to other Anglophone nations too.

Let's keep the 10 Changes, ABCs, mantra and 2035 goal in mind, as we consider the impacts of orthographic disadvantage in this book's 14 insightful research tours.

While much future research is definitely needed, there is already a considerable research base underlying the issues I'm raising. It's well worth exploring, as we need future education changes to be strategic, well considered and well researched (See Figure 1).

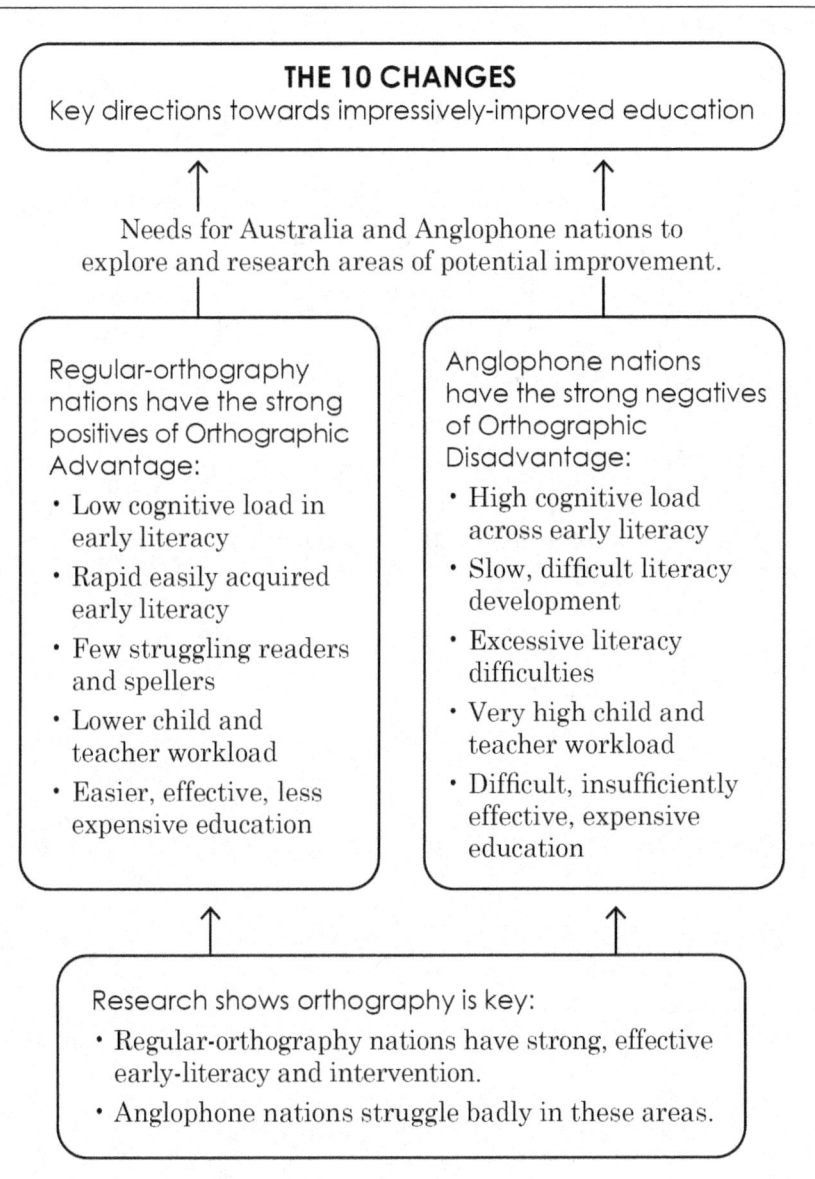

Figure 1. Our needs for the 10 Changes (Galletly 2022a, In press)

Our Education Bunyips

Let's also keep in mind Australia's *education bunyips*: key issues impacting education that many Australians haven't been aware of, that proliferate our needs for the 10 Changes.

In *Bunyips in the Classroom*, a plethora of bunyips were explored. I'll list here just 10 biggest bunyips that we simply can't ignore:
1. Our English Orthographic Complexity Bunyip.
2. Our Too High Cognitive Load Bunyip.
3. Our Widespread Language Weakness Bunyip.
4. Our Too Young Starting Age Bunyip.
5. Our Activated Risk Factors Bunyip.
6. Our Too Much to Teach in Too Little Time Bunyip.
7. Our Too Low Resourcing Bunyip.
8. Our Deficit of Word-Reading Data Bunyip.
9. Our Lack of Needed Research Bunyip.
10. Our Attribution Error Bunyip.

They'd love to be retired, but are currently quite gruesome. They're worth bearing in mind in our discussions across the tours.

We've Swiss-Cheese Research Gaps

Is there an area in cognitive science and cognitive neuroscience that has been more successful than the study of reading? Let us not underestimate the amount that has been learned. ...
My question, then, is this:
*If the science is so advanced, why do so many people read so poorly? ... People who think we should be doing better – I am in this camp – can point to the fact that **66–71%** of [USA] fourth graders and **66–71%** of eighth graders scored at "basic" or "below basic" levels.*
Put another way, there are far too many children scoring in the lowest tier (about a third of the fourth graders and a quarter of the eighth graders are "below basic"), and far too few in the highest (6–8% of the fourth graders and a mere 3% of the eighth graders are "advanced" readers by this measure).

Mark Seidenberg, 2013

Those results Seidenberg discusses are depressing, aren't they? Particularly as Australian children might well show similar results if we were using the same tests.

In my Master of Education studies, I conducted an extensive review of available research on the hows, whys, and ways forward, for word-reading and early-literacy learning difficulties.

I was seeking answers to the three wonderings that have guided my reflecting across my 45 years of working with struggling readers:
- What factors cause our children and adults' reading and literacy difficulties?
- How can we reduce their struggles and suffering?
- What are the ways we can do things better?

Since then, in my research work, four times across the decades, I've widely reviewed the published research literature on reading and learning difficulties, instruction and remediation. This repeated wide reading isn't common, as most researchers build increasingly deep knowledge on relatively narrow areas.

In addition to being usefully knowledge-building, that broad swathe reading has enabled considering changes over time, along with the strengths and weaknesses of our current knowledge base.

Our educational research base that supports education and guides change and improvement, is grossly inadequate in many important areas, whilst seeming excessively comprehensive in others. The extent of ivory-towering (overly researched areas) and Swiss-cheese research (inadequately researched areas) on key topics is really quite appalling.

Swiss-cheese research is my term for when the research bases on important topics highly relevant to practical, school-level needs have more gaps than actual research – more holes than cheese – with a sad lack of knowledge proliferation occurring. It's evidenced in lack of practical research applications for schools and educators to use. It's also evidenced in reviews where the number of actual studies backing up review findings is soberingly small (e.g., Hattie, 2008; Segura-Pujol & Briones-Rojas, 2021; Smith et al., 2021)

Ivory-towering is my term for massive proliferation of experimental research on specific topics, but with that knowledge unfortunately becoming increasingly theoretical, esoteric and academic; and researchers seeming unfortunately detached from school-level issues, and the strong practical school-level focus that's needed. As Solari et al. (2020) comment,

Despite scientific advances that have informed our understanding of reading acquisition and development, a profound gap exists between empirical findings and the implementation of evidence-based practices in the assessment and instruction of reading in school settings. ... the field has yet to invest in the appropriate methodologies and processes to develop an effective model of translational science.

One big issue perpetuating ivory-towering is research budgets being too low. This results in *Publish or perish!*: enormous pressure to have many research articles published, with researchers not paid for time spent sharing their findings, and discouraged from spending time away from research and research writing (Gill, 2004; Merga & Mason, 2021a, 2021b). This widens the yawning gap between theory and practical implementation in schools – the gap we need to bridge.

Ivory-towering abounds on education topics: we've far too many Swiss-cheese research areas. That's particularly the case, given Australia has been *saving* savagely down the decades, spending far too little on educational research (e.g., Gill, 2004).

It's a disappointing, damaging situation, and all too often schools and teachers assume they're using amply evidence-based practice, when the evidence for school applicability is actually incredibly slim.

That's because ivory-towered research often has little practical value for Australian schools, unless it has an accompanying strong school-level focus, e.g., replicating studies in schools to see the extent that findings apply. School circumstances are extremely complicated relative to the controlled conditions of experimental research: all too often, school studies don't show the significant findings of experimental studies, because of the many additional, interacting factors that impact teaching and learning there.

Excessive ivory-towering on topics which are important for schools begs the question, *Who is the hand that feeds reading research?*

Logically, it could be assumed that research funding is for knowledge-building to satisfy school-level needs on education matters – but the lack of practical research, applying experimental findings at school level, makes that assumption seem questionable.

I'm not being critical of researchers involved in this ivory-towering, as budgets are tight, and researchers are so often under pressure.

We need changes to the ways universities prioritise school-level research, and researchers spending time sharing research findings with schools and educators, (e.g., Merga & Mason, 2021a, 2021b).

The Ivory-Towering Vs Swiss-Cheese Contrast

Lest I've given the impression I'm exaggerating, let's explore two practical examples of ivory-towering vs Swiss-cheese research.

The Non-Cambridge "Cambridge Email"

The first, an example of ivory-towering, is research built from that silly email many of us are familiar with:

Aoccdrnig to a rscheeachr at Cmabrigde Uinervtisy, it deosn't mttaer in waht oredr the ltteers in a wrod are, the olny iprmoetnt tihng is taht the frist and lsat ltteer be at the rghit pclae. The rset can be a toatl mses and you can sitll raed it wouthit porsbelm. Tihs is bcuseae the huamn mnid deos not raed ervey lteter by istlef, but the wrod as a wlohe.

The amount of research discussion that email has generated is quite staggering e.g., see discussion in Frost (2012), and that article's appendix of detailed peer commentaries. While of academic interest, the extensive research time and therefore funds expended have little relevance to improving literacy development in schools.

Of course, the email isn't from researchers at Cambridge University and, for beginning readers, letter order is of huge importance.

It's an issue of cognitive load: experienced readers with wonderfully automised word-reading simply don't need all the letter clues. Thus, you and I can read those words quite effortlessly. It's similar to how we can read *A_st_al_a* with many letters missing.

As readers become more automatic, word-reading uses increasingly less cognitive load. It's automaticity that makes reading that email so easy. But it's very different for beginners who lack automised skills.

The proliferation of research on that email, with low applicability to school learning, smacks strongly of unfortunate ivory-towering.

Key Word-Reading Subskills

A second ivory-towering vs Swiss-cheese contrast is the research on phonological-verbal short-term and working memory, and *Rapid Automised Naming* (RAN) – a measure of processing efficiency for retrieving and activating phonological-verbal information.

Because English orthographic complexity makes learning difficult and produces high cognitive load, three cognitive-processing skills are particularly important for Standard-English beginners, being almost vital for word-reading and spelling development (Peng et al., 2022):
- Short-term memory capacity.
- Working memory capacity.
- Processing efficiency for actioning information.

They're easy to measure. Short-term memory, ability to take in and retain memory briefly, is easily tested by e.g., having children repeat back increasingly long lists of numbers or words they hear, to see how many items of information can be remembered.

Working memory, ability to take in and retain information while we manipulate it, is easily tested in a range of ways, often by using increasingly long lists of items, this time said back in reverse order.

To assess processing speed for word-reading, we usually measure children's Rapid Automised Naming (RAN): how many easily-named pictured items they can name as quickly as possible in a short time, e.g., in 30 seconds or a minute (Denckla & Rudel, 1974;

Georgiou et al., 2016; Norton & Wolf, 2012). Numbers, colours or easily named single-syllable words can be used, e.g., the RAN test I've posted on ResearchGate uses six easily-named pictures (ball, car, fish, cat, dog, and boat) in a grid of 36 pictures (Galletly, 2014d).

The three skills, short-term memory, working memory, and RAN as processing efficiency, are important, as skill weakness impacts cognitive load, automisation weakness, and difficulty mastering and becoming automatic at word-reading, spelling, and often maths facts too. Anglophone children weak in one or more of these three skills are consequently at risk of major literacy learning difficulties.

Incidentally, not only are the three skills easy to measure – they can also be easily measured in fun ways with children as young as 4 years old. That's young enough to identify at-risk children before they start school and reading instruction, and implement strategic, fun interventions. Starting early, using fun building of readiness, can make a wonderful difference for vulnerable children.

Now for a quick measure of ivory-towering and Swiss-cheese research on those areas. I used a search on *Google Scholar*, which is easy to do. In less than three seconds, I received just over 9,000,000 results:

- 3,980,000 results for *short term memory*.
- 5,040,000 results for *working memory*.
- 19,600 results for *Rapid Automised Naming* (RAN).

They're the numbers of research articles and publications, website discussions, and so on, that the search provides links to. Numbers of that size indicate a myriad of research on those areas.

Now those numbers don't indicate ivory-towering – we establish ivory-towering and the extent of Swiss-cheese by considering the extent of research done, and comparing it with the extent of useful applications that the research has led to: applications used in practical settings such as our kindies, daycare centres and schools.

With over 9,000,000 results in total, most of which will be research articles discussing research studies, lots should be happening for our children before they start school and at school. But there isn't!

Our schools, kindies and daycare centres don't have fun easy tests of short-term memory, working memory and processing efficiency to identify young at-risk children weak in these areas. Further, the research on school-level applications, while useful, is woefully small – hence the smell of Swiss-cheese pervades.

Looking further, you find that most early-years and primary school teachers haven't had professional development on why the skills are important, and on strategies for children weak in these areas (e.g., Gathercole & Alloway, 2008) – that's a major application gap.

In consequence, many teachers and schools aren't aware of their struggling learners' weaknesses in these areas, and how to support their ongoing information-processing difficulties. Many at-risk and struggling learners thus miss out on supports that are much needed.

People often think it's just word-reading and spelling that are major problems for children with Language, Literacy and Learning Disorder (LLLD, my term), or Dyslexia as it's often termed.

That's actually not the case. In reality, functional working-memory weakness that frequently causes high cognitive load and overload is a separate, major weakness these children have, additional to their reading and writing difficulties. It impacts speaking and listening as well as reading and writing tasks and development

There's far too little awareness across Australia of how often our beginners and older struggling readers have information-processing weakness that causes high cognitive load and overload.

That's sad, inappropriate and unnecessary – and it's largely because schools don't have tests and professional development discussing relevant findings – because that mountain of ivory-towered research hasn't been prioritised for being taken through to school usefulness.

That contrast of 9,000,000 articles vs almost no practical application is a classic ivory-towering vs Swiss-cheese research disparity. We've had many similar dilemmas to resolve, areas with appreciable theoretical research, but woefully insufficient school-level applied research or schools being resourced with useful, valid research information.

I've developed free tests of phonological-verbal short-term and working memory, RAN, and phonological awareness, along with early-years language-skills tests that schools can use (Galletly, 2014b, 2014c, 2014d). Available on ResearchGate, they're easy-to-use criterion-based measures, for which norms can easily be developed, e.g., by schools measuring children's skill levels for a few years and pooling their data for age groups and year-levels.

Let's Build from Available Studies

May I emphasise that ivory-towered research can be extremely valuable. Well-established research findings can provide a strong basis for applied school research that can then end Swiss-cheese research areas, with knowledge gaps replaced by useful findings.

As an example of useful well-established research findings, let me expand the quote of Mark Seidenberg (2013) that I used above – he provides a succinct summary of the knowledge base:

Is there an area in cognitive science and cognitive neuroscience that has been more successful than the study of reading?

Let us not underestimate the amount that has been learned.

We understand the basic mechanisms that support skilled reading, how reading skill is acquired, and the proximal causes of reading impairments.

We understand the fundamental problem facing the beginning reader: how to relate a new code, a written script, to an existing code, spoken language.

We know which behaviors of 4-year-old prereaders are strong predictors of later reading ability, how children make the transition from prereader to reader, and the obstacles that many encounter.

We know what distinguishes good and poor readers, younger and older skilled readers, "typical" readers from those who are atypical because of either constitutional factors (such as a hearing or learning impairment) or environmental ones (e.g., poor schooling or poverty).

We know how basic skills that provide the child's entry into reading relate to other types of knowledge and capacities that support comprehending texts of increasing variety and difficulty.

We understand that some aspects of reading are universal (because people's brains are essentially alike) and that some are not (because of differences among writing systems and the languages they represent).

Neuroimaging studies have been successful in identifying the main brain circuits involved in reading and the anomalous ways they develop in dyslexics, as well as several probable causes of such impairments.

We have computational models that specify the mechanisms that underlie basic reading skills, how children acquire them, and how differences in experience (with spoken language and reading) and individual differences (in learning and memory capacities, motivation and other factors) result in varied reading outcomes.

This vast research base has led to development of intervention and remediation methods that can reliably help many children who need it.

Researchers disagree about many details – it's science, not the Ten Commandments – but there is remarkable consensus about the basic theory of how reading works and the causes of reading successes and failures.

That's a great summary and, yes, there's definitely an impressive experimental-research knowledge base we can work from. Masses of useful empirical research knowledge is there to be used.

We now need to take key findings through to the classroom coalface, exploring the extent to which they apply in school contexts, with strong focus on the 10 Changes and those useful wonderings:
- What factors cause our children and adults' reading and literacy difficulties?
- How can we reduce their struggles and suffering?
- What are the ways we can do things better?

Change 10 is *Build needed research knowledge as quickly as possible: Use collaborative school-based research.* Let's make applied research in schools a key component of future knowledge-building across Australia.

Analogy Time: Pot-Bound Tomatoes

Let's consider tomatoes briefly. I promise you they're relevant.

The message of pot-bound tomatoes is that a single unrecognised factor can have major impacts that are easily overlooked, and that recognising that factor can be powerful in expediting useful, paradigmatically-new thinking and directions.

This one is a true story, well as true as I can arrive at when events happened in the 1950s in the UK and were told to me rather than being my experience.

My dad and mum met while they were studying tomato roots at Manchester University in the 1950s. Dad is a plant geneticist and Mum was a botanist. He was a clever farm boy from Maclean, in New South Wales, educated on Australian scholarships, doing his doctorate in Manchester. She was a clever English lass who went from school directly into war research on camouflage: now a tutor doing Masters studies, she had plans for Doctoral studies – until she met that winsome Aussie lad, my father.

One anecdote about their studies has always stuck with me.

Apparently, all the Doctoral and Masters students went to one student's verbal exam when she was examined for her PhD.

Why? Because her research findings overturned key aspects of the research knowledge one of her examiners had built over many years about developmental characteristics of tomato plants as they age.

It turns out that there was one overlooked variable that completely changed key growth factors, an overlooked but actually extremely important factor that hadn't previously been sufficiently considered.

You see, it was England, with the weather often cold and inclement, so the plants were usually grown in greenhouses. In pots!

But this student studied tomatoes planted in the ground.

And ... you guessed it ... key characteristics of tomato growth that previous researchers had established were actually characteristics only of pot-bound tomato plants. They simply weren't reality in applied circumstances, i.e., in fields on farms. It turns out, a tomato plant in the field differs in key ways from a tomato plant in a pot!

And the research knowledge base on tomato plant characteristics wobbled briefly, then took on new stronger forms.

Not surprisingly, the students were worried this Doctoral candidate might find herself in hot water with the examiner. And she did.

Now, research knowledge-building is alas not always impartial and not personal. Not surprisingly, the external examiner first tried to remove all the Doctoral students, but couldn't as they were entitled to be there, and then made life tricky for the student nonetheless – she had to omit the pot-bound issue from her thesis. Sigh. Such are the vagaries of research politics. Indeed, one of my mother's strong role models of that time was Rosalind Franklin, notoriously under-recognised for her work unravelling DNA mysteries (Lee, 2013).

At least the Doctoral candidate knew she was right and had strong support from her peers that they knew she was right – sometimes research knowledge is transferred informally, rather than officially.

Thus, the tomato research knowledge base grew. And now, decades on, I'm using her experience for ongoing useful research purposes.

Lessons from Pot-bound Tomatoes

That analogy has multiple useful implications. I'll list a few here.

One, it highlights the importance of rigorous fundamental basic experimental research that clearly tracks down all the key variables likely to be impacting a situation. In other words, let's love the educational research knowledge base and the experimental and quasi-experimental knowledge that research has developed. Ivory-towering and all, it's a wonderful and powerful resource.

Two, it highlights the huge importance of applied research in practical settings, including the classroom coalface. Findings from experimental research so often should only be the first step. For functional usefulness, they must subsequently be replicated in a range of practical contexts. That's why it's so powerful for Australia to extract key findings, to research here in school contexts.

Three, it highlights that variables impacting a situation often have a pecking order, an order of importance, with some having far stronger impacts than others. The pot-boundness was not just an overlooked variable; it was also an extremely important underlying variable with major impacts that resulted in lots of other changes.

Now there's every likelihood that (*drum roll, please*) ... the orthography children meet when first learning to read and write is a pot-bound tomatoes variable, a vitally important, insufficiently considered variable, with major impacts on secondary variables.

For us, those impacted secondary variables include, notably,
- The too young age, and hence insufficiently developed cognitive-processing skills, of many of our 5-year-olds.
- The too high cognitive load young Anglophone children live with for too long across early-literacy development.
- The risk factors activated by English orthographic complexity and high cognitive load, in children with insufficiently developed cognitive-processing skills.
- Our at-risk children developing major word-reading and spelling difficulties not seen in regular-orthography nations.
- Quite likely, *Acquired Helplessness* and self-esteem issues our struggling learners develop due to ongoing low success.

I'm far from alone in emphasising English orthographic complexity being of massive importance. The Initial Teaching Alphabet (ITA) researchers certainly felt the same, six decades ago (e.g., Downing, 1969a, 1969b; Mazurkiewicz, 1971, 1973b; Warburton & Southgate, 1969). And so, now, do increasing numbers of recent crosslinguistic researchers, many of whom may not have read the work of earlier crosslinguistic researchers of the 1950s and the ITA researchers of the 1960s and early 70s, as some imply it's only recently been realised (e.g., Ziegler et al, 2010):

Over the past decade, it has become clear that orthographic consistency is the key factor determining the rate of reading acquisition across different languages.

Ageism is a bit of an issue in modern research writing, amidst word count limits of journal articles, which pressure writers to cite recent studies and omit those from decades past. This can lead to knowledge gaps and the wheel being reinvented.

The writers are actually discussing rediscovery. The ITA research provides insights on far more literacy aspects than modern crosslinguistic research seems to have done. And orthographic consistency was well researched, with these impacts well known in the 1950s and 60s, e.g., do read different researchers' discussions in the 1957 *Linguistics across cultures* that Robert Lado edited, and the *Comparative Reading Project* John Downing writes of in 1972.

But such is life in research. The wheel is often reinvented, and this often strengthens findings and opens new research directions.

Now, if English orthographic complexity is established as being a pot-bound tomatoes issue through Australian school-level research, and if we then change so our children first learn to read and write a fully-regular beginners' orthography, this may herald the end of many powerful negatives of current instruction and outcomes.

Our children's long list of risk factors that can derail them would reduce in functional terms from over 50 to the few risk factors that functionally impact regular-orthography children: family history of difficulties, weak Rapid Automised Naming (RAN) and weak letter-sound skills (Clayton et al., 2020; Eklund et al., 2013, 2015; Ronimus et al., 2019).

Using that beginners' orthography, we too might have very few weak word-readers, with low speed their main weakness. And, a wonderful advantage, child and teachers' workload might shrink like Alice to the manageable levels of Taiwan, Japan and China.

We'd actually have far smaller workload than Taiwan, Japan and China. The beginners' orthography we'd use would be highly similar to Standard English, with many words and syllables identical, whereas they've minimal similarity between their beginners' and complex orthographies, and thousands of characters to be learned.

As an example, the figure below shows text written in Stage-1 of Fleksispel, a fully-regular English beginners' orthography.

Fleksispel - Stage 1

Wuns upon u tiem thair wer three litul pigz hooo livd in u kotuj with thair muthu.

Wun dae muthu pig sed tooo her kidz, 'It's tiem for yooo tooo bild yor oen howzuz.' Soe of thae went.

Thu ferst litul pig met u farmu with a loed of stror.

'Pleez cood I hav sum ov yor stror?' thu pig arskt pulietlee.

'Sertunlee, yooo fien yung pig,' ansud thu farmu, hooo gaev thu litul pig az much stror az woz wontud.

Figure 2a. *Text using Stage-1 Fleksispel (Galletly, 2005b, 2023a, In press)*

Analogy Time: Pot-Bound Tomatoes

I've developed Fleksispel to be a single-stage fully-regular beginners' orthography and also a multi-stage transitioning orthography (Galletly, 2005b, 2023a). It's available for free, non-commercial, flexible use by researchers and educators. While decidedly odd at first view, you can see how myriads of words and syllables would be identical, or highly similar, in Standard English and Stage-1 Fleksispel. The figure below shows the GPCs for Stage-1 Fleksispel, a fully-regular beginners' orthography.

41 Grapheme-Phoneme Correspondences (GPCS)

19 Vowel GPCS				22 Consonant GPCS					
ae	m*ae*t	**ar**	m*art*	**b**	*bat*	**n**	*nat*	**sh**	*shat*
a	*mat*	**er**	m*er*t	**d**	*dat*	**p**	*pat*	**ch**	*chat*
ee	m*ee*t	**or**	m*or*t	**f**	*fat*	**r**	*rat*	**th**	*that*
e	*met*	**ow**	n*ow*	**g**	*gat*	**s**	*sat*	**ng**	ta*ng*
ie	m*ie*t	**oo**	f*oo*t	**h**	*hat*	**t**	*tat*		
i	*mit*	**ooo**	m*ooo*	**j**	*jat*	**v**	*vat*		
oe	m*oe*t	**oy**	b*oy*	**k**	*kat*	**w**	*wat*		
o	*mot*	**air**	h*air*	**l**	*lat*	**y**	*yat*		
ue	m*ue*t			**m**	*mat*	**z**	*zat*		
u	*mut*								
u	*sistu (ə)*								

Figure 2b. *Fleksispel: Stage-1 GPCs (Galletly, 2022a, 2023a)*

As you'll see in Research Tour 5, which explores the research on beginners' orthographies, reading and writing a beginners' orthography such as Fleksispel prior to Standard English, means children have vastly faster and easier literacy development, and transition very easily to Standard English.

The 10 Changes: The Nitty Gritty contains detail on Fleksispel and its stages, along with nitty gritty on many other areas. A file on Fleksispel is available on ResearchGate (Galletly 2023a, In press).

Solving Seidenberg's Puzzle

Using computer modelling, Mark Seidenberg and colleagues have impressively researched how English orthographic complexity impedes developing readers' statistical learning (e.g., Bruno et al.,

2007; Harm & Seidenberg, 2004; Seidenberg, 2005, 2013; Seidenberg & McClelland, 1989). Studies of reading and spelling show similarly (e.g., Caravolas, 2018, 2004; Caravolas et al., 2005; Rau et al., 2016).

Seidenberg (2013) outlines a puzzle that Anglophone researchers of literacy learning disabilities need to solve. He emphasises that there's an important factor or series of factors, that researchers aren't currently aware of, and that need to be discovered. He specifies three key characteristics of that missing factor or factors:

- It contributes to children's increasing word-reading and literacy difficulties across the first four years of schooling.
- It lays children low irrespective of their SES (Socio-Economic Status) levels, such that many children with high SES nonetheless develop difficulties, despite effective instruction and strong family support.
- The children's difficulties are often somewhat unexpected: before they started school and reading instruction, they were doing well with no major achievement gaps evident.

It does sound like our Early Years Factory, doesn't it? Enter stage left, wee Australians seemingly destined for success, and exit right a few years later about one third now crushed and crumpled, struggling with both literacy and confidence.

Really, there's every likelihood the answer to Seidenberg's puzzle is English orthographic complexity, plus the high cognitive load and impeded learning it creates across early-literacy development that's too difficult for at-risk children aged 4.5 to 5.0 years.

Three likely associated factors are
- Young age and associated low cognitive-processing skills.
- Risk factors being activated by that high cognitive load and impeded learning.
- Acquired Helplessness and self-esteem factors, through insufficient success being experienced on an ongoing basis.

While I only read about Seidenberg's puzzle more recently, our CQU research team summed up the situation well (Knight et al., 2017a):

> At the present time, Anglophone researchers and schools seem unable to routinely achieve effective word-reading and literacy intervention and catch-up for many struggling learners. ...
> It is likely that the high cognitive load of learning to read and write using Standard-English orthography is the major cause of current large numbers of children with word-reading and word-writing difficulties.

Analogy Time: Pot-Bound Tomatoes

Three types of factors seem related to the cognitive overload and resultant low success of at-risk and struggling learners:
1. Curriculum content load factors, being the high curriculum content load of early word-reading and word-writing; and the challenges of effectively sequencing instruction to keep curriculum content load manageable, to enable automising of reading skills.
2. Statistical learning factors, with confusion created by Grapheme: Phoneme Correspondence (GPCs) being rarely one: one strongly impeding easy effective statistical learning, leading to difficulties automising skills.
3. Child factors, including weak literacy pre-skills and experience, and processing capacity and learning efficiency reduced by younger age and risk factors, anxiety and Learned Helplessness.

Research is needed, as it's definitely a Swiss-cheese research area. I'm happy to be wrong, if I am wrong, but I think research will show the CQU team and I have been heading in the right directions, with orthographic impacts, through high cognitive load and activated risk factors, being the answer to Seidenberg's puzzle.

A Caveat

I'll detail a caveat here before we start exploring research. My knowledge-building is just a start, a stimulus for further, more detailed knowledge-building by others.

I want to emphasise my Australian and largely private-practice background, i.e., the limited research funding and thus less than ample time I've had for deeply exploring different areas.

Further, the theorising I've done and conclusions I've made are doubtless influenced by the fact that I've grown up and lived my life here in Australia, and haven't had extended exposure to the regular-orthography nations I'm discussing.

Yes, I've visited schools and researchers in many nations, and I've read the research widely. However, because research studies differ in the measures and sample sizes they use, findings of available studies may not fully reflect practical realities, thus some conclusions I've developed from reading of studies may only be partially applicable.

Let me give you an example of how that can happen. I recently encountered an interesting and somewhat erroneous assumption that researchers from a non-Anglophone nation had made about Anglophone children in an Australian research journal. They state,

> *Unlike alphabetic knowledge in English which emerges around the age of three and is complete by early school-age, [our nation's regular-orthography alphabetic] knowledge is not a prerequisite ... and is not officially taught until Grade 1.*

It's not a particularly accurate assumption, is it? It doesn't take into account Anglophone children's first year of schooling often not being termed Grade 1, but rather Kindergarten or Prep, and that children are often taught letter-sounds in that first year, prior to Grade 1.

The writers seem to be thinking that children in Australia and other Anglophone nations have to know their letter-sounds before they start school, and that this is very different from how things happen in their nation, where children are taught their regular-orthography letter-sounds in Grade 1, which is their first year of formal education. In reality, we're similar, teaching letter-sounds the first school year.

Apart from that comment, the article was excellent. The writers had simply made assumptions from reading of research articles, but with likely limited exposure to education in Anglophone nations.

I found reading the comment humbling because, as a minimally-funded researcher of far-flung Australia, researching education in distant nations whose culture I've relatively little experience of, it's possibly I may have made similarly inaccurate assumptions at times – as I've simply had too little practical experience of life there.

You'll notice the 10 Changes are largely recommendations for knowledge-building towards possible changes. While that's because research is needed, it's also because I recognise the limitations of my knowledge and experiences, and thus the possibilities that some conclusions I've made may only partially reflect reality.

So here's my caveat. I've read reams of research studies. I've visited and observed at schools in Anglophone, regular-orthography and other nations, and had useful discussions with teachers and researchers in those nations.

I've strong knowledge of teaching, learning and resourcing of Australian schools, and extensive first-hand experience of the difficulties our struggling readers experience.

I've thus been able to relate knowledge built on literacy development in regular-orthography nations to my practical knowledge of children and literacy development here, and the research on Anglophone children and the reading and learning difficulties many experience.

That said, there may be areas where I've somewhat misconstrued aspects of regular-orthography nations' reality. I've accommodated for potential errors through my recommendations being strongly for knowledge-building regarding the changes we should explore.

I view my job as raising awareness of key issues with potential to enormously improve literacy development and education here, and handing the baton on, to educators and researchers of the future.

I'm confident that, into the future, keen readers will find other useful areas and ideas – perhaps using my writings and the studies we'll explore in this book as a basis of future reading and research.

The Research Tours Begin ...

Off we go now on our research tours.

They're a series of individual tours, each focused on a key topic area, e.g., Tour 1 explores studies showing how rapidly word-reading and spelling develop for regular-orthography children, and how slowly they develop in our children.

I've selected studies and research areas for their relevance to 10 Changes issues. They establish the Changes as powerful directions.

In each tour, we'll walk through key research studies that shed light on our current situation and its challenges, our needs for change, and logical directions for change towards improvement.

I'll cite key research studies as we go. For those wanting to gain deeper understanding, do read the original articles to get their nitty gritty: they're listed in the reference section of this book.

Here's the route our research tour will take.

We'll start with the major impacts of orthographic complexity:

Tour 1. Too Slow Standard-English Word-Reading Development.
Tour 2. Orthography Is The Key Factor.
Tour 3. Success Inoculation Vs Acquired Helplessness.
Tour 4. Regular Orthographies and Intellectual Disability.
Tour 5. The Power of Beginners' Orthographies.

We'll then explore language and reading contributions to literacy:

Tour 6. Our Epidemic of Language Weakness.
Tour 7. Literacy Components and Quadrants.
Tour 8. Our Too Many Low Literacy Achievers.
Tour 9. Needs for Workload Research.

We'll next consider key cognitive-processing skills:

Tour 10. A Multiple Deficits Vs Phonological Basis.

Tour 11. Executive-Function Skills Empower Word-Reading.

After that, in our final tours, we'll explore the intransigent difficulties that the Anglosphere has in achieving effective word-reading in Standard-English at-risk and struggling readers:

Tour 12. Our Impeded Statistical Learning.

Tour 13. Unfamiliar Words: Our Standard-English Nemesis.

Tour 14. Our Insufficiently Effective Word-Reading Intervention.

Research Tour 1.
Too Slow Word-Reading and Spelling Development

Most longitudinal studies with English-speaking children did not even include measures of reading fluency but reported development in word-reading accuracy only.
In phonologically more transparent orthographies however, word-reading accuracy is often close to or at ceiling after only a few months of formal reading instruction, and word-reading speed is the only word-reading measure that differentiates between good and poor readers in higher grades.

Karin Landerl & Heinz Wimmer, 2008

Word-reading is the reading of words, and sometimes word-parts. We identify what words say (the spoken word), and, where relevant, attach meaning. Word-reading has accuracy (reading correctly), plus fluency (speed and intonation).

The quote, above, highlights a pertinent contrast: the Anglosphere predominantly studies word-reading accuracy but regular-orthography nations don't. They study fluency, as their children master word-reading accuracy very easily, but a small group lack fluency.

That difference in focus positions us as poles apart. We're distinctly different worlds separated by a massive crosslinguistic gap – with the Anglosphere struggling as regular-orthography nations thrive.

Issues of word frequency, length and word-neighbours (highly similar words with few letters different, e.g., *can-cat-car*) all impact word-reading development across nations (Daniels & Share, 2018; Frost, 2012; Monster et al., 2022; Protopapas & Vlahou, 2009; Seidenberg, 2005). Overwhelmingly, however, the factor that most expedites and impedes word-reading and spelling development is orthographic complexity: the extent to which letter-sounds are consistent, and use one-to-one GPCs (Knight et al., 2017b, 2019; Share, 2008).

At its simplest, word-reading and spelling are *phonemic recoding*, or what's often termed the *Alphabetic Principle*: moving between words and letters via letter-sounds. (Adams, 1990; Byrne, 1998; Galletly, 2004a, 2005b; Hempenstall, 2016; Nation, 2008b; C. Snow et al., 1998a, 1998b; Stuart & Stainthorp, 2015; Wolf, 2007).

For reading and writing, a regular-orthography is the Alphabetic Principle at its simplest, both in learning to read and write, and when reading and writing in everyday literacy tasks.

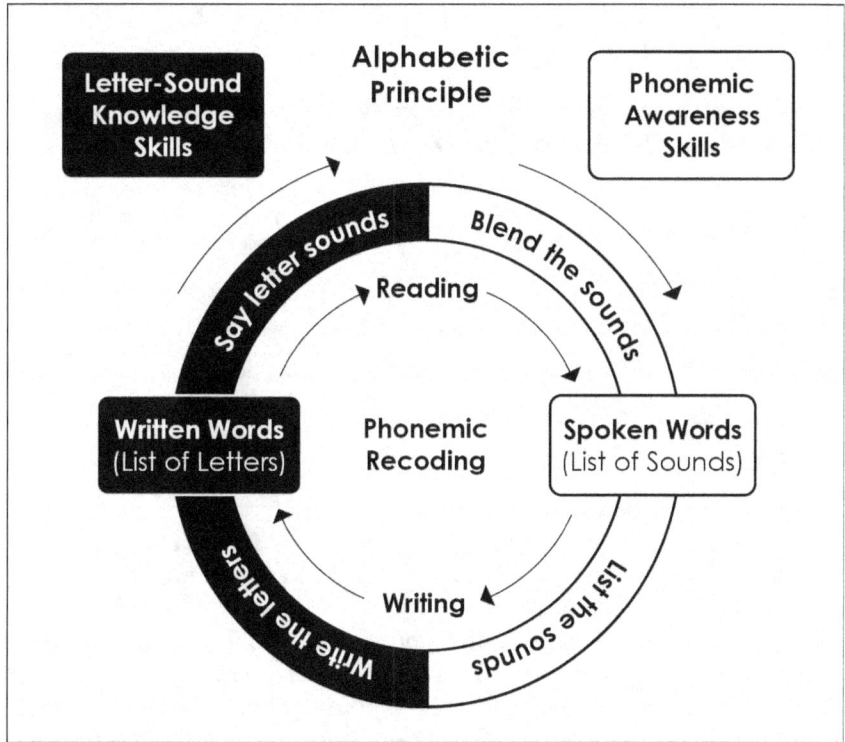

Figure 3. Phonemic recoding (Alphabetic Principle), showing the skills and single-stage learning of regular-orthography word-reading and spelling (Knight et al., *2017b, 2019*)

With all words being regular, once the child knows the orthography's letter-sounds and how to blend sounds to read words, and list sounds, to write words, there's conceptually little more to learn. For Finnish children, that's 23 letters and their sounds, as Finnish has 23 sounds, each represented by a single letter (M. Aro, 2004, 2017a). Confidence and fluency then build as the child reads and writes, using self-teaching (Nation et al., 2007; Share, 1995).

In contrast, reading and writing Standard English is the Alphabetic Principle at its most complex (See Figure 4). With our 26 letters, 40+ sounds and 560+ GPCs, learning commonest letter-sounds and how to read and write regular words is just the start.

Standard-English uses at least three orthographic grainsizes (Galletly 2004a, 2005b, 2008, 2017b, 2018; Goswami, 2002; Ziegler & Goswami, 2005), while a regular orthography has but one. That makes a vast difference in how complex it is to learn to read and write, and to use early reading and writing when learning. As the figure below shows, our children must work through multiple stages as they learn to read and write (Galletly, 2008).

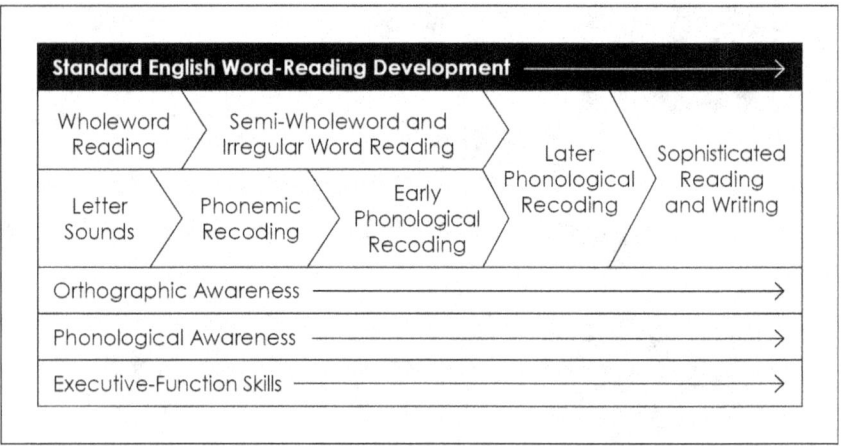

Figure 4. Phonological recoding: the multiple stages of learning to read and write Standard English (Galletly, 2008, adapted)

Regular orthographies use only phoneme grainsize, and thus have just *Regular Words* and syllables, e.g., *bus, crunch, yesterday*, which are read using phonemic recoding (*sounding-out*). While Standard-English has very large numbers of Regular words and syllables, we also have our other grainsizes children must work with.

We have orthographic-unit grainsize: the multi-letter spelling patterns of our many *Pattern Words* and syllables, e.g., *look, car, yesterday*. They're read using rhyme, analogy and *phonological recoding*, e.g., knowing *ball* and rhyming, children can read and write other words with that *-all* pattern, e.g., *tall, small, fall*.

We've also the wholeword and whole-syllable grainsize of our myriads of highly irregular words that use less-frequent GPCs, e.g., *one, was, yesterday, people*. Their learning involves remembering whole words and syllables visually.

Our children thus have prolific learning and concepts to negotiate. As you can see in the figure, integrating these different aspects of learning means children work through multiple sub-stages of learning (Galletly, 2008),

In this tour, we'll explore studies showing how rapidly regular-orthography word-reading develops, that highlight how very slow Standard-English word-reading development is. We'll also explore studies of spelling and phonemic-awareness development.

We'll first tour three key studies:
- Seymour, Aro & Erskine's (2003) report on the European COST-A8 14-nation study of Year 1 word-reading skills.
- Aro's (2004) study of Finnish word-reading and phonemic-awareness development.
- Huang and Hanley's (1994, 1997) studies of Taiwanese children's word-reading and phonemic awareness.

The COST-A8 14-Nation Word-Reading Study

While orthographies differ in diverse ways (Babayigit, 2022; Borleffs et al., 2017, 2019; Lara-Martínez et al., 2022), orthographic regularity, which is also termed transparency, is a characteristic all orthographies share, with extent of regularity significantly impacting ease and speed of learning to read and write.

Seymour et al.'s (2003) word-reading research project, conducted with the COST-A8 (European *Cooperation in Science and Technology Action A8*) network, showed rapid, easy word-reading development widespread in European regular-orthography nations. Equally, it showed English word-reading to be incredibly slow.

Table 1 lists data from that study. It's a table from a 2017 article our CQU team wrote (Knight & Galletly, 2017), which discusses Seymour et al.'s findings with regard to Australian education needs.

The table shows that end-Grade-1 readers of 10 nations with extremely regular orthographies: Swedish, Italian, Spanish, Finnish, Turkish, Norwegian, Dutch, Icelandic, German and Greek children – read real words and pseudowords with 90-98% accuracy, on average.

The children had very strong proficiency. Indeed, while testing for the study was done at end-Grade-1, the authors comment that most of the children in these nations would have been proficiently accurate for word-reading considerably earlier, by mid-Grade-1.

The Research Tours: Impacts of Orthographic Disadvantage

Nation	Orthographic Regularity	Word-Reading Results			Age Levels	
		All Words	Frequent Real Words	Unfamiliar Words	Age	Age Gap UK Yr1
Finland	Extremely Regular	96.7%	98.3%	95.0%	7.9	2.3
Greece		94.8%	97.6%	92.1%	6.8	1.2
Italy		92.4%	95.3%	89.4%	6.9	1.3
Spain		91.8%	94.7%	88.8%	6.8	1.2
Austria		94.7%	97.5%	91.9%	7.6	2.0
Germany		96.0%	97.7%	94.4%	7.4	1.8
Norway		91.3%	91.8%	90.8%	7.9	2.3
Iceland		90.3%	94.1%	86.5%	6.9	1.3
Portugal	Highly Regular	75.2%	73.5%	76.9%	7.0	1.4
Sweden		91.4%	95.1%	87.7%	7.5	1.9
Netherlands		88.8%	95.4%	82.2%	7.0	1.4
Denmark Yr1	Moderately Regular	62.4%	71.1%	53.7%	7.7	2.1
Denmark Yr2		86.9%	92.6%	81.3%	8.6	3.0
France Yr1		82.0%	79.1%	84.9%	6.7	1.1
France Yr2		98.3%	99.2%	97.4%	7.9	2.3
UK Yr1	Highly Complex	31.6%	33.9%	29.3%	5.6	--
UK Yr2		70.0%	76.4%	63.5%	6.6	--

Table 1. Word-reading and child age in nations ordered by extent of orthographic complexity (Knight & Galletly, 2017, using data from Seymour et al., 2003)

The end-Grade-1 readers of somewhat less regular French and Danish read with over 60% and 80% accuracy. The Portuguese children also scored lower, though other factors were likely in play there, as Portuguese is a highly-regular orthography.

These findings of rapid word-reading development in children learning to read highly-regular orthographies are reported by many regular-orthography researchers. Torppa et al. (2016) and Lyytinen et al.

(2021), for example, discuss most Finnish children being proficiently accurate by mid-Grade-1, with accuracy errors rare from then on, even in less-fluent word-readers (Torppa et al., 2016):

> Since word-level decoding reaches a high level of accuracy for most Grade 1 students after only a few months of school, students' commitment and motivation for silent reading to improve their fluency and comprehension are supported daily from Grades 1 and 2 onward, soon after they have acquired the decoding skill.

In contrast, Table 1 shows end-Grade-1 Standard-English readers had barely 30% accuracy. That's sad. That's life in the Anglosphere.

The researchers had anticipated that English readers, with a highly irregular orthography, and French and Danish readers, with somewhat less-regular orthographies, would have significantly slower word-reading development. In consequence, end-Grade-2 children were included for these nations, to explore how well their children were reading after another year of teaching and learning. Those results are also shown in the table.

The Standard-English readers' impeded development was still present, which hammers home the damaging effects of Standard English. Whereas French and Danish children had largely closed the gap after their additional year's learning, the English end-Grade-2 children were still far behind, having just 70% accuracy.

The end-Grade-2 English readers' low reading establishes a key finding: Standard-English word-reading develops extremely slowly relative to regular-orthography nations. It also establishes a key implication, that we have far higher teaching and learning workload across our many years of word-reading development (Galletly & Knight, 2011b; Galletly, 2022a. In press).

After a year's extra teaching and learning, the English readers were still far behind. And whereas French and Danish children caught up to highest-regularity nations within one year, with English orthography of far higher complexity, multiple years of teaching and learning time would be needed for English readers to catch up.

Learning to read English is clearly very difficult relative to regular-orthography nations, with the differences ongoing and long-lasting. Indeed, they're still present in healthy-progress, adult readers, e.g., Paulesu et al. (2000) found marked differences in the word-reading of Italian and English university students, with the Italian readers significantly faster at both familiar and unfamiliar words. They comment on the challenges of learning to read English:

> *In English there are 1120 ways of representing 40 sounds (phonemes) by different letters or letter combinations (graphemes). The mappings between graphemes, phonemes and whole word sound are essentially ambiguous, as illustrated by pairs such as pint/mint, cough/bough, clove/love.*
>
> *By contrast, in Italian, 33 graphemes are sufficient to represent the 25 phonemes of the language, and the mappings from graphemes to phonemes are unequivocal.*
>
> *Young Italian readers can achieve 92% accuracy on word reading tests after only 6 months of schooling, whereas learning to read in English takes much longer. ...*
>
> *Compared to German, another consistent orthography, accuracy levels in English are lower and reading speed is slower even after three years of schooling.*

Clearly, Standard-English readers have very slow, impeded word-reading development. This is a major, ongoing time and workload issue that Anglophone children, teachers and schools wrestle with.

English Readers' Very Young Age

Children's mean ages are included in Table 1, along with the age-gap for the English children. The English readers are far younger, e.g., 2.3 years younger than children in Finland and Norway.

The age data highlights how very young our Standard-English readers are when learning to read, relative to children of many other nations. In the Anglosphere, children learn to read and write at age 5 years, and sometimes from age 4 and 4.5 years.

From many perspectives, that's an unfortunate, inefficient and hence expensive habit, as 4 to 5-year-olds have markedly less-effective learning skills than, e.g., Finnish and Norwegian Grade 1 beginning readers aged 7 to 8 years. And, alas, it's also much harder to overcome difficulties than prevent them, thus our widespread Standard-English literacy difficulties create considerable workload pressure, and time pressure, in Anglosphere schools.

You might think it's just the English readers' young age that's causing their slow progress, however, as you'll see in studies we'll explore in Tour 2, orthographies are a much stronger factor than children being of young age.

While learning to read and spell at a young age has impacts, they're tiny relative to the impacts of orthographic complexity.

Standard-English Test Norms

Seymour et al. (2003) suggest it takes 2.5 to 3 times as long to learn to read English. They're likely referring just to fully-regular words, such as those their research used, however, as the suggestion doesn't match with other studies (e.g., Frith et al., 1998), or the age levels of norms for Anglophone word-reading tests: it takes far more than 2.5 to 3 times longer to be proficiently accurate for Standard English.

Most Standard-English word-reading tests have word-reading ages up to 12.5 to 13 years (Grade 7 or 8), on average. If we subtract from age 5.0 years when children start learning, that means it takes 7.5 to 8.0 years, on average to reach reasonably proficient accuracy in perhaps two thirds of children, with one third still appreciably low.

With spelling test norms often going to 15.0 years (Grade 10), at least 10 years seem needed for adult-level spelling proficiency.

That said, those test-norm upper ages are certainly not at ceiling level, and multiple Standard-English tests have word-reading and spelling ages up to adulthood, without marked ceiling effects. As an example, Torgesen et al.'s (2012) *Test of Word-Reading Efficiency-2* (TOWRE-2) has norms up to 25 years, and shows word-reading still improving appreciably across teenage years and young adulthood.

That shows word-reading taking as much as 20 years, and sadly, as we'll explore in Tour 13, even our high-schoolers with what we'd consider healthy word-reading, would quite likely be considerably less accurate than Grade 1 and 2 regular-orthography children.

Even using a conservative figure of 5 to 6 years (10 to 12 semesters) for English word-reading and spelling development, if most regular-orthography children have proficient, adult-level accuracy by mid-Grade-1 (1 semester), our word-reading and spelling test age-levels suggest it likely takes at least 10 times longer to learn to read and spell proficiently. It's clear that, by international standards, our word-reading and spelling is inordinately slow to develop.

Research is needed to establish the speed and range of children's word-reading accuracy skills across nations, in Anglophone nations, European regular-orthography nations, and Asian nations that use initial regular orthographies prior to their complex orthographies.

Importantly, comparative research needs to move from largely reporting just average achievement, to also reporting on weaker and stronger word-readers, e.g., considering thirds and tenths, plus the lowest and highest 5% and 2% of achievers.

Aro's Finnish Study

Finnish researcher Mikko Aro's (2004) studies of Finnish beginning readers show how fast regular-orthography word-reading develops.

He found Finnish children take four weeks to learn to read, and be accurate word-readers. He discusses word-reading and spelling developing at similarly rapid rates, and the children also developing strong phonemic-awareness skills across that brief 4-week period.

He discusses that Finnish progress in four weeks being akin to that of English readers having two years of classroom instruction. That's a massive time and workload difference.

One key finding of his studies was that, while the Finnish Grade 1 children might vary in their starting point, they all developed word-reading proficiency at a similar rate, in approximately four weeks:

The analysis revealed that in the development of reading and spelling accuracy, there was variation only in the [starting point] of accuracy (intercept), and not in [speed] of development (slope).

The Regular-Orthography "Aha!" Moment

When we visited him in 2005, Professor Aro explained that many Finnish people remember the specific moment that they learned to read. Teachers at a Kindergarten we visited confirmed this. Finnish children have an *Aha!* moment, a moment of enlightenment when they suddenly realise that they can now read and spell.

That *Aha* moment might well be the start of their 4-week rapid word-reading development, from fledgling to accurate word-reader.

We Australians discussed remembering this moment of wonder for learning to swim and ride a bike, but not learning to read. Recently, a teacher friend identified with this experience, when she used International Teaching Alphabet (ITA) in linguistics to read an ancient language translated into ITA. She'd had that feeling of wonder, still vividly remembering the text as suddenly transparent, popping open, such that she could then effortlessly read it, understand it, and *see* its morphemes and grammatical units.

This moment of wonder, which happens for regular-orthography readers, but not English readers, epitomises the ease and simplicity of regular-orthography word-reading and spelling development.

Considering this moment of wonder expedited our team's ride-a-bike vs drive-a-truck analogy (Galletly & Knight, 2013):

Research Tour 1. Too Slow Word-Reading and Spelling Development

- Learning to read and write a highly-regular orthography is incredibly easy, akin to learning to ride a bike on a smooth path in ideal circumstances.
- Learning to read and write Standard English is difficult and challenging, somewhat akin to learning to drive a truck off-road in ever-changing complex circumstances.

Using our ride-a-bike ease analogy, when starting, some regular-orthography children need the bike held a little bit longer, giving time to build letter-sound and sounding-out skills. However, once they take off, they progress with similarly rapid speed, such that four weeks later they've reached appreciably high accuracy.

In addition, conveniently for schools, while progress starts at different time-points, most children have mastered word-reading by Semester 1 of Grade 1. Meanwhile, using conservative estimates, our children take at least 10 times longer, and 5 to 6 years.

Regular-orthography word-reading development taking just 4 weeks, and most children having mastered word-reading by the end of 1 semester of Grade 1 instruction is extremely impressive. Wow!

Our Teachers' Higher Workload

Let's now take a teaching-eye view of these findings and their implications for teaching and learning in Anglophone nations.

Using our word-reading test norms, on average, our children take at least 5 to 6 years (200 to 240 school weeks) to master word-reading – whereas Finnish children take 4 weeks. That's a ratio of at least 200:4 to 240:4 school weeks: our children taking 50 to 60 times longer to develop reasonably accurate word-reading. It also hints at needs for 50 to 60 times more teaching and learning hours.

Importantly, whereas Finnish children make highly homogenous progress that takes only 4 weeks, Standard-English readers have widely different rates of word-reading development, and teachers must deal with a wide range of word-reading and writing skills.

It's homogeneity vs heterogeneity. From Grade 2, Finnish teachers teach to classes where children have highly similar skill levels, with virtually all being proficiently accurate, confident, self-teaching, independent readers and writers.

While their Grade 2 children are not as fluent and fast at reading as Grade 4 children, they have very high word-reading and spelling accuracy. They've also strong, confident self-teaching skills, with relatively little need for help.

Meanwhile, our teachers must work with major heterogeneity, and children having very different instructional needs. This creates a wide crosslinguistic gap in workload and curriculum pressure.

Collaborative research that our CQU team conducted with teachers and schools in our local area showed a very wide range of word-reading levels, with many children below age-level (Knight & Galletly, 2006). Figure 5 shows the range of word-reading ages.

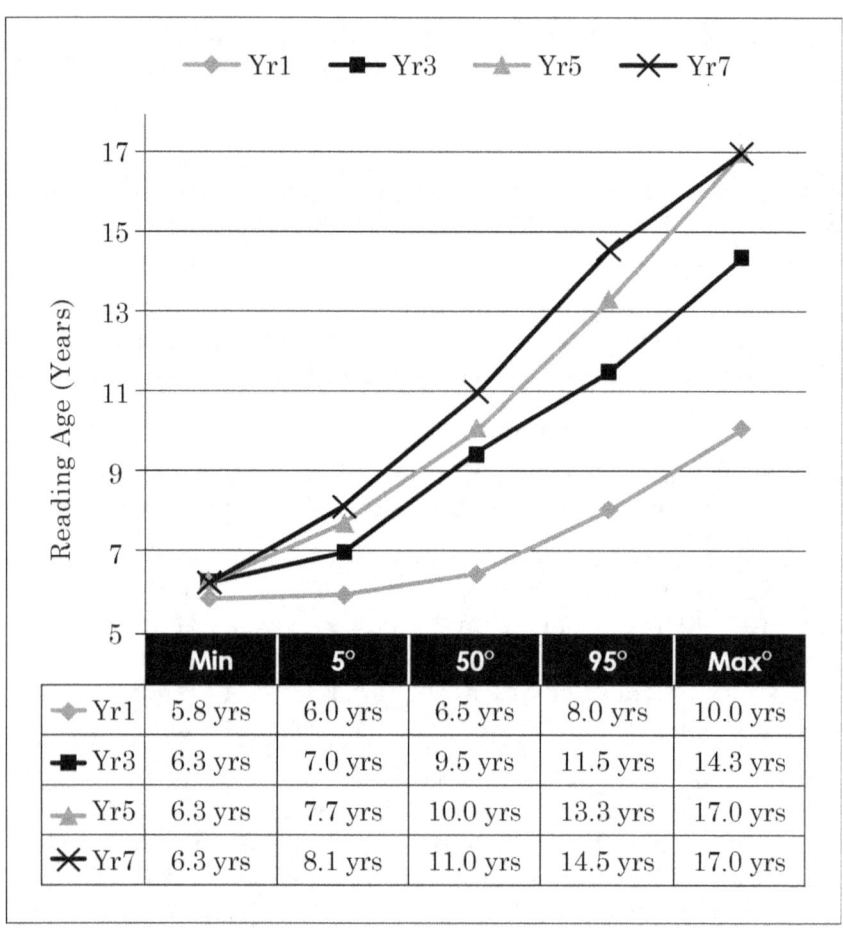

Figure 5. Queensland word-reading age-levels in Years 1, 3, 5 and 7 (Knight & Galletly, 2006; Knight et al., 2017a)

The graph shows the ranges of word-reading ages for a Queensland cohort of 1200 children assessed using the Test of Word Reading Efficiency (TOWRE; Torgesen et al., 1999).

In Year 1, there is a skill range of 4.2 years. This expands to 8.0 years in Year 3, then widens further, to be 11.7 years in Years 5 and 7. The figure shows our best word-readers read extremely well, while, in every year-level, the lowest 30% are appreciably below their classmates, and the weakest 5% and 10% are severely struggling.

From Grade 2, Finnish teachers have a teaching environment conducive to effective teaching and learning, because, with strong literacy skills, children can be efficient, effective, independent readers, writers and learners. In contrast, our teachers of all school years must cater for a challengingly wide range of word-reading and spelling skills, with many children insufficiently skilled and needing considerable help.

Additionally, having such a wide range of rates of development, schools can't easily group children for remedial help. That's because some Year 5s' word-reading and spelling is at Year 1 level, while others are at Year 2 and 3 level, and children at those differing levels of proficiency have quite different remedial needs.

For many teachers, it is their weaker readers who are the challenge for differentiation of instruction. We'd benefit greatly by crosslinguistic studies comparing the range of word-reading and spelling accuracy levels in regular-orthography and Anglophone nations. They would be powerful in revealing the very major challenges teachers in Australia and Anglophone nations have in remediating and supporting weak word-readers, and how this is so much less an issue in regular-orthography nations.

Huang and Hanley's Taiwanese Study

Taiwan, Japan and China use 2-Stage early-literacy development:
- In Stage 1, they use regular orthographies for initial literacy learning, to enable rapid, easy early-literacy development, with easy learning and high levels of success.
- In Stage 2, their children, now confident readers and writers who've developed cognitive-processing and learning skills, transition to learning to read and write their complex morpho-logographic orthographies (Taylor & Taylor, 2014).

This stepped approach works extremely well: two orthographies work much better than one, when the end goal is mastering a complex orthography – as long as the first orthography is regular.

Anglophone nations already use 2-Stage learning: in handwriting. We first teach children to print, then later transition them to using cursive script (*running writing*). This keeps learning conceptually low, able to be managed confidently and competently by young children. This Stage-1 learning also builds needed key subskills and confidence, and these, in turn, scaffold the learning of Stage 2.

If Australia adopted 2-Stage early-literacy development for reading and writing, using a fully-regular beginners' orthography, children would read and write the beginners' orthography initially, and then transition to Standard English.

There's thus strong value in exploring the research of nations that currently use 2-Stage learning. Huang and Hanley's (1994, 1997) research and discussion of literacy development in Taiwanese children sheds useful light on this area. They discuss Taiwanese education using just 10 weeks of regular-orthography instruction before children begin transitioning to their complex orthography.

Taiwan may well prove a useful role model for Australian education in our deciding whether to use a beginners' orthography initially. While we're the world's biggest island, and they're a tiny one, we have similar population numbers. Conveniently, Taiwan is close by, has consistent literacy instruction across schools, and has many researchers interested in reading and literacy development.

Notably, international PIRLS and PISA studies show Taiwanese children to be strong readers, with healthy reading comprehension, and notably few low achievers.

Taiwan's fully-regular orthography, ZhuYin FuHao, is used first as a beginners' orthography, then it's used to transition children to reading and writing Hanzi. It's also called *BoPoMoPho*, the names of its alphabet's first four letters, just as we say *ABC*. When I presented seminars at Taiwanese universities, *ZhuYin FuHao* seemed unfamiliar, while *BoPoMoPho* was immediately recognised.

After children have learned to read and write it, schools use ZhuYin FuHao to support children's transitioning to reading and writing Hanzi, their highly complex morpho-logographic orthography, which has thousands of characters, each to be individually learned.

Huang and Hanley (1994, 1997) discuss it being usual Taiwanese educational practice for schools to hold off all instruction on reading and writing Hanzi characters in the first semester of Grade 1. During this time, they settle children into school, then do 10 weeks of teaching and learning fully-regular ZhuYin FuHao. This 10 weeks is all most children need to usefully master ZhuYin FuHao.

As Huang and Hanley (1997) explain,
> Before they are taught any characters in school, all Taiwanese children learn Zhuyin Fuhao, an alphabetic script similar to Pinyin, the alphabetic system used in mainland China.

> *In Zhuyin Fuhao, each phoneme is represented by a unique visual symbol (in Pinyin, the written symbols comprise letters from the Roman alphabet). There is a total of 37 symbols. Zhuyin Fuhao is taught during the first 10 weeks of the 1st grade in Taiwan. ... It is not permitted to teach any [Taiwanese] characters during [this time]. The only teaching material is a textbook [teaching] Zhuyin Fuhao. ...*
>
> *After 10 weeks, the children learn [Taiwanese Hanzi characters] via Zhuyin Fuhao. A representation of the pronunciation of the appropriate word written in Zhuyin Fuhao appears on the right side of the characters in primary school textbooks.*
>
> *Knowing Zhuyin Fuhao thus helps children to pronounce new characters ... without assistance from the teacher.*

Importantly, in transitioning, Hanzi characters are also written in ZhuYin FuHao in texts children read. This is a powerful support for learning Hanzi characters, as, if the character seems unfamiliar, the word is easily read in ZhuYin FuHao.

This simple, easy, and powerful strategy empowers statistical learning and expedites self-teaching as children read and learn Hanzi. In the same way, it expedites fluency, removing needs to pause to work out unfamiliar words. Through reducing the cognitive load of text reading, it also expedites comprehension. And, of course, it makes school life vastly easier, impressively reducing the teaching and learning time schools need, for children to be confident, fluent, independent readers, writers and learners.

That's a very important finding, that Stage 1 can be as short as 10 weeks before children transition. While we'd not rush, it means that, if we trialled 2-stage early-literacy, most children might need only a term or semester of solely reading and writing the beginners' orthography that we use, before beginning on Standard English.

Huang and Hanley's studies focused on reading development of Hanzi characters, not ZhuYin FuHao, and because of this, they did not assess the children's ZhuYin FuHao progress. They did, however, assess their phonemic awareness, both prior to and immediately after their 10 weeks of learning to read and write ZhuYin FuHao.

Importantly, just as Aro (2004) found, Huang and Hanley found very strong phonemic-awareness development in the 10-week period, from being minimal, to now being quite proficient. This strong phonemic awareness would now support their learning of complex Hanzi.

Further, given that phonemic awareness was the only cognitive-processing skill tested, the children quite likely also developed other cognitive-processing and executive-function skills that weren't tested (e.g., see Papadopoulos, 2001).

Our brains change as we learn, and, most certainly, in that brief 10-week period, very impressive cognitive strengthening took place:

- Impressive orthographic development: the children could now read and write ZhuYin FuHao texts effectively, and were ready to start learning to read and write Hanzi characters.
- Impressive cognitive-processing development: they had impressive phonemic-awareness development, and quite likely development of other cognitive-processing skills.
- Impressive development of self-teaching: they mastered self-teaching as they learned to read ZhuYin FuHao, reading words very slowly initially, then with increasing fluency.
- Impressive use of self-teaching: they used self-teaching to both
    o Learn to read and write Hanzi characters, and
    o Read texts with words in both Hanzi and ZhuYin FuHao.
- Impressive development of independence: the children were so quickly independent readers, writers, learners and self-teachers steadily building increasing confidence, fluency and skills.

And all that in a 10-week period!

That highly successful early-literacy development highlights a key implication: children who need to master a highly complex orthography such as Hanzi or Standard English make far stronger word-reading and literacy progress by learning two orthographies, when the first is fully regular, than if learning just the complex orthography. Studies we tour later show that's very much the case.

Our children too could experience rapid development of orthographic awareness, phonemic awareness, self-teaching, reading and writing, and be independent readers, writers and learners, if we too used a fully-regular beginners' orthography, prior to Standard English.

Wouldn't our teachers and schools just love to be teaching to classes where all children had proficiently mastered word-reading and writing accuracy within a few months, with children taking off at different times, but only taking approximately 4 to 10 weeks from start to finish, with virtually all children being confident highly-accurate readers and writers from Year 2.

That would mean teachers from mid-primary school wouldn't have our many struggling word-readers and spellers, and early-years teachers would have far more time to enrich literacy and learning.

We too could achieve that rapid, easy, homogenous early-literacy development, if we used a fully-regular beginners' orthography.

The Developmental Trio: Phonemic Awareness, Word-Reading & Spelling

Word-reading, spelling and phonemic awareness develop together and support each other's development.

Phonemic-awareness development is extremely slow in children learning to read highly complex orthographies including Standard English (Hanley et al., 2004) and Thai (Vibulpatanavong & Evans, 2019; Winskel & Iemwanthong, 2010).

For monolingual children, there are relatively few alphabetic orthographies more complex than Standard English. Thai is one of them, and studies show phonemic awareness is notably slow to develop in Thai children, just as word-reading and spelling are.

Aro's (2004) Finnish children and Huang and Hanley's (1997) Taiwanese children's rapid phonemic-awareness development took only 4 to 10 weeks, the same brief time it took to build proficiently accurate word-reading, spelling and writing.

That's meteorically fast relative to English readers' phonemic-awareness development, which is very slow to automise (Hanley et al., 2004). It's appallingly slow, really. English spelling drags us down across literacy development and education, and too slow phonemic-awareness development likely plays a big role in this.

As we'll see in exploring other studies (e.g., Papadopoulos, 2001), regular-orthography children develop diverse cognitive-processing and executive-function skills in word-reading development.

It's likely that Aro's (2004) Finnish children and Huang and Hanley's (1997) Taiwanese children would have developed efficient skills in other cognitive-processing areas that weren't assessed, including executive-function skills.

While research is needed to further explore this area, we might well consider phonemic awareness a proxy for cognitive-processing and executive-function skills whose development is similarly stimulated within word-reading and spelling development.

Studies show early phonological-awareness skills, syllable and rhyme skills, develop universally at approximately the same age across most nations, syllable awareness at about age 3 to 4 years, and rhyme awareness at about age 4 to 5 years (Goswami, 2002).

In contrast, phonemic-awareness skills (ability to think about and manipulate the individual sounds of syllables and words) don't develop universally at the same age. Instead, phonemic-awareness development is time-limited in multiple ways.

It's constrained by when children start to learn to read, with children who start reading older being later to start developing phonemic awareness (Goswami, 2002; Ziegler & Goswami, 2005).

Importantly, the time it takes to reach proficiency is also limited, by children's speed and rate of word-reading and spelling development (M. Aro, 2004; Hanley et al., 2004; Huang & Hanley, 1997; Spencer & Hanley, 2003, 2004).

It seems children don't become proficient at phonemic awareness until they're proficient at word-reading and spelling. That's bad news for us, because strong phonemic awareness would be a great help for our children learning to read and write Standard English.

Importantly, studies show lack of development of phonemic awareness in those who haven't learned to read:
- Children in different nations develop phonemic awareness at different ages – depending on the age they learn to read (Goswami, 2002).
- Portuguese adults, illiterate due to low education, had significantly weak phonemic-awareness skills relative to similar adults who'd learned to read (Morais et al., 1979).
- Chinese readers of alphabetic Pinyin, showed healthy phonemic awareness, while readers who'd only learned logographic characters (i.e., no alphabetic reading), had very weak skills (Read et al., 1986; Wagner & Torgesen, 1987).

Five-year-old Anglophone children start to develop phonemic-awareness skills far younger than European regular-orthography children because they start learning to read when much younger.

At first glance, that might seem a strong positive, but it's not, as the regular-orthography children soon overtake Standard-English children then very quickly soar past, leaving them far behind.

That's because regular-orthography children develop proficient phonemic awareness so quickly – as quickly as they develop accurate word-reading and spelling skills.

Sadly, Anglophone phonemic-awareness development can be very

Research Tour 1. Too Slow Word-Reading and Spelling Development

slow to emerge, particularly in struggling readers. Compared to regular-orthography children, it's tortoise-slow, plodding alongside our tortoise-slow years of word-reading and spelling development.

As you'll see in Welsh-English studies we'll explore in Tour 2, our children may well not achieve proficient phonemic awareness until they're quite skilled word-readers and spellers.

Sadder still, because our struggling learners are so slow to develop word-reading and spelling, many never achieve this needed phonemic awareness, or proficient word-reading and spelling: they join our Spelling Generations of struggling readers and writers.

Ironically, phonemic awareness isn't actually prerequisite for word-reading and spelling development of highly-regular orthographies – because children's learning is so easy. It's empowering to have healthy phonemic awareness, with faster word-reading progress, but weak phonemic awareness doesn't prevent successful development of word-reading and spelling (M. Aro, 2004, Cossu, 1999, Cossu et al., 1993; Huang & Hanley, 1997; Wimmer et al., 1991).

It's the opposite for Standard-English readers, alas, as having weak phonological and phonemic awareness virtually guarantees Standard-English word-reading and spelling struggles.

That's very frustrating: regular-orthography readers not needing strong phonemic awareness but having it in abundance, while our poor at-risk learners desperately need it, but are unable to acquire it.

Having strong phonemic awareness from earliest literacy would make an enormous difference for our at-risk word-readers and spellers, expediting their word-reading and spelling development.

It's a nasty Catch-22 situation, as word-reading, spelling and phonemic awareness are a developmental trio, developing together, and supporting each other's development (Goswami, 2002; Perfetti et al., 1987). While research is needed, the options seem to be rapid vs slow development of all three skills, as children aren't able to achieve strongly in one skill without high skills in its partners.

The reciprocity of word-reading, phonemic-awareness, and spelling development is now quite well-established, with the three strands building from each other, and in turn further building each other, e.g.,
- In children's Standard-English learning: Perfetti et al.'s (1987) longitudinal study testing USA children at multiple time-points across Grade 1 showed phonemic awareness enabling reading gains, and reading gains enabling phoneme awareness gains, with more complex phonemic-awareness

skills being the result of, and not the cause of, reading success.
- In regular-orthography children's learning: Silven et al. (2004) found Finnish children's strong growth in phonemic awareness should be considered a consequence of their word-reading development, and not a precursor.

We'd love our children to have quickly developed strong phonemic-awareness and cognitive-processing skills that regular-orthography children develop. We'd achieve that if we changed to 2-Stage learning, with children initially using a fully-regular beginners' orthography. They'd then have strong phonemic awareness early on, enhancing their subsequent progress with Standard English.

Exploring Phonemic Awareness in Cognitive Processing

Australia and the Anglosphere need research that builds deep knowledge of crosslinguistic differences in phonemic-awareness and cognitive-processing skills as word-reading and spelling develop.

We need both cross-sectional and longitudinal data, building knowledge on skill development in our children and regular-orthography children: both Asian dual-orthography children and European single-orthography children.

As part of that, we also need to compare word-reading and cognitive-processing of older struggling readers and younger healthy-progress, *developing readers* with word-reading and spelling at their levels.

I use the term *developing readers* for children making healthy-progress by our standards, and the term *struggling readers* for children experiencing difficulties. For Standard-English word-reading, older struggling readers quite often have word-reading levels similar to those of younger developing readers.

It's important research providing important knowledge for our schools, e.g., as to the impacts of our actioning Changes 8 and 9:
- Change 8. Investigate the potential of fully-regular beginners' orthographies: They're winners.
- Change 9. Play to learn first: Start Standard English word-reading instruction from mid-Year 2.

Slow Vs Rapid Spelling Development

Crosslinguistic studies of spelling development generally show regular-orthography spelling development to be rapid, but usually somewhat slower than word-reading development, with the gap being smallest for highest-regularity orthographies (Babayigit, 2022): *Findings raise questions about the notion of symmetrical transparency: spelling is less transparent and cognitively more demanding than reading even in orthographies considered highly transparent for both reading and spelling.*

Of course, even though it's slower than word-reading, regular-orthography spelling develops far more rapidly than Standard-English spelling.

Marinelli et al. (2015), studying English and Italian children's spelling acquisition across primary school to Grade 5, found the Italian children were highly accurate by end-Grade 2, while the English children were still weak spellers in Grade 5.

In like manner, Caravolas (2004) found Czech children's spelling to be well ahead of English children's, after 8 months of schooling.

With Finnish having highest orthographic regularity, word-reading and spelling both develop rapidly, hence Grade 1 children are soon proficient spellers (e.g., M. Aro, 2004).

Wimmer et al.'s (1991) study of Austrian Grade 1 children showed them to be highly accurate spellers of German by end-Grade-1, but with spelling not as strong as their extremely accurate word-reading. That's because German orthography doesn't have bidirectional regularity: it's highly-regular for word-reading, but somewhat less so for spelling, as multiple graphemes are used for some phonemes.

Cossu et al.'s (1995) study of Italian children similarly found mild but significant differences between rates of word-reading and spelling development, with differences still present in Grade 2, suggesting mild dissociation of word-reading and spelling development.

Babayagit (2022) found for highly regular Turkish, that while both are rapid, spelling lags word-reading development, and discusses spelling being more cognitively demanding than word-reading.

Torppa et al.'s (2017) study of approximately 2,000 Finnish children across Grades 1 to 4 found an interesting dissociation in tiny subgroups. While on the whole children with strong word-reading skills had strong spelling skills, and children with weaker word-reading skills had weaker spelling skills, one tiny group (1.8% of the cohort) had stronger spelling than word-reading, and another tiny group (2.1%) had stronger word-reading than spelling. Only 6.9% had weak word-reading or spelling, with 3.0% having both.

Protopapas et al. (2013) showed spelling for dyslexic and healthy-progress regular-orthography spellers, to be largely a continuum, with dyslexic Greek children in Grades 3, 4 and 7 making more errors than their healthy-progress peers, but with the errors being of the same types, and in comparable relative proportions. This is in keeping with other studies of Greek healthy-progress and dyslexic readers (Diamanti et al., 2018).

Differing Phonological-Awareness and RAN Impacts

Interestingly, in nations where word-reading is fully regular and spelling is less so, while phonological awareness isn't strongly related to the fully-regular skill, it's needed for the less-regular skill.

That's seen in German readers with weak phonemic-awareness skills having highly accurate word-reading but significantly weak spelling (Galletly, 2005b; Wimmer & Mayringer, 2002). Of course, *weak* German spelling is brilliant by our standards.

Another key crosslinguistic difference is how weak Rapid Automised Naming (RAN) and phonological awareness have different impacts across nations, due to differences in orthographic complexity.

For Anglophone children, both phonological-awareness weakness and RAN weakness lead to spelling and word-reading accuracy difficulties, and those with a *Double Deficit*, being weak in both areas, develop far more severe difficulties.

In contrast, for regular orthographies, RAN is strongly associated with reading fluency, but not accuracy (Landerl et al., 2019; Moll et al., 2014; Papadopoulos et al., 2018; Papadopoulos, Spanoudis et al., 2021).

Regular-orthography children weak on RAN have slower dysfluent word-reading and writing, with considerable hesitations as they slowly read and write words – but they're nonetheless highly accurate word-readers and spellers.

Importantly, RAN weakness and its associated fluency weakness have proved very difficult to overcome in regular-orthography children (Hintikka et al., 2008; Huemer et al., 2008, 2010; Landerl & Wimmer, 2008; Thaler et al., 2004).

As with word-reading development, it's mostly only phonological awareness and RAN that have been studied in relation to spelling development.

In future research towards improving early-literacy development, we'd benefit by also researching development and impacts of other cognitive-processing and executive-function skills.

Regular-Orthography Struggles With Learning to Spell Irregular Words

Let's now look at two important findings with strong implications for Australian spelling development, both now and if, in the future, we adopt a beginners' orthography.

Like German, Italian has a small number of words with ambiguous spelling, i.e., words that are less regular, because multiple graphemes are used for a few phonemes. Having so few irregular words, one might expect their children would soon master those spellings. Not so, it seems, and it seems Standard-English readers may have a particular strength for learning irregular spellings.

Irregular Spellings Are Hard to Learn

Notarnicola and colleagues' (2012) interesting study of Italian children's spelling skills across Grades 1 to 8 showed the children very soon mastered regular words, with 90% accuracy in Grade 1 and full accuracy by Grade 4.

In contrast, the children showed vastly slower spelling development for their relatively few ambiguous spelling words, e.g., words using *qu, cu, cqu*, which say the same sound. They had only 65% accuracy for these words in Grade 1, only 85% accuracy in Grade 5, and the words still weren't at ceiling level in Grade 8 with the children having only 90% accuracy. This suggests that even adult Italian readers would likely make errors on some of these words.

The study showed statistical learning was reduced for these more complex Italian words, despite them being relatively few.

Unfortunately, this is another study where only data on average achievement is shown. That alas reduces it to the role of useful preliminary research, as further studies are needed. There was quite likely a range of Italian spelling ability, from some children who quickly mastered spelling of those irregular words, through to children with major difficulties, and we can't tell if, e.g., most children were soon highly accurate but with some weak spellers scoring particularly low. We need, and will benefit by, future research comparing weaker and stronger spellers across nations.

Now, Italian has only a small number of words with ambiguous spelling, so difficulties spelling these words would likely have quite negligible impact in slowing children's independent writing. However, in contrast, Standard English has many thousands of irregular words with ambiguous spelling, and most words can be written multiple ways: *Ostrailya, Australya, Astraylea, Ustrallier.*

Notarnicola et al.'s study therefore has implications for us that are well worth considering.

One, given Italian children had slow spelling development for their few ambiguous spelling words, it's no surprise Standard-English spelling development is so slow, given that irregular words abound.

Two, because we've myriads of less-regular words children are often uncertain of, to encourage rich vocabulary and reduce cognitive load, we need to encourage spelling approximations in first draft writing across primary and high school, with our children focused on the craft of writing, rather than troubled by irregular words, whether to double consonants and our many schwa options, e.g., dep_pend_/dep_end_, min_or_, min_er_, vir_us_. This can heighten creativity, vocabulary and maturity of content and wording, as children think on wording and ideas, instead of so often pausing to ponder spelling.

A third point, this study suggests likelihood that even if we used a fully-regular beginners' orthography and 2-Stage learning, some, and perhaps many, children would nonetheless have difficulties spelling many less-frequent, highly-irregular words.

This implies value in investigating the extent to which multi-stage transitioning would be useful in increasing our children's Standard-English spelling proficiency, e.g., using Fleksispel's transitioning stages might strategically progress spelling (Galletly, 2023a).

Quite likely, the difficulties our children might experience after transitioning would be minimal for reading and more major for spelling. That's because context clues in meaningful texts strongly support reading of unfamiliar words but not spelling them.

It's also because we don't need as many grapheme cues to do effective word-reading. We can read words with quite a few letters missing, mixed or in error, but to spell a word correctly, we must not only know every letter, but also its precise position: while it's easy to read *A_str_l_a*, spelling it is a challenge for many.

If and when Australia uses 2-Stage early-literacy learning, with a beginners' orthography then transitioning, it's highly likely we'll continue to encourage spelling approximations in first-draft writing, while children are transitioning to using Standard English.

Our Children's Strength for Learning Irregular Spellings

While more research is needed, findings from another study, this time of Italian and English readers (Marinelli et al., 2020), suggest hope, as our plethora of irregularly spelled syllables and words may build stronger skills for learning irregular spellings.

Marinelli and colleagues compared English and Italian children in Grades 2 to 5 on their ability to learn to spell new words. They used pseudowords, not real words, to ensure the spellings were completely unfamiliar and new (Strategically chosen pseudowords are well established as being valid and reliable for testing of reading of unfamiliar words). Results showed the English children learned new words far more quickly and efficiently than the Italian children did, with this being the case for both younger and older children.

They conclude that children learning to read a highly irregular orthography are more able to learn new irregular words, which is very good news for us. That said, again, only average achievement was reported, with no comparison of proficient vs weaker learners, with needs for further studies of this area.

Marinelli et al., also found that the English and Italian children relied on different cognitive-processing skills:
- Visual-spatial memory and phonological awareness contributed to all children's writing.
- Phonological short-term memory contributed more strongly to the Italian children's writing (perhaps due to them sounding-out, given that almost all words and syllables are regular).
- Visual attentional capacity contributed more to the English children's writing (perhaps due to focusing on letter units and letter position, as so many words and syllables are irregular).

Confirmatory Supporting Evidence

The results of the studies we've explored so far are in keeping with other findings, e.g.,
- Word-reading developing very quickly to proficiency in Grade 1 for Greek children, with letter knowledge (e.g., perhaps knowing 80% of letter-sounds) stimulating word-reading development (Sarris, 2022).
- GPC consistency for letter-sounds being only 0.72 for English but at high levels for regular-orthographies, e.g., at approximately 0.92 for Czech and Slovak (Caravolas, 2018).
- In later primary school, German and Welsh children being far ahead of English children for reading of unfamiliar words (Frith et al., 1998; Hanley et al., 2004).
- (Highest-regularity) Albanian children's word-reading being ahead of (highly-regular) Welsh children's, with theirs, in turn, being well ahead of English children's (Ellis & Hooper, 2001; Hoxhallari et al., 2004).

- (Highest-regularity) Slovakian children's word-reading being ahead of (highly-regular) Czech children's, with theirs, in turn, being well ahead of English children's (Caravolas, 2018).
- Terms used for Finnish readers (Holopainen et al., 2001) being
  o Precocious: reading well at start of Grade 1 (now approximately 50% of children, Lyytinen et al., 2021).
  o Early: reading well within 4-months.
  o Average: reading well within 9-months.
  o Delayed: not reading well within 18-months.
- Usual school practice in Finnish and German schools consisting of brief Grade 1 systematic word-reading instruction, then speed and fluency built through engaging in authentic reading (M. Aro, 2017a; Wimmer & Mayringer, 2002).
- Word-reading accuracy tests not being used in highest-regularity orthography nations from Grade 2 on, e.g., Finland, Germany and Austria, because children are soon proficiently accurate, with very few word-reading errors being the norm.
- Word-reading efficiency, i.e., speed, being tested instead of accuracy (Lyytinen, Aro et al., 2006; Wimmer et al., 1999), due to approximately 4% of regular-orthography children reading at slower speed (e.g., Wimmer et al., 1999):
  Poor reading speed and an absence of serious reading accuracy problems is quite typical for German children with dyslexia from Grade 2 onward.
- Word-reading fluency takes several years to develop in regular-orthography children, e.g., Furnes et al. (2019), comparing regular-orthography (Norwegian and Swedish) and Standard-English (US and Australian) Grade 2 readers on spelling and reading efficiency (speed of correct word-reading, using the TOWRE *Sight Word Efficiency* test) found the regular-orthography children far ahead in spelling, but to be not yet reading as efficiently as the English readers, who had had several years more reading instruction.
- Finnish researchers using a criterion for word-reading accuracy difficulties of children having less than 90% accuracy on long multisyllabic pseudowords (Lyytinen, Aro et al., 2006):
  We emphasize that although the process of acquiring fluent reading in Finnish can be relatively effortless, a substantial number of children still face problems in learning to master reading completely. Roughly 6% cent of children do not achieve accurate reading skill (at least 90% accuracy in reading pseudo-words) despite 3 or 4 years of schooling, and 4% are still relatively slow in reading. Thus, approximately 8% (due to the overlap of these two groups) of Finnish children still face

reading problems by the time they should be fluent and accurate readers.

Oh dear! As you'll see in later tours, many, if not most, upper-primary and high-school Standard-English children would show severe word-reading accuracy difficulties, using that 90% criterion, whereas it was only 6% of Finnish children.
- Very large numbers of Australian teenagers and adults have insufficient literacy skills, e.g., approximately 40% achieve below the international standard for healthy literacy in PISA and the *Programme for the International Assessment of Adult Competencies* (Australian Bureau of Statistics, 2013).
- Leading regular-orthography nations show impressive teenage and adult literacy levels, e.g., Australian teenagers' literacy levels in PISA 2018 were 1.5 years below regular-orthography nation China, the leading nation (Thomson et al., 2019).

Our CQU research team has explored orthographic complexity issues extensively down the years, in peer-reviewed publications:
- *The high cost of orthographic disadvantage* (Galletly & Knight, 2004).
- *Differential disadvantage of Anglophone weak readers due to English orthographic complexity and cognitive processing weakness* (Galletly & Knight, 2011a).
- *Transition from Early to Sophisticated Literacy (TESL) as a factor in cross-national achievement differences* (Galletly & Knight, 2011b).
- *Because trucks aren't bicycles: Orthographic complexity as a disregarded variable in reading research* (Galletly & Knight, 2013).
- *Managing cognitive load as the key to literacy development: research directions suggested by crosslinguistic research and research on Initial Teaching Alphabet* (i.t.a., Knight et al., 2017a).
- *Effective literacy instruction for all students: A time for change* (Knight & Galletly, 2017).
- *Orthographic Advantage Theory: National advantage and disadvantage due to orthographic differences* (Knight et al., 2019).
- Practical school-level implications of cognitive processing and cognitive load (Knight & Galletly, 2020).
- *The Literacy Component Model: A pragmatic universal paradigm* (Knight et al., 2021).

In our theorising, we've developed multiple models, which are tools for considering different aspects of crosslinguistic differences due to orthographic complexity. They include models of orthographic advantage and disadvantage, *Orthographic Advantage Theory*, *Differential Disadvantage, Transition from Early to Sophisticated*

Literacy (TESL), and the *Literacy Component Model* (Galletly & Knight 2011a, 2011b, Knight et al., 2017a, 2017b, 2019, 2021).

Transition from Early to Sophisticated Literacy (TESL)

The *Transition from Early to Sophisticated Literacy* (TESL) model is particularly useful for considering crosslinguistic differences including school differences in ease of learning, and needs for teaching and learning hours. As can be seen in the figure depicting the TESL model, the features of children's transitioning from Early to Sophisticated Literacy, is a key factor in orthographic advantage and disadvantage, creating the wide crosslinguistic divide between Anglophone and regular-orthography nations (Galletly & Knight, 2011b; Knight & Galletly, 2020; Knight et al., 2017a, 2019).

The upper and lower diagrams show Standard-English and regular-orthography literacy development respectively.

The model emphasises two key aspects of literacy:
- *Continuing Literacy*: literacy across the lifespan.
- *Core Literacy*: when children learn to read, write and spell (Galletly, 2002).

It uses three stages of literacy development, prior to, during, and subsequent to, children learning to read and write:
- *Home Literacy*: literacy development prior to formal instruction, including being read to, writing one's name, and discussing letters, words and favourite books.
- *Early Literacy*: literacy development during early-years word-reading and writing instruction and Core Literacy, when children are being taught to read and write words.
- *Sophisticated Literacy*: subsequent literacy development, with children now having strong word-reading and spelling skills, and being largely independent at reading and writing.

The TESL line is the thick black line with double-ended arrows across it: it shows the efficiency and time duration of children's Transition from Early to Sophisticated Literacy (TESL).

Anglophone and regular-orthography nations contrast markedly on Core Literacy, the TESL line and Sophisticated Literacy.

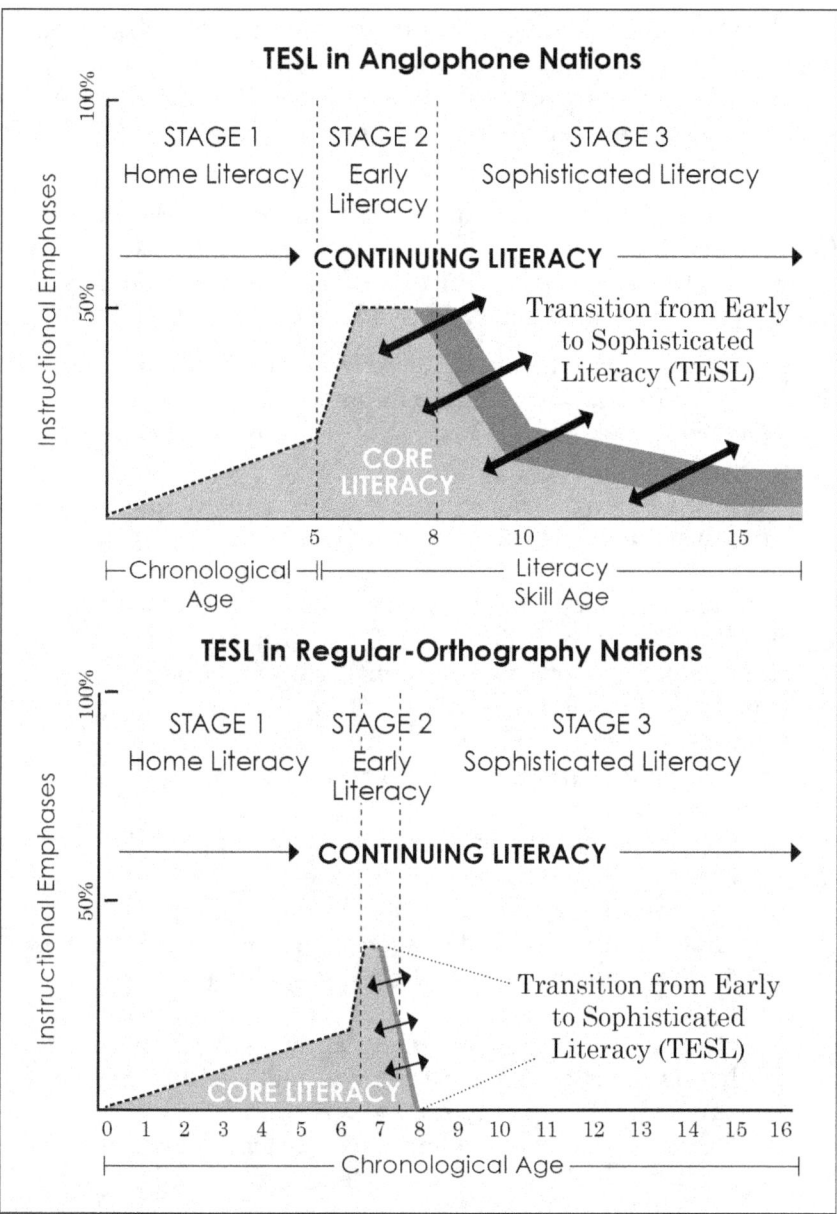

Figure 6. *Transition from Early to Sophisticated Literacy (TESL) for Standard-English and regular-orthography readers (Galletly & Knight, 2011b, Knight et al., 2017a, 2019)*

The time pressure of our schools is evident when one considers
- How large Standard-English Core Literacy is, and how, in consequence, this reduces time for Continuing Literacy.

- How long and wide our TESL line is, showing slow, drawn-out transitioning from Early Literacy to Sophisticated Literacy.
- How the Standard-English Sophisticated Literacy phase is complicated in major ways by so many children still not being proficient readers and writers.

Regular-orthography Core Literacy is delightfully brief, enabling Continuing Literacy to be ongoing, with little interruption. Its tiny size also indicates the low cognitive load children experience across Early Literacy, and low teaching and learning hours needed.

The regular-orthography short, relatively vertical TESL line, with Sophisticated Literacy being clear of Core Literacy intimates
- How virtually all regular-orthography children transition rapidly to Sophisticated Literacy.
- Impressively strong homogeneity, with transitioning happening in a very short space of time, that contrasts strongly with Standard-English heterogeneity.
- How soon children are independent readers and writers.
- How little they need adult help for reading and writing, being strong self-teachers and confident learners.
- How low cognitive load is across Early and Sophisticated Literacy, because word-reading and spelling are so easy.
- Teaching implications of rapid TESL and strong homogeneity:
  o It being so easy to teach word-reading and spelling, with mastery for virtually all, in Grade 1.
  o It being so easy to teach subject-area content when virtually all have proficient reading and writing, and so few have weak word-reading and spelling.
  o How effectively subject-area learning can be achieved.
  o How time-rich regular-orthography nations are, given so little time spent on word-reading and spelling, and supporting weak readers and writers.
  o How education can be improved far more easily, e.g., as shown in PIRLS and PISA, when virtually all children are confident, independent readers, writers and learners from early primary school.

These strong positives are also indicated by the ages used on the bottom axis of the TESL diagrams. The Standard-English figure uses word-reading ages, as children have diverse word-reading levels. In contrast, in the regular-orthography figure, chronological age can be used, as children master word-reading largely homogenously, with little need for word-reading ages. The ages of Finnish and Estonian children have been used: virtually all their children are confident, independent readers, writers and learners in Grade 2, at approximately 8 years.

Using the TESL model, nations are categorised as three TESL types: *Rapid*, *Facilitated* and *Complex*:

- *Rapid-TESL nations*, e.g., Finland, Estonia and South Korea, use single highly-regular orthographies, with fastest, easiest early-literacy development, and potential for strongest orthographic advantage.
- *Facilitated-TESL nations*, e.g., Taiwan, Japan and China, with 2-stage early literacy first use a fully-regular beginners' orthography for Core Literacy then later transition children to their complex orthography as part of Sophisticated Literacy learning. With learning eased and speeded, they too have potential for strong orthographic advantage.
- *Complex-TESL nations*, e.g., Australia, other Anglophone nations, and Thailand, use sole, highly-complex orthographies that creates extremely high cognitive load across literacy development, resulting in slowed early-literacy development, many children becoming struggling readers, and schools experiencing major time and workload pressure. They're guaranteed severe orthographic disadvantage.

The Transition from Early to Sophisticated Literacy (TESL) model suggests many areas of research, where Australia can build valuable research knowledge, towards 10 Changes improvements.

Our Research Needs

In recent decades in crosslinguistic research, there has been very strong research emphasis on word-reading and phonemic awareness, and more recently Rapid Automised Naming (RAN). In contrast, few recent crosslinguistic studies have assessed other aspects of literacy.

In many ways the 1960s ITA research studied literacy much more broadly and in far more detail than modern crosslinguistic research. Unfortunately, Swiss-cheese currently abounds in the research of recent decades for literacy skills beyond word-reading.

We need and will benefit by Australian education engaging in multi-nation research similar to Seymour et al.'s (2003) COST-A8 study, exploring word-reading and literacy skills, including reading of meaningful texts, fluency, reading comprehension, spelling, written expression, vocabulary, ideation and later language skills for writing, plus cognitive-processing and executive-function skills.

We'd also study factors suggested by the TESL model, above, e.g.,
- Timing and duration of Early and Core Literacy, and of transitioning from Early to Sophisticated Literacy (TESL).
- Levels of time pressure and teaching and learning complexity due to complicated, impeded statistical learning.
- Complexities of subject-area teaching when many children lack reading and writing proficiency.

It's disappointing that extensive research on wider aspects of literacy is lacking, particularly as it would be very easy to do multi-nation studies of spelling and written expression. We might compare spelling of a list of common vocabulary, or perhaps study writing samples on a set topic.

When visiting schools and researchers in different nations, I've informally done a writing-sample exercise, with Australian, Ugandan and Estonian children writing for 10 minutes, on the topic, *What I like about school* (Galletly, In press). What quickly became evident, in comparing our children's work with that of children in Uganda, where children have high multilingualism, and Estonia, with its fully-regular orthography, is that there's vastly less difference between their upper and lower achievers as regards text length and content, whereas our children spread out hugely – as our *long sad tail* of low achievers (Galletly, 2022a).

In future research, we'll likely find that, by international standards, our lower third of word-readers and spellers, and even our lower two thirds, will be very weak readers, spellers and writers – quite likely weaker than regular-orthography lowest-tenth achievers.

We need both cross-sectional studies comparing literacy skills and subskills of weaker and stronger readers in all year-levels, and longitudinal studies that follow cohorts over many years.

This research would be valuable and quite easily achieved, in our commitment to Change 10: *Build needed research knowledge as quickly as possible: Use collaborative school-based research.*

Key Findings from Tour 1

Findings and implications of studies explored in Tour 1 suggest the following points are useful considerations towards improving literacy and education in Australia and Anglophone nations:
1. Regular-orthography word-reading development is extremely fast, often complete in less than a semester, sometimes taking only 4 to 10 weeks.

2. Regular-orthography spelling often develops slightly more slowly than word-reading, but is nonetheless very rapid.
3. We can infer that Australian children would similarly master a highly-regular beginners' orthography very quickly.
4. Standard-English test norms show that, on average, word-reading development takes at least 6 years and up to 19 years, with spelling development taking longer.
5. They also show we've many struggling readers and writers who take much longer, and don't achieve adult proficiency.
6. Comparing Standard-English test norms with regular-orthography studies of word-reading suggest likelihood that
   a. Standard-English word-reading and spelling develop extremely slowly, quite likely at least 10 times more slowly than children using highly-regular orthographies.
   b. Whereas virtually all regular-orthography children master word-reading and spelling to adult level in early primary school, many Australians never reach this level.
7. Regular-orthography children are often slow to master spelling of less regular words, and sometimes take many years to master them, despite these words being few in number. This may be partly because irregular words are so few, such that children don't develop effective strategies for learning their spelling.
8. Standard-English children have been shown to be faster at learning new irregular spellings than regular-orthography children, probably because so many English words have less regular spelling and multiple spelling options.
9. Regular-orthography children being slow to master spelling of ambiguously spelt words suggests the likelihood that if we used a fully-regular beginners' orthography initially, some of our children may well be slow to master Standard-English spelling of less-frequent highly-irregular words.
10. Regular-orthography children develop proficient phonemic awareness very quickly, within the brief time it takes to master word-reading, e.g., in 4 weeks for Finnish children, and within 10 weeks of instruction for Taiwanese children.
11. It's likely Australian children would similarly build strong phonemic awareness quickly, if they learned to read and write initially using a fully-regular beginners' orthography. Strong phonemic awareness and associated accompanying skills would then expedite our children's subsequent learning of reading and writing Standard English.
12. It's likely there are strong cognitive-processing advantages to learning to read a regular-orthography. To date, this is strongly evident in regular-orthography children's impressive phonemic-

awareness development.
13. Studies have focused largely on phonemic awareness and Rapid Automised Naming (RAN), rather than other cognitive-processing and executive-function skills.
14. When considering research findings, it's possible phonemic awareness might be considered a proxy for a range of cognitive-processing and executive-function skills: phonemic awareness is often the only cognitive-processing skill tested, however studies show regular-orthography children have rapid development of other cognitive-processing skills.
15. Studies to date largely report mean (average) achievement, without discussion of higher and lower achievers. They also largely focus only on word-reading, with little attention to other literacy and language skills.
16. There is value in Australia engaging in crosslinguistic research on many areas of literacy and language-skills development:
    a. Going beyond word-reading, spelling, phonemic awareness and RAN to also assessing reading of meaningful texts, fluency, reading comprehension, spelling, cognitive-processing, receptive and expressive vocabulary, other language skills, and text writing.
    b. Going beyond mean achievement to carefully considering development of upper, middle and lower-third achievers, perhaps also reporting results for deciles (10% groups) plus our lowest and highest 5% and 2% of achievers.
17. The Transition from Early to Sophisticated Literacy (TESL) model (Galletly & Knight, 2011b; Knight et al., 2017a; Knight & Galletly, 2020) is a useful tool for understanding the impacts of orthographic complexity, and wide crosslinguistic differences between Australia and regular-orthography nations. It highlights many areas of useful research, e.g.,
    a. Timing and duration of Early and Core Literacy.
    b. Timing of transitioning to Sophisticated Literacy.
    c. Time pressure, and complexity of teaching and learning.
    d. Difficulty of subject-area teaching due to heterogeneity and slow speed of word-reading and spelling development.
18. Towards trialling regular orthographies, we need research exploring cognitive-processing development in 2-Stage early-literacy in Taiwan, Japan and China, studying development of phonemic and orthographic awareness, and executive-function skills, as children first read and write their fully-regular beginners' orthography, developing self-teaching, independence and self-confidence, then transition to their complex orthography.

Research Tour 2.
Orthography Is the Key Factor

Cross-linguistic studies have shown that students learning to read in a writing system with unreliable and complex GPC rules, such as English, acquire fundamental reading skills more slowly than typical development in more regular orthographies (e.g., Seymour et al., 2003). This finding has been very consistent, as there has been no cross-language comparison on early word-level reading that provided different findings.

Timothy Papadopoulos, Valéria Csépe, Mikko Aro, Marketa Caravolas, Irene-Anna Diakidoy & Thierry Olive, 2021

While young age certainly reduces learning effectiveness, multiple studies show orthographic complexity has far more major impacts. In this tour, we'll visit studies exploring this area.

Studies in Bilingual Schools

Studies of children in bilingual schools simultaneously learning to read Standard English and a highly-regular orthography provide useful insights into age vs orthography impacts.

Geva and Siegel (2000) studied native English-speaking Canadian children in a Hebrew bilingual school who were learning to read and write Hebrew (a highly-regular orthography) while they were learning to speak and understand it as a second language, at the same time that they were learning to read and write English.

The study showed that although the children's Hebrew verbal skills were very limited, their Grade 1 Hebrew word-reading was very impressive, being well in excess of not just their Grade 1 English word-reading, but also Grade 5 English word-reading:

When the script is less complex young children appear to develop their word recognition skills with relative ease, even in the absence of sufficient linguistic proficiency.

It would be useful to replicate and extend this study in Australian bilingual schools, monitoring development of children's word-reading, spelling, and independent reading and writing of both the orthographies being learned, along with development of children's cognitive-processing, executive-function and language skills.

Importantly, Australia has many indigenous languages that Australians read and write, and virtually all use highly-regular orthographies (D. Moore, 2018). Many isolated Aboriginal communities have bilingual schools where children read and write Standard English plus the highly regular orthography of their first language.

While the current practice in those community schools seems to be for children to learn to read English first, with their regular-orthography introduced later, it may be the case that some schools use the reverse order (first mastering the regular-orthography, then learning to read and write Standard English), or might be prepared to trial it. Certainly, considerable research establishes the reverse order, with children initially learning to read and write their regular-orthography, as producing far more powerful learning (Frith et al., 1998; Knight et al., 2017a; Seymour et al., 2003).

Learning to read and write one's Aboriginal first-language regular-orthography initially would have definite cognitive-processing benefits, and would expedite children's subsequent transitioning to reading and writing Standard English. It would also be a powerful tool enhancing children's second-language learning of English.

Australia also has other bilingual schools where children learn to read both a regular-orthography and Standard English. These regular orthographies vary in orthographic complexity, e.g., they include

- Extremely regular Greek and Italian.
- Extremely regular Hebrew, which changes in mid-primary school, to being somewhat less regular, when children move from fully-regular pointed Hebrew to unpointed Hebrew, which omits considerable orthographic information.
- Moderately regular German, which is fully regular for reading but less so for spelling.
- Somewhat regular French and Danish, which are considerably more regular than English, and have much faster word-reading development (Seymour et al., 2003).
- Regular then complex Taiwanese, Japanese and Chinese orthographies, with children first mastering the extremely regular orthography, then transitioning to the complex one.

Pleasingly, we've also a growing number of Queensland country schools that are teaching their children to speak, read and write endangered indigenous languages. This has important cultural significance, and also offers opportunities for research studying the cognitive-processing skill development of children learning to speak, read and write an indigenous language and its regular-orthography (DSS, 2014). Fully-regular orthographies expedite second-language learning because written words clearly show words' pronunciation.

Second-language learning combined with regular-orthography reading and writing, can build strong literacy and learning skills, plus prevent risk factors being activated (van Daal & Wass, 2017). That would be powerful for at-risk Australian children.

Indeed, in the future, within 10 Changes improvements, Australian children and education might enjoy and benefit significantly from a nationwide project that entertains our littlies while building their skills for speaking, reading and writing one of our indigenous languages that's used across the project.

An Additional COST-A8 Study's Findings

In addition to Seymour et al.'s (2003) COST-A8 14-nation word-reading study, whose data was shown earlier in Table 1, the COST-A8 research team also conducted a further unpublished study.

This study measured word-reading progress of children in multiple nations at sequential time-points. Test Point 1 was at the end of Kindergarten, while Test Points 2 to 4 were across Grade 1. For the English readers, Test Point 5 at end of Grade 2 was also included.

When our CQU team visited these researchers in 2005, they provided us with the study's results for Finnish, Icelandic, and English readers.

It's a useful study because Icelandic children are a year younger than Finnish children when in Grade 1 and learning to read, so it enables consideration of the impacts of starting age for two nations with high orthographic regularity. Mean ages at end-Grade-1 were 7.9 years (Finland), 6.9 years (Iceland), 5.6 years (UK).

Unfortunately, the results can't be interpreted solely with regard to age, as while Icelandic is a highly-regular orthography, it's slightly less regular than Finnish. The Icelandic children are thus younger but also reading an orthography that's slightly more complex, though vastly more regular than Standard English. They nonetheless shed useful light on age vs orthography impacts.

While the Finnish and Icelandic children both read at ceiling level by Test Point 4 (end-Grade-1), on average, the younger Icelandic children did show slower development at the earlier test points:
- On average, for the words used in the study, proficiency was reached earlier in Grade 1 (Test Point 2) for Finnish readers, a little later for Icelandic readers (end-Grade-1, Test Point 3), with English readers much later (end-Grade-2, Test Point 5).
- All Finnish readers reached a point of rapid transition at various times during Grade 1, from which point they moved rapidly to ceiling-level word-reading accuracy.
- The lower 50% of Icelandic readers showed a wider spread of achievement, far less than the English readers, but significantly more than the Finnish readers.
- The trajectories of the lower 50% of English readers showed a significantly wide spread of achievement at all test points.

These are very interesting findings. They show that
- Orthographic complexity and children's age when they learn to read both impact word-reading development.
- Orthographic complexity has stronger effects than age.
- The disadvantaging effects of age and orthography are much stronger on weaker word-readers.
- The *long sad tail of Standard-English word-readers* (Galletly, 2022a) starts from when children first learn to read and write, i.e., from the start of early-literacy development, with large numbers of less successful readers, many with major struggles.

It would be useful for Australia to engage in longitudinal research of this type, perhaps using our schools and working with schools and researchers in nations such as Wales, Finland, and Taiwan, and studying development of cognitive-processing, executive-function, language and other literacy skills, in addition to word-reading and writing.

Role Model Welsh-English Studies

Welsh is a highly-regular orthography, and Spencer, Hanley and colleagues' series of Welsh-English studies (Hanley et al., 2004; Spencer & Hanley, 2003, 2004) quite definitively establishes orthographic complexity having much stronger effects than age.

Their findings are very much in keeping with Ellis and Hooper's (2001) Welsh-English study, which showed Welsh readers well in advance, and English word-reading development being markedly slow. Using parallel word-lists developed with careful adherence to word types and frequency, that study too is well worth replicating and extending in Australian school-level research. Helpfully, both groups of researchers have included the word lists they used, in their articles (Ellis & Hooper, 2001; Spencer & Hanley, 2003).

Importantly, Spencer and Hanley's studies show orthographic impacts to be especially major irrespective of young age. They also establish powerful findings on phonemic-awareness development and the Standard-English long sad tail of underachievers.

Spencer and Hanley explored children's word-reading and phonemic-awareness skill levels longitudinally across primary school, with skills assessed in Grades 1, 2 and 5. Their studies controlled for age, with the Welsh and English readers being the same age, all 5-years-old when in Grade 1. The studies also controlled for sociocultural impacts. The children lived in the same small town, attending very similar government schools, which differed in the language used across school life and instruction: one school using Welsh, and the other using English.

The studies also controlled for multilingualism. At start of school, all the children were monolingual, and all began second-language learning in Grade 2: the English speakers learning Welsh and vice versa. Multilingualism effects were thus not present across Grade 1, and would have been similar from Grade 2.

Many studies show multilingual children have stronger cognitive-processing skills (e.g., Barac et al., 2014, 2016; Bialystok, 2015; L. Kuo & Anderson, 2010; Sparks et al., 2013). While multilingualism was present in the Grade 2 and 5 Welsh and English readers, both groups had similar multilingualism advantage.

Importantly, the researchers explored skill development of high, average and lower achieving readers. As you'll see from the discussion below, doing so produces valuable findings.

The studies are useful, practical school-level research that there's value in replicating and extending, in multiple contexts, including Australian bilingual schools.

With apologies for cultural insensitivity and to avoid confusion, I'll refer to the two Welsh cohorts as English and Welsh readers respectively, referring to their language of school instruction and the orthography they first learned to read and write. The English readers learned to read English, the Welsh readers learned to read Welsh. The studies started with 88 English readers and 74 Welsh readers in Grade 1, dropping to 75 and 70, respectively, in Grade 2, then to 52 and 46, respectively, in Grade 5.

The earlier studies explored the children's word-reading, cognitive and phonological-awareness development across Grades 1 and 2 (Spencer & Hanley, 2003, 2004), while the later study assessed these skills several years later, in Grade 5 (Hanley et al., 2004).

The studies' findings showed the negative impacts of English orthographic complexity to be much stronger on lower achieving English readers, with the English readers with more severe difficulties experiencing the most damaging effects.

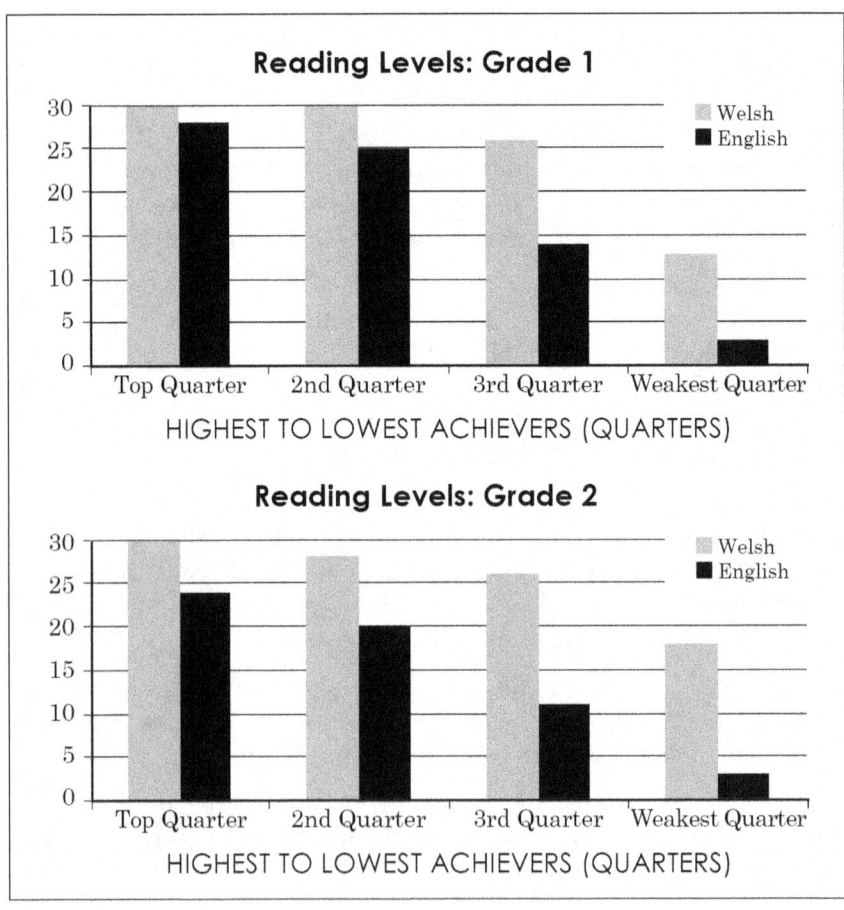

Figure 7. Number of words read correctly by Grade 1 and 2 Welsh and English readers (Spencer & Hanley, 2003)

The study's results were reported for quarters of achievers. They show the lower 50% of English readers developed word-reading difficulties far more than their Welsh-reader peers.

As the figure intimates, there was no significant achievement gap for the top quarter at end-Grade-1, but a definite but relatively mild difference present by end-Grade-2.

For the second highest quarter, a mild end-Grade-1 gap widened significantly by end-Grade-2. By then, English readers in this quarter read only a little better than the Welsh lowest quarter.

Oh dear! That suggests that perhaps about two thirds of our children are struggling, relative to regular-orthography readers.

Importantly, very large differences were evident in the lowest two quarters, with the Welsh readers making impressive progress while the English readers showed increasingly major delay.

Of course, while orthographic complexity shows very strong effects in the studies, young age was likely also having impacts, e.g., Spencer and Hanley's Welsh readers seemed to develop word-reading more slowly, across Grades 1 and 2, than older Grade 1 children in regular-orthography nations in the Seymour et al. (2003) COST-A8 study.

Standard-English Unfamiliar Words: A Major Challenge

Spencer and Hanley's work was both cross-sectional and longitudinal, which adds considerable value to their findings. In their subsequent study of the children when in Grade 5, 3 years later, the English readers were still well behind (Hanley et al., 2004).

While the Grade 5 Welsh readers proficiently read all words, the Grade 5 English readers still struggled with less-frequent, irregular words, with the lowest quartile of English readers struggling badly.

For regular real words and pseudowords (used to test reading of unfamiliar words), the Grade 5 English readers, on average, were now as strong as the Welsh readers, and the two groups were similarly proficient at reading high-frequency, irregular words: these were highly common words, which were only irregular for the English readers, as all Welsh words are regular.

However, when it came to less-frequent, irregular words, the Grade 5 English readers were significantly weak.

By Grade 5, after several years of second-language learning, the English readers would have now been able to speak Welsh, and quite likely read and write it.

That means they'd now have had a level of multilingual and regular-orthography advantage. Alas, any such advantage failed to resolve their difficulties with less-frequent, irregular words (Hanley et al., 2004):

> Even the best readers among the English children read medium- and low-frequency irregular words less accurately than the Welsh children read the Welsh equivalents (which are, of course, regular in Welsh).
>
> By definition, these are words that the English children will have encountered in print less often than the more frequent irregular words, and it appears that many of the children have not yet learnt to recognize the printed form of a substantial number of them.
>
> What this finding demonstrates is how difficult it is to become a fully skilled adult reader of English with a large vocabulary of words that can be read by sight.
>
> It therefore appears to be the case that the opaque nature of the English orthography slows down the acquisition of decoding skills [as seen in the children's Grade 1 and Grade 2 results, Spencer & Hanley, 2003], but even when these skills have caught up, children learning to read English appear to need considerable exposure to irregular words in print before they can be read accurately.

Those are important findings, with strong implications.

One, it highlights the vital importance of effective self-teaching skills, so children can read unfamiliar words (Nation et al., 2007; Share 1995, 1999; Shahar-Yames & Share, 2008; Share & Shalev, 2004). As Ziegler et al, (2014) emphasise,

> The most influential theory of learning to read is based on the idea that children rely on phonological decoding skills to learn novel words. According to the self-teaching hypothesis, each successful decoding encounter with an unfamiliar word provides an opportunity to acquire word-specific orthographic information that is the foundation of skilled word recognition. Therefore, phonological decoding acts as a self-teaching mechanism or 'built-in teacher'

Two, it highlights just how wide the crosslinguistic gap is for self-teaching, between the ease of regular-orthography reading of unfamiliar words, and our children's Standard-English struggles.

Three, it highlights how very difficult it is to rescue Standard-English readers once word-reading difficulties have set in.

Even though they'd by now have developed multilingual advantage, and quite likely be reading Welsh quite well, Hanley et al.'s (2004) lowest quartile of Grade 5 readers were still struggling badly.

Four, it highlights how word-reading instruction is still very much needed in later school years, in Anglophone nations. That's rare in Australian schools.

Five, it highlights unfamiliar, less-regular, infrequent words being a particular challenge for Standard-English readers.

That's bad news, as less-regular, unfamiliar words abound in subject-area texts from mid-primary school (Share and Stanovich, 1995):

> *Whereas just over 100 'heavy duty' words (eg, the, in, was, etc.) account for around half of all the letter strings appearing in printed school English, a very large number of words exist which appear very rarely in print (Carroll, Davies & Richman, 1971; Nagy & Anderson, 1984). In fact fully 80% of English words occur less than once in a million words of running text (Carroll et al., 1971).*

Struggles of Weaker English Word-Readers

In Spencer and Hanley's studies, the Standard-English long sad tail of underachievers was very evident from Grade 1 then continued on. It showed in Standard Deviations (SDs) being extremely large for the English readers, but impressively tiny for the Welsh readers.

Let's briefly explore the Means and SDs for the number of words the Grade 5 English and Welsh readers read correctly of their 110-item word lists. The Mean (and SD) was 102.5 (SD = 6.2) for the Welsh readers, and 87.7 (SD = 18.4) for the English readers.

Let's first consider how Means and SDs are useful for considering the range of achievement in a Normal Distribution, which shows how scores tend to spread in a large representative group for many different factors, e.g., height, and Standard-English reading scores. Because of its shape, it's often called a *Bell Curve*.

The Mean of a distribution is its average, calculated by averaging all scores. The Standard Deviation (SD) is a measure of the extent to which scores vary or are dispersed: while usually calculated by software, it can be done manually, being the square root of the variance: it's complicated but logical.

Means and Standard Deviations (SD) are a great way to compare groups who've completed the same test, or a highly similar one.

They allow thinking on
- Average achievement (the Mean).
- The range of achievement.

- The likely scores that low, average and high-level children would achieve.

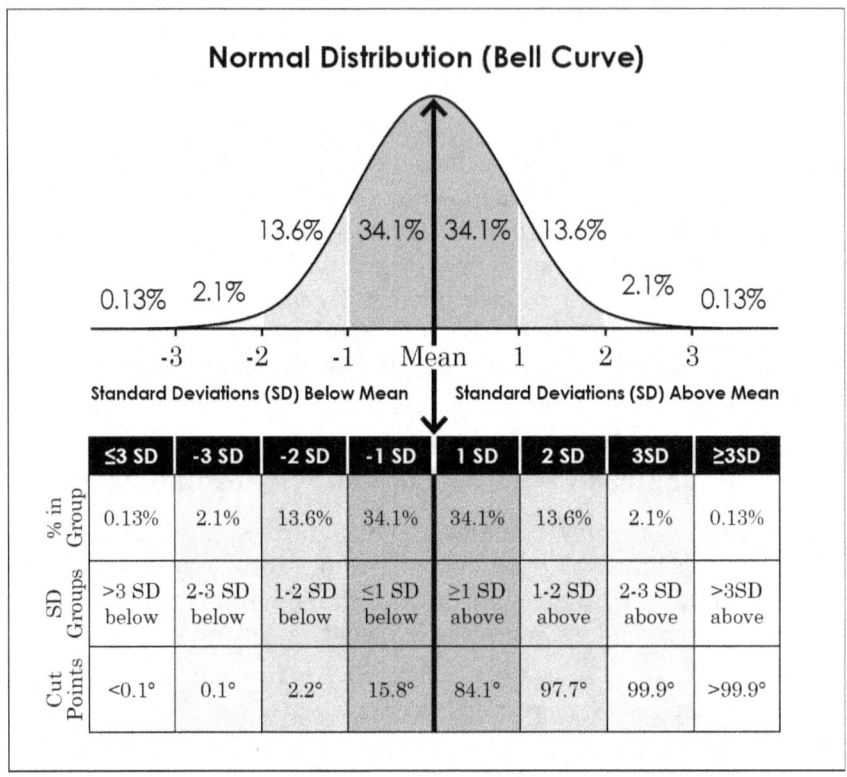

Figure 8. *Standard Deviation (SD) groups (% of population) with percentile cut-points for a Normal Distribution (Bell Curve)*

As you can see in the Normal Distribution in the figure,
- The Mean (Average) is in the middle of the distribution: it divides the half the population above the Mean from the half of the population that's below it.
- Using Standard Deviations (SDs), we can divide achievement into sections: 1, 2, 3 and >3 SDs above and below the Mean.
- Most children (68.2%) achieve within 1 SD of the Mean (34.1% at and above the Mean, 34.1% below it). That's considered Average level: for reading tests, 68.2% of children achieve average scores.
- The next band is between 1 and 2 SDs of the Mean: 13.6% are high achievers, and 13.6% are low achievers. It's 27.2% of the population.
- Thus 95.4% (68.2% + 27.2%) of the population in a Normal Distribution lie in those two bands, being within 2 Standard

Deviations (SDs) of the Mean: 47.7% (34.1% + 13.6%) above the Mean and 47.7% below.
- The third band (between 2 and 3 SDs of the Mean) has 2.1% who are extremely high achievers, and 2.1% who are extremely low achievers. That's 4.2% of the population.
- Only approximately 0.26% of children achieve >3 SDs beyond the Mean. For reading, that would mean 0.13% reading at perhaps genius level, and 0.13% reading at an exceptionally low level relative to their peers. I've calculated the cut-point for >3SDs beyond the Mean as 4SDs below the Mean.

Let's now use these Standard Deviation (SD) groups to consider the lower 50% of achievers in the Grade 5 English and Welsh reader groups. Doing so shows just how poorly the English weaker half were reading, far worse than the Welsh-reader *weak* readers.

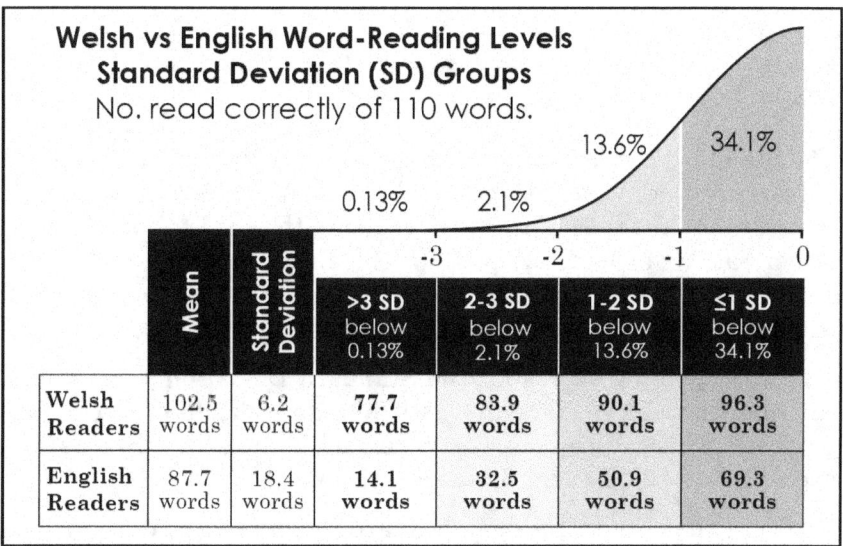

Figure 9a. Word-reading levels of Standard Deviation (SD) groups for Hanley et al.'s (2004) Grade 5 weaker 50% of Welsh and English readers, in table form

As you can see in the figures above and on the next page, we can do this by repeatedly subtracting the SD from the Mean. Subtracting the SD once shows the score for children 1 SD below the Mean, subtracting it again shows the score for children 2 SDs below the Mean, and so on.

You can see how the Welsh readers have a much higher Mean, of 102.5 words correct out of a list of 110 (93% correct), while the English readers' Mean is far lower, at 87.7 words correct (80%).

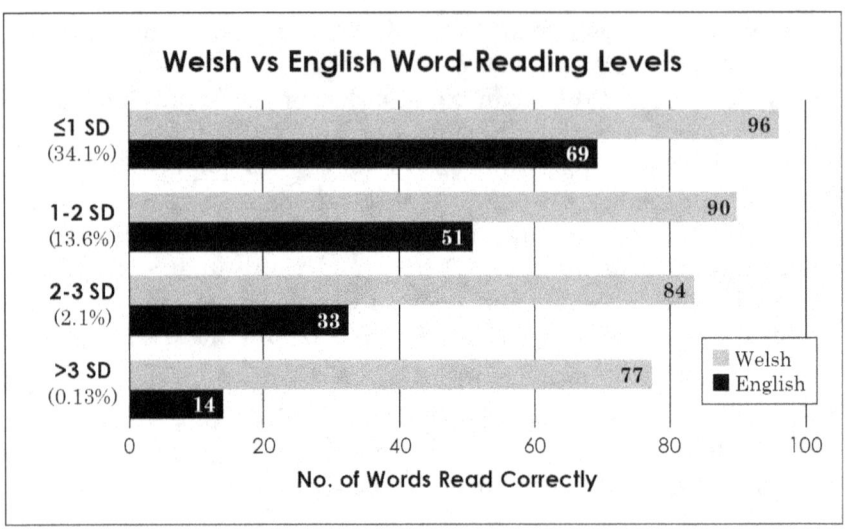

Figure 9b. Word-reading levels of Standard Deviation (SD) groups in bar graph form for Hanley et al.'s (2004) Grade 5 weaker 50% of Welsh and English readers,

The Standard Deviations (SD) show there is relatively little spread of scores for the Welsh readers, with the SD being 6.2 words correct. In contrast, for the English weak readers, the SD is almost 3 times larger, at 18.4 words correct, which shows an extremely large achievement spread. Yes, just as an animal's tail drags behind it, Standard-English weak word-readers form a long sad tail.

The word-reading scores for the Standard Deviation groups show the English weak readers are vastly weaker – the differences really are huge. This can be seen by comparing the number of words read correctly at 1, 2, 3 and 4 SDs below the Mean.

The data shows even the very weakest Welsh readers were reading well by English standards. The range of scores to 3 SDs for the Welsh weak readers is less than 20 words (from Mean of 102.5 to 83.6 words correct at 3 SD), and their weakest readers' score of 83.6 words correct is close to the English Mean of 87.7 words correct. Ouch!

In contrast, the English weak readers' 3 SDs' range is over 55 words: from a low 87.7 down to an abysmally low 32.5 words correct.

Let's now consider how well children in each of the Standard Deviation groups were reading. This usefully estimates how well children in larger populations would be likely to score, e.g., how well Australian and regular-orthography children might be achieving.

Of the Welsh weaker half of readers, using SD groups,

- A 34.1% group (≤1 SD) would have read approximately 96 to 102 words correctly (96.3 words being the 1 SD cut-point), reading better than many of the English upper half of readers.
- The next 13.6% group (from 1 to 2 SDs) would have read at least 90 words correctly, better than many of the English upper half: thus 47.7% (34.1%+13.6%) are reading as well or better than many of the top half of English readers.
- Importantly, even weakest Welsh readers (>3 SDs, with the cut-point actually 4SDs below the Mean, 0.13% of a normal distribution cohort) have appreciably strong reading skills, correctly reading at least 77.7 words.

The Grade 5 English scores quickly move from sad to woeful:
- A 34.1% group (≤1 SD) read only at least 69.3 words correctly, with many achieving lower than weakest Welsh readers.
- The next 13.6% group (from 1 to 2 SDs), with 50.9 to 69.3 words correct, are far lower than weakest Welsh readers.
- The even-weaker English 2.1% (from 2 to 3 SDs) scored between 32.5 and 50.9 words correct.
- Any English readers scoring more than 3 SDs below the Mean read only between 14 and 32.5 words correctly.

The differences really are major, as you can see in this figure:

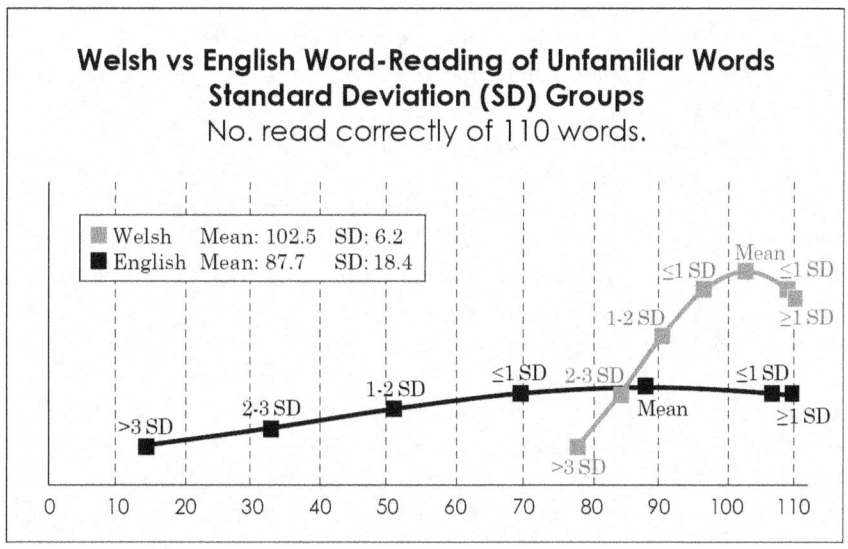

Figure 9c. Unfamiliar-word word-reading levels of Standard Deviation (SD) groups in Hanley et al.'s (2004) Grade 5 Welsh and English readers

The figure shows two approximate bell curves, one each for the

Welsh and English Grade 5 groups for reading of unfamiliar words, with the X axis having reading scores out of 110 words. With a high Mean, and low SD, the Welsh bell curve is narrow, bunched in tightly, and considerably to the right of the much lower English Mean. In contrast, with such a large SD for the English readers, the English bell curve is really quite flat, and spread out hugely.

With the full range of children included, the figure also shows high achievers. Both the English and Welsh groups have appreciable numbers of high achievers, with approximately 16% of children correct on most words. The differences lie in lower-achievers' scores.

Suffice to say, Welsh weak readers were reading well, while English weak readers were very much our long sad tail of underachievers. For Anglophone nations, that's not just humbling: it's horrific. It also highlights a serious ethical issue: the struggles Australia inflicts on its children by using 1-Stage early-literacy development.

It also highlights the importance of all 10 Changes. Briefly perusing the list shows each is relevant and important:

Change 1. Understand how orthographies matter: English spelling is dragging us down.
Change 2. Own our struggling reader woes: End hypocrisy and pretence.
Change 3. Weigh workload: Our children and teachers are working far too hard.
Change 4. One-size education does not fit all: Teach to the decidedly different instructional needs of upper-third and lower-third readers.
Change 5. End our data deficiency: Build strong knowledge on word-reading levels.
Change 6. Enrich every child: Ensure effective supportive tailored education.
Change 7. Insist on easy literacy development: Reach regular-orthography nations' achievement levels.
Change 8. Investigate the potential of fully-regular beginners' orthographies: They're winners.
Change 9. Play to learn first: Start Standard-English word-reading instruction from mid-Year 2.
Change 10. Build needed research knowledge as quickly as possible: Use collaborative school-based research.

Higher English Reading Comprehension

You'll be pleased to know that it's not all bad news for Standard-English readers. There were two bright spots in the Grade 5 study (Hanley et al., 2004). English readers, on average, had higher comprehension than their Welsh peers, and they also read faster.

Higher reading comprehension is a plus. Standard-English readers likely rely far more on context cues to support their weaker word-reading of less familiar words, so it's perhaps not surprising that Standard-English reading comprehension was higher, particularly in stronger word-readers.

The researchers comment (Hanley et al., 2004),
The most unexpected finding was that the English children performed significantly better at answering comprehension questions about stories that they read than the Welsh children. This result suggests that a transparent orthography does not confer any advantages as far as reading comprehension is concerned. As comprehension is clearly the goal of reading, this finding is potentially reassuring for teachers of English. Nevertheless, it would be more reassuring if relatively good reading comprehension could be demonstrated in younger English readers at a point when their decoding skills lag behind those of their Welsh counterparts.
The fact that the comprehension score of the English children actually exceeded the score of the Welsh children might conceivably occur because an opaque orthography fosters greater emphasis on semantic than phonologically based strategies.

The idea that regular orthographies don't confer advantage for reading comprehension seems questionable, as PIRLS and PISA data shows regular-orthography nations to have high reading comprehension and few struggling readers (Galletly & Knight, 2011b; Thomson et al., 2017, 2019). That said, the finding is important, and has been repeated, e.g., Oney and Goldman's (1984) Turkish-English study found strong reading comprehension in healthy-progress Standard-English word-readers.

Alas, both studies provided only averages, with no data on stronger and weaker word-readers – information needed in future research.

Findings of higher reading comprehension align with Australia's strong PISA 2000 results for Reading (reading comprehension), due to our strong readers' high scores. We were sixth of all nations, on average, because their impressively strong scores more than compensated for the sadly low scores of our low achievers.

Higher comprehension in the Grade 5 English readers may also align with Standard-English children being better than Italian children at learning irregular spellings (Notarnicola et al., 2012). So many words being irregular means children focus on spelling idiosyncrasies.

It also means they focus more on meaning and context clues.

So, yes, there are some advantages to Standard English as a sole orthography, including heightened reading comprehension and heightened skills for learning irregular spellings. That said, these advantages seem won through struggles, and are likely to be characteristic only of successful readers. Research is needed.

Watching Our Long Sad Tail Develop

In the Welsh-English studies, the impact of English orthographic complexity on Standard-English word-reading development fell most strongly on the lowest two quarters, the lower 50% of readers.

For us, their performance is worrisome, as there's every likelihood our at-risk children experience similar struggles.

The studies showed that few Welsh readers developed entrenched word-reading difficulties, whereas at least 25% of the English readers were severely struggling.

At end-Grade-2, the English third quarter were reading less than half as well as the Welsh third quarter, while the English lowest quarter were virtually non-readers. Meanwhile, the Welsh lowest quarter had reading almost as good as the English second quarter.

No improvement occurred by Grade 5, with the lowest English quarter still struggling badly. The researchers discuss our long sad tail:
The poorest 25% of the English readers continued to perform much worse than the lowest performing 25% of Welsh readers on both words and nonwords.
An underachieving tail of this kind was not observed in the reading performance of the Welsh-speaking group.
Overall, these findings suggest that in the long term the detrimental effects of an opaque orthography are most damaging to the poorest readers.

Spencer and Hanley used quarters, while I'm using thirds, but we do seem to be discussing the same struggling readers, don't we, and English orthographic complexity being damaging for at-risk readers?

Having worked with a plethora of struggling readers, I know well the chain of events. From the start, weak cognitive-processing skills and impeded statistical learning were dragging the at-risk English readers down, with automisation weakness soon evident – some children are very slow to learn letters and irregular sightwords, and all are far slower to master reading of unfamiliar regular words, with confidence dropping, and Acquired Helplessness usually building.

Weak Phonemic Awareness in Grade 5

Spencer and Hanley's findings on phonemic awareness in the Welsh and English readers are important. They show Standard-English readers' phonemic-awareness skills are still under-developed in later primary school, with weakness present in Grade 5.

In keeping with Aro (2004), and Huang and Hanley (1994, 1997), Spencer and Hanley found Welsh readers' phonemic-awareness skills well ahead of English readers', from early in Grade 1.

Then, four years later, in Grade 5, children's sixth year of schooling, they found the English readers still significantly weaker on phonemic awareness. The Grade 5 Welsh readers were significantly better on phoneme counting, for both Welsh and English words, showing significantly stronger phonemic awareness.

That's a sad finding that aligns well with phonemic-awareness development paralleling word-reading development. It suggests our weak word-readers are restricted to tortoise-slow phonemic-awareness development, with it probably not fully proficient until word-reading and spelling development are relatively complete.

It's a challenge we should consider – our children needing phonemic awareness but not having it. While phonemic awareness isn't crucial for regular-orthography children (M. Aro, 2004; Cossu, 1999; Cossu et al., 1993; Huang & Hanley, 1997; Galletly, 2018), while Anglophone nations use solely Standard English in 1-Stage early literacy, our at-risk readers need it, very much so.

That finding of continuing low phonemic awareness in the Grade 5 English readers adds vigorously to arguments for investigating the potential of fully-regular beginners' orthographies (Change 8), with children reading and writing a regular-orthography first, to expedite early-literacy plus mastering Standard English.

Statistical Learning and Automisation Weakness

To make effective progress, at-risk word-readers need highly strategic teaching and learning, using strong principles of effective practice and learning (Dehaene, 2009, 2021; Seabrook et al., 2005; Rohrer & Hartwig, 2020; Sherrington, 2019; Swanson et al., 1999; Weinstein et al., 2018).

Why is it that Spencer and Hanley's at-risk English readers became the Standard-English long sad tail of underachievers, with effective progress and intervention so very difficult to achieve? Why did the at-risk Welsh readers become strong word-readers despite probably starting school with highly similar risk factors?

Why do major risk factors for our children have such minimal impact on regular-orthography children? Why are so many risk factors activated in Standard-English at-risk children? Those are important questions. Complex learning, weak cognitive-processing skills, high cognitive load and insufficiently effective statistical learning will be involved, as will related automisation weakness.

Statistical learning is our learning from patterns we observe. It develops across childhood, impacted by age, modality (e.g., information being visual, auditory or orthographic), and children's cognitive-processing, executive function and communication skills (Ren & Wang, 2023). Studies show statistical learning relates significantly to word-reading and reading ability: strong-progress readers have strong statistical learning, while weaker readers lack those skills (Arciuli & Simpson, 2012; Knight & Galletly, 2020; Plante & Gómez, 2018).

Weak readers and children with language weakness show similar, and in many cases, identical. areas of weakness (Knight & Galletly, 2020; Plante & Gomez, 2018). As an example, studies show that children with language weakness have difficulty with statistical learning, including feedback-related learning, coping with distracting information, focusing attention appropriately and making sufficiently strong memories of what they've been exposed to and learned: those weaknesses are characteristic of weak readers.

Not surprisingly, and in line with good teaching practices, studies also show both groups benefit significantly from regularity in the input they receive: clear explanations, practice involving lots of exposures and useful demonstrations and examples. Additionally, both struggling readers and children with weak language skills need far more exposures and consistency than healthy-progress children. Importantly, both weaker and stronger learners benefit from implicit as well as explicit statistical learning, i.e., both from relatively passive exposure to examples, and from being actively taught.

For struggling word-readers, automisation skills and teaching which builds automisation are important, supporting them to learn then master reading and writing skills (Dehaene, 2009, 2014, 2021; Jones et al., 2016; Logan, 1997; Logan et al., 1999; Nicolson & Fawcett, 2008, 2011, 2019; Rohrer & Hartwig, 2020; Samuels, 1997; Samuels & Flor, 1997; Sherrington, 2019; Swanson et al., 1999;

Walberg & Wang, 1987; M. Wang, 1987; M. Wang & Walberg, 1983; Weinstein et al., 2018).

Effective attention and memory play a pivotal role in all learning. They're key to healthy learning, supporting children to first begin to understand skills, then master them, and then build fluency and, finally, automaticity. When children are automatic at a skill, they do it easily (skill mastery and automaticity), they continue to be good at the skill without loss of skill over time (skill maintenance), plus they use the skill well in diverse contexts (skill generalisation).

The impacts of orthographic complexity and activated risk factors show in the major difficulties struggling Standard-English readers have in automising word-reading and writing skills.

They struggle to learn the skills in the first place, and often need masses of practice to become even somewhat fluent. But they're not automatic, and, if practice stops, skill levels often slip, with children often forgetting concepts that seemed mastered – including word-reading and spelling skills, and often counting and maths facts too.

Healthy automaticity is evidenced in skills being mastered to a proficient level, with little or no loss of skill over time. Considerable research interest has focused on the challenges of Anglophone weak readers building skill automaticity, their needs for scaffolding in initial learning, extensive practice to build automatic skills (Nicolson & Fawcett, 2008; Samuels & Flor, 1997), and identifying areas where learning breaks down (Gabay et al., 2012a, 2012b; Jones et al., 2016).

Studies show many factors underlie the automisation difficulties children experience. They include not just cognitive-processing and executive-function skills. They also include speech skills, including articulation speed, articulation time and pause time when speaking, and speech-discrimination speed. In addition, some studies show weaker learners have a procedural learning deficit (Gabay et al., 2015a, 2015b; Nicolson & Fawcett, 2008, 2011).

Skill automaticity is a key issue for Australian schools, as skills that become forgotten need re-teaching, and this can consume copious teaching and learning time. In addition, sometimes skills children have forgotten go unnoticed, with it being assumed proficiency has been retained – this can lead to major struggles with subsequent learning relying on subskills that children have learned but now lost.

It's likely there are two levels of automisation weakness: skill accuracy and skill fluency. These two levels become very evident when we consider accuracy and fluency differences in Standard-English and regular-orthography word-reading.

Level 1 Automisation Weakness: Accuracy

Level 1, Standard-English children's first level of automising difficulties, is mastering word-reading accuracy to a proficient accuracy level.

The two key skills of Standard-English word-reading are to develop

- A growing bank of sightwords: regular and irregular words recognised automatically – on sight.
- Increasing skill for decoding (reading) unfamiliar words.

Our children learn letters and their sounds, then reading and writing of highly-regular Consonant-Vowel-Consonant (CVC) words. They also learn highly-frequent irregular words, e.g., *was, one, who* as wholeword sightwords. Over time, they develop increasingly sophisticated skills for working out unfamiliar words. In healthy progress, skills become and remain automatic, staying mastered and not slipping after practice ceases.

Many weak word-readers have Level 1 Automisation Weakness:
- They confuse vowel sounds *e/i* and *a/u*, and this confusion persists, often reappearing later, after practice has ceased.
- They take a long time to master regular CVC words, e.g., *hut, bus, tep, zub*, and words with consonant blends, e.g., *list, flank*.
- They take a very long time to master CVCe words and not confuse them with CVC words, e.g., *bit/bite, cut/cute*.
- They often lose progress in these skills when there's a break from skill-building and practice, e.g., school holidays.
- They have slow, struggling spelling development, that usually parallels their slow word-reading development.
- *Late-emerging*, struggling word-readers struggle mostly with unfamiliar words, while *early-emerging* word-readers struggle to master letters and their sounds, read regular CVC words and to learn highly frequent irregular sightwords.

Many also often struggle to automise counting down by numbers and maths facts, e.g., counting down effortlessly by 2s from 20, 4s from 40, and to easily remember times-tables for those numbers.

Interestingly, studies of Dutch dyslexic university students with reading and writing difficulties showed difficulties for maths facts to be common (Tops et al., 2012), i.e., showing Level 1 Automisation Weakness present in regular-orthography readers. Further, along with reading fluency, Dutch universities use phonological-awareness and spelling tests to identify Dyslexia. This suggests possibilities of Level 1 Automisation Weakness for spelling that's hard to remediate in regular-orthography nations whose spelling is not fully regular.

Regular-orthography nations do have a tiny number of children and adults with continuing word-reading and spelling difficulties, with difficulties in reading fluency, spelling and writing (Tops et al., 2012).

Given some regular-orthography university students have literacy learning difficulties, albeit far less major than ours, regular-orthography nations obviously have some difficulties fully remediating their struggling readers. We need to research the difficulties of Standard-English and regular-orthography adults with literacy difficulties, as these show the teaching challenges school education has struggled with.

While Level 1 Automisation Weakness may well be universal, it's a far lesser issue for regular-orthography word-reading and spelling, impacting only fluency, but not accuracy, of word-reading, and impacting spelling accuracy only where orthographies aren't fully-regular for spelling. That's the case too for children who have developmental difficulties, e.g., intellectual disability (Cossu et al., 1993; Olofsson, 1993; Olofsson & Niedersoe, 1999; Poskiparta et al., 1999; Schneider et al., 1997, 1999).

Level 1 Automisation Weakness is a very big issue for Standard-English struggling word-readers. It was very much evident in the weak English word-readers in the Welsh-English studies (Hanley et al., 2004; Spencer & Hanley, 2003, 2004). It started in Grade 1, and continued, being still very much present in Grade 5.

Letter-Sound Weakness as Universal Level 1 Weakness

Letter-sound weakness in at-risk regular-orthography children may well indicate universal Level 1 Automisation Weakness, with children of all nations perhaps having weakness in this area.

Along with RAN (which impacts fluency, but not accuracy), and family history, letter-sound weakness is one of the three risk factors which functionally derail rapid, effective progress in regular-orthography children (Eklund et al., 2013, 2015; Ronimus et al., 2019).

It's interesting that researchers of regular-orthography nations tend to consider letter-sound weakness a risk-factor rather than it being word-reading difficulties.

In contrast, for Anglophone nations, letter-sound weakness is word-reading difficulty. That's because letter-sound learning is, in effect, sightword learning, and Anglophone children struggling to learn that this new shape, which the teacher has said is B, says *buh*, similarly struggle to master that the *one* 3-letter shape says *wun* (1).

This difference, with researchers in regular-orthography nations terming letter-sound weakness a risk factor, while Anglophone nations include it in word-reading difficulties, perhaps reflects Level 1 Automisation Weakness impacting just letter-sound learning but not word-reading accuracy for regular-orthography children, as all words are regular.

Letter-sound weakness, mastering then automising letter-sounds, is a prioritised issue in regular-orthography nations, with sizeable numbers of children benefiting from Finland's *GraphoGame* (now termed *GraphoLearn*, www.grapholearn.com): digital, interactive intervention building letter-sound knowledge then word-reading with letter-sounds. It's now a routine part of Finnish Grade 1 classrooms, and is now being explored in over 30 nations (Bach et al., 2013; Lyytinen et al., 2015, 2021; Ojanen et al., 2015).

GraphoLearn has a Standard-English version using orthographic units as well as letter-sounds, combined with strategic tailored encouragement (e.g., Kyle et al., 2013; Lyytinen et al., 2021). GraphoLearn might prove useful in automisation research, given its use across nations. In Australia, there's value in exploring automisation weakness in two cohorts, one using solely Standard English, and the other initially using a beginners' orthography.

Level 1 Automisation Weakness as Forgetting of Skills

It does seem that Level I Automisation Weakness may be universal for letter-sound mastery, and also, quite likely, for automising counting down by integers (e.g., by 2s from 20, 7s from 70), and associated maths facts (Dehaene, 2011; Tops et al., 2012).

However, universality is not the case for word-reading and spelling. Level 1 Automisation Weakness for Standard-English word-reading and spelling is evidenced in weak classroom learning, and in studies showing slippage in the skills Anglophone children gain from intervention after intervention ends (e.g., R. O'Connor, 2000).

Regular-orthography studies show slower developing word-readers' learning is automised, with no forgetting or loss of skill over time after intervention ceases, and strong skill maintenance (Cossu et al., 1993; Olofsson, 1993; Olofsson & Niedersoe, 1999; Poskiparta et al., 1999; Schneider et al., 1997, 1999).

It's very different for Standard-English struggling word-readers, who, when practice has been discontinued, often forget vowel-sounds, and how to effectively read regular CVC, CVCe and CCVCC words (e.g., *bit, bite, brink*). Many children learn then forget – with this evident a few months after intervention ends (Knight & Galletly, 2020; R. O'Connor, 2000; Torgesen, 2000). There's every likelihood it was happening in the lower 50% of Spencer and Hanley's weaker English readers, as they moved to join the English long sad tail.

Anglophone studies of what is termed *Summer Slump* are similarly revealing as regards the skills that weak Standard-English word-readers lose when practice ceases for long periods of time, e.g., over school holidays, and particularly the long USA summer vacation (Cooper, 2003; Galletly, 2005b, 2008; Good et al., 2002; Knight et al., 2017a). Catherine Snow et al. (1998a) comment of Standard English,

At least in early acquisition, reading ability is a bit like foreign language ability: use it or lose it, and the more tenuous the knowledge, the greater the loss. Thus, the well-documented and substantial losses in reading ability that are associated with summer vacation are especially marked for younger and poor readers (Hayes and Grether, 1983; Alexander and Entwisle, 1996).

This skill loss can be extensive, e.g., the *Dynamic Indicators of Basic Early Literacy Skills* (DIBELS) norms for weaker readers suggest USA weak word-readers can lose virtually a term's progress over the long summer break: seen in the norms of DIBELS *NonWord Reading* and *Oral Reading Fluency* tests for weak readers in the final term of most grade-levels being very close to the first term norms for the next grade-level.

Skills slipping badly over school holidays in weak readers is very much my experience in the children I work with in clinical practice. I encourage families to continue home practice over the holidays, as skills so often slip if practice isn't continued. I similarly encourage schools not to end interventions just before school holidays, instead continuing them into the next term, in order to identify needs and implement catch-up intervention for lost skills, as it's often needed.

Some skills slip more easily than others. Progress is often lost in children's overcoming of early vowel confusion, particularly of a/u and e/i short vowels, reading of CVC words, and confusing CVC and CVCe words, e.g., mixing up words such as *hat/hut, grant/grunt, pet/pit, check/chick, cut/cute, strip/stripe*.

When Standard-English Struggles Are Entrenched ...

Standard-English weak word-readers forget skills; regular-orthography children don't. Future research may well establish that learning to read and write a regular orthography in earliest literacy produces useful executive function and cognitive-processing skill changes, which enable and expedite Level 1 automisation in regular-orthography children, including slower-developing word-readers.

It's also likely that high cognitive load, impeded statistical learning, and high cognitive-processing needs experienced by our children due to English orthographic complexity exacerbate Level 1 Automisation Weakness for word-reading and spelling accuracy. Acquired Helplessness will also be in play (Maier & Seligman, 2016)

Timing is important, as is preventing children from experiencing difficulties, with ongoing success needed from the start of learning, and motivation and engagement remaining high (Lyytinen et al., 2021).

This seems evidenced in Hanley et al.'s (2004) Grade 5 weak English readers not having overly benefited by regular-orthography and multilingual advantage developed from Grade 2, when they began second-language learning, to speak, read and write Welsh.

Children may acquire regular-orthography and multilingual advantage, in the form of enhanced cognitive-processing skills, when they learn to read and write a regular orthography, or become multilingual.

Perhaps this cognitive-processing advantaging doesn't optimally develop to a sufficient level in Standard-English readers already struggling word-readers prior to regular-orthography or multilingual experience. Certainly, any advantage in Hanley et al.'s weak Grade 5 English readers wasn't sufficiently powerful to overcome impacts of English orthographic complexity, and their word-reading struggles.

Both multilingualism and learning to read and write a regular-orthography produce stronger cognitive-processing skills, and the English readers had been learning Welsh as a second-language since Grade 2, and would have been reading and writing it too.

As a result, by Grade 5, all the English readers should have had a level of cognitive-processing and executive-function advantage, due to now being multilingual plus having mastered reading and writing of a highly-regular orthography. However, the Grade-5 English lowest quarter was severely struggling, and both stronger and weaker English readers struggled to read unfamiliar words. Really, their now being multilingual didn't seem to evidence any appreciable benefits for word-reading. One wonders whether Standard-English difficulties, once entrenched, might even impede development of multilingual advantage in some ways.

In our Early Years Factory that so ruthlessly produces our flood of struggling readers, it seems likely that our main failure to meet our teaching challenges is our providing learning that's too difficult and therefore frustrating when children aren't developmentally ready for it, thus allowing children to enter the slippery slopes of ongoing struggles and defeat. Beginning readers need ongoing success.

Torgesen's 1998 article discussing Standard-English readers is aptly entitled *Catch them before they fall*, and research to date does not refute its opening statement that research studies consistently show that children who develop word-reading difficulties in earliest literacy are rarely caught up to their healthy progress peers.

Clearly, Level 1 Automisation Weakness is a major issue for at-risk Standard-English word-readers. Key issues separating Standard-English and regular-orthography lower achievers seem to be task difficulty, and the extent and duration of confusion and high cognitive load children experience both at the present time and in earlier learning.

It's that learning to ride a bike vs drive a truck contrast (Galletly & Knight, 2013). Whereas regular-orthography word-reading and spelling development is easy, akin to the fun of learning to ride a bike in ideal circumstances, our children's learning is all too often far less predictable and more challenging – akin to learning to drive an off-road vehicle in difficult, ever-changing circumstances.

This contrast deserves focused investigation, exploring cognitive-processing skills and automisation in letter-sound, word-reading, spelling and numeracy learning, to establish universal and orthography-specific aspects of Level 1 Automisation Weakness.

Suffice to say that Level 1 Automisation Weakness for word-reading accuracy is a minimal issue for regular-orthography readers, but a major issue for our lower-third word-readers, schools and teachers, consuming much precious school time, and causing great frustrations.

Level 2 Automisation Weakness: Fluency

Level 2 Automisation Weakness is difficulty achieving fluency, usually in reading of meaningful texts. It's very obvious in regular-orthography nations' small number of dysfluent readers, who've major struggles with speed and fluency, but strong word-reading accuracy.

It's emphasised in Dutch universities' definition of Dyslexia: *'An impairment characterized by a persistent problem in learning to read and/or write words or in the automatization of reading and writing.'*, and fluency tests being used to identify Dyslexia (Tops et al., 2012).

It's a universal weakness linked to weakness in Rapid Automised Naming (RAN) and its subskills (Siddaiah & Padakannaya, 2015; Sideridis et al., 2019). It's obvious and easy to study in regular-orthography dysfluent readers because they have strong accuracy. It's harder to study in our struggling word-readers, as their fluency difficulties are also impacted by their word-reading accuracy difficulties (Level 1 Automisation Weakness).

It's interesting how, while on a much lesser scale, Anglophone difficulties achieving Level 1 automaticity in word-reading accuracy are mirrored by regular-orthography nations' difficulties achieving Level 2 automaticity in their children with fluency difficulties.

Their fluency intervention studies seem to consistently show that while children can build fluency with the words in texts they train on, all too often these skills don't generalise to wider reading of new words and texts (Knight & Galletly, 2020):

In regular-orthography children, RAN weakness shows as relatively intransigent fluency difficulties, with studies consistently showing negligible transfer from interventions to wider reading fluency (de Jong, 2003; Hautala et al., 2013; Thaler et al., 2004). While present in Anglophone children and often showing little improvement, fluency difficulties are often less obvious and a lesser focus because of the major word-reading difficulties accompanying them (Vaughn et al., 2009).

The Struggles of Overcoming Level 2 Automisation Weakness

Failure to achieve proficient word-reading fluency due to RAN weakness, i.e., Level 2 Automisation Weakness, is quite possibly a universal feature of reading disability. Certainly, it underlies the fluency difficulties of dysfluent regular-orthography children.

Regular-orthography studies consistently show major difficulties overcoming Level 2 Automisation Weakness in fluency weakness:
- Landerl and Wimmer (2008) followed German children across Grades 1 to 8, finding 70% of the children who were dysfluent in Grade 1 were still dysfluent in Grade 8.
- Hintikka et al. (2008) explored three different computerised methods to increase fluency in Finnish Grade 2 dysfluent readers with RAN weakness, but found, for all methods, that

gains made happened only for the training materials used, and did not result in increased general reading speed.
- Thaler et al. (2004) working with dysfluent regular-orthography readers found that, even with very large amounts of practice, dysfluent readers improved speed only for the practiced materials, with no wider improvement.
- Huemer et al. (2008) trained consonant-cluster reading fluency in 40 German dysfluent readers in Grades 2 to 4. The children improved for the trained items and words containing them, but showed little generalisation of skills, with no improvement in speed for unfamiliar words.
- Huemer et al. (2010) and Heikkilä et al. (2013) explored fluency training with dysflent Finnish readers, using repeated reading of syllables of different types. Reading speed of trained syllables increased, but this did not transfer generally to reading speed.
- In all studies, RAN weakness linked strongly to dysfluency.

Certainly, Level 2 Automisation Weakness is difficult to overcome.

Our Children Forget, Regular-Orthography Children Don't

Anglophone struggling word-readers are *clever at forgetting*.

That's a term I use when I'm talking with children I'm assessing: *'Do you find you're clever at forgetting things that you've learned? You learn your spellings and know them for the test but two weeks later you can't remember them.'*, or *'Do you find you learned, e.g., the 3-times-tables, and you knew them, but later on, you couldn't remember them?'*

For word-reading, regular-orthography studies show this forgetting doesn't happen, at least not nearly to the same extent as it occurs for our children (Chien, 2010; Olofsson, 1993; Olofsson & Niedersoe, 1999; Poskiparta et al., 1999; Schneider et al., 1997, 1999). As an example, Cossu and colleagues' (1993) study of children with Down Syndrome who made great progress to a healthy level, showed they held their skills and did not regress.

Educators I've talked with, who are working in remote Aboriginal communities, similarly comment that mastery without forgetting is a characteristic of their children's regular-orthography reading.

Standard-English word-readers forget word-reading concepts and spellings, showing Level 1 Automisation Weakness, while regular-orthography children don't. We need, and will benefit greatly, from research investigating our extent of automisation weakness, and also its workload impacts.

Key Findings from Tour 2

Findings and implications of studies explored in Tour 2 suggest the following points are useful considerations towards improving literacy and education in Australia and Anglophone nations:

1. High orthographic regularity has far stronger impacts than young child age in expediting rapid, easy word-reading and spelling development.
2. English orthographic complexity is thus a major factor impeding our children's word-reading and spelling development.
3. When children are particularly young when learning to read, age nonetheless has significant impacts, likely through
   a. Immaturity.
   b. Reduced executive-function skills.
   c. Children not coping well with learning that's confusing.
4. At-risk regular-orthography children master accurate word-reading and spelling quickly and proficiently, with few struggling word-readers.
5. In contrast, English orthographic complexity is damaging for at-risk Standard-English readers, with quite likely at least 25% of children soon moving into entrenched word-reading, spelling and associated literacy difficulties, from earliest word-reading and spelling development.
6. Phonemic-awareness development seems to parallel word-reading development, which makes Standard-English phonemic-awareness development extremely slow.
7. Strong phonemic-awareness skills develop very rapidly in regular-orthography children, but take many years in Standard-English readers.
8. Having strong phonemic-awareness development prior to learning to read Standard English would likely ease and speed our children's word-reading and spelling progress, however the slow speed of Standard-English word-reading and spelling seems to deny them this option.
9. There are significant cognitive-processing advantages to learning to read a regular-orthography initially, in particular, strong building of phonemic-awareness and orthographic-awareness skills, and possibly other associated skills, with likelihood these strong skills would advantage subsequent learning of Standard English.

10. This suggests strong value in our children using a fully-regular English beginners' orthography prior to learning to read and write Standard English, as they would then have cognitive-processing advantages.
11. There's likelihood that many of our upper-primary and high-school children lack proficiency for reading less frequent unfamiliar words, despite words of this type occurring frequently in texts they read.
12. This suggests value in schools including tailored word-reading instruction across primary and high school, to build skill with increasingly complex, unfamiliar words.
13. Automatisation weakness is a major factor for our children, teachers and schools:
    a. Frustrating and impeding children's learning.
    b. Increasing teaching and learning hours needed.
14. It's likely there are two levels of automatisation weakness:
    a. Level 1 Automatisation Weakness: difficulties learning, mastering, maintaining and generalising skills – usually word-reading, spelling, counting and maths facts.
    b. Level 2 Automatisation Weakness: difficulties efficiently actioning learned skills, usually reading, writing and numeracy fluency, associated with weak Rapid Automised Naming (RAN).
15. Level 1 automatisation of regular-orthography word-reading and spelling accuracy is achieved very easily when regular orthographies are used, but is an intransigent difficulty for at-risk Standard-English readers, and their teachers and schools.
16. Studies show that
    a. Anglophone nations struggle with Level 1 Automatisation Weakness (word-reading accuracy), while
    b. Regular-orthography nations struggle with Level 2 Automatisation Weakness (word-reading fluency) in their few dysfluent readers.
    c. It is likely that
        i. Using a fully-regular beginners' orthography initially would greatly reduce Australian children's difficulties in mastering Standard-English word-reading accuracy (Level 1 automatisation).
        ii. A small group of children with RAN weakness would read and write with relatively slow speed.
17. There are strong needs for research exploring these areas, monitoring development of word-reading, writing, phonemic-awareness and other cognitive-processing skills, here and in regular-orthography nations.

Research Tour 3. Success Inoculation Vs Acquired Helplessness

Acquired helplessness is not learned, but instead an automatic default path when success is averted, and failure, stress and difficulties are experienced.

Bruce Knight & Susan Galletly, 2020

Why are there such vast differences between our at-risk word-readers and spellers and regular-orthography at-risk word-readers and spellers? Why do we have our long sad tail of weak word-readers while regular-orthography at-risk children overwhelmingly succeed?

Anxiety and stress compound and complicate our children's difficulties (APPA, 2020). That's evidenced in recent studies showing greater reading gains when reading interventions strategically incorporate interventions to reduce stress (Didion & Toste, 2022; Francis et al., 2021; McArthur, 2022; Vaughn et al., 2022)

Strong success vs lack thereof is doubtless a major factor affecting both children's literacy and executive-function development. Regular-orthography weak readers, while a little slower to take off than their healthy-progress classmates, nonetheless experience *Success Inoculation*, because there's no confusion in their learning, and slower developers have ongoing, albeit slower, earned success. Meanwhile, Standard-English struggling word-readers, with ongoing limited success, have major *Acquired Helplessness* (also termed *Learned Helplessness*; Maier & Seligman 1976, 2016; Seligman & Maier, 1967).

This research tour explores the research on Acquired Helplessness.

Have you heard about Learned Helplessness? Our CQU team terms it Acquired Helplessness, since Maier and Seligman (2016) so

Research Tour 3. Success Inoculation Vs Acquired Helplessness

thoroughly revised their 1976 Learned Helplessness theory.

There's an extensive research base on Learned Helplessness in areas outside education, but quite little on learning difficulties (e.g., Hersh et al., 1996; Valås, 1999, 2001a, 2001b), and almost none on word-reading difficulties in Standard-English readers, or comparing Anglophone and regular-orthography word-readers.

Indeed, the literature is so minimal that Livingston et al. (2018) did not use the term *Learned Helplessness* as a search term in their review of research publications from 1980 to 2018 that investigated emotional impacts and consequences of word-reading difficulties (Dyslexia). Their findings suggest acquired helplessness to certainly be an issue:

Learning disabilities are associated with mental health, behavioural and social difficulties. ... Individuals with learning disabilities have reported anger, stress, embarrassment, aggression, guilt, isolation, insecurity, anxiety and emotional and social problems. ... The memories of these experiences can have lasting damage into adulthood. ...

In individuals with dyslexia, 60% also meet criteria for at least one psychiatric disorder (Margari et al., 2013). Children with dyslexia may be susceptible to becoming withdrawn, anxious and depressed due to their academic underachievement. ... Adolescents with learning disabilities including dyslexia are also found to be at twice the risk of emotional distress, including risk for violence and suicide attempts. ...

Learning disabilities such as dyslexia have far-reaching effects on the emotional health of an individual, in turn having a negative impact on chances of success, for example, in school, jobs or relationships. ... These individuals underestimate their actual abilities ... and can experience less life success due to a potential self-fulfilling prophecy.

Success Inoculation vs Acquired Helplessness will be reducing the effectiveness of Standard-English catch-up remediation, and widening the gap between Anglophone and regular-orthography nations.

Acquired Helplessness will prove a key issue in struggling word-readers: in why remediation is so often insufficiently effective, and why we need to prevent, rather than remediate word-reading difficulties.

Acquired Helplessness is a state of passiveness, often mixed with anxiety and features of depression, that we move into when we find ourselves achieving poorly or unable to achieve in an area, and feel unable to change the situation. It's an inner, subconscious belief that we're not capable of doing or mastering a skill, in keeping with

Henry Ford's maxim, *Whether you think you can, or whether you think you can't, you're right.*

With anxiety and stress markedly reducing processing capacity and executive-function efficiency, Success Inoculation and Acquired Helplessness are important factors impacting children's learning.

That's why it's so important to prevent children experiencing too much difficult or unmotivating learning when they're first learning to read. It's quite likely also a factor in Hanley et al.'s (2004) Grade 5 English struggling readers lacking appreciable multilingual and regular-orthography advantage after learning to speak, read and write Welsh across Grades 2 to 5.

In Learned Helplessness research, it has long been thought that it's helplessness that is learned when unavoidable stressful challenges are experienced (Maier & Seligman, 1976; Seligman & Maier, 1967). Not so, it's now proved, and they've now revised the theory (Maier & Seligman, 2016).

They identified Learned Helplessness in the 1960s, after observing dogs' reactions when the floor of the platform the dogs were on induced mild electric shock, with only a very low fence stopping them from simply walking off the platform.

Two groups of dogs had been mixed together, and their reactions to the shock were very different. Dogs that previously had experienced unavoidable similar shock (mild shock they couldn't get away from), did nothing and simply endured the shock. The other dogs did the logical thing, quickly stepping over the fence, and leaving the floor.

Reflecting on the dramatically different responses of the two groups, Maier and Seligman reflected on how unavoidable trauma can cause passiveness and depressed behaviour, with feelings of inevitability for negative circumstances, i.e., that one is incapable of resolving the situation. Exploring the area further, they developed their theory, labelling it *Learned Helplessness* (Maier & Seligman 1976).

A half-century later, following much research, in their seminal article, *Learned Helplessness at fifty: Insights from neuroscience*, Maier and Seligman (2016) overhaul Learned Helplessness theory, reversing it in major ways. Discussing a plethora of studies, they show it's not helplessness that's learned, but instead the opposite: learning resilience is learned, but helplessness is guaranteed.

Resilience for learning is acquired when learning involves ongoing strong success. Children develop what our CQU team calls *Success Inoculation* (Knight & Galletly, 2020; Knight et al., 2017a): armed with skills and confidence, they confidently engage in and persist at learning tasks, even when subsequent learning is difficult.

Instead of being learned, Acquired Helplessness is more an automatic, default path learners move into when success is averted and failure, stress and difficulties are experienced.

Here's the abstract of Maier and Seligman's 2016 article:

Learned helplessness, the failure to escape shock induced by uncontrollable aversive events, was discovered half a century ago. Seligman and Maier (1967) theorized that animals learned that outcomes were independent of their responses – that nothing they did mattered – and that this learning undermined trying to escape.

The mechanism of learned helplessness is now very well-charted biologically, and the original theory got it backward.

Passivity in response to shock is not learned. It is the default, unlearned response to prolonged aversive events.

For a taste of Acquired Helplessness' sad, impeding impacts on crushed and crumpled, struggling Standard-English word-readers, consider this quote from famous Dyslexic, Richard Branson:

And when my Grade 3 teacher asked me to read out loud, I knew it was going to be another of the worst days of my life.

Yes, that's word-reading he's talking about there – reading aloud, with his sadly weak skills on show to his classmates, leaving him humiliated and ashamed, not just in the moment, but on a continuing basis. You can almost feel his passive resignation, can't you: another poor child enduring reading, rather than being a keen active learner? And, alas, active engagement is crucial for success when learning is complex.

We should probably stop using the term *Learned Helplessness*, instead calling it *Acquired Helplessness* or *Default Helplessness*, perhaps also using terms such as *Success Inoculation*, and *Learned Resilience* or *Resilience for Learning* (Knight et al., 2017a).

In revising Learned Helplessness theory, Maier and Seligman (2016) emphasise the crucial importance of initial success, with inoculating effects empowering learners to confidently persist in later learning.

Given their ongoing low success, most Standard-English struggling word-readers and spellers would have appreciable levels of Acquired Helplessness, which would consequently dampen motivation and engagement and, in turn, markedly impede learning effectiveness.

Our 5-year-old, lower-third, struggling beginners, and our older struggling word-readers, children for whom word-reading isn't easy, show Acquired Helplessness. Some seem depressed by it, while others inwardly take their bat and ball and go home, protecting their self-esteem by inwardly deciding *I don't do reading*, with task avoidance and lack of engagement the order of the day.

Success Inoculation vs Acquired Helplessness will doubtless prove to be a key difference between high and low-progress Standard-English readers and writers, and between lower-third Standard-English and regular-orthography word-readers.

We need studies of Acquired Helplessness and Success Inoculation in our children and regular-orthography children, as we study word-reading, spelling and cognitive-processing development. As part of that, let's explore the impacts on children's cognitive-processing, executive-function, learning and self-teaching skills in weaker and stronger word-readers, including thirds, tenths and the lowest and highest 5% and 2%. That research is much needed.

Australian teachers consider Acquired Helplessness to often be present in children with weak word-reading and spelling: seen, when reading, in relying excessively on adult help, and, in writing, in excessive use of safe words they can spell, rather than taking risks and using more mature vocabulary (Knight et al, 2017a, 2017b). It's also seen in passiveness: all too often, these children are slow to get started, show limited engagement, and are keen to avoid reading and writing, e.g., quickly volunteering for classroom jobs.

Success Inoculation is the norm for regular-orthography children and our upper-third readers, while Acquired Helplessness may well be the norm for our lower-third word-readers.

Acquired Helplessness will doubtless be far more an Anglophone than regular-orthography nation issue, for word-reading and spelling.

As an example, when Torppa et al. (2017) explored task avoidance in Finnish weaker readers, they found no task avoidance in weak word-readers, unless the children were also weak writers:

> *These findings suggest that there is no association between task avoidance and unexpected poor reading, unless poor reading is accompanied by poor spelling.*

That's very different from our schools, where many primary school teachers feel that word-reading and reading aloud are areas where weak readers are so often passive, holding back and hoping that, e.g., the teacher aide they're reading with will read the words instead.

English Readers Need Success Inoculation

Success Inoculation is yet another area where regular-orthography children win hands down. Our healthy-progress readers enjoy Success Inoculation, as they're blissfully unaware of how severely delayed they are relative to regular-orthography children. But, alas, virtually all our struggling beginner word-readers are destined for Acquired Helplessness, with its many negative impacts.

This means it's not just the high cognitive load of learning to read and write that's laying our at-risk children low in our Early Years Factory, activating risk factors that remain dormant in regular-orthography nations. Negative impacts of Acquired Helplessness are also at work, compounding children's difficulties and woes.

Changing to 2-Stage learning using a fully-regular beginners' orthography initially, would provide strong Success Inoculation, and prevent Acquired Helplessness. We'll see strong indicators of Success Inoculation in Tour 5 when we explore the Initial Teaching Alphabet (ITA) research.

The findings of future research will be informative and, quite likely, exciting. Doubtless, executive-function impacts are involved, impacting children's skill development. Acquired Helplessness and lack of Success Inoculation, and their effects on executive-function and learning skills, will also prove key in why so many severely struggling Standard-English word-readers respond so poorly to intervention. It's so much harder to achieve effective intervention when children aren't optimistic and expect continued struggles.

Activation of risk factors will also be involved: because we've so many risk factors likely to move beginning word-readers into slow progress and discouragement, our children are more susceptible to Acquired Helplessness. With Australia's sadly low school supports, and high time and curriculum pressure, generating struggling readers and Acquired Helplessness en masse might be somewhat a specialty of our Early Years Factory.

Anxiety might be another Australian specialty, courtesy of Acquired Helplessness. Many weak word-readers experience high anxiety, and teachers comment that with our national curriculum being so broad and teaching thus needing to move quickly in order to cover it all, many children are feeling pressured, particularly those for whom the curriculum moves too fast.

They feel they're seeing considerably more anxiety in children. I'd have to agree, as in recent years I've seen considerably *Panicked*

Young Word-Readers (Galletly, 2014f; 2015b; Knight et al., 2017b).

Starting formal word-reading and writing instruction in Prep, rather than Year 1, with pressured instruction, may well contribute strongly to increased levels of anxiety and Acquired Helplessness.

Being so young, and thus having low working memory and executive-function skills, our beginners lack resilience and persistence for tasks that aren't easy (Foley, 2017; Gray, 2017). Just watch children at play – they persist forever on things going well, but quickly switch off and move on when things seem difficult or they get bored.

When our beginners experience ongoing low word-reading success, they move into anxiety or passiveness and land on the default path to Acquired Helplessness and ongoing word-reading struggles.

Other work by Seligman, focused on building children's optimism and resilience, offers useful insights for this area, as do intervention programs using his work (Bailey & Challen, 2012; Seligman, 2007).

Needs for Strong Emotional Supports

Revised Learned Helplessness theory likely means Anglophone nations need to include strong emotional supports as a strategic part of effective instruction for at-risk children. That's seen in the *Bridging the Gap* project's emphasis that *Successful Engaged Learning* is pivotal for learning success in at-risk readers, who need to be engaged when learning (Knight et al., 2017b, 2020).

Many studies show Standard-English weak readers have associated emotional difficulties, frequently experiencing significant anxiety and symptoms of depression (e.g., Hendren et al., 2018). Useful research by Australian researcher Andrew Martin (2010) shows strong benefits for children who are taught motivation and engagement strategies. Other studies show working directly on reading difficulties and overcoming them, and preventing reading difficulties through ensuring effective reading development, have very strong effects building motivation and engagement (Freire, 1974; Pitman, 1973; Warburton & Southgate, 1969).

Hamre & Pianta (2005) showed low-achieving USA Grade 1 readers need and benefit from strong emotional support and encouragement:

> *By the end of first grade, at-risk students placed in first-grade classrooms offering strong instructional and emotional support had achievement scores and student-teacher relationships commensurate with their low-risk peers. At-risk students placed*

in less supportive classrooms had lower achievement and more conflict with teachers.

Research on class size supports this idea, with Anglophone struggling learners particularly benefiting from smaller class size (Hattie, 2005, 2008; Mathis, 2017; Zyngier, 2014). Teacher workload is more manageable when classes are smaller, with at-risk children more likely to receive needed instruction and emotional supports.

It's likely Australia's lower-third and perhaps our lower-half, our children who don't find learning easy, are highly at risk of Acquired Helplessness and its depressed passiveness. They're also at risk of task avoidance, boredom, and their resulting negative effects.

There's thus value in also researching the impacts of boredom and task avoidance within research on Success Inoculation and Acquired Helplessness. Children who aren't engaged and listening, when learning a difficult skill, often miss out on crucial learning, then get a bit behind, then further and further, and so on, moving one paddock, two paddocks, three paddocks, four, from the year-level playing field.

There's also value in researching the role of Acquired Helplessness in low effectiveness of English word-reading instruction, and the role of Success Inoculation in remediation that's found successful.

Perhaps overcoming Acquired Helplessness is the reason there are 6,428,693 different word-reading instruction programs that at least two people found effective. I'm joking of course, but, seriously, we have so many different systems advocated as *the cure*, and clearly none works as well as a fully-regular beginners' orthography, given the Anglosphere still has such crowds of struggling readers.

Importantly, one factor these *cures* have in common is that they made a world of difference for some strugglers, reversing Acquired Helplessness, changing *I can't* to *I can*, and achieving not just word-reading progress, but also the pride, confidence and resilience building of Success Inoculation. And from that point, those learners made far more rapid, confident and determined progress, and moved from success to success. Word-reading progress plus Success Inoculation can be decidedly impressive.

Inadequate Education As Possible Neglect

Sadly, large numbers of Australian children start school emotionally vulnerable, and in need of strong emotional supports. Many become struggling readers and learners. Education can and should play an active role in providing these emotional supports, particularly those needed to support children being active, effective, motivated learners.

To what extent is Australian education achieving this at present?

Inadequate education, with children not sufficiently receiving the individual attention, appropriate instruction and tailoring of instruction that they need, is in many ways a form of neglect. Having learning difficulties is traumatic in many ways, with lasting social-emotional effects, making it important that Australia is active in achieving effective instruction, and avoiding instruction which can be characterised as neglect.

When we compare our education outcomes with those of regular-orthography nations in PIRLS and PISA, our much higher numbers of struggling learners show that our Find the Learning Time Challenge is in no way a minor issue. And our Find the Caring Time Challenge accompanies it.

Neglect, through children receiving too little one-on-one attention, deserves serious consideration, given that we're insisting Australian children learn to read and write Standard English at a very young age without benefit of a regular orthography. In effect, this allows English orthographic complexity to add insult to injury, inflicting stress, high cognitive load, and, quite often, severe literacy and learning difficulties to vulnerable children.

Most Australian research on neglect has focused on family neglect, with neglect being associated with increased adolescent and adult life functioning difficulties (e.g., Kisely et al., 2020; Mills et al., 2012).

There's perhaps value in researching inadequate instruction as a form of educational neglect, with associated effects, as we explore the impacts of orthographic complexity, with focus on education being GENTLE vs HEARTSH, and the appropriateness of instruction and supports, along with their impacts on academic and social-emotional functioning.

Motivational-Emotional Struggles of Regular-Orthography Children

Of course, adopting 2-Stage learning and the use of a fully-regular orthography prior to Standard English doesn't mean no problems for our children. It does mean far fewer problems than at present.

Motivational-emotional issues can develop very easily, particularly in children who see themselves as doing poorly relative to their peers (e.g., Valås, 1999). This happens in regular-orthography children too, and there seems value in crosslinguistic research exploring the relationship of self-perception of weakness and objective severity of difficulties, given that the word-reading skills of regular-orthography weaker word-readers would be vastly higher than those of Australian weaker word-readers (e.g., Lyytinen, et al., 2021; Seymour et al., 2003; Torppa et al., 2017).

Some Finnish studies shed light on this area. Poskiparta et al. (2003) found motivational-emotional struggles to be present in Finnish weak readers. They followed children from pre-school through to Grade 2, using tasks which tapped motivational-emotional vulnerability, then looked back to consider the differences between weak and stronger readers. They found no difference in Kindergarten but clear differences in Grades 1 and 2, with weak readers being less task-oriented, more ego-defensive and more socially dependent than the stronger readers.

Further, Tuija Aro et al. (2022), in their study of 579 Finnish children with reading and maths learning disabilities, aged 8 to 15 years, found *alarmingly high levels* of behavioural-emotional symptoms at clinical levels, with over 37% having affective disorders, anxiety, and Attention-Deficit/Hyperactivity Disorder (ADHD) problems. They emphasise the importance of school and teacher awareness of behavioural-emotional issues for children with learning difficulties, and needs to assess these difficulties.

Given Anglophone nations have far greater severity of ongoing literacy learning difficulties (Dion et al., Lyytinen et al., 2021; Scammacca et al., 2016), we have strong needs for crosslinguistic research exploring and comparing the behaviour and emotional difficulties of weak learners in regular-orthography and Anglophone nations.

Studies show regular-orthography struggling learners have internalising symptoms and dysfunctional cognitive-emotional processes that impact literacy skills and learning, e.g., Sideridis et al. (2019), considering Greek beginning readers, discuss

> *A generic shutdown of the system that controls reading performance, caused by the additive effects of limited cognitive resources and print-related skills and compounded by cognitive and emotion self-regulation difficulty. ... Generic shutdown effects, as apparently unpredictable fluctuations in student reading performance, are a major concern for special education practitioners. ... The accumulated effects of failure and frustration may lead to dramatic changes in students'*

behaviors, such as choosing to withdraw from a task, competency, or skill area overall. Educators need to be sensitive to changes in students' emotionality and mood to prevent such episodes and to help students maintain a level of integrity and achievement that is necessary for them to maintain proper levels of engagement.

It seems likely this would be a greater issue in Anglophone weak word-readers and writers, given the much higher cognitive load and impeded learning, frustration and failure that they experience.

It is notable that Torppa et al. (2017) found task avoidance in weak Finnish spellers. This suggests that Acquired Helplessness is experienced, with emotional supports needed across regular-orthography learning – though probably not to the extent of our weak readers and spellers.

Eklund et al. (2013) also found Finnish weaker readers showing task avoidance. In addition, an important finding, they found lack of task avoidance acts as a protective factor for healthy-progress children, enabling stronger reading. They emphasise the crucial importance of keeping children motivated and interested in schoolwork and reading.

Similarly, GraphoLearn researchers stress the importance of setting children up for success, not starting too early as children might become bored, and scaffolding children so they're motivated and engaged (Lyytinen et al., 2021).

Ronimus et al. (2019) found self-efficacy strongly differentiated the progress of Finnish first graders with *severe* word-reading fluency weakness. In their GraphoLearn learning, children with high self-efficacy made good progress, while the progress of children with low self-efficacy was limited – Acquired Helplessness may well have been a factor in their low self-efficacy.

Further, a meta-analysis of GraphoLearn research studies (McTigue et al., 2020), showed that on the whole, from studies considered, GraphoLearn had relatively low success, but this was not the case when strong adult supports were provided, with learning then far more successful.

Clearly, motivational, behaviour and emotional difficulties are universal, present in both regular-orthography and Anglophone nations, i.e., across nations for learning difficulties. Research on crosslinguistic differences is needed, e.g., on how severity of literacy weakness expands behaviour and emotional difficulties.

Research Tour 3. Success Inoculation Vs Acquired Helplessness

Setting Children Up for Success

I'm a keen advocate for setting children up for strong success.

So often, an activity gets a bad reputation when the reason it wasn't successful is less the activity and more that children weren't provided with the scaffolding needed to ensure they experienced Successful Engaged Learning (Knight et al., 2017b, 2020).

As Torgesen (1998) states,
> *The most critical elements of an effective program for the prevention of reading disability at the elementary school level are:*
> *The right kind and quality of instruction delivered with*
> *The right level of intensity and duration to*
> *The right children at*
> *The right time.*

For our at-risk and struggling readers, activities so often need to be used strategically, at the right time, with strong supports and encouragement, if children are to achieve strong success.

I tell families that my job is to give the right activities and, if one seems too hard, skip it and tell me next session – Successful Engaged Learning is crucial for our struggling readers (Knight et al., 2017b).

A strong, trusting working relationship is important for our struggling readers, one where children know they're working with an expert who understands and respects their difficulties, and is confident of their potential to improve and keep improving.

Children's perception of themselves against their peers is also important. Ironically, it's quite likely that
- Our middle and upper-third word-readers have high self-confidence, because they don't know they're extremely slow learners relative to regular-orthography readers, while
- Lower-third regular-orthography readers have much lower self-confidence, despite having much higher skills than our middle and upper-third.

The GraphoLearn Success Inoculation Story

GraphoLearn (previously termed *GraphoGame*) was developed as part of Finland's impressive *Jyvaskyla Longitudinal Study of Dyslexia* (JLD), e.g., Eklund et al., 2013, 2015; Lohvansuu et al., 2021; Lyytinen, 2014; Lyytinen et al., 2004, 2014, 2015; Lyytinen, Aro et al., 2006; Lyytinen, Erskine et al., 2006; Richardson et al., 2003.

Its research provides powerful insights on the needs for learning to be carefully strategic if children are not to move into Acquired Helplessness and ongoing early-literacy struggles.

As Lyytinen et al. (2021) explain,
> Recent GraphoGame studies reveal that severe dyslexia is very difficult to overcome when intervention is started after the child has been affected by the related failures during the first semester (Ronimus, 2019). Thus, the optimal starting time is when children enter school. When adults motivate the child to use GraphoGame, successful learning is more likely to occur (McTigue et al., 2019). ...
> The optimal use of this program includes starting at the time the learner enters school, when children tend to be most interested in developing their reading skills. ... Our studies provide strong evidence that support with GL needs to start early in the primary school grades in order to be optimally effective.
> If learners start the program too early, the risk increases that the child may not be motivated to continue using it; they become bored with the task as too many repetitions are required before the goal is reached.
> This could be because many children with dyslexia have delayed brain development reflected by accompanying delayed development of spoken language (e.g., Lyytinen et al., 2015a); thus, starting this game too early may not be effective because the child is not ready yet to learn the connections without very numerous repetitions. ...
> Only 20% of the trials are chosen to be focused on contents where the learner tends to make repeatedly incorrect choices (i.e., getting thus negative feedback), to keep playing enjoyable. The crux of the program rests on positive feedback, to motivate the learner to continue practicing the task until the goal is reached. GL's effectiveness results from the real-time adaptation to every individual's actual needs rather than on traditional remedial activities that do not directly build the still compromised aspects of literacy-related skills for children who require remediation. ...
> Most children using the GL in transparent writing environments in the developed world get sufficient help, preventively using it to follow the mainstream learning curve in the basic reading/spelling skills. This finding is true concerning children with dyslexia if GL is used when the child first begins school and the game is used for 10–15-min sessions (preferably more than one) per day for several weeks.

Research Tour 3. Success Inoculation Vs Acquired Helplessness

> *Children facing severe difficulties most often require continuation until the third grade especially if the game is used only relatively infrequently (i.e., a few short sessions per week). This program is most effective when the game is used in the context of face-to-face remedial teaching. We have found that remedial teaching is strongly enhanced when the game is utilized as an addition to that remediation. Our studies have revealed that if the training game is used for at least a quarter of the time (10–15 min) the child is in the special education session, learners improve their spelling skills to the level of the mainstream children by the end of the third grade (Saine et al., 2010, 2011, 2013).*

That's a long, but very useful quote. Let's explore it briefly, as it has useful insights for nations starting children on the highly confusing learning of Standard English at age 4.5 to 5.0 years in schools providing considerably less supports than Finnish schools.

It emphasises highly strategic instruction being needed to achieve success in at-risk children even when the learning is notably easy.

It shows that even when children are aged 7.0 to 8.0 years in Grade 1, and only needing to master very simple learning of Finnish, it's highly, and perhaps crucially, important to ensure failure and disappointment are avoided and that children experience highly motivating Successful Engaged Learning on an ongoing basis.

That's the case even in a nation where learning to read and write is so easy that 50% of children are already successfully reading when they start school, and relatively few need strong teaching supports.

That's sadly impressive. It suggests the odds are very much against Australia routinely achieving successful word-reading and spelling in our 4.5 to 5.0-year-old lower-third in our Early Years Factory.

It also intimates that if we enacted Changes 7, 8 and 9, we could improve education exponentially across Australia:

- Change 7: Insist on easy literacy development: Reach regular-orthography nations' achievement levels.
- Change 8. Investigate the potential of fully-regular beginners' orthographies: They're winners.
- Change 9. Play to learn first: Start Standard English word-reading instruction from mid-Year 2.

We'd wonderfully improve our odds by enacting those changes: ensuring rich building of readiness, with children having mature learning skills, and starting with a regular-orthography easing and expediting learning to read and write Standard English.

Just like Finland, we too might have over half of our children learning to read prior to formal instruction, few children needing intervention, and that intervention being highly successful, such that even our weakest 5% and 10% would be proficiently accurate, independent readers and writers well before high school.

It's interesting that Japanese and Chinese weak word-readers are now using GraphoLearn to good effect. That could be us too.

Key Findings from Tour 3

Key principles that can be established from findings on Acquired Helplessness and Success Inoculation include the following:
1. Children need to experience strong success and feel confident about their skills and potential for progress, to achieve success learning. Successful Engaged Learning should be a key focus of Australian early-years education (Knight et al., 2017b).
2. Strong success provides, in effect, Success Inoculation, giving children resilience for later learning, coping well even when that learning is challenging.
3. Ongoing difficulties and low success in initial learning are particularly damaging, especially for young children who lack maturity and resilience.
4. Acquired Helplessness seems an automatic default pathway that struggling readers move into, due to experiencing ongoing low success and difficulties.
5. It's likely there are high levels of Acquired Helplessness in Australian lower-third word-readers and spellers.
6. Success Inoculation and Acquired Helplessness have corresponding positive and negative impacts on children's learning skills and learning.
7. Minimal research has focused on Success Inoculation and Acquired Helplessness impacts on Standard-English word-reading, spelling and early-literacy development, and associated cognitive-processing and executive-function skills.
8. Indicators of Acquired Helplessness are seen in the prevalence of high levels of anxiety and depression in Anglophone children with weak word-reading and learning difficulties, and studies showing that young children with weak word-reading have major needs for strong emotional supports and confidence building in addition to instruction that's highly effective.
9. The importance of Success Inoculation and avoiding default Acquired Helplessness suggests value in exploring the role of

English fully-regular beginners' orthographies in providing Success Inoculation and preventing Acquired Helplessness.
10. Research is needed, exploring the impacts of Success Inoculation and Acquired Helplessness in Standard-English and regular-orthography children.

Research Tour 4.
Regular Orthographies and Intellectual Disability

A transparent orthography treats even a phonologically immature reader in a lenient manner. It helps in explicating the Alphabetic Principle, the correspondence between spoken and written language ... It does not burden the beginning reader with a plethora of correspondence rules; and together with systematic phonics teaching it provides the beginning reader with a simple tool for successful word recognition.

Mikko Aro, 2004

How well do Anglophone nations meet their teaching challenges for our children with intellectual disability? Not nearly as well as regular-orthography nations.

Because regular orthographies are so easy to learn to read and write, there are very few risk factors likely to derail vulnerable children from word-reading, spelling and early-literacy success. That includes children with significant intellectual disability.

In effect, regular orthographies are kind orthographies. One measure of just how kind they can be for beginning readers, is how easily children with intellectual disability master word-reading and spelling, and how, for them, low intelligence is not a major risk factor for word-reading difficulties.

Let's explore that now.

In Anglophone nations, children with moderate and severe intellectual difficulties almost inevitably experience severe word-reading and spelling difficulties, and many never become proficient readers and writers.

That's not the case in regular-orthography nations. Studies show it's routine for children with major disabilities to be proficiently accurate word-readers, including children with moderate to severe intellectual disability and children with severe inherited Dyslexia.

Multiple regular-orthography studies show strong word-reading and phonemic-awareness development in cohorts of regular-orthography children that include children with severe disabilities (Cossu et al., 1993; Olofsson, 1993; Olofsson & Niedersoe, 1999; Poskiparta et al., 1999; Schneider et al., 1999). Similar Anglophone studies show sadly minimal gains relative to regular-orthography children (e.g., Fuchs et al., 2002; Groen et al., 2006; Torgesen, 1998; Torgesen et al., 1997).

Giuseppe Cossu and his team show this gentle, easy word-reading development in their research on Italian children with Down Syndrome learning to read (Cossu et al.,1993, Cossu, 1999).

The children they studied had severe intellectual disability (Mean IQ of 44 and IQ range of 40 to 56), but mastered word-reading relatively easily, correctly reading 93.8 % of real words, and 88% of pseudowords, which were used to test reading of unfamiliar words.

Speaking with Professor Cossu when our CQU team visited researchers and schools in Italy, one big challenge in setting up the study was finding children with Down Syndrome who weren't yet reading well, because word-reading development happens quite easily for Italian children with intellectual disability.

In common with other crosslinguistic researchers (e.g., Jimenez et al., 2003), Cossu (1999) concludes that general intelligence and working memory aren't pivotal for the acquisition of Italian word-reading, a statement that could never be made of English:

Whatever impairments the children with Down's Syndrome undoubtably show ... these deficits have not precluded the children from acquiring the transcoding skills involved in reading. ... despite a mean IQ of 44, these children read (regular words, irregular words and nonwords) with the same proficiency as normal Italian 7 year olds.

Now the children were older, with an age range from 8.0 to 15.8 years, but to be reading with Italian 7-year-old proficiency is simply brilliant by our standards, because 7-year-old Italian readers are virtually fully accurate, just not yet super speedy.

The study also clearly demonstrates how working memory and intelligence aren't big requirements for learning to read a regular-orthography, because learning to read a regular-orthography has such low cognitive load (Cossu, 1999):

> *Since a transparent orthography is mastered with no special effort by normal children, it is not surprising that even [intellectually disabled] children can easily grasp the orthographic principles and become efficient readers and writers (qua decoders).*
> *This particular condition shows that general intelligence, verbal memory or psycho-motor skills are largely irrelevant factors for the acquisition of literacy.*

Reading that statement in the early 2000s caused our CQU team to realise just how paradigmatically different Anglophone and regular-orthography worlds are.

That would be a ridiculous statement, if made about Standard-English reading development, the notion that general intelligence, verbal working memory, and cognitive-processing skill efficiency aren't needed, and are somewhat irrelevant factors when it comes to children learning to read and write.

No, that's a statement for the regular-orthography, easy, expedited education world, the world across the crosslinguistic divide. It's definitely not applicable to learning in Australia at the current time.

Our children need general intelligence, verbal working memory, and cognitive-processing efficiency to effectively learn to read and write Standard English, and weaknesses in those areas set children up to be enormously at risk, with struggles virtually guaranteed.

Down Syndrome is characterised by particularly low working memory, e.g., Bower & Hayes, 1994. Thus, the children in Cossu et al.'s study had severely low IQ plus the additionally low working memory of Down Syndrome – yet, as word-readers, they were thriving!

Those Italian children's effective word-reading skills additionally speak volumes on how early intervention and remediation work extremely effectively in regular-orthography nations.

Cossu et al.'s (1993) findings of strong word-reading development fit with my observations of children with intellectual disability in schools in Italy, Finland and Japan. They're impressively literate by our standards for our children with healthy intellectual ability:

Unfortunately, with rare exceptions, the word-reading levels of Anglophone children with Down Syndrome are low, and their gains from Standard-English word-reading interventions are extremely modest (e.g., Groen et al., 2006). Intervention studies show that word-reading increases, but only incrementally (Burgoyne et al., 2012; Lim et al., 2018, 2019), with most children with Down

Syndrome not achieving beyond a 6- to 8-year-old word-reading age (Groen et al., 2006), a level vastly weaker than that of Italian 7-year-olds (Cossu et al., 1993).

Thus, while making gains, the vast majority of our children with intellectual disability continue to be significantly disabled word-readers and writers.

Groen et al. (2006) studied the word-reading of a girl with Down Syndrome in English with word-reading in the average range, comparing her with a control group of other children with Down Syndrome. The control group showed markedly weak word-reading, despite the data of six children having not been included due to them being unable to score at base level.

The article's title, *A case of exceptional reading accuracy in a child with Down Syndrome* highlights the Standard-English norm being decidedly low word-reading levels for our children who have intellectual disability. The sadly low word-reading and writing levels of Anglophone children with intellectual disability is an extremely serious aspect of our severe orthographic disadvantage, given that it's the opposite story for similar children in regular-orthography nations, who experience the gentle kindness of regular orthographies.

This wide crosslinguistic gap urgently needs addressing. It is unkind, unethically so, positioning our most vulnerable citizens as severest victims of Standard English and orthographic disadvantage.

Regular-orthography intervention studies show word-reading intervention for children of low ability to be brief, relatively non-intensive and highly effective, with it routinely progressing them to reading as accurately as their peers (e.g. Olofsson, 1993; Olofsson & Niedersoe, 1999; Poskiparta et al., 1999; Schneider et al., 1997, 1999).

Anglophone nations would like that. Using a beginners' orthography, we could have it.

Key Findings from Tour 4

Findings and implications of studies explored in Tour 4 suggest the following points are useful considerations towards improving literacy and education in Australia and Anglophone nations:
1. Efficient working memory, general intelligence and cognitive-processing skills are not essential for regular-orthography children learning to read and write.
2. For this reason, regular-orthography children with severe

intellectual disability are able to become highly accurate word-readers and spellers using usual school instruction and intervention, with this enabling them to be effective readers and writers to the level their intellectual and language skills allow.
3. Efficient working memory, general intelligence and cognitive-processing skills are crucial factors for Standard-English children learning to read and write, because of ongoing high learning demands and high cognitive load.
4. In consequence, our children with moderate and severe intellectual disability usually have extremely severe word-reading and spelling difficulties.
5. This positions Australian children with intellectual disability as severest victims of English orthographic complexity.
6. It is likely that using a fully-regular beginners' orthography would immensely empower the word-reading, spelling and literacy development of many Australian children and adults with intellectual disability.

Research Tour 5.
The Power of Beginners' Orthographies

The long uphill grind has been cut out. Reading is more an ordinary part of childhood instead of a chore and so the children take it in their stride. They pick up a book in their free time as they would a paintbrush or jigsaw.

F. W. Warburton & Vera Southgate, 1969

Towards decision-making on whether Australia should use a fully-regular beginners' orthography prior to Standard English, Australia needs to study literacy development in Taiwan, Japan and China, and the extensive 1960s research on the Initial Teaching Alphabet (ITA). In this tour, we explore these areas.

As we're now about to head off on our fifth research tour, it's a useful time to recap briefly, and think on what we've learned so far. We've explored the major impacts of orthographic complexity. We've completed four tours thus far:

- **Tour 1.** Too slow Standard-English word-reading development.
- **Tour 2.** Orthography: The key impacting factor.
- **Tour 3.** Success Inoculation vs Acquired Helplessness.
- **Tour 4.** Regular orthographies and intellectual disability.

Those tours have shown us our current struggles as we try to achieve effective early-literacy development and strong school learning.

We're mired in severe orthographic disadvantage. We've an Early Years Factory in action, alas, with too slow, arduous reading and writing development, that produces our flood of struggling readers. That's largely due to our education habits of:

- 1-Stage early-literacy using solely Standard English.
- Having our children attack this learning far younger than children in most nations, at age 4.5 to 5 years.

Along with other Anglophone nations, we have severe orthographic disadvantage, and are the world of Cs. We're a Chaotic, Cluttered-Curriculum nation that's awash with Confused, Complex learning and too high Cognitive load (Galletly, 2022a).

The tours have also, to a certain extent, shown us our potential for a very strong future. Life doesn't have to be this difficult, and the Anglosphere is but one part of our wonderful wide world. Using regular orthographies, many nations are thriving, with delightfully easy, rapid, early-literacy development.

If and when Australia moves from 1-Stage to 2-Stage early-literacy development, by adding in a fully-regular beginners' orthography for our children's earliest literacy development, we too will enjoy powerful orthographic advantage. We'll join the regular-orthography world of Es: Easy, Expedited, Efficient, Effective Education.

The tours, thus far, have also shown us the potential of the 10 Changes (Galletly, 2022a, In press):

Change 1. Understand how orthographies matter: English spelling is dragging us down.
Change 2. Own our struggling reader woes: End hypocrisy and pretence.
Change 3. Weigh workload: Our children and teachers are working far too hard.
Change 4. One-size education does not fit all: Teach to the decidedly different instructional needs of upper-third and lower-third readers.
Change 5. End our data deficiency: Build strong knowledge on word-reading levels.
Change 6. Enrich every child: Ensure effective supportive tailored education.
Change 7. Insist on easy literacy development: Reach regular-orthography nations' achievement levels.
Change 8. Investigate the potential of fully-regular beginners' orthographies: They're winners.
Change 9. Play to learn first: Start Standard-English word-reading instruction from mid-Year 2.
Change 10. Build needed research knowledge as quickly as possible: Use collaborative school-based research.

They've shown us, too, the power and potential of our ABCs of optimising education (Galletly, 2022a):
A. **ACT** locally while looking globally.
B. **BOOST** the lower-third to benefit everyone.
C. **CHANGE** effectively to work less and achieve more.

We're now on Tour 5, *The Power of Beginners' Orthographies*. Showing us the enormous power and potential of beginners' orthographies, it's most definitely a good news tour.

Early Literacy in Taiwan, Japan and China

To explore the potential of 2-Stage early-literacy development, Australia and Anglophone nations will learn much by considering early-literacy development, difficulties and instruction in Taiwan, Japan and China, nations that last century moved from 1-Stage to 2-Stage early-literacy development, and subsequently experienced extremely impressive literacy, education and economic improvement.

While I've not found lots of studies on early-literacy development in Taiwanese, Japanese and Chinese children, it's important to note that I've only read research written in English. There may well be many useful studies in Taiwanese, Japanese and Chinese journals.

Certainly, available studies show word-reading and writing difficulties occur in only a very small proportion of children.

Japan has three orthographies:
- Fully-regular Hiragana, used for Stage-1 earliest literacy.
- Fully-regular Katakana, used for foreign and scientific words, and learned after Hiragana.
- Highly complex Kanji, whose morpho-logographic characters are learned one by one, in Stage-2 literacy.

Uno et al. (2009) found extremely low levels of literacy difficulties:
- Hiragana: 0.2% reading difficulties, 1.6% writing difficulties.
- Katakana: 1.4% reading difficulties, 3.8% writing difficulties.
- Kanji: 6.9% reading difficulties, 6% writing difficulties.

This minimal extent of difficulties is also evidenced in Makita's (1968) research finding that Japanese teachers considered less than 1% of students to have word-reading difficulties.

Wouldn't we love to be like that, with less than 2% of children having difficulty reading and writing our beginners' orthography, and less than 7% having difficulties with Standard English?

Makita (1968) used an excellent, brief, practical survey of teachers, which is included in the article. Future crosslinguistic research using a survey such as this one would quickly build useful knowledge.

Other early studies of Japanese and Taiwanese reading difficulties also show that few had word-reading and writing difficulties, e.g., Stevenson et al. (1982) discuss findings of Makita in Japan, and W. Kuo (1978) in Taiwan, of very low incidence (e.g., Makita, 1974):

> While [reading disability] comprises a formidable portion of psychiatric practice in western countries, its incidence in Japan is so rare that specialists in Japan do not get any referrals.

Given that Japanese families prioritise seeking supports to boost their children's learning, that's an important finding.

It contrasts markedly with Australia, where both local GPs and paediatricians are inundated with families attending for help with their struggling readers and learners. Rowe and Rowe's (2002, 2004) studies found approximately half of paediatric consultations were for behaviour and attention difficulties, which often incorporate reading difficulties, and that about 20% of referrals were for learning difficulties.

Kuo's (1978) survey of Taiwanese teachers similarly showed only a tiny proportion of Taiwanese weak word-readers:

> The present investigation proclaims that [Taiwanese] children seldom have a problem of reading disabilities. It was found that primary school teachers in Taiwan are unaware of the existence of such an issue. When the characteristics of reading disabilities were explained to them, they remarked that only a very limited number of their students fell into such a category.

Stevenson et al. (1982) also discuss psychologists and educators in Hong Kong and mainland China considering reading difficulties to be very infrequent.

Stevenson et al.'s (1982) study was of reading comprehension, not word-reading. It compared Grade 5 children in the USA, Japan and Taiwan, finding similar numbers of struggling readers in all three nations. As they didn't assess word-reading, the relationship of word-reading to reading comprehension wasn't explored.

It's encouraging that the groups had similar comprehension skills. This might reflect Standard-English reading comprehension from mid-primary school being predicted more by language skills (Adams, 1990; C. Snow et al., 1998a; Stuart & Stainthorp, 2015; Wolf, 2007). Equally, it might reflect Standard-English children developing stronger reading-comprehension skills because they rely far more on context cues in early literacy, because their word-reading skills aren't yet proficient (Hanley et al., 2004; Oney & Goldman, 1984).

Given their impressive achievement levels in PIRLS and PISA, where they achieve at high levels not just in Reading but also in Maths and Science, it seems likely that children in Taiwan, Japan and China have strong reading skills.

With multiple studies showing Standard-English readers' reading comprehension to be equal to or higher than regular-orthography readers (Hanley et al., 1994; Oney & Goldman, 1984; Stevenson et al., 1982), there seems value in researching this area.

It's likely we'll find the high scores of our upper-third children with great reading comprehension compensate well for the low scores of our lower-third children, to give us a healthy Mean score. That's what seemed to be happening in PISA 2000 and PISA 2003 when we achieved respectable Mean reading scores – prior to us declining, as other nations improved.

Australian education would benefit greatly from cooperative research with researchers and schools in nations such as Taiwan, Japan and China, building knowledge on 2-Stage learning, first learning a fully-regular orthography, then transitioning to reading and writing a complex orthography; and how cognitive-processing and literacy factors impact word-reading and spelling development.

Maximising Learning of a Second Orthography

I wasn't able to find studies exploring cognitive-processing skill development of children in Taiwan, Japan and China first learning their regular-orthography then transitioning to their complex orthography. Given there are many Asian journals not written in English, there may well be useful research studies available to interested readers skilled in reading the relevant languages.

If we used a fully-regular initial orthography, our children's transitioning to Standard English would be much faster than that of Taiwanese, Japanese and Chinese children. That's because
- Their beginners' and complex orthographies (e.g., Hiragana vs Kanji) use different sets of characters (graphemes), so there are large amounts of post-transition learning.
- The characters of their complex orthographies are visually highly complex (Verhoeven & Perfetti, 2022), which further heightens the amount of new learning.

- Our beginners' orthography would be very similar to Standard English, with both being alphabetic orthographies, with thus far less additional learning of letters.

The Anglosphere will nonetheless benefit greatly from exploring the learning of children in Taiwan, Japan and China, to build understanding of the factors expediting their success.

With regard to word-reading development, key factors in Taiwanese, Japanese and Chinese children's successful, subsequent learning of their complex orthography seem likely to include the following:

1. The nations holding back their complex orthography during earliest literacy, so children build strong skills and confidence reading and writing their initial fully-regular orthography, and do not experience confusion and frustration in early learning.
2. Statistical learning and self-teaching being heightened through the initial orthography being fully regular.
3. Maximising self-teaching and implicit statistical learning during transitioning through words being written in the two orthographies side-by-side.
4. Ensuring extensive, effective practice and successful statistical learning by providing ample reading materials where new characters currently being learned are also written in the fully-regular orthography.
5. Portioning the learning of the complex orthography into manageable year-level amounts, e.g., Japanese children learn just over 1000 Kanji characters from Years 1 to 6, learning year-level sets of 80, 160, 200, 200, 185 and 181 characters, in Grades 1, 2, 3, 4, 5 and 6, respectively.
6. Expediting learning of their complex orthography by integrating word-reading, spelling, handwriting and vocabulary instruction in children's learning of their year-level sets of characters.
7. Having very manageable child and teacher workload, a relatively streamlined national curriculum, and ample teaching and learning time.
8. Word-reading and spelling difficulties being quite minor, so effective intervention happens quite easily, without children losing considerable class time or confidence.
9. Children being empowered, skilled learners, who are confident about their ability to self-teach, to learn independently.
10. Having calm, orderly classrooms where learning takes place smoothly and efficiently.

Together, these factors enable their children's learning of both their regular and complex orthographies to be extremely efficient.

Research Tour 5. The Power of Beginners' Orthographies

The Initial Teaching Alphabet (ITA)

Let's now explore the prolific research done in the 1960s on the Initial Teaching Alphabet (ITA).

Historically, we Anglophone nations briefly used two companion orthographies in many schools. Children first learned to read and write an experimental fully-regular English beginners' orthography, to develop confident early-literacy skills. Then they transitioned to reading and writing Standard English.

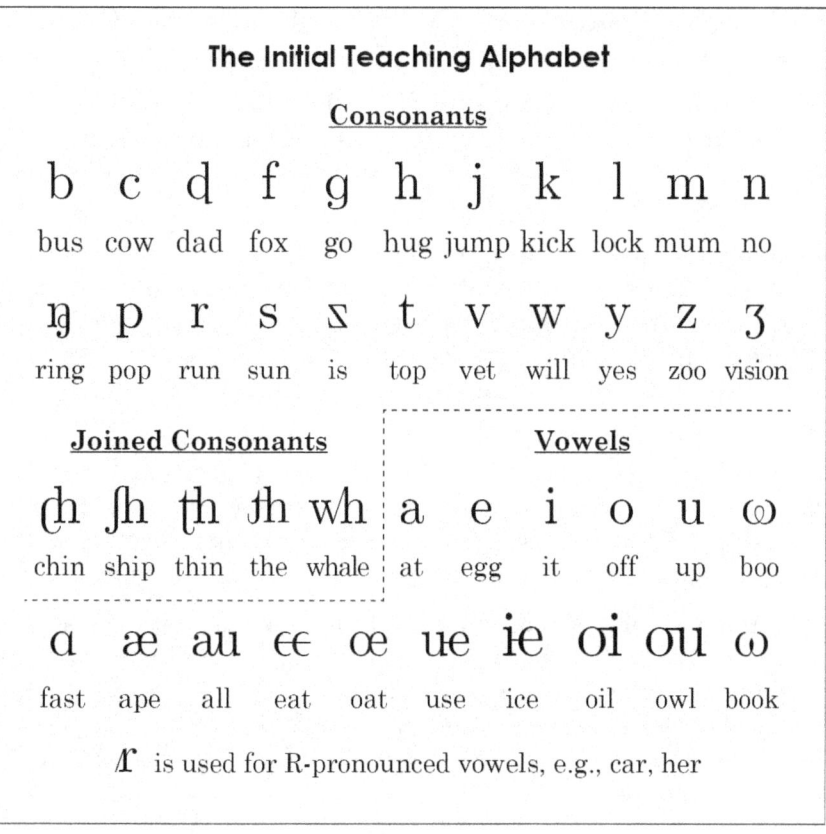

Figure 10. *The Initial Teaching Alphabet (ITA)*

Termed the Initial Teaching Alphabet (ITA), it was virtually fully regular, apart from two additional spelling patterns (GPCs), to ease transitioning: both C and K were used for *kuh*, and there were two Z graphemes, with a reversed letter Z, named *Zes* used for the Z sound we write as S at word ends, e.g., *is has* (Warburton & Southgate, 1969):

> *Pitman's aim was to produce an alphabet which closely approached a one-to-one relationship between spoken sound and*

written symbol, while at the same time endeavouring to ensure that children would experience little difficulty in transferring from reading materials printed in i.t.a. to reading materials printed in our traditional orthography.

In addition, to reduce the extent of letter learning that children needed to do initially, ITA used no capital letters (and ITA's name was written *i.t.a.*). Finland and Estonia do this now, using just all capitals initially.

By today's standards, the research methods used in the 1960s ITA research were particularly rigorous, and the extent of research massive, with many hundreds of studies conducted.

Alas, the ITA research finished abruptly in the late 1960s or early 1970s, for seemingly unknown reasons, with many planned studies not completed, apart from a tiny extent of usage in small pockets across the world.

Despite searching widely, our CQU team didn't find comments from ITA researchers on its abrupt end (Knight et al., 2017a). The timing of its end suggests likelihood it was due to the burgeoning popularity of Whole Language educational philosophy, which positioned word-reading as a relatively inconsequential skill.

Some recent writers comment that ITA ceased because it was a failure, but when one reads the research in depth, that's definitely not the case. Suffice to say the research stopped, with many intended studies not conducted, and with educators largely unable to easily continue its use, as, e.g., typing in ITA font wasn't available.

When one considers recent research on crosslinguistic differences and the PISA and PIRLS success of Asian nations that use beginners' orthographies, it's clear the ITA research was cupboarded far too soon. Indeed, the Anglosphere has quite possibly lost six decades of improved education because of that research's untimely end.

Our CQU team (Knight et al., 2017a) reviewed the ITA research, comparing findings with those of recent crosslinguistic research, while considering key issues impacting Anglophone reading difficulties. That chapter's big name says it all: *Managing cognitive load as the key to literacy development: Research directions suggested by crosslinguistic research and research on the Initial Teaching Alphabet (ITA).* Its abstract reads,

In recent years, orthographic complexity (the complexity of nations' spelling systems) has been established as a key factor impacting ease and speed of early-literacy development through

the extent of cognitive load it creates for beginning readers. This chapter analyses and synthesises research findings from three large bodies of research, using cognitive load and orthographic complexity perspectives, towards useful research directions for optimising Anglophone reading, literacy development and instruction.

The three corpuses are

1. The research on word-reading and literacy development and instruction in Anglophone nations;

2. Research establishing crosslinguistic literacy differences between Anglophone and regular-orthography nations, whose spelling is highly regular; and

3. Anglophone research from past decades on schools using a fully-regular English orthography, the Initial Teaching Alphabet (ITA).

In recent decades there has been considerable research exploring crosslinguistic differences in reading development and difficulties. This establishes Anglophone word reading and literacy development as being much slower and more complicated, particularly for struggling readers. However, regular-orthography nations show expedited literacy development for virtually all children. This difference seems created by the high cognitive load of Anglophone early word-reading development.

In the 1960s and early 1970s, there was considerable research in Anglophone nations exploring the impact of the Initial Teaching Alphabet (ITA) in reducing cognitive load and expediting Anglophone early-literacy development.

While these bodies of research explore Anglophone reading and literacy development, difficulties, and instruction from different perspectives, their findings have much in common and suggest useful directions towards improving Anglophone literacy learning.

For wider reading of the ITA research, useful papers include

- The research chapter our CQU team wrote (Knight et al., 2017a), and references listed there.
- Warburton and Southgate's (1969) large UK review.
- Writings by Downing (e.g., Downing, 1965, 1967a, 1967b, 1967c, 1969a, 1969b, 1972a, 1972b; Downing et al., 1967; Downing & Halliwell, 1964).
- Writings by Mazurkiewicz (1965, 1967, 1971, 1973a, 1973b).

The USA's *Education Resources Information Centre* (ERIC,

https://eric.ed.gov) also lists many ITA research publications that contain useful detail.

ITA Research Findings

Prior to the cessation of ITA research, the ITA studies investigated whether children would learn to read and write Standard English more easily using an initial orthography prior to Standard English.

They most certainly did! As Bushnell (1971) summarises, when discussing Mazurkiewicz and colleagues' work,
> A study conducted in Bethlehem, Pennsylvania, elementary schools, the first schools to adopt the Initial Teaching Alphabet (i.t.a.) approach to teaching basic reading in this country, revealed that children who started with i.t.a. had significantly less reading failure than children with traditional orthography (T.O.) training.
> Although the i.t.a. children were generally highly mobile and less advantaged than the T.O. children, it was found that:
> 1. The rate of failure (as evidenced by repeating grades) was three times higher for the T.O. group,
> 2. Twice as many T.O. pupils received remedial reading training as did i.t.a. pupils, and
> 3. On subtests of a standardized battery, i.t.a. pupils scored higher on capitalization, knowledge and use of references, and spelling.
> Further, T.O. children needed help on word recognition and comprehension, while i.t.a. children needed help only on comprehension.
> It was suggested that i.t.a. children had developed characteristics such as ego-strength, skills development, and learning behavior to produce a higher success rate in reading.

So many individual studies were conducted that review articles were used to summarise and review them, e.g., Block (1971) reviews 70 studies, the ITA Foundation (1971) discusses 42 studies, and ITA conference publications contain hundreds of papers (Block, 1968).

The ITA research has a strong research basis (Knight et al., 2017a):
> ITA's use and research built from strong crosslinguistic awareness that
> - nations using highly-regular orthographies had expedited literacy development;
> - Asian nations using complex [morpho-logographic orthographies] successfully expedited literacy development using

an initial fully-regular orthography; and
- optimal orthographies use GPC ratios as close as possible to one: one (Burt, 1969; Downing, 1972a, 1972b; Lado, 1957).

ITA was designed to ease and expedite Anglophone children's early reading and writing development through minimising the complexity that Standard-English spelling and letters create. With Anglophone nations starting school and reading instruction much younger than most other nations (and young children needing learning to be as simple as possible), the rationale of using ITA was to reduce the cognitive load of learning to a minimum.

This endorsed a simple logical path of reading and writing development, with transitioning from ITA to Standard-English orthography. In the same manner that children are first taught to print and use printing for earliest written expression, ITA would expedite early-literacy development and build strong confident early-literacy skills.

While there are many ITA studies conducted with impressive rigour, two sets of studies provide particularly useful detail. They are the UK studies conducted with many thousands of children from 1961 by Downing and colleagues at London University and the Ministry of Education, and the Pennsylvania USA studies conducted by Mazurkiewicz and colleagues. Their findings have been replicated in many other studies.

In addition, a large 1966 UK inquiry was instigated to review UK research and use of ITA in UK schools (Warburton & Southgate, 1969) – its report provides very useful reading.

At the time of the review, approximately 9% of UK schools were using ITA (1500 schools), with most using ITA after seeing its effectiveness in other schools. Virtually all schools that trialled it then continued with ITA. Only 2% of schools discontinued ITA usage after trialling it, with reasons provided being administrative, not dissatisfaction with ITA (Warburton & Southgate, 1969).

The UK reviewers surveyed and interviewed many hundreds of teachers and other personnel involved in or observing ITA instruction, and also examined ITA research projects and reports.

They found teachers overwhelmingly reported ITA as being very effective in helping children make a strong start in reading and writing: ITA made beginning reading and writing far easier, with children beginning to read earlier and learning to read quickly and easily. They reported children being much happier and more confident: keen to read, write and learn, and positive and confident about their skills.

Not all studies showed strong ITA superiority or long-term effects. As an example, the second major UK study of Downing and colleagues showed the second ITA cohort didn't make as impressive progress after transitioning as was seen in the first study.

Downing (1969b), in his research article, *Initial Teaching Alphabet: Results after six years*, discusses ITA findings from the two large UK Ministry of Education studies: both achieving their primary goals of eased early literacy and reduced difficulties, but only the first study showing strong ongoing gains in later primary school years:

The results of the first phase of the research were conclusive in both experiments. On every test, the reading attainments of pupils who use the initial teaching alphabet were very much superior to those who use traditional orthography.

Indeed, the difference was quite dramatic. For example, in the initial teaching alphabet classes, pupils were able to read by the end of the year on average more than twice as many words of English as children who use traditional orthography.

In the second phase, [results for] tests for the transfer of learning from initial teaching alphabet to traditional orthography were also the same in both experiments. ...

In both experiments, in the middle of the second year the pupils who had learned the initial teaching alphabet were not able to read in traditional orthography as well as they could read in the initial teaching alphabet which they had been learning. This was hardly surprising, but it is noteworthy that their reading attainments in traditional orthography were equal to those of the pupils who had been learning traditional orthography from the beginning of the experiment.

Even more surprising were the later results of the first experiment: by the end of the third year, the pupils who had learned the initial teaching alphabet had traditional orthography reading attainments that were significantly superior to those of the control group pupils who had used only traditional orthography.

The average pupil in the initial teaching alphabet classes was five months ahead of his counterpart in the traditional orthography classes after three years of school.

However, the results for this second phase – the transition from the initial teaching alphabet to traditional orthography – are not as clear as those for the first phase when attainments were

> *measured in the same alphabet as the pupils were learning. One result of the first experiment has not been confirmed as yet by the second experiment. ... [Pupils] did not show at the end of the third year the superiority found in the first experiment. There is some evidence that the teaching pace of the second experiment was slower, and, therefore, the recovery from transition may come later. This second experiment has been extended for two more years to investigate this question.*

As with other intended studies researchers discuss, our CQU team were unable to locate findings on this intended 2-year extension.

Most definitely, a very large majority of studies showed strong findings on ITA's effectiveness in expediting early literacy and preventing word-reading, spelling and early-literacy difficulties.

Importantly, while transitioning to using Standard English was often not a particular focus of their research, studies consistently showed that children transitioned easily and effectively.

When they transitioned, their skill development slowed initially, probably due to high cognitive load, then strong progress returned (Downing, 1967b, 1969b; Mazurkiewicz, 1971, 1973a, 1973b).

As Warburton and Southgate (1969) comment,

> *As soon as children had made the transition to traditional orthography the range of what they read increased enormously, partly because there is so much more reading matter printed in traditional orthography. ...*
>
> *A number of headteachers, relating how they now regularly borrowed large boxes of books from the public libraries in order to cater for these infant children who had become thirsty for books, pointed out that this was a practice which had formerly only been necessary for [much older children].*

Clearly, ITA usage strongly eased and accelerated early-literacy development, and prevented word-reading, spelling and associated early-literacy difficulties – and these would be Australia's primary reasons for using a fully-regular beginners' orthography.

There is prolific research showing ITA was successful for these purposes, and definite value in critically reading multiple ITA studies, with a focus on these two priority areas:
- Reducing the extent of word-reading and writing difficulties.
- Easing, speeding and enhancing early-literacy development.

Block's (1971) review of 70 studies comparing ITA and Standard-English cohorts in Anglophone nations showed that

- Two thirds of the studies found ITA cohorts to be significantly higher achievers.
- The remaining one-third found both cohorts equally successful.
- No studies found adverse effects of using ITA.

Block discusses the results being a strong answer to Reading Wars criticisms ITA research was getting from educators and researchers who weren't involved in ITA:

The report replies to frequently occurring criticisms of the i.t.a. program, such as
1. Children [have] difficulty transferring to [Standard English],
2. Children regress to i.t.a. after they have moved into a T.O. class,
3. i.t.a. materials are expensive, and
4. Children in i.t.a. programs experience the Hawthorne Effect (learn better because they are participating in an innovative program).
It is argued that such criticisms are not supported with evidence or research and that the research on i.t.a. can refute such claims.

Whereas recent regular-orthography research has focused largely on word-reading, ITA researchers included a focus on language skills and written expression skills as part of literacy development. Studies showed enhanced language development, including advanced vocabulary and ideation in writing (Downing, 1969b; Mazurkiewicz, 1971, 1973b; Warburton & Southgate, 1969).

Multiple researchers also discuss how ITA additionally enhanced language development because texts could now use expansive wording, no longer needing to use the contrived simpler vocabulary that Standard-English texts do.

As Ho et al. (1970) comment:

ITA books need not be as limited in vocabulary, scope, and content as the [Standard-English] books for the beginning readers. Thus the child could be helped to develop an enthusiasm for reading and for learning with a wide range of interesting and educationally valuable materials.

ITA wasn't considered to be necessarily the best transitional orthography, with researchers recognising that other transitional orthographies might be equally useful. Oliver et al.'s (1972) study of children's learning of two-letter graphemes explored four English orthographies:

- Joined letters (ITA).
- Underlined letters (e.g., *th*in, *fo*rt, tr*ee*).
- Using spacing between letters (e.g., th I n, f or t, t r ee).

Research Tour 5. The Power of Beginners' Orthographies

- Standard-English orthography.

They found both joined letters and underlined letters created much stronger learning than spaced graphemes and Standard English. ITA uses joined letters for multi-letter graphemes, while underlining is easily used with Fleksispel (Galletly, 2005b, 2023a, In press).

ITA proved highly effective with children of young age, with many ITA cohorts being aged 4 to 5 years. Warburton and Southgate (1969) report a discernible trend, that the younger the children were, the more enthusiastic teachers were about the value of ITA in helping children to read and write, with teachers of Reception classes (Prep) being almost unanimous that ITA had expedited great improvement.

Really, when one considers our so many young struggling readers and writers in our school, that ITA finding speaks as convincingly on how very difficult it is for 5-year-olds to learn to read Standard English, as it does on the benefits of ITA.

This strength of ITA in empowering particularly young children is also evidenced in Ho and colleagues' studies with USA children, many from backgrounds of significant disadvantage (Ho, 1972; Ho & Eiszler, 1970; Ho et al., 1972). Their Kindergarten ITA learners showed significant gains over Standard-English learners, gains that continued through to final testing at end-Grade-3.

As Ho and Eiszler (1970) state,

An investigation is being made of the effects of the interaction between differing socioeconomic backgrounds and two beginning reading programs on the reading achievement of pupils at three ability levels. This report gives the results of data that have been collected for Grades 1 and 2 only.

Participating were 754 pupils in a small city school district in southern Michigan. The Initial Teaching Alphabet (i.t.a.) was used with 350 of the pupils, traditional orthography (T.O.) with the rest. Reading achievement was determined by the Standard Achievement Test; IQ by the Otis Quick-Scoring Test, Form AS; and socioeconomic status (SES) from the fathers' occupations and educational backgrounds.

Data indicated that

1. High SES background seemed to benefit high-ability pupils more than low- or middle-ability pupils;

2. First graders from all ability levels and SES backgrounds using i.t.a. outperformed their T.O. counterparts on sound-symbol association tests;

3. i.t.a. was especially helpful to middle-ability, low-SES second graders; and
4. In no instance did T.O. pupils significantly outperform i.t.a. pupils on all Grade-1 and Grade-2 tests.

ITA children then, and quite likely our children in the future, would have major transitioning advantage relative to Taiwanese, Japanese and Chinese children today. That's because, whereas the Asian beginners' and complex orthographies use completely different characters and systems, English regular orthographies and Standard English are able to be very similar.

The strong similarities of ITA and Standard English made transitioning extremely easy, e.g., Mazurkiewicz (1965), discusses children transitioning easily from ITA to Standard English in Grade 1, with 40-65% of words being spelled identically in ITA and Standard English. Many syllables in multisyllabic words would also have been identical.

Mazurkiewicz (1971) reported on an 11-year study of 14,000 USA children, half in ITA classes, and half in Standard-English classes, in schools in Pennsylvania. He discusses major differences in their reading skills both before and after transitioning.

Eight months into Grade 1, only 6% of the Standard-English cohort were reading above grade-level, i.e., reading Grade 2 or 3 reading materials. In contrast, 75% of the Grade 1 ITA cohort were ahead:
- The top quarter (25%) were two years ahead, and reading Grade 3 materials.
- The middle two quarters (50%) were a year ahead, and reading Grade 2 materials.
- Just 15% were at grade-level, and reading Grade 1 (grade-level) materials.
- Only 11% showed delayed reading, reading materials at Primer level (the year before Grade 1).

That Standard English vs ITA divide is akin to Tour 2's English vs Welsh contrast (Hanley et al., 2004; Spencer & Hanley, 2003, 2004):
- Regular orthographies create reading and literacy success in both at-risk and non-at-risk children, while
- Standard English is damaging, slowing reading and writing development of all children, and causing word-reading and spelling difficulties, and a long sad tail of struggling readers.

Mazurkiewicz's discussion of the advantages of ITA shows definite indicators of robust Success Inoculation, strong executive-function skill development, and ITA children being confident independent

readers, writers and learners (Mazurkiewicz, 1965):
> The most dramatic flowering of all is evident in the large numbers of free, self-expressive, six-year-old writers.
> They write more abundantly and about many more subjects than do children learning the traditional alphabet.
> They write alone, without help or editing from teachers, sounding-out their own spellings and using any words they feel like using in any sentence pattern that occurs to them.

Teacher workload also seemed significantly reduced, with teaching much empowered, creating opportunities for learning to be tailored to individual children's interests and needs (Mazurkiewicz, 1965):
> Other observations indicate that the first grade teacher's complaint about "what to do with the other children when working with one group" seems no longer to be a problem in ITA classes. ...
> While learning may start with whole class activity, this disappears in a short time in favour of individualised activity based on the rates of learning of individual children.
> The range of ability begins to show itself and the teacher finds himself working with individuals within groups.
> It is noted that the teacher with many years' experience in first grade feels that an ITA approach answers the first-grade teacher's cry [that] there must be an easier way of teaching reading.

He lists seven conclusions from the Grade 1 ITA results:
- Traditional spelling of English is a significant source of difficulty in beginning reading.
- Children can learn to read more rapidly with ITA and experience markedly less frustration.
- ITA children wrote easily and expressively, with ITA having a releasing effect on ability to communicate using writing.
- ITA Grade 1 classrooms ran more smoothly, with fewer behaviour and organisational problems, as the ITA children were confident, independent and markedly self-motivated.
- Reading materials could be at individual ability levels, with children pursuing individual interests.
- Post-transition reading of ITA children continued strongly.
- Post-transition spelling achievement was equal to non-ITA children, with indicators of greater gains made in Grade 2.

On the whole, ITA children were strong learners who quickly and easily developed word-reading, spelling and confident independent reading and writing, and ITA worked particularly well for more at-risk children. As Warburton and Southgate (1969) commented,
> So long as the children are tested in the medium which they

have used, those infants who have been taught by ITA appear to make, on average, more rapid progress than those in the control groups who have been taught the old alphabet and spelling. Backward readers, thwarted by the difficulties presented by the traditional orthography, all too often develop a profound and permanent antipathy for anything to do with print.

'Few things,' wrote Matthew Arnold in one of his reports as Inspector of schools, 'create so much unhappiness in the life of the schoolchild as the way he is taught to read'.

With the Pitman alphabet [ITA] many of these difficulties are largely circumvented; and the child's eager interest in the content of his reading books is more readily preserved.

That sounds like today's regular-orthography nations, doesn't it? ITA schools could have easily fitted in play-based learning too, had that been a priority, in the time freed by rapid literacy development.

Mazurkiewicz (1973a) reports that, of the 11-year study of 14,000 USA children, half in ITA classes, half in Standard-English classes,

The advantages of i.t.a. are that it permits the child to:
- advance more rapidly in reading and writing experience;
- achieve significantly superior reading skills at an earlier time;
- read more widely;
- write more prolifically, more extensively, and with a higher degree of proficiency;
- develop high spelling skills fairly early;
- show a lack of the inhibitions in writing which are commonly found early in the first year; and
- write more creatively in terms of the number of running words and the number of polysyllabic words used.
An analysis of subsidiary characteristics indicated:
- a marked reduction in letter confusions,
- fewer restrictions on adhering to [school reading book series],
- reduction in the need for remedial reading, and
- a reduction in failure rate.

Warburton and Southgate (1969) also emphasise ITA's strong effects:
Generally speaking, in ITA schools, almost regardless of the types of organisation, children want to read more than traditional orthography children, and spend a great proportion of all the odd minutes in a day doing so.
Teachers' comments thus represented a general conclusion, which was confirmed by the investigators' observation in schools, that usually children who learn to read by ITA both

> *want to, and do, spend more time on reading than children taught by traditional orthography.*
> *This conclusion refers to all ages and all intelligence levels of children, and covers lesson times, free times, break times and time at home.*
> *Teachers' comments on children's attitudes can be summarised:*
> *1. Children enjoy learning because of the simplicity and regularity of the alphabet;*
> *2. This gives them confidence so that they are eager to try;*
> *3. The regularity of the sounds-symbol relationship means that their attempts are generally successful; and*
> *4. This in turn cuts out frustrations and gives a sense of achievement.*

How lovely to have children reading and writing so easily, with no anxiety and children being highly motivated.

Parents overwhelmingly found ITA a positive experience (Warburton & Southgate, 1969):

> *The majority of parents whose children are taught by ITA had not considered this innovation a cause for concern.*
> *The main impression to be gained regarding the reaction of parents whose children had learned to read and write by means of ITA was that these parents were pleased by the results, having observed that children learned happily, easily and quickly. No instance was reported of parents, whose child had learned to read by ITA, expressing disapproval of it, saying they would have preferred the child to have been taught by traditional orthography or requesting that a younger child should be taught by traditional orthography. In poor socio-economic areas, a number of parents of large families of low ability remarked on the fact that younger children taught by ITA liked reading, in contrast to older siblings who had failed to learn to read.*

Areas ITA Research Did Not Explore

No ITA research or projects were found specifically exploring optimising of ITA advantage across later primary school and high school, although there seemed a definite intention that later research and professional development would focus on this area.

Researchers were very aware of this area of need, with multiple researchers commenting on classes from Grade 2 on not taking advantage of children's robust early-literacy skills and potential for ongoing strong progress, and ITA children consequently losing momentum, with their accelerated progress dwindling.

Lack of focus on optimising later instruction is likely why some studies show no lasting long-term impact from earlier ITA usage.

In like manner, though further research seemed intended, no studies were found exploring optimising timing and duration of transition, or using multiple learning stages in transitioning.

ITA research did not focus on cognitive-processing skills such as phonological awareness and Rapid Automised Naming (RAN), as those concepts weren't being widely explored in the 1960s. Further, most studies didn't include focus on intellectual ability. While many researchers made comments on children being bright or dull (using terms of that era), and teachers were divided on whether ITA worked best with brighter or slower learners, with it working well for both groups, we only found Ho and colleagues' work specifically compared ability groups (Ho, 1972; Ho & Eiszler, 1970; Ho et al., 1970, 1972).

While some studies focused on struggling readers, there's also no mention of learning difficulties or learning disability in children of healthy general ability. There seems little recognition of learning difficulties occurring in intelligent children, or of factors such as cognitive processing and phonological awareness.

In addition, family history of reading difficulties doesn't seem explored beyond teacher and parent comments of successful reading by young children in families whose older children had failed to learn to read (Warburton & Southgate, 1969).

ITA Spelling Development

ITA studies of earliest literacy development, when children were solely using ITA, showed very strong parallel development of word-reading and word-writing, with ITA spelling and writing being fast and accurate. In contrast, the Standard-English cohorts developed spelling and word-writing more slowly than their word-reading.

Our team found variable findings on whether ITA children were better spellers than their Standard-English counterparts, and whether they maintained gains over time. Some studies report ITA cohorts being stronger spellers (Karr et al., 1974; Mazurkiewicz, 1971), while others report them equivalent (Downing & Halliwell, 1964).

The assessments used and the timing of studies seem the basis of these variable findings, e.g.,
- Whether testing was done in Standard English or ITA.
- Children's grade-level.

Research Tour 5. The Power of Beginners' Orthographies

- When they'd transitioned.
- How close to transitioning they were when testing was done.

There was mention of planned studies to more deeply explore spelling, but we couldn't find these studies, and it seems likely this planned research may not have happened.

Differing spelling results are perhaps also influenced by there being little research establishing optimal timing of the ITA-only earliest literacy phase, and timing and speed of transition. Studies vary greatly in the time since children transitioned, and whether testing was done in ITA or Standard English.

Certainly, researchers emphasised a gentle, unhurried, spelling transition, with children encouraged to keep writing freely, and to continue using ITA spellings as needed in draft writing, rather than being over-focused on correct spelling of Standard English.

Hahn's (1965) large Grade 1 study is worth reflecting on, as regards the importance of timing and of the orthography with which children were tested. It's also an example of how negative messages about ITA's effectiveness might inadvertently have started.

It compared an ITA cohort with two Standard-English cohorts: a Language Arts cohort and a basal reader cohort. Hahn found ITA children had superior word-reading and superior spelling when ITA spellings were accepted as correct, but, surprisingly, concluded that *'the spelling problems of ITA children will certainly warrant careful study throughout the primary grades'*.

This is a curious conclusion, perhaps reflecting more Hahn's personal opinion, as it's not supported by the study's facts and data. They show that testing was done after only 20 weeks of teaching (and likely before the children had transitioned to using Standard English), that all testing was done in Standard English, and that, when ITA spellings were included as correct spellings, the ITA cohort achieved as highly as the Language Arts cohort for spelling, with both groups better than the basal reader group.

Warburton and Southgate's (1969) conclusions regarding ITA and spelling development were confident and positive:

1. The overwhelming opinion of infant teachers and all knowledgeable visitors at schools was that the use of ITA as a writing system had enormously simplified the task of spelling for children. It was this factor which was mainly responsible for the increase in children's free writing.
2. It was generally concluded that children's attempts at

spelling in ITA were much more often correct than they would have been in traditional orthography; even young children soon gained confidence in their own ability to spell any word and so became relatively independent of the teacher.

3. Infant teachers did not consider that the transfer from ITA to traditional orthography for spelling caused children any difficulty; a few teachers in junior schools took the opposite view.

4. There was general agreement among infant teachers, as well as among advisers and inspectors, that the transfer in spelling should take place later than the transfer in reading and that mixed traditional orthography and ITA spelling should be accepted for a considerable time. Many infant teachers found some direct instruction in traditional orthography spelling rules to be helpful for children at the transition stage.

5. No infant teacher expressed the view that children who had been taught by ITA, once they had made the transition to traditional orthography spelling, were less able spellers than children who had used traditional orthography from the beginning.

6. Junior school teachers differed in their opinions as to whether spelling had improved in junior school writers, with some feeling it had, and others that it hadn't.

7. There had been no clearly observed deterioration of the spelling of children who had learned to read and write with ITA and later transferred to traditional orthography although such a result had originally been rather widely feared.

Preventing and Overcoming Standard-English Struggles

ITA was highly effective with at-risk readers. Explaining data from schools' six years' use of ITA, Mazurkiewicz (1971) discusses
- Three times more Standard-English children repeating a year-level due to low achievement.
- Twice as many Standard-English children receiving remedial intervention.
- Definite differences in remedial needs, with ITA children needing support only with language skills and comprehension but not word-reading, while Standard-English children required intervention in both areas.

Downing (1969a) discusses the significant research findings of numerous studies of ITA used both upstream, preventing difficulties, and downstream, remediating difficulties (Llamas, 2017):

- Consistently fewer ITA children had reading difficulties, both during initial sole use of ITA, and during and after transition to use of Standard English.
- Older struggling readers made significant reading and literacy gains when receiving remediation using ITA in 30-minute sessions four times weekly, with gains maintained post-transition.
- ITA was found highly effective by schools for children with special needs.
- ITA was used successfully in remediation of adult readers.
- ITA was used successfully with second-language learners learning to speak and read English.

Discussing studies that didn't find ITA more effective in reading remediation, Downing found these tended to use ITA with lower intensity, e.g., considerably less time and fewer sessions per week.

ITA was also used very successfully in remediation of British soldiers with low literacy skills (Pitman, 1973), with powerful Success Inoculation effects accompanying strong literacy progress.

ITA Readers Showed Strong Success Inoculation

In addition to successful readers having Success Inoculation from earliest literacy, effective remediation can also achieve Success Inoculation effects, and seemingly reverse helplessness. Indeed, for many struggling readers, achieving successful reversal of Acquired Helplessness may be crucial if remediation is to be effective.

The ITA research sheds useful light on both early Success Inoculation, and Success Inoculation from effective remediation in older struggling readers.

Acquired Helplessness and associated task avoidance don't seem part of ITA at-risk readers' early-literacy experience. Statements from Warburton & Southgate's (1969) review of ITA use, in 1500 UK schools and associated research studies, suggest strong Success Inoculation in seemingly all beginning ITA word-readers, with this contrasting quite markedly with the Acquired Helplessness of Standard-English weaker word-readers:

> *The majority of teachers interviewed appeared to consider the change in children's attitudes to reading to be at least as important, or even more important, than the increased progress in reading. ...*
>
> *Children don't get blockages as they did with traditional orthography. Even the youngest, [slowest] child can have a go. ...*

> Children feel on top of it instead of struggling. ...
> [Slower-progress] children don't get that defeatist attitude. ...
> The shutters don't go down when the child meets a word he doesn't know. He'll try it. ...
> One doesn't now find children in the middle of infant school who have, as it were, given up. Even if a child is going slowly, he feels he is making progress.

Warburton and Southgate (1969) discuss a headmistress, who'd worked with slower readers for many years, commenting that when Standard-English children finished reading their practised page, they'd edge away from her desk to avoid being asked to read the next page, which they'd not practised. In contrast, the opposite now happened, with slower-progress ITA readers being eager to turn to and read new text, to show her how cleverly they could read it.

That description of even slower-progress ITA readers having notable confidence and motivation seems to bespeak Success Inoculation in ITA at-risk children, with this preventing Acquired Helplessness. Australia and other Anglophone nations would love that Success Inoculation and its positive effects.

It's important to note, of course, that the ITA children would also have had stronger word-reading skills plus the confident self-teaching that children develop in unimpeded statistical learning. Confidence and strong skill development go together and grow together.

Regular-Orthography Citizenship Impacts

Success Inoculation also seemed the order of the day in ITA remediation of older struggling readers. Here's comment on ITA's powerful social-emotional benefits, and even what seem citizenship benefits, for UK soldiers who were struggling readers.

The soldiers made impressively rapid reading and writing progress, and transitioned well to Standard English. They also made strong gains in social-emotional and citizenship areas (Pitman, 1973):

> The rapid success rate induces more controlled emotional responses and gain in self-respect. The students gain self-confidence and a new awareness and independence. The striking increase in morale fosters motivation. There is a surprising carry-over of ability and confidence to arithmetical attainment.
>
> The men concerned have become more cooperative and less anti-social and, therefore, both better citizens and more proficient soldiers.

That's impressive. In addition, the broad swathe impacts of confident literacy listed there have interesting ramifications.

The soldiers gaining both confidence and agency is in some ways akin to the empowerment and confident citizenship that Brazilian peasants developed under Paulo Freire's (1974) skilful tutoring, bringing them first literacy, using highly-regular Brazilian Portuguese, and then socio-political empowerment.

Giving literacy prowess to people who previously couldn't read and write, and have therefore felt incapable in many ways, is clearly immensely empowering.

I recently read a book discussing older weak readers' needs for increasing patriotism and enthusiasm for the USA nation and its government. It outlined a major initiative focused on building patriotism and national pride in weak readers. Reading it caused me to reflect on Freire's illiterate Brazilian peasants and the British-soldier ITA readers. Their progress in literacy and other areas was paralleled by appreciably increased self-confidence and optimism generally, e.g., with the soldiers now having far greater pride in themselves, the military services, and the nation.

Brazilian Portuguese, like ITA, is a highly-regular orthography, and building of both literacy and self-confidence may have been similar in the two groups of adults.

There's an interesting contrast, there.

On the one hand, we could implement initiatives building national pride in teenage and adult weak readers who are crushed because, for them, we failed so badly to meet our teaching challenges.

On the other hand, we could empower them through rectifying our education failures, and belatedly meeting our teaching challenges. Using a fully-regular beginners' orthography, we'd enable our older struggling readers to successfully build their reading and literacy skills, realising, in the process, that they really are the intelligent, capable adults they'd previously thought they never could be.

It can be utterly dispiriting to be a struggling reader – long school years of learning difficulties and feeling unintelligent, and all too often receiving sadly insufficient support and encouragement. Having ongoing struggles and low literacy skills can so easily drag a person down, not just academically but also socio-emotionally.

When Pinyin was introduced nationally across schools in mainland China from 1958, it was used both upstream and downstream:

- Upstream, as an initial orthography for all beginning readers, which successfully prevented them developing difficulties.
- Downstream, as successful intervention for older struggling readers, and literacy training for previously illiterate adults.

In similar manner, ITA was also used both upstream for beginning readers and downstream for older struggling readers.

We need to explore the use of fully-regular beginners' orthographies both upstream and downstream – preventing difficulties in young children as they launch easily into early literacy; and effectively remediating older children and adults who are struggling readers.

It's inspiring, how those British soldiers learned to read and write so quickly, transitioning easily and well to Standard English, and how, in becoming confidently literate, they realised they were intelligent and competent, and were soon using their confidence and skills effectively in diverse positive ways.

Just as Freire and the ITA researchers did, we might reverse our Spelling Generations' struggles, by respectfully empowering them, initially through use of a fully-regular English orthography.

Lack of Research of ITA's Impacts on Later Development

It's interesting that some recent writings about ITA state that ITA was ineffective, emphasising lack of success in later primary school – yet this Phase 2 ITA research largely doesn't seem to have taken place. Further, when we searched for the knowledge base these ITA critics were using, we didn't find any ITA studies they were considering – their criticisms seem based on hearsay, and not on research evidence.

The few studies of later primary-school literacy which are available show mixed findings, with some showing advanced skills in the ITA children, and others showing them doing as well as the Standard-English cohort but no better.

Some discuss the impacts of later primary school teachers not having been adequately prepared to continue expanding and enhancing ITA children's burgeoning literacy and language skills.

Severe orthographic disadvantage is virtually guaranteed for nations that use solely a complex orthography. In contrast, strong orthographic advantage isn't guaranteed, and is instead a readily-available option, taken up by regular-orthography nations, who chose to add teaching excellence after the early years.

With our long history of teachers and schools developing interesting, enticing work units, Australian teaching is often more exciting and enticing than teaching in other nations. We're thus well set up for achieving effective, later education advantaging, if we changed to 2-Stage early literacy, and used a fully-regular orthography initially.

Certainly, similar to Taiwan's Zhuyin Fuhao, Japan's Hiragana, and China's Pinyin, ITA and other English beginners' orthographies would work well in expediting early-literacy development, preventing word-reading and literacy difficulties, and remediating struggling readers: both older children and adults.

Building from that basis, and then being time-rich, our later years education would then have potential for impressive gains.

Regrettably, in the ITA schools of the 1960s, instruction from Grade 2 and 3 continued largely as usual, with little excitement and enrichment. It's thus likely that lack of encouragement and tailored instruction steadily dampened advantage that had been present.

Summing up the available research of the mid to late 1960s, Warburton and Southgate's (1969) comments reflect waiting on Phase 2 research which was to happen:

The evidence is not convincing that ITA is the superior medium after the transition to traditional orthography.

The results obtained from the children [studied] into the third year suggest that the traditional orthography groups catch up. We must await the findings of [ongoing and suggested research studies], to obtain more conclusive evidence.

Our team couldn't find those ongoing and suggested research studies, and it seems likely they may not have been actioned.

ITA use in schools and research stopped, seemingly without explanation and, with little heard of ITA since the early 1970s. It's likely research funding dried up and, quite likely, considerable research data was set aside and never taken through to publication.

Our CQU team only recently sought out and reviewed the research on ITA, after becoming aware of our orthographic disadvantage and the major advantages regular-orthography nations enjoy. We'd assumed previously, from having heard so little about ITA, that the studies must have been small and showed quite minimal effects.

We were therefore astonished when we realised the extent to which ITA had been explored, and the impressive findings consistently found across studies, that ITA was highly effective in expediting literacy development, and preventing word-reading and spelling difficulties,

just as regular orthographies expedite literacy so well in regular-orthography nations now. We were astounded by both
- The abrupt end of ITA research of the 1960s, and
- The lack of meaningful explanation as to why both ITA instruction in schools and ITA research ceased so abruptly.

As late as 1972, research reports term themselves interim reports (Ho, 1972), and many research reports imply research would be ongoing, but the ITA research stopped, seemingly abruptly (Knight et al., 2017a):

Pidgeon (1972) and Pitman (1973) write favourably about ITA in their submission to the 1975 UK Bullock report, 'Language for Life', which also supports ITA (Department of Education and Science, 1975). In contrast, later UK reports on literacy instruction make no comment about ITA.

Multiple ITA researchers made mention of ongoing criticism of ITA across the 1960s. Importantly, Warburton and Southgate's (1969) comprehensive 1966 review, discusses loudest criticisms coming from people with negligible association with schools using ITA:

The majority of the verbal evidence represent favourable reports on the use of ITA with infants. Only a small minority of the people interviewed expressed unfavourable opinions or doubts.

The most noticeable trend in this mass of evidence was that the people nearest to, and most knowledgeable about actual teaching and learning in infant classes, were most favourably impressed, while those who saw dangers and had misgivings were generally those who had neither used ITA themselves nor observed it in use.

The majority group, with favourable impressions of ITA, consisted of most teachers who had used it, a large percentage of HM Inspectors, many but not all local education authority advisors and inspectors with wide experiences of observing it, and the majority of parents concerned. The minority group, of those least favourably impressed, included a few teachers in schools which had always attained good reading standards with traditional orthography, certain of HM Inspectors and local education authority inspectors, College of Education lecturers and university staff with little experience of observing ITA being used, and a few parents.

Yet education, its emphases, likes and dislikes, was in a state of change. The 1960s and 1970s climate was one of educators being influenced strongly by Whole Language philosophy. The whole field was undergoing momentous change.

Research Tour 5. The Power of Beginners' Orthographies

Thus, while Warburton and Southgate emphasise strong positive findings, increasing ITA use, and widespread enthusiasm for ITA in 1966, these findings stand in marked contrast to the educational climate of the 1970s.

There is ample evidence of this strong school and teacher enthusiasm for ITA, e.g., Warburton and Southgate (1969) emphasise, of 1966:
Examples of every conceivable type of school are now using ITA with infants and, with only rare exceptions, the teachers concerned have no desire to revert to the use of traditional orthography. The majority of teachers who have used ITA, as well as knowledgeable visitors to schools, have concluded that, when ITA is used with infants, better progress is made than when traditional orthography is used. Observed results include
- Easier and early reading skills acquired without frustrations for the child,
- An increase
   - In the time children choose to spend on reading,
   - In the number of books they read, and
   - In their understanding of the content of the books,
- An increase in quantity and quality of children's free writing,
- An improvement in children's attitudes and behaviour, and
- Beneficial effects on
   - Other school subjects and
   - The general life of the school.
The teachers who reached the foregoing conclusions [had] many years of experience of using traditional orthography.

Those are very definite, and very positive conclusions being made about enthusiastic ITA schools and teachers. Yet, by the mid-1970s, ITA seems to have largely disappeared. That means most of those teachers and schools so keen on ITA in 1966 must have changed their minds, e.g., the Bullock report (Dept of Education & Science, 1975) comments on teachers generally feeling negative about ITA.

Across many ITA research reports from the mid-1960s, there seems concern about the negative impacts of unfounded criticisms, and hope that the strong positive findings about ITA in many studies would withstand the negative impacts of these critics (e.g., Block, 1966):
Hope is expressed that educators will not disregard the opportunities that are offered by ITA.

Unfortunately, this hope was not realised, with the Bullock report perhaps the last research-based publication speaking positively about ITA (Dept of Education and Science, 1975; Pitman, 1973).

It seems likely that, as criticism flourished, governments and funding bodies lost confidence in ITA and its potential, thus funding ended – and so did the ITA research.

Doubtless, others will find more detailed answers to this curiosity, in uncovering writings that we did not find or explore, and speaking with retired teachers as to why research projects were cancelled and how schools decided over time that ITA wasn't worthwhile.

Suffice to say, the ITA research ended abruptly, with only the first phase of research done, and intended second-phase research not completed or published.

ITA Strongly Achieved Its Primary Goals

People closely involved with ITA, be they teachers or researchers, found ITA highly effective in achieving its primary goals of easing and speeding early-literacy development, and reducing the number of children experiencing word-reading and spelling difficulties, and the extent of their difficulties.

As Warburton & Southgate (1969) discuss,
> The teachers' greatest pleasure came from their observations that ITA made the task of learning to read much easier for children and consequently they found more enjoyment in the process.
> Most teachers laid greater stress on this aspect of enjoyment than on their belief that ITA helped children to learn to read earlier and more quickly, although many such comments were made.
> One headteacher said, "I have no doubts whatever that a gain in reading has been made. The children achieve reading skill earlier with ITA."
> One headmistress stated that "Even [less intelligent] children can begin to read at [age 6 years] with ITA."
> Another headteacher pointed out how advantageous it is to teachers of large classes when children begin to read earlier.
> One teacher, referring to the decrease in time now required to learn to read, said, "The child picks up tremendous momentum in reading."
> The fact that most children learn to read so quickly with ITA was a source of amazement and pleasure to many teachers who had, as they now described it, struggled so long with traditional orthography. One teacher summed up for many when she said, "Children get off to a really good start with ITA."
> If teachers had been asked what infants now read, the replies would undoubtedly have been given in one word – "Everything".

Research Tour 5. The Power of Beginners' Orthographies

One teacher, speaking of children who are still using ITA, said: "Children can read anything almost right from the start. They don't need to have an artificially controlled vocabulary. The teacher can use any of the words of the children's own vocabulary when she writes news items and notices for them." Thus the general trend of teacher's remarks, in nearly all the schools visited, was that children who had learned to read by ITA read many more books and more printed materials of all kinds than had similar children who had been taught by traditional orthography.

Naturally the slower children did not read as many or such difficult books as the brighter children; but even [children of low ability], who with transitional orthography would probably not have begun to read by the end of the infant school, had now read many simple books.

The content of the books read by infants had also increased: longer storybooks, reference books and information books, which would formerly have been read mainly by juniors, were now enjoyed by large numbers of infants. The interviewers' observations in schools using both traditional orthography and ITA supported the conclusions of the teachers on this point.

An overwhelming majority of infant teachers who had used ITA expressed their pleasure in the increase in the quantity and quality of children's free writing; many of them rating this as the chief advantage of ITA. It was particularly emphasised that this free writing arose spontaneously, at an earlier stage than when traditional orthography was used, and that children were able to pursue this form of expression almost independently of the teacher.

Yes, ITA strongly achieved its primary goals of easy, rapid early-literacy development, and confident successful literacy and learning in at-risk children likely not to have succeeded well with Standard English: our long sad tail of underachievers.

Key researchers' conclusions are definite, emphasising how starting with Standard English is seriously inferior, while starting with a fully-regular beginners' orthography builds success (Downing, 1969b):

The unequivocal conclusion is that the traditional orthography of English is a seriously defective instrument for the early stages of reading and writing.

As long as this traditional orthography is used in the early years of schooling in English-speaking countries, children's learning of reading and writing is bound to be much less efficient than it can be with a simplified and regularised writing-system such as the Initial Teaching Alphabet.

Downing's words, there, seem almost prescient, as though discussing our struggles: our too slow word-reading and spelling development relative to regular-orthography nations, along with the trials of all Anglophone struggling word-readers and spellers since the 1960s.

There's every likelihood that, had Whole Language proponents embraced ITA, education would be thriving across the Anglosphere.

My call for the 10 Changes, and leaving HEARTSH behind, instead embracing GENTLE, is in key ways a yen for that powerful combination the 1960s offered – of early Whole Language methods used strategically, in combination with a beginners' orthography.

Independent reviewers Warburton & Southgate (1969), while emphasising needs to wait on research on ITA's long-term benefits, were confident about ITA's effectiveness as regards its primary goals:

There is no evidence whatsoever for the belief that the best way to learn to read in traditional orthography is to learn to read in traditional orthography. It would appear rather that the best way to learn to read in traditional orthography is to learn to read in the initial teaching alphabet.

They also emphatically conclude,

The experimental results so far obtained suggest very very strongly that I.T.A. is, in fact, a more efficient medium for teaching reading to beginners than traditional orthography. The magnitude of the differences found in its favour in many different researches is unusually high.

Those 1960s comments on ITA's effectiveness for beginning readers fit well with the findings of current regular-orthography researchers, e.g., Finland's Mikko Aro's (2004) comment that

A transparent orthography treats even a phonologically immature reader in a lenient manner. It helps in explicating the Alphabetic Principle, the correspondence between spoken and written language. ... It does not burden the beginning reader with a plethora of correspondence rules; and together with systematic phonics teaching it provides the beginning reader with a simple tool for successful word recognition.

Whole Language Minus ITA Couldn't Win

It's immensely disappointing that Whole Language actioners didn't embrace and use ITA. This may well prove the Anglosphere's greatest education tragedy of the past century, as early Whole Language plus ITA had strong potential to optimise education.

Whole Language had, and has, many strengths, but it did not achieve successful word-reading, spelling and early-literacy development in the Anglosphere's many struggling Standard-English word-readers and writers.

It's quite likely that continued flood of struggling readers and writers acutely impeded Whole Language's success, whereas, had ITA and Whole Language worked together, with early literacy easily acquired and schools time-rich, they'd have been an immensely powerful, and perhaps unbeatable, combination.

At the time I did my teacher training, in 1978, Whole Language literacy instruction, incorporating Language Experience emphases (Holdaway, 1979), was in full flow. I found it useful, as did many teachers. They'd been inserviced using Queensland's *Early Literacy Inservice Course* (ELIC) in the 1980s, and loved its emphasis on enriched, individualised, literacy development.

At that stage, Whole Language literacy instruction included systematic word-reading instruction. This was to be conducted on an as-needs basis with small groups developed through common needs, using instruction precisely tailored to those needs. Different groups would work on, e.g., reading and writing regular CVC words, collecting irregular sightwords to explore their spelling vagaries, and writing phonemic approximations when writing.

Literacy instruction also included lots of meaningful reading and writing, which would have been perfect for children doing ITA first then transitioning to reading and writing Standard English.

Really, there's every likelihood that the rocks the Whole Language ship floundered on are Anglophone nations' continuing to have slow, impeded early-literacy development and excessive numbers of struggling word-readers, with schools thus overly time-poor.

Whole Language methods were intended to expedite successful literacy development for at-risk children, and prevent major word-reading and writing struggles, but could not achieve this. After all, they were up against Standard English, one of the world's most complex orthographies, with children only 5-years-old when learning to read and write it.

Alas, Whole Language philosophy then took somewhat unfortunate paths and many educators who'd agreed with earliest Whole Language principles, found themselves at odds with this approach.

Over time, as Whole Language evolved, the use of decontextualised words and word-parts in word-reading tests and instruction unfortunately came to be considered inappropriate and almost anathema. In time, even standardised tests, statistical data and experimental research were also considered inappropriate.

Whole Language's strong focus on enriched, individualised learning remains impressive. Had Whole Language embraced using a fully-regular beginners' orthography, the two would have been a formidable winning combination. We might then have *had it all*, as regular-orthography nations do now – children with powerful literacy skills, very few struggling word-readers who have only minor difficulties, and ample time for rich literacy development.

Certainly, we've potential for prolific improvement in the future, using 10 Changes improvements:
- Insisting literacy development is as easy here in Australia as it is in regular-orthography nations (Change 7).
- Building awareness of our orthographic disadvantage's many facets (Change 1).
- Implementing rich language and learning empowerment until mid-Year 2 (Change 9).
- Investigating the potential of fully-regular beginners' orthographies (Change 8).
- Using the increased teaching and learning time to achieve skilfully differentiated teaching and learning (Change 6).

Let's Ensure Success

Many other ITA studies could be discussed – the more one looks, the more that's found, e.g., one recently discovered treasure trove of ITA studies, a 428-page file, *i.t.a. as a Language Arts Medium*, the proceedings of a 1967 international ITA conference, is packed with papers on diverse use of ITA, including in second-language learning, and with children with disabilities (Block, 1968).

Suffice to say that ITA was found highly successful in many studies, large and small. Hurrah, the sun rises and a new day dawns brightly across Anglophone nations.

The next phase of studies was planned to
- Investigate different transitioning options.
- Compare ITA effectiveness in weaker and stronger readers.
- Explore post-transition spelling and optimising thereof.
- Investigate later-years impacts of ITA, and empowering of later-years teachers for building on ITA advantage.

Research Tour 5. The Power of Beginners' Orthographies

Then, alas, the blinds crash down, with sunshine gone, amidst sounds of dismal rain! For unknown reasons, most likely the advent of Whole Language, ITA research finished abruptly in the early 1970s, with planned second phase research studies not actioned.

Perhaps saddest of all, in the years since the research was conducted, the strong ITA findings on its effectiveness in achieving its major goals of easier literacy development and preventing difficulties have for the most part been overwhelmingly ignored.

It's sad and bad having lost the six decades of potential progress in optimising literacy development since the ITA research was shelved. However, that's nowhere near as bad as the century or so behind we'll arrive at, if we continue to ignore the ITA research and the successes of Taiwan, Japan and China – myopically looking only inward, cruising the Anglophone fishbowl, over-prioritising the Anglosphere and largely ignoring the world beyond.

We've had the suffering of 60 years of our damaging Standard-English Early Years Factory since then – 60 years of crushed and crumpled learners and Spelling Generations, with word-reading, literacy and learning difficulties developed because our children are born in the unlucky *Lucky Country*, Australia, instead of a regular-orthography nation.

The A of our 10 Changes' ABCs: *Act locally while looking globally* is very important, as WYSYAIN (*What You See, You Assume Is Normal*) has played a key role in our education woes being so long-standing and, quite likely, is why ITA research was so quickly ignored.

We've been WYSYAINing carelessly, believing we must use solely Standard English at 4.5 to 5.0 years, with that our only option. Doing so, we've perpetuated massive time pressure, excessive child and teacher workload, and our flood of struggling readers.

The ITA research findings are very impressive, and highly relevant to discussions about optimising reading and literacy instruction in the Anglosphere. It's shocking, really, how long the ITA research and findings have been available, and how little they've been used.

Suffice to say, when ITA was used, easy, expedited reading and early-literacy development were the order of the day for Anglophone children, with far fewer children having word-reading, spelling and early-literacy difficulties, and those difficulties being relatively minor.

Children with weak language skills still had weaker reading comprehension and written expression, as language skills are central to literacy, but they were greatly advantaged relative to children now because they'd mastered reading, writing and independent learning.

I love it when children I work with have strong word-reading and spelling, needing help just with language-skills: intervention is far easier when you don't need to also build word-reading and writing.

That's how schools would have been when ITA was in use, and how we can be in the future. There were far fewer struggling readers, abundant, powerful Success Inoculation effects, and considerably reduced workload. Plus, ITA worked very well in remediating older struggling readers.

Notably, everyone agreed that transitioning to using Standard English happened extremely easily. That was a worry and a big unknown when ITA research began – but it turned out a non-issue.

And ITA was immensely popular, so much so that its usage spread rapidly beyond research project schools to being used in its heyday in 9% of England's schools. May I repeat here my favourite ITA quote, by a teacher interviewed in Warburton & Southgate's (1969) review:

> *The long uphill grind has been cut out. Reading is more an ordinary part of childhood instead of a chore and so the children take it in their stride. They pick up a book in their free time as they would a paintbrush or jigsaw.*

It's impressive, isn't it? ITA had opened the door to easy, expedited education in Anglophone nations – and with 5-year-old children!

Now, please note this: ITA was an orthography, and NOT a method. If and when Australian education does wider trials of a beginners' orthography, I think that should be our approach too. The UK researchers were adamant that teachers could use whichever teaching method they wanted. Both phonics and wholeword reading, the two main word-reading instruction methods then, were fine to use, as both included teaching of ITA letter-sounds.

Similarly, nowadays, Australia's most common word-reading instruction method could easily be used – a small amount of systematic instruction teaching letter-sounds and sounding-out of regular words, combined with lots of reading of texts of manageable difficulty. Our highly-frequent, irregular sightwords would initially be regular, in beginners' orthography, and then later might well be in both orthographies, as children transition to Standard English.

We'll learn much from comparing children's word-reading and spelling development using different instruction methods with the

Research Tour 5. The Power of Beginners' Orthographies

beginners' orthographies we explore, be they modern versions of ITA, Fleksispel and its transition stages, or others.

At the time that ITA was introduced in England, many teachers and schools disliked strong phonics instruction, and prioritised a Language Experience approach, incorporating gentle, more informal instruction on letter-sounds and word-reading. Some ITA studies strategically controlled the reading-instruction methods used with ITA and Standard-English cohorts, while other studies encouraged schools to use their choice of methods.

Importantly, the Warburton and Southgate survey and interviews were with UK teachers using diverse reading instruction methods with ITA, and the teachers and the report emphasise ITA's value, irrespective of the teaching method used.

Resourcing needed for effective instruction was not a specifically researched area, however interviewed teacher comments show teaching of ITA classes to be easier. Because fewer children needed help, and most children were confident, independent readers, writers and learners, teachers had time to achieve effectively differentiated instruction.

Researchers also commented on differing resource needs, e.g., budget needs for far more paper for the extensive enthusiastic writing which ITA children did, and needs for greater diversity of advanced reading materials to meet children's reading interests.

When Whole Language swept through, it created education's paradigmatic Reading Wars shift, from *Reading Wars Past* to *Reading Wars Present*:

- *Reading Wars Past*: arguments about two word-reading instruction methods, phonics vs wholeword sightwords – whether children should be taught to read using phonics (learning letter-sounds and how to sound out words) vs taught wholeword sightwords (learning words as whole units, noticing their visual features).
- *Reading Wars Present*: arguments about whether word-reading is relevant or has importance as a literacy skill, whether and how it should be taught systematically, and whether and how it should be tested.

With Reading Wars Past being vigorously argued in the ITA era, the UK ITA researchers felt it important not to specify instructional methods and instead simply to provide the regular orthography.

With orthography being the factor that eases or complicates word-reading and word-writing development, they simply provided schools professional development on ITA and a series of ITA reading books paralleling the Standard-English reading books the schools already used. And ITA worked well with all methods, with 5-year-olds, including children with strong risk factors.

The ITA research showed children having the strong confidence of Success Inoculation, the enriched language skills of expedited early-literacy development, and an easy effective transition to Standard English, which was expedited by their confident regular-orthography literacy and associated strengths.

If we too used a beginners' orthography, there's every likelihood we could have that too.

Setting Our Beginners' Orthography Goals

While research to clarify the extent to which ITA advantages persisted didn't end up happening, there's no doubt that ITA was highly successful in achieving its primary aims: vastly reducing the number of struggling readers and the extent of their difficulties, and greatly easing early-literacy development for all children.

Those would be our primary aims in exploring a beginners' orthography: reducing difficulties, and easing and expediting literacy development. A secondary aim would be to explore, and work to produce, ongoing advantages in later school years.

We would learn from modern regular-orthography nations and their clearly evident, enduring advantages, evident in how easily they achieve at high levels in PIRLS and PISA studies.

We would learn similarly from the lack of continued gain in many ITA schools after children had transitioned, knowing that we can't assume advantage will continue, and that we'll need to continue extending our children's strong skills.

When we investigate beginners' orthographies, there's strong need to set our priorities clearly, in a definite order of three key primary priorities and one secondary priority:

- **Priority 1 (Key Primary Priority)**: To reduce to a minimum, both our numbers of children experiencing word-reading and spelling difficulties, and the extent of their difficulties.
- **Priority 2 (Key Primary Priority)**: To ensure early reading and writing development is easy, gentle, successful and rapid.

- **Priority 3 (Key Primary Priority):** To ensure efficient, effective transitioning to Standard English.
- **Priority 4 (Secondary Priority):** To achieve ongoing heightened literacy, language and learning development across primary and high-school years, ensuring early-years advantage from a beginners' orthography is continued and extended.

Learning from the ITA fiasco, we would strategically prioritise and not get caught up in confusion, accidentally mistaking Priority 4 as Priority 1, then giving up if we didn't initially achieve Priority 4.

We'd instead celebrate our achieving Priorities 1 to 3 as impressive achievements on our improvement journey. Then we'd implement changes so we also achieve Priority 4, as effectively as regular-orthography nations do now.

It really was a fiasco, wasn't it? ITA achieved well its primary goals of expediting early literacy and massively reducing numbers of struggling word-readers and spellers and their extent of difficulties. But it was then rejected on the basis of a lesser priority, widespread enriched language and literacy skills across later school years, a priority which hadn't even been adequately explored.

It's interesting to note many ITA researchers' ongoing efforts to bring attention back to the primary aims of ITA: that the primary goals were to prevent word-reading and literacy difficulties in at-risk children and make early-literacy development a vastly gentler and easier journey.

Downing (1969b) comments:

To question the worth of the initial teaching alphabet on this basis is to ignore several educational benefits to be derived from the dramatically improved achievements of pupils taught the initial alphabet while still working with that writing system. Because the initial teaching alphabet clarifies the structure of English, the discovery approach to learning is facilitated, the children can express themselves more readily, more fluently, and more creatively in free writing composition.

Moreover, young boys and girls may develop a healthy self-image from the greater certainty of success derived from the simplicity and the regularity of the initial teaching alphabet. Again, it must be added, these gains may result if the benefits of the materials used in teaching the initial teaching alphabet are planned to take advantage of the potential of the new writing system in these respects.

ITA Research Suggests Cognitive-Processing Growth

It's an interesting truth that universally, across the plethora of ITA research studies, ITA children transferred easily and relatively effortlessly to reading and writing Standard English.

The ITA children didn't move immediately into using perfect Standard English spelling, of course, and would quite likely have initially made many errors. But having strong phonological and orthographic awareness, and enhanced executive-function skills, they were ripe for making effective progress.

As an example, in becoming confident with irregular spellings such as *yacht* and *nation*, ITA children already had an orthographic framework for those words, i.e., *y-o-t* and *n-a-sh-u-n*. Being confident, interested learners with strong Success Inoculation who knew that Standard English has many different spelling patterns, with irregular Pattern and Tricky words and syllables abounding, those words and their spelling would likely have seemed interesting and amusing rather than overwhelming. This could lead to further motivated enquiring and learning, particularly if schools de-emphasised correct spelling as a requirement of first draft writing.

It's another interesting truth that the same happens today for children in Taiwan, Japan and China, and would happen for our children too if we used a beginners' orthography initially. Children transition easily and effectively from a regular-orthography to using a complex orthography.

But why? Why is it learning two orthographies, the easy one then the hard one, so much easier than just learning the hard one?

While orthographic-awareness, phonological-awareness and other cognitive-processing skills weren't talked about in the 1960s, and Learned Helplessness theory was in its infancy (Seligman & Maier, 1967), from the available ITA research, it does seem likely that ease of transfer was expedited by
- Phonemic and orthographic awareness developed using ITA.
- Success Inoculation and executive-function skills.
- The children already being confidently literate independent readers, writers and learners when learning Standard English.

Given that studies of children learning to read a fully-regular orthography show they develop executive-function skills (e.g., Papadopoulos, 2001), it's also highly likely that ITA children had strengthened cognitive-processing skills expediting their transition to reading and writing standard English.

Research Tour 5. The Power of Beginners' Orthographies

This could be studied in children in Taiwan, Japan and China today, and in our bilingual schools. As an example, our schools in remote Aboriginal communities might trial
- Children first learning to read and write their first language with its fully-regular orthography,
- Then moving to Standard English, armed with strong cognitive-processing skills,
- With the first-language regular-orthography now a powerful tool for both English second-language learning and mastering Standard-English reading and writing.

We need school-level research in Australia and regular-orthography nations exploring how children's development of phonemic and orthographic awareness, executive-functioning and other cognitive-processing skills relate to their word-reading, spelling and self-teaching skill development – in lower, middle and upper-third readers for Standard-English and regular-orthography readers.

For word-reading and spelling, we need to include the two core skills of Standard-English word-reading development:
- Proficiency with highly frequent words, children meet often.
- Proficiency with unfamiliar words – how well they read and write words they've not yet learned.

More Recent ITA Research

Perhaps because of difficulties making reading materials with ITA font, there's been relatively little use of ITA down the decades. After all, ITA materials in the 1960s were made by commercial publishers, and there were no ITA typewriters.

There have been a small number of studies investigating ITA in more recent years. Their findings consistently show its effectiveness.

Thorstad (1991) compared Italian children with two groups of English readers – one reading Standard English and one reading ITA, finding that the Italian and ITA children acquired reading and spelling at similar rates, and far more quickly than the Standard-English readers, who took three to five years to master what the Italian and ITA children mastered in one year.

Following studies showing its effectiveness, ITA has been used on an ongoing basis in reading remediation coordinated by St Mary's University of Minnesota, with its use found extremely effective (J. Anderson, 2021; Debner & Anderson, 2017; Flynn, 2000),

Jane Flynn (2000, now Jane Anderson) discusses

- Finding ITA remediation to be far more successful than two other remediation methods, with the ITA cohort well ahead on word-reading accuracy, reading fluency, spelling, and writing fluency, despite all testing being done in Standard English.
- The use of Language Experience remediation being highly effective, with children doing daily writing of texts using ITA and considerable repeated reading of ITA texts and their own written texts.
- Major advantages of ITA being ease of mastery, children being able to read and write age-level content and longer texts with ease, and effortless transitioning to Standard English.

ITA has also been used on an ongoing basis by the ITA Foundation in the USA (www.itafoundation.org) down the decades. From early 2021, I've enjoyed discussions with Jane Anderson, a lead member of the ITA Foundation. She had inadvertently stumbled on ITA when looking for an alternative instruction method to use in a research project she was conducting (J. Anderson, 2021; Flynn, 2000).

In doing so, she realised how superior ITA instruction was, with it being far more effective than the other methods she explored. This led to her active, ongoing involvement with the ITA Foundation.

The focus of the ITA Foundation in the USA in recent decades has been downstream not upstream – on ITA use in remediation with struggling readers, not the initial learning of beginning readers. There's also been a major focus on ITA use in second-language learning, e.g., for Puerto Rican children learning to speak and read English, and for children and adults learning to speak and read indigenous languages, e.g., Ojibwe.

I like the term they use: *biliteracy*, e.g., their 2021 annual conference was entitled *Biliteracy: Learning to Read in Different Languages*. They also use the term *Traditional Orthography* where I use *Standard English*, as the term *Standard English* in the USA is generally associated with a spoken English dialect.

The ITA Foundation provides literacy intervention at their St Mary's University clinic in St Paul, Minnesota, and has school projects in various locations. Their website has useful information and resources, e.g., a YouTube channel, ITA font, ITA charts and ITA reading books.

Their intervention programs initially build word-reading, spelling and writing accuracy (Level 1 automaticity), then build fluency (Level 2 automaticity). Their videos usefully detail their methods.

Interestingly, Jane emphasises never using the word *transition*, as transitioning is a nonissue, with all children moving confidently from ITA to Standard English, with virtually no hiccups.

Current projects include intervention clinics, intervention projects in schools, and ITA use in second-language learning: in learning to speak and read Ojibwe, and in Spanish-English literacy.

Regrettably, very little recent research writing has been done as staff numbers are few, with many volunteer hours, and most of them focused strongly on intervention and project work. They've copious intervention and project data that interested researchers might explore and use.

Key Findings from Tour 5

Findings and implications of studies explored in Tour 5, on the use of highly-regular beginners' orthographies prior to reading and writing a highly complex orthography, suggest the following considerations towards improving literacy and education in Anglophone nations:

1. We use 2-stage learning of handwriting, with children first learning to print, then, using the pre-skills and confidence they've developed, to transition to using cursive script.
2. For nations with highly complex orthographies such as Standard English, early-literacy development for reading and writing can also use 2-Stage learning.
3. In 2-Stage early-literacy development, children first learn to read and write a highly-regular beginners' orthography (Stage 1), then transition to reading and writing their nation's complex orthography (Stage 2).
4. This 2-Stage scaffolding keeps learning far more manageable in Stage-1, plus builds learning skills and confidence that empower learning to read and write the complex orthography.
5. Taiwan, Japan and China are role models for 2-Stage early literacy for reading and writing. Since they commenced 2-Stage early-literacy development, by adding in a beginners' orthography for earliest literacy, literacy levels are high, and numbers of children with word-reading and writing difficulties, are extremely low, with their difficulties seeming very mild.
6. There are very strong indicators that it is much easier for children, schools, education and the nation when 2-Stage early-literacy development is used, than when children must learn to read sole highly-complex orthographies such as Standard English, Thai, Taiwan's and China's Hanzi, and Japan's Kanji.
7. The strong advantages of 2-Stage early-literacy development,

where children first learn to read and write a highly-regular beginners' orthography, prior to learning to read and write their nation's complex orthography, create value in Anglophone nations researching and trialling 2-Stage early-literacy.
8. Extensive research findings on the Initial Teaching Alphabet (ITA), a fully-regular English beginners' orthography, align very strongly with the findings of crosslinguistic research of recent decades, while providing additional useful insights (Knight et al., 2017a; 2019).
9. Using ITA or a similarly regular beginners' orthography prior to moving to Standard English is similar to Asian nations' use of fully-regular initial orthographies prior to moving to use their highly complex orthographies.
10. Use of ITA greatly expedited development of early-literacy skills, including word-reading, word-writing, vocabulary and language skills for literacy, reading comprehension and written expression.
11. It greatly reduced the number of children with word-reading and literacy difficulties, and their extent of difficulties.
12. It was highly effective in remediating older struggling readers.
13. It was highly effective in second-language learning.
14. It produced verbal-efficiency effects including enhanced vocabulary, and heightened ideation in children's writing.
15. Recent crosslinguistic research has largely focused on quite narrow aspects of literacy development, including word-reading, phonemic awareness, and Rapid Automised Naming (RAN).
16. ITA research had a much broader focus, including word-reading, reading comprehension, enjoyment of reading, spelling, written expression, enjoyment of writing, extent of independent reading, vocabulary and language usage within writing, and socio-emotional aspects of literacy.
17. ITA research showed strong indicators of children and adults experiencing Success Inoculation, with Acquired Helplessness prevented in slower-developing readers.
18. All studies showed that children transitioned easily and effortlessly to using Standard English.
19. ITA research was conducted as school-level research using separate Standard-English and ITA classes.
20. Whereas Standard-English cohorts had many struggling readers needing support for word-reading and spelling, as well as language skills and reading comprehension, the much smaller numbers of ITA children needing remediation needed it only for language skills and reading comprehension.
21. ITA significantly increased the number of children with advanced word-reading and writing skills, e.g., Mazurkiewicz

(1971, 1973a), discussing an 11-year study of 14,000 Pennsylvania children, half in ITA classes and half in Standard-English classes, comments that

   a. Only 6% of Standard-English Grade 1 children were reading Grade 2 and 3 books, in contrast to 75% of ITA Grade 1 children.
   b. Three times more Standard-English children repeated a year-level, and twice as many needed intervention.
   c. The most dramatic flowering was in children's writing, with very large numbers of ITA children being confident, independent, expansive, enthusiastic writers.
   d. Teacher workload was significantly reduced, with teachers using the increased teaching time available to differentiate instruction.
22. Fully-regular beginners' orthographies are used with strong success, for many purposes, including early literacy, learning to subsequently read and write a complex orthography, second-language learning, remediation of Standard-English struggling readers, and literacy development of previously illiterate adults.
23. There is considerable evidence that ITA achieved its primary goals of easing and speeding early-literacy development, reducing and preventing reading and writing difficulties, and achieving easy transitioning to Standard English.
24. There is relatively little evidence that early ITA advantage continued, as the few studies on this area showed mixed findings, and the ITA research stopped abruptly, with the many intended research projects in this area not completed, including intended projects building later years' capacity for expediting early ITA advantage.
25. There seems strong likelihood that this lack of improvement was due to teachers in later primary school not having been trained on how to continue optimising the flourishing literacy and language skills of the ITA children.
26. Regular-orthography nations currently having robust orthographic advantage, with e.g., high PIRLS and PISA results, suggests early advantage can definitely be continued successfully across primary school and high school when nations put in place appropriate teaching mechanisms.
27. There seems to have been an ITA fiasco: copious findings on ITA use meeting its primary goals, of rapid, easy, early-literacy development and preventing word-reading and writing difficulties, having been completely ignored down the decades, due to general thinking focused on a lesser, insufficiently-researched priority, of achieving advantage in later school years.

28. In future Australian research of beginners' orthographies, it is thus important to circumvent possibilities of this ITA fiasco being repeated.
29. This is likely done best by keeping a clear perspective of four priorities maintained in a definite order of importance, of three key primary priorities and one secondary priority, in line with children's rights to an effective education developing healthy literacy and learning skills:
    a. Priority 1 (Key Primary Priority): To minimise both our numbers of children experiencing word-reading and spelling difficulties, and their extent of difficulties.
    b. Priority 2 (Key Primary Priority): To ensure easy, gentle, successful, rapid development of reading and writing.
    c. Priority 3 (Key Primary Priority): To ensure efficient, effective transitioning to Standard English.
    d. Priority 4 (Secondary Priority): To achieve ongoing heightened literacy, language and learning development across primary and high-school years, ensuring early-years advantage from a beginners' orthography is continued and extended.
30. There is value in prioritising actioning of researching the effectiveness of 2-Stage early-literacy and a beginners' orthography for achieving Priorities 1 to 3, as delays can unfortunately continue hardship, e.g., the Anglophone world may well have lost 60 years of impressive progress through the ITA research findings having been unfortunately ignored.
31. Research studies on the impacts of ITA on early-literacy development and transitioning were very rigorous by research standards then and now.
32. ITA research may well have been discontinued because of the philosophical emphasis of the times, notably the advent of Whole Language, as there are insufficient findings of it being inadequate from evidence-based perspectives when the extensive ITA research is reviewed.
33. It is most unfortunate for Australian education that ITA was not embraced as part of Whole Language actioning in the 1980s, as Whole Language plus ITA would have been an immensely powerful and empowering combination, expediting early-literacy development, with few struggling readers and ample time to achieve enriched empowered literacy learning.
34. The strength of this combination is seen in Freire's (1974) highly effective literacy work with Brazilian adults who'd previously been illiterate (Brazilian Portuguese is highly regular).

35. There is great value in Australian education revisiting the research on ITA as part of educational improvement initiatives.

Research Tour 6.
Our Epidemic of Language Weakness

For many, the seeds of academic failure are sown early and are evident in early reading struggles. Despite sustained efforts by educators, an achievement gap persists between the reading skills of children from more and less advantaged homes. Language ability at ages three and four predicts later reading comprehension through high school, and later language ability builds directly on earlier competencies.

Differences in children's language ability and associated capacities emerge early, relate to social demographic factors, and foreshadow future reading success.

David Dickinson, 2011

In considering our learners' strengths, weaknesses and needs, we need to include a strong focus on language skills. In this tour, we'll explore key aspects of the language skills that our children need for effective literacy and learning. We'll also explore the supports that Australia provides children with language-skills and literacy weakness, and our major needs for improvement in this area.

Language skills that children use for communication and learning include their receptive and expressive vocabulary, their language comprehension and language expression skills used in listening, speaking, reading and writing, and their language reasoning and inferencing skills, including social reasoning.

They also include cognitive-processing skills: information-processing skills children use endlessly, including phonological and phonemic awareness, processing speed and rapid naming, short-term and working memory, and executive-function skills.

Language-skills weakness is a major aspect of many children's literacy difficulties. It's a universal issue from early childhood, present in regular-orthography and Anglophone nations, though the effects are stronger on Standard-English readers (Galletly & Knight, 2011a; Knight et al., 2017a, 2021).

Finland's *Jyvaskyla Longitudinal Study of Dyslexia* (JLD) showed weak infant speech perception skills and language skills at 2 years old predicted later literacy difficulties (Lyytinen, 2014, Lyytinen et al., 2004, 2015; Lyytinen, Aro et al., 2006; Lyytinen, Erskine et al., 2006; Richardson et al., 2003; Torppa et al., 2010).

Findings are similar for Anglophone children: neonatal speech perception predicts early-childhood language skills, and both predict later literacy skills (Espy et al., 2004; Molfese et al., 2001).

As with word-reading and executive-function skills, the picture is clearer for regular-orthography children. Regular-orthography studies show children with Dyslexia, with and without diagnosed language weakness, have language deficits in key areas, e.g., vocabulary, syntax, and phonological cognitive-processing skills.

Hämäläinen et al.'s (2009) useful study of speech perception in Finnish children with reading difficulties found weak speech perception linked to weak phonological awareness and spelling, with results suggesting a path of children's auditory processing abilities affecting their speech perception skills, which in turn lead to phonological processing weakness and dyslexia.

Perhaps, in the future, particularly if we're initially using a regular-orthography, we will have highly effective identification of babies at risk of language weakness in early childhood, then later literacy difficulties. We'll perhaps use early-intervention computer games and neuropsychological interventions that appreciably resolve difficulties before their impacts spread (Ahmed et al., 2020; P. Anderson et al., 2018; Apfelbaum et al., 2013; T. Aro et al., 2015; Carson, 2020; Crippa et al., 2015; Engel de Abreu et al., 2014; Fawcett & Jones, 2020; Gandolfi et al., 2021; Gathercole et al., 2012; Georgiou et al., 2020; Jacob & Parkinson, 2015; Knight & Galletly, 2020; Koponen et al., 2013; Kyle et al., 2013; Papadopoulos et al., 2004; Pascoe et al., 2013; Roberts, Quach et al., 2016; Traverso et al., 2015).

We've Widespread Language Weakness

Numerous Australian studies show language weakness to be a major public health issue. It's increasingly discussed as a *language weakness epidemic*, given such high numbers of children and adults have language-skill weakness (e.g., S. Anderson et al., 2016; Lamb et al., 2020; Law et al., 2010, 2015, 2017; Schoon et al., 2010; P. Snow, 2016; P. Snow et al., 2020; Walker & Haddock, 2020):

- Undetected language weakness is widespread, in pre-schoolers, school children and groups of vulnerable adults, e.g., in unemployed and jailed Australians.
- Low socio-economic status (SES) has an extremely strong association with language weakness.
- Language weakness at young ages has damaging impacts on children's literacy and academic achievement, flowing through to major adult disadvantage in many forms.
- Speech language pathologists and families consider lack of free services a massive problem across Australia.
- Children's communication difficulties are an increasingly urgent Australian public-health issue, due to significant language weakness being so widespread.

Jessup et al.'s (2008a, 2008b) studies of children starting school with language weakness in one Australian region, showed 41% starting school with significant language weakness, and 85% of those children not having been previously identified as having language weakness (Jessup et al., 2008a, 2008b).

We'd benefit by replicating this study across Australia, additionally exploring availability and need for speech language pathology services. We'd quite likely find similarly significant findings in most states and territories, of up to 40% of children starting school with notable language weakness, with most not previously identified as having language weakness.

We'd also likely find that this is due in large part to allied-health services for pre-school children being so meagre, education departments only taking responsibility from start of school, and schools not assessing children's language skills.

Language Disorder (children having significant communication difficulties), which is quite often termed Developmental Language Disorder, is a lifelong disorder that needs and deserves respect and strong supports. Estimates in Australian children at school entry range from 7% and 14%, to 20% and higher. There's likelihood all schools and daycare centres should anticipate and be resourced to support language weakness in at least 25-30% of their enrolment.

Harrison and McLeod's (2010) study, using data for 4,329 children in the 2009 *Longitudinal Study of Australian Children* (LSAC; Daraganova & Joss, 2019) explored the impact of risk factors, establishing 19 significant factors. They discuss a core set of significant predictors, including parent and family factors, which hint at generational disadvantage, plus child factors, including being a boy, having hearing problems, not persisting at activities, being less sociable and having a more reactive temperament.

Other Australian studies discuss the cumulative effect of health and education disadvantages (Kikkawa, 2014; Quach et al., 2017), with, on average, the number of risk factors having more effect than the extent of any individual factor (Quach et al., 2017):

Number was more important than type (physical, psychosocial) of adversity. ... The accumulation of health adversities predicts poorer academic achievement up to 2 years later.

Interventions might need to address multiple domains to improve child academic outcomes. ...

Coordination across the health and education interface might be crucial to optimising outcomes.

Studies of prison populations and flexible learning programs for children who've been excluded or diverted from mainstream school show depressingly high proportions of children with major language weakness and associated severe literacy weakness (S. Anderson et al., 2016; P. Snow et al.). As an example, Pamela Snow et al. (2020) found 72% of such Australians had major language weakness, with almost half having reading comprehension at least four years below age level.

Australia's 2020 Educational Opportunity report (Lamb et al., 2020; Macklin & Pilcher, 2020) has a depressing, though apt, title: *Educational opportunity in Australia 2020: Who succeeds and who misses out.* It discusses key issues being clear from school entry and expanding over time. The report includes revealing data:

- Over 20% of Australian children start school not on track in all key domains, with over 15% decidedly not on track for healthy literacy and numeracy development.
- Almost 25% start school socially vulnerable, with 20% having insufficient emotional maturity, and almost 15% having difficulties respecting others and behaving appropriately. Importantly, it's not just the children in need of help: it's also their teachers, as children's difficulties can drastically reduce the effectiveness of teaching and learning in their classes.
- Almost 25% of middle-school children don't achieve above our *National Minimum Standard* for both literacy and numeracy in NAPLAN (and those National Minimum Standards are sadly low, especially by regular-orthography nation standards).

- Over 30% of middle-school children don't meet international benchmarks in science, with 27% not meeting them for Maths, Science and Reading.
- Over 30% lack healthy self-efficacy and self-belief.
- Almost 20% of high-school students don't complete Year 12.
- Of our young adults, almost 30% aren't engaged full-time in education, training or work, 27% aren't gaining any post-school qualification, and almost 30% lack confidence in themselves and the future.
- Socio-Economic Status (SES) has very major impacts, with over 50% of children with low SES not achieving above the National Minimum Standards for both literacy and numeracy.

That's sad, isn't it? It's even sadder when we use a Finnish contrast that shows how well educated Finnish young adults are. Ronimus et al. (2019) describe a sample of Finnish parents that's fairly representative of national levels: 27% of mothers and 16% of fathers having a Masters or Doctoral degree, almost 40% of mothers and 30% of fathers having a bachelor's degree, and 23% of mothers and 36% of fathers having upper-secondary education qualifications.

The Educational Opportunity report comments,

Those who are doing well achieve all that the national goals say will be achieved. There is another sense, however, that also stands out from the results of this report: our education and training systems are dogged by inequality. No matter which way you turn, which measure you use, parts of our population are missing out and falling behind.

There are very uneven levels of academic learning across different groups of young Australians and wide gaps in achievement as learners progress from stage to stage. Young people from poorer backgrounds, indigenous Australians, and rural students experience high rates of noncompletion of school, and poor outcomes.

For these Australians, our systems are not functioning well, raising a question about the quality of education and the capacity for meeting the needs of all young Australians.

The results are at odds with the very first goal expressed in the Alice Springs Declaration which commits Australian governments to promote excellence and equity in education and provide 'all young Australians with access to high-quality education that is inclusive and free from any form of discrimination' and 'recognise the individual needs of all young Australians, identify barriers that can be addressed, and empower learners to overcome barriers.

Australia and Australian education are definitely struggling, and our language weakness epidemic plays a very strong role in our struggles. Our Act, declarations and agreements deliver many promises, but these too often prove to be rhetoric, given we don't deliver the required services implied in those promises (Galletly et al., 2010; Knight & Galletly, 2017).

Geoff Masters (2016) in his very readable report, *Five challenges for Australian education*, discusses one in five Australian children being developmentally vulnerable at the start of school and locked into a trajectory of long-term low achievement.

He notes 22% of Australian children being found developmentally vulnerable in the 2015 *Australian Early Development Census* (AEDC, Commonwealth of Australia, 2016), in one or more key domains – physical health and well-being, social competence, emotional maturity, and language and cognitive skills:

> *By Year 3, there are wide differences in children's level of achievement in learning areas such as reading and mathematics. Some children are already well behind year-level expectations and many of these children remain behind throughout their schooling. Many are locked in the trajectories of 'underperformance' that often lead to disengagement, poor attendance and early exit from school.*

Alas, our 2018 AEDC report showed similar levels of vulnerable children (Commonwealth of Australia, 2019). Studying our 900,000 Australian children who started Prep in 2018, it discusses improvements, but also a continuing 22% of vulnerable children:

> *Since the first census in 2009, more children have consistently had access to high-quality preschool in the year before they commence full-time school. As a nation, we have seen a steady improvement in the language and cognitive skills of children starting school. By continuing to focus on preschool attendance, our children will be better prepared for school.*
>
> *The AEDC found 21.7 per cent of Australian children were developmentally vulnerable on one or more domain. While the development of Australian children as a whole is improving, there is still work to do to give young Australians the best possible start.*

Masters (2016) sets five key challenges needing overcoming:
- Declining reading and maths achievement.

- Growing disparities between schools, strongly linked to Socio-Economic Status (SES).
- Too many learners achieving significantly below year-level.
- One fifth of Australian children being at risk of difficulties at school entry and vulnerable for long-term low achievement.
- Teaching being decreasingly desirable as a career option.

He emphasises twin early-childhood challenges:
- Supporting the progress of all children in the pre-school years, particularly those lagging in development, and
- Ensuring they cope well in their first year of school by meeting their individual points of need from the start of school.

Needs for Strong School Services and Supports

Australian teachers' estimates show increased numbers of children starting school with speech and language weakness. They discuss children who have special health-care needs, with up to 5% having *established needs*, but almost four times that number having so-called *emerging needs* – difficulties that don't yet have a formal diagnosis, or that are milder but nonetheless significant (M. O'Connor et al., 2019, 2020).

Using data from the 2009, 2012 and 2015 Australian Early Development Census (AEDC), Meredith O'Connor et al. (2019) found speech language difficulties increased by 14.7% for children with emerging needs, and that emotional problems rose by 13.7% for children with established needs. They emphasise that it's less the children's need for a diagnosis, and more their major need for school supports. That's very true.

Our children with emerging needs are a serious issue for Australian schools (Angus et al., 2004, 2007; APPA., 2008a, 2008b, 2020; Galletly et al., 2010; Garvey et al., 2020). All too often, children with emerging needs don't receive required supports, and this can add greatly to child and teacher workload. They need our schools well resourced and able to support them, and alas, all too often, that's not the case.

It's also inappropriate that we have this dichotomy of children having established vs emerging needs, as both groups need, and are entitled to, the highly effective education our Act and agreements promise, and which our schools should be resourced to provide.

That's particularly the case when our Education Act and disability documents promise our children a strong, well-supported education (Australian Government, 2005a, 2005b, 2015; Galletly et al., 2010).

In a 2010 research article, *When tests frame children*, our CQU team explored this issue (Galletly et al., 2010). Its abstract reads,

> *Decision-making regarding intensive instructional support for children with special needs should build from children's instructional needs, and not from diagnostic labelling and criteria for funding eligibility.*
>
> *Cognitive referencing, the use of results on intelligence and language quotients to decide children's academic options and funding eligibility, is established as inappropriate practice yet continues to be used by many education systems.*
>
> *This paper discusses systemic practices in Australia, UK and USA, and then details four cases of children "framed" by their tests, i.e., experiencing unwarranted disadvantage due to how they were positioned by their tests and diagnoses.*
>
> *The final section makes recommendations for considerations needed in the improving of Australian education of children with special needs.*

Our Education Act and disability documents don't require children to have diagnostic labels for their schools to achieve Special Education funding, and many children are better off without a label, except perhaps Learning Disability, the missing category from our governments' disability funding system.

Australia needs change, to ending requirements for diagnostic labels, and schools instead being well resourced to meet children's individual intervention and support needs.

Meredith O'Connor and colleagues (2020) used school entry data on 42,619 Australian children, from the Australian Early Development Census (AEDC), along with the children's Year 3 NAPLAN data. They found children who started school with established or emerging needs had significantly lower reading and numeracy outcomes in Grade 3.

They also found savage Socio-Economic Status (SES) impacts, with SES having multiplicative, not additive effects, markedly exacerbating children's literacy and numeracy difficulties. Low SES's enormous effects on Australia and Australian education is a nemesis we must resolve. Using 10 Changes improvements, loosening, then removing, the linkage of low SES to low achievement is quite likely achievable.

The studies above highlight the generational disadvantage that Anglophone nations live with, and our Early Years Factory in action. For as long as Australia uses solely Standard English with vulnerable

4.5 to 5-year-olds, we'll continue both our Spelling Generations and generational disadvantage: excessive numbers of children who are insufficiently literate, and become adults with low income and SES, who struggle as parents to support the next generation who, in turn, also struggle with language, literacy and academic development.

O'Connor et al. (2020) emphasises our needs for improved supports:
The education system is an important universal platform for meeting children's additional health and developmental needs. Children are exposed to an average of 950 hours of schooling each year, and school professionals regularly administer mediations, provide counselling, implement behavioural intervention plans, and monitor behavioural and emotional issues. ...
A particular challenge facing education systems is how to support children whose health and developmental difficulties emerge as they transition to school. Teachers play an important role in early identification; increased social, language, and cognitive demands of the classroom environment often highlight children's need for greater support. ...
In addition, not all health and developmental difficulties that have been identified qualified children for special-needs programs, and the degree to which the needs of children who fall outside this scope (18% of the school entrance population in Australia ...) are recognised and met is unclear.

Our flood of children with unresolved language difficulties swells our flood of struggling readers and learners. Given our language weakness epidemic's major education impacts, we need to position overcoming language weakness as very much an education system challenge and responsibility.

We've Widespread Insufficient Services

Let's now explore our Australia-wide lack of Speech Language Pathology services.

While it's not something that's ever cured, when appropriate supports are provided (Cirrin et al., 2010; Ebbels et al., 2019), children with Language Disorder can do well, moving successfully into healthy, rewarding, productive adult life. They need supports across childhood, including the pre-school years, and across primary school and high school.

Alas, a very large number of Australian studies show that these supports aren't being provided at an appropriate level, and that consequently children and adults with language weakness overwhelmingly struggle – at school, in the workforce, and in adult life generally.

Let's briefly explore the findings of a range of these studies.

McCormack et al.'s (2011) study, of the same 4,329 children in the 2009 LSAC study found that 24% of children aged 4 to 5 years had communication impairment, with 76% of these children not having been previously assessed and identified as having language weakness. They discuss provision of services to school-aged children being extremely variable, and access and provision of services being markedly inconsistent across states and localities.

They also discuss there being limited relationship between children having communication difficulties and children having received services. Now, that's a major negative investment in our children and education – one worthy of national shame.

In my region, it's common for families to wait 18 months and more for speech language pathology and allied-health services, and before NDIS began, it was much longer.

It's disappointing that it's far easier to research the lack of services in Australia, and families' views thereof, than it is to research well-resourced interventions.

We've many studies discussing our lack of services and the negative consequences thereof (e.g., McGill et al., 2020; McLeod et al., 2020).

McGill et al.'s (2020) study is aptly titled *Many wasted months: Stakeholders' perspectives about waiting for speech-language pathology services*. It analysed written submissions to an Australian Government Senate Inquiry. It discusses families' very high needs for speech language pathology services, and services being insufficient, such that most families endure very long waiting lists, with

- Families often waiting 12 months for an assessment and then up to 2 years for follow-up.
- Families finally making it to the top of one list, but unfortunately moving to another location, where they must start again at the bottom of waiting lists.
- Children being on the Community Health waiting list until they become ineligible due to starting school, and then being on the school waiting list – if their state has school services.

They detail the detrimental impacts of lack of services, with burdens on physical health, finances, time, emotional well-being and relationships, continuity of care, and intervention needs.

The situation McGill et al. describe has certainly been the case in my local region over the years. In recent decades, the hospital has only offered inpatient services, saying children are provided services by Community Health (which only sees pre-school children), and the Education Department. Then, alas, children can be still on the Community Health waiting list when they start school. Then, far too many children don't receive school speech intervention, because school speech language pathologists are too few. NDIS has changed things for the better for those children accepted for NDIS funding, but far too many children in need still miss out.

McGill et al.'s (2020) introduction sums up our situation well:
Waiting for speech-language pathology services is a common reality, and poses risks for consumers, professionals, and organisations. Waiting lists often occur in health care when demand for services exceeds the supply and the limited resources available must be rationed. Long waiting lists can prevent access to early intervention and may deter [people] from seeking speech-language pathology support at all, meaning those who need support may miss out.

Failure to receive timely speech-language pathology intervention can lead to long-term impacts on academic, occupational, and emotional outcomes. In under-resourced organisations, speech-language pathology services may be rationed based on priority, with individuals considered higher priority receiving services faster than those considered lower priority.

Individuals who are considered low priority for services may be left on waiting lists until their difficulties "become more pressing, or until more resources are available".

Not surprisingly, McGill et al. conclude that existing services are inadequate in meeting stakeholders' needs, with action needed to reduce waiting-list time and increase services, towards minimising the negative consequences too many Australians experience.

McLeod et al. (2020) explored waiting-list options for families of 222 children who'd already waited eight months on waiting lists at two regional New South Wales (NSW) Community Health centres. They screened the children, all aged 3 to 6 years, finding 111 with significant speech and/or language difficulties, who were then allocated to one of three options:

- *Therapy*: 12 x 45-minute individual weekly sessions of direct intervention over a 14-week period.
- *Advice*: a 45-minute individual session to discuss results, set joint goals, and provide resources and caregiver training.

- *Website*: referral to the NSW government *Waiting for Speech Pathology* website, which has numerous family-friendly fact sheets discussing strategies for improving children's speech and language skills.

Having a dedicated *Waiting for Speech Pathology* website seems a strong comment on insufficient services. Not surprisingly, the study found that while all three options were found useful, family satisfaction was highest for the therapy group, and speech improved most in that group. Language scores showed little difference across the options – quite likely because language skills are such a big area, and most children with weak language skills need far more than 12 weeks' intervention.

A key reason I've included this study is its focus on children working one-on-one with speech language pathologists. While small group interventions can be effective, all too often children with speech or language difficulties need one-to-one intervention and all too often they don't get it. Even in states where there are school speech language pathologists, one-to-one intervention often isn't possible, because much of their time is used on assessments and report writing, and preparing programs for school staff to implement.

Specially trained speech language pathology aides can make a strong positive difference. Currently, few or no states use trained aides widely in schools. This is unfortunate, reducing practice between speech language pathology sessions, and its effectiveness.

Many children only need occasional one-on-one time with a speech language pathologist, e.g., weekly, fortnightly or monthly sessions, depending on their progress and needs – as long as they receive strategic practice between sessions. For children of school age, practice on a daily to weekly basis is needed, preferably at least 90 minutes per week.

They'd benefit greatly from one-on-one practice with a trained aide who knows them well, works well with them, is very encouraging, and works closely with the school's speech language pathologist.

Murdoch Children's Research Institute's policy briefs (MCRI), *Developmental Language Disorder: A public health problem?* (Law et al., 2017), and *Social disadvantage and early language delay* (Law et al., 2015) are packed with useful information, all of it rather sad. So is the Deeble Institute's evidence brief *Developmental Language Disorder: A disability, health and education challenge* (Walker & Haddock, 2020). They're worthwhile reading.

Law et al. (2017) used Medicare session numbers to highlight needs:

- Access to funded Medicare support for speech language pathology sessions being meagre, with limited sessions (up to five sessions maximum per year) and refunds often covering only a small proportion of fees paid.
- Medicare claims for sessions increasing markedly, e.g., from 3,051 sessions claimed in 2004-5 to 115,167 sessions claimed in 2012-13.
- Families being desperately in need of speech language pathology support but not receiving it.
- Free or fully-funded services rarely being available except to children with NDIS funding.

Australia needs greatly increased speech language pathology and allied-health services for our children, both in and out of school. It's curious, and disappointing, that children can have considerably more than five Medicare sessions for occupational therapy or psychology, additionally accessed on a mental health plan, but for speech language pathology, it's five sessions maximum.

Into the future, we need to be focusing strongly on overcoming language-skills weakness, as strongly as we focus on overcoming literacy and learning weakness – because language skills are the central core of all learning and academic achievement.

We also need our schools well-resourced, so they're organised and able to meet children's needs from start of school and across the school years.

Australian Research Is Insufficiently Resourced

Research funding inadequacies reduce the power of Australian research on our children's language, literacy and learning skills in major ways.

As an example, one of our biggest studies is *Growing up in Australia, The longitudinal study of Australian children* (LSAC; Daraganova & Joss, 2019): it studied two cohorts of approximately 5000 Australian children, who in 2004 were aged 0 to 1 years and 4 to 5 years, respectively.

Many researchers use LSAC data as the basis of their research (e.g., Harrison & McLeod, 2010; McCormack et al., 2011), but alas, LSAC data on children's skill levels is sadly minimal. The only language test was a modified short-form of *Peabody Picture Vocabulary Test-3*, used at just one time-point, when children were aged 4 to 5 years.

For language-skills researchers, LSAC's power is significantly reduced through only minimal language testing being conducted, with the lack of testing likely due to insufficient research funding.

Relative to other nations, Australia saves savagely on research funding, with education and our struggling readers the sad victims of our research insufficiencies.

In the LSAC study, while children's NAPLAN data can be used to provide useful data on reading comprehension, spelling, written grammar and written expression, we've no data on word-reading or language skills. LSAC didn't include testing of word-reading, and no testing of language skills beyond that one brief vocabulary test.

Other nations conduct longitudinal studies in projects that are far more optimally resourced, and far more powerful in the findings they provide. We'll explore two of those projects here, Finland's *Jyvaskyla Longitudinal Study of Dyslexia* (JLD), and the USA *Early Childhood Longitudinal Study: Kindergarten Cohort* (ECLS-K; Mashburn & Myers, 2010),

The Jyvaskyla Longitudinal Study of Dyslexia (JLD)

Tiny Finland has a quarter of Australia's population, and quite likely far less government funds. Finland nonetheless conducted the extremely impressive Jyvaskyla Longitudinal Study of Dyslexia (JLD). It incorporated extensive assessments of children across early childhood and school years, from birth to Grade 9, using this data in a multitude of useful research studies (e.g., Eklund et al., 2013, 2015; Lohvansuu et al., 2021; Lyytinen, 2014; Lyytinen et al., 2004, 2015; Lyytinen, Aro et al., 2006; Lyytinen, Erskine et al., 2006; Richardson et al., 2003).

The researchers screened over 8000 families having babies between 1993 and 1996 to find families with a dyslexic parent and a close dyslexic relative, eventually narrowing down to a group of just over 100 babies with familial risk for Dyslexia and a similar-sized control group of babies without Dyslexia risk. They then followed these babies and families across early childhood and the school years, monitoring their skill development.

Assessments started within five days of birth, with measures of heart rate and speech perception, then continued with multiple assessment instances each year. The list of tests used is detailed on the project website: by Australian standards, it's massive.

Very large numbers of individual studies have been conducted using JLD's delightfully comprehensive data. Importantly, at least 13 researchers actioned Doctoral studies within the project.

The JLD results shed considerable light on underlying difficulties of regular-orthography children who experience literacy difficulties (e.g., Lohvansuu et al., 2021; Lyytinen, 2014; Lyytinen et al., 2015):

- Children with a family history of Dyslexia being four times more likely to have Dyslexia (literacy difficulties).
- Speech perception of infants within a week of birth identifying those who would have Dyslexia.
- Speech perception related to phoneme length identification at six months of age predicting both those who would have Dyslexia, and also children's reading speed.
- Early oral-language skills, phonological-processing skills, Rapid Automised Naming (RAN) and letter knowledge differentiating Dyslexia and control groups from ages 2.5 to 3.5 years on, and predicting Dyslexia and reading development through to adolescence.
- Home environment, children's interest in reading, and task avoidance did not differentiate the two groups, but were found to be additional predictors of reading development.

The JLD study focused both on establishing best-practice early identification of at-risk readers, and achieving effective prevention and intervention: GraphoLearn was developed in JLD research.

As Lohvansuu et al., (2021) summarise,

The JLD revealed that the likelihood of at-risk children performing poorly in reading and spelling tasks was fourfold compared to the controls.

Auditory insensitivity of newborns observed during the first week of life using brain event-related potentials (ERPs) was shown to be the first precursor of dyslexia.

ERPs measured at six months of age related to phoneme length identification differentiated the family risk group from the control group and predicted reading speed until the age of 14 years.

Early oral language skills, phonological processing skills, rapid automatized naming, and letter knowledge differentiated the groups from ages 2.5–3.5 years onwards and predicted dyslexia and reading development, including reading comprehension, until adolescence.

The home environment, a child's interest in reading, and task avoidance were not different in the risk group but were found to be additional predictors of reading development.

Based on the JLD findings, preventive and intervention methods utilizing the association learning approach have been developed.

It would be extremely powerful for Australia, if we replicated the Jyvaskyla longitudinal study. It would be even more powerful if we included larger subject numbers, to the extent that we could study four strands from start of school, to explore impacts of an initial orthography vs Standard English at start of school, and learning to read at age 4.5 to 5.0 years vs doing 2.5 years of language and learning enrichment then learning to read from mid-Year 2.

We'd also learn much by engaging in both GraphoLearn and Comprehension Game research.

The "Early Childhood Longitudinal - Kindergarten Cohort" Study

The USA Early Childhood Longitudinal Study: Kindergarten Cohort (ECLS-K; Mashburn & Myers, 2010), one of many such USA studies, is a useful example of another Anglophone study with aims comparable to our under-resourced LSAC study.

Conducted by the Department of Education, it followed a nationally representative sample of 20,000 children from Kindergarten in 1998 through to Grade 8 in 2007. It used ongoing surveys of teachers and families, as LSAC used. Unlike LSAC, the USA study also used comprehensive longitudinal one-to-one testing of a wide range of relevant skills, with children assessed at seven time points: twice in Kindergarten and Year 1, then once in Grades 3, 5 and 8.

Its respectable extent of testing has provided useful data for many USA studies (e.g., Lubotsky & Kaestner, 2016), and contrasts sadly with LSAC's affording just one brief language test at one time point.

We limit our researchers savagely when our research funding is so meagre (Gill, 2004). In doing so, equally savagely, Australia is limiting both education and our children.

Dyslexia Is Language Disorder!

Many studies have established that word-reading and language skills are two key components underlying reading comprehension and proficient independent reading (Adlof & Hogan, 2018; Alloway et al., 2017; Catts et al. 2005, 2015; Hoover & Gough, 1990; Hulme et al. 2015; Knight et al., 2019; P. Snow, 2016; Snowling et al. 2015).

There are many major overlaps between language weakness and reading difficulties. The two have high comorbidity both with each other and other developmental disorders, including Attention Deficit/Hyperactivity Disorder (ADHD), auditory processing weakness, coordination weakness seen in handwriting weakness, behaviour weakness, anxiety and depression, and Autism Spectrum

Disorder (ASD) or traits thereof (Galletly & Knight, 2011a; Hendren et al., 2018; Moll et al., 2020; Wagner et al., 2019).

Mashburn and Myers (2010), considering changes in the primary diagnosis of a large cohort of USA children receiving Special Education services, found a steady increase in the numbers of children with a primary diagnosis of Learning Disability (from 11% in Kindergarten, 25% in Grade 1, to 50% in Grade 3, and 60% in Grade 5), but a seemingly parallel reduction in the number of children with a primary diagnosis of speech or language impairment (from 42% in Grade 1, and 25% in Grade 3, to 14% in Grade 5). It's likely our struggling readers will receive more effective supports from well-coordinated support services involving speech language pathologists and learning-support teachers rather than from separate services.

Now, while current consensus is generally that Dyslexia (word-reading and associated difficulties) and Language Disorder (weakness in language skills) are highly overlapping but nonetheless separate disorders, it's time to challenge that notion.

It's a Swiss-cheese research area, but there's likelihood that virtually all Standard-English readers with word-reading and literacy difficulties, whether or not it's called dyslexia, have pre-existing weakness in language skills. That's evident from considerable research, e.g., Finland's Jyvaskyla Longitudinal Dyslexia Study's (JLD) findings, and my practical experience, e.g., having assessed many hundreds of children who've come for literacy intervention without mention of communication difficulties, but nonetheless have major language weakness.

Their language-skills weakness commonly includes
- Word-finding and expressive vocabulary weakness.
- Associated verbal expressive language weakness, which includes hesitations, pausing and rephrasing when speaking.
- Stronger expressive language skills for narrative retells and general conversation.
- Much weaker expressive language skills when required to give precise wording and succinct explanations, e.g., in school tests and assignments, and tasks such as *TILLS Vocabulary Awareness* subtest, and the *Renfrew Word Finding Test*.
- Expressive vocabulary being much weaker than receptive vocabulary, which is a relative strength.
- Greater use of Simple and Compound Sentences, and early Complex Sentences (e.g., those using the conjunction *because*).

Research Tour 6. Our Epidemic of Language Weakness

- Reduced use of both complex description and Complex Sentences with advanced conjunctions.
- Errors on irregular past tense verbs, e.g., *catched, drived*, and irregular plurals, e.g., *mouses*.
- Language difficulties in editing and honing written work.
- Language expression and language comprehension difficulties reflecting functional working memory weakness more than pure language-skills weakness.
- Language sequencing difficulties that interact with automisation weakness, e.g., difficulties mastering the alphabet, and counting down by numbers, e.g., from 20 by 2s, 30 by 3s, 70 by 7s, and associated times-tables.
- Phonological-awareness impacts on similar sounding words, e.g., often confusing teen/ty numbers such as 13/30, 19/90, which in turn leads to difficulties building a strong number sense of numbers 1 to 100, and numeracy difficulties.

Included within their weak language skills, they also have the phonological-verbal information-processing weakness of Language Disorder, impacting both communication and literacy development:

- Weak phonological-verbal short-term and/or working memory using tests of digit span, e.g., TILLS *Digit Span Forward* and *Digit Span Backwards* subtests.
- Functional weakness coping with high cognitive load, which is exacerbated by tasks with high cognitive load, including coping with larger amounts of information, e.g., in the TILLS *Following Directions* subtest.
- Phonological-awareness weakness, including lack of automaticity for syllable and rhyming skills, and well delayed phonemic-awareness development.
- (Often) Rapid Automised Naming (RAN) weakness.
- Automising weakness, with difficulty initially mastering new phonological-verbal concepts, and building them to an automatic level.
- Weaker statistical learning.
- Weaker executive-function skills.
- Strengths in functional visual-spatial areas which stand in strong contrast to children's weak phonological-verbal skills, e.g., high skills in creativity, imagination, caring for animals, science, dance, drama, construction, machinery, art, sports athletics, and maths reasoning (but often not maths facts).

The children also frequently have mild articulation weakness:

- Errors on later developing sounds, usually TH, e.g., *wif/ with, firty/thirty*, and sometimes R, e.g., *wed twuck bwoke*.

- Errors on occasional longer multisyllabic words, e.g., kitar/guitar, jewry/jewelry, micaphone/microphone.

It's interesting that, in scrutinising studies showing Dyslexia and Language Disorder being separate disorders, one often finds the areas of language-skills weakness listed above haven't been tested. Instead, strength factors have been used as language measures:
- Narrative retell.
- Receptive vocabulary, or expressive vocabulary combined with receptive vocabulary to form a single vocabulary score.
- Working memory tested just by nonword repetition, rather than also by other tests, e.g., digit-span forward and reversed, and sentence span tasks.

Use of strength rather than weakness factors can unfortunately reduce the power of studies' findings, with value in considering which language skills are tested. As an example, Gutiérrez et al.'s (2023) findings of USA Grade 1 predictors of Grade 4 weak reading are empowered through both Grade 1 language tests being tests of weakness factors: one an expressive vocabulary test, and one a test of listening comprehension that involves cognitive load.

While weak language skills usually produce weak literacy skills, the reverse is also true – weak literacy skills produce weak language skills. Weak literacy skills delay subsequent development of literacy-enriched language skills in significant ways, e.g., beginners starting school with adequate narrative skills, who have the above areas of weakness, are usually well below average for the content of narratives they write by later primary school.

For these and many other reasons, there are strong arguments for positioning our children's word-reading and literacy struggles within language and communication weakness. Further, there are strong arguments for speech language pathologists playing a key role in school intervention for these children.

Here's how I often describe the difficulties of children I work with, who usually show the weakness patterns listed above in addition to having major word-reading, spelling and literacy difficulties:

As evidenced in her results today, Jessie has Developmental Language Disorder along with severe Dyslexia as part of having Developmental Language Disorder and its associated information processing difficulties.
Her Dyslexia (literacy difficulties), in addition to reading and spelling difficulties also includes Dysgraphia (writing difficulties) and Dyscalculia (difficulties with number and

counting skills).

Dyslexia and Developmental Language Disorder occur together so frequently that researchers have investigated whether the two are one disorder or two separate disorders, often considering them to be separate but hugely overlapping disorders. Dyslexia develops due to the phonological-verbal information processing difficulties which are part of Developmental Language Disorder. I have marked with # below the areas of weakness that fit what I consider a classic profile of Dyslexia occurring as part of and alongside Developmental Language Disorder.

A sample assessment report showing these marked (#) areas of weakness is available on ResearchGate (Galletly, 2023d).

Research into the future, using tests of relevant expressive-language and cognitive-processing language skills, such as those I've listed above, is likely to increasingly establish most children with dyslexia having significant language weakness.

Language Weakness and Reading

Language skills and literacy skills are intricately interrelated. Not least, that's evidenced in many neuro-psychological factors similarly impacting language and literacy skills (Knight & Galletly, 2020).

It's also evidenced in infant language weakness, in the form of infant and early childhood speech perception weakness, underlying both word-reading and language comprehension aspects of reading. Infant speech perception predicts children's strength of language skills as pre-schoolers and also their strength of later word-reading, and literacy skills. Weak speech perception is also found present in many parents of at-risk children (Espy et al, 2004; Lyytinen, 2014; Lyytinen, Aro et al., 2006; Lyytinen, Erskine et al., 2006; Molfese et al., 2001; Richardson et al., 2003).

Studies of school children show speech perception continues to mature in children aged 7 to 10 years, and relates strongly to their language-skills development (Kwok et al., 2018).

Studies also show multiple aspects of early-childhood language skills underlie both language comprehension aspects and word-reading aspects of reading difficulties (Peng et al., 2022). This is seen in Hulme et al.'s (2015) longitudinal study of Anglophone children, that found early oral language skills predicted phoneme awareness and grapheme-phoneme knowledge just before school entry, with these in turn predicting their word-reading skills at school.

Hulme et al.'s (2015) findings validated Hoover and Gough's (1990) Simple View model (*Reading Comprehension = Word-Reading x Language Skills for Literacy*). They found that both children's language skills at 3.5 years and their word-reading skills at 5.5 years predicted reading comprehension at 8.5 years, with these patterns similar for children at familial risk of Dyslexia, those with pre-school language difficulties, and typically developing children.

Other studies show early-childhood language skills and vocabulary have particularly strong impacts on Anglophone children's reading and literacy development (Biemiller, 2003; D'Apice & von Stumm, 2020; Hart & Risley, 2003; Sparapani et al., 2018), and weaker impacts for regular-orthography children (Protopapas, Mouzaki et al., 2013; Suggate et al., 2014).

Literate Cultural Capital (Prochnow et al., 2013; Tunmer et al., 2006), is the reading-related experience and skills children have at start of school, built in home and pre-school activities supporting early-literacy development. Sometimes referred to as children's *backpack* of early-literacy experiences, it includes experience with books, listening to stories, and related discussions with adults.

Language skills are a huge part of Literate Cultural Capital: the two go together and grow together, expedited by Socio-Economic Status. Our numbers of young children with Language Disorder are tellingly not so different from our numbers of teenage and adult weak readers. Language and literacy development go together and grow together, before and across literacy development (D'Apice & von Stumm, 2020; Isoaho et al., 2016; Lohvansuu et al., 2021; Lyytinen, 2014; R. O'Connor et al., 2010; Snowling et al., 2016, 2019; Spanoudos et al., 2019).

Vocabulary development research by Hart and Risley (2003) showed this clearly. They found a gap of 30-million words by age 4 years:
In a year, children in professional families heard an average of 11 million words, while children in working class families heard an average of 6 million words and children in welfare families heard an average of 3 million words.
By age four, a child from a welfare-recipient family could have heard 32 million words fewer than a classmate from a professional family.

They also found that children's vocabulary levels as 3-year-olds predicted their vocabulary levels at age 5 and 8 years.

At the present time, the linkage of SES, low Literate Cultural Capital, weak language skills and low literacy and academic achievement is immensely strong, and very difficult to overcome. Using current resourcing and funding, it's impossible for our schools and teachers to uncouple this linkage. That's particularly the case, when we start Standard-English word-reading instruction at such a young age, with English orthographic complexity then activating our children's many risk factors for Standard-English reading and writing development.

We most certainly can remove that linkage of low SES to school struggles: regular-orthography nations have, and so can we.

We could do that by working with each child and family, which would be an immensely expensive exercise. Alternatively, and an option offering long-term savings, we could use 10 Changes improvements, and reform early reading instruction to include extensive, early language and literacy enrichment and a fully-regular beginners' orthography.

The vocabulary research also fits with Australian research showing children's intelligence dwindles across the early childhood years, for children experiencing poverty (Najman et al., 2004, 2009). Najman and colleagues (2009) followed approximately 7000 Australian children from birth to age 14 years, finding longer duration and repeated episodes of poverty to be significantly associated with lower results on cognitive tests. Ouch!

Further, studies in other Anglophone nations show that, to be really effective, language enrichment for highly at-risk children needs to start when children are born, and to be highly intensive, involving, e.g., weekly one-to-one intervention sessions playing with and developing children's communication, creativity, imagination and thinking skills, plus building strong parenting skills. This works very well, with dividends of strong child and adult success that breaks the cycle of Generational Disadvantage (Campbell et al., 2012, 2014; Duffy, 2020; Heckman, 2020a, 2020b). While expensive, this intensive intervention actually results in savings, because of reduced expenses in areas such as the costs of prison, unemployment, and mental-health services.

Importantly, it's not just vocabulary differences that would have been present in Hart and Risley's (1995) 3-year-olds. Vocabulary weakness is usually accompanied by other weak language skills, e.g., difficulty understanding longer sentences and instructions that include unfamiliar terms, and use of immature grammar, phrases and sentences used when speaking. Vocabulary and language weakness is consequently a major risk factor for reading and literacy struggles.

Clearly, speech language pathology intervention in early childhood is important for our children with language weakness. This creates value in monitoring children's language development across early childhood and the school years.

We also need Australian cognitive-processing research exploring
- The role of early childhood speech perception, vocabulary and language skills as predictors of reading and school difficulties.
- Development across childhood, infancy to adulthood, of speech perception, language, executive-function, and literacy skills.
- The relationships of infant and early-childhood language skills with later word-reading and literacy development.
- Early childhood interventions reducing risk of school difficulties.
- Prevalence and impacts of language weakness at school entry.

They Go Together and Grow Together

Communication skills and literacy development go hand-in-hand.

As an example, Hayiou-Thomas et al. (2017), followed children with speech sound disorder at age 3.5 years, assessing their literacy skills at ages 5.5 and 8.0 years. They found early speech difficulties conferred a small but significant risk of poor phonemic-awareness and spelling skills at age 5.5, and poor word-reading at 8.0 years.

Co-occurring language weakness and speech sound disorder predicted weak literacy skills at both time points, as did having a family risk of Dyslexia. Hayiou-Thomas et al. (2017) conclude that early speech sound disorder has only modest impacts on literacy development, but stronger impacts when extra risk factors are present.

Disordered speech difficulties were more strongly associated with word-reading difficulties than delayed speech difficulties. They found persistence of speech difficulties to be significant – children whose speech difficulties were still present at start of school had poorer literacy skills. My experience is that difficulties with the TH sound, and sometimes also the R sound, and continued difficulties with multisyllabic words are very common speech difficulties in children with word-reading difficulties.

In a somewhat similar vein, Lewis et al.'s (2000) longitudinal study comparing children with speech difficulties with children who additionally had language difficulties, found the speech-language group had much weaker speech, word-reading and literacy skills at follow-up (age 8 to 10 years), 11 times more word-reading difficulties, lower SES and more prevalent family histories of communication and learning weakness than the speech-only group.

Harrison et al. (2009), using LSAC and survey data, similarly found combined speech-language weakness an important predictor of school literacy difficulties, finding that parent reports of speech-language impairment in early childhood are useful for identifying children at risk of literacy difficulties, to provide early intervention by speech language pathologists and specialist teachers.

Language weakness, far more than speech weakness, begets literacy weakness, and language and literacy skills do indeed go together and grow together in many ways. That said, it's very common to find very mild speech weakness in children with literacy difficulties: errors on occasional multisyllabic words, TH words, and sometimes R words, e.g., *kitar/guitar, wif/with, gwab/grab*.

The language skills children start school with predict their later reading comprehension and written expression levels. Children with language weakness often continue to struggle with language weakness across the school years, and longitudinal studies show reading comprehension and written difficulties accompany each other in children who start school with weak language skills (Hogan et al., 2014; Knight et al., 2021; Nation et al., 2006b, 2010).

While many assume children develop weak reading comprehension and written expression due to instructional factors, e.g., poor teaching, it's more often the case that they start school with weak language comprehension that causes them to develop language-based reading comprehension and written expression difficulties quite early, and then continue on with both weak language skills and weak reading comprehension skills.

That's a good reason for schools to assess language skills on school entry, to establish underlying levels of language skills. So often, struggling readers I assess show parallel patterns of weakness:
- Weak content of spoken explanations highly similar to weak content of their written expression.
- Weak listening comprehension highly similar to their weak reading comprehension.

For our struggling readers, the telling linkage of early language-skills weakness to later weak literacy skills is unfortunate in many ways. Early-childhood vocabulary and language weakness reduces odds of successful word-reading and early-literacy development, and that in turn impedes development of the independent reading skills children need to develop later vocabulary and language skills.

While there is little crosslinguistic comparative research on language skills development, language weakness seems impacted quite profoundly by orthographic disadvantage (Galletly & Knight, 2011a). That's because ease and speed of Standard-English vs regular-orthography independent reading and writing creates major differences in the extent to which children with pre-existing language weakness, when starting school, will experience ongoing language and literacy weakness.

As proposed in our model of differential disadvantage, (Galletly & Knight, 2011a), all Standard-English weak readers are severely disadvantaged relative to regular-orthography weak readers. That's due to cognitive-processing weakness and the high cognitive load of learning to read and write, and working on tasks that use reading and writing. It's also due to their weak literacy skills impeding subsequent language development.

Regular-orthography children and adults with the language-skills weakness of dyslexia also have expressive language difficulties, and weakness for text structure and clarity in discussion of ideas when writing (e.g., Tops et al., 2013). That said, they've much lower cognitive load in literacy tasks than we have, due to being highly accurate readers, and most words being very easy to spell. We'd learn much, on the impacts of orthography, cognitive load, and language weakness, and their interactions, through crosslinguistic research studying written expression, e.g., of primary-school, high-school and university students completing the same writing task.

Our children with pre-existing weakness in language and cognitive-processing skills, experience heightened disadvantage with early language weakness blocking literacy development, then impeded language development continuing across the school years.

Because most regular-orthography children with language weakness will develop effective literacy skills, they've excellent potential for overcoming earlier language weakness through the reading and writing they do, that then builds language skills.

In contrast, our Anglophone children with language weakness have high likelihood of failing to develop effective literacy skills (Galletly & Knight, 2011a; Peng et al., 2022).

Indeed, many struggling readers experience a *Triple Whammy* disadvantage (Knight et al., 2017a, 2019, 2021):

1. They start school with weak language skills, often via generational disadvantage – being children of parents with weak literacy skills who then have difficulty building their children's early language and pre-literacy skills.
2. Their weak phonological-awareness and language skills result in word-reading, spelling, and literacy difficulties.
3. Their low literacy skills then block later language development.

Adding insult to injury, communication difficulties and behaviour difficulties also go together and grow together (Chow et al., 2018; Conti-Ramsden et al., 2018; Horbach et al., 2020; Law et al., 2015, 2017). When not provided with appropriate supports, all too often, communication difficulties become behaviour difficulties.

There's likelihood that high levels of undiagnosed language weakness play a considerable part in our unruly classrooms, our children who don't finish high school, our adults with long-term unemployment, our justice system and prison populations – and Australia ranking eighth worst in the world for having unruly classrooms (OECD, 2019).

Our children who start school with weak language skills consequently end up victims of our severe orthographic disadvantage and our Early Years Factory.

We need crosslinguistic research comparing literacy and language-skills development of Anglophone and regular-orthography children who start school with language weakness.

Language, Literacy & Learning Disorder (LLLD)

What's in a name? Lots, actually (Wehmeyer, 2013), particularly if we want to emphasise the commonalities and overlaps of language disorders, reading and literacy disorders and learning disorders.

Serry and Hammond's (2015) survey of Australian allied-health professionals and educators, found that while the term, *dyslexia*, is used increasingly by Australians, as regards formal terms, many professionals prefer alternative terms, and prioritise reference to *reading, language, processing* and *learning*.

Further, there was strong preference for the term *difficulties* rather than *disorder* or *disability*, and for funding to be allocated for supports. In contrast, there was little preference for requirements for formal diagnoses. As a clinician, those are my preferences too.

They include one response that perhaps reflects the views of many:
Funding is totally necessary. I call dyslexia the hidden

> disability. ... Children should be funded in terms of their functional impairment, not on a diagnosis.

But what terms should we use. Dyslexia is a useful informal term, but can be confusing, given there are so many differing views on what it entails.

The problem is that all too often the terms we use push us in associated directions, some of which aren't optimal.

Should we be emphasising literacy and learning difficulties? Yes, we should. After all, building literacy skills is often schools' major emphasis for struggling readers and learners?

Should we be emphasising language disorder? Yes, we should, as those literacy and learning difficulties almost always sit within language disorder and underlying communication difficulties including information-processing weakness present from infancy.

Terms also tend to push us in specific intervention directions. If the term emphasises language disorder, intervention is often provided more by speech language pathologists, many of whom don't work closely with children's teachers and learning-support staff at school. Similarly, if the name emphasises learning disorder, often the child's language skills difficulties are overlooked.

That can be the case even when definitions include definite emphasis on language, e.g., the definition of *Specific Learning Disability* used in the USA's *Individuals with Disabilities Education Improvement Act* (IDEA, US Govt, 2004a). It's considered a disability of reading, not language, despite its definition emphasising language weakness:

> *A disorder in one or more of the basic psychological processes involved in understanding or in using language, spoken or written, which disorder may manifest itself in the imperfect ability to listen, think, speak, read, write, spell or do mathematical calculations.*

We also need to consider words such as *Difficulties, Disability, Disorder, Impairment, Delay, Developmental* for terms we'd use.

The terms *developmental* and *delay* can be unfortunate, and sometimes confusing, building assumptions that the difficulties must be temporary, and that children will outgrow them later.

Disorder seems the best term currently, as it can incorporate the permanent nature of language, literacy and learning difficulties. It's also the term now used by the *World Health Organisation* (WHO, 2007), its *International Classification of Functioning, Disability and Health* (ICF, Ma et al., 2008; Westby & Washington,

2017; WHO, 2007), and the DSM-5 (*Diagnostic and Statistical Manual of Mental Disorders*, Fifth edition; APA, 2013), which are used internationally by governments and education professionals.

We'd benefit from carefully choosing terms we use, and by including the words *Language, Literacy, Learning* and *Disorder*.

Nations such as France and Finland strongly emphasise the language basis of literacy and learning difficulties (e.g., Dion et al., 2010; Hubert-Dibon et al., 2016; Lyytinen et al., 2021). This dual emphasis expedites neatly coordinated intervention services. As an example, France has regional *Learning Disabilities Reference Centers*, with intervention provided by multidisciplinary teams that include specialised teachers, a paediatric neurologist, neuropsychologist, speech language pathologist and psycho-motor therapist.

I suggest the term *Language, Literacy and Learning Disorder* (LLLD) may prove useful for Australia and the Anglosphere, because of its emphasis on the three key aspects of weakness in struggling readers.

Some nations use the term *Dyslexia* (New Zealand Govt, 2008; Rose, 2009; Serry & Hammond, 2015), e.g., New Zealand has its excellent *4D for Dyslexia* program and Dyslexia handbook, and the term Dyslexia may work well there (Dyslexia Foundation of New Zealand, 2008; New Zealand Government, 2008; Nicholson & Dymock, 2015; Tunmer & Greaney, 2010).

I often use the term Dyslexia with children, families and schools, for its reassuring connotations of healthy ability, i.e., that, just like Richard Branson, this is a bright child with major reading difficulties.

However, all too often, people don't associate dyslexia with language weakness: indeed, it's commonly thought that to be dyslexic is to have excellent language skills, with weakness predominantly in visual areas, e.g., often reading letters in reverse order. Dyslexia thus seems a less useful overarching term for Australian education. Importantly, the term Language, Literacy and Learning Disorder (LLLD) doesn't preclude additional use of other terms, including Developmental Language Disorder (DLD) and Dyslexia.

Let's Build Awareness of Language Disorder

Failure to associate language weakness with literacy and learning difficulties is not surprising, really.

That's because, internationally, both the general public and educators lack awareness of language weakness as a specific entity.

Thordardottir et al. (2021), in a European COST research project, surveyed 1500 people across 18 European nations. They found far lower awareness of language disorder than of other childhood disabilities including autism, Dyslexia, AD/HD and speech disorder, and definite needs for increasing international awareness of language disorder.

Given such low awareness, many nations are strategically implementing public awareness campaigns to develop far more widespread awareness of language disorder, including likelihood that at least two children in every class have Language Disorder, plus awareness of Language Disorder's impacts and needs for intervention (Bishop et al. 2016, 2017; Bowen, 2018). Indeed, the world now even has *International Developmental Language Disorder Day*, each October (www.thedldproject.com).

School Usefulness of the Term *Developmental Language Disorder*

The term Developmental Language Disorder (DLD) is currently promoted as the international term for children with significantly weak language skills (Bishop et al., 2016, 2017; Bowen, 2018, SPA, 2018). For schools and school-aged children, however, I suggest it's likely the term Language, Literacy and Learning Disorder (LLLD) would prove more useful.

Bishop et al. (2017) list 12 key statements about DLD that in effect are part of its definition. While DLD's a useful term for speech language pathologists and families, it's not sufficiently practical to be education's overarching term for children with language-skill weakness, and associated weakness in literacy and learning.

While the term DLD has strengths, and avoids the disadvantages of many alternative terms (e.g., Reilly et al., 2014), for school children with language weakness, it also has disadvantages.

One, the DLD category only includes quite minimal emphasis on literacy difficulties. DLD includes literacy and learning difficulties, but doesn't overly emphasise them, certainly not to the extent our schools need, if we're to consider language, literacy and learning difficulties collectively.

Two, DLD is unfortunately somewhat exclusive, as children with additional disorders aren't diagnosed with DLD but instead *Language Disorder associated with (Name of Disorder)*. DLD is thus separate to language disorder associated with other conditions, including autism, cerebral palsy, and hearing loss.

This dichotomy seems unfortunate in key ways. It means DLD isn't available as a single broadly-encompassing category. It also makes DLD somewhat exclusive, e.g., why shouldn't a child with Autism also have DLD, particularly given that he may well have had a DLD diagnosis for many years prior to being diagnosed with autism? As regards needs for intervention, the dichotomy seems unnecessary and somewhat akin to that of cognitive referencing, as intervention needs of children with DLD and children with *Language Disorder associated with X* are overwhelmingly more alike than different.

Given that schools benefit from collectively considering all children in need of support for weak language skills, an inclusive term such as Language, Literacy and Learning Disorder seems preferable as the overarching category for school use, with DLD and *Language Disorder associated with X* then being subgroups.

Three, including the word *Developmental*, with its implications of childhood-only, seems curious, given DLD is a lifelong condition, with our teenagers and adults also having DLD. *Developmental* doesn't sufficiently add power to DLD's definition to warrant its inclusion, and isn't used for other similarly lifelong conditions, e.g., autism and AH/HD, which seem easily as developmental as DLD.

Four, while the term DLD, with its definition and 12 factors, is presented as a multi-national model, input from experts from non-Anglophone nations, including regular-orthography nations, was decidedly minimal. While using impressive cycles of discussion that built consensus on the term DLD, the international team members were from Anglophone nations, and discussion on DLD's definition and factors seemed focused on the Anglosphere.

Anglocentrism as regards literacy and language skills development is extremely disappointing (e.g., Daniels & Share, 2018; Share, 2008). In this instance, it seems to reduce the rigour of the Developmental Language Disorder category for children with language weakness in the school years.

Had language disorder experts from regular-orthography nations been involved, DLD and its 12 factors might well be somewhat different, as language, literacy and learning are so often considered together in regular-orthography nations (e.g., Hubert-Dibon et al., 2016; Lyytinen et al., 2021).

Literacy difficulties and school learning might be emphasised more effectively, children with other disorders might well have been included, and a stronger whole-of-life perspective taken in place of

DLD's developmental emphasis.

Further, we'd be confident that decision-making had included thorough consideration of crosslinguistic differences in language disorder in Anglophone vs regular-orthography school children.

There seems value in continuing the building of the Developmental Language Disorder category, by
- Consulting language-weakness experts of regular-orthography nations: nations using sole orthographies, e.g., Finland and Iceland, and nations with the higher cognitive load of learning a complex orthography, Taiwan, Japan and China.
- Exploring crosslinguistic differences in language disorder in primary-school, high-school and university students.

In practical terms, schools need an inclusive term for all children with language, literacy and learning weakness and support needs, and Developmental Language Disorder is not sufficiently inclusive.

Let's End Cognitive Referencing

One of Developmental Language Disorder's definition statements usefully and directly addresses cognitive referencing (Bishop et al., 2017): the antiquated requirement that, to be eligible for school funding in the communication-disorder category, intelligence test results must show a distinct gap between higher *performance* skills and lower *language* skills.

Ethically, cognitive referencing is a seriously inappropriate criteria for Education Departments to be using, having long been discredited by ample research. Its use discriminates against many with major language weakness (Galletly et al., 2010; Washington, 2007).

Statement 8 on Developmental Language Disorder and its discussion is usefully clear and definite (Bishop et al., 2017):
A child with a language disorder may have a low level of non-verbal ability. This does not preclude a diagnosis of DLD. ... This statement confirms that a large discrepancy between non-verbal and verbal ability is not required for a diagnosis of DLD.

In decades past, both learning disability and language disorder used cognitive referencing. Then, over time, both researchers and practitioners realised that in many ways it was both inappropriate and discriminatory. Interestingly, whilst USA legal battles ensured cognitive referencing was removed there, Australian Education Departments have quietly continued its use for language disorder.

Doing so, they've saved impressively on funds not delivered to schools for supporting severely struggling children, while exacerbating the woes of the children and their schools (Galletly et al., 2010):

> Psychometric tests are useful as contributors to multiple lens views of assessment, however their use as a prioritised [eligibility criteria] is established as being highly inappropriate. ... Considerable research has focused on building knowledge showing the inappropriateness of basing educational decision-making on cognitive referencing (Aaron, 1997; Catts et al., 2006; Catts et al., 2002; Siegel, 2003.) ...
>
> Inappropriate circular reasoning seems present: IQ scores dictate allocated diagnoses (Specific Language Impairment vs Non-specific Language Impairment; Learning Disability vs Intellectual Impairment) yet many children in the discrepancy groups are differentiated more by their IQ-discrepancy than by their functional literacy and language levels, instructional needs, and response to intervention.
>
> Researchers cognizant of the area inevitably conclude that discrepancy-defined and nondiscrepancy-defined groups of poor achievers are more alike than different. (Aaron, 1997; Catts et al., 2006; Catts et al., 2002; Fletcher et al., 2005; Francis et al., 2005; Siegel, 2003; Swanson, Hoskyn, & Lee, 1999).

Key assumptions underlying cognitive referencing that are now established as flawed include the following (Galletly et al., 2010):

- That intelligence test results are needed for deciding children's diagnoses and intervention needs.
- That children with major difficulties will clearly show needed intelligence test profiles, rather than results often being variable.
- That language and literacy weaknesses have different aetiologies in children with different intelligence test profiles, and that these groups of children require decidedly different kinds of remedial treatment.
- That children's intelligence test profiles more effectively suggest children's responsiveness to intervention and optimal educational intervention options than does information provided by schools and teachers on children's responsiveness to different forms of instruction and intervention.

Australia needs to move away quickly and decisively from cognitive referencing, and its damaging impacts on our children and schools.

Receptive Vs Expressive Weakness? Perhaps Not!

For decades, speech language pathologists and teachers have discussed and emphasised two categories of language skills, receptive language skills (input skills) and expressive language skills (output skills).

That said, these two categories are largely a useful convention for thinking about language skills, rather than actual reality (Nelson, 2016; Tomblin & Zhang, 2006).

The two categories are also used by education systems for allocating disability labels and school funding. Often, children must show a particular level of severity for either an expressive-language deficit, a receptive-language deficit, or a deficit in both areas. Only then will they receive a disability label, with their school then receiving additional intervention funding.

This can be discriminatory in major ways, because many children don't show these neat profiles of major weakness in receptive and/or expressive language. In testing, subskill scores are added together and averaged, and this means children's areas of relative strength can be mixed in with their areas of major weakness, with their averaged results then not low enough to meet the restrictive cut-offs our governments use.

That's particularly the case when the tests used are of fundamental language skills, e.g., those used in the *Clinical Evaluation of Language Fundamentals-5* (CELF-5, Wiig et al., 2013), rather than also testing functional language skills children use at school in communication and learning, e.g., those tested in the *Test of Integrated Language and Literacy Skills* (TILLS; Mailend et al., 2016; Nelson et al., 2016; Nelson, 2016).

Tomblin and Zhang (2006) usefully explored this area, investigating whether children's results on language tests reflect expressive vs receptive language categories. They assessed two large samples of children on receptive and expressive vocabulary, and receptive and expressive sentence use; and followed 600 USA Kindergarten children longitudinally, testing their language skills in Kindergarten and Grades 2, 4 and 8.

Importantly, they found language skills considered as a single factor represented the children's results much more effectively than did using two factors of receptive and expressive language skills. Language disorder as a collective category is certainly my clinical experience with children with language and literacy weakness.

They considered that while there was a developmental trend for grammatical abilities and vocabulary abilities to be two separate factors, the children's results did not show significant differences reflecting receptive vs expressive language skills.

Tomblin and Zhang are not alone in language skills being considered not as separate receptive and expressive language skills. The Literacy Component Model emphasises a single category of *Language Skills for Literacy* (Knight et al., 2021). Further, many clinicians don't find the dichotomy of receptive and expressive language skills helpful, either for children being assessed for eligibility for funded support at school, or for intervention purposes.

Towards not discriminating against our children with disabilities, while further research is needed, there seem arguments for Australian education departments moving away from emphasising receptive and expressive subcategories as criteria for diagnoses, severity levels, and eligibility for supports, and no longer rejecting applications due to children not having sufficiently low scores in receptive vs expressive skill categories.

We need to consider children's difficulties by focusing on their individual profiles of strengths and weaknesses in language, literacy and learning skills. In practical terms, the receptive vs expressive dichotomy isn't helpful, whereas a single category of language skills, in which children have strengths and weaknesses, is more useful (Knight et al., 2021; Nelson et al., 2016).

Nelson and colleagues emphasise needs to move away from receptive vs expressive language categories if we are to more fully understand the strengths, weaknesses and instructional needs of school children with language, literacy and learning weakness (Mailend et al., 2016; Nelson, 2016).

In developing the Test of Integrated Language and Literacy Skills (TILLS; Mailend et al., 2016; Nelson et al., 2016), the two dimensions of language subskills they used were
- Phonological skills (Sound/Word ability) and
- Nonphonological (Sentence/Discourse ability) skills.

The TILLS' 15 subtests focus on communication as listening, reasoning, cognitive-processing, speaking and writing skills. They provide a useful profile of functional as well as key fundamental language skills. Not surprisingy, TILLS is being used increasingly by speech language pathologists across Australia.

As Nelson (2016) usefully comments,
> *Reading disorders are language disorders and not separate or parallel. ... disorders affecting oral language and literacy development, although heterogeneous, depend on a common foundation of cognitive-linguistic abilities and overlap sufficiently that they should be assessed together and treated as*

integrated, intertwined abilities. ...
Widespread agreement is unlikely to converge on checklists of behaviours for diagnosing language disorders during the school-age years, because not all children demonstrate all symptoms, and many children demonstrate some symptoms at some ages and not others. In fact, research has shown that growth trajectories can shift to such an extent that the same children may appear to demonstrate typical development at one age and atypical development at another. ...
Failure to acknowledge overlap between language disorders and learning disabilities ... leads to an artificial sense of distinction between them. This is not in the best interest of children and adolescents with language/literacy disorders.
It is possible, in fact, that students with language impairments and learning disabilities are the same children and adolescents, but with different labels depending on when they are identified and by whom ... Problems affecting language and literacy learning lack a recognisable, agreed-upon label and a clear identity.
[We] suggest a model of assessment of language and literacy abilities that can form the basis for heightened awareness and less artificial separation of language/literacy disorders. This newer model suggests that language be assessed and described across modalities at sound/word and sentence/discourse levels, replacing older models that attempt to assess and explain disorders as receptive and expressive difficulties, which are not supported by scientific evidence.

The TILLS is a useful test battery for school use in allied-health and learning-support assessments, particularly if the TILLS authors substituted Australian words and items for the few which aren't familiar to Australian children.

How Intensive Should Intervention Be?

We need research exploring optimal patterns of intervention for Australian children with language, literacy and learning weakness.

It's interesting that other Anglophone nations view their school speech language pathology services as meagre, despite them being vastly more extensive than ours. If their services are meagre, ours are appallingly low.

High needs for services for school children with language weakness is likely due to Standard-English readers with language weakness rarely being *cured*, instead continuing to have intervention needs, in keeping with language disorder being an ongoing disability

(Conti-Ramsden et al., 2012; Ebbels et al., 2019; Knight et al., 2017a; Norbury et al., 2019; Reilly et al., 2014; Stothard et al., 1998).

Our children's needs are high. It may well be that factors such as starting children too young on a highly complex orthography induces significant Acquired Helplessness, cognitive-processing and executive-function challenges, resulting in ongoing language difficulties as well as literacy difficulties.

It does seem likely that Language, Literacy and Learning Disorder (LLLD), will be ongoing and expensive while we continue with just Standard English at age 4.5 to 5 years.

But what level of intervention is optimal? Ebbels et al. (2019) reviewed the research on intervention for children with language disorder, finding a modified Response to Intervention (RTI) model to be most effective. The conventional RTI model uses three tiers:

- *Tier 1. Core Instruction*: differentiated instruction for all children, usually being classroom instruction.
- *Tier 2. Skills Building Intervention*: focused intervention, usually in small groups.
- *Tier 3. Intensive Remediation*: intensive, highly-tailored intervention, usually conducted one-to-one.

Ebbels et al.'s (2019) modified form of RTI strategically separates Tier 3, individualised intervention, into two forms:

- *Tier 3A, Indirect Individualised Intervention*, led by a speech language pathologist, but with practice between sessions conducted by trained aides or trained family members.
- *Tier 3B, Direct Individualised Intervention*, with speech language pathologists working one-on-one with children with more severe needs.

Interestingly, that division, of indirect intervention and skilled practice support vs direct intervention, is equally useful for literacy intervention by specialist support teachers and trained aides.

RTI is a useful, practical model for both school learning support and allied-health intervention, particularly when schools are resourced well and able to provide needed services.

For language disorder with speech language pathology input in schools, Tier 1 prevention is high-quality teaching and interactions for all children supported by professional development that speech language pathologists provide. Studies show this professional development needs to be intensive, e.g., 50-60 hours, and preferably include follow-up sessions and ongoing coaching.

Tier 2 intervention is small-group intervention led by teachers, speech language pathologists or well-supported, trained aides.

Importantly, in Anglophone nations, quite often Tier 2 intervention has relatively limited effects (e.g., Ebbels et al., 2019; Lonigan & Phillips, 2016), with suggestions made that, to be effective, instruction needs to be highly intensive and focused on specific areas of need, with very small groups, with highly similar needs.

As an example, Lonigan and Phillips (2016) conducted two studies of Tier 2, teacher-led, small-group intervention in USA government funded pre-Kindergarten programs, with at-risk children who had received high-quality Tier 1 instruction. They compared control groups receiving just Tier 1 instruction, with experimental groups, who also received 11 weeks of Tier 2 small-group intervention.

In Study 1, of 93 children attending 12 government Preschools, Tier 2 instruction was provided to groups of 2 to 6 children for 44 sessions (80 mins per week for 11 weeks). Intervention activities built phonological-awareness, word-reading and language skills.

Limited effects were found for the Study 1 cohort – following intervention, the Tier 2 group did not achieve overly higher than the Tier 1 control group. As we'll see in Tour 14, this low effectiveness of relatively light intervention, while common in Anglophone nations, is not the case in regular-orthography nation intervention for at-risk readers (Chen et al., 2015; Chen & Tzeng, 2019; Chien, 2010; Cossu et al., 1993; Olofsson, 1993; Olofsson & Niedersoe, 1999; Poskiparta et al., 1999; Schneider et al., 1999).

Lonigan et al.'s Study 2, of 184 children attending 19 Preschools, provided more intensive Tier 2 instruction and used smaller groups and instructional activities that were more narrowly focused:
- The curriculum used emphasised scaffolding activities, so they met individual children's particular instructional needs.
- Groups had a maximum of 4 children.
- Intervention focused on children's specific needs, and omitted activities not focused on their areas of need.
- Numbers of sessions were tailored: 60 to 160 minutes weekly.

Importantly, the tailored, more intensive instruction of Study 2 showed significant, moderate-to-large effects.

Neither study followed children longitudinally post-intervention, so we don't know the extent to which the stronger skills were retained, i.e., their extent of Level 1 automisation.

As regards Tier 3 intervention, there's stronger evidence for the effectiveness of one-to-one direct intervention than indirect intervention involving trained aides and families, and evidence that home programs work if ample home practice happens and parents receive direct skilful coaching from a speech language pathologist (Ebbels et al., 2019; Tosh et al., 2017).

More studies of this area are needed, e.g., Tosh et al. (2017) found no studies of home program intervention for children aged above 7 years, and found that effective home programs were as expensive as direct one-to-one intervention, perhaps because home programs often used insufficiently effective coaching, and direct one-to-one intervention thus showed a more consistent treatment response.

It's likely the fallout from Australia's long-standing lack of speech language pathology and other allied-health services is many children needing frequent, ongoing one-to-one intervention sessions with allied health professionals. It's equally likely our state and national budgets can't afford that ongoing intensity.

We need research on the effectiveness of intervention models using different combinations of allied-health professional, trained aide, and family home practice.

That's particularly so now that NDIS clients with ample funding have moved allied-health intervention to a *sufficiency model*, and away from our previous decades-long *paucity model*. Alas, the paucity model continues for many who don't have NDIS funding.

Using private speech language pathology and occupational therapy as examples, in decades past, prior to NDIS, most families couldn't afford optimal frequency and duration of private practice sessions.

This resulted in cutting corners: less frequent and shorter sessions, intermittent periods of intervention with long breaks between them, and often ending intervention because children had made appreciable progress, despite them still having ongoing difficulties.

The continuing nature of language, literacy and learning difficulties is strongly evidenced in children with adequate NDIS funding who now receive ongoing intervention to needed levels, to the extent that service availability allows.

There's value in comparing costs and effectiveness of allied-health services for children with and without NDIS funding, and extent of use of Tier 3A (direct) and 3B (indirect) intervention models.

Value in Education Department Oversight of Services

There seems value in investigating the extent to which allied-health intervention would benefit from Australia moving to the model many leading nations use, wherein government education departments oversee allied-health intervention for children from age 1 year to 18 years, for public and private services, both in-school and out-of-school.

Studies will likely show many allied health professionals feel school-aged children with major *Language, Literacy and Learning Disorder* (LLLD) don't need solely Tier 3B: direct individualised intervention, with frequent one-to-one sessions. Instead, at lower cost but continued effectiveness, children might have considerably fewer 3B sessions. They'd instead receive combined 3A and 3B intervention, with many progressing well with effective, less-expensive Tier 3A intervention: indirect intervention led by the allied-health professional, with intensive, strategic practice between sessions with trained family members, aides or support workers.

Unfortunately, currently, particularly in private-practice services, there seem insufficient allied-health aides and support workers to provide that practice guided by allied-health practitioners.

Those studies will also find that, with language weakness and intervention needs all too often ongoing, too much government funds, in this case NDIS funds, are spent on Tier 3B, direct allied-health intervention, where lesser funds would be needed if Australia was effectively organised for Tier 3A, indirect individualised intervention.

As many private allied-health practitioners do, I use both Tier 3A and Tier 3B: indirect and direct intervention, using family coaching and working closely with NDIS support workers who do weekly home practice. This means I seldom see clients weekly, instead usually seeing them fortnightly, or once or twice each term. This continues effective progress, at lower expense. It's also meant I can work with many more children and their families.

Cost-benefit considerations are important, particularly given that we have so many children with Language, Literacy and Learning Disorder (LLLD), and those on NDIS funding seem mostly to be receiving expensive, Tier 3B, one-to-one, allied-health sessions.

There may well be value in Education Departments coordinating both in-school and out-of-school allied-health services for children with communication weakness from age 1 year to adulthood.

With a firm focus on our children's rights to appropriate supports as part of achieving an effective education (McLeod, 2018), and using trained aides and support workers, we'd likely achieve a useful, highly effective balance of in-school and out-of-school services.

Importantly, using 10 Changes improvement, particularly Changes 8 and 9, there's likelihood the allied-health intervention needs of our struggling readers will be considerably reduced.

Language Disorder as Executive-Function Disorder

Multiple studies purport to establish Dyslexia and language disorder as being overlapping but separate difficulties. However, these studies usually haven't included the weak cognitive-processing skills of Language Disorder, which at school become the weak cognitive-processing skills of literacy difficulties.

It lacks logic to exclude cognitive-processing and executive-function skill weakness from communication weakness. Ability to read and write is an add-on skill: while speaking and listening are used universally, not all societies have developed reading and writing.

Struggling readers' information-processing weaknesses are pre-existing, there from infancy, impacting and part of communication weakness (e.g., Lyytinen et al., 2021; Richardson et al., 2003).

While many discuss the notion of expected vs unexpected school difficulties (Catts & Petscher, 2022), in reality, most children's struggles are only unexpected in their families not anticipating difficulties prior to reading instruction starting. If we'd more speech language pathologists working with children prior to school, the difficulties of many children would have been identified far earlier.

I'm not alone in including cognitive processing and phonological-verbal information-processing in Language Disorder (e.g., Hayiou-Thomas et al., 2004; Knight & Galletly, 2020; Tomas & Vissers, 2019). Hayiou-Thomas et al.'s insightful study on the impacts of raising the cognitive load that children experience, which we'll explore in Tour 14, provides useful insights on this area.

Tomas and Vissers, in their 2019 article, *Behind the scenes of Developmental Language Disorder: Time to call neuropsychology back on stage*, make an excellent case for it being multiple deficits in neuropsychological development that underlie and form the basis of language weakness and Language Disorder.

Reviewing the role of perception, executive-function, and attention skills in the statistical learning and communication difficulties of children with language-skills weakness, they consider DLD as a complex neuropsychological syndrome, and recommend that assessment and treatment be developed aligned with this neuropsychological basis:

> *Alternative accounts of DLD have observed the children suffering from this impairment often have additional neuropsychological deficits accompanying language problems. ...*
>
> *It has recently been put forward that DLD is not only closely associated with neuropsychological deficits, but occurs when [multiple] cognitive processes are disrupted. ...*
>
> *This observation is in line with what has long been claimed by the proponents of neuropsychological approach to speech pathology going back to the 1930s (Vygotsky, 1934) and later expanded in the 1950s-1960s (Luria, 1962, 1966).*
>
> *Neuropsychology is concerned with the behavioural expression of brain dysfunction and it thus suggests deep interconnections between the various higher cognitive processes, including, for example, language and executive functions.*
>
> *Within this framework the causes underlying the observed behavioural problems are thus thought to be rooted in multiple neurophysiological deficits.*

In their abstract, Tomas and Vissers emphasise widespread frustrations with current categorisations, and make a clear case for the neuropsychological executive-function basis of language disorder:

> *Although Developmental Language Disorder (DLD), also known as Specific Language Impairment, in children has been the focus of unceasing scientific attention for decades, the nature and mechanisms of this disorder remain unclear.*
>
> *Most importantly, we still cannot reliably identify children requiring urgent intervention among other 'late talkers' at an early age and understand the high prevalence of comorbidity with psychiatric phenomena such as Autism Spectrum Disorder. One of the main reasons for this is the traditional 'diagnosis-by-exclusion,' resulting in heterogeneity of the DLD population.*
>
> *This paper proposes an alternative approach to the diagnosis, treatment and research of DLD, claiming that it is these children's multiple deficits in neuropsychological development, which impede the spontaneous acquisition of their first language.*
>
> *Specifically, this review of the state-of-the-art in DLD research demonstrates deep and systematic interconnections between the speech and other higher cognitive functions developing in early childhood, including perception, attention and executive functions.*

In the proposed framework, [speech and language ability] is, therefore, considered as one of neuropsychological abilities, and the delay in its development is explained by other neuropsychological deficits, resulting in highly individual clinical profiles.

By considering DLD as a complex neuropsychological syndrome, whose successful treatment depends on a holistic approach to diagnosis and intervention, we may significantly increase the efficacy of speech therapy, and also better understand the flexibility of the developing brain, its compensatory mechanisms and hence the comorbidity of DLD with psychiatric symptoms. Implications for using this paradigm in future scientific research are discussed.

There really are strong arguments for Dyslexia, with its word-reading and language difficulties, being part of language disorder, given the phonological-verbal information-processing difficulties inherent to language disorder. And the term Language, Literacy and Learning Disorder (LLLD), incorporating all these aspects, seems a useful term for Australian education.

Improvement: Hugely Expensive Vs Far Less So

How shall we best overcome generational disadvantage, with too many Australian children having major language weakness, and associated literacy, learning and life difficulties?

We have two role models for those directions.

While both have their substantial research base, they're very different, and to a certain extent epitomise the wide crosslinguistic and achievement divide between regular-orthography and Anglophone nations.

They also epitomise our needs for 10 Changes improvement, and the value of our ABCs:

A. ACT locally while looking globally.
B. BOOST the lower-third to benefit everyone.
C. CHANGE effectively to work less and achieve more.

Let's term them the *Effective Education Road* and *Pre-School Child Road*, respectively.

The Effective Education Road

On the one hand, we could take the Effective Education Road.

It's a regular-orthography nation model – the one used by Taiwan,

Japan, China and Korea. It emphasises changing education so the risk factors children start school with aren't activated, and effective early-literacy and independent learning develop quickly and easily, irrespective of disadvantage children might have at start of school.

Taking the Effective Education Road, we would use Change 8, a beginners' orthography, and focus on education and early-literacy development here in Australia being highly efficient and effective, to the extent that children who've started school with major risk factors still easily master word-reading, spelling, reading and writing, with these in turn arming them for effective subject-area learning. Then, with an effective education and strong literacy skills, they can continue successfully on into adult life.

Taiwan, Japan, China and Korea did this, quickly and decisively ending both their previously struggling education and their numbers of illiterate citizens. They did this by implementing fully-regular orthographies that expedited literacy and learning development for all children who started school from that point on. They also used them in remediation of older struggling readers and adults who had limited literacy. This inexpensive reform worked impressively well, with outstanding educational and economic benefits.

Certainly, the inexpensive Effective Education Road has value.

The Pre-School Child Road

On the other hand, we could take the Pre-School Child Road.

An Anglophone nation model, it emphasises major efforts to have our beginners ready for effective learning at start of school.

As Macklin and Pilcher (2020) comment, of our 2020 *Educational Opportunity* report (Lamb et al., 2020):

> Failure to address educational inequality reproduces and amplifies existing poverty across generations. It saps productivity, undermines social cohesion and costs governments and communities billions of dollars. On an individual level, it hampers young people's search for secure employment and is connected to poorer health and lower quality of life.
> There are no quick ways to fix educational inequality, but there are several key improvements that will make a difference.
> Closing gaps in participation and lifting the quality of early childhood education services – particularly in disadvantaged communities where services tend to be lower quality – should be one of our highest priorities.
> Early childhood education is critical to giving every child the

best possible start. Evidence shows preschool raises children's chances of being developmentally ready for school in key areas by around 12 percentage points.
Addressing educational inequality is as much about what happens outside the classroom as inside. Nurturing every child's development and well-being is best achieved through a partnership between schools, families, communities and other support services.

The Pre-School Child Road uses the Heckman Equation to achieve improvement (e.g., Campbell et al., 2012, 2014; Doyle et al., 2009).

James Heckman is famous for his work overcoming the effects of poverty and low SES in Anglophone nations. His Heckman Equation is *Invest + Develop + Sustain = Gain*:

Invest: Invest in educational and developmental resources for disadvantaged families to provide equal access to successful early human development.
+ Develop: Nurture early development of cognitive skills in children from birth to age five.
+ Sustain: Sustain early development with effective education through to adulthood.
= Gain: Gain a more capable, productive and valuable workforce that pays dividends to America for generations to come.

Quite likely, the reason it's largely an Anglosphere model is because the Anglosphere has widespread generational disadvantage, with many at-risk from infancy, for major school and adult struggles.

Heckman's model is highly effective. While resource intensive and very costly, it makes for impressive savings overall, because of later savings on extremely expensive areas of adult life: unemployment, our justice system, and teenage and adult mental health supports.

While research is needed, it's likely that, even with its impressive savings, the Pre-School Child Road is vastly more expensive than the Effective Education Road. After all, readying children for meeting one of the worlds' most challenging orthographies at close to the world's youngest age is a formidable challenge.

Using the Pre-School Child Road and the Heckman equation, we'd focus on the years before school:

The best investment is in quality early childhood development from birth to five for disadvantaged children and their families.

The Pre-School Child Road is somewhat a starfish on the beach model – it makes a great difference for the individual children involved. Implementing it, we'd focus on making a massive positive difference for individual Australian preschoolers.

Chittleborough et al. (2016) estimates this intensive early intervention would be valuable for perhaps 10% of Australian families, and would perhaps reduce by a quarter, our number of children starting school at major risk of school difficulties.

Now, that's a sadly sobering finding, as reducing our at-risk children by just a quarter still gives us far too many struggling readers, relative to the numbers struggling in regular-orthography nations with similar education and intervention standards.

The Middle Path: The Enhanced Effective Education Road

Research is needed to explore and compare the Effective Education Road and Pre-School Child Road. Logically, we'd also explore a strategic middle path, which integrates those two options within 10 Changes improvement. Let's name it the *Enhanced Effective Education Road*.

Implementing Change 8, we'd explore a fully-regular beginners' orthography, the many advantages of 2-stage early literacy, and the costs and benefits of the Effective Education Road.

Additionally, implementing Change 9, we'd explore 2.5 years of play-based enrichment prior to starting formal literacy and numeracy instruction from mid-Year 2, and the extent to which this reduces our numbers in need of the Pre-School Child Road.

Together, implemented across our schools, those changes would drastically reduce the impacts of risk factors our children start school with, including low SES. With risk factors not activated, just as happens in regular-orthography nations now, we'd have children effectively ready for early-literacy learning at start of school far more easily.

Importantly, without these changes, Australia will still have hordes of struggling readers, no matter how enriched their pre-school lives become. With the changes, impressive success may be achieved.

Of course, in doing so, we'd not neglect severely at-risk pre-schoolers. Recognising the damage we're doing through depriving children of allied-health supports needed in early childhood, for children in need, we'd provide allied-health intervention as needed from infancy. That would likely work very well, especially as implementing Changes 8 and 9 will lower the readiness levels children need to reach at start of school, if they're to become effectively literate, active learners.

Research Tour 6. Our Epidemic of Language Weakness

We'd similarly ensure robust allied-health supports across the school years, including integrated Tier 3A and 3B intervention. That too would work well as, again, Changes 8 and 9 would likely reduce numbers needing high levels of intervention.

The middle road with its four changes – Change 8, Change 9, and providing ample allied-health supports prior to and across school – would likely be found far more effective than either the Effective Education Road and Pre-School Child Road on their own.

Nicely, our success would give us big savings. Taking the middle road would be much cheaper and more effective than the Pre-School Child Road taken without Changes 8 and 9. While it's dearer than the Effective Education Road, in adding robust allied-health supports, they'll be a rewarding investment that pays dividends.

We'd have the wins and ample advantaging that Japan, Taiwan and China have achieved in exchanging their previous overwhelming orthographic disadvantage for powerful orthographic advantage enjoyed at child, family, school, education, adult and national economic levels – because, using 2-stage early literacy, most children would easily acquire strong literacy and learning skills.

We'd also have extended our children's *early childhood* by 2.5 years, by holding back formal education until mid-Year 2 and insisting on play-based enrichment from start of Prep.

No longer having to have children ready for Standard English by age 4.5 to 5 years will ease both teaching and learning, e.g.,

- We'd be rich in school time, with child and teacher workload much reduced, as we'd leave behind the mega-hours of learning to read and write solely Standard English.
- We'd have solved our Find the Learning Time Challenge.
- We could end our Find the Caring Time Challenge, with powerful mentoring and supports.
- We'd have closed down our Early Years Factory.

We'd probably also make great progress in empowering our Spelling Generations, and in doing so, end our Spelling Generations, as high literacy levels become the norm across our children and adults. We'd have all the wins of strong education and allied-health supports enriching our children's lives. We'd also be able to leave behind our current HEARTSH, with its Hugely-Exhausting, Actually-Rather-Tedious Schooling Heaviness, and instead achieve GENTLE: Gentle, Engaging, Never-Tiring, Learning Enrichment.

Yes, a strategic middle path using 10 Changes improvements seems a delightful, time and cost-effective, extremely powerful way forward into strong success.

Key Findings from Tour 6

Findings and implications of studies explored in Tour 6 suggest the following considerations towards improving literacy and education in Australia and Anglophone nations:
1. Australia is not providing sufficient speech language pathology and other allied-health services, both before and across the school years.
2. Many of our children thus miss out on needed supports.
3. Children with serious language weakness are often denied additional services and school funding because of overly restrictive criteria being used, including cognitive referencing, a practice long discarded in other nations.
4. Language Disorder is a lifelong condition that contributes to major school and academic difficulties, including severe Standard-English literacy difficulties, poor academic outcomes, behaviour difficulties, and disadvantaged adult life, with high unemployment, social-emotional difficulties and justice system issues.
5. When provided with appropriate supports as needed, before school and across primary and high school, children with language weakness can do well and achieve adult advantage.
6. It's therefore extremely important that children with language weakness receive appropriate intervention of sufficient intensity and duration, so their needs are adequately met.
7. Children with language-skills weakness are highly at risk of word-reading, literacy and academic learning difficulties.
8. In many ways, Australia can be considered as having an epidemic of language weakness, with quite likely 20-40% of children starting school with significant language weakness.
9. Language and literacy skills go together and grow together, and so do language and literacy difficulties.
10. The term Language, Literacy and Learning Disorder (LLLD) is recommended for systemic use as it emphasises and highlights the separate and integrated difficulties of language weakness, literacy weakness and associated learning difficulties so many struggling readers have.
11. Our children's language development continues and is important across all school years:
    a. Language skills are pivotally important from start of school, building literacy, communication and learning.

b. In turn, being literate then expedites building of later language skills.
12. With language skills so important, there is clear advantage in monitoring our children's development of key language skills.
13. We need to monitor children's language skills before and across school years, providing intervention and enrichment as needed.
14. Language skills which might be monitored include
    a. Receptive and expressive vocabulary, language expression skills and listening and language comprehension skills used in listening, speaking, reading and writing.
    b. Language reasoning, including inferencing and social reasoning.
    c. The cognitive-processing and executive-function skills that underlie effective communication and learning, including phonological and phonemic awareness, processing speed and rapid naming, short-term and working memory, and additional executive-function skills such as cognitive flexibility and inhibition control.
15. Such testing needn't add to class teacher workload, e.g., it can be carried out by learning-support and allied-health staff, and trained teacher aides; and might become part of online NAPLAN testing.
16. While some argue that literacy weakness and communication weakness are separate but overlapping disorders, there are compelling arguments for literacy weakness being considered part of communication weakness. Importantly, the weak executive-function and cognitive-processing skills underlying word-reading and literacy difficulties are part of early-childhood language weakness well before literacy difficulties begin.
17. Failing to adequately address the communication needs of children prior to school entry and across the school years, adds in major ways to our education difficulties, including our having continuing high numbers of struggling readers, writers and learners, and troubling behaviour and attention difficulties.
18. We have the option of supporting our children appropriately, so they are successful across school and achieve success as adults.
19. We also have the option, currently taken, of not adequately supporting them, which gives us excessive learning and behaviour difficulties in schools; excessive numbers of unsuccessful youth and adults with language weakness in our cohorts of long-term unemployed, prison and justice system populations; with many having associated mental health and life adjustment issues.
20. Choosing the latter option, we also perpetuate low SES and

generational disadvantage.
21. Having a language weakness epidemic in Australia that is not being adequately addressed means that our Education Act, UN Agreements, disability documents and education declarations are, to a certain extent, rhetoric: they promise our children an effective education and the supports they need, but fail to provide them, with children's needs insufficiently addressed.
22. Consequently, Australian schooling has many children needing major supports but receiving inadequate supports, widespread language weakness, behaviour difficulties and unruly classrooms.
23. In resolving our language weakness epidemic and our associated major literacy and education difficulties, two options seem worthy of deep consideration.
    a. One option is an *Effective Education Road*, which would enable strong advantaging from the start of school:
        i. Using Taiwan, Japan and China as role models, we'd implement Change 8, and no longer have our major literacy and learning difficulties, by implementing use of a fully-regular beginners' orthography that children and older struggling readers use in learning to read and write before transitioning to Standard English.
        ii. We'd also implement Change 9: 2.5 years of language and learning enrichment prior to formal literacy instruction commencing in mid-Year 2, with this including strategic early intervention and skill boosting.
    b. Another option is the *Pre-School Child Road*, using Heckman Equation intervention, which focuses on removing disadvantage prior to start of school, by providing intensive intervention from infancy. This in turn reduces to a certain extent the proportion of children experiencing school difficulties.
    c. There seems strong value in taking a strategic middle path, *The Enhanced Effective Education Road*, as part of 10 Changes improvements, with Australia embracing both options and implementing
        i. Change 8: An initial fully-regular beginners' orthography.
        ii. Change 9: 2.5 years language enrichment to mid-Year 2.
        iii. Pre-school supports and early-childhood enrichment.
        iv. Strong allied-health supports across the school years.
24. Australian education needs research comparing the costs and effectiveness of these options.

Research Tour 7.
Literacy Components and Quadrants

> *If we have learned anything about reading in recent years, it is that it is far more complex than anyone thought. In fact, reading may be the most complex cognitive activity that we humans learn. Therefore, we will likely need complex models and intervention programs. However, models need to rest on a solid foundation. We feel that the Simple View of Reading and its linguistic underpinnings provide a start to such a foundation.*

Hugh Catts and Tiffany Hogan, 2003

Across nations, children's word-reading and language skills work together, in integrated fashion, to empower reading comprehension, while word-writing and language skills similarly empower writing.

In this tour, we'll explore the relationships between language skills and word-reading, as well as children's needs for tailored instruction optimising component skills. Our focus will be reading, as there's considerable research on reading, and little on written expression.

We'll first explore the Simple View model (Gough & Tunmer, 1986; Hoover & Gough, 1990), and then the Literacy Component Model, which incorporates and expands from the Simple View model (Knight et al., 2021). We'll then tour studies that usefully explore the balance of word-reading and language skills in reading comprehension, using Simple View and Literacy Component concepts.

The Simple View Model

Building from the extensive research showing word-reading and language comprehension to be key to reading comprehension, Gough and Tunmer (1986) proposed the *Simple View of Reading* (SVR), which is now often termed the *Simple View* model:

> *To clarify the role of decoding in reading and reading disability, a model of reading is proposed, which holds that reading equals the product of decoding and comprehension.*
>
> *It follows that there must be three types of reading disability ... an inability to decode (dyslexia), an inability to comprehend (hyperlexia), or both (reading disability).*

The relationship in the *Simple View* model is often expressed as
> *Reading Comprehension = Word-reading x Language Skills.*

In beginning readers, word-reading skills most strongly predict and limit reading comprehension, with this changing over time as word-reading skills become proficient, to language skills most strongly predicting and limiting reading comprehension (Garcia & Cain, 2014; Hogan et al., 2014; Knight et al., 2021; Torppa et al., 2016; Wagner et al., 2015).

While, at times, the subject of controversy, the Simple View model is much researched and well established as a model with robust usefulness for schools and researchers.

It has generated considerable love-hate Reading Wars divisiveness down the decades, with many loving it and many loathing it.

While it has its shortcomings, it's a logical, practical model, built from a strong research base and straightforward premises (Hoover & Gough, 1990):

> *The simple view does not deny that the reading process is complex. Linguistic comprehension is certainly a complicated process, whether accomplished in reading or auding; and decoding, as evidenced by the extreme difficulty some have in acquiring it, is also no simple matter.*
>
> *The simple view simply holds that these complexities can be divided into two parts. Moreover, the simple view holds that these two parts are of equal importance.*
>
> *The simple view does not reduce reading to decoding, but asserts that reading necessarily involves the full set of linguistic skills, such as parsing, bridging, and discourse building; decoding in the absence of these skills is not reading.*
>
> *At the same time, the simple view holds that decoding is also of central importance in reading, for without it, linguistic comprehension is of no use.*
>
> *Thus, a second central claim of the simple view is that both decoding and linguistic comprehension are necessary for reading success, neither being sufficient by itself.*

In various forms, the Simple View model has survived and thrived down the decades (Adlof et al., 2006; Cadime et al., 2017; Catts et al., 2006, 2015; Ebert & Scott, 2016; Florit & Cain, 2011; Garcia & Cain, 2014; Georgiou et al., 2008; Hempenstall, 2016; Hoover & Gough, 1990; Joshi & Aaron, 2000; Joshi et al., 2015; Kendeou et al., 2013; Kim, 2017; Kirby & Savage, 2008; Knight et al., 2017b, 2020, 2021; Konold et al., 2003; Leach et al., 2003; Lonigan et al., 2018; Nation, 1999, 2008a; Nation & Norbury, 2005; Nation et al., 2010; Norbury & Nation, 2011; Pimperton & Nation, 2014; Protopapas, Mouzaki et al., 2013; Ricketts, Bishop et al., 2008; Ricketts, Lervåg et al., 2020; Ripoll Salceda et al., 2014; Sabatini et al., 2014; Savage et al., 2015; Silverman et al., 2013; Spencer et al., 2014; Tobia & Bonifacci, 2015; Torppa et al., 2016; Tunmer & Chapman, 2012; Wagner & Ridgewell, 2009; Wagner et al., 2015).

Tunmer and Hoover's (2019) *Cognitive Foundations Framework* uses the Simple View model, while specifying important underlying subskills of word-reading and language skills for literacy. So does Wren's useful *Cognitive Foundations of Literacy* framework (2001). In conjunction with writing, and key impacting factors, it's also a key aspect of the *Literacy Component Model* (Knight et al., 2021), and was used in the *Bridging the Gap* project and report (Knight et al., 2017b).

A key issue that has created divisiveness amongst educators with regard to the Simple View model is that it has not positioned reading comprehension as a separate important skill, instead subsuming it within language skills. It's felt this underemphasises the huge amounts of literacy instruction that schools do, focused on reading comprehension strategies, many of which aren't specifically language skills, but instead strategies for dealing with text in order to build reading comprehension.

Recognising this issue, the Literacy Component Model deliberately includes Reading Comprehension and Written Expression as key literacy components.

The Literacy Component Model

The Literacy Component Model, shown below, is a flexible, pragmatic model our CQU team developed for use by educators and researchers (Knight et al., 2021).

Our children's literacy proficiency builds from the combination of all the different aspects in the figure. As shown in the figure, the model includes reading, writing and key factors which impact them in skill development, skill actioning, children's reading and writing difficulties and instructional needs, and our tailoring of instruction to optimally meet those instructional needs.

The model includes Gough and Tunmer's (1986) Simple View model as an equation: *Reading Comprehension = Word-Reading x Language Skills*. It has a similar equation for writing (Juel, 1988; Nicholson & Dymock, 2015): *Written Expression = Word-Writing x Language skills*.

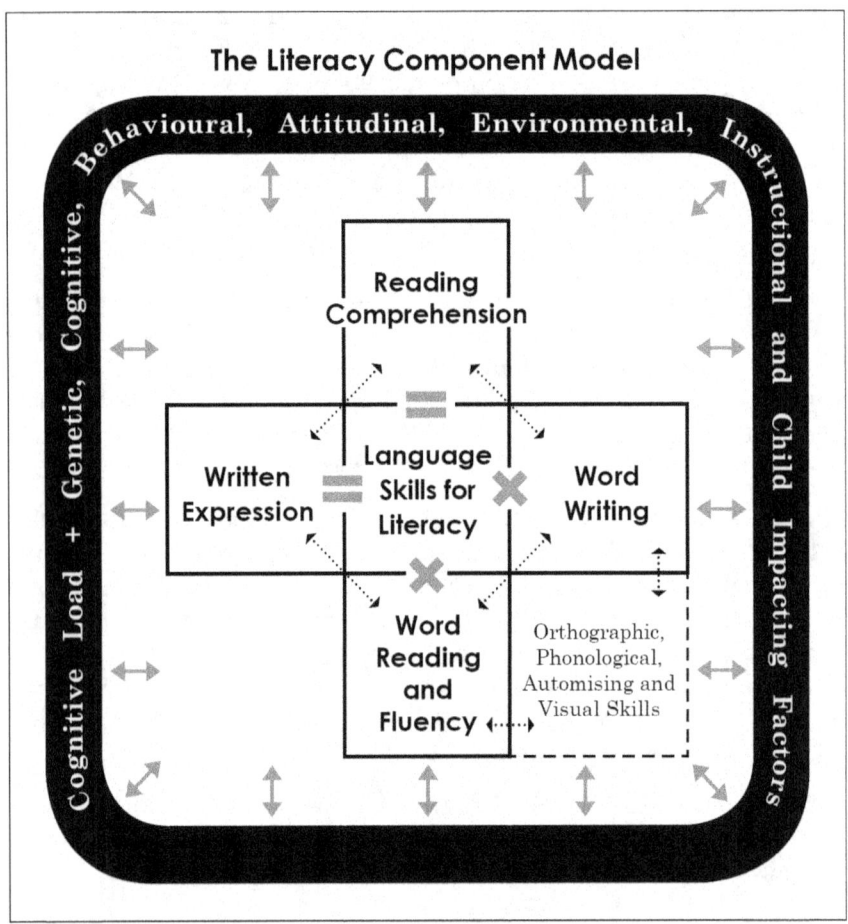

Figure 11. The Literacy Component Model (Knight et al., 2021)

The model deliberately positions *Language Skills for Literacy* in the centre of literacy in the diagram. In part this is to emphasise the importance of language skills in literacy development and school instruction, (e.g., Catts, 2018):

> We generally give the complexity of comprehension "a nod" and go on to measure it with a single test (or construct) and talk about it as if it were a single entity.

> In reality, comprehension is a multidimensional cognitive activity and one of the most complex behaviors that we engage in on a regular basis.

The reading equation highlights how Reading Comprehension skills (Capital-R Reading, how well we understand what we read) build from the integration of Language Skills for Literacy (how well we understand things generally) and Word-Reading skills (small-r reading, how effectively we read the words in the text), in the context of cognitive-processing efficiency and the extent of cognitive load being experienced.

Its writing equation similarly highlights how Written Expression skills (how well we express ourselves in writing) build from the integration of Language Skills for Literacy (how well we organise and express our thoughts) and Word-Writing skills (spelling and spelling approximations, and handwriting, typing or speech-to-text skills), in the context of cognitive-processing efficiency and the extent of cognitive load involved.

The model also emphasises *orthographic, phonological, visual and automising* skills: key subskills that word-reading and word-writing share, which directly impact their development (Knight et al., 2021):

> In the Literacy Component Model, automisation skills can be used as a catch-all category for other factors beyond cognitive processing which are likely to impact mastery and automisation of word-reading and word-writing. This catch-all role is supported by SVR studies showing much unexplained variance after key factors are considered. It is likely other factors less frequently highlighted are also involved.
>
> These include the cognitive load of the required learning, prior learning, learning rate, spoken-language features, monolingualism and multilingualism, age when commencing word-reading instruction, attention, motivation, and, using Maier and Seligman's (2016) revised Learned Helplessness theory, Learned Helplessness and resilience developed in early literacy development.

The more peripheral factors that impact reading, writing and literacy are in the model's border, showing them to be impacting all aspects of literacy contained by that border. Those factors include

- The cognitive load of literacy tasks.
- Genetic, cognitive, behavioural and attitudinal factors.
- Environmental and instructional factors.
- Child factors, e.g., children's language-skill levels and literacy readiness at start of school and currently.

Teachers and schools prioritise reading comprehension as a separate subskill, strategically building children's skills on multiple specific reading comprehension strategies across the school years. Written expression is similarly a major school priority area. In the Literacy Component Model, Reading Comprehension and Written Expression are positioned as specific, separate, literacy components, e.g., Catts (2018) usefully comments:

> One false impression I believe the Simple View of Reading has contributed to is the notion that comprehension, both language comprehension and reading comprehension, is unidimensional and not nearly as complex as it really is.
> By displaying comprehension alongside decoding in a comparable fashion, we have often been led to think that comprehension, like decoding, is a "single thing."

The Literacy Component Model thus emphasises five key areas of literacy instruction, each of which can be expanded further, as needed:
- Reading comprehension.
- Word-reading.
- Language skills for literacy.
- Written expression.
- Word-writing.

The model's double-headed arrows emphasise literacy development and actioning being highly interactive, with subskills interacting with each other and supporting each other's development.

The model emphasises how key literacy skills parallel each other, having much in common (Kim, 2022). Reading comprehension and written expression parallel each other, with both being higher-order literacy skills (Capital-R Reading and Capital-W Writing), building from language skills, and actioning a print-accuracy skill (word-reading and word-writing).

In similar vein, word-reading and spelling also parallel each other, both being print-accuracy skills, and needing, using and building orthographic, phonological, automising and visual skills.

Our Knight et al. (2021) article that explains the model, *The Literacy Component Model: A pragmatic universal paradigm*, emphasises the model being deliberately flexible and pragmatic. Researchers and educators are encouraged to use the model flexibly, adjusting it strategically to highlight focus areas they wish to include. As examples,
- While handwriting can be considered as being part of *orthographic, phonological, automising, visual and coordination skills*, schools might add it as a specific area.

- Researchers and schools might choose to expand *Language Skills for Literacy* to include specific language skills, such as vocabulary or genre skills.
- Specific cognitive-processing and executive-function skills might be added, e.g., working memory.
- An additional component might be added, e.g., *Literacy Task Actioning Skills* might be used, for focus on how children's motivation, engagement and executive-function skill efficiency supports them taking their reading and writing skills through to effective skill use in subject-area reading, writing, studying, and planning and completing assignments.
- In crosslinguistic research, fluency and accuracy might well be included for word-reading and word-writing.

From 2013 to 2017, our CQU research team worked with local teachers and schools in the *Bridging the Gap* research project to establish principles of effective reading instruction for at-risk readers in the early school years (Knight et al., 2017b, 2020).

We used a simplified version of the Literacy Component Model and emphasised the three key subskills: reading comprehension, word-reading, and language skills for literacy.

Using the Literacy Component Model, the project report includes four sections of reading-development principles (Knight et al., 2017b):
- Literacy Component Model strategies.
- Reading-comprehension strategies.
- Word-reading strategies.
- Language Skills for Literacy strategies.

The report details hundreds of principles, with major overarching principles, subprinciples, individual strategies and activities. They are principles towards optimising reading instruction, many of which are found in other useful texts (C. Snow et al., 1998b), and all are deliberately practical. The project was a strong learning experience for both university and teacher-researchers, epitomising the strengths of collaborative research. Notably, an impressive number of teachers and schools adopted the Literacy Component Model as their school framework for their literacy and English programs. The report, and associated research article, are available from ResearchGate (Knight et al., 2017b, 2020).

Components' Impacts Start Early

We'll now briefly explore studies showing the robust, strong predictiveness of children's skills in the two key components of reading comprehension: language skills and word-reading. They highlight the importance of giving children a strong start from earliest school learning, and preventing literacy and learning struggles.

Children's language skills and readiness for learning to read and write when they start school hugely predict their school progress. Tunmer et al.'s (2006) seven-year longitudinal study of New Zealand children found children's levels of *Literate Cultural Capital* (pre-school language and literacy-readiness skills) at school entry strongly predicted later Standard-English reading achievement. Harshest fallout was on the most disadvantaged, including children with lowest SES. Importantly, children in the lowest Literate Cultural Capital quarter at start of school were, on average, 2 years 4 months behind in reading when in Year 7.

That finding is confirmed in other studies showing low extent of print exposure and pre-school literacy and language enrichment significantly impacts Standard-English readers, limiting their reading, spelling, vocabulary, language skills and academic progress (e.g., Hindson et al., 2005; Sparks et al., 2013).

As regards both word-reading and language skills, Juel's (1988) study, which we'll explore shortly, showed that Standard-English readers' Grade 1 word-reading and language skills clearly predicted their Grade 4 skills in these areas. Children with strong Grade 1 skills continued with robust skills, while children weak in Grade 1 remained behind, and were notably weak in Grade 4.

In similar vein, Cunningham and Stanovich's (1997) study *Early reading acquisition and its relation to reading experience and ability 10 years later* found children's Grade 1 reading levels firmly predicted their Grade 11 reading levels, and that levels of print exposure firmly predicted reading-comprehension levels across the school years.

Sparks et al. (2013) replicated Cunningham and Stanovich's (1997) study, following Grade 1 children to the end of Grade 10, with highly similar findings. They found Grade 1 reading skills strongly predicted Grade 10 outcomes, and that differences in extent of print exposure predicted differences in development of reading, spelling, vocabulary and listening comprehension.

Other studies show similarly, e.g., Christopher et al. (2015), in a twin study that assessed literacy and language skills before start of Kindergarten, and at end-Grade-1 and end-Grade-4, found Grade 1 literacy skills strongly predicted Grade 4 levels, with genetic and environmental factors both being in play.

Literate Cultural Capital, the metaphorical backpack children start school with, packed with their pre-school literacy experience and literacy readiness, clearly makes a massive difference when it's Standard English they learn to read and write.

While there are many predictors of later reading and literacy skills, from schools' perspectives, there's strong usefulness in children's early word-reading and spelling being such strong predictors of later skills, as word-reading and spelling skills are easily measured and monitored.

Importantly, it's not just giving children a strong start at school that's crucial. When it's Standard-English and 1-Stage early literacy without a beginners' orthography, it's a major disadvantage to start school with weak language skills (Galletly & Knight, 2011a; Hogan et al., 2014; Nation et al., 2010). In Anglophone nations, it's thus particularly important that children's language skills are strong at school entry.

When needing to identify at-risk children prior to formal word-reading instruction, other measures are needed (Catts et al., 2015; Gutiérrez et al., 2023; Lubotsky & Kaestner, 2016; P. Thompson et al., 2015). As an example, Catts et al. (2015), investigating useful screening and progress monitoring tools to identify children in Kindergarten who are highly likely to have later word-reading difficulties found a screening battery containing measures of letter naming fluency, phonological awareness, rapid naming and nonword repetition accurately identified good and poor readers at the end of Grade 1.

They also found response to instruction for learning of letter names added usefully to identifying of at-risk children. Letter naming is often used in early identification, however schools often prefer to focus more on letter-sounds, given that letter-sound skills directly underlie reading and writing. It's useful to note that testing letter-sounds can work as effectively as letter names (Galletly, 2008).

Nation et al. (2010) investigated the origins of weak reading comprehension in mid-primary school children with healthy word-reading skills. They followed 245 UK children, assessing reading and language skills at five time-points, (ages 5.0, 5.5, 6, 7 and 8 years), twice in Reception (the first year of schooling), then annually in Grades 1, 2 and 3.

At age 8, they found 6% of children (15 children) had poor reading comprehension in combination with healthy word-reading. They then matched these children with 15 children with healthy skill in both areas, and then considered earlier language and reading skills.

They found those poor in comprehension to have had weak language skills, and hence weak reading comprehension, at all time points, with ongoing weakness in expressive and receptive language, listening comprehension and grammatical understanding.

The children started school with weak language comprehension and thus developed reading comprehension difficulties early, and continued with weak language and reading comprehension skills. Had their writing been tested, they'd have shown written language difficulties, given the central role of language skills in both reading and writing.

That's seen in Cragg and Nation's (2006) study of the written expression of another group of UK children, 10-year-olds with age-level word-reading and spelling, but weak reading comprehension.

They found significantly weak language in narratives the children wrote based on stimulus pictures: weak genre skills (immature story structure), lack of detail, with much information not included.

Quadrants Show Children's Instructional Needs

In supporting teachers and schools to prioritise building language skills and word-reading, as part of building reading-comprehension and written-expression skills, there's huge value in schools being able to explore the relationships between word-reading, language skills and reading comprehension using their children's data.

By testing reading comprehension and written expression's subskill components, schools and researchers can then consider children's balance of language skills and print-accuracy skills, and precisely establish their instructional needs. The Simple View and Literacy Component models both encourage use of scatterplots and quadrants as useful, practical tools for research and school use, for establishing children's strengths, weaknesses and instructional needs.

As shown on the next page, testing the two subskills of reading comprehension, using a word-reading test and a language-skills test, then using a scatterplot to show children's scores, establishes which of the four quadrants each child will be positioned in.

Similarly, by testing language skills and word-writing (usually spelling), and using a scatterplot, we arrive at four quadrants for written expression that show children's strengths, weaknesses and needs.

Research Tour 7. Literacy Components and Quadrants

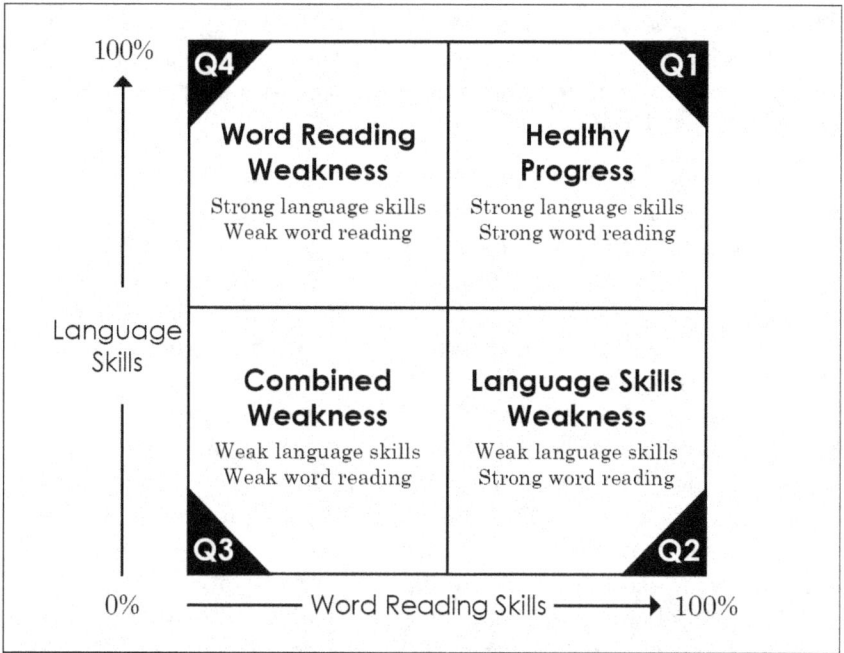

Figure 12a. *Quadrants for reading-comprehension subskills: word-reading and language skills (Knight et al., 2021)*

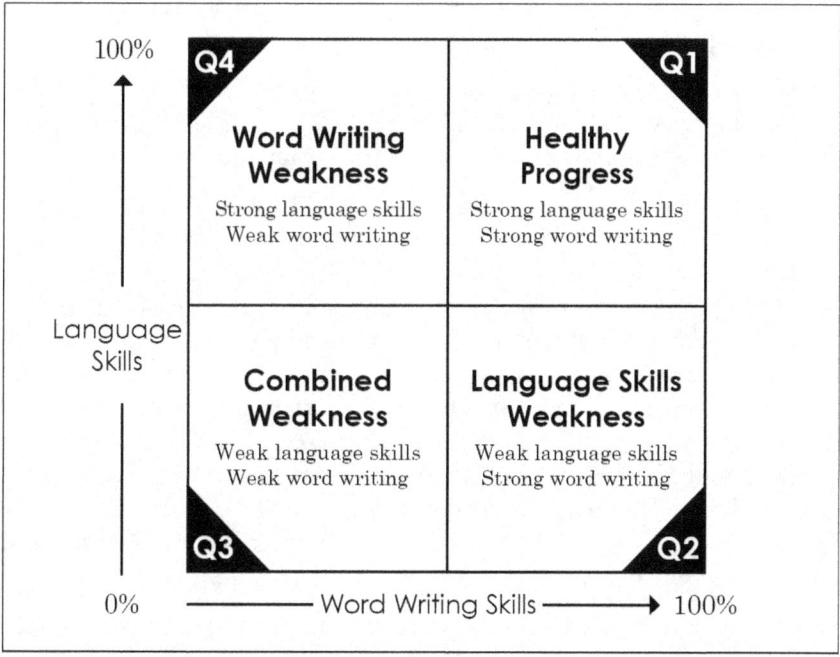

Figure 12b. *Quadrants for written-expression subskills: word-writing (spelling) and language skills (Knight et al., 2021)*

The figures above show quadrants for (a) reading-comprehension, and (b) written-expression subskills. Each quadrant is a group of children, whose instructional needs for word-reading and language skills are largely similar.

The quadrants for reading and writing are similar in many ways:
- Quadrant 1 (Q1) is healthy progress in both areas.
- Quadrant 2 (Q2) is isolated language-skills weakness: it's sometimes termed Hyperlexia, as children's word-reading and spelling is advanced relative to their weak language skills, with some having superb word-reading and spelling.
- Quadrant 3 (Q3) is combined weakness with children struggling in both areas.
- Quadrant 4 (Q4), which is often termed Dyslexia, is
    o Isolated word-reading weakness, for reading quadrants.
    o Isolated spelling weakness, for writing quadrants.

When teachers and schools test whole classes or year-level cohorts, and create scatterplots, children's scores spread across the quadrants. Schools find this powerful towards tailoring instruction to more precisely meet instructional needs (Knight et al., 2017b).

Quadrants can also be as easily used for individual children, e.g., speech language pathologists often use a quadrant figure such as those above to indicate where a child is positioned, as part of explaining the child's strengths, weaknesses and needs.

Ebert and Scott (2016) used quadrant research and the Simple View model in a very useful, practical study, which is a useful role-model for school and clinic-based research and practice.

They analysed the assessment results of 112 school-aged children, aged 6 to 16 years, in USA, who'd been referred for speech-language evaluation at a single urban clinic. Using children's scores for language comprehension, word-reading, reading comprehension, and expressive language skills, they examined the distribution of children across subtypes and the relationships among the four constructs. They found the children distributed across the four quadrants. In keeping with the referrals having been for communication weakness, they found few children in Quadrant 4 (isolated word-reading weakness), and most children to be in Quadrants 2 and 3 (isolated language-skills weakness and combined weakness).

It's likely many Australian speech language pathology practices would have useful databases of children's results on language and literacy skills, which would be useful for research using quadrants.

My database of results on over 500 children, with personal details de-identified, is available to approved researchers for this purpose.

In clinical practice, I use quadrants to explain children's strengths, weaknesses and needs, in reports and discussions with families and teachers. It's found extremely useful.

I also quite extensively use a handout I developed for workshops I conducted with educators and allied-health professionals in Canberra and Queensland. In it, I've listed key subgroups of weak readers and their instructional needs, positioned in Quadrants 2 to 4 (Galletly, 2014f; Knight et al., 2017b):

- Quadrant 2 (Language Skills Weakness) has two categories:
  - Hyperlexic Readers.
  - Late-Emerging Weak Comprehension Readers.
- Quadrant 3 (Combined Weakness) has two categories:
  - Language Disorder Readers.
  - Mixed Weakness Readers.
- Quadrant 4 (Word-Reading Weakness) has three categories:
  - Dyslexic readers.
  - Panicked Young Dyslexic Readers.
  - Late-Emerging Dyslexic Readers.

Teachers in the *Bridging the Gap* project identified strongly with these categories, finding the descriptions of areas of strength and weakness, and specific instructional needs for each of the categories particularly useful. That handout, *Three categories & seven 'types' of weak readers: common patterns of strengths and weaknesses in children with reading difficulties* (Galletly, 2014f) is available on ResearchGate, and included in the *Bridging the Gap* project report.

Because testing word-reading and language skills hasn't been overly encouraged in Australian schools, many schools don't know which quadrants their struggling readers sit in. When only reading comprehension is assessed, it's difficult to establish struggling readers' specific instructional needs – whether they're needing intervention for language skills, word-reading, or both.

There's strong value in Australia moving to wide use of Simple View and Literacy Component Model quadrants in research and practice. In doing so, schools may strategically use sets of tests that lend themselves to quadrant use, being easy and efficient to administer, score and analyse (Cain & Oakhill, 2006; Chan & Rao, 2022; Claessen et al., 2020; Desiree et al., 2014; Fawcett & Jones, 2020; Galletly, 2005a, 2014b, 2014c, 2014d, 2015a; Gandolfi et al., 2021; Gutiérrez et al., 2023; Mashburn & Myers, 2010; Nelson, 2016; Torgesen et al., 2012; Z. Wang et al., 2020).

Studies Using the Simple View Model

Let's now examine five useful Simple View studies that explore the interrelationships of word-reading, language skills and reading comprehension. The studies discussed in our Literacy Component Model article (Knight et al., 2021) are also useful reading.

Study 1. Juel's 1988 Study

Juel's (1988) study, *Learning to read and write: A longitudinal study of 54 children from first through fourth grades* is a practical school-level study conducted at a single, low-SES, USA school. It's easily replicated for school and research use. Juel used both the Simple View of Reading and the *Simple View of Writing* that it implies. Juel assessed cognitive, language, reading and writing skills across Grades 1 to 4. The study began with 129 children in Grade 1, but by Grade 4, only 54 of the children remained at the school, and the analysis is of these 54 subjects with full data.

Juel asked useful, practical research questions:
- Do the same children remain weak readers and writers year after year?
- What skills do weak readers and weak writers lack?
- What factors seem to keep weak readers and weak writers from improving?

The children's results showed that yes, strong readers and weak readers overwhelmingly continued to be strong readers and weak readers, respectively, with an identical pattern for writing.

Of the 30 healthy readers in Grade 1, 26 were still healthy readers, with only 4 now having become weak readers. The 24 weak Grade 1 readers continued as weak readers: 3 had word-reading weakness, 2 had language weakness, and 19 were weak in both areas.

Juel's findings were in keeping with other studies (e.g., Christopher et al., 2015). Her study validated the Simple View model, finding
- Word-reading and language skills were major factors contributing to reading comprehension skills.
- Spelling and language skills were major factors contributing to written expression skills.
- Weak readers and writers fitted neatly into the three quadrant subgroups: of language skills weakness (Q2), word-reading and spelling weakness (Q4), and combined weakness (Q3).

Juel also found marked differences between strong and weak readers in their attitudes to reading, the amount of reading they did out of school, and print exposure generally.

Weak readers read little at home, and considered reading boring:
Poor fourth-grade readers seemed to read little because they hated reading (which several children said) or because of the failure experiences associated with reading. The most common response of the poor readers to why they did not like to read was that it was boring.

Juel also explored and discusses phonemic awareness and Literate Cultural Capital and their impacts on literacy development. Her writing also hints at factors akin to Success Inoculation and Acquired Helplessness.

Juel emphasised the importance of at-risk word-readers staying motivated, and developing effective phonemic awareness and word-reading, with it seeming quite critical that they stay motivated and experience strong success in Grade-1 word-reading.

Similarly, she emphasised the importance of reading to children, and children engaging confidently in reading out of school:
Good readers simply read more and over time have experienced more ideas and vocabulary that can be incorporated into their writing. In the words of Stephen Spielberg (1987 Academy Awards), 'Only a generation of readers will spawn a generation of writers'.

Juel's is an excellent study, and one that our schools could easily replicate, as could NAPLAN researchers, towards us tailoring instruction effectively. It's well worth reading.

Study 2. Hoover and Gough's 1990 Study

Hoover and Gough's (1990) study, establishing the validity of the Simple View model was quite likely conducted close to when Gough and Tunmer (1986) proposed the model. Its findings are very similar to those of many other studies, prior to and since that time.

The researchers analysed the data of 254 English-Spanish bilingual children whose early-literacy development had been monitored across the early school years, in five Texas locations.

Cognitive, language, word-reading, and reading comprehension skills were assessed several times annually, from Kindergarten through Grade 4. Subjects included 206 children followed from Kindergarten, plus 48 children followed from Grade 1.

In line with many other studies, analysis of results showed
- Steady growth of all three skills, word-reading, language skills and reading comprehension across the 5 years.

- A relatively weak relationship between word-reading and language skills, i.e., them being relatively independent skills.
- Both word-reading and language skills contributing strongly to reading comprehension.
- The relationship of word-reading to reading comprehension being strongest in the earlier years with this changing to language skills having the strongest relationship with reading comprehension in Grades 3 and 4.

Hoover and Gough discussed the variance shared by word-reading and language skills, with them not being completely separate and independent of each other. While related, they're separate enough to be considered as independent when taking a simple view.

Study 3. Lonigan et al.'s 2018 Study

Lonigan et al.'s (2018) study, *Examining the Simple View of Reading with elementary school children: Still simple after all these years,* analysed the cognitive, language and reading skills of 757 children in Grades 3, 4 and 5, using multiple tests of each skill area.

It found the model to be sound. Word-reading and language skills accounted for most of the variance in reading comprehension, with developmental trends over time for their importance: word-reading contributed most strongly to reading comprehension for younger and weaker readers, while language skills were the strongest contributor for older and stronger readers.

Similar to other studies, it found word-reading and language skills largely separate, and overlapping each other, being related to each other most likely through cognitive and linguistic skills.

Whereas Hoover & Gough's (1990) study was longitudinal, following the same group of children as their skills developed, Lonigan et al.'s study (2018) was cross-sectional, studying children of multiple year-levels at a single time point. In line with other longitudinal and cross-sectional studies, both studies showed word-reading and language skills to be the key subskills of reading comprehension.

Study 4. Torppa et al.'s Finnish Study

Torppa et al. (2016) explored how well the Simple View model worked for Finnish children, and the predictive value of phonological awareness, letter knowledge, rapid naming, and vocabulary on children's word-reading and language skills. They followed 1,815 Finnish children from Kindergarten (where children learn letters and their sounds) to Grade 3.

Not surprisingly, given Finnish is a highly-regular orthography, and in line with other studies (Cadime et al., 2017; Kendeou et al., 2013; Protopapas, Fakou et al., 2013; Tobia & Bonifacci, 2015), they found reading fluency, not reading accuracy, contributed decisively to reading comprehension, as did children's listening comprehension, i.e., their language skills.

They also found the developmental order of importance, with the predictive effect of reading fluency only present in Grade 1, and language skills predicting reading comprehension from Grade 2 on.

They found phonological awareness, letter knowledge, rapid naming, and vocabulary predicted reading comprehension mostly indirectly, through Grade 1 reading fluency and language skills.

Study 5. Gutiérrez et al.'s Prediction Study

Schools are empowered when able to use strategic assessment at the start of school to identify children at risk of later difficulties. Ideally, schools need minimal testing, tests that are easy to administer and score, and test batteries with strong sensitivity (correctly identifying at-risk children) and selectivity (not incorrectly *identifying* children not at risk of difficulties).

Considerable research has focused on achieving these ends. Crosslinguistic research shows RAN, phonological awareness, and letter-sound knowledge to be predictors of progress in both Anglophone and regular-orthography nations (Georgiou et al., 2012; Landerl et al., 2013, 2019).

Family history and response to instruction are also strong predictors, as are attention, behaviour and language skills (Gooch et al., 2014; Lervåg et al., 2009; Lohvansuu et al., 2021; Lonigan & Phillips, 2016; Lyytinen, 2014).

Benefits from identifying Anglophone at-risk children at a young age are certainly present (Catts et al., 2015). Gutiérrez et al. (2023) discuss USA needs for effective early intervention in the context of,
- Early academic difficulties persisting across high school.
- Achievement gaps widening across the school years.
- Numbers of struggling readers expanding across school years.
- Worrying levels of low literacy, e.g., in 2019 National Assessment of Educational Progress (NAEP) tests, with
  - Only 35% of Grade 4 children at proficient level.
  - Achievement levels dropping from 2017 to 2019.
  - Numbers of low achievers increasing.

o   Mean achievement lower, with lower results for both Average and Low achievers.

Gutiérrez et al.'s study establishing Grade 1 identifiers of weak Grade 4 readers, in a cohort of 450 children assessed in Grade 1 and 4, achieved high (.91) sensitivity but lower (.75) selectivity. It used useful tests that schools would find useful.

The study found key predictors of children's Grade 1 reading included a mix of early word-reading and language skills, including letter-naming, phonemic awareness, early word-reading, expressive vocabulary, and listening comprehension.

That said, the Gutiérrez et al. (2023) study has appreciable limitations. Firstly, it seems likely that some children with reading-comprehension difficulties were included in the study's Grade 4 not-at-risk group, and secondly, the study did not explore the power of each individual test in their battery, which might mean more tests may have been used than were needed.

There's value in future research in this area, in conjunction with research exploring the extent to which English orthographic complexity activates children's risk factors.

We'd also benefit by researching our potential for reduced activation of risk factors, if and when Australia actions Changes 8 and 9, investigating the potential of 2-stage early literacy using a beginners' orthography; and of 2.5 years of language and literacy enrichment prior to starting formal word-reading, writing and numeracy instruction in mid-Year 2.

Quadrants of Early and Late-Emerging Difficulties

Let's now explore Leach et al.'s (2003) *Late-emerging reading disabilities* study. It's a useful USA school-level study exploring the distributions of struggling readers, and the extent to which children have early and late emerging reading difficulties.

It used quadrants to explore the extent to which struggling readers sit in the three quadrants of weak reading comprehension: word-reading weakness (Q4), language skills weakness (Q2), or combined weakness in both areas (Q3).

In using quadrants, the researchers explored the *Fourth Grade Slump* (Chall & Jacobs, 2003; Hirsch, 2003): how quite a few children do well in early years but are struggling by mid-primary school. To do this, they investigated the extent to which struggling readers in later years have early-emerging and late-emerging weakness.

Research Tour 7. Literacy Components and Quadrants

Children with *early-emerging* difficulties have difficulties from very early on, after starting school, while those with *late-emerging* difficulties have healthy-progress and skills in early school years, and develop difficulties later, by or in middle primary school.

Many consider the Fourth Grade Slump to be due to language weakness: difficulties with the vocabulary and mature language and wording used in texts.

Language weakness being exclusively the cause isn't actually not the case, however, as numerous studies have found word-reading weakness to also be a factor in later-years difficulties (Galletly et al., 2009; Z. Wang et al., 2020; Yovanoff et al., 2005).

Their study had two stages. They first tested children and looked at proportions in each quadrant, as shown above.

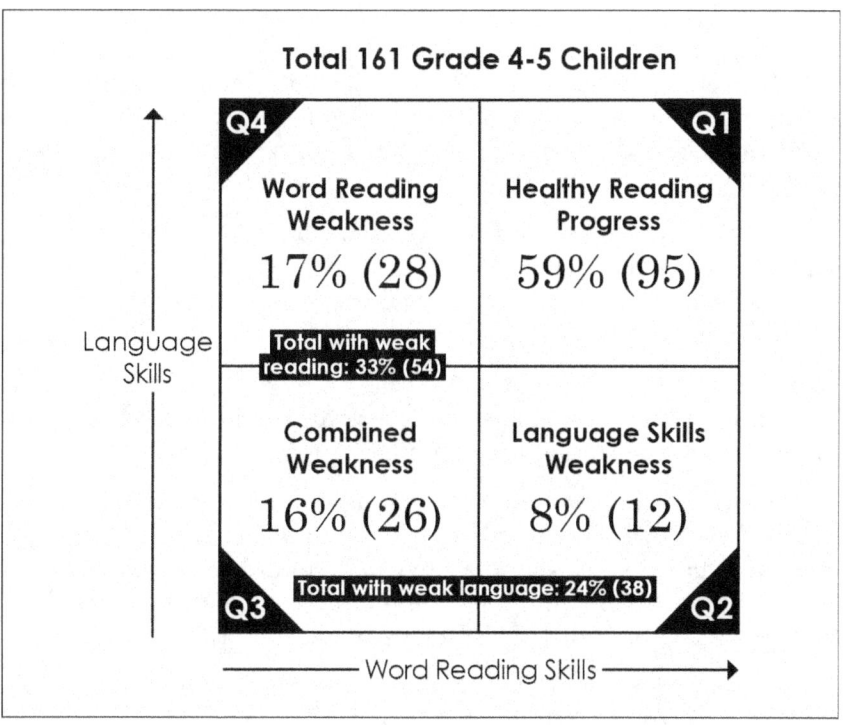

Figure 13a. Quadrant distributions of Leach et al.'s (2003) Grade 4-5 readers

Leach et al. tested 161 Grade 4-5 children, finding 95 (59% of the cohort) in Quadrant 1 (Q1), with healthy reading comprehension.

The 66 children with weak reading comprehension were in the three skill-weakness quadrants:

- 12 children (8% of the total 161 children) were in Quadrant 2 (Q2), with isolated language skills weakness.
- 28 children (17%), more than twice as many, were in Quadrant 4 (Q4), with isolated word-reading weakness.
- 26 children (16%) were in Quadrant 3 (Q3), having combined weakness in both language skills and word-reading.

The study thus found both word-reading difficulties and language-skills difficulties to be key factors in the Fourth Grade Slump: with weak word-reading more prevalent than weak language skills:
- Word-reading: 33%, using rounding, Q3 + Q4 = 54 children.
- Language-skills weakness: 24%, Q2 + Q3 = 38 children).

Proportions of Early and Late-Emerging Reading Difficulties

In the next stage, Leach et al. considered the origins of the Fourth Grade Slump for these 66 weak readers.

They did this by looking back at the children's early-years reading achievement to establish whether their difficulties were early-emerging or late-emerging,. They had longitudinal data, and knew how well the children had done in reading-comprehension tests in their early years of schooling.

Of the 66 children now showing reading-comprehension weakness, 35 had early-emerging weakness (present now plus present back in Grades 1-3) and 31 had late-emerging weakness (present now, but not present in Grades 1-3).

Leach et al. then explored the spread of subskills of early vs late-emerging groups by considering their word-reading and language skills. Here's the spread they found.

In the early-emerging group, almost all children had word-reading difficulties (95%, with numbers rounded): 49% had isolated word-reading weakness (Q4), plus 46% had combined weakness (Q3). Early-years word-reading instruction and remediation hadn't been effective enough, and their word-reading difficulties continued on.

Considerably fewer of the early-emerging group had language-skills weakness (52%): 6% had isolated language weakness (Q2), and 46% had combined weakness, also having word-reading difficulties (Q3).

In the late-emerging group, Grade 4 and 5 children who'd had healthy reading comprehension when younger, weakness in word-reading and language skills was in reasonably even thirds:
- One third had isolated language skills weakness (Q2, 32%).
- One third had isolated word-reading weakness (Q4, 35%).

Research Tour 7. Literacy Components and Quadrants

- One third had combined weakness (Q3, 32%).

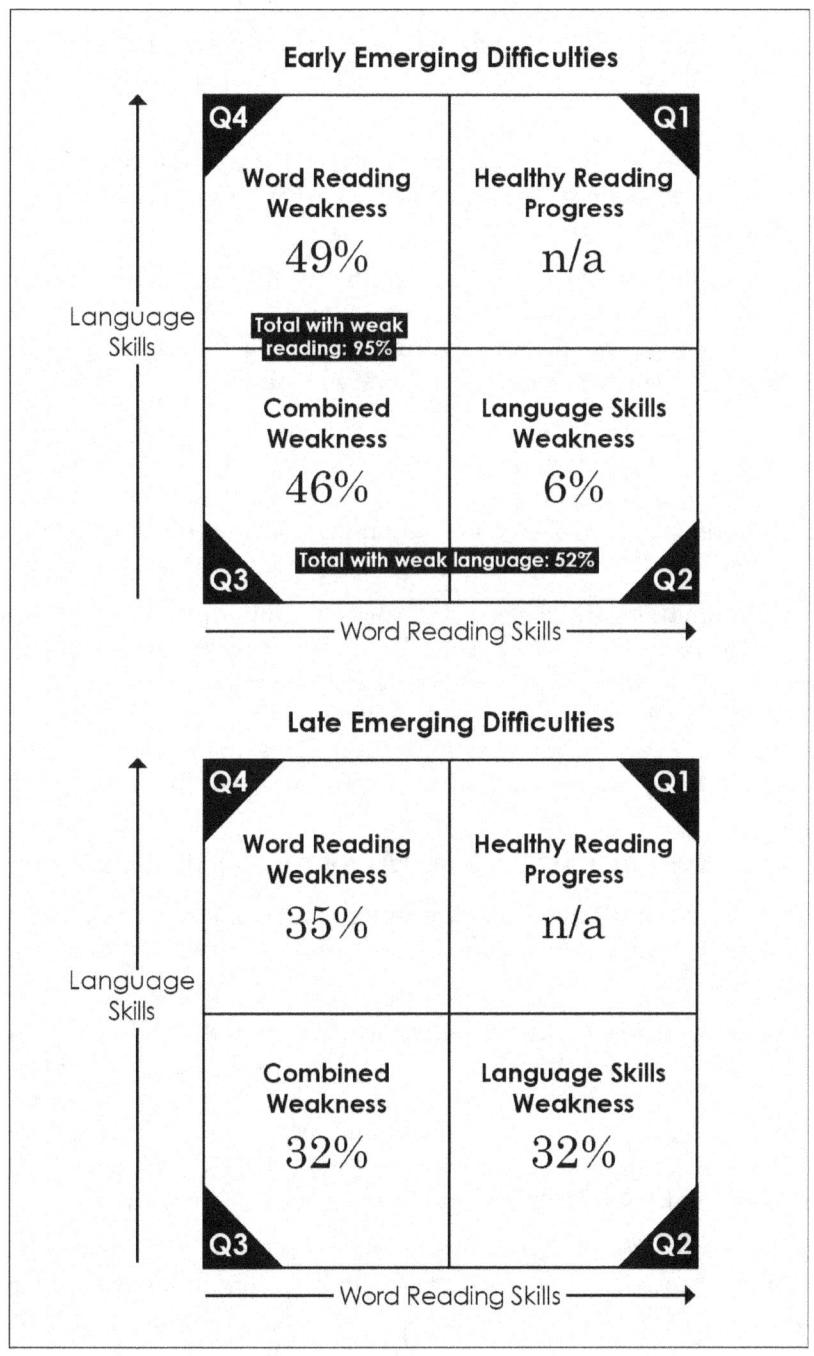

Figure 13b. Quadrant distributions of Leach et al.'s (2003) children with early vs late-emerging reading difficulties

As the figure shows, two thirds (64%) of the late-emerging group, had language weakness, and two thirds (67%) had word-reading weakness.

Clearly, while language weakness is a definite factor in late-emerging reading difficulties and Fourth Grade Slump, for this study, word-reading difficulties was easily as big a factor.

Australia needs research studies establishing our proportions of early and late-emerging difficulties and the balance of language-skills and word-reading needs.

I've chosen to use Leach et al.'s study for its simple yet powerful research method, which Australian schools and NAPLAN could easily use. We'd learn much by replicating and extending it here in Australia, in schools, regions and systemically.

I'm not using the study because of the proportions of children it established in weak word-reading, language skills and combined weakness quadrants. After all, it's an American study. With reading instruction in Australia differing from USA instruction in many ways, our quadrant proportions may be quite different.

Testing reading comprehension, word-reading and language skills down the years, we could establish the extent to which our children develop early and late-emerging reading-comprehension difficulties. That way, we could also explore how the Fourth Grade Slump develops. There'd be value too in extending crosslinguistic research on these areas (e.g., Kendeou et al., 2013; Torppa et al., 2016).

Evidence from Other Anglophone Studies

Other USA studies of late-emerging weak readers show higher numbers having language-skills weakness and fewer having word-reading weakness.

Catts et al. (2012), using a weighted sample, found 52% had isolated language skills weakness (Q2), 36% had isolated late-emerging word-reading weakness (Q4), and 12% had combined weakness (Q3). Adding together the numbers for word-reading weakness (Q3 + Q4) and language weakness (Q2 + Q3), that's 48% with word-reading weakness, and 64% with language-skills weakness.

Cirino et al. (2013), exploring literacy skills in USA high-school children, including language and reading comprehension, word-reading accuracy, and word-reading and text-reading fluency, found 47% were below the 25th percentile for word-reading accuracy, and 49% below the 25th percentile on three or more areas.

Solis et al. (2022) also found word-reading important in older readers, with USA high-schoolers' pre-existing word-reading levels predicting their responsiveness to literacy intervention.

Interestingly, a Canadian study, which is potentially a useful model for Australian school-level research, showed markedly low numbers of weak word-readers. Etmanskie et al. (2016), using school-level data from one Canadian district, where schools had assessed word-reading, found only 0.7% had weak word-reading. They found 12.6% had weak reading comprehension, approximately equal groups of early and late-emerging readers, plus impressive progress, with, e.g., most late-emerging weak readers recovering by Grade 7.

The study did have noteworthy limitations: 12.2% of the children were designated as *borderline*, having scored at healthy level for either reading comprehension or word-reading; and in addition, the children with poor reading comprehension showed weaker word-reading. However, even though total numbers with word-reading difficulties were likely somewhat higher than the 0.7% they cite, they still seem likely to be appreciably lower than other studies e.g., Catt's et al. (2012), and Leach et al.'s (2003) large numbers.

Etmanskie et al.'s study also hints at the Canadian advantage we see in PIRLS and PISA results, with value in Australia inviting collaborative research to explore our similarities and differences. The study's useful, practical research design is one that Australian schools, regions and systems could readily replicate and extend, e.g., testing of other language and literacy skills, and perhaps more deeply analysing performance of that *borderline* category of readers.

Of course, findings of studies are impacted not just by children's skill levels, but also by the tests used, and cut-off criteria used to define subject groups (Sabatini et al., 2014). They're also influenced by the skills researchers choose to assess, e.g., if only language skills that are relative strengths for weak word-readers are assessed, e.g., receptive vocabulary and narrative retell, children with language disorder may seem to have healthy language skills.

It would be powerful for our teachers and schools to know the proportions of children they have in each quadrant. When teachers and schools in our Bridging the Gap project had tests they could easily use, they loved quadrants and how usefully they highlighted whether weak readers' instructional needs were for word-reading, language skills or both (Knight et al, 2017b). The project focused on reading quadrants, but schools could similarly explore writing quadrants, using tests of spelling, written expression, and language skills, e.g., expressive vocabulary and narrative-retell skills.

Let's Conduct Component and Quadrant Research

While there has been considerable research on the Simple View model, currently, there's an Ivory-towering vs Swiss-cheese research contrast, with most research articles exploring the model as a theoretical construction, and relatively few studies being of schools using the model to establish children's strengths and weaknesses more precisely, for tailoring of differentiated instruction.

This is disappointing as the Simple View and Literacy Component models are a powerful tool for teacher and school use (Connor, Adams, et al., 2020, Connor, Kelcey, et al., 2020b; Knight et al., 2017b). It is an area of extremely useful research, with potential to quite quickly build powerful knowledge on children's strengths, weaknesses and instructional needs.

It would be very useful to establish Australian quadrant proportions across the year-levels, in different schools and regions, and, initially, a 10% NAPLAN sample whose word-reading and language skills are assessed.

It would also be very valuable to establish our proportions of children with early-emerging and late-emerging difficulties.

Certainly, as we'll explore in Tour 8, the way our numbers of low achievers for reading, writing and spelling steadily increase across the NAPLAN years, from lowest numbers in Year 3 to highest numbers in Year 9, suggests late-emerging difficulties to be as much a challenge as early-emerging difficulties for Australia, in our meeting our teaching challenges.

In replicating Leach et al.'s (2003) study, reading-comprehension tests such as Pat-R Reading Comprehension or NAPLAN reading tests could be used, and a word-reading test such as TOWRE-2. To assess language comprehension, PAT-R Vocabulary test or a test of expressive vocabulary might be used, or, alternatively, a multiple-choice test of reading-comprehension changed to a language-comprehension test by the text being read aloud to children without them seeing the words, then using multiple-choice questions which are read aloud while also being viewed. Other measures used in Anglophone nations might also be used (e.g., Etmanskie et al., 2016; Gutiérrez et al., 2023; Z. Wang et al., 2020).

Importantly, there'd be huge value in establishing reliable cut-off criteria for the tests we use. It's common for tests, schools and researchers to use Standard Deviations (SDs) in deciding which children are *Low* achievers and which are not.

Where that cut-point is set can make a very big difference in numbers:
- If set at 1 SD below the Mean, for a full population, approximately 16% of children would be Low achievers (1 SD is 34.1% of achievers, so 84.1% of children would be above that cut-point: 50% being the upper half of achievers and 34.1% being children below the Mean and within 1 SD of the Mean.
- If set at 1.5 SD below the Mean, for a full population, only about 13% of children would be Low achievers (1.5 SD is 36.6% of achievers, so 86.6% of children would be above that cut-point: 50% being the upper half of achievers and 36.6% being children below the Mean and within 1 SD of the Mean.
- If set at 2 SD below the Mean, only about 2.2% are Low achievers. A cut-point that low is ethically highly questionable. That said, I've included it as multiple Australian states use cut-points as low as the 1st and 2nd percentile for eligibility for Special Education funding for language disorder.

You can see that the numbers of Low achievers in Leach et al. (2003) would change if cut-points changed from 1 SD to 1.5 SDs, etc. So too would numbers in future Australian studies of this type.

Internationally, and in Australia, we need rigorous discussions to establish relatively standardised cut-points for deciding which groups of children are Low, Healthy, and High achievers.

The cut-points we arrive at for different skills may vary in type and form. They might use Standard Deviations. They might be criterion based. As an example, the cut-point I've used in our 2035 goal has criterion and SD aspects. It required *at least 98% of Australian school children* to be able to read *90% of the 10,000 most-frequent words*. The *98%* means I've used a 2 SD cut-point: I'm saying we consider it acceptable to have 2% of school-children who have word-reading weaker than that level. The *90% of the 10,000 most-frequent words* is a criterion-based measure, which is likely to be useful to use across nations as well as in Australia.

Using it, we might develop tests somewhat similar to my *Galletly Most-Frequent Words 50-Word Probes* for testing children's reading of the 200 most frequent words (Galletly, 2005a). I've used every fourth word, in random order, in multiple sets. We might have a series of tests we use, e.g., of the first 200, first 500, 500-1000, then a set for every 1000 to 10,000 (Galletly, 2008).

Recommended, standardised cut-points for research studies and education will make comparing the results of different studies far easier, and enable Australia to have a central educational research data bank, where results of studies are compiled and compared. They're useful for practice, and the research we need that will empower practice. Setting recommended cut-points is thus powerful and much needed.

Key Findings from Tour 7

Findings and implications of studies explored in Tour 7 suggest the following considerations towards improving literacy and education in Australia and Anglophone nations:

1. There is enormous value in using children's data on word-reading, language skills and reading comprehension to explore the relationship between these three variables.
2. All three are important reading subskills warranting strong instructional focus, e.g., in the regional Queensland Bridging the Gap project report (Knight et al, 2017b) listing principles towards effective instruction, four sections of practical strategies are included:
   a. Literacy Component Model strategies.
   b. Reading-comprehension strategies.
   c. Word-reading strategies.
   d. Language Skills for Literacy strategies.
3. The *Simple View of Reading* or *Simple View* model (*Reading Comprehension = Word-Reading x Language Skills*; Gough & Tunmer, 1986), that's incorporated in the Literacy Component Model (Knight et al., 2021), is a useful concept for schools and education. It implies a simple view of writing (*Written Expression = Word-Writing x Language Skills*; Juel, 1988; Knight et al., 2021), which the Literacy Component Model includes.
4. The Simple View model does not disparage reading as being simple, but instead emphasises that when taking a simplest perspective of reading, the two key subskills underlying effective reading comprehension are children's word-reading skills and their language skills used in literacy.
5. The Literacy Component Model encourages flexibility, e.g., schools wanting to emphasise all three reading and writing subskills, might include in the model, both
   a. *Reading Comprehension = Word-reading x Language Skills + Reading Strategies.*
   b. *Written Expression = Word-Writing x Language Skills + Writing Strategies.*
6. There is considerable experimental and quasi-experimental

research exploring the relationships between word-reading, language skills and reading comprehension. It shows consistently that
   a. Both word-reading and language skills contribute substantially to reading comprehension.
   b. On average, and for healthy-progress word-readers, word-reading most strongly predicts reading comprehension in the early school years, with this changing over time to language skills most strongly predicting reading comprehension, once children have acquired a reasonable level of word-reading skills.
   c. Both word-reading and language skills predict children's academic progress.
   d. Three prevalent areas of weakness underlying weak reading comprehension are isolated word-reading weakness, isolated language skills weakness, and combined weakness in both areas.
7. By using tests of word-reading and language skills and creating scatterplots which show four quadrants, schools can establish children's instructional needs:
   a. Children with healthy reading comprehension need ongoing enriching instruction building word-reading, language skills and reading-comprehension strategies.
   b. Children with weak language skills additionally need tailored remediation building language skills.
   c. Children with weak word-reading skills additionally need tailored remediation building word-reading skills.
   d. Children with combined weakness additionally need remediation building word-reading and language skills.
8. Australia has major needs for research exploring the relationships between word-reading, language skills and reading comprehension.
9. This could be done in individual schools and in NAPLAN research that perhaps initially uses a 10% sample of Year 3, 5, 7 and 9 children.
10. While some children show early-emerging word-reading and language skills weakness, other children have late-emerging weakness in these areas.
11. The *Fourth Grade Slump* refers to children with late-emerging weakness who did well in early school years but are struggling by later primary school.
12. While many have thought it is weak language skills which causes the Fourth Grade Slump, studies show that weak word-reading can contribute as much as weak language skills, and

sometimes more so.
13. Monitoring children's language skills, word-reading and reading comprehension across the school years enables schools and researchers to
    a. Explore early and late-emerging weakness in language skills, word-reading and reading comprehension, and investigate the Fourth Grade Slump,
    b. With the focus on developing effective instruction that remediates early-emerging weaknesses and prevents later-emerging weaknesses.
14. Multiple studies are potentially useful, for replicating and extending in Australian school-level research, e.g., Leach et al.'s (2003) school-level study, Etmanskie et al.'s (2016) district-level study, and Ebert and Scott's (2016) data-base analysis.
15. While word-reading, spelling and language skills are highly important skills, it is important to remember that there are many other factors that impact reading comprehension, expression, literacy and academic development, and to consider and research these other factors, e.g., the *Cognitive Load + Genetic, Cognitive, Behavioural, Attitudinal, Environmental, Instructional and Child Impacting Factors* that the Literacy Component Model includes (Knight et al., 2021).

Research Tour 8.
Our Too Many
Low Literacy Achievers

Overall, vast sums have been spent throughout the English-speaking world over the last 20 years, in an attempt to raise standards and meet the needs of the lower-achieving students. However, there is little evidence that anything has changed, or is changing, for these students.

Jonathan Solity, 2015

Too many Anglophone children are struggling with literacy and learning, e.g., Gutiérrez et al. (2023) discuss only 35% of all USA fourth graders showing proficient reading skills in the 2019 National Assessment of Educational Progress (NAEP) tests, and average achievement being lower than previous years, commenting that the statistics are worrying, given primary-school difficulties tend to persist and widen across the school years.

Let's fly in now to consider Australian children's early-literacy levels, and, where available data permits, use the perspectives of the Simple View and Literacy Component models, of reading comprehension building from word-reading and language-skill levels, and written expression building from language skills and writing accuracy, including spelling.

Australia doesn't have systemic word-reading and language-skills data, alas, which restricts the insights we can gain. Our dearth of data on word-reading and language skills disadvantages education greatly here in Australia, with change badly needed. For now, we do what we can, and trust that, into the future, data on all three reading literacy skills will be available, providing us far more powerful insights.

We'll first consider PISA and PIRLS data, then NAPLAN data. All three provide sobering food for thought.

PISA and PIRLS Anglosphere Struggles

Regular-orthography and multilingual nations with strong focus on education consistently achieve high standards in PIRLS and PISA, while few Anglophone nations are high achievers.

Australia's PIRLS Performance

The *Progress in International Reading Literacy Study* (PIRLS) tests reading comprehension of 10-year-olds in many nations every five years (Thomson et al., 2017):

> Year 4 students are the focus of the PIRLS assessment because they are usually at a key transition point in their schooling, during which they move from learning how to read, to reading in order to learn. PIRLS aims to inform policies and practice while there still is an opportunity to improve students' performance in reading.

PIRLS began with PIRLS 2001, with subsequent rounds in 2006, 2011 and 2016. PIRLS is paralleled by the *Trends in International Mathematics and Science Study* (TIMSS), which tests maths and science skills every five years.

With PIRLS 2021 data not yet available, until May 2023, we'll consider just data from PIRLS 2001 to 2016 (Thomson et al., 2017).

PIRLS 2016 involved over 580,000 children in 61 nations. Australia's contingent was 6,341 Year 4 children from 286 primary schools across Australia: at least one full class, and all indigenous Year 4 students at those schools were included.

In PIRLS, only reading comprehension is assessed, with no testing of reading-comprehension subskills. While this is quite possibly adequate for regular-orthography nations, where children have proficient word-reading accuracy, and language-skill levels correlate strongly with reading-comprehension levels, it is insufficient for the needs of Anglophone nations, where word-reading is still developing, and language skills more strongly impact reading development.

Anglophone nations would benefit by PIRLS adding in brief, online testing of word-reading, spelling and language skills, including cognitive-processing and executive-function skills. This additional testing could be conducted within PIRLS, or as testing by individual nations or a cooperative of nations. That testing would be conducted after usual PIRLS testing was completed, to ensure it did not impact conventional PIRLS results.

Our PIRLS and PISA performance and trends have been rather similar across the years, with Australia continuing to have excessive numbers of low achievers, and a distinct lack of progress in reducing those numbers, and the extent of difficulties experienced.

In PIRLS 2016, Australia was at 21st position by Mean score, being
- Lower than 13 nations, including Ireland, Northern Ireland and England,
- At a similar level to 12 nations, including the USA, Canada and Italy.
- Higher than 24 nations, including New Zealand and France.

Australia showed modest improvement (20 points) for average and higher achievers from 2011 to 2016, which is pleasing. Alas, there was no improvement as regards our weaker readers.

PIRLS uses four achievement levels: Advanced (625 points), High (550), Intermediate (475) and Low (400). Australia has set Intermediate (475) as our proficient level, i.e., our pass standard.

The Australian Mean in 2016 was 544 points, in the Intermediate range, and close below High. As regards our spread of achievers,
- 16% of children were in the Advanced category (≥625 points).
- 35% were at High level (550 to 624 points).
- 30% were at Intermediate (475 to 549 points).
- 12% were at Low (400 to 474 points).
- 7% were below Low (<400 points).

In comparison, leading nations Russia and Singapore had Means close to Advanced level (625 points), with about 25% of children in the Advanced category, and almost no children achieving below Low level (1% and 3%, respectively).

Australia's PISA Performance

The *Program for International Student Assessment* (PISA) assesses the Reading, Science and Maths skills of our 15-year-old high-school students (Thomson et al., 2019).

Australia's involvement in PISA is major, e.g., over 14,000 students and their teachers, in 740 high schools were involved in PISA 2018.

As with PIRLS, for reading, only reading comprehension is assessed, and Australia and other Anglophone nations would benefit greatly by also using brief, online, testing of language-skills, word-reading and executive-function skills, after PISA testing.

In PISA 2018, we were positioned 16th of 79 nations, ordered by Mean score, with 10 nations significantly ahead of us, nine at a similar level, and 58 nations significantly below us

PISA uses Levels to report student achievement. Reports state that six proficiency levels are used, but given the lowest level, Level 1 is reported at three sub-levels, numbers are actually reported at eight levels. Using United Nations *Sustainable Development Goals*, Level 2 proficiency is set internationally as the minimum level of proficiency, which all children should reach by end of high school.

Nations decide the PISA level they will use as their national criteria for minimum proficiency: Australia uses Level 3. In PISA 2018, 59% of Australian children achieved at or above Level 3 competency (≥Level 3). Of the 41% of children below competency level, half were at Level 2, and half were below it.

Importantly, from 2000 to 2018, Australia's numbers of High achievers (Levels 5 and 6) have steadily dropped as our numbers of Low (< Level 2) achievers have increased, a pattern that's present in all test areas: Reading, Maths and Science.

The OECD Mean and Standard Deviation for PISA 2018 were 487 and 99 score points respectively. Australia's Mean was 503 points, and equalled our 2015 Mean. This means we did not continue the decline Australia has had across previous PISA rounds.

That said, our 2018 Mean is markedly lower than our PISA 2000 Mean of 528. For reading, OECD estimates 33 points as equivalent to a year of schooling, so a drop of 25 points is sizeable.

Not surprisingly, Australia was considerably below PISA leading nations for reading, e.g., was, on average, 1.5 and 1.3 years of schooling, respectively, below leading China (BSJZ) and Singapore.

While Australia's scores have declined over time, many nations have progressed, improving significantly across the years.

As examples, in their first PISA round, Canada, Hong Kong (China), Ireland and Korea achieved at the same level as Australia, while Estonia, Macao (China) and Poland were significantly below. All seven nations have progressed across PISA cycles, and achieved significantly above Australia in PISA 2018.

In addition, Taiwan, Denmark, Germany, Norway, Sweden, UK and USA, seven nations that previously were significantly below Australia, have also progressed significantly, to now achieve at the same level as Australia in PISA 2018.

Research Tour 8. Our Too Many Low Literacy Achievers

The figure below shows Mean PISA Reading scores from PISA 2000 to 2018 for Australia and other Anglophone nations.

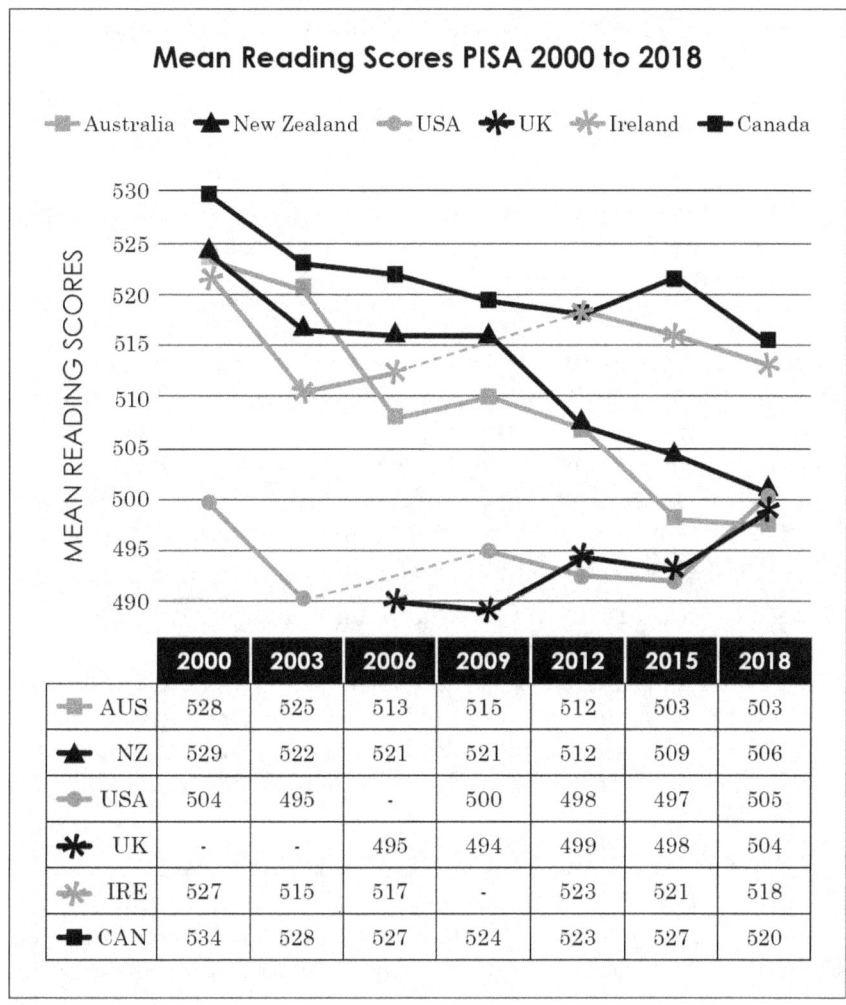

Figure 14. Mean reading scores of Anglophone nations, PISA 2000 to 2018

Canada and Ireland consistently achieve higher, and may have much to teach us. The UK and USA are trending upwards, which is encouraging, though they're still well below many high-achieving nations. And Australia and New Zealand continue downwards.

Australia achieved well, on average, in PISA 2000 and 2003, as our high-achievers' scores compensated for the low scores of our large numbers of weak readers. Then, from 2006, we dropped, relative to both our PISA 2000 levels, and other nations' superior levels.

In contrast, many regular-orthography nations improved from PISA 2000, not just in Reading, but also in Science and Maths. It doesn't seem an education expenditure issue, as nations with quite small economies, e.g., Estonia and Poland, show good improvement. For nations with strong orthographic or multilingual advantage, with their highly literate school populations, it's much easier to improve education.

As PISA results show, Anglophone nations struggle, achieving Mean scores well below top level. Our lower achievement quite likely reflects our too slow early-literacy development, too high workload, and too many struggling learners.

Canada and Ireland consistently achieve highest of Anglophone nations, and case-study research of their education and early-literacy teaching and learning would be valuable. They possibly experience multilingual advantage, as children learn two national languages from start of school (French, in Canada; Irish in Ireland). It's also possible that more effective instruction is involved. Further, they may well have stronger word-reading (Etmanskie et al., 2016; Parrila et al., 2005).

New Zealand is also a bilingual nation and thus should experience similar multilingualism advantage, but doesn't evidence Canada's and Ireland's high achievement. That may be due to insufficiently effective word-reading instruction for at-risk learners (Prochnow et al., 2013; G. Thompson et al., 2008; Tunmer et al., 2013). It may also be due to Māori and Standard-English vowel sounds differing in confusing ways.

Excessively high numbers of struggling readers seem an integral aspect of Australia's intransigent difficulties in improving reading instruction and outcomes. As an example, in 2009 PISA, which, like PISA 2018, focused in depth on reading, Australia was ninth of 48 nations, equal to New Zealand and Netherlands, and significantly below six nations (Shanghai-China, Korea, Finland, Hong Kong-China, Singapore and Canada).

While that might seem respectable, when numbers of weak readers are considered, it's less so: whereas Shanghai-China, the highest performing nation, had 6% of readers at or below Level 2 (baseline proficiency level), with only 3% actually below Level 2, Australia had 33% at or below Level 2, and 13% below Level 2. With our increasing numbers of Low achievers, by PISA 2018, that 33% has expanded to 41%.

By considering our PISA 2009 results, we can also think on

generational disadvantage, the extent to which our parents with weak literacy struggle to support our current generation of school children. The PISA 2009 15-year-olds turn 29 in 2023, and many would now be parents of current school children. In PISA 2009, 27% of girls and 43% of boys were at or below Level 2, and 9% of girls and 20% of boys were below Level 2, i.e., severely struggling.

Those 2009 statistics show three pertinent findings:
- Australia has excessive numbers of struggling readers in both primary and high-school years.
- We've excessive numbers of weak readers in our current generation of parents, who will be having difficulty supporting their children's language and literacy development.
- Given that high-school results build from the effectiveness of all earlier school years, optimising reading instruction and outcomes is an issue for all school years.

Our low achievers, our Spelling Generations, are our nemesis, our flood of struggling Australians for whom education has failed. Too many of that PISA 2009 generation, today's parents, missed out on effective literacy instruction, and Australia's PISA 2018 results show the same sad tale continues. We've not improved, and too many Australians are struggling. Improvement is certainly needed.

Major NAPLAN Struggles

Australia's annual reading-comprehension results in NAPLAN (*National Assessment Program – Literacy and Numeracy*) continue to show our many struggling readers and writers, with Standard Deviations (SDs) for all states and territories being extremely large.

Our 2021 and 2022 NAPLAN results show girls achieving higher than boys, far too many indigenous children severely struggling, and Socio-Economic Status (SES) a major restrictive factor, with children with parents of less education and lower earnings achieving much lower than children of high SES.

Importantly, our NAPLAN reports seem to exaggerate our number of successful learners, e.g., our PIRLS and PISA results show significantly more struggling readers and fewer high achievers.

Using 2021 NAPLAN data, let's consider first our Year 3 children's results. They're products of our Early Years Factory, the effectiveness of our education across our first school years. The table below shows the percentage of Australian Year 3 children at or below our National Minimum Standard (≤NMS) on the 2021 NAPLAN tests. I've included scores for the full Year 3 cohort, and also those for gender, indigeneity and SES. As regards SES, I've compared scores for children whose parents completed university with children whose parents finished school prior to or in Year 11, and did not complete high school.

2021 % Yr3 Students ≤ NMS		Reading	Writing	Spelling	Grammar & Punctuation	Mean % Literacy	Mean % Numeracy
All Students		11%	8%	14%	13%	11%	15%
Gender	Boys	14%	10%	17%	15%	14%	14%
	Girls	9%	5%	12%	10%	9%	15%
Indigeneity	Indigenous	37%	30%	41%	41%	37%	44%
	Non-Indigenous	10%	6%	13%	11%	10%	13%
SES (Parent Education)	Low SES	33%	25%	37%	37%	33%	40%
	High SES	4%	3%	6%	5%	5%	6%

Table 2. 2021 NAPLAN Year 3 low achievers (≤NMS)

The table shows our percentage of children in the lowest two NAPLAN bands, plus children exempted from NAPLAN on the basis of being recent immigrants still struggling with English, or children with severe disabilities, i.e., severely struggling learners unlikely to achieve beyond the lowest band. It's important to include numbers in the exempt category in our numbers of low achievers, as it's common for parents of struggling readers and their schools to request that struggling readers seek exemption.

For all year levels, NAPLAN results use six bands, two each for low, healthy and high achievement. Severely-low children in the lowest band are below the National Minimum Standard (<NMS) and those in the second band are at the National Minimum Standard (=NMS).

The table shows, on average, girls achieve higher than boys on literacy skills, with significantly fewer girls in the bottom band (<NMS). It

Research Tour 8. Our Too Many Low Literacy Achievers

also shows how low SES and being indigenous are strongly linked to very low academic achievement. With low-SES and indigeneity numbers being similar, it's likely many indigenous children are disadvantaged largely through factors related to low SES.

While I've analysed 2021 NAPLAN data, the 2022 data is similar, e.g., the ACARA press release announcing the 2022 results commented,
> Results [are] mostly stable at a national level from 2021 to 2022, apart from a decrease in Year 5 numeracy and Year 9 spelling. When looking at the National Minimum Standard (NMS), the percentage of Year 9 boys achieving the NMS in reading has fallen to its lowest level, below 90 per cent, with 13.5 percent not achieving the NMS this year, compared to fewer than 8.5 per cent in 2008. It is certainly concerning that we have so many students who are not demonstrating the capacity to read at this basic level only a few years before they leave school.

Let's now consider our 2021 weak achievers in Years 3, 5, 7 and 9.

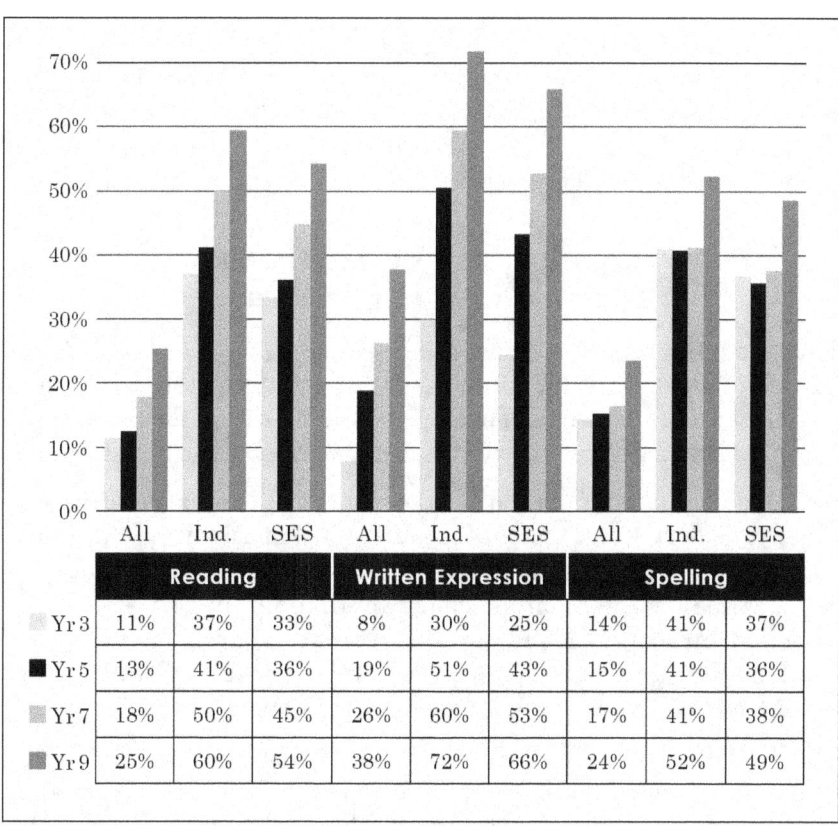

	Reading			Written Expression			Spelling		
	All	Ind.	SES	All	Ind.	SES	All	Ind.	SES
Yr 3	11%	37%	33%	8%	30%	25%	14%	41%	37%
Yr 5	13%	41%	36%	19%	51%	43%	15%	41%	36%
Yr 7	18%	50%	45%	26%	60%	53%	17%	41%	38%
Yr 9	25%	60%	54%	38%	72%	66%	24%	52%	49%

Figure 15. *2021 NAPLAN Year 3, 5, 7, 9 low achievers (% of cohort ≤NMS) for reading, written expression and spelling*

The Research Tours: Impacts of Orthographic Disadvantage

I've used a reduced amount of data for ease of viewing in the figure, and the results for indigenous children and children with low SES can only be compared with the full-cohort results. The indigeneity and SES contrasts are actually much higher, when they're contrasted with non-indigenous and high-SES groups.

Oh dear! That data is depressing. Not only does Australia have excessive numbers of low achievers, but we're also a consistent pattern of increasing numbers of struggling learners across year-levels – numbers achieving in our lowest two bands increase from Year 3 through to Year 9, in all areas assessed in NAPLAN.

There are a few possible reasons for that trend.

One is that we've a flood of struggling learners – that's quite likely true, as it fits well with our PIRLS and PISA results.

Another, less-likely, scenario is that our tests might not be optimally normed, with those increasing numbers consequently somewhat artificial – a product of the cut-offs used.

We'd learn a great deal if we conducted an Anglophone nation study, inviting other Anglophone nations to have samples of children do our NAPLAN tests, while samples of our children do their national tests. We'd learn even more by including tests of word-reading, and language skills, including associated cognitive-processing skills.

Large Standard Deviations Show Many Struggling Learners

Let's now explore the information we can gain from considering Standard Deviations (SDs). As discussed in earlier tours, it's useful to consider the lower half of achievers by subtracting the SD from the Mean to show the scores achieved by Standard Deviation (SD) subgroups.

You'll recall from our early discussion, that in a Normal Distribution, when considering test scores of the lower 50% of achievers, the SD cut-points show the scores children in the SD groups are likely to achieve:
- 1 SD below the Mean is where approximately 34.1% of children score: they're our low-average group.
- 1-2 SD is a further 13.6% group of significantly low achievers.
- 2-3 SD is a 2.1% group of very low achievers.
- >3 SD is a minute 0.13% group of extremely low achievers.

Quite a few tests and research studies use 1 SD below the Mean as their cut-point to identify children with significant weakness. That 15.9% group that's more than 1 SD below the Mean can be considered as struggling learners. We'll explore that struggling learner group now. Rounding up, we can say that, when using a 1 SD cut-point, 34% of a full population are in the low average range, while 16% are struggling *Low* achievers.

Thus, using the Means and SDs for our full 2021 cohorts of Year 3, 5, 7 and 9 children, by Australian standards, 34% of the children are above the cut-point, at low-average level, and the 16% of children below it can be considered struggling learners.

We can then use that information to explore how our vulnerable subgroups measure up against that 16% standard: our indigenous children and our children with low SES backgrounds.

We've no NAPLAN or other systemic word-reading data to use, so I'm using the 2021 NAPLAN spelling data here instead. Many studies establish spelling as somewhat a proxy for word-reading: it's not a replacement or preferred choice, but can suffice as a stand-in when a nation, incredibly, has no systemic word-reading data.

2021 Cohorts		Year 3	Year 5	Year 7	Year 9
Full Cohort	*Mean*	421	504	548	580
	SD	89	73	70	69
	1SD Score	332	431	478	511
	% ≤ NMS	14%	15%	17%	24%
Indigenous Cohort	*Mean*	344	443	492	524
	SD	104	85	77	74
	1SD Score	240	358	415	450
	% ≤ NMS	41%	41%	41%	52%
Low SES Cohort #	*Mean*	358	456	502	534
	% ≤ NMS	35%	36%	38%	49%

% ≤ NMS: Proportion of the cohort achieving at or below the NAPLAN National Minimum Standard (NMS).
SD: Standard Deviation
1SD Score: NAPLAN score for children who achieve at 1SD below the mean
No data on Standard Deviation (SD) was provided for this area.

Table 3. 2021 NAPLAN Year 3, 5, 7 and 9 low achievers for spelling (% of cohort ≤NMS)

Word-reading and spelling are similar skills in many ways, and children's spelling levels are often close to their word-reading levels for reading unfamiliar words, e.g., using the TOWRE-2's *Phonemic Decoding Efficiency* subtest. Spelling is sometimes not overly close to reading of familiar words: children with late-emerging word-reading often have strong word-reading for familiar words, but weakness for spelling and reading of unfamiliar words.

The table shows our Standard Deviations (SDs) to be large, e.g., for the 2021 Year 3 children, the SD is 89 points, and, for Years 5 to 9, SDs range from 73 for Year 5 to 69 for Year 9. Then, the SDs for indigenous children are larger still, from 104 to 74. Unfortunately, no SDs were reported for SES factors, e.g., for parent education.

Now, as regards high achievers, SDs of that size are encouraging, e.g., they show we've at least 16% who are doing impressively well. For our lower achievers, however, they clearly show our weakest 16% of children are seriously struggling. They're struggling for spelling, and, using spelling as a proxy for word-reading, it's highly likely they are also significantly weak word-readers.

The Means for our indigenous children in each year-level are sadly low. Indeed, they're actually very close to the 1SD cut-points for the full year-level cohort: that indicates that it's not just our weakest 16% of indigenous children who are struggling, but also the next 34% as well. Quite likely, at least half of our indigenous children are seriously struggling spellers, and, by proxy, also struggling for word-reading of unfamiliar words.

While the NAPLAN report didn't provide SDs for parent education, the figures for the percentage of children achieving at or below the National Minimum Standard (NMS) are extremely high. That suggests, we've quite likely at least 40-50% of children who've low SES struggling with spelling, using Australian standards.

From considering SDs and the percentage achieving at or below our NMS, it's clear that, even by Australian standards, we've excessive numbers of weak spellers. Then, with spelling a proxy for word-reading, we quite likely have similarly excessive numbers who struggle to read unfamiliar words: at least 16% of all children, 50% of indigenous children, and 40-50% of low-SES children.

That seems in keeping with findings of Australian small word-reading studies, e.g., our CQU team explored the use of a range of quick-to-use word-reading efficiency tests in collaborative research with schools in one Queensland region. The *Dynamic Indicators of Basic Early Literacy Skills* (DIBELS, Good et al., 2002) was used with children in Years 1 to 3 (Galletly & Knight, 2006), while the Test of Word Reading Efficiency was used with children in Years 1 to 8 (Galletly, 2008; Galletly et al., 2009; Knight & Galletly, 2006).

We found our children's word-reading results were quite similar to those of USA children, with perhaps 20% of children having major difficulties, and one third considerably below healthy progress.

Our Increasing Numbers of Weak Learners

If our tests are well normed for establishing our children in the lowest two bands – and our large SDs suggest they quite probably are – the tables and figures above, showing our percentages of low achievers really are quite frightening. They show our percentages of struggling readers and writers steadily increasing across year-levels for the 2021 cohort, from Years 3 to 9. For reading, writing and spelling, the proportion of children at or below our NMS rises steadily upwards: starting from Year 3, it rises to Year 5, then rises further to Year 7 then further again to Year 9.

Those rising percentages are a very compelling statement on the ineffectiveness of Australian education for our at-risk children. We're failing to rescue children and provide effective intervention, plus we're also steadily and drastically adding to their numbers across the school years. The numbers say it all, with our early-years flood of struggling readers seeming but a trickle relative to our flood of struggling high-school learners.

Our 10 Changes improvements are clearly vitally needed.

Of Word-Reading and Language Skill Struggles

Let's now try to consider our Australian situation using Simple View model perspectives, of
Reading Comprehension = Word-Reading x Language Skills.

Alas, we've no systemic word-reading or language skills data, so it's time for proxies again.

We can use spelling as a proxy for word-reading, as we did, above. We can also use reading-comprehension and written expression as proxies for language skills, as both reading comprehension and written expression build strongly from language skills.

So let's consider children's spelling, reading-comprehension and written-expression skills, in their NAPLAN Reading and Writing results, as to what they suggest on word-reading and language skills.

If our NAPLAN tests are well normed, we've an appreciable number of struggling spellers who quite likely also have word-reading difficulties: a quarter of Year 9 children, and, from Year 5 on, about two fifths of indigenous and low-SES children.

They show, as per Figure 15, above, that, by Year 9, we've a quarter of children struggling with reading comprehension, and almost 40% struggling with written expression. For our indigenous and low-SES children, 40-50% of children are seriously struggling by Year 5. Written expression seems to impact our indigenous and low-SES children harder than reading does: about 10% more children are at low level for writing.

Importantly, our having far more weak writers than weak spellers suggests weak language skills are an issue for many weak writers. That seems in keeping with the Australian Education Research Organisation's (AERO, 2022) report analysing a decade of NAPLAN writing results. It found declining skills for persuasive writing (which build strongly from language skills). It also found declining NAPLAN writing achievement, widening gaps between high and low achievers, and greater declines across high school years.

Our NAPLAN data does show quite firm indicators that we've considerable word-reading and language-skills weakness especially in older children and our indigenous and low-SES cohorts.

Is our steady increase in numbers of struggling readers a Fourth Grade Slump issue? Are word-reading and spelling a major issue? Is weakness in language skills a major issue. Most likely, it's all of these. Research is needed.

Let's Reset our National Minimum Standard (NMS)

In our 10 Changes, Change 2 is *Own our struggling reader woes: End hypocrisy and pretence*. As part of that, in Australia's actioning of Change 2, we need to investigate the appropriateness of levels we've set for our NAPLAN National Minimum Standards (NMS).

Our National Minimum Standards (NMS) seem set embarrassingly low. Whereas USA reports speak openly of e.g., 66-71% of Grade 4 and Grade 8 children scoring at or below basic, Australia confidently asserts that 95.9% and 95.91% of our 2021 Year 3 and Year 5 children achieved higher than our NMS.

Figures such as those are a nonsense. They hide the realities of our children's, teachers' and schools' struggles, and fuel cynicism. As an example, the only comment on literacy and education in the

Australian Institute of Health and Welfare's 2020 *Australia's Children* report implies Australian education is thriving, stating in the executive summary (AIHW, 2020):

The proportion of Year 5 students achieving at or above the national minimum standard for reading and numeracy increased between 2008 and 2018. Reading increased from 91% to 95% and numeracy from 93% to 96%.

That comment epitomises the Change 2 hypocrisy and pretence that Australia needs to address. AIHW is quite likely a victim of confident reporting, that focuses overly on NMS data.

Given our too many low achievers in international PIRLS and PISA comparisons, setting our NMS so low seems highly inappropriate. Many recommendations have been made in recent years to rebrand NAPLAN (e.g., McGaw et al., 2020). In achieving useful reforms, let's align NAPLAN reading-comprehension and numeracy levels with PIRLS, *Trends in International Mathematics and Science Study* (TIMMS; maths) and PISA achievement levels, so that NAPLAN's low, average and high achievement bands align with PIRLS, TIMMS and PISA low, average and high achievement levels.

Until then, let's end our NAPLAN reports detailing just our numbers *below* the NMS (our numbers achieving at appallingly low levels), and instead report numbers *at and below* the NMS: children in the lowest two NAPLAN bands. That's practical and useful, given that healthy achievement starts at the third band. It may also reduce the low esteem many have for NAPLAN (Fachinetti, 2015).

Importantly, it seems inappropriate that NAPLAN data doesn't align with the large numbers of weak readers Australia has in PISA and PIRLS. PIRLS and PISA reading data has far more low achievers:

- Figures as low as 11.4% for NAPLAN Year 3 low achievers (in 2021) contrast markedly with 19.0% of PISA Year 4 low achievers (in 2016), suggesting NAPLAN's cut-point is too low.
- Figures as low as 25.4% for NAPLAN Year 9 low achievers (in 2021) contrast markedly with 40.7% of PISA 15-year-old low achievers (in 2018), again suggesting a too-low cut-point.

There does seem value in resetting NAPLAN NMS cut-offs, to more adequately report our numbers of struggling learners.

Key Findings from Tour 8

Findings and implications from considering lower achievers in 2021 NAPLAN testing suggests the following considerations towards

improving literacy development and education:
1. In literacy development,
   a. Word-reading and language skills are key skills integral to effective reading comprehension, and
   b. Spelling and language skills are key skills integral to effective written expression.
2. In our systemic NAPLAN testing of our children's literacy skills in Year 3, 5, 7 and 9, we assess reading comprehension, written expression, spelling, and grammar and punctuation, thus
   a. We assess the key skills for written expression, but
   b. We fail to assess the key skills for reading comprehension.
3. Given English orthographic complexity has major impacts on word-reading and language-skills development and literacy development, and many children start school with language weakness, we need to add systemic testing of language skills and word-reading skills to NAPLAN testing.
4. Our 2021 NAPLAN results show our numbers of struggling learners increase steadily and markedly across the school years. In addition, while our numbers also rise in this steady fashion for our indigenous children and children with low-SES, they show vastly more struggling learners:
   a. For Reading Comprehension, they rise from
      i. 11% in Year 3, to 25% in Year 9, for all children.
      ii. 37% in Year 3, to 60% in Year 9, for indigenous children.
      iii. 33% in Year 3, to 54% in Year 9, for children with low SES.
   b. For Writing, they rise from
      i. 8% in Year 3, to 38% in Year 9, for all children.
      ii. 30% in Year 3, to 72% in Year 9, for indigenous children.
      iii. 25% in Year 3, to 66% in Year 9, for children with low SES.
   c. For Spelling, they rise from
      i. 14% in Year 3, to 24% in Year 9, for all children.
      ii. 13% in Year 3, to 52% in Year 9, for indigenous children.
      iii. 35% in Year 3, to 49% in Year 9, for children with low SES.
5. Our 2021 Standard Deviations (SDs) were high for our all-children totals, and extremely high for our indigenous children and children with low SES. This suggests that while we have healthy-progress and high achievers doing well, we also have at least 16% of children with major literacy difficulties, including

at least 50% of indigenous children and children with low SES.
6. If our NAPLAN tests are well normed and valid, our numbers of struggling learners increasing so consistently from Year 3 to Year 9 in 2021 seems evidence of severely ineffective education for our at-risk learners, to perhaps an unethical level, with needs to improve education and supports, and research this area.
7. Australia needs research to establish our children's word-reading levels for reading of both familiar and unfamiliar words.
8. If we consider spelling a proxy for children's word-reading (due to there not being systemic word-reading data to consider), using systemic spelling numbers, it's likely we have perhaps a quarter of all children, and half of our indigenous children and children with low SES, significantly weak on word-reading for reading of unfamiliar words.
9. Our numbers of struggling writers being so much higher than our numbers of struggling spellers suggests that
   a. Weak language skills contribute strongly to our children's weak written expression skills, and
   b. We need strong assessment and instruction emphases focused on building children's language-for-literacy skills.
   We need research to clarify this.
10. Our failing to systemically assess and emphasise word-reading and language skills may mean we've many children in primary and high school with weak skills in these areas.
11. This undetected weakness may be a factor in
    a. Why so many of our indigenous children and children with low SES are struggling so badly, and
    b. Why we have increasing numbers of struggling learners as children progress through school.
    We need research to clarify this.
12. Indigenous achievement levels being similar to low-SES achievement levels suggests that disadvantage for our indigenous children is likely largely through low-SES factors, with educational disadvantage from start of school being currently a massive factor impeding our children's learning.
13. It also shows that Australian education is not overcoming the disadvantage that our children start school with.
14. This must change, given that
    a. Our Education Act, UN Agreements and Alice Springs (Mparntwe) Declaration promise our children an effective education, and
    b. In regular-orthography nations, low SES and other factors that are major risk factors in Anglophone nations don't impede literacy development and academic progress.

15. Australia would benefit from studies re-norming our NAPLAN tests against the levels of other Anglophone nations, and PIRLS and PISA studies, to ensure we are using appropriate cut-offs for low, average and high achievement, e.g., with a large sample of Australian children doing the national tests of other Anglophone nations, and samples of children from those nations doing NAPLAN tests.
16. Our National Minimum Standard (NMS) is inappropriately low.
17. It seems ethically questionable for reports to publish only numbers below the NMS, (numbers in the lowest NAPLAN band), rather than our numbers at and below the NMS (numbers in the two lowest bands), as this reporting can give an inappropriate sense that Australia is doing particularly well, e.g., it seems that 95.9% and 95.91% of our 2021 Year 3 and Year 5 children are thriving. Far more children have major difficulties, and these figures contrast markedly with our numbers of low achievers in PIRLS and PISA studies.
18. There seems value in aligning NAPLAN reporting of Years 3 and 5 with PIRLS achievement bands, and aligning reporting of Year 9 with PISA achievement bands.

Research Tour 9.
Needs for Workload Research

> *Australian children spend vastly more hours at school than children in many higher-achieving nations ... and Australian teachers have far more teaching hours than teachers in those nations. ... Australian funding of education is respectable, as are Australian teacher salaries. Yet outcomes are not improving. ...*
>
> *PISA results show Australia to be a very low-progress nation ... Australia, with its deep and complex orthography, is experiencing major difficulties optimising reading and literacy instruction ... Failure to address students' instructional needs has major long-term ramifications ...*
>
> *Australian primary-school teaching conditions are challenging given our high learning and teaching hours. Our student: teacher ratio (15.6) and class sizes (17.9) are considerably higher than [many nations with vastly easier early-literacy learning], e.g., Finland (13.2, 12.3) and Estonia (13.0, 13.9).*
>
> Bruce Knight & Susan Galletly, 2017

Ouch! That quote is somewhat depressing. The good news is that the difficulties it lists are certainly not set in cement. It's showing us our starting point, where we are now, before Australia actions 10 Changes improvements (Galletly, 2022a, In press).

We're about to head off on our ninth research tour. Having toured a considerable amount of research and discussion across the last eight tours, let's recap briefly, on what we've learned so far.

Tours 1 to 4 explored the major impacts of orthographic complexity:
- **Tour 1.** Too slow Standard-English word-reading development.
- **Tour 2.** Orthography: The key impacting factor.

- **Tour 3.** Success Inoculation vs Acquired Helplessness.
- **Tour 4.** Regular orthographies and intellectual disability.

Tour 5, *The power of beginners' orthographies*, then showed us the power and potential of fully-regular beginners' orthographies.

It showed us, too, how our story is not all sad and bad. By moving from 1-Stage to 2-Stage early literacy, initially using a fully-regular beginners' orthography, prior to Standard English, Australia and Anglophone nations have enormous potential for improvement, in early-literacy development, school learning and school life.

Then off we went on Tours 6 to 8:
- **Tour 6.** Our epidemic of language weakness.
- **Tour 7.** Literacy components and quadrants.
- **Tour 8.** Our many low literacy achievers.

They showed us our current reality, with Australia having definite needs for improvement. We've far too many at-risk and low achievers, and sad impacts of generational disadvantage (Galletly, 2022a, In press; Knight et al., 2019): too many children starting school with language weakness and other risk factors that set them up for failure.

Nicely, Tour 7 also showed us the power of quadrants: empowering education by establishing children's instructional needs more precisely, towards strategically tailoring the instruction we provide.

Fortunately, in showing our problems and potential, all eight tours build the importance, value and potential of each of the 10 Changes. They're strategies for expediting improvement (Galletly, 2022a):

Change 1. Understand how orthographies matter: English spelling is dragging us down.

Change 2. Own our struggling reader woes: End hypocrisy and pretence.

Change 3. Weigh workload: Our children and teachers are working far too hard.

Change 4. One-size education does not fit all: Teach to the decidedly different instructional needs of upper-third and lower-third readers.

Change 5. End our data deficiency: Build strong knowledge on word-reading levels.

Change 6. Enrich every child: Ensure effective supportive tailored education.

Change 7. Insist on easy literacy development: Reach regular-orthography nations' achievement levels.

Change 8. Investigate the potential of fully-regular beginners'

orthographies: They're winners.
Change 9. Play to learn first: Start Standard-English word-reading instruction from mid-Year 2.
Change 10. Build needed research knowledge as quickly as possible: Use collaborative school-based research.

The tours have shown us, too, the ABCs' power and potential, as tools for our future improvement journey (Galletly, 2022a):
A. **ACT** locally while looking globally.
B. **BOOST** the lower-third to benefit everyone.
C. **CHANGE** effectively to work less and achieve more.

So off we go on Tour 9, *Needs for Workload Research.* It's practical, interesting, useful and important. Workload, our children's and our teachers', will prove a key factor in our current difficulties and needs for improvement, and in the improvements that we achieve.

Workload: A Key Factor Towards Improving Education

Change 3 of our 10 Changes is *Weigh workload: Our children and teachers are working far too hard.*

If we're to improve education here in Australia, we desperately need research on workload impacts. They're a massive aspect of our education woes. That's the case for both child and teacher workload. They're a key reason why education is ineffective in so many ways.

Our children have rights (McLeod, 2018). Australia has an Education Act that clearly requires us to provide a rich, well supported education for all children, including those with difficulties. We've also an inspiring 2019 *Alice Springs (Mparntwe) Education Declaration* (Council of Australian Govts Education, 2019), and are signatory to the UN *Convention on the Rights of the Child* and *Convention on the Rights of Persons with Disabilities* (UN, 1989, 2006).

It seems common for high-achieving regular-orthography nations with similar documents to provide the education that they promise to their children, thus meeting their teaching challenges.

We're not delivering, however. Australia has vastly more struggling learners and higher severity of learning difficulties than regular-orthography nations, along with massive difficulties improving education and academic achievement levels.

The chapter's introductory quote is from our 2017 research article, *Effective literacy instruction for all students: A time for change* (Knight & Galletly, 2017). It's a useful read, detailing the complexities and challenges Australian education struggles with. Its abstract reads

Australia's 2016 Senate report is highly critical of current Australian government support for children with disabilities, including children with reading and literacy difficulties, and children with language weakness and communication difficulties (Senate Standing Committee on Education and Employment, 2016). It reveals serious inadequacies of current instructional supports, inappropriate lack of transparency by education systems, and a major need to improve instruction and increasing government transparency. This paper explores the Senate report in the context of children's rights and Australian legal requirements for supporting children with literacy learning difficulties. It discusses the complexities facing Australia and other Anglophone nations endeavouring to provide effective instruction for at-risk and struggling readers.

There's every likelihood that excessive child and teacher workload lies at the heart of our struggles. It's workload that's proliferated by

- English orthographic complexity and its impacts on our developing and struggling readers.
- Word-reading and spelling development taking excessively long for all children, including our upper and middle-third.
- Our too many struggling readers.
- Our language weakness epidemic.

The workload impacts our children and teachers experience are excessive, e.g., they're not compensated for by our children being at school for 300 more hours annually than leading nations (Knight & Galletly, 2017; OECD, 2015, 2022).

Australia has the usual workload all nations have for subject-area learning. Then we've the additional workload acquired through, e.g.,

- Using solely Standard English, instead of starting with a beginners' orthography.
- Starting our children so young on this complex learning.
- Insufficient allied-health supports prior to and at school.
- Requiring teachers to do much longer class-teaching hours.
- The time pressure these factors create.
- Inadequately resourcing our schools, with particularly major insufficiencies for at-risk and struggling learners, e.g., relative to Finnish and USA schools (M. Aro, 2017b; US Govt, 2004a, 2004b).

We thus need research, both locally and with regular-orthography nations, investigating child and teacher workload and its impacts.

In that research, we could use hours of teaching and learning as a proxy for child and teacher workload, as, logically, work takes time. Hours needed to achieve common learning goals here in Australia and in regular-orthography nations will likely prove a useful workload measure – with value added when we report on hours needed for thirds, tenths, and the lowest and highest 5% and 2% of achievers.

Within workload research, we'll also benefit by studying the extent of stress and cognitive load that children and teachers experience in those workload hours, e.g., using physiological measures including sweat levels and eye responses (Knight & Galletly, 2020).

Let's also study resourcing as part of workload impacts, given additional resourcing can reduce teacher workload.

Importantly, let's also compare the workload impacts of
- Australia using current resourcing and requirements.
- Australia using estimated levels of needed resourcing.
- Other Anglophone nations using different types and levels of school resourcing.
- Nations using sole regular orthographies, e.g., Finland, Estonia and South Korea.
- Nations using 2-stage early literacy, regular-orthography then complex orthography, e.g., Taiwan, Japan and China.

Research We Could Work From

I'd love to be discussing rich research with detailed findings on
- Child and teacher workload, in Australia and other nations.
- The workload impacts of nations' curriculum expectations.
- The impacts of ongoing high cognitive load Anglophone children experience due to Standard-English word-reading and spelling requiring much effort in primary and high-school years.

It's Swiss-cheese research time, alas, with many gaps to fill.

For many decades, Australian school leaders have been calling for urgent action (Angus et al., 2004, 2007; APPA, 2008a, 2008b; Galletly et al., 2010). Fortunately, momentum is building, showing change is necessary, with recent Australian reports being useful towards filling gaps and establishing directions (e.g., Gallop et al., 2021; Hunter et al., 2022; Productivity Commission, 2022).

The 2022 report, *Review of the National School Reform Agreement* (Productivity Commission, 2022) is very useful reading on this area.

Working from its 2021 survey of 5,000 teachers and 442 school leaders, the Grattan Institute's 2022 report, *Making time for great teaching: How better government policy can help,* usefully emphasises the role of government responsibilities (Hunter et al., 2022; Sonnemann & Joiner, 2022), and needs for urgent reforms:

> Governments should commit to ensuring all teachers have the time needed for great teaching [and] adopt three reform directions:
> • *First, let teachers teach, by better matching teachers' work to teachers' expertise:* Improve the integration of specialist and support staff in schools to help teachers focus on high-quality classroom instruction, and to ensure that non-teaching staff can perform duties that don't require teaching expertise.
> • *Second, help teachers to work smarter, by reducing unnecessary tasks:* Examine administrative activities, but also core teaching activities. Reduce the need for teachers to 're-invent the wheel' in curriculum and lesson planning.
> • *Third, rethink the ways teachers' work is organised in schools:* Ensure industrial agreements give school leaders the flexibility to strike a sensible balance between class sizes and teachers' face-to-face teaching time, and to smooth out workloads over the school year by scheduling more time for teachers to work together on preparation activities in term breaks.

While adding holiday work to our already time-stressed teachers is a concern we'd need to address, the recommendations are pertinent, plus they make a further recommendation, for governments to action a $60,000,000 5-year research project on these reform directions, which would quite likely focus on achieving effective workload.

The New South Wales Teachers Federation report, *Valuing the teaching profession: An independent inquiry* (Gallop et al., 2021), building from its investigation into changes implemented in teaching practices in New South Wales public schools since 2004, also usefully provides pertinent information and recommendations regarding workload and resourcing.

Internationally, OECD reports including *Education at a Glance* (OECD, 2015, 2022) and the *Teaching and Learning International Survey* (TALIS), e.g., TALIS 2018, provide useful information, as do PIRLS and PISA reports (Thomson & Hillman, 2019, Thomson et al., 2017, 2019). Towards planning future research, these resources may also prove useful:

- Kennedy's (2005, 2010) work on attribution error, and needs to include teaching-situation characteristics in teaching studies.

- Sweller and colleagues' *Cognitive Load Theory* (Centre for Education Statistics and Evaluation, 2017; Sweller et al., 1998, 2019).
- Research on executive-function skills and statistical learning (e.g., Arciuli, 2018; Arciuli & Simpson, 2012; Knight & Galletly, 2020; Plante & Gómez, 2018; Ren & Wang, 2023).
- Directions suggested in Louden et al.'s (2006) Australian study, In teachers' hands: Effective literacy teaching practices in the early years of schooling.
- Pressley et al.'s (1998, 2001) work on effective and less effective literacy teaching and learning.
- Connor et al.'s work on achieving effectively tailored instruction (e.g., Connor et al., 2009, 2011, 2013, 2014, 2018; Connor, Adams, et al., 2020, Connor, Kelcey, et al., 2020; Connor & Morrison, 2016; Crowe et al., 2009; Day et al., 2015; Guo et al., 2015; McLean et al., 2016; Piasta et al., 2009; Sparapani et al., 2018, 2019; Toste et al., 2015).
- Studies on impacts of reduced class size (Hattie, 2005, 2008; Mathis, 2017; Shen & Konstantopoulos, 2017; Zyngier, 2014).
- Case study research of curriculum, teaching and family aspects of education in different nations (e.g., Stevenson, 1998; Stevenson et al., 1982, 1990; Stevenson & Nerison-Low, 2002).

Certainly, we need to be adding up the workload and stresses of upper, middle and lower-third learners and their teachers. Kennedy's (2005, 2010) useful model's including of *teaching and learning situation characteristics* is insightful, as is her work on *attribution error* and inappropriate blaming of teaching quality. She emphasises how common it is for the impacts of individual teacher quality to be overestimated by researchers and policy makers:

> *The qualities teachers bring with them to their work are not enough to ensure better teaching practices. It is what teachers actually do that is most relevant to student learning. It is time to look beyond the teacher to the teaching situation itself: the school, the classroom, the teacher's schedule, and the teacher's resources. ... We need to change our tacit model of teaching from one that looks something like this:*
> *(a) Teacher Characteristics → Teaching Practices*
> *→ Student Learning*
> *to one that looks something like this:*
> *(b) Teacher Characteristics & Situation Characteristics*
> *→ Teaching Practices → Student Learning*

Australia's currently excessive numbers of teaching improvement initiatives that schools action in response to pressure for improved NAPLAN results (*NAPLAN bullying*, Galletly, 2022a, In press), seems strong evidence that currently Australia is inappropriately actioning the first model: it positions teachers' skills as fully responsible for our children's academic results. We need to instead use the second model, which includes teacher skills but sensibly positions teaching within the teaching situation, i.e., what can be achieved in current circumstances.

Tools developed by researchers studying teaching and learning in schools will likely also prove extremely useful in workload research, e.g., Connor et al.'s observation systems, *Optimizing Learning Opportunities for Students* (OLOS) and *Creating Opportunities to Learn from Text* (COLT, Connor, Adams, et al., 2020, Connor, Kelcey, et al., 2020).

Let's Research Workload Impacts of Word-Reading and Spelling Development

Word-reading and spelling development have very major workload impacts: they lie at the heart of the wide crosslinguistic divide between regular-orthography and Anglophone nations. (Knight et al., 2019).

Where many regular-orthography nations take weeks to months for children to be confidently accurate readers, writers and self-teachers, our children take many years. Across those years, we spend hundreds of teaching and learning hours for our healthy-progress readers, in literacy and subject-area lessons, supporting and building early-literacy skills – and many hundreds more for struggling readers.

Child workload and literacy stress levels similarly differ greatly across the crosslinguistic gap. With word-reading and spelling soon accurate and automising steadily from early in primary school, regular-orthography children experience low cognitive load from literacy demands in subject-area learning.

This reduces workload as reading and writing are easy, quickly-acquired tools. In contrast, our children are slow, laborious readers and writers, who are so often working with high cognitive load, due to pausing to think on, and work out, individual, unfamiliar words. The crosslinguistic child-workload gap is consequently wide and well worth exploring.

Let's measure the teaching and learning hours involved in children learning to read and write to an *adult proficiency level*, in Australia and elsewhere, gathering data on thirds, tenths, and the lowest and highest 5% and 2% of achievers.

Let's also compare hours needed for 1-Stage and 2-Stage early-literacy development: time needed by Australian cohorts that
- Use solely Standard-English or
- Initially use a regular-orthography, prior to Standard English.

The term *adult proficiency level* is used deliberately there, rather than e.g., *healthy year-level accuracy*, in order to be ethically appropriate, as our children are entitled to the high skill levels that so many regular-orthography nations routinely achieve.

If children in many regular-orthography nations reach adult-level word-reading and spelling accuracy (Level 1 automisation) in less than a year, and adult-level fluency (Level 2 automisation) within a few years, our children are entitled to similar ease – and our actioning of research should reflect this.

Let's Research the Impacts of Orthographic Advantage and Disadvantage

Easy vs impeded word-reading and writing development leads to a host of national advantages and disadvantages (TESL; Galletly & Knight, 2011b; Knight et al., 2017a, 2019; Knight & Galletly, 2020).

As shown in Figure 16, below, our CQU team has developed Orthographic Advantage Theory to support reflection on the massive crosslinguistic differences between Anglophone and regular-orthography nations (Knight et al., 2019).

The abstract of our Orthographic Advantage Theory article reads,
Considerable research shows nations differ in orthographic complexity (regularity and consistency of spelling patterns used); that this impacts ease and speed of reading and writing development; and that, in contrast to the world's many regular-orthography nations, English word-reading and word-writing development is extremely slow, with difficulties more frequent and severe.
Orthographic Advantage Theory proposes that, according to their level of orthographic complexity, nations experience disadvantage and potential advantage in multiple areas of education and national functioning.
Building from current crosslinguistic theories and research on crosslinguistic differences, it proposes six key dimensions of orthographic advantage and disadvantage, namely:

1. Ease of early-literacy development;
2. Simplified school instruction and learning across primary and secondary school;
3. Ease of improving education;
4. Impacts of reduced workplace illiteracy;
5. Increased adult life advantage; and
6. Generational advantage through confidently literate parents being able to effectively support their children's literacy development.

This article details Orthographic Advantage Theory, reviewing research findings that show the major differences in reading development and outcomes in regular-orthography and Anglophone nations. The theory is offered as a tool for educators and researchers towards optimising reading and literacy outcomes.

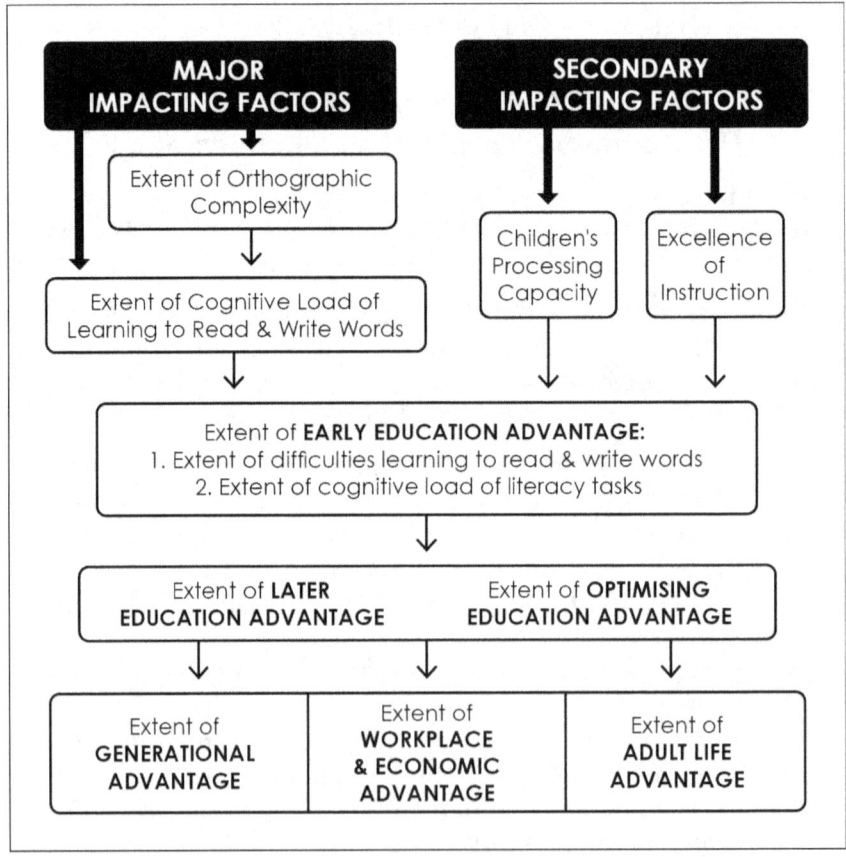

Figure 16. Orthographic Advantage Theory (Galletly & Knight, 2004; Knight et al., 2017a, 2017b, 2019)

Let's research the workload impacts of orthographic advantage and disadvantage. They're prolific, e.g., *The 10 Changes: The Nitty Gritty*, which partners this book, details 50 aspects of severe orthographic disadvantage we experience, and most of them involve workload.

Let's include focus on factors that Orthographic Advantage Theory emphasises, in particular, the workload hours associated with
- Ease of learning to read and write, and becoming confident highly-accurate independent readers and writers.
- Ease of teaching and learning across primary and high school.
- Ease of improving reading and education outcomes.
- Adults having the life advantages of high literacy.
- Generational advantage, through parents being proficiently literate and thus able to read to their children and support their literacy development.

Let's also explore workload aspects of associated factors, including
- National literacy levels.
- Extent of risk factors impacting learning to read and write.
- Extent of cognitive load children and teachers experience as children learn to read and write.
- Ease of developing phonemic awareness, and other cognitive-processing skills, within word-reading and spelling development.
- The impact of these cognitive-processing skills on children transitioning to learning a complex orthography.
- School and home hours used in learning to read and write.
- Child and teacher workload for using fledgling literacy skills in subject-area lessons.
- Numbers of children and adults with word-reading and writing difficulties, and the severity of their difficulties.
- Extent of early-years resourcing needed to achieve effective literacy in at least 98% of our school children.
- The extent of resourcing needed for remediation of literacy learning difficulties.
- Socio-Economic Status (SES) impacts increasing likelihood of learning difficulties.
- Ease of improving education.
- Workplace literacy levels.

Let's Take Account of Hurdles Nations Have Overcome

In considering workload impacts in regular-orthography nations, let's appreciate the major hurdles high-achieving nations have endured, as many have achieved massive improvement despite immense adversity.

Japan and Korea had huge infrastructural, cultural and personal struggles during and following World War II, and Taiwan only began as a nation from that time, yet all three nations quite quickly achieved outstanding national economic and literacy levels. It's not coincidental that for all three nations, their improvement began from the time they enacted 2-Stage early-literacy, and introduced beginners' orthographies.

Achieving so well despite such major adversity makes these nations powerful role models for just how strongly regular orthographies can contribute to, and expedite, strong improvement.

Estonia's disadvantaging is more recent, making it a useful role model. Following World War II, Estonia was under Russian occupation and had a communist economy from 1945 until 1991, when it moved back to democratic rule. Despite its small economy, its improvement over the past two decades has been massive.

I first visited Estonia in 2005. While far ahead of us for reading and writing development, from resourcing perspectives, education in Australia seemed well ahead of Estonia, then, where

- Class size was big, often well above 35.
- The curriculum in many ways seemed unexciting.
- Support for children with difficulties seemed minimal.
- Classroom resourcing seemed relatively poor.

When I subsequently visited in 2017, there'd been massive improvement, with class size now much smaller, classrooms far better equipped, and a strong focus on children receiving needed supports, with allied-health support staff much involved.

Estonia's PISA improvement over time has thus been impressive to watch. Estonia joined PISA in 2006, the third PISA round. It started as a comparatively low achiever in PISA 2006 and was low in PISA 2009 – lower than Australia, in fact. Since then, it's improved greatly, to now being a leading nation.

PISA 2009 and 2015 data analysis focused strongly on reading gains. Reading improvement gains from PISA 2009 to PISA 2015 showed Estonia achieved 2.7% fewer lower achievers and 5.0% more higher achievers. We did the opposite, lost in both areas, with 3.8% more lower achievers and 1.7% less higher achievers.

In having achieved such successful improvement despite such disadvantageous national circumstances, Estonia, Taiwan, Japan and South Korea seem valuable role models for 10 Changes improvements in Australia and Anglophone nations.

They've achieved it by making early-literacy development and education so much easier, through the use of a regular orthography, and its associated very manageable child and teacher workload.

Let's Research the Impacts of GENTLE

Our children too often have HEARTSH (Hugely-Exhausting, Actually-Rather-Tedious Schooling Heaviness). In contrast, regular-orthography nations Finland and Estonia prioritise achieving GENTLE (Gentle, Engaging, Never Tiring, Learning Enrichment).

There's need for, and value in, Australia and Anglophone nations researching the costs and benefits of GENTLE vs HEARTSH, and the extent to which they're present in schools, as they have major workload impacts and implications.

I developed my sense of education being GENTLE vs HEARTSH in reflecting on my visits to Finnish and Estonian schools, talking with teachers and teacher educators there, and considering their extent of school supports (e.g., M. Aro, 2017b).

They view their children as needing and benefiting from effective, gentle education, particularly in the early years of school. They prioritise learning breaks and playtime.

It's likely GENTLE can only be achieved when time is ample, as it can be in regular-orthography nations, with their rapid, easy literacy development and children so soon being confident independent readers, writers and learners. Managing orthographic complexity well plus having a GENTLE attitude is a powerful combination.

There seem six factors that are key to nations achieving GENTLE:
1. Prioritising and esteeming the nation's children and their development, insisting education must be gentle, well-rounded and not overly arduous, while being highly effective, for all three thirds of achievers.
2. Treating the nation's teachers highly professionally in multiple ways, including
   a. Workload being appropriate and far from excessive.
   b. Teaching time being balanced with ample off-class time for lesson preparation, professional development, working with allied-health professionals, and providing one-on-one support.
   c. Postgraduate studies being encouraged and supported.
3. Choosing a kind orthography for early-literacy development, one that gently and effectively expedites children's literacy

development.
4. Providing appropriate, effective word-reading and word-writing instruction well matched to its orthography's characteristics (For us, we'd use a regular orthography then transition children to Standard English).
5. Strongly supporting weaker learners, providing ample, gentle, effective intervention and support.
6. Funding appropriately, so these purposes are achieved.

We'd benefit by comparing Australian education with Finnish and Estonian education, as to the child and teacher workload impacts incurred in GENTLE vs HEARTSH, and those six factors.

We'd also benefit by exploring workload impacts of other enabling factors that Finland and Estonia use:

- A 15-minute break after each lesson, when children can play.
- The education system managing education from infancy across childcare centres and Kindergarten.
- Providing early childhood allied-health intervention across pre-school years.
- Starting formal education when children are older, e.g., their children are 7 to 8-years-old when in Grade 1.
- Reducing the cognitive load of learning letters, and keeping first learning simple, by children reading and writing with just capital letters in Kindergarten and Grade 1.
- Having shorter school days for Grade 1 and 2 children, which reduces pressure and enables out-of-school play hours.
- Using half-class literacy lessons in Grade 1 and 2, to enable more individual support, achieved through staggered starting times – half the class starts one hour earlier, the other half finishes one hour later, and the half-class literacy lessons take place in the first and last hour of the day.
- Enabling ample time before and after school for intervention lessons, without children missing class lessons, by using shorter school days and staggered start times.
- Having allied-health support staff as a key part of education, e.g., Estonian speech language pathologists are also trained learning-support teachers.
- Having ample student-free time for teachers' off-class duties:
  o Estonian and Finnish teachers have approximately 260 and 200 fewer class teaching hours than our teachers (OECD, 2015, 2022).
  o Schools have the option of student-free weeks during the summer break for teacher professional development, which most schools don't use, as education is going well.

- Having primary-school teachers take the same class for three years, in Grades 1-3 and 4-6.
- Using financial incentives and fee relief for teachers doing post-graduate education studies.
- Having primary school principals often also being classroom teachers, teaching a reduced number of subjects.
- Having high parent literacy, with parents confidently helping children learn to read, and supporting their school learning.
- Having a highly-effective national curriculum, appropriately deep and not too broad, with ample time for subject-area learning, and relatively minimal curriculum development done at school level.
- Using national-curriculum textbooks for all subject areas, with a textbook and matching student workbook for each year-level, empowering teachers and families.

The workload factors involved there are well worth researching.

Let's Research the Impacts of Low School Resourcing

Nations vary greatly in the supports they provide their schools, and particularly in the resourcing provided for early-literacy instruction and supports for at-risk and struggling learners.

As an example, learning support and special education in Australia focuses mostly on children with significant difficulties, whereas, in other nations, supports are provided for all children, including higher achievers. In Finland, approximately 35% of children access *Special Education* for some time across the years, and children move in and out of Special Education, as needed (M. Aro, 2017b).

We need research exploring the extent of resourcing that schools have, in early and upper-school years, and the extent of supports and resourcing that seem needed, here, in Australian states and education systems, and in other nations. In that research, let's focus on the needs of children in our three thirds of achievers: advanced vs. average vs lower achievers.

Let's research the adequacy of resourcing provided and associated workload impacts of Inclusion here – for our children with disability labels who do most learning in mainstream classes. Let's compare teacher estimates of their workloads for their healthy-progress children vs their funded children with disabilities.

Let's also research the workload impacts of schools gathering data and making funding applications for children, e.g., for our states' funded disability categories:

- Measuring the time spent by teachers, families and allied-health professionals here, as they work to achieve disability labels and associated additional funding.
- Comparing those hours with the time spent in nations such as Finland, Estonia and the UK that provide resourcing based on school needs, with no requirement for disability labels.

Let's also assess workload aspects of our Nationally Consistent Collection of Data (NCCD), the extent of workload involved in gathering that data, and the extent of workload relief provided for class teachers from NCCD-linked funding.

Let's also compare class teacher workload for funded and nonfunded children with learning struggles, i.e., Special Ed funding allocated for individual child vs supports from general learning-support funding. That's important, as we've far too many children with severe difficulties who fit definitions of disability, but miss out on disability funding and supports (Galletly et al., 2010; Knight & Galletly, 2017; M. O'Connor et al., 2019, 2020; Senate Standing Committee, 2016).

M. O'Connor et al. (2019), explored *established* and *emerging* needs in teacher data on Australian children starting schools, i.e., children identified vs not identified by government agencies as having disabilities and associated education needs, likely to include school disability funding, and perhaps also NDIS funding. They used data from the 2009, 2012 and 2015 rounds of the Australian Early Development Census (AEDC): teacher-reported information on all children starting school (M. O'Connor et al., 2019).

From workload perspectives, it's highly notable that they found almost four times more non-identified children than identified children (18.9% vs 4.9%). Our schools are not being effectively resourced for very large numbers of children with major education needs but insufficient official recognition. This is a sadly negative investment in child and teacher workload, Australian education, and our children's academic achievement levels. There's quite likely a significant relationship between our numbers of children receiving inadequate supports and numbers of low achievers in NAPLAN, PIRLS and PISA.

M. O'Connor et al. found needs increased significantly from 2009 to 2015:
- A 14.7% increase in children with communication difficulties, with 43.7% having communication weakness in 2015.
- A 5.3% increase in children with learning disability, with 10.4% having learning disability in 2015.

- A 7.0% increase in children with emotional problems, with 16.3% having emotional problems in 2015.
- A 4.7% increase in children with behaviour difficulties, with 17.1% having behaviour problems in 2015.
- No decrease in children having home disadvantage, with 21.2% having disadvantage in 2015.

Those figures bespeak our major needs for increased resourcing for schools to support our at-risk children from start of school.

Let's Research Allied-Health Supports

Let's assess the workload impacts of allied-health supports prior to and across the school years, while considering both needed vs provided supports.

For our children starting school, let's compare teacher estimates of workload and supports needed for both our healthy-progress readers and struggling readers, reporting for thirds, tenths, and the lowest and highest 5% and 2% of achievers. Let's also compare teacher estimates of workload and supports needed for children with healthy language skills and those with significant weakness.

We may well find our figures for reading difficulties close to our figures for language weakness, with both groups having Language, Literacy and Learning Disorder (LLLD) in various expressions.

Let's also compare different measures and estimates of workload:
- The class-teacher workload, which is needed, for children to be successful readers as per our 2035 goal.
- Current class-teacher workload for healthy-progress readers.
- Current class-teacher workload for struggling learners both those with and those without identified disabilities.
- Likely workload for those struggling learners, shared by teachers, allied-health professionals and aides, if disability funding was revised, with school resourcing provided to the needed extent.

Let's Research Impacts of Automisation Weakness

As we discussed in Tour 2, developing and mastering a skill involves two levels of automisation:
- We first acquire accuracy, being correct in using the skill (Level 1 Automisation).
- We then build ease and fluency (Level 2 Automisation).

A major crosslinguistic workload difference builds from the difficulties that large numbers of Standard-English at-risk readers have in achieving word-reading accuracy, i.e., Level 1 automisation.

Standard-English readers forget words they've learned for reading and writing. Regular-orthography children don't.

Importantly, workload in Anglophone nations builds markedly when children are *clever at forgetting*, and alas, many of our children with Level 1 Automisation Weakness, forget word-reading concepts and spellings they've learned at great length. They've used many school hours learning the skill, but have only mastered it to a lesser level but not to consistent accuracy (Level 1 automaticity).

Many of our children also forget maths facts they were previously accurate on (Dehaene, 2011; Joyner & Wagner, 2020). We need research on the extent this is a crosslinguistic issue, perhaps happening more in our children, due to young age, slow success in literacy and school learning, plus Acquired Helplessness.

There's value in researching Level 1 Automisation Weakness, and measuring and estimating workload and hours involved, e.g., for

- Teaching the 2, 3 or 7-times-tables in Term 1 to a level where as many children as possible are correct, then, after teaching has ended, and revision ceased, testing skills after increasingly long periods, e.g., 2-weeks, 1-month, 1-term.
- Similarly testing sets of spelling words children have learned and been correct on in spelling tests.
- Similarly testing reading of lists of irregular sightwords and lists of regular words that have been mastered, after practice is ceased.
- Exploring numbers of high schoolers still not automatic at spelling words which are often misspelt, e.g., Wednesday, February, could've, government, library, restaurant, signature, its/it's, who/how, who's/whose, woman/women, you're/your, they're/their/there, we're/where/wear/were, sure/shore.

We could easily extend this research by coordinating with partner researchers in regular-orthography nations.

It's an important issue – we've too many who are *clever at forgetting*, and automisation weakness and skill loss adds insidiously to our workload and education woes. Overlooking and reteaching forgotten basic skills reduce the effectiveness of education in many ways, adding teaching and learning time, and child and teacher workload.

Automisation weakness amidst rushed learning likely plays a major role in our crowded national curriculum not working sufficiently well, and in having so many low achievers in NAPLAN, PIRLS and PISA.

It may prove a major aspect of our contrast with regular-orthography nations, of them having Es (Ease) and Easy Expedited Efficient Effective Education, while we and other Anglophone nations have Cs, being *Chaotic, Cluttered-Curriculum* nations awash with *Confused, Complex* learning and too high *Cognitive* load, ever wrestling with our *Complicated, Cluttered-Curriculum Conundrum* (Galletly, 2022a).

Automisation weakness also expands the contrast of GENTLE vs HEARTSH. Being far less time-pressured, regular-orthography nations can easily achieve GENTLE (Gentle, Engaging, Never-Tiring, Learning Enrichment). With skills here far more difficult to acquire, our Australian schools, in contrast, are pressure cookers, amidst our ever present Find the Learning Time Challenge. This can often leave us mired in HEARTSH (Hugely-Exhausting, Actually-Rather-Tedious Schooling Heaviness). And alas, it's our most vulnerable children, our struggling learners, who are hit with automisation weakness and HEARTSH the hardest.

Our Children Forget Word-Reading Skills

It's extremely common for automisation weakness to impede our struggling word-readers and spellers' mastery of early vowels and words using those vowels. They often find mastering of *a/u*, and *e/i* sounds, and CVC, CCVCC and CVCe words a challenge and can need masses of practice before they're confidently reading and writing words using them, e.g., *hat/hut, pet/pit, grant/grunt, check/chick, cut/cute, strip/stripe.*

These lower-third word-readers and spellers need ample, encouraging, motivating, unstressed practice within early-literacy development. Our schools need that time, but alas don't have it.

Importantly, our national curriculum developers don't seem to have sufficiently accommodated the time needed for this learning.

Our Children Forget Maths Facts Too

Our children with difficulties in Level 1 automisation (accuracy difficulties) for word-reading and spelling often struggle similarly with counting and maths facts, e.g., they have difficulty counting down by 2s from 20, 7s from 70, etc., and aren't able to readily answer associated maths facts, e.g., in the 2-times and 7-times-tables.

In future research, these difficulties may prove a universal area of automisation weakness, with lesser crosslinguistic differences.

Failure to master crucial numeracy basics causes our teachers and children major struggles. Recently, I was working with two high schoolers with severe Dyslexia and numeracy weakness (dyscalculia), who are finding simplifying fractions and fraction calculations impossibly difficult. That's because, despite very long hours of learning over many years, they're still too weak on the times-tables that are needed for working with fractions.

When our schools are so pressured and busy, our struggling learners miss out in major ways. Because they've never been given sufficient teaching and learning time to master and automise the times-tables, they've been learning them then forgetting them down the years. Their teachers have mostly been too busy to do more than give homework practising times-tables. That hasn't worked, and consequently, in many areas of maths, the children haven't been able to progress.

Just ask any primary school teacher about automisation weakness – the difficulties our children have mastering word-reading and maths facts, both learning them in the first place, and retaining them long-term. Then ask high-school teachers about it: so often, the Year 2 and 4 children who struggled with those skills become the Year 9 children who've still not mastered them.

Our national curriculum doesn't seem to take automisation weakness into account and this needs to change. Let's consider 2-times maths facts from national curriculum perspectives. It's a very common area of automisation weakness.

The 2-times maths facts include understanding that $8+8 = 2 \times 8 = 8 \times 2 = 16$, plus the ability to apply them in extended and practical situations, e.g., 20×80 and calculating flooring needed for a hall 8m wide and 20m long. They're crucial number skills that are needed for, and enable, the building of many subsequent maths skills.

They're also a classic area of automisation weakness that impedes subsequent learning across many maths areas.

Some maths textbooks aligned to national curriculum expectations seem to expect mastering 2-times skills to take just a few weeks. While many healthy-progress learners master them quickly and easily, for our many children with automisation weakness, building confidence and automised skill with 2-times-tables can take years.

Counting down is simply listing integers (the maths facts answers) in order, a useful and needed skill – but a major area of difficulty for many children: when you ask them to count down, e.g., by 2s from 20 or 7s from 70, they really struggle. First struggling with counting down by 2s and 2-times facts, especially 2 x 7, 2 x 8 and 2 x 9, they then proceed to struggle to learn and master 3, 4, 6, 7 and 8-times-tables.

Our schools lack the learning time that young, immature, lower-third mathematicians need to master these key skills. That then creates maths mayhem, as when children lack automatic counting and maths facts, maths progress continues to be severely impeded. It's our *Complex, Complicated, Cluttered-Curriculum Conundrum*: too high early-literacy and early-maths workload creating major time pressure, so we've not the time we need for the numeracy-skills practice that's needed for mastering crucial basic skills.

All too often, assessing high-schoolers who attend for assessment of literacy difficulties, I find weakness not just for 2 x 800, but also 2 x 8, and marked hesitancy when counting down, e.g., by 20s from 200.

They've low functional working memory and automisation weakness, plus they lack early numeracy proficiency. That's a nasty combination for children expected to do high-school maths – and all too common in our children with literacy and numeracy difficulties.

When one considers the amount of maths content our national curriculum expects to be covered each year, there seems definite lack of recognition of the amount of time schools need for at-risk children to master important maths basics. We need to change that.

Let's Research National Curriculum Impacts

There's likely also value in researching the extent to which our national curriculum expands workload here in Australia, perhaps including focus on assignment and assessment workload.

It does seem inappropriate that children with severe automisation weakness are expected to complete all usual national curriculum expectations, including associated assignments and assessments, when they've missed out on crucial basics – partly because our time-poor schools are so pressured by those expectations.

For those who've fallen behind, so much of subject-area learning and assignments involves excessive stress and virtually no strong learning, as they struggle to deliver on assignments and tests.

Students lacking 3Rs basics – competent reading, 'riting and 'rithmatic skills – desperately need a streamlined national curriculum strand with multiple options. This could end learning and assessment tasks being at stressed survivor level, making them instead very manageable, with useful learning. And time saved from subject-area learning can be used in learning support that builds needed basic skills. This could move many of our struggling learners from surviving to thriving, achieving the effective education they'd like and need. We've not had this strand, and change is needed.

Impossible? Not at all. Exploring time-saving, more motivating formats will achieve at least equivalent levels of subject-area learning to those currently achieved, and quite possibly more. Whereas the rest of the class might, e.g., read multiple texts on ancient China and complete lengthy associated assignments, for those needing 3Rs skill-building lessons, this might reduce to short videos then discussions on key topics. And strategically reducing subject-area learning-task time for selected subjects can enable time for neatly tailored, daily, supported instruction that builds important, needed skills.

Too big an ask? Definitely not, particularly when we consider our children's rights for appropriate supports and effective education.

Currently, our high-school education for struggling readers is too often ineffective, and, really, quite nasty, making SCHOOL *S*ad *C*ruel *H*ours *O*f *O*ur *L*ives. It's not the education our Education Act promises and what our teachers want for our children.

Let's Research the Impacts of Class Size

As part of workload research, let's explore the impacts of reducing class size across primary and high school. Given regular-orthography nations find daily half-class lessons needed and beneficial for their much easier early-literacy instruction for their 7 to 9-year-olds, there's likelihood it's inappropriate for us to have 25 and more, much younger children in our classes for early-literacy learning and subject-area tasks that use reading and writing. Children need and thrive on individual attention, and Australian children currently get far too little of it.

The research on class size supports this (Hattie, 2005, 2008; Mathis, 2017; Shen & Konstantopoulos, 2017; Zyngier, 2014). In particular, smaller class size benefits Anglophone lower-achieving children, as teachers' workload is more manageable when classes are smaller, and tailored instruction and individual attention are more easily achieved. As Hattie (2008) comments, in his review of research on this area,

Most research studies reported here agree that class size

reductions do not affect all children equally. Both American and English evidence shows that children in the early years of schooling and those in the lowest ability groups ... appear to benefit the most from reducing the number of students in front of teachers.

Interestingly, research in regular-orthography nations shows far more minimal effects of reduced class size (e.g., Shen & Konstantopoulos, 2017). That's no surprise, given their already-reduced workload.

While class size of 25 is likely too big here in Australia, Japanese Grade 1 classes work well with 37 children. The strong orthographic disadvantage of the Anglosphere, which creates our many severely struggling readers, also creates our greater needs for, and benefits from, reduced class size.

Let's Research Impacts of Teaching Classes for 2-3 Years

We likely add workload in major ways through our entrenched habit of teachers teaching classes for only one year, rather than keeping the same class for multiple years. Every year teachers start new classes, and must work hard to build understanding of their children's skill levels and social-emotional needs. Thus Term 1 can involve extensive testing. Then in Term 4, there's wind-down as teachers and children get ready for farewells. There's every likelihood this habit decreases the efficiency of teaching and learning, especially in Terms 1 and 4.

We could research this area quite easily, perhaps starting with survey and observation research of teachers here in Australia and in nations where teaching is across multiple years. In Estonian primary schools, for example, it's common to teach classes for three years (Grades 1-3 and 4-6), and some teachers take classes through for even longer cycles, e.g., Grades 1-5.

Let's ask Estonian and Australian teachers about the workload and other impacts of starting work with a new class, then ask the Estonian teachers how that workload differs from their workload in years when they continue with last year's class.

Let's also ask both sets of teachers their opinions on advantages and disadvantages of classes lasting one year vs two and three years.

We'll likely find Estonian teachers strongly reject the idea of having a new class every year, on the basis of it being highly inefficient, and reducing their depth of understanding of the children they teach.

Let's Research Excessive Testing and Report Cards

While comparing education in Australia and overseas, let's also research the extent that schools do in-class testing associated with report-card writing, in primary school and high school.

Other nations, e.g., Finland and Estonia, do far less in-class testing and report writing, particularly in primary school. In discussions, their teachers seemed horrified at our extent of testing and reporting, feeling it's not needed, plus unnecessarily heightens workload.

Further, many Australian teachers feel much in-class testing is superfluous, providing information teachers already know, while reducing teaching time and increasing marking and reporting.

Let's Research the Impacts of Our Young Starting Age

Let's also research the workload impacts of our starting formal education at so much younger an age than most nations.

It's likely our children's young age has strong negative effects on both literacy and numeracy development, through immaturity and low cognitive-processing and executive-function skills.

We start our children at close to the world's youngest age on learning to read and write one of the world's most complex orthographies. We've also number wording which adds cognitive load and relies on mature auditory processing, so 'teen' and 'ty' numbers don't seem identical or interchangeable, e.g., 13/30, 19/90, impeding development of counting and numeracy skills.

There's every likelihood that young age, through immaturity and weak cognitive-processing skills, both heightens and activates children's risk factors and likelihood they'll develop significant learning difficulties.

Let's Research the Impacts of Behaviour Issues

We also need to study the workload and stresses of our unruly classrooms and behaviour difficulties (OECD, 2019). There's value in comparing literacy, attention and behaviour levels of children in Australia and other nations, longitudinally across all school years.

Certainly, our unruly classrooms start early, quite likely at school entry with e.g., 16.3% of Prep children having emotional problems and 17.1% having behaviour problems (M. O'Connor et al., 2019). Further, our schools being insufficiently resourced to provide these children with the education and supports they need to be successful, engaged learners (Knight et al., 2017a, 2017b). Notably, many other nations have far more minimal school behaviour difficulties (Ding et al., 2008; Duesund & Ødegård, 2018).

It's likely studies will show our unruly classrooms are in place by the end of Prep and Year 1, and then worsen across the years, with major workload impacts, and strong association of unruly behaviour and weak word-reading and early-literacy skills.

Our PISA 2018 data showed Australia ranked 69th out of 76 nations for classroom climate and unruly high-school classrooms, i.e., eighth worst in the world (OECD, 2019). In like manner, our PIRLS 2016 data showed major behaviour issues and unruly classrooms here are well in place by Year 4.

PIRLS 2016 involved over 50 nations. We had 6,341 Year 4 children in our representative sample, including at least one full class from 286 schools across states and territories. The children did PIRLS tests, and questionnaire data was also gathered (Thomson et al., 2017).

First, the good news: we had pleasing improvement for average and strong readers, nicely reflecting our schools' improvement efforts.

Now, the sad news: we'd no improvement for our low achievers, and dismal outcomes as regards social-emotional factors. PIRLS 2016 findings included the following (Thomson et al., 2017):

- A strong relationship between reading achievement and behaviour, with weaker readers having significantly more disciplinary issues.
- A strong relationship between reading achievement and teachers considering their school safe and orderly, with more weak readers in schools considered unrulier.
- Almost a fifth of children (19%) reported being bullied about once per week, with much stronger reading in children reporting little to no bullying.
- Close to half of our sample (43%) reported not having a strong sense of belonging, with much stronger reading in children who reported a strong sense of belonging.
- The teachers of 65% of children reported their teaching being significantly limited by student needs, and reading scores being significantly higher for children whose teachers didn't consider their teaching limited by student needs.
- Many children (36%) attended schools where reading instruction was reported as affected by resource shortages.
- Fewer boys were high achievers, and more boys were low achievers, with 23% of boys vs 15% of girls at low level.

- Our indigenous children showed major disadvantage, having a very low Mean, with 43% of indigenous children vs 17% of non-indigenous children achieving at low level.
- SES factors, including number of books at home, related strongly to reading achievement: 35% of children with few books vs 11% with many books achieved at low level.
- Absenteeism and arriving at school hungry related strongly to low reading achievement, with 24% coming to school hungry.
- Almost a quarter (24%) attended schools with significant disadvantage, and the teachers of 40% of those children didn't consider their schools safe and orderly.

That's very sad. It's also a logical outcome of education here being ineffective, and supports for vulnerable children being too few.

There's value in researching the child and teacher workload impacts of virtually all those listed factors, e.g., of
- Catch-up learning for children with higher absentee rates, and children who've recently changed schools.
- Homework efficiency for advantaged and disadvantaged high-schoolers.
- Reduced learning efficiency in children who are hungry and children from disadvantaged backgrounds.
- Reduced teaching and learning efficiency in unruly classrooms.

Let's Go Well Beyond PIRLS and PISA

In exploring child and teacher workload, teaching and learning hours, and the factors creating and impacting them, let's move beyond NAPLAN, PIRLS and PISA to doing detailed observation of and discussions with schools and teachers, and detailed case-study exploration of teaching and learning in schools in different nations.

Towards this end, Harold Stevenson and colleagues' case-study research is valuable reading, in particular, their 1990 *Contexts of achievement: A study of American, Chinese, and Japanese children*, and their 1998 *To sum it up: Case studies of education in Germany, Japan, and the United States* (Stevenson et al., 1990, 1998, 2002).

Their work explores many factors worth considering, e.g.,
- Differing national curriculum designs.
- How some nations use highly-specified national curriculum lessons, with teachers and families then easily knowing the content that's taught.
- How, in some nations, much teacher off-class time is spent honing and optimising those lessons, to make them

increasingly effective for both stronger and weaker learners. (This contrasts markedly with how Australian teachers and schools so often must develop new curriculum, e.g., new units, activities and lessons, which leaves minimal time to hone them.)
- The impact of Chinese and Japanese teachers having far more off-class time, often focused on improving lesson effectiveness.
- The different ways nations encourage family involvement and participation in achieving education goals.
- Differing behavioural expectations, e.g., Chinese and Japanese children often being responsible for classroom behaviour.
- How China and Japan achieve children experiencing minimal embarrassment about errors they make in front of the class. (Quite possibly, having confident literacy and Success Inoculation, their children feel more capable, and errors are viewed as merely part of the learning process, particularly given teachers hone the efficiency of individual lessons.)

While PISA, PIRLS and OECD international comparison data provides much useful information, that information is actually just a start. There's so much more to learn by spending time in schools and doing in-depth observation, interviews and discussions.

Using PISA, PIRLS and OECD information as a useful basis, we want to build needed knowledge. There is immense power in e.g., Australian teachers and speech language pathologists observing in regular-orthography classrooms and talking with teachers, speech language pathologists and researchers there, and vice versa, with teams from other nations similarly spending time in schools and discussions here in Australia.

Case-study visits, with strategic, deep observation and discussions can be highly revealing, as so often, reality is very different to our assumptions. What we see, we assume is normal.

As an example, in talking with Finnish teachers in 2005, I found myself utterly unable to persuade them that Finnish spelling is actually very good, as their reality was that their children's spelling was atrocious. Their vehemence made me realise how easy it is to assume our school worlds are highly similar, e.g., given Finnish and Australian teachers both feel children's spelling is atrocious, but the reality is different: Finnish spelling is magnificent by our standards.

Similarly, a Finnish PISA researcher I spoke with was adamantly confident that Finland's highly-regular orthography and rapid, easy word-reading and spelling development would make no difference in advantaging Finnish education relative to Anglophone nations.

Comments such as these made me realise the need for, and the power of, case-study research where observers cross the crosslinguistic gap, with e.g., Australian teachers and speech language pathologists observing in Finland, Estonia, Taiwan, Japan and South Korea, and groups of their educators observing here in Australia, with ample reflection and discussions taking place.

Case-study research can be formal or informal, and informal observations and discussions can be a useful start. Importantly, it can bring attention to factors not previously considered.

With their strong practical focus, practitioners often notice factors that haven't necessarily been explored in research. I found this in things I noticed, and in comments of regular-orthography teachers.

As an example, in Estonia, I spoke with an Estonian teacher educator, discussing a study's finding that Estonian children start ahead of Finnish children, being stronger readers at the start of Grade 1 (having had reading instruction in Kindergarten), but with Finnish children then catching up quite quickly, in Grade 1, and soon being ahead (Torppa et al., 2019).

She immediately raised an issue not mentioned in that study's discussion: that Estonia perhaps has too strong an emphasis on teaching cursive script in Grade 1, with extensive handwriting lessons reducing time available for literacy enrichment. Other Estonian teachers agreed, with all reflecting on how they'd loathed those handwriting lessons, and how children still dislike them.

It's likely that informal then formal in-depth case-study research at school and classroom level, here in Australia and in other nations, will enhance a strong start on 10 Changes improvements. That's particularly the case if we use researchers with strong practical education experience from both sides of the crosslinguistic divide:

- Our teacher and speech language pathologist researchers doing ample classroom observations and discussions in regular-orthography schools, focused on skill levels and workload issues, and the factors that impact them.
- Regular-orthography teacher and speech language pathologist researchers doing the same in Australian schools.

Let's include practitioners with strong experience with children and schools in our research teams, as e.g., teacher researchers. In those teams, let's include speech language pathologists and teachers with a range of expertise, e.g., in early-literacy, sophisticated literacy, struggling learners, advanced learners, class-teaching, learning-support and special education.

Research Tour 9. Needs for Workload Research

Key Findings from Tour 9

Implications from exploration of workload impacts in Tour 9 suggest the following considerations towards improving literacy and education in Australia and Anglophone nations:

1. Because of our severe orthographic disadvantage, our teachers and children have much higher workload than teachers and children in regular-orthography nations.
2. This workload seems excessive, e.g., our children doing 300 more school hours each year than many leading nations doesn't offset this disadvantage (OECD, 2015, 2022).
3. The impacts of too high child and teacher workload likely play a major role in current education difficulties.
4. Our excessive child and teacher workload and their impacts build from orthographic disadvantage factors, including
    a. English orthographic complexity and its impacts on our developing and struggling readers.
    b. Word-reading and spelling development taking too long for all our children.
    c. Our too many struggling readers.
    d. Our language weakness epidemic.
5. Australian education has exacerbated workload impacts through factors such as
    a. Using solely Standard English, instead of starting with a beginners' orthography.
    b. Starting children so young on this complex learning.
    c. Providing insufficient allied-health supports prior to and at school.
    d. Inadequately resourcing our schools, with major insufficiencies for at-risk and struggling learners.
    e. Requiring our teachers to do much longer class-teaching hours than many leading nations.
    f. The time pressure these factors create.
6. While there is research Australia can build from, there's little research on child and teacher workload and its impacts.
7. Australia thus has major needs for workload research.
8. This workload research should include
    a. Quantifying workload and its impacts.
    b. Comparing workload across multiple nations, including
        i. Australia, using estimates of needed resourcing vs resourcing currently provided.
        ii. Other Anglophone nations using different types and levels of school resourcing.
        iii. Nations using sole regular orthographies, e.g.,

Finland, Estonia and South Korea.

    iv. Asian nations using a regular-orthography prior to a complex orthography, e.g., Taiwan, Japan, and China.

9. Considering teacher and child workloadimpacts for achievers at different levels, including thirds, tenths, and the lowest and highest 5% and 2% of achievers.
10. Comparing different forms of workload estimates, including
    a. The class-teacher workload, which is needed, for children to be successful readers, as per our 2035 goal.
    b. Current class-teacher workload for healthy readers.
    c. Current class-teacher workload for struggling learners (a) with and (b) without identified disabilities.
    d. Likely workload for those struggling learners, shared by teachers, allied-health professionals and aides, if disability funding was revised, with school resourcing provided to the needed extent.
11. We need research on the workload impacts of a wide range of areas including
    a. Word-reading, spelling and early-literacy development here in Australia, and in regular-orthography nations.
    b. Our starting formal literacy and numeracy instruction at a very young age, without using a regular orthography.
    c. Our teachers' workload requirements.
    d. Weak language skills and other risk factors at start of school.
    e. Level 1 Automisation Weakness for literacy and numeracy, and needs for re-teaching required skills.
    f. Aspects of the orthographic advantage of regular-orthography nations vs the orthographic disadvantage we experience, which build from differences in early-literacy development and associated workload impacts.
    g. Factors associated with achieving Finland and Estonia's GENTLE (Gentle, Engaging, Never-Tiring, Learning Enrichment).
    h. School resourcing levels, allied-health supports, class size, national curriculum characteristics, in-class testing and report card writing, and associated factors, here and in other nations.
    i. Too many children starting school at risk, but schools not having the resourcing needed to meet their needs.
    j. Classroom climate and behaviour, social-emotional and attention difficulties, and unruly classrooms from start of school and across the school years.
12. It is likely that a strong focus on weighing workload and achieving equitable manageable workload for our children and

teachers is vitally needed if we are to improve education and outcomes. It will play a strong role in improving education, meeting our teaching challenges, and achieving our 2035 goal.

13. Estonia, Taiwan, Japan and South Korea are high-achieving nations which have made extremely impressive gains despite major cultural and economic hurdles. Using regular orthographies has quite likely played a pivotal role in their marked improvement. These nations are compelling role models for Australian education in many ways, including trialling use of a beginners' orthography.

Research Tour 10.
A Multiple Deficits Vs Phonological Basis?

Reading problems are often found in children who have other diagnoses. So developmental dyslexia overlaps ... specific language impairment ... attention deficit disorder ... Asperger's syndrome and autism. ... Often the diagnosis children end up with is really just a consequence of the kind of specialist they first happened to be referred to.

John Stein, Joel Talcott, & Caroline Witton, 2001.

It's time to move away from positioning phonological-awareness weakness as the universal basis of weak word-reading and spelling.

As a clinician, I do considerable work building phonological and phonemic awareness while I'm building word-reading, spelling and numeracy in the children I work with. I'm also the author of *Phonological Fun*, systematically sequenced games and activities building phonological and phonemic-awareness skills, and *Sounds & Vowels* and *Two Vowels Talking*, books and games building word-reading, which also build phonological-awareness (Galletly, 1999b, 2000, 2001).

I build rhyming and syllable awareness for reading and writing in most weak word-readers and spellers I work with, as they almost invariably lack automaticity for these skills. And of course, with phonemic awareness, word-reading and spelling being that three-stranded rope, developing alongside and expediting each other's development, I also work to build phonemic awareness for word-reading and spelling (Scarborough, 2001).

For phonemic awareness, I use activities aligned to the sequential levels of phonemic-awareness skill of *Rosner's Test of Auditory Integration* (TAAS, Rosner, 1993), which match well to children's skills for reading and writing unfamiliar words. I've posted that test, along with discussion and parallel versions on ResearchGate (Galletly, 2022c).

Virtually all Standard-English readers with weak word-reading or spelling have weak phonological and phonemic awareness (Galletly, 2005b, 2008; Knight et al., 2017a; Knight & Galletly, 2020). While in part, that's because phonemic awareness can't become proficient in children who are still weak at word-reading and spelling, many have wider phonological-awareness weakness, e.g., in syllable and rhyming skills. In consequence, they benefit from intervention building phonological and phonemic awareness that's needed for word-reading and spelling.

However, it does seem time to move away from positioning phonological and phonemic awareness as the basis of word-reading and spelling development and difficulties.

Importantly, crosslinguistic studies find phonological awareness of low importance for regular-orthography readers. It predicts strength of word-reading and spelling development and difficulties for both regular-orthography and Standard-English readers.

However, while strongly predicting Standard-English difficulties across our many years of word-reading and spelling development, it's only a predictor for regular-orthographies for the brief time it takes children to master word-reading and spelling.

In effect, it is a strong predictor for both regular-orthography and Standard-English readers for the period of word-reading and spelling development, however, for us, that's a period of many years.

A Multiple Deficits or Phonological Basis

For many decades, researchers have positioned weak phonological awareness as the basis of word-reading and spelling difficulties (Chirkina & Grigorenko, 2014; Liberman et al., 1989). The widespread popularity of this view is evidenced in many practical applications, e.g., it's emphasised in the First Step Act definition of Dyslexia, from the USA Senate (Miciak & Fletcher, 2020):

Dyslexia means an unexpected difficulty in reading for an individual who has the intelligence to be a much better reader, most commonly caused by a difficulty in the phonological processing (the appreciation of the individual sounds of spoken language), which affects the ability of an individual to speak, read, and spell.

However, that primary role of phonological-awareness weakness has been challenged in recent years, e.g., by weak phonological awareness not blocking word-reading and spelling development in regular-orthography children (e.g., Torppa et al., 2016), and some Anglophone weak word-readers not having weak phonological awareness (e.g., J. M. Carroll et al., 2016; Knight & Galletly, 2020).

Increasingly, studies are supporting Pennington's (2006) Multiple Deficits Basis model of reading difficulties (Daucourt et al., 2020; Hayiou-Thomas et al., 2016; McGrath et al., 2020; Pennington, 2006). Using studies of genetics and comorbidities of reading disability, speech sound disorder and Attention Deficit/Hyperactivity Disorders (AD/HD), and their overlapping features, it emphasises multiple factors underlying word-reading difficulties.

Notably, the model accommodates automisation weakness and the comorbidities that are so often present in weak readers – children with word-reading disability having other disabilities as well, e.g., AD/HD, autism, auditory-processing disorder, behaviour disorders. These can't be explained by single-cause models such as phonological-awareness weakness.

The findings of Pennington et al. (2012), J. M. Carroll et al. (2016) and other researchers, that significant proportions of weak Standard-English word-readers don't have phonological-awareness weakness, also support the multiple deficits perspective.

Further, findings of studies of regular-orthography at-risk readers, which often provide a clearer perspective than Standard-English studies, given far fewer factors impact early-literacy development, increasingly support a multiple deficits basis (Kornilov & Grigorenko, 2018; Mascheretti et al., 2015; Rakhlin et al., 2013; Wimmer et al., 1998; Zuk et al., 2020).

I suspect that, increasingly, Australia will use the Multiple Deficits Basis. We'll likely find executive-function difficulties, rather than phonological awareness, are a universal feature of Language, Literacy and Learning Disorder (LLLD), with the high cognitive load of learning to read and write Standard English being a key factor that both activates and exacerbates impacts of multiple risk factors, including phonological-awareness weakness (Knight et al, 2020):

It may be that phonological-processing weakness, now usually termed cognitive-processing weakness or executive-function weakness, is a more universal feature of literacy difficulties than phonological awareness weakness (Diamond, 2013; Pennington, 2006). Wagner and Torgesen (1987) integrated phonological awareness, phonological recoding (word-reading, using recoding from letters through sounds to words), and phonological working-memory as phonological processing. Within this wider view of phonological processing, they emphasised that the question is less whether phonological skills play a causal role in the acquisition of reading, and rather establishing the particular aspects of phonological processing (phonological awareness, phonological recoding in word reading, and recoding in working memory) that causally relate to particular aspects of reading, the time points of their interacting, and the directions of causality.

Many researchers now use the term or discuss 'phonological processing' for what other researchers now term cognitive processing and executive functioning (Morris et al., 1998; Vandewalle et al., 2010; Wimmer, Mayringer, & Landerl, 1998). ... They focus less on phonological awareness aspects, and more on cognitive processing aspects such as phonological-verbal working memory (verbal working memory), and rapid automised naming (RAN), which includes phonological components.

As such, while adhering to a phonological deficit perspective, they are discussing phonological processing rather than phonological awareness weakness.

There seems value in cognitive-processing research elucidating the extent to which phonemic-awareness development parallels word-reading and spelling development, and the reasons why this occurs; and exploring the applicability of multiple deficit and phonological limitation models.

Importantly, the Multiple Deficits Basis model can be integrated with other useful perspectives, both simple and complex, including

- Most Standard-English struggling word-readers having weak phonological awareness (Landerl et al., 2019, 2022).
- Catts and Pertcher's (2022) delightfully pragmatic risk-resilience model which positions *Dyslexia* for Standard-English readers as a label for unexpected reading disability, due to cumulative effects of risk and resilience factors, which schools may act on early, as soon as weakness is indicated.
- Nicolson and Fawcett's (2019) complex, insightful *Delayed Neural Commitment* framework, building from their work on the major difficulties that struggling Standard-English readers have in automising skills, and their needs for such extensive practice. It proposes that, in addition to slow skill acquisition, dyslexic readers take longer to build the neural networks that underpin the acquisition of reading.

- The strategic research methodologies recommended by eminent regular-orthography researchers (Papadopoulos, 2022; Papadopoulos, Csepe, et al., 2021).
- Word-reading difficulties so often being part of comorbidities (Galletly & Knight, 2011a; Stein et al., 2001).
- Executive-function weakness being a key aspect of comorbidities (Christoforou et al., 2023).

Given that Australian reading and literacy instruction is conducted with all children, including many with disorders that disadvantage word-reading and literacy development, there's value in Australian research using a multiple deficits perspective in researching word-reading, spelling and early-literacy development and difficulties.

Our Children Experience Differential Disadvantage

Elsewhere, we've proposed a model of differential disadvantage due to cognitive-processing weakness and the high cognitive load of learning to read and write Standard English (Galletly & Knight, 2011a). It takes automisation weakness and comorbidities into account, and also the non-automised skills of comorbidities.

---

1. Differential disadvantage against regular-orthography weak readers

Disadvantage through not experiencing the strong expediting of early-literacy development that children who learn to read and write regular-orthographies experience. They miss out on the following benefits:

• Ease of learning to read and write words once letter-sounds are known.
• Cognitive-processing weakness and low intelligence not preventing mastery of word-reading and word-writing.
• Word-reading and spelling being mastered in the first school years.
• Very low magnitude of word-reading and spelling difficulties.
• Word-reading remediation being of short duration and highly successful.
• *Early Literacy* mastery expediting
  - Independent reading, writing and learning.
  - Language development.
  - *Sophisticated Literacy* learning.

Figure 17a. Model of Differential Disadvantage of Anglophone children: Part 1: Disadvantage against regular-orthography weak readers (Galletly & Knight, 2011a, adapted)

As proposed in Part 1 of the model, above, all Anglophone weak readers are severely disadvantaged relative to regular-orthography weak readers because they miss out on the many benefits of regular-orthographies, and reading and writing being easily acquired skills.

Research Tour 10. A Multiple Deficits Vs Phonological Basis?

The disadvantage is considerably more major for at-risk children. As shown in Part 2, those starting school with pre-existing language weakness, including cognitive-processing weakness, experience much greater disadvantage relative to their peers, because their early language-skills weakness more severely impedes literacy development and language development across the school years.

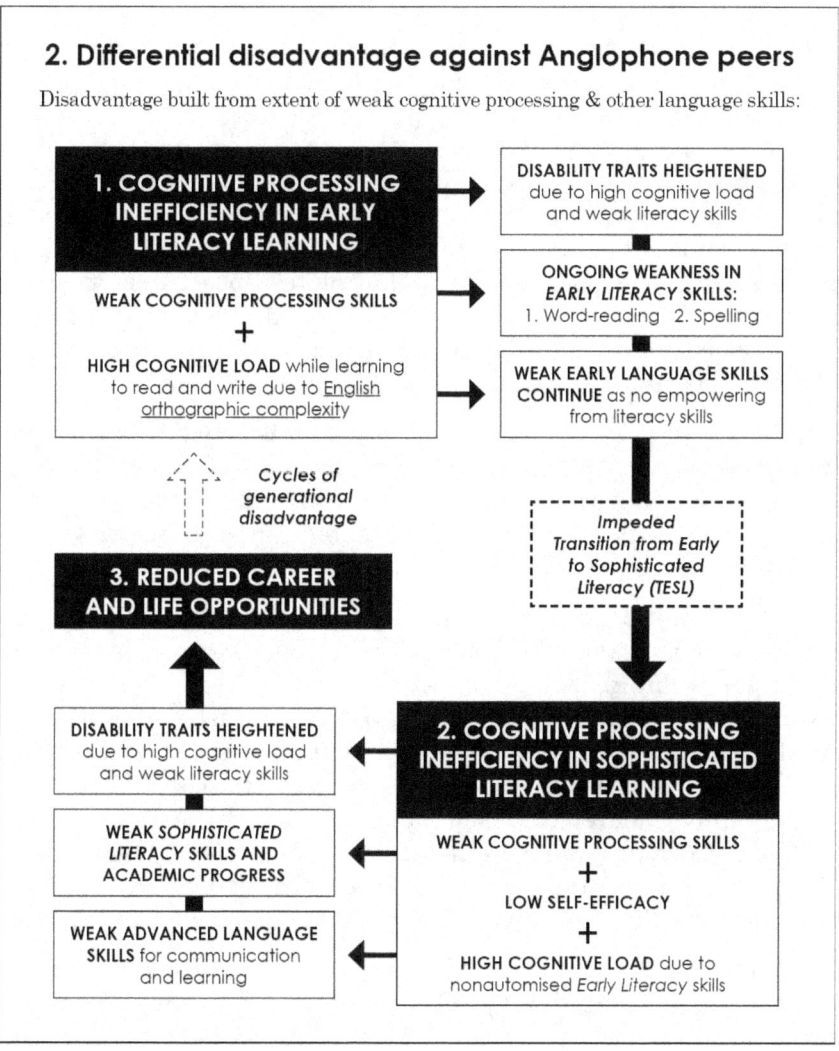

Figure 17b. Model of Differential Disadvantage of Anglophone children, Part 2: Disadvantage relative to Standard-English peers (Galletly & Knight, 2011a, adapted)

Single and Double Deficits

Rapid Automised Naming (RAN), ability to name well-known items such as colours, numbers, letters, and objects as quickly as possible, has also been the focus of many recent studies (e.g., Georgiou et al., 2012, 2013, 2016; Papadopoulos et al., 2016; Sideridis et al., 2019; Wimmer & Shurz, 2010; Younger & Meisinger, 2022).

While RAN weakness universally predicts reading difficulties, the difficulties differ, being accuracy vs fluency weakness (Level 1 vs Level 2 Automisation Weakness). Studies show RAN weakness underlies continuing fluency weakness in regular-orthography children with slower reading. RAN influences fluency directly, and also indirectly through phonological and orthographic processing (Papadopoulos et al., 2016), as RAN uses coordination of cognitive-processing, phonological, orthographic, motor, speech and attention processes (Georgiou et al., 2016; Wolf et al., 2000). Of interest, Papadopoulos et al.'s (2016) review found RAN predicted reading aloud but did not predict silent reading.

Further, a *Double Deficit* of RAN plus phonological-awareness weakness universally predicts more severe difficulties (Wolf & Bowers, 1999), with children in both regular-orthography and Anglophone nations experiencing more major difficulties than children weak in just one of these areas.

Those difficulties are relatively minor in regular-orthography nations, but major for Standard-English struggling readers (Wimmer & Shurz, 2010; Landerl et al., 2019), e.g., whereas word-reading accuracy is measured for Standard-English children, given weak readers have major accuracy weakness, only word-reading fluency is measured in double-deficit studies of regular-orthography children, as their accuracy is high. For Anglophone children, isolated weakness in either phonological-awareness or RAN produces accuracy difficulties for word-reading and spelling, with a double deficit producing difficulties of higher severity.

Landerl et al. (2019) explored the strength of RAN and phonological awareness as longitudinal predictors of reading in five alphabetic orthographies with varying degrees of consistency (English, French, German, Dutch, and Greek), in a longitudinal study of 1,120 children across Grades 1 and 2. They found RAN to be a consistent predictor of reading fluency in all orthographies, but the relationship of phonological awareness with reading to be complex and varying, impacted by many factors, such as age and maturity, the tasks used, and orthographic complexity. Georgiou et al., (2012) exploring predictors in Greek, English and Finnish children also found letter-sound skills to be a very strong predictor.

Regular-orthography double-deficit studies can be particularly useful in revealing subtle influences that often aren't evident in Standard-English studies (Torppa et al., 2013; Wimmer et al., 2000; Papadopoulos et al., 2009; Shany & Share, 2011).

That's because more factors impact our early-literacy development. For regular-orthography children, isolated weakness results in different areas of difficulty, as shown in the table below (Galletly, 2005b; Wimmer & Mayringer, 2002; Wimmer et al., 2000; Wolf & Bowers, 1999; Wolf et al., 1994).

	Phonological Deficit	Rapid Automised Naming Deficit	Double Deficit
Standard-English Readers	Weak word-reading accuracy and fluency	Weak word-reading accuracy and fluency	Very severe word-reading weakness
Regular-Orthography Readers	Healthy word-reading accuracy and fluency	Healthy word-reading accuracy and low fluency	Healthy word-reading accuracy and very low fluency

Table 4. Double Deficit features of Standard-English and regular-orthography weak readers (from Galletly, 2005b)

Furnes et al. (2019) did crosslinguistic investigation of double-deficit groupings in two regular-orthography nations and two Anglophone nations, using data from the *International Longitudinal Twin Study* (ILTS) on early-literacy development in Norway, Sweden, Australia, and USA. They followed large samples of children in these nations from Preschool and Kindergarten to Grade 2, assigning children to single, double and no deficit groups. In line with other studies, they found the double-deficit model to be universal and present in all four nations.

Further, multile studies are exploring the neurological basis of the RAN and phonological awareness single and double-deficit weakness (Ashkenazi et al., 2013; Boivin et al., 2015; Knight & Galletly, 2020; Lohvansuu et al., 2021, Norton et al., 2014). Norton et al. (2014) found
- Dissociation between brain regions sensitive to phonological awareness (left inferior frontal and inferior parietal regions) and rapid naming (right cerebellar lobule VI).

- As regards brain regions sensitive to rapid naming, double-deficit weak readers showing significantly weaker fronto-parietal activation than weak readers with isolated phonological-awareness weakness, who, in turn, had weaker activation than healthy readers.
- As regards brain regions sensitive to phonological awareness, double-deficit weak readers show significantly weaker cerebellar activation than those with isolated rapid naming weakness, who had weaker activation than healthy readers.
- Bilateral prefrontal regions were pivotal in linking brain regions associated with phonological awareness and rapid naming, and the double-deficit group showed strongest weakness in this connectivity.

Several American studies show instability of group membership over time, with children moving between isolated weakness and double-deficit groups as regards their RAN and phonological-awareness levels (Steacy et al., 2014; Younger & Meisinger, 2022). In addition, anxiety, motivation, negative affect and depression can significantly impact test scores (Sideridis et al., 2019).

This suggests that while it's valuable for schools to measure and monitor phonological awareness and RAN in at-risk and weak readers and writers, a main focus on the children's reading and writing skills is needed. As a clinician, I find phonological-awareness and RAN tests particularly useful for establishing a diagnosis of Dyslexia in highly intelligent beginning readers who've a Language, Literacy and Learning Disorder (LLLD) profile, and who are at risk of having their intervention needs overlooked due to their high skills in many other areas of life functioning.

Once working on intervention, however, while working to build needed phonological and phonemic-awareness skills, my focus is strongly on improving written and spoken communication, with little ongoing formal RAN and phonological-awareness testing.

Papadopoulos et al.'s (2009) longitudinal study following Greek children from Kindergarten to Grade 2, similarly showed double-deficit groups. Their literacy difficulties weren't obvious in Kindergarten but were evident in Grades 1 and 2. Children with RAN weakness had ongoing fluency difficulties, those with phonological-awareness weakness had slow word-reading and spelling development that resolved over time, and double-deficit children had ongoing, more severe fluency and spelling difficulties.

Studies showing the proportions of weak readers and spellers are also

revealing: Torppa et al (2017), using double-deficit groups in a longitudinal Grade 1 to 4 study of 1800 Finnish children, found
- 2% had spelling difficulties but healthy reading fluency, and phonological-awareness weakness.
- 2% had healthy spelling but fluency and RAN weakness.
- A 3% double-deficit group had fluency and spelling difficulties.

Anglophone nations would love those tiny percentages. Torppa et al. also found that both the phonological-awareness and combined-weakness cohorts had weak letter-sound knowledge.

The Power of Displaying Instructional Needs

The double-deficit model (Wolf et al., 1994) shares with the Simple View (Gough & Tunmer, 1986), and Literacy Component models (Knight et al., 2021) a key principle: ease of seeing strengths, weaknesses and instructional needs for two focus skills, when skill levels are shown in scatterplots, to make quadrants of achievers.

While using different terminology, the Simple View model (Reading Comprehension = Word-Reading x Language Skills for Literacy) also uses double-deficit groupings: of word-reading weakness, language skills weakness, and combined weakness.

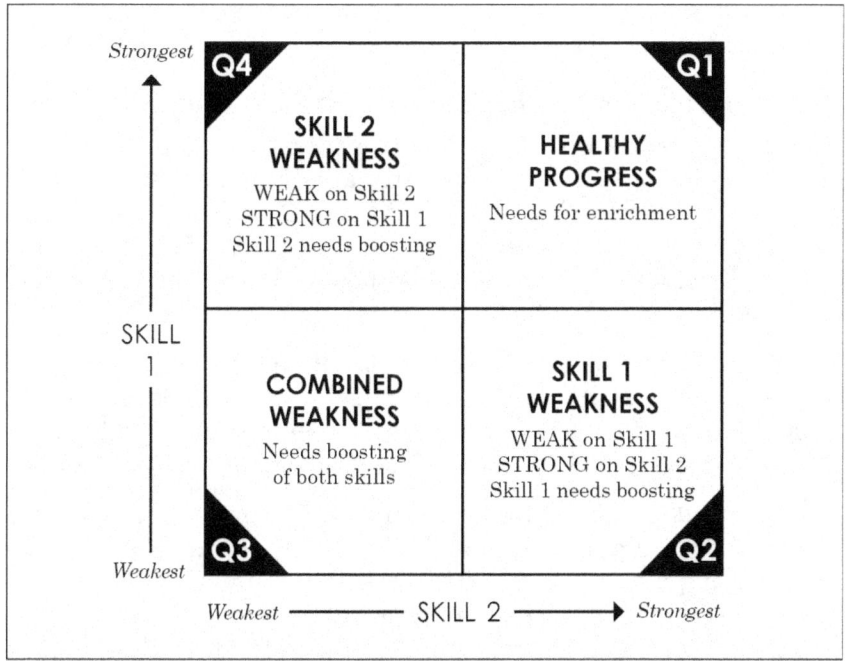

Figure 18a. Double-deficit quadrants for Skills 1 and 2

The figure above shows how scatterplots can display children's strengths, weaknesses and instructional needs on two focus skills by the quadrants they're positioned in.

As can be seen in the figure,
- Quadrant 1 (Q1) is healthy progress in both areas, with children perhaps likely to benefit by enrichment.
- Quadrant 2 (Q2) is isolated weakness in Skill 1, with needs to boost skill levels.
- Quadrant 3 (Q3) is combined weakness in both Skill 1 and 2, with needs to boost skill levels for both skills.
- Quadrant 4 (Q4) is isolated weakness in Skill 2, with needs to boost skill levels.

Earlier, we considered the reading and writing quadrants of the Literacy Component Model (Knight et al., 2021): Skill 1 was language skills for literacy, while Skill 2 was word-reading (for reading-comprehension) or spelling (for written expression).

In Australia, teachers in Bridging the Gap project schools, which we worked with, found those quadrants extremely useful for forming intervention groups (Knight et al., 2017b, 2020). There seems value in researching the usefulness in schools, of the Literacy Component Model, and double-deficit groupings for relevant factors impacting literacy development, for identifying instructional needs and tailoring instruction.

Quadrants for Early Identification of At-Risk Children

Quadrants made by testing Skill 1 and Skill 2 can be used to identify children at major risk, towards commencing strategic *Response to Intervention* (RTI) Tier 2 and 3 early intervention as quickly as possible, catching children before they fall, and before Acquired Helplessness exacerbates their learning woes (Gutiérrez et al., 2023; Torgesen, 2009).

The figure on the next page shows how Rapid Automised Naming (RAN) and phonological awareness might be used as Skills 1 and 2, with children's test scores on those skills plotting in scatterplots using quadrants, to show both risk status and intervention needs.

As confirmed by considerable research (e.g., discussed in Galletly, 2005b, 2008; Knight & Galletly, 2020; Knight et al., 2017a, 2021; Steacy et al., 2014), Standard-English children with isolated RAN or isolated phonological-awareness weakness are at risk of developing major word-reading and spelling difficulties, while children with a double deficit are at risk of much more severe word-

Research Tour 10. A Multiple Deficits Vs Phonological Basis?

reading, spelling and early-literacy difficulties.

Importantly, we can test these skills in fun, easy ways when children are 4-years-old, towards achieving pre-school readiness building, well ahead of when children start school and commence word-reading instruction.

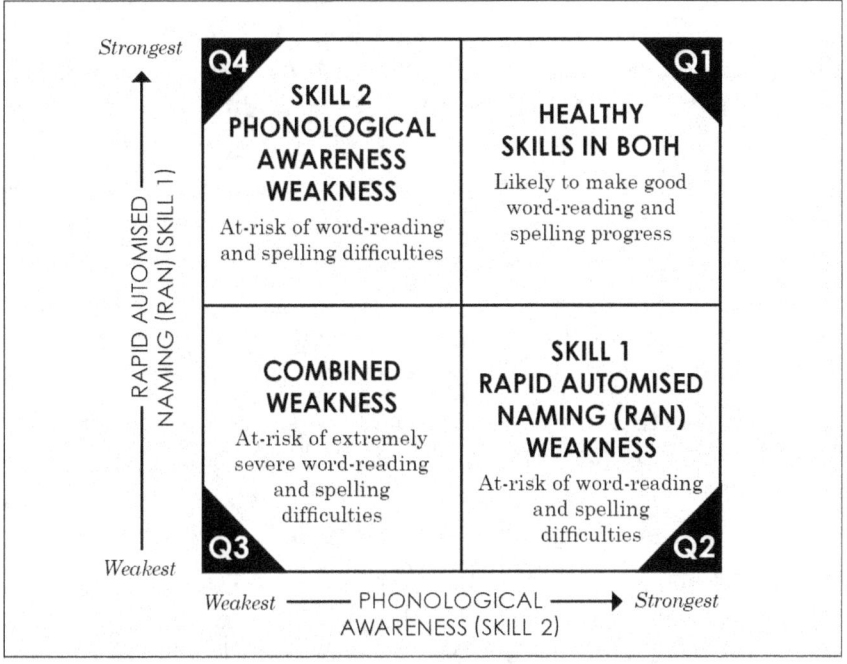

Figure 18b. Standard-English double-deficit quadrants for phonological awareness and Rapid Automised Naming (RAN)

Quadrant 2 and Quadrant 4 children, who have a single weakness in RAN or phonological awareness, need, and would benefit from, strong Tier 2 or 3 intervention strategically building word-reading pre-skills. There's value in research exploring that intervention.

That said, while continuing current early-literacy instruction, we may well find we can't win through sufficiently for these children with a double deficit of RAN and phonological awareness. For them, we may well need to take on Change 8 (2-Stage early literacy that uses a fully-regular initial orthography), and Change 9 (2.5 years of language and learning enrichment prior to formal literacy and numeracy instruction). Our early intervention would then have heightened effectiveness: research is needed.

Currently, for Quadrant 3 children, with their double-deficit weakness in both RAN and phonological awareness, preventative intervention should be an immediate and major priority. While we start our 4.5 to 5-year-olds on Standard English, we guarantee major struggles for our double-deficit children (Steacy et al., 2014).

Tier 3 intensive intervention should start as quickly as possible, perhaps using a combination of Tiers 2 and 3, i.e., strategically using both small-group and one-to-one intervention.

Instead of waiting for these children to fail, having RAN and phonological-awareness data means our schools could act quickly, providing preventative intervention before reading instruction and reading difficulties begin (Compton et al., 2012; Torgesen, 1998).

We wouldn't use just children's RAN and phonological-awareness results at start of school, of course. We'd also consider family history, and teachers' impressions of progress and risk status.

We'd also consider results on other tests, e.g., writing one's name and knowing a few letters and their sounds, and phonological-verbal short-term and working memory.

Australia has had very little school-level research exploring early identification and intervention. It's needed.

Let's Explore Other Double Deficits

The double-deficit concept of choosing two key factors and exploring subgroups of children with and without these factors is a useful one. We might find quadrants made from RAN (Skill 1) and their lowest score on short-term or working memory tests (Skill 2), useful in identifying at-risk readers, well before difficulties start.

Multi-factorial statistical analyses can usefully establish the impact of multiple factors simultaneously and, if desired, show results as quadrants (Kornilov & Grigorenko, 2018; Mascheretti et al., 2015; Rakhlin et al., 2013; Reilly et al., 2014; Zuk et al., 2020).

Quite a few studies have explored weakness in two factors.

Reilly et al. (2014) used two quadrant figures showing their results, in exploring the inappropriateness of using cognitive referencing as a criterion for language disorder. Skill 1 was non-verbal intelligence for both figures. Skill 2 differed, being receptive language skills in one set, and expressive-language skills in the other.

Nelson et al. (2016) used the quadrant model with Sound-Word ability and Sentence-Discourse ability as Skills 1 and 2, in their research developing the Test of Integrated Language and Literacy Skills (TILLS; Mailend et al., 2016; Nelson, 2016; Nelson et al., 2016).

Gathercole et al. (2008) explored the executive-function skills and working memory skills of children with low working memory, as Skills 1 and 2, with potential for use of quadrants. They didn't, however, use groupings of children with isolated and combined weaknesses. They found inattention, behaviour difficulties and working memory problems often co-occur, and that working memory weakness likely plays a causal role in the behaviour difficulties of children with low working memory (Chow et al.2018).

There have also been many studies looking at two factors within comorbidities (e.g., Galletly & Knight, 2011a; Knight et al., 2021). Importantly, researchers often find more severe educational difficulties when children have combined weaknesses, e.g., Meredith O'Connor and colleagues' (2020) findings showed that low SES compounds Australian children's educational disadvantage in multiplicative, not additive, fashion.

In addition, multiple studies, including some Australian studies, show it is often the number of disadvantaging factors, even more than the extent of each, which exacerbates children's educational disadvantage (e.g., Hayiou-Thomas et al., 2017; Kikkawa, 2014; M. O'Connor et al., 2020; Quach et al., 2015, 2017).

Craig et al. (2016) also found additive effects, when using double-deficit concepts in their review of 26 studies that compared executive-function weakness in children with AD/HD, ASD, and combined AD/HD and ASD, by testing executive-function skills in children aged from 3 to 18 years. They found

- The children with AD/HD had weak inhibition control.
- Those with ASD had weak cognitive flexibility and planning.
- Those with ASD plus AD/HD were weak in all three areas.
- Attention, working memory, preparatory processes, fluency, and concept formation didn't discriminate between the groups.
- Executive-function deficits reflect additive comorbidity.

Their findings align with DSM-5 no longer categorising ASD and AD/HD as mutually exclusive.

There does seem value in Australian school-based research that explores impacts of other double deficits beyond the RAN + phonological-awareness combination to explore the impacts of other sets of Skills 1 and 2, i.e., the impact of single and combined factors.

As an example, so many of the children I work with who have severe word-reading and spelling difficulties also have word-finding difficulties and associated expressive-language weakness that impact written language and answering questions during tests.

There would be value in double-deficit research exploring these factors as Skills 1 and 2, and establishing the specific executive-functioning and cognitive-processing skills that underlie these common overlapping difficulties.

Studies of children with isolated expressive language difficulties (including word-finding), isolated short-term or working memory difficulties, and combined weakness might also prove highly informative. So might studies using receptive and expressive vocabulary skills as Skills 1 and 2.

We need to explore key interacting factors in children's literacy development and difficulties, and their impacts. That's one reason our Literacy Component Model includes the cognitive load of learning and literacy tasks, and genetic, cognitive, behavioural, attitudinal, environmental, instructional and child impacting factors, along with reading and writing skills (Knight et al., 2021). It incorporates many factors which might be explored as double-deficit, interacting factors (Knight et al., 2021):

> *Rather than restricting comparison to a single pair of variables (such as in the Simple View of Reading and the Double Deficit models), the Literacy Component Model (LCM) considers that double deficits can logically occur across many variable pairs. The LCM enables sole-dual comparison of many variables as, for example, Brandenburg et al (2015) used word-reading and spelling in sole-dual comparisons of German children (isolated word-reading weakness, isolated spelling weakness, and combined reading-spelling weakness).*
>
> *Other variable pairs which might be explored using sole-dual comparisons include word-reading and executive-function skills, word-reading and written expression, word-reading and numeracy, written expression and reading comprehension, working-memory and short-term memory, handwriting accuracy and speed, spelling and phonemic-approximation writing, and executive-function and reading-comprehension skills.*
>
> *The LCM enables this exploration across diverse variables.*

The Literacy Component Model is a universal model, applicable to Standard-English and regular-orthography literacy development and difficulties. It is useful for schools and for research, and is a flexible model, enabling users to include additional relevant factors, which similarly can be explored in double-deficit research:

> *Somewhat akin to Grigorenko and Dozier (2013, p.11) discussing the increasingly well-researched human genome as*

being "both structurally malleable and functionally dynamic," we propose the LCM as being a malleable model, not always restricted to its [provided] form and equations.

The LCM has potential to take on varied forms in different contexts. ... In proposing flexibility, we suggest some users might add factors such as processing speed, cognitive processing and vocabulary as additional components.

Joshi and Aaron (2003) reported processing speed added significant additional variance, suggesting a relationship of Reading Comprehension = Word-Reading x Language Skills + Processing Speed. Mellard and colleagues (2015), in their work with adult-education participants, established both working memory and processing-speed added significant additional variance, such that Reading Comprehension = Word-Reading x Language Skills + Cognitive-Processing Efficiency.

Other educators might prefer vocabulary positioned separately to language skills, so both areas are prioritised instructional foci. As such, Reading Comprehension = Word-Reading x (Language Skills + Vocabulary). This is supported by findings that vocabulary, language skills, and word-reading skills each have similarly strong relationships with reading comprehension (Protopapas, Mouzaki et al., 2013).

Students using highly-regular orthographies rapidly develop proficient word-reading, spelling and phonemic-awareness skills, and thus have access to independent reading and written expression earlier (Ziegler et al., 2010). Speed of acquisition might become an additional component in studies comparing Anglophone and regular-orthography literacy development. This suggests that Reading Comprehension = Word-Reading (Skill level + Rate of development) x Language Skills (Skill level + Rate of development) x Automatising Skills.

This equation might also be used in studies of multilingual students (Bonifacci & Tobia, 2017) and those with inherited literacy disability (Eklund et al., 2015; Hulme et al., 2015). Spoken language factors that vary across nations also create differing strengths of LCM relationships (Li et al., 2009; McBride-Chang et al., 2005; Ziegler et al., 2010).

Morphemic awareness might be an additional factor for Chinese and Finnish children, given many Chinese words are compound words and long Finnish words are morphemically dense. As such the equation might become Reading Comprehension = Word-Reading x Morphemic Awareness x Language Skills. Studies find morphological awareness and vocabulary more

> strongly impact Chinese (Li et al., 2009; McBride-Chang et al., 2005), and Finnish word-reading development (Ziegler et al., 2010). ... There are many diverse theories and models of reading, writing and literacy development, at a range of behavioural, cognitive, neural systems, brain area and genetic levels (Frost, 2012; Grigorenko & Dozier, 2013; Stuart & Stainthorp, 2015). Using the LCM's flexibility, multiple components, processing skills and impacting factors, the LCM is compatible with, and supports discussion of diverse models of literacy and learning (Frost, 2012; Gabay et al., 2015; Goswami, 2002; Konold et al., 2003; Nicolson & Fawcett, 2011; Seymour et al., 2003; Shahar-Yames & Share, 2008).

The Multiple Deficits Basis model plus the Literacy Component Model, with its flexibility, are a practical and useful combination, and are powerful tools for research and practice into the future.

Key Findings from Tour 10

Findings and implications of studies explored in Tour 10 suggest the following points are useful considerations towards improving literacy and education in Australia and Anglophone nations:

1. Phonological-awareness weakness is a frequent area of weakness in Standard-English struggling word-readers and spellers.
2. For many years, researchers have considered phonological-awareness weakness as a primary universal basis of word-reading and spelling difficulties.
3. However, phonological awareness does not prevent regular-orthography children from mastering word-reading and spelling, and some weak Standard-English word-readers don't have phonological-awareness weakness.
4. Increasingly, researchers are advocating Pennington's (2006) Multiple Deficits Basis model that emphasises word-reading and spelling difficulties being due to multiple underlying factors, as a more useful model than those proposing phonological-awareness weakness as the underlying cause.
5. The Multiple Deficits Basis model accommodates not just phonological-awareness weakness, but also many other factors associated with word-reading and spelling difficulties, including other cognitive-processing difficulties, and comorbidities, including Attention Deficit/Hyperactivity Disorder (AD/HD), autism, auditory-processing weakness, and other disorders.
6. There seems value in using the Multiple Deficits Basis in Australian research exploring word-reading and spelling

Research Tour 10. A Multiple Deficits Vs Phonological Basis?

development and difficulties.

7. Copious research has focused on *Double Deficit* difficulties: children having weakness in phonological awareness, Rapid Automised Naming (RAN), or combined weakness in both areas.
8. Standard-English readers with phonological-awareness weakness or RAN weakness have word-reading and spelling difficulties, and children with combined weakness have far more severe difficulties.
9. In regular-orthography children, RAN weakness does not affect word-reading accuracy (Level 1 automisation), but impedes word-reading fluency (Level 2 automisation).
10. There is value in researching the many other double deficits present in weak readers, e.g., expressive language weakness and word-reading weakness, or expressive language weakness and executive-function weakness.
11. The Literacy Component Model (Knight et al., 2021) offers strong practical usefulness for both schools and researchers.
12. In future research, the Literacy Component Model's flexibility is useful for considering the many factors which impact literacy development, and the separate and combined impacts of multiple factors, including the cognitive load of learning and literacy tasks, and genetic, cognitive, behavioural, attitudinal, environmental, instructional and child impacting factors.
13. The Multiple Deficits Basis model plus the Literacy Component Model, with its flexibility, are a practical, useful combination, and powerful tools for Australian education, able to incorporate many current theories and emphases.

Research Tour 11. Executive-Function Skills Empower Word-Reading

Executive functioning is essential for social, occupational and academic functioning, physical and mental health and quality of life, and comprises top-down neuropsychological functions such as inhibition (of behaviour, attention or cognition in order to achieve a goal), shifting (changing internal perspectives or adjusting behaviour to new demands), and working memory, that is, mentally manipulating information held in mind (Diamond, 2013). Built on these domains, higher-order executive processes (problem-solving and planning) underpin decision-making and behaviour.

Marina Christoforou, Emily Jones, Philipa White & Tony Charman, 2023

What do our children with word-reading difficulties have in common with our children with language skills difficulties? On the surface it's literacy difficulties and academic struggles. Below that, it's weak cognitive processing, poor statistical learning, and quite likely, Acquired Helplessness. It's also the executive-function skills which underlie and are integral to learning.

Children's development of executive-function skills is a key aspect of communication, literacy and learning, and research over coming decades will build compelling knowledge on this area.

The tests used in research studies, and also those that aren't used, can very much limit the findings that studies can show (Knight et al., 2017a, 2017b; Papadopoulos, Csepe et al., 2021; Peng et al., 2022). As research further explores executive-function skills, we'll learn increasingly more on subtle aspects of learning (Knight & Galletly, 2020).

At present, we often work more with generalities. As an example, Ritchie et al. (2015) in a Welsh-English twin study, of 1,890 pairs of twins, assessing reading and intellectual skills at 7, 9, 10, 12, and 16 years, found reading ability at each age test-point significantly associated with intelligence differences a few years later, with this not linked to extent of reading exposure.

Queensland's longitudinal *Mater-University of Queensland Study of Pregnancy* (MUSP) study of over 7000 mothers and their children, ongoing since 1981 (Najman et al, 2015), also found damaging impacts on intelligence, with poverty at any childhood stage linking strongly to drops in intellectual and academic skills, including reading and numeracy, with more severe loss in those who experience poverty more frequently (Najman, 2015; Najman et al., 2004, 2009).

Some might assume low Socio-Economic Status (SES) is the cause of this lowering intelligence and academic achievement. That's not the case, of course, given many high achievers have low-SES childhoods (Education Queensland, 2000).

Instead, executive-function skills will be a major plank in the bridge of that relationship: children in poverty are more likely to have less cognitive, literacy and language enrichment, and thus miss out on needed executive-function enrichment across childhood.

Replicating these studies while extending them, by adding in tests of executive-function skills, might well reveal the linkages of this relationship. In Australian educational research into the future, let's focus on subtleties as well as generalities, and ensure we include a robust focus on executive-function skills.

Crosslinguistic studies of the past few decades have overwhelmingly focused just on word-reading of lists of words, phonemic-awareness development, and more recently, Rapid Automised Naming (RAN). It's therefore exciting in recent years to see increasingly more studies exploring other aspects of cognitive processing, albeit within word-reading development.

They show significant development of executive-function and other skills within word-reading development (Knight & Galletly, 2020; Morgan et al., 2019; Papadopoulos, 2001). This does suggest likelihood that, as discussed in Tour 1, in word-reading studies that have only assessed phonemic awareness, we might consider phonemic awareness as being a proxy for additional cognitive-processing and executive-function skills.

Using this concept, it's likely that Finnish, Welsh and Taiwanese readers don't just rapidly develop proficient phonemic-awareness skills (M. Aro, 2004; Hanley et al., 2004; Huang & Hanley, 1994, 1997), but instead also develop proficiency in other cognitive-processing and executive-function skills (Papadopoulos, 2001).

Let's fly in now to look at studies of cognitive-processing and executive-function development that go beyond phonemic awareness and Rapid Automised Naming (RAN).

Cognitive-Processing and Executive-Function Skills

Cognitive-processing skills are our information-processing skills. They include our more obvious surface-level information-processing skills, including reading, writing, communicating, thinking, and phonological and orthographic awareness. They also include our executive-function skills, a subset of cognitive-processing skills.

Executive-function skills include concentrating, planning, problem solving, coordinating aspects of a task, choosing between options, selecting the most appropriate strategy to use, monitoring its effectiveness, doing self-regulation, inhibiting less useful responses, ignoring distractors, keeping relevant information in mind, switching between task goals as needed, integrating information, building understanding, developing rules and generalisations, learning implicitly and explicitly, behaving appropriately, and monitoring the environment, e.g., listening for instructions. Children action executive-function skills endlessly in reading, literacy, learning and school functioning generally.

Childhood dysfunctions and disorders very much involve and impact children's executive-function skills, e.g., Attention Deficit/Hyperactivity Disorder (AD/HD) is an executive-function disorder, and executive function difficulties are strong features of autism, and communication and literacy weakness (Christoforou et al., 2023; Galletly & Knight, 2011a; Knight & Galletly, 2020; Nicolson & Fawcett, 2019; Pennington et al., 2012).

Executive-function skills also include phonological-verbal and visual-spatial short-term memory, working memory, long-term memory, and the interplay between them and other learning skills.

Increasingly, executive-function research is being focused on diverse aspects of child development, e.g., in Knight & Galletly (2020), we list executive-function studies focused on

- Social behaviour areas, including self-control, self-regulation, anxiety and emotion regulation.
- Attention and distractibility, e.g., in AD/HD.

Research Tour 11. Executive-Function Skills Empower Word-Reading

- The role of working memory in reading and academic difficulties.
- The separate and overlapping executive-function profiles of different developmental disorders, including AD/HD, Autism Spectrum Disorder (ASD), language disorder, dyslexia and reading disability, mathematics disability, developmental coordination disorder and behaviour disorders.
- Specific and interacting aspects of different cognitive-processing and executive-function skills.
- Brain areas associated with specific aspects of reading and executive functioning (Morken et al., 2014; Rueckl et al., 2015).
- Preventative enrichment in pre-reading teaching and learning, and interventions for children with executive-function weakness.
- Developing useful executive-function tests and checklists.

Executive-function skills organise, co-ordinate and action the strategies children use in reading and literacy tasks, e.g., Nguyen and colleagues' (2020) series of studies showed weaker executive functioning increased the likelihood of miscues, particularly in more complex texts (Nguyen, Pickren et al., 2020), and that executive-function weakness contributed separately to higher numbers of miscue errors in Standard-English weak word-readers, beyond the contributions of their weak reading and weak language skills (Nguyen, Del Tufo & Cutting, 2020). They discuss executive functioning's role in co-ordinating the reading and language-skill processes of text reading and likely reasons for the relationship of executive functioning to reading (Nguyen, Pickren et al., 2020):

> One speculation as to why EF contributes to poorer reading performance is that poor readers face challenges in executive coordination across word-, sentence-, and passage-level processes. ... When word-level skills such as sight word recognition and decoding are automatized, readers are able to attend to higher-level factors of the written text (sentence and passage), as well as dedicate their cognitive resources (e.g., working memory and the ability to plan and organize) toward online linguistic comprehension. ...
> Via reasoning, individuals comprehend and draw inferences, as well as predict incoming information (e.g., words), based on the cues that are drawn from prior text and stored within working memory. ...
> Yet, in order to achieve proficient comprehension during oral reading, readers must also identify and/or suppress irrelevant idea units (via inhibitory control and monitoring), which are

then used to construct a coherent mental representation of the current text. ...
Such mental representation then informs word-level abilities through lexical retrieval and the spreading of semantic activation, a cognitive process that is often known as contextual facilitation (Stanovich, 1980).

Three Key Executive-Function Skills

Considerable cognitive-processing research has focused on three key executive-function areas, with many considering them the pivotal components of executive functioning:
- Working memory: holding information in mind while mentally manipulating it.
- Inhibitory control: ability to resist usual or automatic responses when they aren't relevant to the task one is doing.
- Cognitive flexibility (shifting): adjusting thinking and switching behaviours and goals, in response to changes in task priorities.

For Anglophone children, it's phonological-verbal working memory – holding information in mind while thinking on it, which usually has the strongest relationship with Standard-English reading and early-literacy, and academic progress (Galletly, 1999a, 2003, 2004b; Knight & Galletly, 2020). That's logical, really, as English orthographic complexity creates very high cognitive load for our children learning to read and write, and that, in turn, creates a clash of our children having low processing capacity and processing skills (working memory and cognitive processing), against the high cognitive load and thus needs for high processing capacity and processing skills that Standard English creates. Our children have to vastly more thinking than regular-orthography children, when trying to read and write words they're not yet fluent on: effective working memory is needed and helps manage this cognitive load.

Working memory is connected to but separate from short-term memory. Short-term memory, children's ability to take in and store memory briefly, is a key subskill of Standard-English word-reading development, as children need to hold letter-sound information in mind, while working out unfamiliar words, and learning irregular sightwords (Galletly, 2004a, 2004b; Peng et al., 2022). Working memory uses short-term memory (Peng et al., 2018):

Working memory (WM) refers to the capacity to store information for short periods of time while engaging in cognitively demanding activities (Baddeley, 1986). In contrast to

> short-term memory (STM), which is a passive information storage system, WM is the system responsible for storing and processing information simultaneously.
> Theoretically, WM plays an important role in reading performance because many reading tasks involve simultaneous information processing and storage. ... to comprehend a text, individuals first visually process the words; then match the words to the phonological, orthographic, and semantic representations in long-term memory; and finally combine these representations with the context to construct an understanding. ...
> WM is purported to be involved in this process by keeping relevant information in STM, retrieving information from long-term memory, and integrating all sources of information to form an accurate representation of the situation described by the text.

Quite often, we measure phonological-verbal short-term memory by asking children to say aloud increasingly longer lists of numbers, and we measure working memory by asking children to say the lists in reverse order, thus mentally manipulating information. Comparing the two, you can see how short-term memory is storing the information without acting on it, while working memory is both taking in the information and working with it.

When children do functional literacy tasks at school, there's sometimes very little practical difference between the impacts of weak short-term and weak working memory. When the struggling readers I work with are doing complex literacy tasks such as reading for comprehension or writing purposefully, irrespective of whether they show only short-term memory weakness, only working memory weakness, or weakness in both, they all show major functional working-memory weakness in listening, reading and writing tasks, and often experience too high cognitive load and overload. The key factor, in functional terms, is that in tests, the children show weakness in at least one of these areas.

This is in keeping with studies showing that tasks used to test short-term and working memory largely measure subcomponent processes they have in common, including executive-function skills such as controlled attention, rehearsal, maintenance and updating, and differ more in the extent to which these skills are involved (Galletly, 2004b; Unsworth & Engel, 2007).

The next few decades will be an exciting time in neuropsychological research, and we'll quite possibly see useful, practical, school-level applications, e.g., (Knight & Galletly, 2020):

In addition to sole interventions, there seem options of multiple pronged interventions being developed, e.g., combining computerised interventions with options such as
- Event-Related Potential (ERP) and fMRI brain mapping (Molfese et al., 2010; Preston et al., 2016),
- Transcranial Direct Current Stimulation (tDCS; Au et al., 2016; Shin, Foerster, & Nitsche, 2015),
- Physiological measures of cognitive load (Zagermann, Pfeil, & Reiterer, 2016), and
- Use of medications such as those for managing attention difficulties (Diamond, 2013; Rabipour & Raz, 2012).
With recent studies showing value in factors as diverse as self-talk empowering learning, saying words aloud enhancing vocabulary development, and sleep consolidating learning (Durrant et al., 2011; Ehri, 2014; Schiff & Vakil, 2015), it's likely that over time, the range of associated useful factors will expand. ... Event-Related Potential (ERP) brain-mapping, which does electroencephalogram recording of brain waves, may well become commonly used in schools in the future, with it being relatively inexpensive, portable, and non-invasive. ERP responses from specific tasks are now being found to be valuable predictors of the likelihood of later learning difficulties. Transcranial Direct Current Stimulation (tDCS) is increasingly found useful. ... Research is establishing useful practical means of measuring the extent of cognitive load individuals are experiencing ... these measures include blood pressure, heart rate, electrodermal activity, electrical activity in facial muscles, and eye movements (Krzysztot et al., 2018; Zagermann et al., 2016).
[In addition] eye measurement research is becoming increasingly sophisticated, with studies showing extent of cognitive load experienced can be measured with diverse aspects of eye movements. ... These measures can be used in practical contexts such as schools.

There's every likelihood that in the future, schools will use these different measures and interventions to enhance the effectiveness of identification, instruction and intervention.

Executive-Function Skills Develop Across Childhood

Children's cognitive-processing skills improve as they get older, e.g., numerous studies show working memory capacity steadily increases from ages 4 to 8 years, with development continuing into teenage years (Cowan, 2016; Gathercole et al., 2004, Gathercole &

Research Tour 11. Executive-Function Skills Empower Word-Reading

Pickering, 2000a, 200b, 2001a; Gooch et al., 2016; Majerus & Cowan, 2016; Swanson & Howell, 2001).

Chan and Rao's (2022) crosslinguistic study of children aged approximately 4.5 years, in Bangladesh, China and India learning to read Bengali, Chinese and Hindi, respectively, showed the universality of executive-function development (Nicolson & Fawcett, 2019; Wolf & McCoy, 2019). It explored how the three key executive-function skills (working memory, cognitive flexibility and inhibitory control) relate to children's language and early-reading skills (letter-recognition, name writing and early word-reading).

It found all three executive-function skills were significantly associated with children's language and pre-literacy skills, beyond the impacts of age and socio-cultural factors, in all three nations. For all nations, inhibitory control was more strongly associated with oral language, and working memory with literacy. Of interest, cognitive flexibility (shifting) was not as strongly related to language skills for the Chinese cohort.

Chan and Rao's study used practical easy-to-use executive-function tests. There's value in it being replicated in Australia and other nations, along with longitudinally following skill development.

Gathercole et al.'s (2004) study of working memory skills in approximately 600 UK children aged from 4 to 14 years showed that verbal and visual-spatial short-term and working memory develop steadily across ages 4 to 14 years without reaching ceiling level, and that significant differences are present between the short-term and working memory capacity of children aged 4 to 5 years, children aged 6 to 7 years, children aged 8 to 9 years, and so on.

Other studies show that inhibitory control and cognitive flexibility, the two other major executive-function skills, also increase quite markedly across the school years (Diamond, 2013; Knight & Galletly, 2020; Morgan et al., 2019; Ober et al., 2020; Rocha et al., 2022).

These findings suggest that Anglophone children would do far more effective learning if word-reading instruction was delayed a few years until executive-function skills were more developed. Given we start our beginners at close to the world's youngest age on one of the world's most complex orthography, it's important we build deeper knowledge on the cognitive-processing and executive-function aspects of our starting when children are so young.

In future Australian research, we need to explore cognitive-processing differences between our 5-year-olds and older children, here and in regular-orthography nations. We'd explore not just short-term and working memory but also other cognitive-processing and executive-function skills, including inhibitory control, cognitive flexibility associated with the behaviour, maturity, resilience and more effective learning of older children.

Our Children Need Strong Executive-Function Skills

Increasingly, studies are finding that all three of the key executive-function skills (working memory, inhibitory control and cognitive flexibility) impact children's word-reading and reading development (Diamond, 2013; Knight & Galletly, 2020; Morgan et al., 2019; Ober et al., 2020). Not surprisingly, with literacy and language skills highly related, studies find all three executive-function areas impact both language and literacy skill development and difficulties (Knight & Galletly, 2020).

While studies show somewhat variable findings, on the whole, they lean towards all three skills (working memory, cognitive flexibility and inhibition control) being significantly related to Standard-English readers' word-reading, literacy and academic achievement. Children with strong executive-function skills have strong achievement, while children with weak executive-function skills become struggling readers and learners.

Ober et al.'s (2020) meta-analysis of studies on this area found all three executive-function skills related moderately strongly to Anglophone children's word-reading skills.

Morgan et al. (2019), studying 11,000 USA children, explored how weakness in the three areas when children were in Kindergarten predicted subsequent academic difficulties across Grades 1 to 3:
- Working memory weakness virtually tripled the odds of severe Standard-English word-reading difficulties.
- Inhibitory control weakness doubled these odds.
- Cognitive flexibility weakness didn't specifically predict word-reading difficulties.
- All three increased likelihood of maths and science difficulties.
- Gender (being male), socio-economic status (SES) and prior reading achievement level also predicted later reading difficulties.

Age-related differences will of course also be a major factor for our 4.5 to 5-year-olds, learning to read and write with significantly less developed executive-function skills than e.g., Grade 1 European children who are 7 to 8 years when learning to read and write.

Research Tour 11. Executive-Function Skills Empower Word-Reading

They may also be a factor in why it's so difficult to catch up our children with weak word-reading to healthy-progress levels.

Working Memory Is Important

Children's working memory skills predict differences in Standard-English word-reading and reading comprehension, with low working memory strongly associated with low literacy and academic achievement (e.g., Swanson and Howell, 2001).

Gathercole and Pickering (2001) studied the relationship between multiple working memory skills and academic achievement on national curriculum tasks and tests, in UK children aged 6 and 7 years. They found children with weak academic achievement showed significant working memory weakness, and discuss the importance of effective working memory skills if Anglophone children are to achieve effectively in the early school years.

Other studies they conducted also found weak working memory strongly associated with low literacy achievement in at-risk children (Pickering, 2000a, 2000b). Their studies highlight the importance of schools knowing children's short-term and working memory levels from the start of school.

Inhibitory Control Is Important

Inhibitory control, the ability to block responses that aren't relevant, develops from prior to school, initially quite rapidly then more slowly across the school years. Inhibitory control weakness increases likelihood of reading and academic difficulties, with children having difficulty ignoring irrelevant information and habitual responses, and struggling to avert inattentive, impulsive and disruptive behaviours (Christoforou et al., 2023; Craig et al., 2016; Diamond, 2013; Morgan et al., 2019; Ober et al., 2020).

When they're younger, children have weaker inhibitory control. This makes them more likely to experience mind-wandering, impulsiveness, goal neglect when tasks are complex and involve multitasking, and *action slips*, where, while knowing the correct strategy they should use, they instead use an incorrect strategy.

It's logical that weak inhibitory control would be a major risk factor for Australian and Anglophone beginning readers aged only 4.5 to 5 years learning to read and write complex Standard English with its Regular, Pattern and Tricky words and syllables (Galletly 2004a, 2005b, 2008; Goswami, 2002; Ziegler & Goswami, 2005).

Inhibitory control weakness, rather than guessing, may underlie children's action slips, e.g., why Frith et al.'s (1998) Standard-

English readers made real-word substitutions for pseudowords so often, despite having been told the words weren't real words.

Cognitive Flexibility Is Important

Cognitive flexibility, which some researchers term *shifting*, is the ability to shift attention between different aspects of complex tasks. It too is a big issue for our beginners learning to read and write. Developing from approximately 4 years of age through adolescence, cognitive flexibility builds from, and in turn builds, both working memory and inhibitory control.

Children weak in cognitive flexibility struggle to shift attention to different task aspects, and hence do less efficient problem-solving. Learning to read Standard English has high demands for effective cognitive flexibility, which is much needed when trying to read and write less-familiar words: children must flexibly think about what type of word it might be, and which word-reading strategies would be most effective, e.g., on whether the word is

- A Regular Word, for which they'd use sounding-out.
- A Pattern Word, where they'd think on patterns they know, then perhaps use rhyming to work it out.
- An irregular Tricky Word: one they've already learned that they need to recall, or a completely new one they need help for.

It's a nasty Catch-22 situation, with our beginners needing ample cognitive flexibility to negotiate orthographic demands, but with cognitive flexibility being in very short supply at age 4.5 to 5 years. Doubtless, having less-mature cognitive flexibility skills increases our children's risk of word-reading and writing difficulties.

The Impacts of High Cognitive Load

There seems minimal research comparing the cognitive load of early-literacy development in regular-orthography and Standard-English children. I wasn't able to find any studies of the area.

Certainly, high cognitive load on an ongoing basis across early-literacy development is the norm for Standard-English children, and multiple studies show that high cognitive load stresses student functioning (Galletly & Knight, 2011a; Knight & Galletly, 2020).

There's considerable value in research exploring the impacts of high and low cognitive load across literacy and numeracy development in our children and regular-orthography children for thirds, tenths, and the lowest and highest 5% and 2% of achievers.

High Cognitive Load Induces Language Weakness

One interesting study sheds light on the impacts of high cognitive load on our at-risk readers. While many studies reveal existing weakness in tasks with high cognitive load (Galletly & Knight, 2011a), this study showed that deliberately increasing cognitive load can actually induce language and learning weakness temporarily in healthy-progress children.

Hayiou-Thomas et al. (2004) increased cognitive load for 138 6-year-old Grade 1 and 2 children in the UK in two ways, in their study, *Simulating SLI: General cognitive processing stressors can produce a specific linguistic profile*:

- Slowing the information the children listened to, and
- Extending sentence length by adding redundant information.

They found that in these situations of higher cognitive load and task demands, the children's communication and learning skills reduced considerably. Both methods of increasing load produced a pattern of language disorder, i.e., error patterns often seen in children with Language Disorder, but not seen in healthy-progress children.

Given that that English orthographic complexity produces ongoing high cognitive load in early-literacy tasks, Hayiou-Thomas et al.'s finding has multiple interesting findings, e.g.,

- Executive-function weakness' strong role in children's actioning of language skills, and, quite likely, literacy skills.
- Executive-function weakness likely being a basis of Language Disorder (Knight & Galletly, 2020; Tomas & Vissers, 1999).
- High cognitive load directly impacting, and reducing, communication and learning efficiency.
- High cognitive load likely to be particularly damaging for young Anglophone children given its ongoing nature, across the many years of Standard-English early-literacy development.
- Children with low cognitive-processing skills, particularly short-term and working memory, being particularly vulnerable for impacts of higher cognitive load (Galletly & Knight, 2011a)
- Likelihood that Anglophone children with Language, Literacy and Learning Disorder (LLLD) have far greater difficulties than regular-orthography children with similar profiles prior to starting school because of the ongoing high cognitive load of Standard-English early-literacy (Galletly & Knight, 2011a).

The High Cognitive Load of Our Number Wording

It's likely our children's maths development would also benefit significantly by us holding off formal maths instruction until they're older, and have stronger working memory and cognitive flexibility.

Currently factors such as our number wording add cognitive load, and this disadvantages young children with low working memory. Indeed, it's possible Australia and Anglophone nations needlessly induce maths difficulties by starting maths instruction when at-risk children are too young.

Taiwanese, Japanese and Chinese children have cognitive load advantage from their number wording, which enables considerable numeracy progress as pre-schoolers informally enjoy maths fun. Studies show they're well ahead of Anglophone children by the time they start school (Dehaene, 2011). It's largely due to their number wording which kindly reduces cognitive load, and doesn't burden young children's low working memory.

They say *six-hundred four-tens three* for 643, *one-ten three* for 13, and *five-tens three* for 53, with their number wording including place value *(tens)*, and only the digits 0-10. This makes their numbers brilliantly transparent, while ours are relatively opaque. The wording lays out the tens, units and place value of each numeral, ready for addition, e.g., *three-tens four plus five-tens two* makes it far easier for children to add up the ones and tens than our *thirty-four plus fifty-two*. – it's ideal for mental computation. Meanwhile, our numbers are abstract terms that don't organise the numerals neatly for our children, with *thirteen, thirty, fifteen* and *fifty* often causing confusion. Their low cognitive load gives maths advantage while our high cognitive load can create difficulties.

China and Taiwan have additional cognitive load advantage, through their numbers being easy to say more rapidly, with each a two-sound Consonant-Vowel (CV) syllable: 1 to 10 in Taiwan sounds akin to *yi, er, san, si, woo, liu, ki, ba, jiu, shi*. Timing oneself counting 1 to 10 three times, as quickly as possible, then timing saying e.g., *da pa ta* quickly 10 times, hints at this time difference.

That's a working memory issue: it creates lower cognitive load. Being quickly said, their children can easily fit appreciably more numerical information in working memory than our children can. That gives maths advantage.

We'd may well benefit from research exploring a beginners' number system for our children. That's particularly so, given we start maths instruction at age 4.5 to 5.0 years, when working memory is low.

We might use 1-syllable beginners' numbers, e.g., *wa, ta, tha, fa, fie, si, se, ay, ni, te* for 1 to 10, and also the place-value hundreds-tens-one system, with e.g., 21 being *two-tens one*, i.e., *ta-te wa*.

Research Tour 11. Executive-Function Skills Empower Word-Reading

Just as we use printing first, until children are comfortably writing, then move on to cursive writing, we'd start with our beginners' number system then, later, when children have skills and confidence, we'd transition them to our standard number wording of *one, two, three, teens/tys, thirteen, fifty-one* and so on.

Importantly, very large numbers of our struggling word-readers have automisation weakness for counting and maths. They struggle with

- Numbers with abstract wording (e.g., 30 being *thirty* not *three-ty*).
- Teen numbers being said *backwards*: right to left, not left to right like all other numbers, e.g., 13 is *(3)thir-(1)teen*, not *(1)teen-(3)thir*.
- Confusing teen/ty numbers that sound alike (e.g., 13/30, 14/40, 19/90).
- Struggling with counting, and making errors on 12, 20 and 100, because of that teen/ty confusion, e.g., children often say *70-80-90-20*, counting up, and *50-40-30-12-11-10*, counting down.

We may find a beginners' number system a worthwhile help, reducing mixing-up of teen/ty numbers (13/30, 19/90), difficulties mastering 1-100, and counting up and down. Combining that with holding formal maths instruction off until mid-Year 2 would be a strong help: with 2.5 years of early numeracy enrichment play, children would have stronger executive-function skills, and it's likely far fewer would develop Acquired Helplessness, and instead achieving Success Inoculation.

Certainly, Australia would benefit from engaging in crosslinguistic research studying cognitive-processing, executive-function and cognitive-load aspects of numeracy development as we study literacy development here and in regular-orthography nations.

High Cognitive Load Activates Risk Factors

It's notable that many risk factors that lay our children low often aren't activated in regular-orthography children. That seems a kindness from the low cognitive load of learning to read regular orthographies, with this reducing demands for strong executive-function and statistical learning skills.

There's value in Australia and Anglophone nations engaging in crosslinguistic research exploring the extent to which risk factors are activated in young Standard-English readers but not in regular-orthography children who at age 4-5 years have similar risk factors.

The Reading Skills of Children with ASD and AD/HD

Weaknesses in individual executive-function skills are risk factors for Standard-English word-reading and early-literacy difficulties well worth exploring in research on early-literacy development. So too are easily-included factors such as gender (being a boy is a risk factor, as girls usually achieve higher on literacy skills), having a family history, and being young in one's year-level. Immaturity, and Autism Spectrum Disorder (ASD) and Attention Deficit/Hyperactivity Disorder (AD/HD) traits at start of school are further risk factors.

Future crosslinguistic research that Australia might engage in, exploring the impact of risk factors such as executive-function weakness and traits of ASD and AD/HD on word-reading and early-literacy development would enable gaining rich insights on the extent to which English orthographic complexity activates these and many other risk factors, through the high cognitive load it creates as children learn to read and write.

While the executive-function weakness of many children only becomes obvious once reading instruction commences, children with strong traits of ASD and AD/HD have marked executive-function weakness that's in place in early childhood, prior to starting school.

Craig et al. (2016) found marked executive-function weakness in children aged 3 to 18 years with AD/HD, ASD, or combined AD/HD and ASD, with inhibition control weaker in AD/HD, cognitive flexibility and planning weaker in ASD, and all three weaker in combined AD/HD plus ASD, with working memory weakness being present but not discriminating the three groups. They comment,

Executive dysfunction has been shown to be a promising endophenotype in neurodevelopmental disorders such as autism spectrum disorder (ASD) and attention-deficit/hyperactivity disorder (ADHD). ... Although there are important differences in core symptom definition, the co-occurrence between ASD and ADHD is supported by clinical, common biological, and nonbiological risk factors and neuroimaging studies.
Several authors believe that ASD and ADHD share a common genetic basis. Both family and twin studies provide support for the hypothesis that ADHD and ASD originate from partly similar familial/genetic factors. Approximately 50%–72% of the contributing genetic factors in both disorders show overlap. These shared genetic and neurobiological underpinnings form an explanation why both disorders occur so frequently within the same patient and family. ... Both ADHD and ASD are

Research Tour 11. Executive-Function Skills Empower Word-Reading

childhood-onset neurodevelopmental disorders affecting key [brain circuits] that are important for EF.

A better understanding ... of the co-occurrence of ASD + ADHD is important because it could not only provide clues for enhanced treatment options but could also highlight the existence of a combined phenotype. EF impairments have been considered as central deficits in ADHD or ASD.

For pre-school children, findings are similar. Christoforou et al. (2023) reviewed executive-function studies of pre-school children with and without Autism Spectrum Disorder (ASD, 21 studies) and Attention-Deficit/Hyperactivity Disorder (AD/HD, 10 studies) that used tests or survey measures. Results showed that both ASD and AD/HD were strongly associated with significant executive-function weakness, but with profiles of skill-weakness to be somewhat variable (possibly due to methodological issues across studies). Their review findings showed cognitive flexibility (shifting) more consistently impaired in autism; and inhibition control, planning and working memory to be more consistently impaired in AD/HD.

They found informant-based measures often revealed executive-function impairment more robustly than laboratory-based tasks. That seems in keeping with the variable nature of the behaviours of executive function impairment that clinicians encounter, with parents reporting their child being perfectly behaved in a clinical setting, in marked contrast to usual behaviours at home and school.

With regular orthographies making it so easy to learn to read and write, regular-orthography children don't need strong working memory and other executive-function skills to the extent that Standard-English readers do.

In the 10 Changes, both Changes 8 and 9 are highly relevant towards Australia aiming to reduce the impacts of executive-function weakness on children's literacy and learning development:
- Investigating the potential of a beginners' orthography and 2-Stage early literacy (Change 8), and
- Adding in 2.5 years of executive-function and learning enrichment, and delaying formal literacy instruction until children are older with stronger executive-function skills (Change 9).

Anglophone nations need crosslinguistic research comparing the word-reading and literacy development of regular-orthography and Standard-English children with and without ASD, AD/HD, and combined ASD and AD/HD. This will empower decision-making regarding Changes 8 and 9, while adding useful insights on the impacts of executive-function weakness and high cognitive load on both activation of risk factors, and early-literacy development.

Word-Reading Instruction Methods Change Executive-Function and Language Skills

Regular-orthography studies are useful for Australia and other Anglophone nations as they show what happens in relatively *pure* regular-orthography environments where children develop word-reading, spelling and early-literacy skills quickly and easily, usually within one school year, with relatively few external factors impacting their development.

In contrast, with word-reading and spelling proficiency taking many years here in Australia, our children have a myriad of factors that impact skill development, e.g., being taught by multiple teachers, with different methods. The more factors there are which impact a situation, the more the waters are muddied, in research studying skill development.

This makes the crosslinguistic research and the findings of research in regular-orthography nations particularly useful for Anglophone nations. They can provide diverse insights which can then be explored in Standard-English children, e.g.,

- There may be considerably-less direct impacts of executive-function weakness on reading-comprehension development, and much stronger executive-function impacts on word-reading and spelling development (Dolean et al., 2021).
- It's likely executive-function skills support development of handwriting and written expression not just in early primary school, but also across later school years (Rocha et al., 2022).

Let's now explore the changes in language skills and executive-function skills that occurred in Cyprian and Greek children as they learned to read and write Greek, a highly-regular orthography.

Papadopoulos's (2001) study of Grade 1 children shows that learning to read and write a regular-orthography builds executive-function, cognitive-processing and language skills. He studied two groups learning to read and write highly-regular Greek. They were taught with different methods, those of Cyprus and Greece.

The children in Cyprus learned to read using Whole Language methods with strong emphasis on rich literature and meaningful reading. Sounding-out words wasn't an explicit instruction focus, but was discussed and used incidentally during reading.

In contrast, the children in Greece had systematic explicit word-reading instruction, including explicit instruction in letter-sounds and practising sounding-out to read and write words.

Testing conducted 8 months into Grade 1 showed the two groups, on average, achieved similarly for word-reading of familiar real words. In contrast, there were major differences for reading unfamiliar words and other skill areas.

The Greek children, who'd been taught specific decoding strategies, achieved markedly higher for reading unfamiliar words.

Importantly, they also achieved significantly higher on specific executive-function and language skills, being significantly higher on short-term memory, working memory, language reasoning and speech rate.

Papadopoulos concluded that even for Greek, a highly-regular orthography, systematic word-reading instruction usefully builds cognitive-processing, executive-function and learning skills.

The study's findings that different forms of instruction result in stronger skills in diverse aspects of executive-function and language-skills suggest value in also studying instructional emphases in research exploring executive-function and language-skills development: as the brain changes as children learn, it seems that different instructional methods produce different changes.

Those findings of increased executive-function and language skills are in keeping with Perfetti's (2007) *Verbal Efficiency Theory*, which emphasises the positive developmental impacts of literacy development on other skills – though it's interesting that these skills developed so significantly only in the Greek children.

Papadopoulos's (2001) study seems well worth replicating with our children, and children doing 2-Stage early-literacy development in e.g., Taiwan. Studies might test executive-function, cognitive-processing, word-reading, reading-comprehension, spelling, written expression and language skills, and explore development differences in high achieving and lower achieving children.

We would, of course, bear in mind that some areas of improvement might only be visible in regular-orthography children, given more risk and instructional factors impact Standard-English beginning readers, and this can muddy the waters of research findings.

Building Executive-Function Skills Can Build Word-Reading Readiness

Interestingly, the findings of some studies suggest that building executive-function skills first, without focusing on word-reading skills, can boost subsequent word-reading development.

Again, the findings are of regular-orthography children, in another study by Papadopoulos and colleagues (2004). Their research article, *Kindergarten cognitive intervention for reading difficulties: The PREP remediation in Greek* contains useful appendices detailing the intervention used.

The study used the *Planning, Attention, Simultaneous and Successive Processing* (PASS) Reading Enhancement Program (PREP). Developed by J P Das, PASS does not focus on word-reading or its subskills of phonological awareness and orthographic awareness (letter-sound knowledge). Instead, using largely implicit learning, it builds executive-function and learning skills: problem-solving skills that underlie word-reading and reading comprehension (Das et al., 2008; Georgiou et al., 2020; Mahapatra,2016).

Based on Vygotskian principles, it emphasises inductive reasoning, with children supported to work out key concepts. Building simultaneous processing and successive processing executive-function skills logically relevant to later success in reading, the activities used are far removed from letter-sounds, phonological awareness and word-reading.

The Papadopoulos et al. (2004) PREP study involved two sequential studies, with a group of Greek beginning readers.

In Study 1, an experimental group of 15, 5-year-old, Greek children at risk of developing reading difficulties, and a control group of 15 children who weren't at risk, were assessed before and after the at-risk group did four weeks of PASS PREP intervention.

At the end of the intervention, the at-risk children had made significant progress, and achieved at similar levels to the control group on phonological and cognitive-processing measures.

Study 2 was longitudinal, exploring the long-term effects of that four weeks of PASS PREP intervention. They found the experimental (at-risk) PASS PREP group showed healthy word-reading development, achieving as well as the control group on word-reading, alphabet and letter-sound knowledge skills.

The researchers conclude that the inductive training of key

executive-function skills, notably planning, focused attention, and simultaneous and successive processing skills was effective in expediting later letter-sound learning and word-reading development, in the absence of school training of these skills.

Those are interesting findings, which we might well replicate in our at-risk children, particularly if doing 2-Stage early literacy, and initially learning to read and write a beginners' orthography. There'd be value in comparing the executive-function growth in Standard-English vs regular-orthography cohorts – we may well find more minimal effects in the Standard-English at-risk children.

We might also find that combined interventions, e.g., of PASS PREP and GraphoLearn, might have heightened efficiency.

PASS research studies have shown success with Standard-English readers, however, those studies seem to be largely of remedial intervention rather than PASS being used preventatively with beginning readers (Georgiou et al., 2020).

The Papadopoulos et al. (2004) PREP study of Greek children is a particularly useful read for building understanding of PASS and PREP, and the value of building executive-function skills in at-risk children prior to word-reading instruction commencing, towards preventing difficulties occurring.

This program may well be worth investigating in future Australian research exploring word-reading development of Standard-English vs a beginners' orthography. We may find the muddied waters of solely-Standard-English early literacy reduce intervention impacts.

Powerful Byproducts of Effective Cognitive Processing

Differences in children's executive-function and cognitive-processing skills create differences in how effectively they learn to read and write, and build literacy and learning skills. In turn, learning to read and write creates improvement in various cognitive-processing skills.

Together, they create the major learning differences we see between Standard-English and regular-orthography readers, and between our strong-progress upper-third readers, and our struggling lower-third readers and Spelling Generations.

We may well find that learning to read and write a regular-orthography expedites building of children's executive-function and cognitive-processing skills.

In contrast, when we only use Standard English, we may find that executive-function and cognitive-processing skills' growth is lacking in our lower-third struggling readers, whilst happening, albeit slowly, for our upper-third strong readers.

This is suggested by another interesting study by Papadopoulos, Spanoudis et al., (2021), that's also well worth replicating and extending. It explored linguistic and executive-function differences between advanced and average Greek readers.

The study followed a cohort of Greek children from Kindergarten through Grade 2, assessing at multiple time-points on a range of language, literacy, linguistic and executive-function skills.

Not surprisingly, they found the advanced readers had significantly higher executive-function skills, in addition to higher phonological-awareness and Rapid Automised Naming (RAN) skills:
*Results showed that precocious readers exhibited superior performance in phonological awareness, naming speed, and reading fluency across development, whereas their early advantage in letter knowledge disappeared by Grade 1.
A cognitive advantage specific to executive function (planning) was also observed for the precocious readers early on and was maintained through Grade 2.*

We need to bear in mind that those Greek weaker word-readers with weak executive-function skills would be far ahead of our weak word-readers, riding Express Trains to success while our weak Standard-English word-readers have the slow arduous work of riding Railway Handcarts (Galletly, 2022a). Crosslinguistic studies of the full range of word-readers may well show executive-function weakness to be a major issue for Australian weak readers.

There's value in replicating that Papadopoulos et al. (2004) study with Standard-English and regular-orthography groups, exploring thirds, deciles and the lowest and highest 5% and 2% of achievers.

Starting Age Cut-Offs Can Be Punitive

With young age being strongly associated with lower executive-function skills, and associated immaturity and weaker learning, there's also value in considering the impact of education systems using a set date as their cut-off for children starting school.

All Australian states and territories have a compulsory upper-limit for starting age, by which children must have started school. Most states have it set at 6.0 years, while it's 6.5 years in Queensland.

In addition, all states and territories start the school year in late January, with children required to turn 5 by a set cut-off date.

Alas, just as names for the first school year (officially *Foundation*) differ in confusing fashion, the age cut-off dates also vary greatly.

We've actually an 8-month range for starting dates, as shown in the table below. In addition to being awkward for families who move between states, this range may mean we have *age-disadvantage effects*: children in states with later cut-off dates being disadvantaged as regards year-level academic learning, expectations and achievement, relative to children in states with earlier cut-off dates.

State	Cut-off date	Name used for Foundation year
Tasmania	January 1	Prep
Victoria	April 30	Prep
Australian Capital Territory	April 30	Kindergarten
South Australia	May 1	Reception
Queensland	June 30	Prep
Northern Territory	June 30	Transition
Western Australia	June 30	Kindergarten
New South Wales	July 31	Kindergarten

Table 5. *States and territories' entry dates for Foundation year-level*

International research on *age-disadvantage effects*, impacts of being older vs younger in one's year-level, shows that children are likely to experience disadvantage in school learning if particularly young (Bedard & Dhuey, 2006; Depew & Eren, 2016; Gladwell, 2008; Lubotsky & Kaestner, 2016).

That finding has major useful implications for the Anglosphere and Australia:
- Anglophone children are likely to be considerably, and perhaps unethically, disadvantaged by being of much younger age (4.5 to 5 years) when required to learn to read highly-complex Standard-English orthography, given that many European nations start formal education for early-literacy learning that is vastly easier, when children have

considerably higher maturity and executive-function skills, at age 7 to 8 years.
- Australia might best set a single age cut-off date for starting school, to be used across all states and territories.

Lubotsky and Kaestner (2016) studied younger vs older USA child-achievement effects from Kindergarten through Grade 8. Using data from the *Early Childhood Longitudinal Study* Kindergarten Class of 1998–99 (ECLS-K) cohort, they found appreciable differences between older and younger Kindergarten and Grade 1 children for reading and maths.

In their study, the age-advantage effects reduced after Grade 2, to be less strong in Grades 5 and 8. (That wasn't the case for the Socio-Economic Status (SES) gap, which they also explored, comparing richer vs poorer children: it started wide and stayed wide.)

Research by Bedard and Dhuey (2006) study, using cross-national data, found age-advantage effects that stayed strong. Their findings showed strong indicators of persisting disadvantage from starting school at younger age, with Grade 4 and Grade 8 younger children scoring significantly lower than older classmates in the 2003 *Trends in International Mathematics and Science Study* (TIMSS) study. Importantly, they also found younger children significantly less likely to achieve at highest levels at high school.

Age effects are executive-function efficiency effects, and it does seem likely that they would impede younger children. They would impact teaching and learning in many ways, and, quite likely, increase children's likelihood of developing Acquired Helplessness. Also, younger children's age-disadvantage, once begun, would quite likely be perpetuated across the years (Bedard & Dhuey, 2006, 2012; Gladwell, 2008).

As an example, in busy classrooms, it's easy for immaturity effects to be perceived as ability effects, with older Prep children placed in advanced reading groups, and younger children in lower groups. It's common for children's skills to build accordingly, with stronger progress in children receiving extension, and progress limited for those in more remedial streams.

With their stronger learning, the older children are then more likely to continue in advanced groups, while the younger children, lacking impressive progress, are more likely to continue as, and be treated as, lower achievers.

Other studies exploring child age at start of school, also show starting older has empowering effects, e.g., even reducing likelihood of juvenile crime in vulnerable children (Depew & Eren, 2016).

Bedard and Dhuey (2012) discuss many positive impacts of
- Children starting school later.
- Schools changing cut-offs so all children are older.
- Children being older, rather than younger, in their year-level.

While likely to be much stronger for at-risk and struggling learners, the impacts are certainly also present in children with strong skills. Gladwell (2008) explored the birth months of outstanding sportspeople, finding most to have been among the oldest in their year-level when starting sport, and very few born in the youngest three months prior to cut-off. There's likelihood those younger children were unfortunately perceived as being weaker at sports, instead of simply just younger than their older and stronger peers, and were treated, and thus progressed, accordingly.

With youngest children in New South Wales being almost 8 months younger than the youngest Tasmanian children, it's possible we have age-advantage effects present, for all three thirds of children, with our at-risk and struggling learners impacted more severely.

Further, there's every likelihood that future research will show that Anglophone children experience major age-advantage effects in having to do complex formal learning when far younger than children of many other nations. Table 1, in Tour 1, lists the major age-differences between Anglophone children and children in many European nations (Knight & Galletly, 2017; Seymour et al., 2003).

If and when age effects are found present, it behoves us to make early-years education far easier and more manageable, to make education easier and more effective for our children e.g., using 10 Changes improvements, particularly Change 9.

Thus, in addition to research exploring age impacts on early-literacy development in Australian classes, we need cross-national research that compares our children and older European children, and also includes focus on young vs older subgroups. It will quite likely be found that being young in one's year is a much greater risk factor for Standard-English readers who learn to read when very young.

Key Findings from Tour 11

Findings and implications of studies explored in Tour 11 suggest the following points are useful considerations towards improving literacy and education in Australia and Anglophone nations:
1. Executive-function skills, including working memory, inhibition

control and cognitive flexibility, increase across the school years, being significantly low at age 4 to 5 years, when Australian children start formal literacy and numeracy instruction, and significantly higher at age 6 to 8 years when children in many other nations start formal instruction.
2. Australian children are disadvantaged when learning to read and write through their executive-function skills being insufficiently developed.
3. It is likely that many at-risk children are compromised by their executive-function skills being insufficiently developed, when they're trying to learn to read and write words.
4. Because English orthographic complexity creates ongoing high cognitive load in reading and writing tasks, the low working memory our children have at age 4.5 to 5 years is likely to be additionally disadvantageous, through them experiencing high cognitive load in all subject areas involving reading and writing tasks, while they have relatively weak word-reading and spelling skills.
5. In addition to rapid phonemic-awareness development, regular-orthography word-reading development can also expedite development of executive-function and linguistic skills, including short-term memory, working memory, language reasoning and speech rate.
6. Studies of regular-orthography children show that different instruction methods differentially develop executive-function and language skills, e.g., explicit word-reading skills instruction resulted in Greek beginning readers developing significantly higher short-term memory, working memory, language reasoning and speech rate than Cyprian children who didn't receive explicit instruction, when both were learning to read and write highly-regular Greek. Explicit skills instruction seems to build higher levels of executive-function skills and skills for reading unfamiliar words.
7. Preventative early-intervention focused directly on building executive-function skills, and not on word-reading skills and subskills, notably J P Das' *Planning, Attention, Simultaneous and Successive processing* (PASS), can result in regular-orthography at-risk children making healthy word-reading progress when they later learn to read.
8. PASS has been used with Standard-English readers, though largely in remedial contexts.
9. Differing levels of executive-function skills differentiate regular-orthography high and low achieving word-readers – stronger word-readers have stronger executive-function skills while

weaker word-readers have weaker skills.
10. This suggests the likelihood that executive-function skill differences may well be a factor in Australian children becoming upper-third vs lower-third readers.
11. There is strong value in Australian education assessing a range of executive-function skills and monitoring their development across the school years from start of school, and exploring their relationship with literacy skills and instructional methods.
12. Because executive-function skills can be measured at young ages, e.g., 4 years, it may be possible to identify children with executive-function skills weakness before they start learning to read, and provide useful intervention.
13. It may well be the case that if our children first learned to read and write a fully-regular beginners' orthography, they'd develop strong executive-function, linguistic and learning skills prior to transitioning to Standard English, with these skills enhancing their subsequent learning.
14. Studies show that high cognitive load can temporarily induce language weakness in healthy-progress children.
15. This suggests the likelihood of damaging effects from the ongoing high cognitive load learning to read and write Standard English creates for our children, particularly children with weak cognitive-processing skills.
16. It also suggests the likelihood that Anglophone children with language, literacy or learning weakness have far greater school difficulties than regular-orthography children.
17. There are indicators that age differences have strong impact on early-years learning, with children older in their year-level achieving far higher than children younger than most peers.
18. There is value in investigating the impacts of young vs older age, particularly as our states differ markedly in the age cut-offs used for children starting school, with an 8-month range.
19. There is strong value in studying cognitive-processing and executive-function skill development as part of studies of word-reading, spelling, literacy and language skill development in Standard-English and regular-orthography children.

Research Tour 12.
Impeded Statistical Learning

Statistical learning (SL) is an ability comprised of multiple components that operate largely implicitly. ...
Individuals vary in terms of the efficiency of these underlying components ... and tasks differ from one another in how they draw on [statistical learning] components.

Joanne Arciuli, 2018

It's common to consider *statistical learning* as being solely implicit learning, without explicit teaching. In reading and early-literacy research, and in school instruction, it's valuable to focus on implicit, explicit, and combined implicit-explicit statistical learning. We'd learn much from studying these areas as we also study executive functioning in word-reading and early-literacy development.

It doesn't take much to divert our at-risk word-readers off the path to success, into weak statistical learning, and associated poor word-reading progress. For a start, young children who don't find word-reading easy can be easily diverted from effective learning by situation cues, which can seriously impede their learning.

Gough and colleagues' (1992) *Thumbprint Experiment* showed this well. They taught beginning Standard-English readers to read sightwords with words on cards, with one card having a somewhat obvious thumbprint on it. Then they tested the children on their reading, with the thumbprint now moved to a different word. And, you guessed it, lots of children read the thumbprint, saying the word previously written on the thumbprint card instead of correctly reading the current word: they'd focused overly on the reading situation, rather than the words and their individual letters.

Relying on situation cues (*contextual facilitation*) happens all too often for our Standard-English weak word-readers (Nguyen et al.,

2020), e.g., they read *purple* correctly because it's the only long word starting with *p* in the word set that they've practised. Sometimes the focus is word position, e.g., reading *purple* correctly by remembering it's the P word on the second line. They read *people* correctly too, knowing it's the one far right on the next line – then are flummoxed when meeting the words in other contexts or when word-order changes.

On the whole, that impeded learning doesn't happen for regular-orthography children. They read every word and syllable accurately using phonemic recoding (sounding-out) – because words are so utterly trustworthy, with all being Regular Words, with nary a Pattern, or Tricky word or syllable, crossing their path.

It's interesting that Papadopoulos's (2001) Cyprian Grade 1 Greek readers, with implicit learning, were weaker on unfamiliar words. I suspect they'd close that gap reasonably soon, and become strong readers of unfamiliar words (Frith et al., 1998; Landerl et al., 1997).

Basically, regular-orthography children keep practising their one extremely useful word-reading strategy, phonemic recoding, and they soon become extremely good at it.

In contrast, our children look for easy ways to remember words, and often use situational cues – because word-reading of unfamiliar Standard-English words is complex until you've quite a strong level of confidence and skills.

They focus on visual features such as word order and flashcard colour and, in doing so, shoot themselves in the foot because instead of focusing on words and their letters, they're actually practising word-reading avoidance strategies.

Explicit word-reading and spelling instruction helps our children confidently focus on words, and steadily builds their skills for reading unfamiliar words. It works for regular-orthography children and it works to an appreciable extent for our children too. For at-risk children, explicit instruction can be hugely beneficial.

All three thirds of our children benefit from systematic word-reading instruction – it's just the extent that differs. Explicit teaching focuses learners on key concepts and skills, showing them what to do, guiding them and supporting their practice so they steadily build mastery.

Explicit teaching and practice are particularly useful because they reduce likelihood that children will get the wrong idea and, with misconceptions ruling, head off down less useful learning paths, such as the thumbprint, the green flashcard, and *purple* being the first word on the bottom line.

Upper-third word-readers need very little systematic instruction – a word to the wise is often enough. In contrast, lower-third word-readers can benefit tremendously from clear explanations and lots of guided practice, including games, and reading strategic lists of words, e.g., my *Sets of 10* and *Rapid Read* sets, available on ResearchGate (Galletly, 1999b, 2000, 2001, 2003, 2023c, e, f, g).

Towards optimising word-reading development of all three thirds of achievers, Australia needs to study instructional methods and their effectiveness, as differing methods are often shown to have quite marked differences in effectiveness (J. Anderson, 2021; Apfelbaum et al., 2013; AUSPELD, 2019; Boyle et al., 2019; Chall, 1967, 1999; Chard et al., 2000; Colenbrander et al., 2022; Connor, Adams, et al., 2020; Connor, Kelcey, et al., 2020; Connor, Phillips et al., 2018; Denton et al., 2013, 2014; Dykstra, 1968; Dyson et al., 2017; Filderman & Toste, 2022; Galletly, 1999b, 2000, 2001, 2014a, 2017a, 2023c,d,e,f; Galletly & Knight, 2005, 2010; Goldfeld et al., 2017, 2022; Knight et al., 2018; Knight & Galletly, 2016; Kyle et al., 2013; Landerl, 2000; Lyytinen et al., 2021; Mazurkiewicz, 1971, 1973a; Middleton et al., 2022; Nicholson & Dymock, 2015; Papadoloulos et al., 2003, 2004; Pressley, 2006; Reed & Vaughn, 2012; Roberts, Torgesen et al., 2008; Ruotsalainen et al., 2022; Scammacca et al., 2007, 2015, 2016; Seabrook et al., 2005; Serry et al., 2007; Shapiro & Solity, 2008, 2016; Stuart & Stainthorp, 2015; Torgesen et al., 2010; Vaughn et al., 2019; Vousden et al., 2011; Wanzek et al., 2013, 2016, 2018).

A Study of Implicit Statistical Learning

Let's now explore a useful, insightful study that raises important questions about the impeded statistical learning that our Standard-English beginning readers can experience when not provided with explicit instruction. In the same way that Papadopoulos' (2001) study showed instructional methods resulted in appreciably different learning in Greek children, this American study shows it happens too in Standard-English word-reading development.

It's Apfelbaum et al.'s (2013) study, *Statistical learning in reading: Variability in irrelevant letters helps children learn phonics skills.*

It investigated the effectiveness of two different word-instruction methods on children's learning to read regular Consonant-Vowel-Consonant (CVC) words (phonemic recoding). It's a role model study, i.e., worth replicating and extending in Australian school research, likely to produce interesting findings.

Phonemic recoding is the word-reading strategy that regular-orthography children master so quickly, e.g., with Finnish and Taiwanese children usually needing only 10 weeks of instruction (M. Aro, 2004; Huang & Hanley, 1994, 1997) to be impressively accurate word-readers and spellers. Alas, it's a very different story for our children, as is evidenced in Apfelbaum et al.'s study.

The school-level USA study used computerised learning with 224 Grade 1 children. The focus was implicit statistical learning – the extent to which children did direct, unimpeded, unconfused learning, i.e., picked up patterns, concepts, and strategies by themselves, without having had any explicit teaching or explanations.

The children were in two groups, each exposed to just one of the two methods. They were exposed to, and worked with, different word-reading examples, which induced implicit statistical learning.

One method used mixed Consonant-Vowel-Consonant (CVC) words, with a small range of final consonants, e.g., *d, t, n, p*, likely to encourage that group of children to think on Regular Word strategies, i.e., phonemic recoding – reading words by sounding-out their letter-sounds and blending them.

The other method used *-ad* and *-oat* word families, and included many of those words, to encourage that group of children to think on rimes, the part of the word that rhymes, and use Pattern Word strategies. (Did you know we spell the part of a word that rhymes, a *rime*? That's English orthographic complexity at its finest.)

In effect, the word sets encouraged children to think on different orthographic grainsizes (Goswami, 2002; Ziegler & Goswami, 2005):
• The first group, a mixed CVC words cohort, experienced phoneme grainsize: phonemic recoding (*sounding-out*) of Regular Words.
• The second group, a word-family cohort, experienced orthographic-unit grainsize: Vowel-Consonant (VC) units at the end of syllables, which encouraged Pattern-Word reading, using rimes and rhyme.

The words for both strategies used just two vowels: *a* as in *sad, hat*, and *oa* as in *boat, float*.

The goal of the learning was to build the children's skills for reading similar unfamiliar words that used those same vowels with mixed final consonants. However, the children weren't told the goal: that's common in implicit learning studies.

The study's findings are very interesting. The researchers found
- Strong learning for the mixed CVC words cohort, for both stronger and weaker word-readers – they did well at reading new unfamiliar words as well as learned words.
- Far weaker learning for the word-family cohort, especially for weaker word-readers – they read learned words well, but showed notably weak skills for reading unfamiliar words.
- Girls' learning stronger than boys' for both cohorts.
- The word-family format particularly disadvantaging boys and weaker word-readers.

It was a study of solely implicit learning, and one wonders what might have happened had a small or large amount of explicit learning been added, e.g., learning might have been boosted, simply by adding metacognition, through telling children that the aim of the game was to be clever at reading new words.

It's interesting that the word-family (Pattern Word) implicit learning didn't work nearly as well as the mixed CVC words (Regular Word) implicit learning, and that boys and weaker learners did so poorly with them. Apfelbaum et al. comment,

Despite theoretical support for both similarity and variability, under our task conditions, results were unequivocal. Children exposed to items with greater variability in consonant frames [mixed CVC words] learned vowel GPC regularities better than children exposed to items with similar frames [word families]. This benefit extended to novel tasks and words, showing that variability [mixed CVC words] significantly improved generalization.
It also held for both students who entered the study with greater reading abilities and those who began at a lower level, showing that variability can help both early acquisition of regularities and later refinement of learned categories. ...
Not only did stimulus variability increase learning, but in some cases it was essential for learning to occur at all: similar words [word families] produced little measurable benefit for low initial performers, while learners at both performance levels exhibited learning when trained with variable stimuli (mixed CVC words). Girls learned in both conditions (though more so with variability), whereas boys only learned with variable stimuli (mixed CVC words).

The results are thought-provoking. Why did children do such poorer statistical learning using word-families (Pattern Words), and why did boys do so poorly? What factors are involved? It's highly likely that executive-function research would shed useful light on this area.

Other studies show that while boys, on average, are weaker than girls for multiple aspects of literacy learning, they nonetheless benefit similarly from systematic word-reading instruction (e.g., Limbrick et al., 2011, 2012). That makes it relevant to consider why boys showed such poorer implicit learning in this study.

In clinical practice, I certainly find reading of regular CVC words is best taught using mixed CVC words with varied last consonants. That's because word families can be a distracting situational cue, with children over-focusing on word families and under-focusing on phonemic recoding (sounding-out). In consequence, in working with struggling readers, we do ample mixed CVC word-reading. For children who find it difficult, I initially reduce cognitive load by using 2-letter VC words, e.g., moon monster names such as *ub, ed, oz*, along with real words such as *at, egg, if, it, in, is, on, us, up*.

I don't use Pattern Word reading (orthographic grainsize) and word families) for regular words because I want children to focus strongly on the individual letter-sounds of CVC words, and do phonemic-recoding – blending the letter-sounds to make the word.

In contrast, I do use Pattern Word reading and word families for words with common multi-letter rime endings, e.g., *-ook, -all, -aw, -ar, -ee, -ea, -oy*. That's to build focus on those word-end patterns and do phonological recoding: blending beginning letter-sounds onto the sounds of multi-letter units, e.g., *l-ook, ch-ook, d-ay, str-ay*.

I first teach children nine key-word Pattern Words visually as wholeword, sightword Tricky Words: b*all*, l*ook*, s*ee*, pl*ay*, b*oy*, c*ar*, n*ow*, m*e*, m*y*. Then I use rhyme reading activities to build skills to read and write other words that use those patterns, e.g., *-ar-car-far, all-ball-tall*. It works very well. My Pattern Word unit is available for free use on ResearchGate (Galletly, 2023b).

It would be very useful to replicate Apfelbaum et al.'s study in Australian school settings, exploring a wider range of factors, including explicit learning and metacognition, and exploring the executive-function skills that children develop using the different formats. We could explore implicit, explicit and combined statistical learning in our upper, middle and lower-third children, while exploring the executive-function skills they need, and the ones that develop as they learn.

Additional variables might include
- A larger range of vowels and word families.

- Metacognition, including explaining that the aim is to read unfamiliar words, not just the given words, using the skills children have developed.
- Practising generalising, e.g., showing children how to generalise from e.g., -*oat* family to -*oad* family words.

Unfortunately, time and expense are big issues in experimental and quasi-experimental research. The main reason most studies restrict variables used is to keep research time and expenses low.

That's because, if working to establish each variable's precise impacts, so often, this requires a major increase in the number of subjects (e.g., children) and the number of subject groups. High subject numbers in each group increases the power of research, while numbers being too low can result in results being non-significant and factors being dismissed as possibly irrelevant, when actually they're important.

That's why PISA, PIRLS and other large studies can be more confident in their findings. It's also a strong reason for NAPLAN online testing to include tests of word-reading and executive-function and other language skills: assessing 10% of children, high subject numbers would enable confidence about findings.

So increasing variables usually means increasing subject numbers. Then, in turn, that increasing of subject numbers and subject groups increases the extent of testing and intervention to be done, often quite exponentially. Adding variables can thus increase time and expense, often to a prohibitive extent.

So why didn't Apfelbaum et al. (2013) include those extra variables or tell children the aim of the game, given that their knowledge-building may have been much stronger?

Quite likely it's because the aim of the study was to measure children's implicit learning in different learning contexts. Its findings on implicit statistical learning are indeed powerful. They were able to study extent of learning from two methods, plus the learning of boys vs girls, and stronger vs weaker learning.

Additionally, the researchers probably couldn't justify the time and costs of adding more subject groups and the additional testing and training that would entail. Just adding in metacognition (e.g., the aim of the game), would have meant twice as many groups were needed; with either doubled subject numbers, to maintain research rigour, or halved numbers in each group, with rigour thus reduced.

Further, it's often hard to say when enough is enough. After all, even if they'd added the above variables, other USA states might say *but that was only Florida schools and education, and just Grade 1 children – it might have worked differently with Kindergarten children in Ohio* – and increasingly more subject groups might be added so state and grade-level factors could be explored.

Suffice to say, it was a good study, and its findings are provocative, such that it's well worth replicating and extending. It could even be explored informally, initially, with groups of teachers trying the two methods, with and without metacognition and explicit teaching, and comparing their findings. Prof Apfelbaum can be contacted at the University of Iowa (his email is in the article): when I asked, the research resources were potentially available for further use.

Most definitely, the study showed that different teaching methods can increase and decrease statistical learning, and that vulnerable learners can easily be derailed by situational cues. In that way, it's similar to the different skill development of Greek and Cyprian children receiving different instruction (Papadopoulos, 2001).

Different Findings in a Similar Study

It's useful to note that Kyle et al.'s (2013) small GraphoLearn study of computerised learning with UK Grade 2 children, found quite different findings to Apfelbaum et al. (2013), with stronger learning by children receiving Pattern Word instruction. While not stated, it's likely that both combined implicit-explicit statistical learning.

They studied the learning of 31 UK children aged 6 to 7 years, using appreciably low subject numbers:
- A control group of 10 children who had no intervention.
- An experimental group of 11 children who did Regular-Word training using *GraphoGame Phoneme* (GG-Phoneme).
- An experimental group of 10 children who did Pattern-Word training using *GraphoGame Rime* (GG-Rime).

The experimental groups played the computer games daily, for 10 to 15 minute sessions for a 12-week period, to a maximum 60 sessions. The children were tested prior to and at the end of the 12-week intervention period, and also, usefully, 4-months post-intervention, to assess longer-term gains.

Both intervention groups made appreciable gains in word-reading, spelling and phonological awareness relative to the control group. However, the results were opposite to those of Apfelbaum et al.: the GG-Rime group made stronger gains than the GG-Phoneme group.

Of interest is the fact that a lack of Level 1 automaticity seemed present: while children's gains 4-months post-intervention were still significant, there was appreciable loss of gains over the 4 months post-intervention. Loss of skills after intervention ceases (Level 1 Automisation Weakness) is an ever-present issue for Standard-English but not regular-orthography intervention: this makes it important that testing at one or several time-points post-intervention is included in Standard-English intervention studies.

Kyle et al. (2013) had very low subject numbers, and this makes findings less conclusive as regards applicability in our schools. They also did not compare learning of stronger vs weaker learners, or girls vs boys. That said, their study had a clear finding: the Pattern Word group (GG-Rime) did appreciably stronger learning.

Standard-English research on GG-Rime has continued. Ahmed et al. (2020) conducted a much larger study with 398 UK Year 2 children identified with word-reading difficulties by their Grade 1 *Phonics Check* results. Ahmed et al. only used GG-Rime, and not GG-Phoneme (Regular word strategies), so the study doesn't provide further insights on the differing findings of Kyle et al. (2013) and Apfelbaum et al. (2013).

Ahmed et al., found GG-Rime played on its own, without extensive adult support, to progress moderately struggling Standard-English readers to make stronger word-reading progress than control group children who didn't play GG-Rime. That said, the Standard-English children's results are notably low relative to results of GraphoLearn studies of regular-orthography children, e.g., Finnish children using GraphoLearn achieve age-level word-reading and spelling proficiency (Lyytinen et al., 2021).

Certainly, it would be useful to have Australian research extending Apfelbaum et al.'s, Kyle et al.'s and Ahmed et al.'s studies, to build knowledge on the effectiveness of different word-reading strategies.

It's interesting to reflect on the differences between the computerised learning experiments. The difference in results might be due to explicit teaching vs implicit learning. It might also be due to the GraphoLearn intervention perhaps including extra factors:
- Use of a larger range of vowels and word families.
- Implicit plus explicit learning, plus metacognition, with students knowing the aim is to read new words.
- Giving students ample practice at generalising Pattern Word reading to reading unfamiliar words, including words using differing final consonants.

All three studies are useful in encouraging reflection on the range of strategies that can be included in word-reading instruction to build children's skills for reading unfamiliar words and syllables. They are useful baseline studies that are well worth replicating, with additional variables.

Boys Are More Vulnerable

It's interesting that, in Apfelbaum et al.'s (2013) study, the boys did far better when provided with stimuli that provoked consideration of all three sounds of the 3-sound CVC words and phonemic recording, with many of them failing to make effective generalisations from Pattern Words and onset-rime thinking.

Motivation will be a factor and PISA, PIRLS and Australian studies show girls have higher motivation than boys (Martin, 2004, 2010).

But what underlies that lack of motivation? It's possible that word-reading and reading being difficult in earlier reading development is an underlying factor. Quite likely, weaker statistical learning and executive-function skills are part of this. In turn, they'd perhaps create more likelihood of boredom and Acquired Helplessness.

On the whole, boys are far more vulnerable than girls when it comes to reading difficulties (Morgan et al., 2019). That's the case for word-reading (Quinn & Wagner, 2015). It's also the case for reading comprehension, e.g., in all nations in PIRLS and PISA studies, and in NAPLAN testing, on average, girls almost invariably achieve higher than boys for reading. Just being a boy is a risk factor, alas.

Importantly, in addition to more boys than girls being struggling readers, the proportion of boys becomes higher as the severity of difficulties increases.

Wheldall and Limbrick (2010) showed this for Year 3 and Year 5 Australian children's reading-comprehension levels in a large study of more than one million children, using data from New South Wales state testing. The ratio of boys to girls in the lowest achievement band was 1.66:1 for Year 3, and 2.26:1 for Year 5, and their graphs of the proportions of boys and girls at each band level show an almost picture-perfect progression in both year-levels, with the proportion of boys steadily increasing as band levels drop.

Quinn and Wagner (2015) showed relatively similar findings for Grade 3 Standard-English word-reading. They used Florida state data, and found the same steady pattern of increasingly more boys at increasingly severe levels of word-reading weakness.

It's thus important for future research studies to consider gender differences in cognitive-processing and executive-function skills involved in reading and writing, and how these are differentially impacted by the high cognitive load and high conceptual content of learning to read and write Standard English.

In the Galletly Report, I discuss factors underlying why so many boys struggle (Galletly, 2005b):

While many studies exploring the association of boys and weak literacy are working strongly from sociocultural perspectives, it is highly likely that cognitive factors are also involved. In addition to far higher proportions of boys having difficulties with literacy, and attention and behaviour (areas where it is more difficult to decide whether constitutional or environmental factors are in place), there is also higher male incidence of speech-language difficulties, autism spectrum disorders, and auditory processing weakness, areas which are far more likely to have constitutional, not environmental, origin (Bamiou et al., 2001; Blackburn, 2003; Root & Resnick, 2003; K.J. Rowe & Rowe, 2002; K.S. Rowe & Rowe, 2004, Shaywitz, 2003b; Westwood & Graham, 2000).

It is interesting that so many of the 52 recommendations to Senate on school reforms required to engage boys in schooling by Ian Lillico (2000) seem equally valid recommendations for the schooling of students with attention deficits and/or auditory processing weakness.

Research on boys and word-reading needs to be approached from behavioural, cognitive and biological levels. It is possible that word-reading development may prove a significant factor in male underachievement in reading ...

While currently, sociocultural solutions to gender differences are being emphasised (Blackburn, 2003; Englert & Mariage, 2003; Gee, 2000; Griffin, 2001; House of Representatives Standing Committee on Education and Training, 2002), it seems more likely the boys' difficulties are also due to interactions of instructional, constitutional and sociocultural factors (K.J. Rowe & Rowe, 2002; Shaywitz, 2003b).

As with the impact of SES, one wonders if there may be an interaction between gender and orthographic complexity variables. When visiting Finnish schools, there did not seem to be a perception that boys had more difficulty mastering word-reading than girls. When asked about different reading progress in boys vs girls, the Finnish teachers quickly and confidently stated that there were no differences present, and seemed to find our question rather odd.

We need to be doing far better for our boys' word-reading, reading and literacy development. We'd benefit from studies exploring
- Boys' and girls' word-reading, reading and literacy development.
- The involvement of executive-function skills in their learning, and differences in achievement.
- The executive-function impacts of Success Inoculation vs Acquired Helplessness in their learning and progress.
- Gender differences in ways boys and girls flourish with implicit, explicit and combined statistical learning.

Regular-Orthography At-Risk Children and Impeded Statistical Learning

At-risk regular-orthography readers show indicators that they don't just benefit from explicit statistical learning, e.g., their teachers explaining word-reading systematically and giving lots of scaffolded practice – they also need it (Lyytinen et al., 2021).

Explicit teaching helps children get the right ideas and master them, whereas relying on implicit learning can mean children get wrong ideas and mistakenly pursue them.

This is indicated to a certain extent in the Papadopoulos' (2001) study that compared Cyprian children, who did only implicit learning, with Greek children, who did explicit learning. The Greek children were much more powerful at reading unfamiliar words, and had additionally built stronger executive-function skills.

GraphoLearn research similarly suggests the value of explicit learning and scaffolded practice (e.g., Lyytinen et al., 2021). It's also evidenced other intervention studies in regular-orthography nations, that we'll explore shortly, in Tour 14.

This suggests strong value in regular-orthography at-risk children doing explicit learning and scaffolded practice, with schools not relying on implicit learning, and instead proactively providing explicit teaching and learning, to the extent that it's needed.

When Regular Orthographies Include Complexities

Orthographies differ in many dimensions, including many nations using orthographies that aren't alphabetic. As part of studying early-literacy development in Australia, there is value in considering the impacts of differences in orthographic design. As Daniels and Share (2018) emphasise,

The full spectrum of the world's writing systems needs to be considered. The global picture reveals multiple dimensions of complexity. We enumerate 10 such dimensions: linguistic distance, nonlinearity, visual complexity, historical change, spelling constancy despite morphophonemic alternation, omission of phonological elements, allography, dual purpose letters, ligaturing, and inventory size.

When orthographies don't provide needed information, confusion and impeded statistical learning can abound. Just as it occurred for Standard-English readers in Apfelbaum et al.'s (2013) study, and Gough et al.'s (1992) thumbprint experiment, focusing on wrong or less-important cues also occurs with regular orthographies, which have ambiguous features. This makes explicit focus invaluable.

Let's now briefly consider two nations where the inclusion of a complexity can complicate children's learning. Perhaps, future, collaborative research with these nations might shed light on the extent to which complexities complicate literacy development in regular-orthography and Standard-English readers.

Israel: Unpointed and Pointed Hebrew

In Israel, children do 2-Stage early literacy as they learn to read Hebrew orthography, which has two forms:
- A highly-regular version: *pointed Hebrew*, used in Stage-1.
- A complex version: *unpointed Hebrew*, used in Stage-2.

Children first use the fully-regular pointed Hebrew in Stage-1 earliest reading and writing (Share & Bar-On, 2017):

The rapid early mastery of Hebrew's phonologically transparent pointed script is now a well-established finding, confirmed in numerous studies (reviewed in Share & Levin, 1999) and reaffirmed in recent years, notably by Shany, Bar-On, and Katzir's (2012) definitive study of a large nationally representative sample.

When proficient in reading and writing pointed Hebrew, children move in second grade to Stage-2, and transition to using somewhat ambiguous unpointed Hebrew, their much more complex orthography, which uses just consonant letters.

In the highly-regular pointed Hebrew of Stage 1, all vowels are present: they're written as diacritical points and dashes usually positioned below words' consonant letters, and sometimes above.

In complex, ambiguous, unpointed Hebrew, no vowels are present and thus homophones abound. Because of this, both children and adult readers need to rely far more on context to work out words.

Share and Bar-On (2017) describe a triplex model of Hebrew word-reading development:

> Our triplex model emphasizes three phases of early Hebrew reading development: a progression from
> (a) lower-order, phonological (sublexical) sequential spelling-to-sound translation (Phase 1, Grade 1) to
> (b) higher-order, string-level (lexical) lexico-morpho-orthographic processing (Phase 2, Grade 2),
> followed, in the upper elementary grades, by
> (c) a supralexical contextual level (Phase 3) essential for dealing with the pervasive homography of unpointed Hebrew.

From perspectives of 2-Stage early-literacy and Transition from Early to Sophisticated Literacy (TESL, Galletly, 2022a, In press; Galletly & Knight, 2011b), these three phases would seem to equate to the stages of the TESL model, which is shown as Figure 6, in Tour 2:

1. Stage 1, *Early Literacy*: Initially learning to read and write pointed Hebrew, developing accuracy then progressing with fluency.
2. Stage 2. *Early and Sophisticated Literacy*: Transitioning to using an ambiguous, complex orthography with strong needs for language skills and language processing.
3. Stage 3. *Sophisticated Literacy*, with somewhat impeded learning due to needs to focus on words.

From observing in schools and discussing literacy development with researchers in Israel, after word-reading and writing are mastered steadily in Grade 1, children's progress then pauses for a while when they first transition to unpointed Hebrew. They then progress steadily onwards.

The very large extent of homographs, which they have, means that Hebrew readers experience impeded statistical learning for reading comprehension but not written expression, having to pause at times while reading for meaning, to focus on an individual word, to work out just which word it is of its many homograph options. In reading, they'd thus likely experience higher cognitive load (Abu-Rabia, 2001; Share & Bar-On, 2017).

There seem likely to be interesting similarities and differences in the impeded learning of Hebrew and Standard-English readers, and our mutual use of context to empower word-reading of unfamiliar words that children are unsure of.

Australia and Anglophone nations might learn much by asking to do collaborative research involving Israel as a 2-Stage early-literacy nation, in addition to nations such as Taiwan, Japan and China.

There are a large number of researchers investigating many different aspects of literacy development, difficulties, learning and instruction in Israel (Abu-Rabia, 2001; Aram et al., 2014; Bar-Kochva & Breznitz, 2012; Daniels & Share, 2018; Frost, 2012; Gabay et al., 2012a, 2012b; Gabay, Thiessen et al., 2015; Gabay, Vakil et al., 2015; Joshi et al., 2015; Kasperski et al., 2016; Nevo & Breznitz, 2013; Nevo et al., 2020; Rapoport et al., 2016; Schiff & Ravid, 2013; Shahar-Yames & Share, 2008; Shany & Share, 2011; Share, 2008; Share & Bar-On, 2017; Vakil et al., 2012, 2015; Vakil & Heled, 2016; Weiss et al., 2015, 2016; Yael et al., 2015; Yagon & Margalit, 2016).

In the same way that Australia would benefit by collaborating with Finnish researchers, e.g., in replicating and extending aspects of the Jyvaskyla Longitudinal Dyslexia Study (JLD), we'd benefit too from collaborative work with Israeli researchers and educators.

South Korea: Hanguel Using Syllable Block Units

It's notable that most regular-orthography nations do strong explicit word-reading and word-writing instruction in Grade 1, for the brief time it's needed.

In contrast, in South Korea, Whole Language methods are used with negligible explicit instruction building children's skills for sounding-out words. Schools and the nation are thus relying on effective implicit learning.

Alas, this causes difficulties for at-risk word-readers as, while Korean Hanguel is fully regular, it has a visual situational cue that bumps many at-risk children onto the path of struggling word-reading and spelling.

The situational cue is Hanguel being written in neat, syllable-block units, with the vowel and consonants of each syllable included together in a single square space, one for each syllable.

These syllable units are great for readers who know to decode each syllable block, but alas, because children don't get ample explicit word-reading instruction and practice, many at-risk readers decide those squares must be logographic whole-syllable units. They then try to learn each individual syllable and word as sightwords, which causes them to fall behind.

Talking with South Korean teachers and researchers when I've visited, their intervention studies show that brief explicit instruction plus practising sounding-out of syllable units is very effective in rescuing struggling word-readers, and putting them on the path to success. They find this gentle intervention, teaching letter-sounds then phonemic recoding to read and highly effective, making an appreciable difference, particularly for children between the 5th and 40th percentiles, i.e., children in the lower-half and lower third, with more intensive intervention needed for weakest word-readers and writers.

It's interesting too that much of this South Korean research has been done by speech language pathologists working with schools. In somewhat similar manner, speech language pathologists in Australia moved into working on word-reading and literacy in the 1980s and 1990s when Australia was similarly using a predominantly Whole Language approach, with less explicit instruction and stronger reliance on implicit learning.

This finding is similar to those of other studies (Apfelbaum et al., 2013; Papadopoulos, 2001).

We likely all agree that explicit instruction works well, very well, with it just being the extent of explicit instruction that's debated. And when we're strongly aware of the differing needs of lower and upper-third children for lots vs little explicit instruction, because of their very different levels of cognitive-processing and executive-function skills, differing needs for explicit instruction become even more logical.

South Korea is another nation that it would be valuable for Australia to partner with, in collaborative research exploring early-literacy development in a range of nations.

Key Findings from Tour 12

Findings and implications of studies explored in Tour 12 suggest the following points are useful considerations towards improving literacy and education in Australia and Anglophone nations:
1. Whereas regular-orthography children do much stronger statistical learning, Standard-English beginning readers experience significantly impeded statistical learning, due to English orthographic complexity and the extent of high cognitive load and confusion they experience across early-literacy development.
2. This makes Standard-English beginning word-readers particularly vulnerable to being sidetracked by less-relevant situational cues.
3. This can result in children over-focusing on situational cues,

such as word position, and flashcard colour, practising what are in effect word-reading avoidance strategies.
4. Gough et al.'s (1992) *Thumbprint Experiment* showed beginning readers were easily sidetracked by the situation cue of a thumbprint, with many *reading* the thumbprint instead of the word, i.e., saying the word they'd previously seen with the thumbprint, after it had been moved to a different word.
5. This suggests we need to be aware of children using inappropriate visual situational cues that sidetrack them into less effective learning.
6. Apfelbaum et al.'s (2013) word-reading study showed different instruction methods can make a major difference for at-risk word-readers. Their study used only implicit learning, i.e., no explicit instruction, and word sets that focused children on particular orthographic grainsizes, and associated strategies:
   a. Regular Words and phonemic recoding (listing sounds of CVC words then blending to work out the word), vs
   b. Pattern Words using word-families, rhyme and onset-rime reading.
7. They found that
   a. The phonemic-recoding Regular Word group showed much stronger learning, for both stronger and weaker word-readers.
   b. Girls did far stronger learning in both groups.
   c. Boys and weaker word-readers did particularly poorly using the onset-rime Pattern Word reading.
8. These studies show how very easily children move into weak statistical learning, being sidetracked by situational cues, including word families, and visual aspects of reading tasks, e.g., flashcard colours, and words' positions in word lists.
9. While Anglophone nations use just Standard English, without a beginners' orthography, children experience impeded statistical learning over many years, often across primary school and in high school. While the Apfelbaum et al. (2013) and Thumbprint study, to a certain extent, explored cross-sectional *moments in time*, it's important to emphasise impeded statistical learning being ongoing across the many years of Standard-English word-reading and spelling development.
10. Other studies using *GraphoGame Rime* (GGRime) showed weaker readers doing quite strong learning using Pattern Words. The different findings may well be due to additional instructional factors being included in use of GGRime.
11. There is value in exploring statistical learning and self-teaching in word-reading and spelling development, the impact of

Research Tour 12. Impeded Statistical Learning

situational cues, and the impacts of implicit learning, explicit teaching and learning, and combined learning.
12. There also seems value in further research exploring different instructional methods and their impact on healthy-progress and at-risk children's learning.
13. There additionally seems strong value in exploring gender differences in word-reading, spelling and early-literacy development, and impacts of different instructional methods.

Research Tour 13.
Unfamiliar Words:
Our Standard-English Nemesis

Eye halve a spelling checker. It came with my pea sea.
It plainly marques for my revue miss steaks eye kin knot sea.
Eye strike a key and type a word and weight four it to say
Weather eye am wrong oar write, it shows me strait a weigh.
As soon as a mist ache is maid, it nose bee fore two long,
And eye can put the error rite – it's rare lea ever wrong.
Eye have run this poem threw it. Eye am shore your pleased two no
It's letter perfect awl the weigh: My checker tolled me sew.

Margo Roark, *Candidate for a Pullet Surprise*

English orthographic complexity is far from kind to our beginning readers. With words such as those above, it's no wonder it takes so long to master reading and writing Standard English.

While Standard English orthography does have more regular words and syllables than irregular ones, our GPCs overlap to excess in our many less-regular words, and this creates confusion that impedes our children's learning, and literacy development.

To read the word *could*, for example, children who don't know it to read might ponder which of *ou*'s sounds is used, e.g., its different sounds in *out, would, you, enough, cough, bought, touch, thorough*. Then, to write *could*, many would ponder its *ou* sound, and which spelling to use, e.g., *oo u ou, o,* (in *good, full, would, woman*).

One reason orthographic confusion remains ongoing across so many years for our children is because we've so many less regular, *rare words* that occur quite infrequently, e.g., *yacht, antique, clerk, indict, choir*, with many subject-area terms being long, multisyllabic words, such as *metamorphic, physics, sedimentary*.

Research Tour 13. Unfamiliar Words: Our Standard-English Nemesis

We've many words with seldom-used GPCs: GPCs that occur in just a few words. As an example, these seven words, *of, was, people, who, write, one, two* all occur frequently and thus have strong impact on children's statistical learning. However, the underlined letters use GPCs that occur in very few other words that beginning readers encounter. Indeed, using more-frequent GPCs, children might expect them to be written as *ov, woz, peepul, hoo, rite, wun, too*, which is how young children often write them.

In early reading and writing, children are confused by the overlapping GPCs of these and our many other highly-frequent irregular words, and this confusion impedes learning (Bruno et al., 2007; Harm & Seidenberg, 2004; Seidenberg, 2005, 2013).

We do have rules, in fact, we've hordes (e.g., Adams, 1990; Dewey, 1970, 1971, 1978; Fry, 2004; Fry et al. 2004; Galletly, 2005b, 2008; Kessler et al., 2013; Pollo et al., 2008; Scragg, 1974; Stanback, 1992; Treiman et al., 1995; Venezky, 1967; Vousden, 2008). However, every rule has its list of exception words. In practice, this means there's much that seems random, e.g., for children deciding whether consonants should be single or double in multisyllabic words, and which of our 20+ schwa spellings should be used (Hanna et al., 1996; Okrent, 2014).

Some might think USA spelling is kinder, but it's changed very few of the irregular words that beginners struggle with. It's interesting how, while we accept spelling reform for words such as *hiccup/hiccough, thru/through, program/programme*, we've not researched the impacts of remediating spelling of the many highly-frequent irregular words that drag down our many at-risk beginners.

While it's obvious more in our developing and struggling readers, we're surrounded by spelling anomalies, e.g., do read the myriad of spelling contrasts in Gerard Nolst Trenité's 1922 classic poem, *The Chaos*. It's interesting just how often those overlapping GPCs are presented in fun poems. Given the excessive workload and struggles that English orthographic complexity inflicts on children, schools and families, their ever-smiling tone is perhaps a little misplaced. It reflects our widespread needs for Change 1, *Understand how orthographies matter: English spelling is dragging us down.*

Standard-English words so often using overlapping and seldom-occurring GPCs creates havoc for children's reading of unfamiliar words in texts they read, and similarly impedes their writing. Alas, this happens often, when meeting orthographically unfamiliar words: words that are often familiar, everyday words used in speaking and listening, but which are not yet familiar for reading and writing.

For beginners and the severely delayed, the unfamiliar words are usually less-regular Pattern and Tricky words and syllables (Galletly, 2004a, 2005b, 2008; Knight & Galletly, 2011). Then, across primary and high school, it's our many less-frequent and less-regular words that create challenges for all readers, healthy and delayed alike.

Of course, regular-orthography nations have many rare words too, but, being regular, they're not orthographically unfamiliar, and are easily read and spelled. For Standard English, many content-carrying words are orthographically unfamiliar, and thus a challenge for word-reading and spelling.

Less-frequent words are often termed *rare* words. Our children meet them all too frequently. Kamil & Hiebert's (2010) finding that over 4% of words in Grade 4 reading materials are rare, not being in the *common words* corpus of 5,580 to 10,000 words is not incompatible with J. B. Carroll et al.'s (1971) estimation that 80% of English words in school reading materials are rare words, occurring less than once in a million words (Share & Stanovich, 1995):

> *Whereas just over 100 'heavy duty' words (eg the, in, was, etc.) account for around half of all the letter strings appearing in printed school English, a very large number of words exist which appear very rarely in print (Carroll, Davies & Richman, 1971; Nagy & Anderson, 1984). In fact fully 80% of English words occur less than once in a million words of running text (Carroll et al, 1971).*

Clearly, regardless of definition, rare and unfamiliar words abound.

Alas, those rare words are often key content words in subject-area reading and writing, e.g., it makes a big difference thinking a text is about *addition altitudes*, when actually it's about *addiction attitudes*.

Unfamiliar words for reading and writing create high cognitive load, impeded statistical learning, slowed self-teaching, and sadly slow word-reading and spelling development. They also impede and slow independent reading and writing. We see that in our nasty, ubiquitous, Standard-English pause. Now, our children pausing to think on words as they work to read and write them might seem pauses of no concern, particularly as we're so used to them.

However, when we compare our advanced vs struggling readers, and regular-orthography and Anglophone children, it's clearly evident that our Standard-English pause is far from being merely an inconsequential pause. It's an irritating, abrupt interruption, and also a major crosslinguistic difference.

In the same way we adults are irritated when someone starts

chatting to us while we're engrossed in a novel, interruptions to have to work out words abruptly cut across our children's trains of thought. This can interfere greatly with the transferring of meaning between thoughts and print that's the crux of reading and writing. It can also be tiring, and reduce motivation and engagement.

Now, why do I term it a *nasty, ubiquitous, Standard-English pause*? Because those pauses, and the cognitive load they generate, aren't experienced by regular-orthography children across early literacy:
- Not by European children with sole regular orthographies who learn to read and write in easiest 1-Stage learning.
- Nor by Asian children, doing 2-Stage learning, with empowered cognitive-processing built in Stage 1, and words written in both their regular and complex orthographies.
- Nor by Anglophone children of the 1960s, using the Initial Teaching Alphabet (ITA), who similarly did 2-Stage learning, and coped well without words being written in both orthographies, given that most highly-regular words and syllables were identical in both orthographies, and children had empowered cognitive-processing skills.

Regular-orthography children cope well with reading and writing unfamiliar words, while these words are a massive hurdle for Standard-English readers, and Anglophone nations.

We've already explored the difficulties Standard-English readers have in reading unfamiliar words, in Tours 2 and 12. In this tour, we'll take a deeper look at the characteristics and impacts of Anglophone children's difficulties with unfamiliar words. The contrast with European regular-orthography children, who don't have irregular words, is striking. It establishes English orthographic complexity as being damaging across all school years.

Needs to Research Reading of Unfamiliar Words

The two key skills of Standard-English word-reading are
- Having a growing bank of *sightwords*: words recognised immediately, on sight.
- Becoming increasingly skilful at reading unfamiliar words.

The two skills, while similar in many ways, also differ in key ways, e.g., showing different brain activation patterns (Espy et al., 2004).

The two subtests of the Test of Word Reading Efficiency-2 (TOWRE-2; Torgesen et al., 2012) assess these skills extremely well across primary and high school, taking little testing and scoring time:

- The Sight Word Efficiency subtest assesses reading of familiar words, i.e., sightwords.
- The Phonemic Decoding Efficiency subtest assesses reading of unfamiliar words (pseudowords).

While building sightword skills is challenging for many struggling word-readers, reading unfamiliar words is our major Standard-English word-reading challenge, impacting virtually all our children.

You'll recall that in Spencer and Hanley's Welsh-English studies, which we explored in Tour 2 (Spencer & Hanley, 2003, 2004; Hanley et al., 2004), when the children were in Grade 5, most English readers, even high achievers, struggled to read less common irregular words, i.e., unfamiliar words (Hanley et al., 2004). Additionally, the lowest quarter of English readers were severely struggling for all words: they'd have been weak in both of the two key word-reading skills.

You'll also recall that in Apfelbaum et al.'s (2013) study of Grade 1 implicit word-reading learning, that we explored in Tour 12, most children coped with reading familiar words, and it was the unfamiliar words where weaker-progress readers really struggled. That's a consistent finding in Anglophone and crosslinguistic studies: English readers struggling with less common, irregular words.

Z. Wang et al. (2020), monitored 800 USA children across Grades 6 and 7, assessing word-reading four times across three years. They too found Standard-English healthy readers to be markedly less efficient on unfamiliar words, with much slower response times. Importantly, they found that children's response times (how quickly they read each word), predicted their word-reading progress:

> Poor decoders may be trapped in a vicious cycle: poor decoding skill combined with less time spent attempting to decode novel words interferes with decoding development.

It's clearly no mean feat to become a highly proficient English word-reader of unfamiliar words. For many, it's a laborious struggle.

We'll now explore useful studies that compare Anglophone children who are reading Standard English with children of regular-orthography nations.

English-Czech-Slovak Word-Reading Differences

Slovak is a highest-regularity orthography and Czech is highly regular, and both are vastly more regular than Standard English.

Caravolas' (2018) study compared the speed of word-reading development from end-Grade-1 to end-Grade-2, for English, Czech

Research Tour 13. Unfamiliar Words: Our Standard-English Nemesis

and Slovak word-readers, who'd first been assessed at school entry.

There were 165 English children, 124 Czech children, and 173 Slovak children. The groups were well matched at school entry on cognitive abilities and pre-literacy skills. All were of healthy ability and monolingual.

With children starting school younger in Anglophone nations, the English children were a year younger, and had completed an extra year of reading instruction. It's possible the extra year's teaching and learning might compensate for the children being younger.

The research team assessed reading of the two key word-reading skills, frequently encountered words (real words), and unfamiliar words (pseudowords), at three time-points, six months apart, using word-reading efficiency tests (words read correctly in one minute), using lists of frequent real words and unfamiliar words.

As with many other studies, pseudowords were used for unfamiliar words. They're a very effective proxy: while it's often extremely difficult to select real words of a particular orthographic form that are unfamiliar for all readers, pseudowords are easily formed by changing a letter or two of selected real words. They then have the same orthographic form as the real words, but, being non-words, are unfamiliar to children. Pseudowords are a powerful tool both in research and for school testing of word-reading.

The real words and pseudowords in Caravolas' study were carefully matched, to be similar on form, length and syllables. The lists, of 140 to 144 words, had many easier words, plus they deliberately included many complex, more difficult words, as they wanted to avoid potential ceiling effects (many of the Czech and Slovak children reading almost all words correctly).

Not surprisingly, the study showed Slovak readers having fastest word-reading development, and Slovak and Czech word-reading development being markedly faster than that of the English children.

Differences were less marked for real words. That's not surprising, as they were high-frequency words seen often in class reading materials in all three nations. The English children made slower progress, e.g., only 80% of the progress of the Czech and Slovak children in the 6 months to mid-Grade-2. However, their scores for real words weren't excessively below Czech and Slovak children.

Slovak vs English Word-Reading Levels Standard Deviation (SD) Groups
No. read correctly of 140-144 words

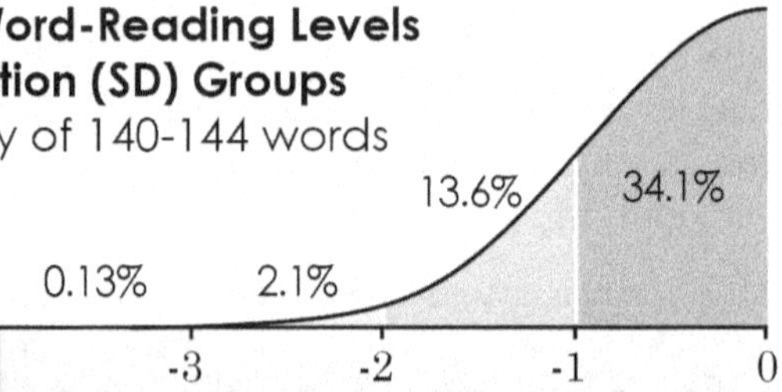

	Mean	Standard Deviation	>3 SD below 0.13%	2-3 SD below 2.1%	1-2 SD below 13.6%	≤1 SD below 34.1%
Slovak Real Words	77.9	18.0	5.8	23.9	41.9	59.9
English Real Words	71.1	23.6	0	0.4	24.0	47.5
Slovak Unfamiliar Words	52.2	12.7	1.5	14.2	26.9	39.5
English Unfamiliar Words	34.6	16.7	0	0	1.1	17.9

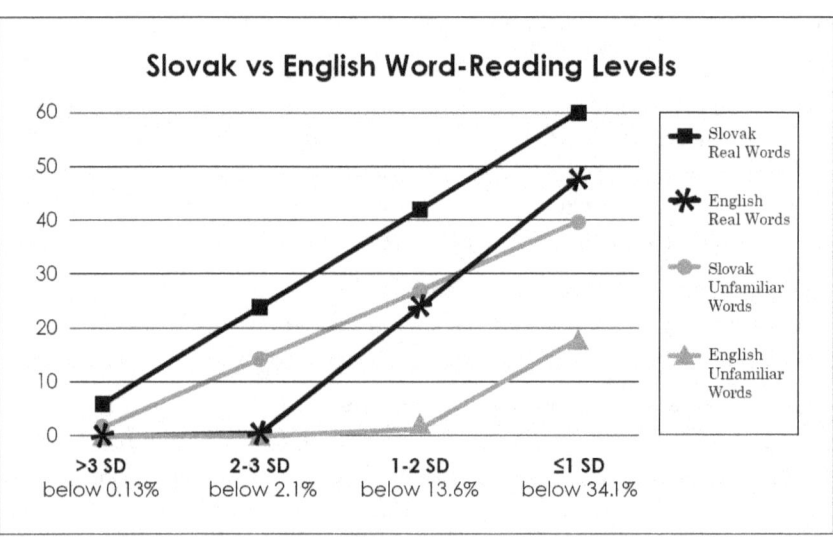

Figure 19 a. & b. Word-reading levels of Standard Deviation (SD) groups for Caravolas' (2018) Grade 2 Slovak and English readers, in (a) table, and (b) line-graph form

In contrast, for unfamiliar words, the crosslinguistic gap was very

Research Tour 13. Unfamiliar Words: Our Standard-English Nemesis

large, with the Czech and Slovak children far ahead of the English children at all time-points.

The figures show the children's end-Grade-2 word-reading levels. For clearer viewing, I've included just the Slovak and English results (the Czech results were highly similar and slightly lower than the Slovak results).

You'll recall from our early discussion, that in a Normal Distribution,
- 0-1 SD measures how widely approximately 34.1% of low-average children score below the Mean, and another 34.1% of high-average children score above the Mean.
- 1-2 SD is further 13.6% groups of higher and lower achievers.
- 2-3 SD is 2.1% groups of highest and lowest achievers.
- >3 SD is minute 0.13% groups of extremely high and abysmally low achievers.
- When using as our measure the number of words read correctly, the SD cut-points show the range of words that children in each SD group would be likely to read correctly.
- Because research subject groups approximate normal populations of similar subjects, by using SD groups, we can estimate the likely achievement levels of much larger, similar populations, e.g., Australian and regular-orthography children.

You can see in the table, above, that for the lower half of achievers, almost all the Slovak children are reading well, while many of the English children have major difficulties. The line graph shows how real-word reading is easier for both groups, and that the Slovak readers are far stronger readers for unfamiliar words.

The figures also highlight the struggles of Standard-English word-reading for unfamiliar words. The weakest 16% of English readers, all children more than 1 Standard Deviation (SD) below the Mean, quite likely didn't read any words correctly. In contrast, the Slovak children 1SD below the Mean were progressing well: they could read unfamiliar words better than the English children could read real words (27 vs 24 words correct).

It's a similar story to that of Hanley et al.'s Welsh and English Grade 5 readers, in Tour 2: a story of orthographic advantage vs disadvantage. Despite a year's less instruction, the Slovak readers are reading well, with perhaps only 2% of children having severe difficulties. And the low English Mean shows that, despite having had three years of teaching and learning, at least half the English readers have major difficulties reading unfamiliar words, and quite likely at least 16% have very severe difficulties.

Those results suggest that it's not just the lower-third of Standard-English readers who are struggling word-readers for reading unfamiliar words, and instead, quite likely, the lower two thirds.

Effectiveness of teaching and learning in each year of schooling also seems a key crosslinguistic issue. There's value in considering the implications of the English children having completed three years of school, a whole year more than the Czech and Slovak children:

- An extra year's instruction may have reduced effects when children are young and read Standard English in 1-Stage early-literacy development, without a beginners' orthography.
- Had the groups been matched by years of learning, with end-Grade-1 English children compared with end-Grade-2 Czech and Slovak children, the achievement gap would have been ferociously wider.
- The cost-benefits of years of teaching are vastly more positive when a regular orthography is used and children are older.

There's every likelihood Australian children would score similarly to the English children in Caravolas' study: it's our story too that's visible in that study.

Years of teaching and learning, and their effectiveness are a key crosslinguistic issue that Anglophone nations very much need to consider. Education is expensive, with every year of teaching and learning a major expenditure of time, money and effort by children, teachers and families. It does seem time to weigh the cost-benefits of

- Starting children at a very young age on highly complex Standard-English orthography.
- Using 1-Stage learning (solely Standard-English orthography) vs using 2-Stage learning (reading and writing a fully-regular beginners' orthography initially, to expedite early-literacy development and empower mastering of Standard English.

The scales tip alarmingly, when we weigh, on one side, the massive time and effort of three years teaching and learning, against the sadly delayed skill development which Standard-English readers achieve. Research comparing word-reading, early-literacy and learning efficiency across nations has potential to quite quickly build knowledge on this area.

English-German Word-Reading Differences

Frith, Wimmer and Landerl's (1998) article, *Differences in phonological recoding in German- and English-speaking children*, details two useful studies that offer powerful insights on the specific difficulties that Standard-English readers have in reading unfamiliar words. With relatively small subject numbers, they could perhaps be considered useful preliminary research, which Australia, working with other nations, might replicate and extend.

Building on earlier work in this area (Wimmer & Goswami, 1994; Wimmer & Landerl, 1997), the studies compared German and English readers' word-reading of single syllable and multisyllabic real words and pseudowords. Study 1, of 7 to 9-year-olds, included the full range of word-readers, while Study 2, of 8 and 12-year-olds, was of solely healthy readers.

German orthography is highly regular for reading, and both studies clearly show how orthographic impacts overwhelm learning-time impacts: despite a year's extra schooling, the English children were still far behind.

As in Caravolas' (2018) study, age-matching was used, and with English children starting school and learning to read a year younger, they'd completed an additional year's schooling. And again, just as in Caravolas' (2018) study,

- No advantage was evident from that extra whole year of teaching and learning, and,
- Had groups been matched by years of learning, the English struggles would have shown markedly greater severity.

Frith et al.'s (1998) Study 1 and 2 are particularly useful for how they highlight Standard-English readers' difficulties reading unfamiliar words. Their results align with findings of other studies the authors discuss: whereas Turkish, German, Dutch and Greek early-years children made errors on 10% or less on unfamiliar words (pseudowords), English readers made errors on 40% to 80%, with particular weakness when reading longer and more complex words.

Study 1 Word-Reading Development

Study 1 compared the real-word and pseudoword reading of 45 English and 50 German readers aged 7 to 9 years, measuring word-reading accuracy and speed.

The children each read 48 words, in two carefully matched lists. The 24 real words were frequent words in both languages: for the English words, half were regular and half were irregular (all the German words were regular as it's a highly-regular orthography for reading). The 24 pseudowords were formed by changing beginning consonants and recombining syllables, with, e.g., *summer* becoming *rummer*: the pseudowords and real words being very similar.

Before they started reading each small set of words, the children were told whether the list's words would be real words or not.

For the German readers, each pseudoword had just one possible pronunciation. For the English readers, very lenient criteria were used, with all possibly correct pronunciations accepted as correct.

Both groups found the real words easier, and, as in Caravolas' study of Slovak, Czech and English readers, over time the English readers' scores closed the gap: in Study 1, by age 9 years, the differences were no longer significant. Not surprisingly, for both real words and pseudowords, word-reading improved with age in both groups, with more errors in 7-year-olds and less in 9-year-olds.

In all instances, the German readers were vastly more accurate, e.g., German error rates for harder, unfamiliar pseudowords were less than half the English error rates for the much easier, real words. This suggests the German readers had Level 1 automaticity (strong word-reading accuracy), while the English children hadn't.

English vs German error rates, totalled for the three age groups, were 20% vs 5% for real words, and 41% vs 12% for pseudowords.

For word-reading speed, the researchers measured latency – the pause time before children said each word they read. The German readers were faster for all ages and word types. With age-groups combined, German vs English latencies were 1.0 vs 2.6 seconds for real words and 1.4 vs 4.1 seconds for pseudowords.

That's very significant, the German readers being 2.5 times faster for real words and almost 3 times faster for pseudowords. It shows regular-orthography Level 1 automaticity (accuracy), with healthy Level 2 automaticity (fluency) now building. It also aligns well with Paulesu et al.'s (2000) finding that Italian university students read both real and unfamiliar words faster than English university students.

The study has interesting implications for the real-word and unfamiliar-word reading of our healthy-progress readers.

For the real words they were correct on, the English children were fast: 55% of the English readers read all real words correctly and they read real words faster (0.6 seconds) than the 76% of German readers fully correct on real words (0.8 seconds).

However, when the researchers analysed this supposedly proficient 55% of English children on their skills for reading unfamiliar words (pseudowords), similar to the Welsh-English studies we explored in Tour 2, they found major Standard-English weakness, with both far higher error rates than the German children (22% vs 8%) and much

Research Tour 13. Unfamiliar Words: Our Standard-English Nemesis

slower reading (latency being 2.2 vs 1.3 seconds).

There's every likelihood that that will also be the case for our supposedly healthy-progress Australian word-readers. That finding highlights the importance of schools including testing of children's reading of both real words and unfamiliar words, and providing word-reading instruction in later school years to those who need it.

Frith et al., discuss the English readers' difficulties with unfamiliar words, and likelihood that different reading strategies are being used:

This particularly revealing comparison throws light on the question of whether there are qualitatively different phonological recoding processes.

Even though the English-speaking children were able to read the [real] words without errors, they misread 1 in 5 [pseudowords]. This is surprising because the nonwords were very similar to the [real] words ... e.g., rummer for summer. ... We suggest that the English-speaking children relied far less on segmental recoding strategies and instead tended to rely on instant recognition of familiar words ... Had they used representations of phoneme or rime segments to recode words, they would have also recognized all of the corresponding [pseudowords].

In contrast, we suggest that the German-speaking children used a recoding strategy that involved phoneme or rime representations. This made these children slower at [real] word reading but faster and more accurate at [pseudoword] reading.

Importantly, Study 1's Standard Deviations (SDs) hammer home the challenges of Standard English: the SDs reveal a massive range of English errors, and few errors by the German children.

When one considers that the English children had received a whole extra year of teaching and learning, and that only 45% made errors for real words (55% of children being fully correct), it's clear that weaker word-readers made a very large number of errors.

The German 7-year-olds made few errors, with the Means (and SDs) being only Mean 7.5% (SD 10%) and Mean 15% (SD 15%) errors made, for real words and pseudowords, respectively.

In contrast, for the 7-year-old English readers the Means (and SDs) for errors made were Mean 30% (SD 30%) errors made for real words and Mean 50% (SD 33%) errors for pseudowords, i.e., on average half the unfamiliar words were read incorrectly. As with Caravolas' (2018) study, it intimates we've perhaps two thirds of children markedly delayed by regular-orthography standards.

The Research Tours: Impacts of Orthographic Disadvantage

Let's compare those differences now using Standard Deviation (SD) groups, as we did for Welsh vs English in Tour 2 (Hanley et al., 2004) and for Slovak and Czech vs English in Caravolas' (2018) study, above. The measure we're using is the average number of words children read correctly out of a possible total of 24 words for each of the two lists: one of real words and one of pseudowords.

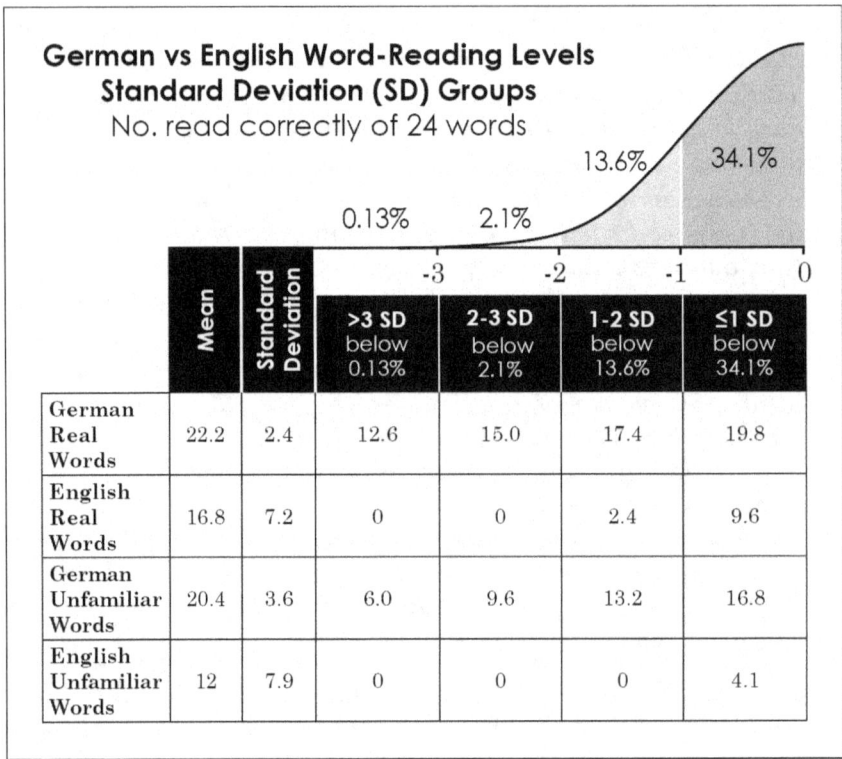

Figure 20a. Word-reading levels of Standard Deviation (SD) groups for Frith et al.'s (1998) weaker 50% German and English 7-year-old readers, in table form

For real words for the English readers, with a Mean of 16.8 words correct, out of 24 words, the top half of achievers, on average, made between 0 and about 7 errors. With the English SD for real words being 7.2 words correct, when we subtract the SD from the Mean, we see that, for the lower 50% of children, on average, for real words,
- 34.1% (0-1 SD below the Mean) read 9.6 to 16.8 words correctly.
- About 13.4% (1-2 SD below) read 2.4 to 9.6 words correctly.
- The weakest 2% (>2SD below) read no words correct.

In contrast, the German Mean was far higher, at 22.2 words correct,

and the SD much lower, at 2.4 words correct. That high Mean shows the upper 50% of achievers made only 0 to 2 errors, on average. Of the lower 50% of German children, on average, for real words,
- 34.1% (0-1 SD < Mean) read 19.8 to 22.2 words (5 errors).
- 13.4% (1-2 SD) would have read 17.4 to 19.8 (7 errors).
- 2.1% (2-3 SD) read 15 to 17.4 words correctly (9 errors).
- Even the weakest 0.13% (>3SD) read over half the words correctly (12.6 to 15 words).

Given that the English Mean was 16.8 words, those results show that only about 2% of the German readers made as many errors as every child in the entire English lower half.

Ouch! While bearing in mind that Means and SDs are averaging, so the subjects in this small study may not have spread out neatly into these precise proportions, there's no doubt the English weaker half of readers were a long sad tail with major difficulties.

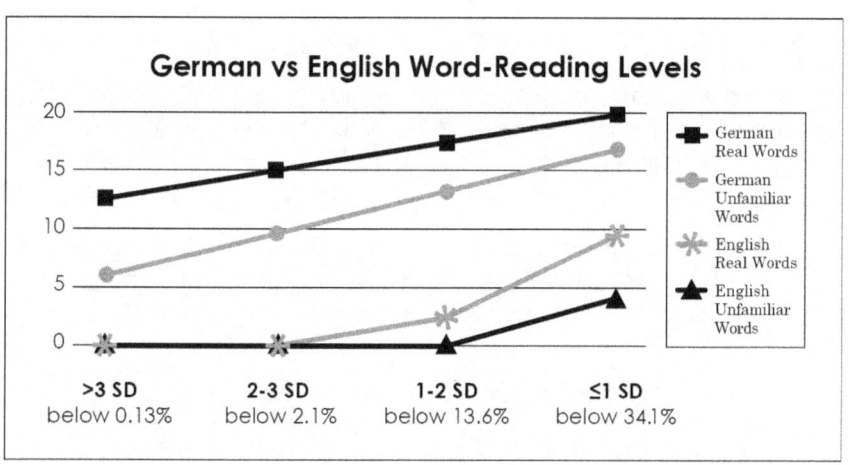

Figure 20b. *Word-reading levels of Standard Deviation (SD) groups for Frith et al.'s (1998) weaker 50% of German and English 7-year-old readers, in line-graph form*

The line graph above clearly shows the English readers well below the German readers. The two lines for the German reading are far higher than the English lines. The English real-word reading is well below the German readers' unfamiliar-word reading. The Standard-English long sad tail is evident in the English scores bottoming out, with appreciable numbers not correct on any words.

For real words, virtually no German children made 30% errors, whereas, on average, half the English readers did so, despite an extra year's teaching and learning, and 55% of children reading all real words correctly and thus likely to be considered strong readers.

For unfamiliar words, the English readers' Mean of 12 words correct, out of a total of 24 words, means the upper 50% of achievers made 0 to 12 errors. Then for the weaker 50%, the scores sadly peter out.
On average, for that lower half of English readers,
- 34.1% (0-1 SD) read about 4 to 12 words correctly (12 to 20 errors).
- The remaining 16% (>1SD) read no words correctly.

The German story for unfamiliar words is very different, with their pseudoword reading well ahead of both real word and pseudoword reading of the English children. With Mean of 20.4 words, the upper 50% made fewer than 4 errors. Of the lower 50% of children, on average,
- 34.1% (0-1 SD < Mean) read 16.8 to 20.4 words (4 to 7 errors).
- The next 13.4% (1-2 SD) read 13.2 to 16.8 (7 to 11 errors).
- The next 2.1% (2-3 SD) read 6 to 9.6 words (15 to 18 errors).
- The weakest 0.13% (>3 SD) read 3.6 to 9.6 words correctly, almost equalling the 0-1 SD English group (34.1% of the cohort).

It's a sad and massive contrast that bespeaks needs to prioritise investigating Change 8: use of 2-Stage early literacy, using a fully-regular beginners' orthography initially, to empower both early-literacy development and subsequent mastery of Standard English.

There's every likelihood that, just like the English children, our Australian weaker word-readers would make very large numbers of errors, particularly on unfamiliar words.

Our Major English Vowel Troubles

The study also explored error types, with useful findings.

Vowels are the most inconsistent feature of English orthography but they're highly consistent for German word-reading. Not surprisingly, the English readers made excessive vowel errors while the German readers made very few. The English children made about 19 times more errors: on the 1 and 2-syllable easier real words, the English vs German 7 to 9-year-olds made 170 vs 9 errors.

The English readers also made lots of word-substitution errors. Those errors reflect either guessing, or impulsiveness and inhibitory control issues: difficulties coping with interference from known vocabulary. Given the children had been told that the words weren't real words, inhibitory control weakness seems more likely.

The researchers conclude that the high regularity of German

Research Tour 13. Unfamiliar Words: Our Standard-English Nemesis

orthography means children systematically use phonemic recoding to read words because this method works so well for them, whereas the massive complexity of English leads to error-prone strategies.

Study 2 Healthy-Progress Readers' Errors

Frith et al.'s (1998) Study 2 explored in more depth the word-reading development of healthy-progress readers. Whereas in Study 1, they considered the full range of 7 to 9-year-old readers with both weaker and stronger readers included, in Study 2, they excluded potentially weak readers, to focus only on healthy readers.

They assessed the real-word and pseudoword reading of 8 and 12-year-old healthy-progress children: 36 German readers and 40 English readers. They were children who were healthy-reading controls for another study, with standardised tests showing them to have healthy text reading, spelling and nonverbal intelligence.

The researchers strategically chose the 4-year age gap as they considered that 8-year-old Standard-English readers would still be developing word-readers, while 12-year-olds might have quite proficient word-reading skills and perhaps ceiling-level proficiency.

Similar to Study 1, they assessed the children using sets of matched German-English words, but this time they included a greater range of complexity. They used 1, 2 and 3-syllable real words and pseudowords, plus a set of simple CVCVCV pseudowords, e.g., *surimo*, as, while this word type isn't common in German or English, it allows quite straightforward application of word-reading skills.

For the 1 and 2-syllable real words, half were low-frequency and half were high-frequency, while all the 3-syllable real words were low-frequency. For the English real words, half were regular and half irregular (all German words are regular for reading).

As in Study 1, matched pseudowords were formed by exchanging initial consonant letters and exchanging and rearranging syllables. Again, the words were presented in small sets, with the children told, prior to each set, whether the words were real words or not.

For the German readers, results showed relatively little difference between 8-year-olds and 12-year-olds: both groups were highly proficient word-readers.

In contrast, there were major differences between the 8-year-old and 12-year-old English readers, and the 12-year-olds were not yet at proficiency. Clearly, healthy-progress Anglophone children are nowhere near ceiling level at 8 years of age, and do a lot of word-reading development between ages 8 and 12 years. That's an important finding: it suggests Australian schools need to include strong word-reading instruction in all primary-school years, and to continue it in high school for many students.

There were strong differences between the German and English 8-year-olds for all words and word types, with the German readers far more accurate, and much faster. Even when only the speed of correctly read words was compared, the English children were significantly slower: while they might be accurate on these words, they'd not yet developed fluency (Level 2 automaticity).

The Major Errors of English 8-Year-Olds

The English 8-year-olds' error rates were relatively low for high-frequency real words (9% errors vs 5% errors by German readers). In contrast, they made far more errors for low-frequency real words and pseudowords, and vastly more errors when words were longer:

- For 2-syllable words, they made over three times more errors for both low-frequency real-words (28% vs 9%) and pseudowords (23% vs 7%).
- For 3-syllable real words and pseudowords, they made almost six times more errors for real words (47% vs 8%) and over three times more errors for pseudowords (57% vs 17%).

Results for the CVCVCV pseudoword task, of words relatively easy to decode, really drive home the challenges of reading unfamiliar Standard-English words. While German 8-year-olds made almost no errors, with a less than 1% error rate (0.5%), the English 8-year-olds made errors on close to a third of words (Mean 30%, SD 22%).

Ouch! If Australian children are similar to those English readers, then most of our 8-year-olds, in their fourth year of learning, still have masses of word-reading development to work through, with our struggling readers experiencing enormous difficulties with both unfamiliar and multisyllabic words.

The errors the 8-year-old English readers made reflected strongly impeded statistical learning that often involved close neighbour words, e.g., 18 children read *sweet/sweat*, four read *bear/beer*, and nine read *counter/contour*. Guessing, or cognitive flexibility difficulties suppressing similar real words, was a factor, with many 1- and 2-syllable pseudoword errors being real-word substitutions.

The Major Errors of English 12-Year-Olds

For real-word reading, the 12-year-old English readers had achieved Level 1 automaticity, with German and English 12-year-

Research Tour 13. Unfamiliar Words: Our Standard-English Nemesis

olds not significantly different for accuracy and speed of word-reading, and the error rate gap being only 2% (4% vs 2%).

In contrast, and despite being *healthy-progress* readers, as decided by healthy reading of meaningful texts, the English 12-year-olds' reading of unfamiliar words was still a problem.

On the easy CVCVCV pseudoword reading task, while errors were low, the English readers' 7% error rate was nonetheless more than twice the German readers' 3% error rate. That's high, really, given that the children were healthy readers, and the words were highly regular and quite simple.

For pseudoword reading, children's reading of unfamiliar words, the differences were much more major. While both groups were equally fast for all words, the English 12-year-olds made far more errors: 22% vs 12% errors by the German 12-year-olds.

That's a striking, and indeed quite shocking finding: that supposedly healthy-progress 12-year-old Standard-English readers have an error rate of over 20% for unfamiliar words.

It suggests likelihood that our high schoolers who we consider strong readers may be making errors on over a fifth of 3-syllable unfamiliar words, with weaker word-readers making far more.

That 22% error rate establishes a lack of Level 1 automaticity for reading longer unfamiliar words in those healthy-progress 12-year-old English readers – and quite likely in our Australian 12-year-olds and high schoolers.

Vowel-Error Rates and Whole Word Substitutions

Study 2 also had useful findings on vowel errors and wholeword substitutions made by the English readers.

How often do healthy-progress Standard-English readers make vowel errors and substitute other words? Extremely often!

The authors provide vowel error rates for combined age groups and combined word groups. Together, the German readers made a total of 8 errors on the first vowels of words. The English readers made far more – 338 errors, in fact.

That's virtually no German vowel errors, but floods of errors by supposedly healthy-progress English children – 44.5 times more errors. Now, hopefully, most errors were made by the 8-year-olds – but the fact that the authors combined the groups suggests that both groups made sizeable numbers of errors.

In Study 1, you'll recall that the ratio of vowel errors was also high. On 1 and 2-syllable easier real words, the 7 to 9-year-old English vs German children made 170 vs 9 errors, almost 19 times more vowel errors. This time it's 44.5 times more, in healthy-progress readers. Clearly longer words, in this case 3-syllable words, result in a lot more errors.

These findings suggest many and varied vowel errors are a major impediment for Standard-English primary-school and high-school developing readers, and a minefield for struggling word-readers.

Wholeword substitutions also seem an issue. The researchers don't give specific figures for the 8-year-old and 12-year-old readers, only what seems to be general statements. They comment that German readers made very few errors, because their systematic word-reading using letter-sounds was excellent.

In contrast, for the English readers, they discuss real-word substitutions being used for 30% of errors on 1 and 2-syllable pseudowords, and 10% of errors on 3-syllable words.

The fact that the children so often said real words when they'd been told the words weren't real words, suggests less that it's guessing, and instead, a cognitive flexibility issue, with the children experiencing interference from known words.

Researchers term this the *Lexicality Effect*, the impact of known words on children's word-reading (Caravolas, 2018; Caravolas et al., 2013) – it's a major issue for Standard-English children, but of minimal impact for regular-orthography readers.

Frith et al. (1998) discuss Berent and Perfetti's (1995) two-cycle model of phonological recoding for Standard-English readers, with possibilities that top-down interference interacts across these two cycles. They also hint at Success Inoculation:

Berent and Perfetti's (1995) two-cycle model of phonological recoding provides an explanation for the difficulties experienced by the English-speaking children. This model suggests that, in English, two cycles are necessary in recoding: first, the consonant skeleton is derived; second, the vowel pronunciation is elaborated ...
One key orthographic feature might be responsible for this difference – the consistency of [GPCs] for vowels.
We hypothesize that the high consistency of vowels in German permits immediate on-line [sequential] assembly of [sounds and syllables].
We suggest that another reason for the ease of acquisition of recoding skills in German is the repeated experience of success

that arises from the normally close match between on-line assembled phonemes and whole-syllable or wholeword sound. It is plausible that teachers capitalize on this close match between subsyllabic and syllabic codes and find frequent occasion to reward a young child's attempts at phonological recoding in the early stages of learning.

In contrast, in English, the correct vowel sound is usually not available until the second decoding cycle. The consonant context has to be decoded before the vowel can be pronounced unambiguously [i.e., it's the letter "r" in "fur, herd, shirt, jar, hear" that signals what sounds those vowels will say], and hence on-line [sequential] syllable formation is rarely possible. As a result, phonemic information acquired in the first decoding cycle might be lost, resulting in omissions and substitutions. The tendency to substitute other words suggests a stronger reliance on top-down processes in phonological recoding than is evident in German.

Rau et al.'s (2016) eye-movement study of German and English child and adult readers with healthy word-reading skills, also showed insights on this area. Rau et al., found German children had stronger, focused, first-pass reading, with far less rereading and regressions, while English children used an *explorer* style, with many regressions to previous words, more word-skipping and more reading of large units of words, and style differences, with these also present, to a smaller extent, in the German and English adults.

Certainly, Frith et al.'s (1998) Study 1 and Study 2 show Standard-English upper-primary and high-school word-readers lack adult proficiency, with value in Anglophone nations monitoring word-reading across the school years: word-reading of both familiar words and unfamiliar words, including longer multisyllabic words.

It's not just our struggling readers who experience major difficulties with vowel errors and wholeword substitutions, i.e., seriously impeded statistical learning. Those errors seem also a major factor in supposedly healthy-progress word-reading development. It seems we need to rescue all our children.

Quite likely, Australia needs both a beginners' orthography and appropriate, explicit instruction, as multi-stage transitioning using tailored, explicit instruction may make an appreciable difference in our children's ability to read unfamiliar words.

That's suggested by explicit teaching being a key difference in Papadopoulos's (2001) study of Greek and Cyprian Grade 1 children, that we explored in Tour 11. The Greek children, who'd had explicit word-reading instruction, were much stronger at reading unfamiliar words than the Cyprian children who'd largely done implicit learning.

Currently, tailored word-reading instruction definitely makes a difference for our children (e.g., Landerl, 2000), but quite likely only to the level that most are on the Slow Train, not on the Express and Bullet Trains that regular-orthography children ride (Galletly, 2022a).

Study 3: German Vs English Dyslexic Readers

Frith, Wimmer and Landerl conducted another German-English study that focused solely on weak word-readers. Using a different order of authors, it's reported in Landerl, Wimmer & Frith's (1997) article, *The impact of orthographic consistency on dyslexia: A German-English comparison*.

Using similar assessments to their Frith et al. (1998) studies, they compared the word-reading errors of the English and German weak word-readers. This study, too, contrasts the molehill word-reading difficulties of regular-orthography children with the Everest-level difficulties that too many of our struggling readers have to endure.

They compared 54 English and German readers, with each cohort having three groups of about 18 children, a group of dyslexic children, an age-matched control group, and a reading-age matched control group. Notably, both dyslexic groups had considerably more boys, with four times more boys than girls.

It's a useful practical study we can learn much from. Along with Frith et al.'s (1998) Study 1 and 2, it would also be extremely easy to replicate, comparing our lower-third word-readers with lower-third word-readers in multiple other nations.

The children, aged 10-12 years, read real words and pseudowords of 1 to 3-syllables. Not surprisingly, orthographic complexity powerfully impeded the struggling Standard-English word-readers:
- The German weak readers made relatively few errors, while the English weak readers made hundreds.
- The German weak readers read the hardest words (long pseudowords such as *quaduktrisch, miktanie, usision, plauferfant*) with much greater accuracy than the English weak readers had for much easier, short, simple pseudowords, e.g., *foo, bish, zeer, swost*.
This contrast highlights how the English weak readers (and Australian weak readers) would have huge difficulty reading

unfamiliar words in class texts, while weak readers of regular orthography nations would likely read them correctly.
- The German weak readers used sounding-out (phonemic-recoding) for all words; whereas the weak English readers used sightword recognition, sounding-out and wholeword substitutions.
- The German weak readers were equally accurate on highly frequent and infrequent words.
- The English weak readers were much stronger on highly frequent words, but had very major difficulties with infrequent words, making 40% more errors than the German readers.
- The English weak readers substituted real words for pseudowords six times more often, i.e., their word-reading skills for unfamiliar words were extremely poor and they often guessed, and substituted real words, despite having been told the list of words wasn't comprised of real words.
- English vowel difficulties were massive, while German vowel difficulties were extremely minimal – the English weak readers made 16 times more vowel errors on words' first vowels (342:20 errors).

It's clear that Standard-English orthography is far from kind, and that unfamiliar words and English vowel GPCs are quite likely our children's most major challenges, for both our struggling readers and our supposedly healthy-progress developing readers.

Perhaps, we need *Workplace Health And Safety* signs saying, *Caution! Dangerous Damaging Spelling!*, also written as *Corshun! Daenjurus Damajing Speling!* to ensure the words are easily read.

That 16-times finding clearly shows the damaging impacts of Standard-English vowel GPC confusion. Importantly, that 16-times more vowel errors for struggling readers is quite tiny relative to the 44.5-times more vowel errors that the healthy-progress English readers made, in Frith et al.'s (1998) Study 2.

The number of vowel errors will vary according to word-complexity, and the 44.5-times more errors were made on more complex words – but they were made by supposedly healthy readers!

Developing and Struggling Readers Show Similar Skills

Standard-English word-reading development is a continuum children progress through, with older *struggling readers* often showing the weak word-reading skills of younger healthy-progress *developing readers* (e.g., Catts et al., 2008). Spelling development is similarly a continuum. Because of this, 14-year-old struggling word-readers may be at the same point on the continuum as 7-year-old healthy-progress developing readers. That's a key reason why schools often find word-reading and spelling ages useful.

Struggling and developing word-readers and spellers can be highly similar not just for achievement levels, but also for the skills and strategies they've mastered and the types of difficulties and error patterns they show. That's why research studies often have reading-age control groups in addition to chronological-age control groups (Diamanti et al., 2018; Landerl et al., 1997).

It's also why word-reading intervention with 12-year-olds is similar in many ways to intervention with 8-year-olds, and the difference being more the level of explanation and extent of practice provided, than actual content (Knight et al, 2017a, 2017b).

Certainly, intervention building word-reading of unfamiliar words in Standard-English struggling readers can be effective (Adams, 1990; Byrne, 1998; Colenbrander et al., 2022; Didion & Toste, 2022; Dyson et al., 2017; Nicholson & Dymock, 2015; O'Connor, 2000; C Snow et al., 1998a; Stuart & Stainthorp, 2015).

It's just that, by regular-orthography standards (Lyytinen et al., 2021), it's simply not effective enough, as so often it's not able to catch children up to healthy levels (Compton et al., 2014; O'Connor, 2000; Roberts, Torgesen et al., 2008; Savage et al., 2018, 2020; Scammacca et al., 2007, 2015, 2016; Wanzek et al., 2013, 2016, 2018).

It's quite likely the error patterns the English readers showed in the German-English studies are part of the extremely slow drawn-out word-reading and spelling development of our healthy-progress readers too. That's because all Standard-English children are slow developers, not just struggling readers (Seymour et al., 2003).

It's Swiss-cheese research time here as regards Australian word-reading error patterns as we don't have word-reading data. Research comparing word-reading skills and error patterns at different ages for developing and struggling word-readers would be invaluable.

Now, low subject numbers can limit the power of studies' results and findings, thus while the German-English studies (Frith et al., 1998; Landerl et al., 1997) are extremely useful, with less than 50 children in each subject group, subject numbers were quite low.

Australia could perhaps term these studies *preliminary* studies useful for replicating. They're preliminary because their findings don't apply directly to Australian children, or even to English children, currently, given we're now decades on from that study.

That said, the power of well-designed research studies is impressive: it's thus highly likely our children will show similar characteristics. There's huge value in similar studies involving Australian children.

English-Turkish Word-Reading Differences

Oney and Goldman's (1984) Turkish-English study explored the word-reading and reading-comprehension skills of healthy-progress Grade 1 and 3 readers at two schools in Turkey, with 20 children in each group. One was a Turkish school where monolingually Turkish children learned to read and write in highly-regular Turkish. The other was an American school, on a USA military base in Turkey where monolingually English children learned to read and write Standard English.

Interestingly, the children were close to each other in age, being just over 7 years old in Grade 1, with children at the USA military base starting school older than children in the USA. It's thus a useful study in that, like Spencer & Hanley's (2003, 2004) Welsh-English studies we explored in Tour 2, controlling for impacts of age allows impacts of orthographic complexity to be more clearly seen.

In order to study healthy readers, Oney and Godman deliberately excluded the weakest 20-25% of readers in each class by teacher rating, and all children who'd repeated a year.

The study used two reading tasks, one a list of pseudowords of increasing length, and the other a reading-comprehension test involving reading two texts and answering questions about them.

This study too showed that healthy-progress Standard-English word-readers struggle with reading of unfamiliar words.

On the pseudoword task, they found
- Turkish Grade 1 readers were as proficiently accurate as the Turkish Grade 3 readers, but significantly slower – they'd achieved Level 1 automaticity (accuracy), but not yet Level 2 automaticity (fluency).
- USA Grade 1 readers were well behind the Grade 3 USA readers.
- USA Grade 3 readers were not as accurate as the Grade 3 Turkish readers (87% vs 94%), though this difference was not significant (which may be due to the low sample size).
- USA Grade 3 readers were much slower than the Grade 3 Turkish readers: they lacked Level 2 automaticity (fluency).

- There was a major word-length effect for the USA readers, with accuracy steadily decreasing as words got longer (from close to 100% accuracy for 3-letter words to 75% accuracy for 9-letter 3-syllable words).
- There was a major speed difference, with the USA readers being far slower, even for correct words, and the USA Grade 3 readers' speed being close to that of Turkish Grade 1 readers.

Oney and Goldman (1984) discuss Frederiksen's (1978) comparison of strong and weak high-school Standard-English word-readers, which showed faster reading for high-frequency words and significantly slower reading of low-frequency words, i.e., unfamiliar words. Oney and Goldman's pseudowords were unfamiliar words for both the Turkish and USA readers, but, with proficient word-reading, the Turkish readers weren't slower for the unfamiliar words.

As regards reading comprehension, the Turkish Grade 1 readers had significantly better reading comprehension than the USA Grade 1 readers, in keeping with having stronger word-reading skills. The Turkish Grade 3 readers had significantly better comprehension than the Turkish Grade 1 readers: with the two groups having equivalent, high word-reading accuracy, this stronger comprehension was attributed to higher age, maturity, and fluency.

This study also showed some good news, similar to the Welsh-English studies we explored. The USA and Turkish Grade 3 readers had equivalent reading-comprehension skills, with USA Grade 3 scores not significantly higher.

Oney and Goldman include useful discussion of automisation and its impacts, using LaBerge and Samuel's theory of automisation (e.g., Samuels & Flor, 1997). They also discuss children's needs to manage cognitive load while reading.

Word-reading and reading comprehension did not correlate significantly for the USA Grade 3 readers. That's not surprising given the study was of healthy readers – from mid-primary school, children's language comprehension skills, not their word-reading, are the strongest predictor of their reading comprehension.

The authors discuss likelihood that different reading strategies are used by regular-orthography and Standard-English readers. Whereas proficient phonemic recoding (sounding-out) is an effective route to meaning for regular-orthography readers, it's less so for Standard-English children. They discuss Standard-English readers' reliance on context cues likely building strongly across early reading development, because of their weak word-reading.

Oney and Goldman's study would be easy to replicate. Nicely, the article includes the words and reading-comprehension passages and questions used.

Australian Needs for Strong Word-Reading Instruction

The studies we've explored across this tour show consistent findings of Standard-English readers having major difficulties reading unfamiliar words, with this being an issue for both healthy progress and struggling readers, and children in upper-primary and high school. With children's spelling skills tending to be at similar levels to their levels for reading unfamiliar words, it's likely to be an issue not just for reading, but also for writing and spelling.

The implications of ongoing difficulties with unfamiliar words are many. As discussed in Tour 2, they include

- Unfamiliar, less-regular, infrequent words being a particular challenge for Standard-English readers.
- The universally crucial role of effective self-teaching skills, so children can read unfamiliar words (Shahar-Yames & Share, 2008; Share 1995, 1999; Share & Shalev, 2004; Ziegler et al, 2014).
- How English orthographic complexity impedes statistical learning, and the development of self-teaching.
- The power of regular orthographies in expediting self-teaching, and, in turn, the reading of unfamiliar words.
- The incredibly wide crosslinguistic gap between the word-reading and writing of Standard-English and regular-orthography children.
- How very difficult it is to build word-reading of unfamiliar words in Standard-English readers.
- How difficult it is to rescue children with word-reading difficulties when using solely Standard English.
- Word-reading instruction being needed across the school years, in Anglophone nations, as needed, rather than only being prioritised in early primary-school years.
- English having extremely large numbers of unfamiliar words, which children encounter in subject-area learning (Share & Stanovich, 1995).
- Likelihood that difficulties reading unfamiliar words is impeding the reading-comprehension skills of many upper primary-school and high school children.
- Subject-area learning quite likely being made more complex in Anglophone nations because of difficulties reading and writing less-regular, unfamiliar words.

- Australia and Anglophone nations having major needs to research the extent to which the above issues are present.

That 22% error rate in supposedly healthy-progress English 12-year-olds in Frith et al.'s (1998) study certainly suggests strong needs for research on this area. We need data on the extent to which Australian children across all primary and high-school year-levels have Level 1 and Level 2 automaticity (accuracy and fluency) for reading and writing of less-frequent (*rare*) words, and, in particular, on how well they read longer multisyllabic, less-regular rare words.

We can intimate similar findings from other research writing, e.g.,
- Finnish and other regular-orthography researchers stating confidently that their children have adult-level accuracy for reading and writing all words in Grade 1 (Torppa et al., 2016).
- Word-reading of orthographically unfamiliar words being so easy in Finnish, and other highly regular orthographies, that approximately half of Finnish children have already mastered reading and writing of Finnish before formal instruction begins in Grade 1 (Lyytinen et al., 2021).
- Finnish children being considered delayed readers if not reading proficiently by mid-Grade-2 (Holopainen et al., 2001).
- Word-reading accuracy tests not being used in highest-regularity orthography nations from Grade 2 on, because all children are so quickly proficiently accurate.
- In like manner, regular-orthography research on word-reading all being done with fluency measures, again because children have such high accuracy, with very few errors being made.
- Finnish researchers using a criterion for word-reading accuracy difficulties of children having less than 90% accuracy on long multisyllabic pseudowords (Lyytinen, Aro et al., 2006).

Needs for Crosslinguistic Research

Difficulties reading unfamiliar words is a serious issue for our children and schools in Australia and Anglophone nations, given that rare words and long, multisyllabic, less regular words abound across subject-area learning, e.g., words such as *metatarsals, multiplicative, metamorphosis, miscellaneous, mitochondria*. So often, in the words in texts children read in Science and Humanities subjects, just one letter being different can result in errors that reduce reading comprehension, e.g., whether the word is *reverent* or *relevant; attitude, aptitude* or *altitude; addition* or *addiction*.

However, particularly at high school, we assume our children are expert readers. We expect them to read and write independently and effectively. For strong subject-area learning, we need our children to be strong readers of unfamiliar words, as strong as children in regular-orthography nations, yet this may not be the case. Research is needed.

It's an orthographic disadvantage issue and also an issue of ethics. Are we meeting our children's rights to an effective education, when regular-orthography children have high accuracy for unfamiliar words from very early in primary school, but high-schoolers in Australia and other Anglophone nations still aren't proficient, with many making sizeable numbers of errors?

You'll notice that of the studies explored in this tour, only Caravolas (2018) is recent. Anglophone nations need to be engaging in collaborative crosslinguistic research establishing current realities of early-literacy development in Standard-English vs regular-orthography children.

Our situation is not all bad, as while we've problems, there are also impressive solutions to pursue. The 10 Changes are hows, whys and ways forward.

Standard English is going to remain a fixture of Australia and Anglophone nations, and the available studies we've explored are of children in European nations which use a sole regular orthography. We thus need to take that research and extend it, in areas applicable to improving literacy development in Australia and Anglophone nations.

We need research in 10 Changes directions. It's likely our early research priorities should be research that explores

- The literacy and learning development of children in nations such as Taiwan, Japan and China, nations which have moved to 2-Stage early literacy, by implementing use of a beginners' orthography, to meteoric effect.
- The Initial Teaching Alphabet research base, with studies then exploring use of English beginners' orthographies.
- The impacts of factors such as young-age, Acquired Helplessness, and weak executive-function skills, in impeding progress of at-risk, struggling and healthy readers.
- Crosslinguistic differences in Anglophone, European sole-regular-orthography nations, and Asian nations that now use beginners' orthographies, monitoring development over time of

- Many aspects of both early-literacy development, including reading, writing, and language skills, including cognitive-processing and executive-function skills.
- Workload and time-usage factors.
- Factors that impede healthy early-literacy development including impeded statistical learning, Acquired Helplessness, and associated factors.

Australia's Big-20 List for Positioning Word-Reading

While we're still using solely Standard English, we need to build knowledge on word-reading and improve the effectiveness of our Standard-English word-reading instruction.

We also need to think on how best to reduce the impeded statistical learning our children experience. Towards that end, I'm including, below, a list of 20 key principles I've compiled, which is likely to be helpful for Australian exploration of word-reading. They're listed below as Set B of the findings from this research tour.

Despite loving working with language skills more, over the decades I've built strong knowledge on word-reading. The Galletly Report (Galletly, 2005b) uses research of that time to make recommendations for Australia as regards word-reading development and difficulties, instruction and intervention. Further, my Doctoral studies explored Australian use of USA word-reading tests (Galletly, 2005b, 2008; Galletly & Knight, 2006; Galletly et al., 2009; Knight & Galletly, 2006).

From my investigating of the impact of regular orthographies since that time, I'm confident we'll find implementing a fully-regular beginners' orthography our strongest way forward (Knight et al., 2017a). That's particularly so if we start with 2.5 years of language enrichment, and start formal academic instruction from mid-Year 2. They'll be powerful factors enabling us to resolve our language weakness epidemic (Law et al., 2015, 2017; Walker & Haddock, 2020).

Anglophone children's struggles to develop effective early-literacy skills underlie current education struggles. Further, early mastery of word-reading and writing lies at the heart of the massive crosslinguistic divide between Anglophone nations' severe orthographic disadvantage, and the strong advantage many regular-orthography nations achieve.

Unfortunately, while Australian education emphasises and monitors spelling development, unfortunately, at the current time, it largely ignores word-reading and language skills. We thus need to build knowledge on our situation now, whilst also engaging in crosslinguistic comparisons.

It lacks logic to simply decide to move to 2-Stage learning and a regular-orthography, without investigating optimising of 1-Stage early-literacy instruction, given that early-literacy instruction and intervention of recent decades has been so poorly resourced.

In investigating 10 Changes improvements, we need to explore both
- The extent to which we can optimise Stage-1 Standard-English word-reading instruction using decidedly increased resourcing and tailoring of instruction to meet children's instructional needs.
- The effectiveness of 2-Stage learning and use of a beginners' orthography, prior to Standard English.

Key Findings from Tour 13

Findings and implications of studies explored in Tour 13 suggest the following points are useful considerations towards improving literacy and education in Australia and Anglophone nations:
- **Set A**: findings from crosslinguistic studies comparing regular-orthography and Standard-English word-reading of familiar and unfamiliar words.
- **Set B**: 20 key principles for positioning word-reading appropriately in Australian education.

Set A: Findings and implications of studies explored in Tour 13:
1. The two key skills of Standard-English word-reading are
   a. Having a growing bank of *sightwords*, words recognised immediately, on sight, and
   b. Becoming increasingly skilful at reading unfamiliar words.
2. Unfamiliar words occur frequently in subject-area reading, e.g., as Share & Stanovich (1995) discuss,
   Whereas just over 100 'heavy duty' words (eg the, in, was, etc.) account for around half of all the letter strings appearing in printed school English, a very large number of words exist which appear very rarely in print (Carroll, Davies & Richman, 1971; Nagy & Anderson, 1984). In fact fully 80% of English words occur less than once in a million words of running text.
3. Reading unfamiliar words, and perhaps unfamiliar long multisyllabic words in particular, seems a specific major challenge of Standard-English word-reading development.
4. Both Standard-English developing readers and struggling readers have difficulties reading long unfamiliar words.
5. Their difficulties are severe, and contrast markedly with how easily regular-orthography readers read long unfamiliar words.

6. There are indicators that high-school readers haven't achieved Level 1 automaticity, i.e., highly accurate word-reading, and still make many errors on longer unfamiliar words.
7. Even healthy-progress Standard-English developing readers seem to have major difficulties with unfamiliar words, e.g., Frith et al. (1998) found
   a. English 8 and 12-year-olds, established as healthy readers, made 44.5 times more vowel errors than same-age German readers, despite having an extra year's teaching and learning.
   b. They also made frequent real-word substitutions on unfamiliar words (pseudowords), despite having been told the words weren't real words.
   c. The English 12-year-olds made errors on over a fifth of unfamiliar multisyllabic words (22%).
8. This suggests needs for Australian research exploring reading of unfamiliar words in healthy-progress and struggling readers, perhaps starting by replicating Frith et al.'s (1998) study.
9. It also suggests value in Australian schools assessing children's skills for reading both familiar and unfamiliar words, across primary and high school.
10. The two subtests of the Test of Word Reading Efficiency-2 (TOWRE-2) assess these skills extremely well, taking little time, and being useful across primary school, high school, and adult literacy contexts:
    a. The Sight Word Efficiency subtest assesses reading of familiar words, i.e., sightwords, while
    b. The Phonemic Decoding Efficiency subtest assesses reading of unfamiliar words (pseudowords).
11. Regular orthographies are immensely kind to at-risk readers, e.g., even children considered to have Dyslexia, i.e., major word-reading difficulties, have minimal difficulties with unfamiliar words, e.g., making 16 times less vowel errors, and being able to read hardest pseudowords such as *quaduktrisch, miktanie,* more accurately than Standard-English struggling readers could read short pseudowords such as *foo, bish.*
12. Given Standard-English readers' difficulties with unfamiliar words, Australia needs to consider the extent to which word-reading instruction is needed across year-levels. There may be considerable value in systematically teaching word-reading across primary and high school, for children whose word-reading skills lack proficiency.
13. In early primary school and in remediation of older, struggling readers, there is value in word-reading instruction

systematically building skills reading more regular words of specific orthographic types.

14. There may be value in integrating vocabulary, word-reading and spelling instruction for long multisyllabic words, e.g., using later-years science and humanities multisyllabic words such as *metamorphosis, government, legislation* for practice reading of unfamiliar words in earlier years, with them then subsequently being studied in later years, as part of integrated vocabulary, word-reading and spelling instruction.

15. Taiwan, Japan and China integrate vocabulary, word-reading and spelling instruction when children learn the characters of their complex orthography, and may prove useful role-models for this area.

Set B: These 20 key principles are useful for positioning word-reading appropriately in Australian education:

1. Word-reading is accuracy and fluency of reading of words and word-parts:
   a. Accuracy of reading both isolated words and words in meaningful texts, including
      i. Quickly recognised words and unfamiliar words.
      ii. Real words and pseudowords, such as *hit, chart, summerly, it, sharn, rummerly, bamasho*.
      iii. Whole words and word-parts, including syllables, spelling patterns and individual letters.
   b. Fluency is an indicator of how automatic children are at word-reading:
      i. Fluency also has aspects beyond word-reading, including intonation.
      ii. In focusing on word-reading proficiency, fluency is usefully measured as word-reading efficiency, e.g., the number of words read per minute. This can be fluency of reading a meaningful text or high-speed reading of a list of words. Words per minute is a valid easy means of measuring this aspect of fluency.

2. It is useful to teach beginning word-readers to use three word-reading strategies matched to English orthography's three grainsizes (Goswami, 2002; Ziegler & Goswami, 2005):
   a. Phonemic recoding (*sounding-out*) of Regular words and syllables, using phoneme grainsize.
   b. Pattern reading using rhyme for Pattern words and syllables of orthographic-unit grainsize, e.g., b-*all*, h-*igh*.
   c. Wholeword reading of highly irregular Tricky words and syllables, e.g., *one, was, eight*.

3. The two partner skills of word-reading are
   a. Developing an expanding number of sightwords, words recognised instantly; some being irregular words learned as wholewords, others being regular words initially read using decoding:
      i. This skill is assessed by testing children's skill reading real words, e.g., the Sight Word Efficiency subtest of the Test of Word Reading Efficiency-2 (TOWRE-2).
   b. Becoming increasingly skilful at working-out and reading unfamiliar words:
      i. Pseudowords, e.g., *dit, sharn, rummerly, bamasho* are a proxy for unfamiliar words children meet in reading.
      ii. This skill is assessed by testing children's skill reading pseudowords, e.g., the Phonemic Decoding Efficiency subtest of the Test of Word Reading Efficiency-2 (TOWRE-2).
4. Early emerging and late emerging word-reading difficulties are both common:
   a. Some children with word-reading difficulties struggle with both building sightwords and reading unfamiliar words – they develop early-emerging word-reading difficulties.
   b. Other children have late-emerging word-reading difficulties – they do reasonably well with early sightwords but have difficulties reading unfamiliar words, often accompanied by spelling difficulties. They cope quite well during earliest reading development when texts are often highly predictable and sightwords are a big help. Their difficulties emerge later, when texts become more complex, and unfamiliar words abound.
   c. It is common for late-emerging word-reading difficulties to go undetected.
   d. Schools' testing reading of unfamiliar words, e.g., using the Phonemic Decoding Efficiency subtest of the TOWRE-2, in addition to its Sightword Efficiency subtest, will identify these difficulties earlier in reading development, with early-intervention provided.
5. Word-reading is a crucial factor in literacy development in all nations, strongly related to development of other literacy skills and academic progress.
6. Word-reading and language skills are the two main subskills of reading comprehension, in a relationship that can be written as *Reading Comprehension = Word-Reading x Language Skills*. There is great value in schools testing all three skill areas: reading comprehension, word-reading and language skills.

7. All children benefit from explicit instruction in word-reading, and practising word-reading strategies using decontextualised words. However, they differ markedly in the extent needed. High-progress (*upper-third*) children often need little explicit instruction, while at-risk and low-progress (*lower-third*) children often need extensive, strategically tailored word-reading instruction and practice.
8. Word-reading takes many years to develop in Anglophone children, thus it is both appropriate and important for word-reading instruction to be included in all primary and high-school year-levels, for children whose skills are still developing, with this instruction tailored to student needs.
9. Word-reading difficulties play a major role in the reading and literacy difficulties many Australians experience, and are quite likely a significant factor in Australia's low achievement for reading at school, state, national and international levels.
10. Word-reading tests are useful at multiple levels, including
    a. Monitoring progress in word-reading development.
    b. Tailoring word-reading instruction to children's needs.
    c. Generating useful data for education systems, and for research that guides systemic decision-making.
11. Most word-reading tests are one-to-one tests, involving an adult testing an individual child. This can be time-consuming, making time efficiency a pertinent factor to consider when selecting word-reading tests. Whole-class and group tests of word-reading tend not to be as useful and powerful as one-to-one word-reading tests:
    a. The Test of Word Reading Efficiency-2 (TOWRE-2) overcomes the time factor well.
        i. Available from Pro-Ed Australia and used extensively internationally in schools, educational systems and research, the TOWRE-2 involves each child reading two lists for 45 seconds each: one list of real words, and one of pseudowords.
        ii. Used in national testing, standardised test procedure could be simplified to reduce test time to perhaps 4 minutes per child, e.g., by reducing practice lists to three items, and using software apps to record scores and results, instead of paper record forms.
        iii. The TOWRE-2 is normed for ages 6 to 25 years, so can be used across primary and high school, and has four parallel forms, so can readily be used for retesting.
        iv. With speech-to-text software becoming more sophisticated, it is likely computerised testing with the

TOWRE-2 and other word-reading tests will become increasingly a possibility.
  b. There are many useful one-to-one word-reading tests schools would find useful, for which it would be relatively easy to develop current Australian norms, e.g.,
      i. Tests of paragraph reading, which also test reading comprehension, e.g., the *Neale Analysis of Reading Ability: Third Edition* (Neale, 1999), has 1999 norms, which are now out-of-date. There is value in developing new norms for this test, particularly given its previous norming data is one of Australia's few word-reading data sets.
      ii. Tests of sentence reading, e.g., the *Holborn Reading Scale* (Watts, 1948), which seems out of print and hence perhaps free to use, has norms now out-of-date, with value in developing new norms. I've posted a modified version on ResearchGate (Galletly, 2013).
      iii. Tests of single word-reading, e.g., TOWRE-2, and free criterion-based tests of word-reading such as *Galletly Most-Frequent Word Probes*, and *Galletly Diagnostic Vowel Words Reading Tests* (Galletly, 2005a, 2015a).
12. There is currently insufficient data available on Australian word-reading achievement:
  a. For school use, e.g., to effectively guide word-reading and reading instruction, and to identify children with word-reading difficulties.
  b. For education system use, e.g., to fund word-reading instruction effectively, e.g., through knowing the numbers of children with significant word-reading difficulties, and the levels of instructional intensity and school resourcing needed to achieve both effective classroom instruction and effective intervention.
  c. For Australian government use, e.g., to establish, categorically, word-reading's role in Australia as a factor in reading comprehension, other aspects of literacy, and academic and career achievement.
13. Word-reading data in the form of word-reading test results is urgently needed in Australia to address this knowledge gap, it being highly inappropriate for a modern nation to be negligent in this way.
14. The Australian federal and state governments and education departments do not sufficiently advocate for word-reading testing, and there is inappropriately-inadequate national gathering of word-reading data, e.g.,

a. National NAPLAN tests for children in Years 3, 5, 7 and 9 test written expression, reading comprehension, spelling, grammar and punctuation, but not word-reading. There are needs for word-reading testing to be included, perhaps starting with a 10% sample across states and territories.
b. At government request, the Australian Council of Educational Research (ACER) has developed Progressive Achievement Tests for assessing children across Years 1 to 10 in science, maths and multiple literacy areas. Word-reading is not included, which contrasts markedly with the other literacy skills these tests assess. There are needs to develop Australian word-reading tests, e.g., perhaps tests similar to the TOWRE-2's two subtests that test the two key skills of word-reading development.
c. There is strong value in Australia testing the word-reading skills of all children involved in international PIRLS and PISA testing.
d. Recently a national phonics test has been proposed for Year 1 children, however, word-reading develops over many years, and this word-reading testing has only been proposed for Year 1, ignoring other year-levels. There are needs for more comprehensive monitoring of word-reading development across the school years.

15. Word-reading instruction and testing is a highly contentious topic in Australia and other Anglophone nations, with this contention often termed the Reading Wars. Its divisiveness seems the reason why the Australian government has twice committed to systemic word-reading testing as part of national testing of literacy skills, in the 1970s and in 2005, and in both instances not acted on this commitment, with word-reading testing still omitted from systemic assessment of literacy skills.

16. It is likely that much contention about word-reading instruction could be resolved if Australia implemented a national testing and research focus, building knowledge on children's word-reading skills; and the relationship of word-reading to reading comprehension, other literacy skills, and academic progress.

17. The Australian government needs to implement a national word-reading assessment program using both subtests of the TOWRE-2 or an equivalent test of efficiency of word-reading of real words and pseudowords:
a. In all schools, including annual testing of children making healthy-progress, and testing at least twice yearly for children making below-average progress.
b. In national and international testing programs, including

NAPLAN testing of Year 3, 5, 7 and 9 children, and PIRLS and PISA tests.
18. Word-reading difficulties create major international differences. There are indicators that most Anglophone nations have about one third of children and adults who have weak word-reading skills while, in contrast, regular-orthography nations have very few children with word-reading difficulties. This creates orthographic advantage and disadvantage experienced by nations: our huge lag behind regular-orthography nations, our superfluity of struggling readers, and our children having much more severe word-reading and spelling difficulties.
19. Ethically, Australian children seem entitled to word-reading and spelling development as easy and rapid as regular orthography children experience, and also to similar very-low likelihood of word-reading and spelling difficulties.
Our current too slow word-reading and spelling development, and too many struggling readers with too severe word-reading and spelling difficulties seem the result of
   a. Standard-English orthographic complexity impacts, including confused complicated learning and ongoing high cognitive load across early-literacy development.
   b. Time pressure from word-reading and spelling development taking so much time, combined with insufficiently effective classroom word-reading instruction and early intervention.
   c. Insufficient school resourcing for building optimal word-reading instruction and remediation.
   d. Lack of alternative national curriculum strands accommodating children with word-reading and spelling difficulties, through increasing time available for word-reading intervention and remediation.
20. A strong national focus on word-reading assessment, instruction, knowledge-building, and appropriate resourcing of these areas has potential to
   a. Markedly reduce the learning, academic, social-emotional, behavioural, and career disadvantaging impacts currently experienced by Australians with word-reading difficulties.
   b. Expedite improving Australia's reading outcomes and education.

Reflections As The Tours End

There are no such things as reading difficulties.
There are only teaching challenges.

Jackie French

Just as when enjoying the best of holiday tours, all great tours must come to an end. On the final days of touring, we've usually mixed emotions as we reflect on new ideas and experiences we've engaged in along the way, and reflect forward, often pondering changes we'd like to make in life and work habits, into the future, after touring has ended, when we're back busily actioning learning and life.

To support usefully reflecting on the research touring that we've done, while actively contemplating the future, and improvements, let's consider briefly where we've toured thus far and where we're at now, before we head off on our final tour, **Tour 14**.

Each tour has its useful list of key points at chapter end, and at the end of this book, there's a detailed Table of Contents, where section headings can be reviewed.

You've quite likely seen the title of **Tour 14**, *Insufficiently Effective Word-Reading Intervention*, and can predict, from what we've toured thus far, that this tour will also show Anglophone nations achieving poorly.

Importantly, from the tours we've completed, you know much about why this is happening.

Our first tours explored the major impacts of orthographic complexity:
- **Tour 1**. Too Slow Standard-English Word-Reading Development.
- **Tour 2**. Orthography: The Key Impacting Factor.
- **Tour 3**. Success Inoculation Vs Acquired Helplessness.
- **Tour 4**. Regular Orthographies and Intellectual Disability.

We're struggling because we're wrestling with Standard English in 1-Stage early-literacy development. We're not managing English orthographic complexity well enough. We require our young 4.5 to 5-year-olds to learn to read and write Standard-English, without the empowering effects of 2-Stage early-literacy, as Taiwan, Japan and China, our role-model nations, use.

And while these youngsters are armed with initial enthusiasm and pre-literacy experiences, they're sadly lacking in the mature cognitive-processing and executive-function skills they need if they're to cope well with the complexities of Standard English and the high cognitive load it creates for their learning and literacy.

You can also probably predict that, in **Tour 14**, we'll explore very good news for regular-orthography nations, with powerful, effective early intervention.

Fortunately, that's not all bad news. It shows the strong potential Anglophone nations have for improvement, if we too move to 2-Stage early-literacy development and a beginners' orthography, with our children and schools then reaping the powerful benefits of orthographic advantage.

After all, we've seen that effectiveness earlier. Both **Tour 4**, *Regular Orthographies and Intellectual Disability*, and **Tour 5**, *The Power of Initial Beginners' Orthographies*, showed us the enormous strengths of fully-regular beginners' orthographies. When difficulties mastering word-reading and spelling are minimal, they're easily overcome. Nations then can meet their teaching challenges, with very few children being struggling word-readers.

Tours 6 to 11 focused on literacy components, and our needs for improvement not just in reading comprehension and written expression, but also in language skills and word-reading: key literacy subskills that Australia hasn't been emphasising in school instruction and skill-monitoring.

Tour 6, *Our Epidemic of Language Weakness*, explored Australia's widespread high levels of language weakness:
- How we've too many children with Language, Literacy and Learning Disorder (LLLD).
- How language skills underlie both the print-accuracy (word-reading and spelling) and verbal-language skills components of reading and writing.
- How too many children arrive at school with weak language skills and are thus highly at risk of developing reading and writing difficulties.

We also considered the costs and benefits of three paths towards improvement:
- The *Effective Education Road*, a path using 2-Stage early literacy and a beginners' orthography (Change 8).
- The *Pre-School Child Road*, a more expensive path, where we'd work with our children from early-childhood to increase likelihood of healthy school achievement.
- A middle road that combines the above two roads, using both Changes 8 and 9, and pre-school supports as needed.

Tour 7, *Literacy Components and Quadrants*, explored the power of schools and education systems testing reading and writing components and using scatterplots and quadrants to more precisely establish children's strengths, weaknesses and instructional needs, at child, class, school and system level.

It showed indicators that we may have many children in upper primary and high school who have weak word-reading and language skills. It also showed the value of Australia using component and quadrant research in exploring these areas, e.g., to establish how well children are doing and the extent to which weak word-reading and language skills underlie our children's literacy difficulties.

Tour 8, *Our Many Low Literacy Achievers*, explored PIRLS, PISA and NAPLAN data. We had to do a considerable amount of inferring, e.g., using spelling, reading-comprehension and written-expression data to suggest insights on our children's word-reading and language skills, as we've no systemic data on these skills. Certainly, it's clear that Australia has excessive numbers of low achievers, and that weak literacy skills are widespread. It's also clear we need data on the word-reading and language-skills levels of our PIRLS, PISA and NAPLAN children.

Tour 9, *Needs for Workload Research*, focused on the excessive child and teacher workload that's a key aspect of the severe orthographic disadvantage of Australia and Anglophone nations. It showed our needs for research investigating the extent to which our children and teachers are stressed and overworked.

Differences in how easily and effectively children develop word-reading and word-writing are the crux of our current, wide crosslinguistic differences in literacy, learning and academic achievement. Thus, in the next tours, exploring available research we zeroed in more closely on word-reading.

Tour 10, *A Multiple Deficits Vs Phonological Basis*, explored value in Australia largely using Pennington's Multiple Deficits model (McGrath et al., 2020; Pennington, 2006), and the Literacy Component Model (Knight et al., 2021) as useful models for both research and practice.

Given the high cognitive load that Standard English creates is a major factor activating our children's risk factors and proliferating reading and writing difficulties, our need for effective cognitive-processing skills is another area of major crosslinguistic difference.

Tour 11, *Executive-Function Skills and Word-Reading*, explored this area, showing the power of effective cognitive-processing skills, and how weak skills increase likelihood of Standard-English reading and writing difficulties.

It also showed likelihood that learning to read and write a fully-regular orthography expedites development of cognitive-processing, including executive-function skills: that's an important area where Anglophone nations need to build knowledge, when exploring the power of 2-Stage early literacy and using a beginners' orthography prior to Standard English.

Then, the tours focused in on the intransigent Standard-English word-reading struggles that our children have, which make the crosslinguistic divide between us and regular-orthography nations so very wide.

In Tour 12, *Our Impeded Statistical Learning*, we explored the difficulties at-risk children experience in learning to read, and needs to research this area.

Then, most recently, in **Tour 13**, *Unfamiliar Words: Our Standard-English Nemesis*, the penultimate tour of our journeys, we explored the wide crosslinguistic divide for reading of unfamiliar words: how they're a massive area of struggle for Standard-English readers, but not for regular-orthography children, who can read and write virtually all words with adult-level accuracy from Grade 1 (Lyytinen et al., 2021; Seymour et al., 2003; Torppa et al., 2016).

Importantly, the studies we explored showed it's not just our young and struggling Standard-English readers who have difficulties with unfamiliar words: difficulty reading unfamiliar words is quite likely an issue for large numbers of primary and high-school children, including those with supposedly healthy reading skills. There's value in considering the studies we explored, preliminary research, with needs for future crosslinguistic research investigating this area, and value in replicating the studies we explored.

Reflections As The Tours End

It really is a tale of our potential vs our status quo:
- Our potential: the orthographic advantage we'd have, with few struggling readers and easy, expedited literacy development, if we moved to 2-Stage early literacy, vs
- Our status quo: struggling children, teachers, schools, families and education, severe orthographic disadvantage, and our long sad tail of underachievers.

As said elsewhere (Galletly, 2022a; Galletly & Knight, 2004; Knight et al., 2019),

When a nation's children learn to read quickly and easily, with few experiencing difficulties, this offers proliferating advantages for individuals and the nation, including
- *Ease of learning to read and write.*
- *Ease of teaching and learning across the school years.*
- *Ease of improving reading and education outcomes.*
- *Adults having the life advantages of high literacy.*
- *Generational advantage, through parents being proficiently literate and thus able to read to their children and support their literacy development.*
- *Workplace and economic advantage.*

When a nation's children are slow to learn to read and write, with many experiencing severe ongoing literacy difficulties, this creates corresponding disadvantage.

Australia and the Anglosphere have enormous potential for improvement: we just need to be brave enough to action the steps that need to be taken.

Across the tours, we've covered much content that showed the importance of each of the 10 Changes, as being key strategies for expediting improvement:

Change 1. Understand how orthographies matter: English spelling is dragging us down.

Lack of awareness of the impacts of orthographies in expediting vs impeding development of reading and writing is a massive factor currently limiting the progress of Anglophone nations. There's power in building widespread awareness of crosslinguistic differences and how these show the savage impacts of English orthographic complexity. Into the future, please do help build wider awareness of how major orthographic impacts are.

The **A** of our improvement ABCs is **ACT** locally while looking globally. Let's build awareness of the current, massive crosslinguistic gap that's present between Anglophone and regular-orthography literacy and academic achievement, then work to close that gap.

Change 2. Own our struggling reader woes: End hypocrisy and pretence.

We need to be brutally honest about
- The difficulties our children are experiencing.
- How our children's difficulties are disproportionately severe compared to those that regular-orthography children experience.
- How inappropriately high our teachers' workload is.
- How inadequately we resource our schools for supporting at-risk and struggling learners.
- How incredibly wide the crosslinguistic gap is, as regards the word-reading, spelling, reading and writing of our most vulnerable children: children with highest risk levels, those with severest learning difficulties, and those with intellectual disability.
- The extent to which education here is HEARTSH (Hugely-Exhausting, Actually-Rather-Tedious Schooling Heaviness) rather than GENTLE (Gentle, Engaging, Never-Tiring, Learning Enrichment).

The **B** of our improvement ABCs is **BOOST** the lower-third to benefit everyone. That starts with Australia owning our *Aussie Reading Woes*, and other Anglophone nations doing similarly.

Pretending all is well, when it isn't, is another massive factor that limits the progress of Anglophone nations. Let's encourage honesty and openness. This will, in turn, build interest and enthusiasm for pursuing improvement that enriches our children, improves and eases their education, and closes the crosslinguistic gap.

Change 3. Weigh workload: Our children and teachers are working far too hard.

Anglophone children, teachers, schools and families have far higher workload for learning to read and write, and for achieving effective subject-area learning, than is the case for the world's many regular-orthography nations that have strong orthographic advantage.

The extra workload is created by, and builds from, severe orthographic disadvantage. It's demonstrated by
- Our children's excessively slow, arduous mastery of learning to read and write.

- Our consequent struggles and difficulties achieving effective teaching and learning across the school years, with needs to
  o Fit in our additional early-literacy workload.
  o Cater for large numbers with severe literacy difficulties.
  o Work to achieve the comprehensive, subject-area education that most nations desire.
- Our resultant failure to improve education, early-literacy development, and school effectiveness.

Unfortunately, there's been little awareness and consideration of this exceptionally high workload, and the major crosslinguistic differences in child and teacher workload between Anglophone and regular-orthography nations. In working towards improving, we need research on workload.

The **C** of our improvement ABCs is CHANGE effectively to work less and achieve more. Let's measure child and teacher workload to establish our starting point, then monitor workload changes, across our improvement.

Change 4. One-size education does not fit all: Teach to the decidedly different instructional needs of upper-third and lower-third readers.

If Anglophone nations had effective early-intervention, we wouldn't have our flood of struggling readers. In achieving **B**, our BOOSTing the lower-third to benefit everyone, and in empowering our upper-third to soar, we must respect and explore the major differences our upper and lower-third groups have in literacy subskills, and tailor education accordingly.

Importantly, our excessive numbers of weak learners, who struggle with literacy and learning, and our struggles to achieve effective progress for them, are a further, major crosslinguistic difference.

Our improvement mantra is Jackie French's wise words,
There are no such things as reading difficulties.
There are only teaching challenges.

Many regular-orthography nations meet their teaching challenges for all three thirds, for word-reading, spelling, reading and writing.

Anglophone nations don't, and there's every likelihood that the excessive workload they have in battling to support so many struggling learners is a key reason they're not able to optimise education for middle and upper thirds.

We really do need to boost the lower-third to benefit everyone, and that starts with Change 4. Where relevant differences exist, let's empower our children by treating them differently in our instructional emphases, so we meet their instructional needs.

Change 5. End our data deficiency: Build strong knowledge on word-reading levels.

Houston, we have a problem; Australia, we've a problem too. Amidst Reading Wars wrestling, we've no systemic data on our children's word-reading levels.

We need it for our upper-third, who need to soar, and not be restricted to basic, skills-building instruction if it's instruction they don't need. And we need it for our lower two-thirds, given it's really quite likely that two thirds of Standard-English word-readers would have significant word-reading difficulties, using international word-reading standards, e.g., the levels routinely achieved across schools in regular-orthography nations.

Change 6. Enrich every child: Ensure effective supportive tailored education.

Let's tailor education effectively, to boost all our children. In doing so, let's respect and monitor language and thinking skills. It's an area where too many Anglophone children are struggling. Let's improve.

Change 7. Insist on easy literacy development: Reach regular-orthography nations' achievement levels.

It's an issue of ethics and our children's rights. If schools in European regular-orthography nations achieve word-reading and spelling skills at adult-level proficiency in Grade 1, that sets an international standard worthy of great respect.

Now, it's most unlikely that Anglophone nations would move to being sole-regular-orthography nations, as, e.g., Turkey and South Korea, have done. (After all, English is an international language, and, quite likely, future research will show that most children and adults who use English as a second language, read and write it more proficiently than our lower-half or lower-third of achievers.)

So the goal for Anglophone nations then becomes the levels that nations actioning 2-Stage early-literacy development achieve. That includes Taiwan, Japan and China, and the levels Anglophone nations achieved in the 1960s, using the Initial Teaching Alphabet (ITA).

Here's our 2035 goal that sets the specifics of the improvement we need to achieve:

By 2035, Australian education will be

*routinely, efficiently, gently and easily
achieving highly effective, rapid development of children's
word-reading, spelling, writing and early-literacy skills,
in GENTLE manner,
in every early-years classroom,
in all schools across our nation,
as efficiently as is achieved routinely
across schools in regular-orthography nations
such as Taiwan, Japan and China,
with at least 98% of Australian school children
being confident, independent readers and writers,
able to read 90% of the 10,000 most-frequent words,
by age 8.5 years, or within 18 months of starting formal word-reading instruction.*

Change 8. Investigate the potential of fully-regular beginners' orthographies: They're winners.

The first three words of Change 8 are important: *Investigate the potential!* They emphasise not jumping willy-nilly into using regular orthographies. They also emphasise how, given extensive evidence, use of fully-regular beginners' orthographies is very much an area that we need to explore.

We need to move forward strategically. We should first read the research, then ask if we might visit Asian nations to observe 2-Stage early-literacy and education in action, plus have discussions with teachers and researchers. In doing so, we'd consider work samples of all three thirds of achievers. We'd also deeply consider the lower-third and weakest 5% and 10% of readers and writers, to explore the extent to which 2-Stage learning really does reduce and remove word-reading and writing difficulties.

We'd then ask if we might do collaborative crosslinguistic research exploring early-literacy development with partner nations.

Then, with appreciable knowledge built, we may well be ready to start careful, strategic research that explores the use of beginners' orthographies with children here in Australia.

Beginners' orthographies and 2-Stage learning offer the potential of the *Effective Education Road*, that we explored in Tour 6.

That's the path Taiwan, Japan, Taiwan and Korea took in the middle of last century, by changing

- From 1-Stage literacy with each nation having just its highly complex morpho-logography, and high levels of illiteracy,

- To 2-Stage early literacy, with schools starting children on a fully-regular beginners' orthography, which expedited and empowered early-literacy development in Stage 1, plus built learning skills for the children subsequently learning to read and write the complex orthography in Stage 2.

The education and economic improvements those nations have achieved from the time they moved to 2-Stage early literacy is extremely impressive. Changing from using a highly complex orthography on its own, to easy, empowering 2-Stage early-literacy can be very effective indeed.

Change 9. Play to learn first: Start Standard-English word-reading instruction from mid-Year 2.

Australia currently has widespread, high incidence of language weakness in children starting school. In addition, our schools are pressure-cookers, with education too often being largely ineffective for our lower-third achievers, evidenced in swelling numbers of low achievers from Year 3 to Year 9, shown in Tables 2 and 3, in Tour 8.

We need to take action that will rescue our children, schools and teachers from the trauma of our current, sad Early Year's Factory: our early-years education, that alas, produces our ongoing flood of struggling readers (Galletly, 2022a).

We need to remove pressure, by freeing up both workload and time pressure. We can do this by implementing Change 9:

- Ending our current practice of formal instruction for word-reading, spelling, writing, counting and number skills commencing from close to the start of Prep.
- Replacing it with 2.5 years of tailored language and learning enrichment, with formal reading, writing and maths instruction commencing in mid-Year 2.

Actioning Change 9, our children would have more mature learning skills, from older age and maturation, plus they'd have the skills and empowerment they'd build in those learning-enrichment years. To heighten the effectiveness of that 2.5 years of enrichment, we'd also address and improve teacher workload and school resourcing.

At age 7.0 to 7.5 years, our children would be the same age as children in many European nations when learning to read and write.

As detailed in *Bunyips in the Classroom: The 10 Changes* (Galletly, 2022a) and *The 10 Changes: The Nitty Gritty* (Galletly, In press), we'd reap many appreciable benefits. As examples,

- We'd have 2.5 years more time for readiness building for all children, and for language and learning interventions for children who start school with weak language skills.
- We'd end our current early-years Find the Learning Time Challenge and Find the Caring Time Challenge.
- We'd end our too-frequent HEARTSH, and achieve GENTLE.

Implementing both Changes 8 and 9 would also enable taking the *Enhanced Early Education Road*, discussed in Tour 6: a gentler path with more-guaranteed effectiveness.

Change 10. Build needed research knowledge as quickly as possible: Use collaborative school-based research.

Australia has saved savagely on education research funding across recent decades. This has proved a significant contributor to our current difficulties. In addition, across those decades, Anglophone nations have paid too little attention to orthographic impacts, and how our current practices, working with solely Standard English, build our severe orthographic disadvantage.

It's two decades since Seymour et al.'s (2003) seminal COST-A8 study highlighted the severe delays Standard-English readers experience, but there seems little to no evidence that Anglophone nations have taken strong research action, such as in-depth longitudinal studies of early literacy development in Anglophone and regular-orthography nations.

It is overwhelmingly obvious that, if we're to improve education and our children's education and literacy development, Australia needs strategic, well-focused research.

There's prolific research happening on many fronts in regular-orthography nations, e.g., just using three authors in my reference list, I can list 15 very useful articles discussing research studies:
- Lyytinen, 2014; Lyytinen et al., 2004, 2015, Lyytinen, Erskine et al., 2006; Lyytinen, Aro et al., 2006.
- Papadopoulos, 2001, 2022; Papadopoulos et al., 2003, 2004, 2012, 2016, 2018, 2021.
- Torppa et al., 2010, 2013, 2015, 2016, 2017, 2019.

All those discussed studies have useful knowledge towards optimising early-literacy and education in Anglophone nations. And there are many more studies those researchers have engaged in, that I've not included, which are equally useful reading. Australia would benefit greatly by engaging in similar, collaborative studies.

So let's ask politely. It's time for our new season of research to begin.

Research Tour 14.
Our Insufficiently Effective Word-Reading Intervention

One of the most compelling findings from recent reading research is that children who get off to a poor start in reading rarely catch up ... the poor first-grade reader almost invariably continues to be a poor reader.

Joseph Torgesen, 1998

The findings of the studies we've explored, and the extent of our current PISA, PIRLS and NAPLAN struggles, offer us a before and after contrast. Australia and the Anglosphere are struggling now, but have potential to do far, far better, by enacting the 10 Changes, and associated improvements.

In there being *no such thing as reading difficulties*, and only *teaching challenges*, the two key ways to meet those challenges are to
1. Prevent difficulties from starting.
2. Provide highly effective early-intervention which ends difficulties quickly and effectively.

Our very large numbers of struggling readers and learners show we fail to effectively prevent difficulties developing in many children.

Our tours have shown us that word-reading is a key factor creating the wide crosslinguistic gap between Anglophone and regular-orthography nations. They've also shown possibilities that the difficulties that Standard-English readers have in reading and writing orthographically-unfamiliar words is a major factor in Australia's education struggles: they may prove a key aspect of why we have such difficulty improving lower achievers' literacy skills and seem unable to prevent word-reading skills developing in many children.

In this tour, we explore another relatively solid brick wall: our

Research Tour 14. Our Insufficiently Effective Word-Reading Intervention

massive difficulties achieving effective word-reading remediation. We'll fly in to explore how insufficiently effective Standard-English word-reading intervention is, relative to the highly effective intervention achieved when regular orthographies are used.

Standard-English struggles have not diminished. Al Otaiba and Fuchs' 2006 comment of English readers is equally relevant today:

The gap between proficient and less proficient readers widens over the elementary years (Stanovich, 1986), and remediation of reading problems becomes increasingly difficult after third grade ... We join a growing number of researchers and educators who have expressed concern that as many as 30% of children at risk for reading difficulties ... may not benefit from generally effective early literacy interventions ...

These students have been called "Treatment Resisters" or "Nonresponders" ... Our work and investigations by others ... have suggested that the percentage of nonresponders among children with learning disabilities may be as high as 50%.

It's clear that Anglophone nations have major difficulties achieving effective intervention that catches children up to healthy progress and keeps them there (Middleton et al., 2022; R. O'Connor, 2000).

We've likely masses of primary-and high-school children not proficient at reading and writing Standard-English, unfamiliar words, particularly long multisyllabic words for these words.

Meanwhile, Finnish and German researchers confidently use a cut-off criterion for word-reading accuracy difficulties, of children having less than 90% accuracy on long multisyllabic pseudowords (Lyytinen, Aro et al., 2006) to decide healthy vs. delayed word-reading. That's perhaps a criterion Australia might use in research.

It's actually very difficult to rescue Standard-English children from word-reading struggles. Prevention, not cure, definitely seems the answer, as Standard English intervention too often is not working sufficiently well. That's the case even when intervention is provided by experts, in intensive, well-funded research studies. Prevention, through introducing and using a beginners' orthography, may well prove our strongest way forward.

It may well prove an issue of prevention being imperative because the cure is simply too hard to achieve, when we use our current practice of children learning to read and write solely Standard English in 1-Stage early-literacy development. Quite likely, we'll find a fully regular beginners' orthography our cheapest and most effective form of prevention.

Currently, our beginners with weak word-reading make many errors. Those errors wouldn't be a problem if we had wonderfully effective intervention – if we could routinely rescue our strugglers from our long sad tail of underachievers, and have them confidently and proficiently accurate.

Unfortunately, while successful for some, Standard-English word-reading intervention is insufficiently effective for far too many struggling word-readers, both in research and in our schools.

The Challenge of Achieving Then Maintaining Healthy Word-Reading

Anglophone nations do have word-reading interventions that enable many struggling word-readers to make appreciable progress, and some go from strength to strength (e.g., Nicholson & Dymock, 2015; Stuart & Stainthorp, 2015). As an example, Australia's MultiLit and MiniLit studies show many children making appreciable gains (Buckingham et al., 2012, 2014; Reynolds et al., 2021; Wheldall et al., 2016, 2017, 2019).

Quite often, without intervention, our severely struggling word-readers make minimal progress. They might make one month's growth of word-reading age in six calendar months at best. In consequence, they steadily slip further and further behind, one paddock, two paddocks, three paddocks, four, further and further away from the year-level playing field.

To catch up, we need children to make more than six months reading progress in six calendar months, and to do this on an ongoing basis, until they're level with their peers.

Effective intervention achieves catch-up gains. As examples, severely struggling Australian word-readers receiving MultiLit and MiniLit intervention make appreciable progress, e.g., 15 months word-reading progress and 11 months reading-comprehension progress in 6 months (Buckingham et al., 2012, 2014; Reynolds et al., 2021):
- Buckingham et al. (2014) found children attending a MultiLit clinic plus doing home practice typically made about 7 months word-reading progress in 9 weeks of intervention.
- Wheldall et al. (2017) using data on 194 socially disadvantaged individual students who completed the MiniLit program in small-group sessions, showed significant gains in word-reading and spelling, with strong effect sizes, with participants making at least 6 months spelling progress and 7-10 months word-reading progress from that 15 weeks of intervention.

Research Tour 14. Our Insufficiently Effective Word-Reading Intervention

- Wheldall et al. (2019) showed students of remote indigenous communities receiving MultiLit training at school, similarly made significant gains in word-reading, with strong effect sizes, and also made progress in receptive vocabulary.

The gains made in those studies are appreciable. Further, it's likely that children participating in other school intervention programs that use similar principles of remediation, also make useful gains.

Unfortunately, our gains are hard-won, plus we've a consistent finding across Standard-English intervention studies that, while children make gains, many don't achieve healthy-progress levels.

Multiple Standard-English studies show that once intervention has ceased, many children don't continue to improve on their own, and later need further intervention (e.g., Al Otaiba & Fuchs, 2006). They also show that an appreciable amount of the gains made during intervention is often lost later, due to Level 1 Automisation Weakness (e.g., R. O'Connor, 2000). They also show a proportion of children making sadly little progress (Al Otaiba & Fuchs, 2002, 2006; Compton et al., 2014; Middleton et al., 2022; Torgesen, 2010; Torgesen et al., 1997; Vellutino, 2000; Vellutino et al., 1996).

Our Anglophone norm seems for us to be pleased children have made progress, but with the children still appreciably behind. Importantly, that finding of insufficient catch-up is using Standard-English healthy-progress as the goal, e.g., average level on Standard-English word-reading tests. By regular-orthography standards, that goal is sadly meagre: by international standards, our struggling word-readers are appallingly delayed.

Reviews of word-reading interventions show Standard-English interventions achieve only modest gains. They often discuss needs for research on children who make little progress (Roberts, Torgesen et al., 2008; Scammacca et al., 2007, 2015, 2016; Wanzek et al., 2013, 2016, 2018).

Too many Standard-English readers are struggling. As an example, Roberts, Torgesen et al. (2008) comment of USA children,

> Over a quarter of 8th-grade students and more than one-third of 4th graders do not read well enough to understand important concepts and acquire new knowledge from grade-level text. For students with learning disabilities, the numbers are more troubling.

Certainly, Standard-English early and remedial intervention isn't sufficiently effective when over a third of USA Grade 4 children are seriously struggling. Australian numbers are likely similar.

Anglophone researchers are increasingly recognising the major challenges of achieving healthy reading and literacy in our struggling Standard-English word-readers (Compton et al., 2014):

> Unfortunately, our best attempts at developing potent interventions to treat Reading Disability can best be described as producing limited successes. For instance, our most powerful researcher delivered code-based interventions aimed at ameliorating early word-reading problems leave as much as 10 to 15% of the population of children emerging from treatment with inadequate word-reading skills. ... In addition, many individuals identified as poor readers in high school or as adults still have significant word-reading difficulties ... Children who are "unresponsive" to our best word-level reading interventions pose serious challenges to our educational system ... There is growing skepticism among researchers over our present prescription of strategy-based instruction to improve the comprehension skill of children with Reading Disability.

Regular-orthography nations do have a small number of children with continuing word-reading and spelling difficulties, and adults with dyslexia usually have difficulties with fluent reading and writing, and spelling of some words. Tops et al. (2012) discusses Dutch universities using tests of reading fluency, spelling, and phonological awareness to identify dyslexia, and Dutch dyslexic adults having expressive language difficulties, and weakness in text structure and clarity of discussion when writing.

Given some regular-orthography university students have literacy learning difficulties, it does seem that regular-orthography nations have some difficulties fully remediating their struggling readers. There's value in crosslinguistic research exploring the difficulties of Standard-English and regular-orthography adults with literacy struggles: they show where school remediation lacked effectiveness.

Perhaps the strongest indicator of the negative effects of English orthographic complexity is how frequently Standard-English word-reading intervention is insufficiently effective for lowest-tenth word-readers – those with severest word-reading difficulties.

The Regular-Orthography Intervention Success Story

Let's take time now to explore remedial studies of the weakest 10% of word-readers in regular-orthography and Anglophone nations.

Intervention studies with the weakest tenth of readers in regular-orthography nations show children making steady progress, and mastering word-reading accuracy proficiently with skills being retained and not slipping after intervention has ceased. This shows regular-orthography delayed word-readers thus achieve strong Level 1 automisation, and proficient word-reading accuracy. While not on the Bullet Train, they're nonetheless on the Express Train, relative to our children.

Observation of intervention in schools in regular-orthography nations shows it to be delightfully brief and simple. Often, it's simply more practice of the same activities used in classroom learning – learning-support staff are holding the bike a little longer till children have got their balance and can take off.

And when regular-orthography children take off, they soar. They never forget how to *ride the bike* and it's the same for their word-reading – they stay fully proficient.

Importantly, they stay in the same literacy and learning playing field as their classmates, with Level 1 automisation delays quite minor and easily overcome.

We want their world of learning difficulties, not ours – and really our children are entitled to it. Their highly effective education is also so much less expensive.

Let's now explore a few regular-orthography intervention studies with their most at-risk children.

Successful Intervention with Taiwanese At-Risk Readers

Intervention in various forms seems to work very well for children who learn just a regular-orthography, or learn one prior to learning a complex orthography.

Taiwan, Japan and China do have a small proportion of children slower to learn to read and write their regular orthographies, and some children are slower at learning the many characters of their highly complex morpho-logographic orthographies (Tzeng, 2007).

When remedial intervention is provided for these children, it works impressively well. Let's now visit three studies of Taiwanese word-reading intervention (Chen et al., 2015; Chen & Tzeng, 2019; Chien, 2010), to consider the effectiveness of interventions there.

Study 1. Remedial Reading Materials

Chen et al. (2015) evaluated the effectiveness of two types of remedial reading materials for low-achieving and disadvantaged Taiwanese children in Grade 2. Two experimental groups of 10 and 19 children received tailored intervention using two different sets of materials, while the control group of 27 children received usual school instruction.

Results showed that both experimental groups showed significantly improved skills for reading comprehension and the language skills focused on, to now being at close to healthy age levels for these skills, while the control group made minimal progress.

Study 2. Long-Term Intervention

Chen and Tzeng (2019) provided a 2-year intervention program to 33 Taiwanese Grade 1 poor readers, whose progress was compared with a control group of 19 children who did not receive intervention.

They found the intervention group significantly outperformed the control group in reading of both fully regular ZhuYin FuHao and Taiwanese characters at the end of Grade 1, when both types of reading were assessed, with 97% and 40% of the intervention group now reading at grade-level, for ZhuYin FuHao and Taiwanese characters, respectively.

Only character reading was assessed at the end of Grade 2, and again, the intervention group significantly outperformed the control group, with 42% of children now reading at grade-level.

Interestingly, after intervention had ceased, some children did show a loss of character reading skill in Grade 3, suggesting a lack of Level 1 automisation for learning Taiwanese characters.

Study 3. Differing Intervention Foci

Chien (2010) explored the impacts of three intervention programs on low-SES disadvantaged Taiwanese kindergarteners.
- One group of 57 children received Zhuyin Fuhao regular-orthography word-reading instruction (phonological-awareness, letter-sound and word-reading training).
- The second group of 88 children received Taiwanese character-recognition training.
- The third group of 67 children received picture-book reading training that emphasised reading comprehension.

The study also included 104 children in low-SES and high-SES control groups, which did not receive intervention.

The interventions were implemented for 40-minute sessions, 4 days per week for 30 school weeks. Relative to the low-SES control group, all three experimental groups showed significant gains, which were still present six months post-intervention, i.e., showing powerful Level 1 automisation. The effects were specific to the treatment method:

- Reading comprehension improved significantly only in the picture-book-reading training group, where intervention emphasised reading comprehension.
- Character reading improved significantly only in the Taiwanese character-recognition training group.
- Phonemic awareness and regular word-reading improved significantly only in the Zhuyin Fuhao word-reading group.

Importantly, the three intervention groups improved relative to only the study's low-SES control group, but not the high-SES group.

There seem multiple possibilities for why the high-SES group did better than all three experimental groups. The children may have experienced stronger home support and out-of-school support. This might have built readiness, which enabled them to progress and catch up their delayed skills within usual class instruction. With families taking responsibility for children's progress, some may have had tutoring. Further, they may have been more self-confident in life and thus in learning, and less likely to develop Acquired Helplessness. These possibilities are enabled through regular-orthography learning being simple and straightforward.

Certainly, all three studies show pleasing effectiveness.

Successful Intervention with German Weakest Readers

In Germany, Schneider et al. (1997, 1999) explored phonological-awareness training with letter-sounds within word-reading development for German children in two groups, one with high and one with low phonological awareness prior to the intervention starting. Children in both groups received daily 10 to 15-minute sessions for six months. Following the intervention, the children's skill development was followed for two years.

The low phonological-awareness group included many children with intellectual and other disabilities. They made excellent progress, and certainly achieved Level 1 automaticity, not only holding their gains over the 2 years they were followed, but also showing significantly higher achievement on reading and spelling tests in late Grade 2. They'd not only progressed, but then used their effective self-teaching to go from strength to strength.

Schneider and colleagues found the performance gap between low and high groups did not increase over time, and although the low group readers performed lower on the reading and spelling measures than the high group, the Mean differences were small. By our Standard-English standards, both groups were impressively strong word-readers and writers.

It is possible the children's strong progress may also stem from an interaction of a transparent orthography with their older age and thus increased maturity of executive-function and learning skills.

That's the case for all the regular-orthography intervention studies we'll explore here. While orthographic complexity has much stronger impacts than age, it's an area where we need future research.

Successful Intervention with Danish Weakest Readers

In Denmark, Olofsson (1993) explored phonological-awareness intervention within word-reading development, which included letter-sounds, on children in the lowest tenth of pre-schoolers for a phonological-awareness task, then followed their reading and spelling over several years. Danish is a somewhat more complex orthography than German and Finnish, but far more regular than Standard English (Seymour et al., 2003). The intervention group included children with significant disabilities.

It was notably successful, with the intervention group achieving significantly higher than the control group on word-reading speed, sentence reading, and spelling, and the gap between them and the control group continued to increase over time (Olofsson, 1993; Oloffson & Niedersoe, 1999).

Successful Intervention with Italian Weakest Readers

Cossu and colleagues' study of Italian children with Down Syndrome, which we explored in Tour 4, similarly showed impressive word-reading skills, and the children maintaining their strong gains over time (Cossu, 1999; Cossu et al., 1993).

Indeed, a big challenge they experienced was finding sufficient children for the study who weren't already reading well.

Successful Intervention with Finnish Weakest Readers

Finnish studies similarly show strong success in intervention with the weakest tenth, including children with major disabilities.

Poskiparta et al.'s (1999) intervention with the weakest 10% of Finnish readers, many of whom had intellectual disability, showed they became healthy word-readers, and after intervention, continued to read at a healthy level, with gains well maintained over the next two years.

The intervention was relatively non-intensive by our standards, given the children's disabilities, being one school year of daily 10 to 15 minutes training on phonological awareness and word-reading. The study had two control groups: one was of low-progress readers who had low intelligence, and the other was of low-progress readers who had average intelligence.

At the end of the intervention, some children were still somewhat behind, and might officially be termed *Low* achievers, being at or below 1 Standard Deviation (SD) of the Mean. The Low achievers included 4% (i.e., 0.4% of the student population) of the group for spelling, and 8% (0.8% of the student population) for word-reading.

Of course, the Finnish children being 1-2 SD below is a relatively minor issue, by Anglophone standards, with their Low achievers making impressively few word-reading and spelling errors.

Poskiparta et al. describe their cohort as being a representative population of low achievers, with them having low verbal intelligence, working memory, counting skill, and letter knowledge.

The children who received intervention made significantly stronger progress than the control group of low-intelligence, low-progress readers who didn't receive intervention.

However, the experimental group's progress was less than that of the second control group: average-intelligence low-progress readers who didn't receive intervention.

These children became close to average decoders and spellers without any additional help, i.e., they were making low-progress at the start of the study, but with regular orthographies mastered so easily, they caught up without need of intervention – that seems akin to Chien's (2010) Taiwanese high-SES control group doing better than the intervention groups.

Poskiparta et al.'s results seem similar to those of other studies (e.g., Saine et al., 2010, 2013), which also show intervention to have strong effectiveness.

Saine and colleagues conducted Tier 2 intervention for 166 Grade 1 Finnish weak word-readers, in a comparison of three groups: one a GraphoLearn computerised-intervention group, one a mainstream-instruction control group, and one receiving usual school remedial intervention. The intervention children, in groups of five, had four 45-minute sessions weekly for 28 weeks. Results showed the computerised intervention had strongest effects, with those children achieving grade-level word-reading in Grade 2 and grade-level spelling in Grade 3. Lyytinen et al. (2021) discuss consistent GraphoLearn findings of Finnish weak Grade 1 readers and writers being at grade-level in Grade 3.

Silven et al. (2004) explored factors expediting Finnish healthy

progress. They followed 61 Finnish children from infancy to start of school (age 1 to 7 years). At start of school,
- 30% were precocious readers, reading above Grade-1 level.
- 43% were emergent word-readers, reading quite a few words correctly though somewhat slowly, i.e., well on their way to mastering word-reading.
- 27% were non-readers, who weren't reading yet.

They found it was children's early-childhood language skills, not their intelligence or SES, that was the key factor differentiating the non-readers from the two reader groups. The precocious and emergent readers had shown significantly more rapid vocabulary and grammatical skill development than the non-readers.

The authors comment that early mastery of Finnish words and word inflections increases children's likelihood of awareness of sound patterns in words, which readies them for healthy word-reading progress. That conclusion is in keeping with other Finnish studies showing auditory processing in infancy predicts how easily they'll master word-reading (e.g., Richardson et al., 2003).

The Anglophone Insufficient-Success Story

When it comes to nations' most vulnerable, weakest tenth of readers, regular-orthography children win while Standard-English children lose.

Let's now consider Standard-English studies of children with disabilities and children in the weakest tenth of word-readers, and compare their success with that of regular-orthography nations.

Rolanda O'Connor and colleagues (1993) examined the feasibility of teaching phonological-awareness skills to USA pre-school students with disabilities. They found the children learned the skills effectively but demonstrated little or no generalisation of those skills, both for highly similar tasks (e.g., from one blending task to another) and dissimilar tasks (e.g., from blending to segmenting).

Anglophone studies of children with Down Syndrome similarly achieve only very modest gains, with the children still far below healthy average achievement (e.g., Burgoyne et al., 2012; Lim et al., 2018, 2019).

Similarly, my work with children with major word-reading and literacy weakness shows children making gains, but still having word-reading and spelling ages well below their chronological ages.

Other Standard-English word-reading intervention studies show similarly (Compton et al., 2014; Roberts, Torgesen et al., 2008; Scammacca et al., 2007, 2015, 2016; Wanzek et al., 2013, 2016, 2018).

Torgesen et al.'s (1997) intervention study with USA word-readers in the weakest tenth found that, after intervention, 24% of those struggling word-readers were at least 1 Standard Deviation (SD) below the Mean.

Now, statistically, that seems similar to Poskiparta et al.'s (1999) Finnish children, so it might seem acceptable progress. It's not.

As we've seen in our Standard Deviation analyses of Welsh, German, Slovak, Czech, and English children, regular-orthography children 1 Standard Deviation (SD) below the Mean are highly accurate word-readers and spellers, while Standard-English children at that level, in comparison, are struggling severely (Caravolas, 2018; Frith et al., 1998; Hanley et al., 2004; Landerl et al., 1997).

In addition, the intervention that Torgesen et al.'s (1997) USA children received was highly intensive, extensive, and time-consuming: daily 30-minute one-to-one intensive intervention by expert interventionists, provided for 2.5 years. That's vastly more intensive than Poskiparta's Finnish intervention.

That's a very important workload finding: the USA children's intervention hours being so high, for such comparatively little gain, given many of the USA children were still well below age-level.

Importantly, quite a few children had made virtually no progress.

Severely low-progress children (also termed Nonresponders and Treatment Resisters) don't seem an issue in regular-orthography and Initial Teaching Alphabet (ITA) children. Unfortunately, their struggles are a very major issue for Standard-English intervention studies, and our schools (Al Otaiba & Fuchs, 2002, 2006; Compton et al., 2014; Middleton et al., 2022; Torgesen et al., 1997, 2010; Vellutino, 2000; Vellutino et al., 1996).

The Anglosphere is really struggling when it comes to closing the intervention gap, and catching up seriously struggling word-readers and spellers. While research is needed, perhaps it really is the case that prevention is imperative, because the cure is proving too difficult and elusive, to consistently achieve.

Torgesen et al.'s (1997) intervention with lowest-tenth Standard-English readers was actually five times as intensive as the intervention Poskiparta et al. (1999) used so successfully with the Finnish lowest-tenth word-readers. Yet the gains made were so much weaker. Quite a few of Torgesen et al.'s children made minimal progress. Three times more were 1 Standard Deviation (SD) below the Mean than in the Finnish study (24% vs 8%). Plus, that 24% who were 1 Standard Deviation (SD) below the Mean were years behind their healthy-progress classmates, whereas the Finnish children at that level were quite proficient readers.

Let's Research Intervention Effectiveness

Research is needed, deeply exploring costs, benefits and effectiveness of intervention with
- Regular-orthography weak word-readers and spellers.
- Standard-English weak word-readers and spellers, doing 1-Stage early literacy, with solely Standard English.
- Standard-English weak word-readers and spellers, doing 2-Stage early literacy, first learning to read and write a fully-regular beginners' orthography, then transitioning to reading and writing Standard English (Downing, 1969a, 1969b; Mazurkiewicz, 1971, 1973b; Warburton & Southgate, 1969).

Anglophone nations need the findings of that research quite desperately. Regular-orthography nations don't need it overly, as early literacy is going well for them, however, if we ask politely, international, collaborative research networks may ensue.

In that research, we also need to use easily compared measures of word-reading, with carefully thought out cut-points for what constitutes healthy vs low skill levels.

You can see how there'd be value in future studies of the lowest tenth of word-readers, in not just comparing Means and SDs on nations' very different word-reading tests, but also establishing commonality using the methods of the researchers who conducted the Welsh-English, German-English, and Czech-Slovak-English studies we've explored in Tours 2 and 13, with strategic use of similar sets of words. Word-reading of nations' most frequent words might also be included. As much as possible, we need to be comparing apples with apples.

Let's Reflect on Workload and Resourcing Implications

It's interesting to consider the school resourcing implications of that Finnish-USA contrast (Poskiparta et al., 1999; Torgesen et al., 1997): the massive crosslinguistic divide that's present as regards time and money expended for extent of gain achieved.

Standard-English orthography really is damaging for our vulnerable beginning readers, when we insist they start with solely Standard English at age 4.5 to 5 years.

Instead of meeting our teaching challenges, we're inflicting on our children extremely major word-reading and writing difficulties, which often respond poorly to intervention. Our children seem entitled to us using a beginners' regular-orthography, so that our intervention studies will similarly be spectacularly effective.

Let's Include Children with Other Disabilities

Another important crosslinguistic difference is that regular-orthography studies often include children with disabilities beyond literacy, while Standard-English studies so often don't.

Anglophone nation studies usually exclude all children with disabilities, or behaviour or attention weakness from their word-reading research cohorts, whereas regular-orthography nations often include their disabled children – quite likely because they know those disabilities won't prevent word-reading progress.

Restricting subject characteristics, e.g., by excluding children with disabilities, is not a bad thing in itself, as it enables clearer cause-effect findings. That said, so many Standard-English intervention studies not including children with more complex needs does make it less likely that their findings would transfer easily to usefulness in in Australian schools, where all children, disabilities included, are in need of instruction, and no children are excluded.

The regular-orthography intervention studies with weakest readers that we've explored, included children with other disabilities and risk factors, and their intervention worked extremely well (Cossu 1999; Cossu et al., 1993; Olofsson, 1993; Olofsson & Niedersoe, 1999; Schneider et al., 1997, 1999). Their children routinely progressed to reading as accurately as their peers, and maintained their gains.

That's the norm for schools in regular-orthography nations. It's routine for children with major disabilities to become proficiently accurate word-readers, including children with moderate to severe intellectual disability, those with language disorder, and those with attention and behaviour difficulties.

In contrast, Standard-English studies consistently show low gains, despite excluding many children likely to have severe difficulties.

It's notable that Finnish high schoolers using Special Education services use them predominantly for maths and second-language learning, not reading and literacy (M. Aro, 2017b). That's not the case in Australia: entrenched word-reading, spelling, reading, writing, and literacy-related difficulties and ongoing, high support needs for building literacy skills are overwhelmingly our primary-school and high-school norm (Angus et al., 2004, 2007; APPA., 2008a, 2008b, 2020; Galletly et al., 2010; Louden et al., 2000; Munro, 2017; Quick, 2020a, 2020b; van Kraayenoord, 1999, 2006, 2007; van Kraayenoord et al., 2001; Woods et al., 2005).

Prevention and effective early intervention seem the crux of effective reading instruction and nations meeting their teaching challenges. Regular-orthography nations achieve this and meet their challenges well. For too many struggling readers, we don't.

Our many children with word-reading and spelling weakness in upper primary school and high school are testament to our insufficiently effective early and later interventions, and major needs for improvement.

Let's Research Intervention Responsiveness

Let's research Australian weak readers' response to intervention.

Slowest-progress word-readers and so called *Treatment Resisters* or *Nonresponders*, who make minimal progress despite intensive instruction highlight likelihood that Australia and other Anglophone nations have many severely struggling word-readers for whom intervention has been unsuccessful in their schools (Al Otaiba & Fuchs, 2002, 2006; Compton et al., 2014; Torgesen et al., 1997, 2010; Vellutino, 2000; Vellutino et al., 1996).

Al Otaiba and Fuchs (2006) explored the responsiveness to intervention of 104 at-risk USA children receiving intervention across Kindergarten and Year 1. They studied the lowest 30% of achievers for gains made from best-practice instruction, e.g., being unable to sound out more than 12 sounds in words per minute, or name over 11 letter-sounds per minute at end of Kindergarten. They confirmed this <30% criteria with teachers, finding it matched teachers' opinions that children achieving at this level were severely at risk of continuing difficulties.

Responsiveness vs non-responsiveness status was then decided at end-Grade-1, after 2 years of intervention, with three groups then formed:
- *Always-responsive* students met responsiveness criteria in both years.
- *Sometimes-responsive* students met criteria in only one year.
- *Non-responsive* students did not meet criteria in either year.

They then considered the children's scores on the range of language, cognitive-processing and literacy skills they'd monitored over time.

They found the three groups reliably different on verbal memory, sentence imitation, syntactic awareness, vocabulary, naming speed, phonemic awareness and problem behaviour. A combination of naming speed, vocabulary, sentence imitation, problem behaviour, and extent of intervention correctly predicted 82% of non-responsive students, 30% of sometimes-responsive students, and 84% of always-responsive students.

They then assessed 50 of the children from Kindergarten and first grade at the end of Grade 3, finding all but one of the non-responsive children had been identified for Special Education, i.e., now having disability status and associated supports, and ongoing difficulties.

That's sadly different to the efficiency of regular-orthography word-reading and writing development, and the effectiveness of regular-orthography intervention.

Reviews of studies of lowest progress Standard-English readers find them to have severe information-processing and automisation weakness, with many having weak verbal language skills, cognitive processing, behaviour difficulties and developmental delays (Al Otaiba & Fuchs, 2002, 2006; Compton et al., 2014). Their markedly low progress bespeaks major Level 1 Automisation Weakness.

Those findings also have a crosslinguistic divide: they're factors which lay Standard-English at-risk readers low, but don't prevent effective word-reading and early-literacy development when a regular-orthography is being used.

Let's Talk about "Nonresponders"

I was extremely surprised the first time a highly skilled teacher said to me that their school was thinking of dropping word-reading intervention for their children with severest word-reading difficulties – because they'd found it so minimally effective.

Talking together, I realised many Australian teachers and schools haven't heard of *Nonresponders* and *Treatment Resisters* being a well established, recognised group of extremely slow progress word-readers (Al Otaiba & Fuchs, 2002, 2006; Compton et al., 2014; Torgesen et al., 1997, 2010; Vellutino, 2000; Vellutino et al., 1996).

Ongoing systematic word-reading instruction is still the answer for those weakest Standard-English word-readers, but for children with severest difficulties it needs to be very systematic, intensive, ongoing and of long duration, and include lots of encouragement and confidence building, with children and teachers having a strong confident working relationship.

Quite frankly, our schools usually don't have the budgets needed to achieve that level of intensive intervention.

That's another reason Australia and Anglophone nations need to explore using a beginners' orthography prior to Standard English – because ethically it's highly inappropriate that our children should struggle so severely – and, quite possibly, prevention using a regular orthography is imperative, as we can't provide the cure.

Let's Reflect on Insufficiently Effective Intervention

A USA school-level study by Rolanda O'Connor and colleagues highlights the challenges that schools experience due to Level 1 Automisation Weakness – children's skills slipping after intervention is completed, plus schools' huge resourcing needs if they're to provide optimal intervention for all children (R. O'Connor, 2000).

It also sheds light on how neat findings from research studies conducted in well-controlled research settings often don't translate well in the messy complexity of schools' teaching and learning.

O'Connor's study was of school and university personnel working together to provide intervention to weak readers over a 2-year period.

She discusses the challenges schools face:
- Needing to remediate all children, some with Special Education funding but many without it.
- Interventions being less intensive than preferred due to resourcing insufficiencies.
- Children prevented from receiving interventions due to teachers and parents not giving permission.
- Different teachers using different reading programs.
- Children changing to a new teacher and possibly different reading instruction each year.
- Differing teacher expertise.
- Low responders making minimal progress.
- Difficulties adequately supporting low responders who make minimal progress despite schools' highest intensity intervention.
- Major difficulties catching children up to grade-level.
- Major difficulties then keeping the children at grade-level.

O'Connor discusses the difficulties experienced moving struggling readers up to grade-level, even children who made the highest progress, and the subsequent major difficulties they had keeping those children at grade-level after intervention ceased, as many would subsequently drop below, and then need further support.

That's a world away from regular-orthography effectiveness, isn't it? And Kennedy's (2005, 2010) teaching-situation factors, e.g., child and school factors additional to teaching, seem strongly in play.

O'Connor's (2000) study is particularly useful, being school-level research in usual school circumstances.

The findings of Anglophone reading research done in controlled settings all too often don't transfer well to school settings, and the research findings we have are often from controlled studies conducted in far more ideal circumstances than those of schools (Galletly, 2008).

O'Connor's conclusion speaks volumes:

The most important implication of this work may be the effort necessary to maintain nearly normal progress for the children with an initial difficulty in reading ...
Within just a few months, most of the children with disabilities and several others lost ground in comparison with the children not at risk when reading instruction retreated to the status quo. These findings are sobering because we may be seriously overestimating the effects of our short-term interventions on the long-term trajectory of reading growth.

That's a strong statement and one that many of our teachers and families would agree with.

Over-estimating the extent to which research-study interventions will work in the messiness of school situations is a serious issue. It can also be nasty, particularly amidst attribution error, and our inappropriately blaming teachers and their teaching for all our woes.

It's likely that research intervention studies should report not just children's extent of improvement, but also if they're still below age-level at the end of intervention, and how far behind they still are.

Let's Compare Apples with Apples

In intervention studies of the future, let's make sure we compare apples with apples. Many Anglophone intervention studies establish effectiveness of their intervention method by comparing their subjects only with subjects who've not received any additional attention or intervention.

In effect, they're comparing apples with oranges. They've not compared their intervention's effectiveness with the effectiveness of other interventions. The researched intervention might be no better than other interventions, but the findings suggest strong effectiveness – because no other interventions are compared.

It's thus quite appropriate for schools to be cautious in taking on interventions with a supposedly strong research base. Yes, the children improved in studies on those interventions. However, they might have improved as much or more on other programs. That includes school-developed instruction, where schools have been provided with similar funding, staff resourcing, time-release, professional development, and prioritising of, and time to implement intervention, do data collection and publish results.

In addition, and importantly, no Standard-English word-reading intervention studies show improvement anywhere near the strong positive impacts of prevention using a beginners' orthography prior to Standard English, as the ITA studies evidenced (e.g., Downing, 1965, 1967a, 1967b, 1967c, 1969a, 1969b, 1972; Ho, 1972; Ho & Eiszler, 1970; Ho et al., 1970, 1972; Knight et al., 2017a; Mazurkiewicz, 1965, 1967, 1971, 1973a, 1973b; Warburton & Southgate, 1969).

Suffice to say, currently, as soon as we use the levels of achievement schools routinely achieve across regular-orthography nations as our standard, our Standard-English word-reading interventions are insufficiently effective, and inadequate, for far too many children.

As our 2021 NAPLAN spiralling numbers of low achievers from Year 3 to Year 9 show (see Figure 15 and Table 3), and in line with our too many low achievers in PIRLS and PISA, we're not just failing to meet our teaching challenges, we're also investing strongly in Railway Handcarts – masses of hard work and massively impeded early-literacy development. That's an absolute travesty, and a tragedy, given the massive potential we have for meteoric 10 Changes improvement.

There's huge value in us comparing apples with apples as we build knowledge on effective instruction and intervention, by providing equal resourcing for school-developed programs, as we provide for commercial intervention programs (e.g., Hill & Crevola, 1999; Quach et al., 2018), with data gathered and shared from the different interventions. We need to be comparing interventions matched for extent of professional development, intervention group sizes, extent of professional expertise in those delivering intervention, administration time provided, and so on.

Too many researched intervention programs have never been compared with the logical equivalent: other commercial and researcher-developed interventions, and schools receiving the same funding for resourcing and professional development, so they can implement school-developed methods and programs.

Let's move from *this or nothing* options to *this or that*, with different intervention programs explored in volunteer schools, comparing a range of commercial and school-developed programs.

Our Intervention Resourcing Needs Are Huge

There seems a lack of research exploring the teacher workload and resourcing levels that our schools need for achieving effective Standard-English word-reading in all their children, including their weak word-readers. While we've useful writings discussing our resource inadequacies (Angus et al., 2004, 2007; APPA, 2008a, 2008b; Galletly et al., 2010; Gallop et al., 2021; Hunter et al., 2022; Sonnemann & Joiner, 2022), we also need reports summing up and quantifying our needs, at child and teacher levels.

With research lacking, there's value in considering the research on various impacting issues.

Reduced Class Sizes

To a certain extent low class size can create more manageable teacher workload and thus enable more effective teaching, including teaching efficiently tailored to children's needs. In that sense, lowering class size in effect reduces teacher workload (Hattie, 2005, 2008; Mathis, 2017; Shen & Konstantopoulos, 2017; Zyngier, 2014).

There's thus value in us researching the workload impacts of class size on our teachers and their teaching. While doing so, let's look at the range of children in each class, including the number of children with disabilities and significantly weak skills.

Australian researcher David Zyngier (2014) reviewed studies of the impacts of class size on academic achievement, particularly studies in Australia and New Zealand. He discusses class size being a very political issue, and policy advisers perhaps using a rather selective review of the literature. Zyngier discusses smaller class size in the first four years of school being extremely valuable, particularly for at-risk and struggling learners, especially when low class size is combined with teacher professional development on optimising differentiated instruction.

John Hattie (2008) similarly emphasises class size reductions having strong positive impacts for early-years classes, and struggling learners in all year-levels.

Effective Intervention-Resourcing Levels

Reading Recovery intervention resourcing levels are impressive relative to most schools' resourcing for intervention. It includes funding for intensive professional development prior to teachers conducting intervention, plus children doing ongoing 30-minute one-to-one daily sessions with a constant, trained, supportive teacher. That resourcing is the intervention model used in quite a few research studies (e.g., Torgesen et al., 1997; Vellutino, 2000).

Please note I'm not recommending the Reading Recovery program (Clay, 1993), just its resourcing model. Alas, Reading Recovery is seriously ineffective in many ways for struggling word-readers, and many if not most early-years struggling readers have word-reading difficulties (Al Otaiba & Fuchs, 2002, 2006; Leach et al., 2003).

Many studies show Reading Recovery's major lack of effectiveness for word-reading, with Reading Recovery graduates still having major difficulties, and that gains too often slip markedly after intervention ceases, such that relative to children who receive no intervention, long-term gains can be rather minimal.

When you look at the program, you can see why – for struggling word-readers, while it's nicely enriching, there's too much repeated reading of easily-remembered reading books packed full of meaning cues and situation cues that reduce needs for children to use focused word-reading, and too little fun practice reading isolated words.

Online, there's a useful Open Letter by 27 word-reading researchers, summarising those negative findings. Just search, Baker et al. (2002) *Evidence-based research on Reading Recovery*.

That report is in keeping with the findings of a useful Australian study by Serry et al. (2014): *Reading Recovery teachers discuss Reading Recovery*. Yes, teachers love it, but on the whole, they find it's best for children with mild delays, rather than children with major word-reading difficulties. That's my experience too – when Reading Recovery was used in Queensland, I worked with too many Reading Recovery graduates who still had severe word-reading difficulties, to afford its word-reading remediation much respect.

Thus, while it's often been endorsed and enacted here in Australia and also in New Zealand, for our children with weak word-reading, Reading Recovery is not the answer – it's part of the problem.

On the other hand, the school-resourcing levels provided within Reading Recovery are very useful – children receiving daily one-to-one sessions on an ongoing basis with a dedicated teacher they know well and are comfortable with.

There's perhaps value in using a similar resourcing model across Australia, with schools having ample funding for both professional development and administrative aspects as well as intervention funding for extensive one-to-one intervention with struggling readers. Teachers strongly agree, and so do parents. That's why schools loved Reading Recovery – as a this or nothing option, it had huge strengths.

Let's Amply Resource Intervention

As part of identifying children in need of remedial support, let's work out what constitutes effective school resourcing.

Finland is a useful role model for intervention supports and resourcing. Lots of Finnish children receive Special Education support (learning support). They move in and out of Special Education as needs emerge and are met. About 35% of Grade 1 children have Special Education support, usually for reading, or speech and language. So do about 15% of Grade 9 children, usually for support for maths or foreign languages (M. Aro, 2017b).

Notably, Finland doesn't use test eligibility criteria, and thus no formal tests and diagnoses are required to establish children as eligible for support. Instead, schools, teachers and children decide when support is needed and the type of support to be provided. We'd like that. Nicely, about 15% of teachers in primary schools are Special Education teachers. We'd like that too.

We might also model ourselves on Finland, as regards early childhood education being our government education departments' responsibility from infancy, not start of school.

Certainly, we've strong grounds for hugely improved intervention supports and associated increased resourcing (Angus et al., 2004, 2007; APPA, 2008a, 2008b; Galletly et al., 2010).

Through too low resourcing for too many years, we've exacerbated our schools' struggles (Gallop et al., 2021; Gonski et al., 2011, 2018; Hunter et al., 2022; Sonnemann & Joiner, 2022).

From my deep knowledge of both our struggling readers' support needs and the gross inadequacy of the school supports they currently receive, it's likely that, to achieve major improvement, for every 500 children, our primary schools and high schools should be allocated

- One highly skilled learning-support teacher and four learning-support teacher aides.
- One speech language pathologist with education training, and four communication aides.
- One occupational therapist with education training, with four occupational therapy aides.
- One social worker with education training.
- One educational psychologist with education training.

I know, at present, that seems a lot. Indeed, most teachers to whom I list it off are laughing incredulously before I'm halfway through, finding such richness utterly beyond belief.

Let me emphasise, however, that there'd be no laughter, only nodding heads, if I listed that level of resourcing in Finland, Estonia and many USA states. That's particularly the case if they were well informed of our low levels of school resourcing, our insufficient skill monitoring, and our children's massive needs, including at least a fifth of children starting school severely at need, and about a third of primary and high-school students struggling in major ways (Lamb et al., 2020; Masters, 2016; T. Moore & McDonald, 2013).

They'd also certainly be nodding, not laughing, at my suggestions, below, for 200 less teaching hours, a teachers' aide, and a well-resourced national curriculum.

In addition to highly skilled learning-support teachers and allied-health professionals with post-graduate studies in education and language, literacy and learning disorders, we also need well-trained teacher aides, as many studies show that well-trained aides supported by skilled professionals can be powerfully effective in providing intervention and support (e.g., Scammacca et al., 2007).

These allied-health and learning supports I'm suggesting would provide intervention meeting our struggling learners' needs. Children would receive intervention as schools decide, including, for some, 30 to 90-minute one-to-one or small-group intervention sessions five times weekly.

They'd also play a major role in school assessment programs, thus ensuring class teacher workload is not excessively increased by skills-monitoring assessment programs.

Using this resourcing, we'd start to reshape our current sad gourd-like *Response to Intervention* (RTI) reality, with far too many severely struggling learners in need of Tier 3 intervention, due to inadequacies of school resourcing, instead of RTI's intended small numbers in need of intensive supports (Angus et al., 2004, 2007; APPA., 2008a, 2008b, 2020; Galletly et al., 2010, Louden et al., 2000; Quick, 2020a, 2020b; K. J. Rowe & Rowe, 2002; K. S. Rowe & Rowe, 2004; van Kraayenoord, 1999, 2006, 2007; van Kraayenoord et al., 2001).

In subsequently implementing 10 Changes improvements, Australia might well achieve RTI's intended, neat, inverted-triangle shape, and an optimally efficient RTI model, as regular-orthography nations achieve for early literacy skills (M. Aro, 2017a, 2017b):

- Most children thriving in effective Tier 1 classroom instruction.
- Tier 2 small group intervention and extension working extremely well.
- Only a tiny number of children needing Tier 3 intensive intervention.

We won't achieve this level without major education changes, including using a fully-regular beginners' orthography, plus using the first 2.5 years of schooling for play-based learning and language enrichment, holding back formal instruction until mid-Year 2.

Doing that, we'd likely move away from disability labels and needs for long applications for additional intervention funding.

We also may combine *Special Education* and *Learning Support* intervention in schools, as many regular-orthography nations do (e.g., M. Aro, 2017b). Currently in Australia, they're often separate, with Special Education staff supporting children with disability labels who've disability funding, while Learning Support staff support all non-funded children with difficulties and disabilities.

Using 10 Changes improvements, combining Special Education and Learning Support would work well.

We might also combine our school intervention and allied-health intervention systems. The reason they're separate here in Australia at present is most probably our separate Special Education and Learning Support funding systems.

The reason they're combined in regular-orthography nations is because effective, efficient education and literacy development can be achieved so easily for all children, including many children with major disabilities.

Towards more effective, efficient intervention and supports, our Education Departments might well take responsibility for all in-school and out-of-school allied-health intervention for all school children, including, for many, the supports provided currently through the National Disability Insurance Scheme.

This should include funding of well-coordinated services using allied-health professionals and trained aides in and out of school.

Currently, NDIS is financially pressured by the ongoing nature of language disorder, and it not being a quick fix, with our struggling readers having ongoing needs for intervention and supports. Very large amounts of NDIS funding are currently expended on frequent one-to-one allied-health sessions for children with NDIS funding.

For many children, this intervention could likely be conducted less expensively and more effectively using integrated services that efficiently coordinate Tier 3A and 3B indirect and direct intervention. They'd quite likely reduce one-to-one sessions with allied-health professionals from weekly, to fortnightly or monthly; and add in less-expensive twice-weekly practice sessions with highly-trained aides; with coordinated emailed discussions or meetings to liaise in-school and out-of-school supports as needed.

We could achieve that less-expensive, well-coordinated national intervention system quite easily, particularly if we also did language and learning enrichment for the first 2.5 years of school, holding off formal instruction until mid-Year 2, and used a fully-regular beginners' orthography prior to Standard English.

After all, really, using our Education Act, Alice Springs (Mparntwe) Declaration and UN agreements, our children are entitled to the easy, effective, early-literacy development, with lower likelihood of difficulties, that they'd have, if we too became a regular-orthography nation, using an English beginners' orthography. with our children playing to learn richly till nicely mature and ready for literacy, armed with empowered learning.

Let's Amply Resource Our Class Teachers

If we're to achieve effective education, we need highly effective class instruction. Our teachers and their teaching are our strongest investment in our children and indeed, our future.

I've been considering Australia's needs for strategically eased and supported teacher workload from many perspectives, for many years. I've done that as part of considering school and intervention

resourcing. Those perspectives include
- My experience as a researcher considering resourcing in schools in Australia and other nations.
- Talking with teachers and observing in classrooms here and in those nations.
- My experience working with struggling readers and understanding both their needs and their schools' needs.
- Talking with our allied-health professionals about the extent of intervention levels needed.

From this broad consideration of our needs, I make the following recommendations. For our children in all thirds of achievers to have the effective education they're promised and entitled to, our teachers and schools need the following four resourcing items:

1. Fewer Teaching Hours

We need to reduce our class teachers' annual class teaching hours to those of Finland, i.e., 677 hours of class teaching time each year (OECD, 2015, 2022), and set that as our maximum. Our teachers would gain, on average, at least 200 hours additional off-class work time for preparation, administration, meetings, and working one-on-one with children. That's one extra hour per day, five hours per week for each of our forty school weeks.

2. A Full-Time Teacher Aide

We need to allocate each class teacher a full-time teacher aide. That aide would support classroom teaching and learning, and work with individual students and small groups, and also do relevant aspects of administration.

3. Effectively Resourced Learning Support

We need to provide schools with the learning-support and allied health supports I've listed above, so our children receive ample intervention from learning-support teachers, speech language pathologists, occupational therapists, social workers, educational psychologists and trained intervention aides.

These resources would strongly support our class teachers and their teaching, and, hence, our children and the education they receive.

4. A Strong National Curriculum and Resourcing

We need to reduce teacher workload that's due to our national curriculum currently being insufficiently resourced.

Our schools and teachers' workload is already excessively large relative to many leading nations, but then we've add extra workload because our national curriculum is insufficiently specified and insufficiently resourced.

We need our national curriculum to be as streamlined and well-resourced as those of leading nations, e.g., Finland, Estonia, Taiwan, Japan and China.

Let's insist on streamlined options for our children with learning disability, and for extending our high-progress learners.

Let's have textbooks and workbooks for every subject in every year-level, not compulsory but available, and useful, realistic options.

Let's have curriculum resourcing for subject-area units organised at national curriculum level, not school level. We need to stop the wheel being reinvented endlessly, ad nauseum, as our individual Australian schools and teachers develop curriculum and resources, which would be far more efficiently provided at national level.

Let's also ensure that strategic remedial and advanced reading and literacy remediation resources are developed, matched to each subject-area unit.

Those four improvements – reduced class teaching hours, a full-time teachers' aide, strong intervention services, and a strategically resourced national curriculum – would make an appreciable difference, expediting 10 Changes improvements and enabling the improved education our children need.

Let's Research Upstream and Downstream

There is a massive difference between regular-orthography and Standard-English word-reading and spelling development, instruction and difficulties. There are also major differences in the school difficulties that children with language disorder experience.

Because of this, ethically we need to research upstream as much as we research downstream – because our children have rights to literacy development that is as easily achieved, as schools across regular-orthography nations routinely achieve.

Upstream, we need to investigate the potential of fully-regular English beginners' orthographies prior to reading and writing Standard English.

We need to explore a range of issues:
- The extent that a beginners' orthography reduces the impact of risk factors, and word-reading and spelling difficulties.

- How effective it makes word-reading and spelling intervention.
- How well it eases and speeds word-reading and spelling development for all children.
- The social-emotional, motivational and cognitive-processing benefits of using a beginners' orthography initially.
- The extent of resourcing needed to achieve effective regular-orthography, then Standard-English, instruction and any needed intervention, routinely across Australian schools.

Downstream, we need to investigate the effectiveness of optimised Standard-English instruction and intervention, using Standard English as a sole orthography.

We need to explore
- The extent to which optimised Standard-English instruction can achieve word-reading, spelling and early-literacy development to the levels achieved in regular-orthography nations such as Taiwan, Japan and China, which like us, have a highly complex orthography.
- The extent to which Standard-English word-reading and spelling difficulties can be prevented and reduced, to the level that regular-orthography nations achieve.
- The extent to which early intervention and later remediation are successful to the level of regular-orthography nations.
- The social-emotional, motivational, cognitive-processing, word-reading, spelling, literacy and learning advantages and disadvantages of using solely Standard English.
- The extent of resourcing needed to achieve highly effective word-reading, spelling and early-literacy development using solely Standard English, in all children, including our weakest 5% and 10% of word-readers.
- A requirement that instruction and intervention must be as effective as regular-orthography nations such as Taiwan, Japan and China routinely achieve, as Australian children should not experience significant disadvantage relative to children in regular-orthography nations.

It's Time to Rethink Cut-Off Criteria

What criteria should we set for optimal Standard-English word-reading now?

What criteria should we set for it in the future, if we use a fully-regular initial orthography prior to Standard English?

That second question might be easier to answer than the first. Logically, after using a fully regular orthography, our children would read well. We might use a criteria similar to Finnish and German researchers, of healthy-progress word-reading accuracy being above 90% proficiency for reading long multisyllabic words.

But what criteria should we use for our current situation?

Defining difficulties using percentages, cut-offs and benchmarks is an age-old and ongoing problem (e.g., Makita, 1968; Scammacca et al., 2015; Wagner et al., 2019). Modern researchers, e.g., Wagner et al. (2019) discuss these dilemmas with almost identical thinking to those of decades past, e.g., Makita (1968):

The criteria for reading disability differs so much between various investigators in many countries that the comparison of its prevalence is a difficult task to carry out properly.

That's true. Comparison of prevalence is a massive challenge. We'll do well, in future Australian research, by establishing clear definitions and criteria useful across Anglophone and regular-orthography nations.

We need definitions and benchmarks that enable thinking on what constitutes healthy progress by regular-orthography vs Anglophone standards.

Quite likely, in studying early literacy here in Australia, and comparing early-literacy development here and in other nations, it would be useful to include both

- Percentages, e.g., the 20% of children scoring below the 20th percentile on the TOWRE-2 subtests, and
- Skill levels and error rates for reading specific word groups (Galletly, 2008), including perhaps sets of multisyllabic words, or words from the 200, 500, 1,000, 5,000 and 10,000 most familiar words of one's nation.

Importantly, the Test of Word Reading Efficiency-2 (TOWRE-2) may be useful as multiple non-Anglophone nations have versions of TOWRE-2.

As a starting point for considering the findings of research studies, we need definitions and there's huge value when studies use similar criteria and measures.

In cross-national comparisons and in ethical decision-making about the rights of our children, it's quite likely that, in addition to percentiles, we need to use accuracy scores and error rates, e.g., similar to those used in the German-English studies (Frith et al.,

1998; Landerl et al., 1997). That's because we need details on types of errors made, percentage of words read correctly and so on.

Perhaps we might set up standard tasks, e.g., those used by Seymour et al. (2003) or Frith et al. (1998), perhaps combinations of words from the 5000 most frequent words. Perhaps we might use tests like the Test of Word Reading Efficiency-2 (TOWRE-2) adapted for different languages.

We may still want cut-offs of some type, for school decision-making on children needing intervention and school resourcing needs.

If we're to improve reading and literacy levels both ethically and impressively, we need to set the bar high, at regular-orthography nation level, and do that soon. Ethically, by regular-orthography standards, it's likely that both our lower and middle-third have word-reading and spelling levels too low to be considered healthy.

Given the studies we've explored show Standard-English children to be appallingly weak word-readers compared to European regular-orthography children, if using cut-offs, we might well set the 50th or 66th percentiles on current word-reading and spelling tests as the cut-off for identifying children requiring support. The intervention needed for our middle-third may not be onerous, perhaps simply a teaching emphasis building children's skills at accurately reading each and every unfamiliar word they encounter.

Before making any decisions of that type, however, we need to gather a lot of word-reading and spelling data, on our children and regular-orthography children.

Ethically the benchmark should be word-reading, spelling and early-literacy development acquired as quickly and easily as children do in Taiwan, Japan and China, nations with orthographies far more complex that ours.

That's a high goal but a needed one, and there's every likelihood we won't get there without using a fully-regular beginners' orthography.

Sometimes, Standard Deviations (SDs) are used as criteria to create cut-offs to identify children in need of disability funding. That said, SDs need to be considered carefully, as e.g., when crosslinguistic differences in word-reading achievement aren't considered, SDs can blur what in reality are huge differences. There's a massive difference in the literacy skills and support needs of children below a 1.5SD cut-off, when children are Japanese, e.g., in Uno et al.'s, (2009) study, vs Standard-English readers, e.g., in Shaywitz et al.'s

(1990) study – while both these studies used a 1.5 SD cut-point, it's a learning to ride a bike vs drive a truck extent of difference.

In addition to broader definitions of difficulties, disabilities and instructional needs, there is also likely huge value in simply reporting on behavioural measures, e.g., rather than talking about subjects with dyslexia, instead talking about children with word-reading difficulties, achieving in, e.g., the lowest 20% of word-readers on the TOWRE-2.

Key Findings from Tour 14

Findings and implications of studies explored in Tour 14 suggest the following points are useful considerations towards improving literacy and education in Australia and Anglophone nations:

1. There are paradigmatic differences between Standard-English and regular-orthography word-reading intervention, because regular-orthography children have extremely mild word-reading and spelling difficulties relative to the difficulties our children experience.
2. Studies of the weakest 10% of word-readers in regular-orthography nations, show that they make very impressive progress from intervention of low intensity, becoming highly accurate word-readers.
3. In strong contrast, studies of the weakest 10% of word-readers in Anglophone nations show that, e.g., (Torgesen et al., 1997),
    a. A quarter continue to have major difficulties.
    b. A significant number make minimal progress.
4. Studies show that Standard-English children with extremely severe word-reading difficulties need and benefit from systematic word-reading instruction, however this needs to be extremely strategic, intensive, ongoing and of long duration, for even quite small gains.
5. It's likely most Australian schools have insufficient budgets to afford this level of intervention.
6. There are indicators that Anglophone research studies overestimate the extent to which word-reading intervention will be effective in usual school circumstances.
7. Australian education has very major needs for research on word-reading and spelling instruction, intervention, workload and resourcing needs in and across schools.
8. Ethically, we need to consider the rights of our at-risk children, given that Standard-English intervention is so often insufficiently effective, and that using a fully-regular beginners'

orthography would hugely reduce both the number of children who experience word-reading and spelling difficulties and their extent of difficulties.
9. Numerous Australian reports detail the inadequacies of Australian school resourcing, and our vital needs to increase resourcing and improve teacher workload, if education is to improve (e.g., Angus et al., 2004, 2007, APPA, 2008a, 2008b; Gallop et al., 2021; Gonski et al., 2011, 2018; Senate Standing Committee on Education, 2016; Hunter & Sonnemann, 2022; Sonnemann & Joiner, 2022).
10. There is strong need for our schools to receive appropriate resourcing to provide effective instruction and intervention, e.g.,
    a. Class teaching hours being reduced, e.g., to the level of Finnish schools.
    b. Class teachers having a full-time teacher aide.
    c. Our national curriculum being strategically resourced, to reduce teacher workload.
    d. For every 500 enrolled students, in every Australian primary school and high school, our schools need to have at least
        i. One learning-support teacher and four learning-support teacher aides.
        ii. One speech language pathologist and four communication aides.
        iii. One occupational therapist and four occupational-therapy aides.
        iv. One social worker.
        v. One educational psychologist.
    e. Children receiving the tailored intervention they need, which might include 30 to 90-minute intervention sessions, up to five times weekly, using one-on-one, or groups of two or three.
11. There is also value in aiming to improve school resourcing and instruction, so we achieve effective instruction and intervention using a *Response to Intervention* (RTI) model with three tiers of well-resourced, highly effective instruction:
    a. *Tier 1. Core Instruction*: strategic differentiated reading instruction used for all children, usually in well-resourced classroom instruction, including differentiated instruction focused on children's areas of instructional need.
    b. *Tier 2. Skills Building Intervention*: focused more-intensive instruction, usually in small groups, being early intervention for children not progressing well with Core Instruction alone.
    c. *Tier 3. Intensive Remediation*: highly-intensive

intervention, often one-to-one, for students not progressing well with Intervention.
12. We are unlikely to achieve this level of effective instruction and intervention without major changes, quite likely including
   a. Using a fully-regular beginners' orthography.
   b. Using the first 2.5 years of schooling as a time of play-based learning and language enrichment, and commencing formal literacy and numeracy instruction from mid-Year 2.
13. Ethically, because of the strong evidence that fully-regular orthographies are so effective in meeting children's rights for effective early-literacy development, we need to research *upstream*, i.e., the potential of fully-regular beginners' orthographies, as strongly as we research *downstream*, i.e., our ability to improve Standard-English instruction and intervention.
14. Upstream, we need to investigate the potential of fully-regular English beginners' orthographies prior to children reading and writing Standard English, as to
   a. The extent that a fully-regular beginners' orthography and 2-stage learning reduces the impact of risk factors, and word-reading and spelling difficulties.
   b. How effective 2-Stage learning makes word-reading and spelling intervention.
   c. How well it eases and speeds word-reading and spelling development for all children.
   d. The social-emotional, motivational and cognitive-processing benefits of using a fully-regular beginners' orthography initially, and 2-stage learning.
   e. The extent of resourcing needed to achieve effective regular-orthography then Standard-English instruction and any needed intervention, routinely in all Australian schools.
15. Downstream, we need to investigate the effectiveness of optimised Standard-English instruction and intervention, using Standard English as a sole orthography, as to
   a. The extent to which optimised Standard-English instruction achieves word-reading, spelling and early-literacy development to the levels achieved in regular-orthography nations such as Taiwan, Japan and China, which like us, have a highly complex orthography.
   b. The extent to which Standard-English word-reading and spelling difficulties can be prevented and reduced, to the level that regular-orthography nations achieve.
   c. The extent to which early intervention and later

remediation are successful to the level that regular-orthography nations achieve.
   d. The social-emotional, motivational, cognitive-processing, word-reading, spelling, literacy and learning advantages and disadvantages of using just Standard English and 1-Stage early-literacy development.
   e. The extent of resourcing needed to achieve word-reading, spelling and early-literacy development to the level regular-orthography nations achieve, in all children, including our lowest tenth, when we use solely Standard English, in 1-Stage early literacy.
16. Australia needs to set a standard that instruction and intervention must be as effective as regular-orthography nations such as Taiwan, Japan and China routinely achieve across schools, as Australian children should not experience excessive disadvantage relative to children in regular-orthography nations.
17. There is strong value in Australia adopting the following 2035 Goal, towards actioning and achieving effective improvement:
By 2035, Australian education will be
routinely, efficiently, gently and easily
achieving highly effective, rapid development of children's word-reading, spelling, writing and early-literacy skills,
in GENTLE manner,
in every early-years classroom,
in all schools across our nation,
as efficiently as is achieved routinely
across schools in regular-orthography nations
such as Taiwan, Japan and China,
with at least 98% of Australian school children
being confident, independent readers and writers,
able to read 90% of the 10,000 most-frequent words,
by age 8.5 years, or within 18 months of starting formal word-reading instruction.

Let's Research Together

Our perspective on what to do when they're only a few quantitative studies, which often is the case ... is as follows: make as much of whatever data you have, especially data collected in well-controlled, carefully conducted studies. That is, data in excellent studies are definitely much better than no data. After all, by definition 'the cutting edge' has only been studied a little.

Michael Pressley, Steve Graham & Karen Harris, 2006

Each and every one of us is a researcher. Every time we ponder on an issue and seek confirmatory facts and data, we're researching (Stanovich & Stanovich, 1995).

Sometimes we publish our research, often we don't.

I've done extensive research observing in schools in other nations and talking with researchers and teachers there. While in many ways it's been informal knowledge-building, it's research.

There's huge value in us moving into decades of constructive, useful research, building the knowledge we need to optimise early-literacy development and education (Galletly, 2017b, 2018; Galletly & Knight, 2011a, 2011b, 2013; Knight & Galletly, 2017, 2020; Knight et al., 2017a, 2017b, 2019, 2021).

Let's Resource Research Impressively

As discussed in *Bunyips in the Classroom: The 10 Changes* (Galletly, 2022a), and elsewhere (Galletly, In press; Knight et al., 2017a, 2017b), Australia needs to greatly increase financing and supporting of educational research.

In Bunyips I detailed four needed items of research resourcing Australia needs if we're to usefully fill our current Swiss-cheese

Let's Research Together

research knowledge gaps, using strategically empowered research:
- Increased research funding, to perhaps four times Finland's average, annual, research budget.
- An Australian strategic research project focused on optimising early-literacy development towards meeting our 2035 goal, which coordinates, resources and supports associated, strategic, collaborative, school-level projects.
- Many teachers being researchers: our education system providing supports, including appreciable off-class time, and supported, funded paths to Masters and Doctoral studies, so that many Australian teachers and schools choose to be part of our focused research, with many working in school and district-level projects of value to their schools.
- Exemplary, open sharing of past, present and future research knowledge, with a central agency coordinating gathering, collating and reporting of relevant knowledge, including data and findings of current research projects.

Let's engage in large, strategic projects that conduct useful research in Australia and with other nations. Let's focus strongly on school-level research, building knowledge that directly supports education and instruction.

In addition to large strategic projects, let's also encourage bricolage research across Australia as we take the 10 Changes forward, using many and varied research methods, in many and varied studies, both large and small (Knight et al., 2017b):

Bricolage Research builds from the French word, bricoleur, a handyperson, who works towards and achieves set goals, using available resources and tools, and an overriding spirit of ingenuity (e.g., Kincheloe & Berry, 2004). It is pragmatic, mixed-methods research, open to using diverse data forms and research methods, thus lending itself well to the Australian situation where schools are strongly focused on optimising reading instruction, in the context of low research funding. Whereas experimental and quasiexperimental research can be prohibitively expensive when there are many variables to control for, Bricolage Research need not be expensive, as it seeks and finds opportunity within what is available.

In educational settings, Bricolage Research focused on establishing principles of effective reading instruction might perhaps be better termed Consensus Research.

Consensus Research (e.g., Bishop et al., 2016, 2017; Knight et al., 2017b) may well guide our 10 Changes improvement research. It's collaborative bricolage research, with university and teacher researchers working together in multiple strategic cycles of knowledge-building – considering the knowledge gained thus far, offering insights and deciding upon further projects, to achieve additional needed facts and data.

Many teachers and schools might decide to gather facts and data on their Prep to Year 3 children's skill levels for e.g., language skills, word-reading, spelling, short-term and working-memory, phonological and phonemic awareness, and Rapid Automised Naming (RAN), to explore how those skill levels relate to each other and to children's NAPLAN scores. That's research.

Other teachers and schools might gather word-reading data and keep records of time spent on explicit skills development vs reading books of manageable difficulty, to explore the extent to which upper, middle and lower-third children differ in the balance they need.

An Australian teacher, staying the Christmas holidays with cousins in e.g., Taiwan, might spend several days visiting and observing in schools and talking with teachers, seeking out information to answer questions built from considering the 10 Changes, using this book, its partners (Galletly, 2022a, In press), or simply the 2-page key concepts sheet on the books' website (Galletly, 2022b). A politician or journalist might do similarly. That's research.

In the next chapter, I list 100 useful research questions we might explore, as part of 10 Changes improvement research.

Importantly, let's be organised, and work together so we build knowledge efficiently in shareable forms.

Five groups of teachers heading off to Estonia, Wales, USA, Taiwan and Japan, staying with teachers there, conducting research during Australian school holidays, would gather masses of facts and data.

Now, while that's good news, the data might be in many and varied forms, and an Everest of different data types can be difficult to use efficiently.

Strategically using organising frameworks so data from multiple studies can be easily collated and compared is the answer: this can hugely empower the effectiveness of research and knowledge-building.

When our schools and travelling teacher researchers all have the same guiding research questions and requested data forms, their individual sets of data can be usefully collated and shared.

We'd similarly gather powerful shareable knowledge when groups of teachers from Estonia, Wales, USA, Taiwan and Japan come to stay with teachers here in Australia. (One advantage of being *Down Under* is that northern hemisphere schools are in action while we're on holidays in December and January, whereas they'd love to visit us in July and August in their school summer holidays. Quite likely these visits could be organised within existing exchange programs.

Within our facts and data, we'd want lots of opinions from our travelling teachers – their thoughts about the information and observations that they've made. That's research too – evaluating and interpreting information.

While less powerful for low subject numbers, collectively opinions and evaluations can have strong value, e.g., if we found that 54% of teacher travellers considered that teacher workload in regular-orthography nations is *far less* relative to Australian workload, 38% considered it *somewhat less*, only 8% felt it was *no less* and no teachers felt it was *higher than* Australian workload.

The future will be interesting, that's certain. Perhaps we'll have collaborative research conferences, with our groups of travelling teachers, and groups of schools who've gathered data on children's skills. Multiple groups would present their findings, with this followed by Consensus Research discussions, collating findings and making suggestions on future knowledge-building. The information might also be published online by our central agency that coordinates knowledge building, enabling others to evaluate information and add contributions. It might even be the *My State, My Nation* website suggested in *Bunyips* (Galletly, 2022a, In press).

Importantly, in evaluating information, we'd work hard to be objective, and try to reduce as much as possible, the impacts of passionate beliefs we might hold dear.

Let's Prioritise Factful Thinking

To be human is to be gullible.

The research is in. Studies of human nature show we humans are gullible, incredibly gullible (Gladwell, 2005; Kahneman, 2013; Rosling et al., 2018). We are easily persuaded into opinions that seem so right at the time, but actually aren't. They're actually deluded thinking.

Delusions are entrenched beliefs that are strongly owned as truth but are actually wrong, and can be highly resistant to reason and facts. We all do a lot of somewhat deluded thinking, so it's good to be aware of how easily it happens.

Nobel Prize winner Daniel Kahneman (2013) explains clear and deluded thinking in his book, *Thinking, fast and slow*. We have two thinking systems, *System 1 and System 2 thinking*, and also, at times, use sidestep default thinking.

System 1 is fast automatic thinking that tends to rule us. It renders all of us astonishingly gullible at times. System 1 is extremely useful, indeed essential, in many ways, so it's definitely not to be rejected. However, because System 1 thinking makes us so gullible, for education issues, we need to be far more aware of when System 1 is ruling our thinking.

System 2 is controlled logical reasoned thinking. It can control our rapid default gullible System 1 thinking IF it chooses to. Alas, System 2 is rather lazy at times, and so defaults to System 1. This makes us gullible to the extent that we lie at times, even to ourselves, confidently adamant we're functioning in rational System 2, while facts clearly show System 1 is firmly in control.

Sidestep default thinking is something we also do often. Instead of dealing with a central question or issue using safe System 2 thinking, we allow System 1 to be in action, and often rapidly sidestep, replacing the focus issue with a default issue that's easy to talk on, and focusing strongly on that one instead.

We notice politicians doing this routinely in media interviews, but we've massive blindspots when we do it ourselves. Clear vision and fact-focused peers are needed in education, if we're to resolve our current difficulties and make efficient progress.

System 1 leading System 2, and let's-reframe-the-topic-to-the-one-I-like-to-talk-about are a serious issue. Importantly, experts are as gullible as everyone else: research shows even the most intelligent and clear thinking of us are easily tricked.

Our gullibility sets the scene for us to easily use deluded thinking and WYSYAIN (*What You See You Assume Is Normal*, Galletly, 2022a), assuming what we see is either acceptable or unchangeable, when actually that can be far from being the case.

As we engage in 10 Changes improvement research, we need metacognition about clear and deluded thinking, so we're aware of the types of thinking that we do.

Thomas Edison wisely said, *The most necessary task of civilisation is to teach men how to think* (Juma, 2022). He's right.

Let's be Possibilists and Factfulists, not Ideologists

Have you read Hans Rosling's book, *Factfulness* (Rosling et al., 2018)? It's an inspiring read.

The world is not going from bad to worse, and, in many nations, life is improving immensely. And, as per Kahneman (2013), we often use majorly deluded thinking as our default.

See if you can do better than me on Rosling's 13 question survey – I got only a few correct! Then take heart, as Rosling discusses virtually everyone achieving well below chance, then being curious to find out why we systematically *know* the world so incorrectly.

And curious we certainly become, as we realise we've been systematically thinking inappropriately negatively about the world, even the best of us. At one session where Rosling was presenting with Bill and Melissa Gates to well-established experts on world facts and improvement, that audience did no better.

Hans discusses 10 aspects of erroneous thinking, and techniques to use to avoid them. We systematically think erroneously: too negatively, too dramatically, too them and us, too fearfully. We overgeneralise too much, we think through our feelings, we react intuitively while sure we're acting on facts.

And when do we do this erroneous thinking most spectacularly well? (*Drum roll, please ...*) It's when we don't have data readily available, to confront us with the facts!

That does sound like our ongoing *Reading Wars* controversies, doesn't it, lots of strong statements on word-reading when Australia has a word-reading data dearth – virtually no facts and data?

It also shows why WYSYAIN can flourish in education when we've virtually no facts and data on our children's skill levels for word-reading, and language and cognitive-processing skills.

In thinking on education issues, we need to first embrace our deluded thinking, then move on to sorting strong beliefs that are valid from those that aren't.

Rosling emphasises, not being simply optimists, but instead fact-based possibilists:

People often call me an optimist, because I showed them the enormous progress they didn't know about ...
I'm not an optimist. That makes me sound naive.
I'm a very serious possibilist ... someone who neither hopes without reason, nor fears without reason, someone who

constantly resists the overdramatic worldview ...
It is having a clear and reasonable idea about how things are.
It is having a worldview that is constructive and useful.

There are powerful parallels for improving reading and education here in Australia and across the Anglosphere.

The world is getting a whole lot better, it's immensely better than the majority of us are thinking. In like manner, we really can improve early literacy and education here meteorically, and do this using logical System-2 decision-making, nicely avoiding inappropriate naysaying and rose-coloured glasses hype.

But to do so, we need paradigmatically new mindsets and clear thinking. Into the future, let's be possibilists, who neither hope without reason, nor fear without reason, who constantly resist the overdramatic worldview, who have clear reasoned ideas and a constructive useful worldview, and strong convictions that massive improvement is possible.

In doing so, let's be highly aware how easily we can default to WYSYAIN and deluded thinking. Let's work with keen deliberation to be and remain clear-sighted.

Crucial for Heightened Clear Thinking: Facts and Data

In Factfulness, Hans emphasises a crux issue – the crucial role that facts and data play in revealing deluded thinking and enabling us to move to clear thinking instead.

That's why Hans called his book Factfulness. He'd tried logical reasoning for many years but it just didn't work, as people's deluded thinking was too entrenched. He then shifted to facts and data, and quick surveys that invoke culture shocks – and, from that point, achieved strong success! That's because, when facts and data are out there on the table, it's so vastly easier to do clear thinking.

So, let's be not just possibilists, but also factfulists, using facts and data to build and maintain clear thinking.

Of course, Hans is not alone on the importance of thinking clearly and using data. Drucker and Edison were similarly facts and data aficionados.

Let's use mantras developed from Peter Drucker's ideas: *What gets measured, gets managed* and *What's measured, improves.*

Let's achieve ample useful facts and data by measuring children's word-reading and language skills, including their cognitive-processing skills, across the school years, in Australia and other nations, to achieve powerful facts and data – and also measuring child and teacher workload, and school resourcing.

Let's use Thomas Edison's mantras with strong System 2 emphases:
Faith, as well-intentioned as it may be, must be built on facts not fiction – faith in fiction is a damnable false hope.
Truth is governed by natural laws and cannot be denied.
I cannot see that unproved theories or sentiment should be permitted to have influence in the building of conviction upon matters so important.

The world's greatest inventor, who died in 1931, foresaw solar, wind and wave power – and also, it seems, he foresaw the ITA research cupboarded and ignored, and the mountainous rhetoric of Anglophone nations' Reading Wars, with overgeneralisations abounding and academics and educators arguing about word-reading instead of gathering needed data on children's word-reading and language skills:
Proof, proof! That is what I always have been after; that is what my mind requires before it can accept a serious fact.
I cannot accept as final any theory which is not provable.

Our current situation can relatively accurately be summed up using the downside of Edison's and Drucker's wise words. For the past six decades, Anglophone management of early-literacy development has been sadly insufficient, with word-reading and language skills unmeasured, attribution error rife, and society vigorously blaming our overworked teachers, ignoring other key impacting factors.

Our actions seem based, at least in part, more on Edison's *fiction* with a *damnable false hope* that literacy outcomes would improve magically despite ignoring word-reading's and language skills' crux cruel roles in impeding Anglophone literacy development.

Fortunately, since the Covid-19 epidemic, as a society, we're more accepting of change when facts and data show the need, and are keen for change built from sensible, efficient, data gathering. Into the future, in 10 Changes improvement research, let's use Drucker and Edison's thinking (Drucker, 1994; Juma, 2022).

Let's also use the work of educational-change researchers, e.g., Frank Crowther, Peter Senge, Andy Hargreaves, Brian Caldwell and their teams (Caldwell, 2016; Caldwell & Spinks, 2008; Crowther, 2011, 2017; Hargreaves, 1994, 1997, 2021; Senge, Cambron-McCabe et al., 2000; Senge, Lucas et al., 2000).

Most importantly, let's end our well-intentioned rhetoric that, lacking needed facts and data, lies far too close to fiction.

In our context, I think Edison would've said insist on word-reading and language-skills testing, data and evidence for Standard-English and regular-orthography children, and instigate a baseline rule that discussions include strong focus on data or needs to gather data we currently lack. Hans Rosling would have agreed.

Let's Avoid Ideological Thinking

Let's avoid ideological thinking. Let's also avoid Semmelweis reflex, reflex rejecting of evidence and knowledge simply because it doesn't fit well with current established norms, beliefs, and expectations (e.g., Kadar, 2021). Ideology and rhetoric reign when we won't legitimately consider facts and data.

Let's judge evidence on its own merits instead of just accepting groupthink. Let's keep our rhetorometers clicking (Galletly, In press), and aim to explore options and wonder deeply.

Let's also be alert for our all too common WYSYAIN. We assume our current norm is how life should be, in myopic Anglophone fishbowl style. That's not correct, and it's also highly inefficient and ineffective. Spending time observing education in schools in other countries soon shows how, with strategic changes, Anglophone education can be vastly improved.

So let's add a WYSYAIN alert to our rhetorometers, and be on the alert for rhetoric and WYSYAIN, both collectively and individually: noticing when they're happening and moving instead to reflecting on possibilities, and then how to explore issues using facts and data.

And where needed, let's be the small child in *The Emperor's New Clothes*, making a loud call that things are not as they should be, and that facts and data would improve the situation.

Indeed, watch the reactions over time to the *Aussie Reading Woes* trilogy (Galletly, 2022, 2023, In press).

You'll notice most of my calls, in the 10 Changes I'm recommending, are simply for knowledge-building in 10 Changes areas. That's because I'm confident that, with objective research in these areas, ample facts and data will be gathered, leading to logical decision-making on both (a) using a fully-regular beginners' orthography initially, and (b) holding back formal word-reading, spelling and numeracy education, with the first 2.5 years of schooling being language and learning enrichment, hopefully with an enriching play-based emphasis.

That said, my calls may well initially be rejected. Do watch for weapons of relativism and double delegitimising: ignoring major truths while finding fault on minor issues where I may not have been sufficiently precise; then rejecting me as the messenger, while simultaneously dismissing the messages I'm handing on. My works, too, may be cupboarded and ignored, in the manner the ITA research has been.

That might be sad, but such is life. I view my task as being to alert current and future researchers and educators to key truths worthy of deep investigation, whose time will come, later, if not sooner.

Let's Keep the Discussion Going

Australian education deserves improvement, and our children are entitled to it.

Do keep the discussion going on 10 Changes issues. In those discussions, do include comment on the 10 Changes, our 2035 goal, ABCs and mantra.

Our 2035 goal is worthy, reflecting our children's entitlements:
By 2035, Australian education will be
routinely, efficiently, gently and easily
achieving highly effective, rapid development of children's
word-reading, spelling, writing and early-literacy skills,
in GENTLE manner,
in every early-years classroom,
in all schools across our nation,
as efficiently as is achieved routinely
across schools in regular-orthography nations
such as Taiwan, Japan and China,
with at least 98% of Australian school children
being confident, independent readers and writers,
able to read 90% of the 10,000 most-frequent words,
by age 8.5 years, or within 18 months of starting formal word-reading instruction.

Our ABCs of improving education are logical and needed:
A. ACT locally while looking globally.
B. BOOST the lower-third to benefit everyone.
C. CHANGE effectively to work less and achieve more.

Our 10 Changes are a strong way forward into the future:
Change 1. Understand how orthographies matter: English

spelling is dragging us down.
Change 2. Own our struggling reader woes: End hypocrisy and pretence.
Change 3. Weigh workload: Our children and teachers are working far too hard.
Change 4. One-size education does not fit all: Teach to the decidedly different instructional needs of upper-third and lower-third readers.
Change 5. End our data deficiency: Build strong knowledge on word-reading levels.
Change 6. Enrich every child: Ensure effective supportive tailored education.
Change 7. Insist on easy literacy development: Reach regular-orthography nations' achievement levels.
Change 8. Investigate the potential of fully-regular beginners' orthographies: They're winners.
Change 9. Play to learn first: Start Standard-English word-reading instruction from mid-Year 2.
Change 10. Build needed research knowledge as quickly as possible: Use collaborative school-based research.

Let's also keep in mind our education bunyips, important issues we've too much ignored – issues we want to reduce and retire:
1. Our English Orthographic Complexity Bunyip.
2. Our Too High Cognitive Load Bunyip.
3. Our Widespread Language Weakness Bunyip.
4. Our Too Young Starting Age Bunyip.
5. Our Activated Risk Factors Bunyip.
6. Our Too Much to Teach in Too Little Time Bunyip.
7. Our Too Low Resourcing Bunyip.
8. Our Deficit of Word-Reading Data Bunyip.
9. Our Lack of Needed Research Bunyip.
10. Our Attribution Error Bunyip.

Additionally, do keep reflecting on my three wonderings that have guided my enquiries and thinking down the decades:
- What factors cause our children and adults' reading and literacy difficulties?
- How can we reduce their struggles and suffering?
- What are the ways we can do things better?

There are no such things as reading difficulties.
There are only teaching challenges.
Jackie French, *2015 Senior Australian of the Year*

The 100 Research Questions

It seems appropriate to end our tours with research questions that Australians and others might use to guide research into the future. They're useful, practical questions towards turning our many Swiss-cheese knowledge gaps into wonderfully solid cheddar.

The 100 research questions are useful questions for all involved in education, particularly those who might consider postgraduate Masters and Doctoral studies, while being equally useful for experienced researchers and academics, education systems, and governments.

A limit of 100 questions forced brevity on topics, and many pertinent factors aren't included. For detail on further pertinent research areas, I refer you to these writings by myself and our CQU research team:
- The findings listed at the end of each of this book's 14 Research Tours: in their summing up each tour's key implications, many findings are worthy research topics. They are also available as a separate file on the trilogy's website.
- Our 2017, 89-page book chapter, *Managing cognitive load as the key to literacy development: Research directions suggested by crosslinguistic research and research on Initial Teaching Alphabet (i.t.a.;* Knight et al., 2017a). It analyses research on Standard-English, regular-orthography and Initial Teaching Alphabet (ITA) reading development and instruction and concludes with detailed lists of findings, which need research.
- Our 2020, 90-page book chapter, *Practical school-level implications of cognitive processing and cognitive load* (Knight & Galletly, 2020). It discusses many aspects of early-literacy development, and associated research studies, with particular focus on cognitive processing, executive-functioning skills, statistical learning, and self-teaching. These are discussed with regard to the severe difficulties experienced by Standard-English struggling readers relative to the far milder difficulties of regular-orthography weaker readers, along with

advances in neuropsychological investigations and interventions. It discusses many areas worthy of research.
- The 2017 123-page, project report, *Principles of reading instruction towards optimising reading instruction for at-risk readers in Prep to Year 3: Principles developed through teacher reflection on research and practice in the ARC project 'Bridging the gap for at-risk readers: Reading theory into classroom practice* (Knight et al., 2017b): this discusses key factors in reading instruction, and includes extensive lists of principles towards effective reading instruction for at-risk and struggling readers, many of which are worthy research areas.

Where possible, I've worded questions to be more easily read, so some lack the careful wording research practices often require. The list isn't exhaustive: they're a sample of questions towards research for improving early-literacy and learning.

The questions use this book's conventions, e.g., of terms such as *developing readers* and *struggling readers* having specific meaning, and the term *reader*s standing in at times for *readers and writer*s.

The 100 questions are in 20 sections, under these topics:
1. Generic questions for use in all sections below.
2. Our research drought, needs, and future directions.
3. Our status quo: Current levels of literacy skills.
4. Language skills for literacy.
5. Literacy components and quadrants: Our balance of word-reading and language skills.
6. The crosslinguistic gap: Major differences between Anglophone and regular-orthography nations.
7. Orthographic advantage and disadvantage.
8. Beginners' orthographies and 2-stage early literacy.
9. The roles of word-reading and spelling in crosslinguistic differences.
10. Our teachers' high workload.
11. Our children's high workload.
12. Differential disadvantaging of our at-risk learners.
13. Motivation, engagement, persistence, and resilience.
14. Young vs older starting age when learning to read.
15. Models for guiding research and practice.
16. School instruction and assessment practices.
17. Executive-function skills and learning.
18. The ethics of our status quo.
19. The impacts of beliefs on change.
20. Our education future.

By considering these questions I've listed, it's likely readers will think of other, useful, relevant research examples and questions, including ones they'd personally find more directly of interest, being pertinent and applicable to their specific education context. That's often how research starts: reflecting on a relevant area of interest.

I've deliberately included a range of applied-research questions with direct applicability to schools and education settings.

Research Questions Section 1: The Generic Research Questions

The first four of the 100 are questions that could be included at the end of every category below. They're generic questions that might be used as subpoints of research questions in future studies – final research questions have often evolved to be quite detailed, with multiple subpoints.

While we won't separately consider any of the next 96 questions, let's briefly consider each of these first four questions, and how each might be actioned.

Q.1 What research studies, findings and discussions are available on this area, which have relevance towards schools optimising early-literacy development for Anglophone children?

Q.2 To what extent, and in which ways, is the available research knowledge relevant, of practical use, and applicable to, Australian and Anglophone school situations?

Q.3 How might teachers and schools do data-keeping, investigations, and knowledge-building for school purposes that is also useful for research purposes, with value for all parties, in building knowledge that supports improving education across Australia?

Q.4 How does this knowledge-building relate to, use, and apply the 10 Changes, ABCs of improvement, Thesis Statement, 2035 Goal, Mantra, and the 20-item list towards positioning word-reading effectively, which are tools for use in Australia's education improvement journey (Galletly, 2022a)?

Question 1, above, is the starting point for most research: reading widely, having discussions, doing observations, then compiling a summary of research studies, and knowledge gained and developed.

Really, this whole book, *The Research Tours*, addresses Question 1. It's a summary of the available knowledge, thinking and theorising, that I've compiled. Virtually all large books, small research articles (research-journal word counts are often highly restrictive), and all the informal notes and documents that researchers compile, build from reading and reflecting on research publications. One finds an interesting article, and, while reading it, highlights potentially useful, referenced articles discussed there, then locates those articles, and reads on.

There's great value in systematically summarising the information read and noting down reflections at that time. In the 1950s, for my father's doctoral studies, he had a box of cards, one per article, with strategic topic holes punched in the top of each card.

To search a topic, he inserted a probe in the relevant hole, to extract all articles on that topic: that was cutting-edge then. Now, we've wonderfully useful bibliographic programs, such as *Endnote*, the program I use.

Each of the almost 800 references cited and listed in this book was entered in Endnote (laboriously in early years, and more recently, directly imported from online library databases). So too, are the 7,500 other entries there. In Endnote, I paste in relevant text, e.g., potential quotes, write summaries, and add comments. I'm happy to share my Endnote collection with interested others.

Question 2 considers the research gathered and contemplated in Question 1, reflecting on its strengths in current form for schools and improving education. Whilst most research is valuable, some is more theoretical: where findings seem important, this creates value in further applied-research, replicating or extending it to explore its applicability and value in schools and in improving education.

In addition, while we can gain considerable useful knowledge from studies conducted in other nations, often decades ago, we acquire far more powerful and relevant knowledge when we replicate and extend those studies in Australian schools and contexts.

With Australia having had a long research drought due to restricted funding, we've enormous needs for research, including very large amounts of applied research in schools.

Needs for, and practicalities of, school-level research, are explored in
- The *10 Changes: The Nitty-Gritty*, Book 3 of the Aussie Reading Woes trilogy which partners this book.
- Section 4 of our CQU report on the *Bridging the Gap* project, which identified principles of instruction towards optimising early-years reading instruction for at-risk Standard-English readers, developed by CQU researchers and teachers working together in one Queensland region (Knight et al., 2017b).

Question 3 considers the value of data we have currently, and how we might gather data into the future.

Currently, we've quite likely large amounts of data in Australia, that could be of use establishing knowledge of our status quo. While we've no systemic NAPLAN data on our children's levels for word-reading, and language skills, including cognitive-processing skills, there'd be considerable useful data in the records and databases of individual teachers, schools, and allied-health professionals.

Ebert and Scott's (2016) study, discussed in Tour 7, a useful example of this type of research, analysed the reading and language-skills data of 112 children attending a USA allied-health clinic, with many pertinent findings.

There's value in Australian teachers, schools and allied-health professionals using their data in this way, with permissions established for use of carefully de-identified data. Publishing these results, working on one's own, or collaboratively with university academics, or colleagues who enjoy statistics, would provide valuable knowledge for Australia. That's even more the case if Australia actioned a cooperative research project (see below) that values, uses and incorporates findings of many smaller studies.

Descriptive statistics (Means and Standard Deviations) are useful, with particular value when e.g., school data on the full range of achievers is reported for thirds, tenths, and the lowest and highest 5% and 2% of achievers. Also valuable is reporting of correlations of sets of scores, e.g., how strongly children's word-reading and language-skill levels relate to their NAPLAN results.

There's value too in reporting on Standard Deviation (SD) groups, as I've done in Tours 2 and 13, to consider the spread of the word-reading levels of Welsh vs English, Slovak and Czech vs English, and German vs English children (Caravolas, 2018; Frith et al., 1998; Hanley et al., 2004; see Figures 8, 9a,b,c, 19a,b, and 20a,b).

Microsoft Excel is a useful program for these purposes: it's added increasingly more applications across the years. Further, it's likely education systems or schools would provide advanced statistical programs such as SPSS Data Analysis software, where needed.

There's value in having overarching models and frameworks that guide research, and **Question 4** brings knowledge-building back to the 10 Changes, ABCs of improvement, Thesis Statement, 2035 Goal, Mantra, and 20-item list for Australia positioning word-reading. While other frameworks will also be used, these tools for Australia's education improvement journey may also prove useful.

Let's now move steadily through the topics and research questions.

Research Questions Section 2: Our Research Drought, Needs, and Future Directions

Q.5 Using literature review, and contacting of agencies in Australia and internationally, how does Australia's spending, per capita, on researching of early-literacy development, associated school needs, and instruction for optimising early-literacy development, compare, at the current time, and across the past five decades, with other nations, including the USA and Finland?

1. How do Australian levels compare with those of USA and Finland, as regards the extent of assessments used and data gained in research studies regarding children's skill levels, and effectiveness of instruction, for early-literacy skills including reading comprehension, word-reading accuracy and fluency, and language skills, including the cognitive-processing and executive-function skills used in reading and writing?
2. In what ways has a long-term lack of dedicated Australian research on early-literacy development impacted the current levels of knowledge we have on Australian early-literacy levels, child and teacher workload, and the improving of early-literacy skills, in both healthy-progress, at-risk and weak readers?
3. With Australia needing considerable catch-up in knowledge-building, due to low research funding, and thus having limited research across recent decades, to what extent would an annual early-literacy-education research budget four times that of Finland's be appropriate and needed, given the effectiveness of Finnish research across the decades, Australia's population being well over four times larger than Finland's, and our paucity of research knowledge built in recent decades?

Q.6 What value is likely to be found in the Australian government establishing both

1. A large, dedicated research project building knowledge in Australia and cross-nationally about current challenges in Standard-English early-literacy development in *developing* and *struggling readers*, and ways forward?
2. A central agency for encouraging, supporting and co-ordinating knowledge gathering, which
   a. Collates, shares, and disseminates gathered knowledge,
   b. Co-ordinates, encourages and supports cycles of research, including bricolage research that uses a range of research methods, and quasi-experimental studies,

c. Invites and co-ordinates discussion reflecting on gathered knowledge, as to the uses to which current data can be applied, needs for further knowledge-gathering, and methods that would enable this knowledge generation in next cycles of research, and
d. Provides information on key education aspects, such as
   i. Research data, findings and discussion points,
   ii. Data on e.g., children's word-reading and language-skill levels, including cognitive-processing skills,
   iii. Factors explored in OECD's *Education at a Glance*,
   iv. Useful data shown for all Australian states and territories, e.g., numbers of children receiving Special Education disability funding, and criteria used for eligibility, and
   v. Data on literacy-skill levels for Australia, its states and territories, other Anglophone nations, and regular-orthography nations using 1-Stage and 2-Stage early literacy?

Q.7 To what extent might Australia's knowledge-building on early literacy be more quickly achieved by Australia collaborating with Finnish researchers to replicate, and, where indicated, extend, aspects of international research studies and projects, including the Jyvaskyla Longitudinal Study of Dyslexia (JLD; Lohvansuu et al., 2021; Lyytinen et al., 2015, 2021) and use of *GraphoLearn* and *Comprehension Game*, developed from the JLD research findings?

Q.8 What types of knowledge will be built by Anglophone teachers with expertise in teaching both *developing* and *struggling readers*, visiting regular-orthography nations to observe and consider teaching, work samples and data on literacy levels, and have discussions with researchers and teachers, in both
1. Sole-orthography nations using 1-Stage early literacy, e.g., Estonia, Finland and South Korea, and
2. Taiwan, Japan or China, nations currently using 2-Stage early literacy, and fully-regular beginners' orthographies?

Q.9 In what ways can cooperative teacher-researcher knowledge-building be enhanced, e.g., by
1. Including use of standardised summary forms for recording information, which include both survey and open-ended questions?
2. Knowledge gathering and collation of knowledge being coordinated and supported by a national organisation established in Australia?

3. Developing ongoing cross-national partnerships of teachers, schools, towns and districts that enable deep cross-sectional and longitudinal knowledge to be gathered?
4. Building networks across a range of Anglophone and regular-orthography nations so wider experience of nations' practices and achievement levels is built?
5. Having annual conferences, to discuss findings and observations in conjunction with exchange visits?
6. Encouraging and supporting post-graduate Diploma, Masters and Doctoral studies within this program?

Research Questions Section 3: Our Status Quo: Current Levels of Literacy Skills

Q.10 What are Australian children's levels of early-literacy skills in individual primary and high-school year-levels, with reference to thirds, tenths, and the lowest and highest 5% and 2% of achievers, as regards accuracy and fluency of

1. Functional literacy skills, including accuracy and fluency of word-reading, spelling, vocabulary and language skills used in literacy, and independent reading and writing?
2. Language skills used in literacy, including those listed in Research Questions Section 4, below?
3. Key literacy subskills including orthographic knowledge and skills, phonological and phonemic awareness, and executive-function skills, including inhibition control, cognitive-processing, working-memory efficiency, statistical learning efficiency, and the ability to action and complete tasks independently and effectively?

Q.11 Using school data, to what extent do Australian children's word-reading levels align with the norms of standardised tests used internationally, including the *Test of Word Reading Efficiency-2*'s two subtests that assess reading of common real words, and reading of unfamiliar words (TOWRE-2. Torgesen et al., 2012)?

Q.12 What are the relationships between word-reading levels on the TOWRE-2's two subtests and children's spelling, reading-comprehension and written-expression levels?

Q.13 Using longitudinal monitoring of skills, using the TOWRE-2's two subtests, along with monitoring of spelling, phonological and phonemic awareness, letter-sound knowledge, Rapid Automised Naming (RAN), and other executive-function skills, what evidence do schools find of

1. Early vs. late-emerging word-reading difficulties?
2. Difficulties with unfamiliar words being more associated with late-emerging difficulties?
3. Difficulties with all words being more associated with early-emerging difficulties?
4. The strength of the relationship between children's word-reading and writing skills, and the extent to which word-reading of common-familiar words vs unfamiliar words are associated with spelling?
5. Double-deficit subgroups for RAN and phonemic awareness, with children with weakness in both areas having more severe word-reading and spelling difficulties?
6. Children of healthy ability who make extremely low progress in developing word-reading skills (often discussed as Nonresponders and Treatment Resisters in research studies, e.g., Al Otaiba & Fuchs, 2006)?
7. The extent to which these children have factors such as family history, more severe cognitive-processing and letter-sound difficulties, lower Socio-Economic Status (SES) and lower Literate Cultural Capital?

Research Questions Section 4: Language Skills for Literacy

Q.14 In what ways are the following, and other, language skills used by children to communicate and learn, in both informal and formal ways, including assessment contexts:

1. Receptive vocabulary, for words, phrases and concepts, including idioms and colloquialisms,
2. Expressive vocabulary and word-finding skills,
3. Expressive language skills, including precision and maturity of answers and extent of detail provided, in verbal and written contacts, both informal and formal (e.g. when being assessed),
4. Language comprehension, at literal and inferential levels,
5. Language reasoning, including use of subtlety, social reasoning, and pragmatics,
6. Cognitive-processing skills needed for and used in literacy and learning, including auditory perception, phonological awareness, short-term and working memory, and other executive-function skills, and
7. Ability to cope with high cognitive load, including the extent to which the above language skills are impacted when children experience high cognitive load when reading, writing, and planning and actioning literacy tasks?

Q.15 What are Australian children's levels of these language skills, in specific contexts, including
1. Language skills used in written expression across school years?
2. Language skills at school entry, built prior to school?
3. Language skills schools build prior to commencing learning to read and write, both currently, when time is short, and when trialling Change 9, with 2.5 years of executive-function, language and learning enrichment, with formal early-literacy instruction delayed until children are older and have higher levels of maturity and executive-function skills?
4. Language-skill levels and progress while reading and writing are developing?
5. Language skills developed through being proficiently accurate, fluent independent readers and writers?

Q.16 In what ways do language and literacy skills go together and grow together, advantaging and disadvantaging each other's development?

Q.17 To what extent should reading and writing difficulties, and the cognitive-processing and executive-function skill difficulties that underlie them, be considered part of language disorder, given that
1. Cognitive-processing skills, including executive-function skills, are used extensively in communication across early-childhood prior to children commencing school,
2. Reading and writing are print-communication skills which use and build from existing communication skills, and are added onto and integrated into those skills, and
3. Children with literacy difficulties almost invariably have difficulties with language skills, either
   a. The cognitive-processing skills underlying word-reading and spelling development and actioning,
   b. The language skills of verbal communication, or
   c. Both these skill areas?

Q.18 As discussed in Tour 6, to what extent might the term *Language, Literacy and Learning Disorder* (LLLD) be useful as an overarching category for Australian education systems, for considering children with literacy and learning difficulties, given that, for example,
1. It highlights the primary role of language skills in, or underlying, literacy and learning difficulties,
2. It emphasises the three key aspects: language skills, literacy skills, and learning difficulties,
3. The current primary term for communication difficulties, Developmental Language Disorder (DLD) is not an overarching

category, as its tenets emphasise multiple school-based categories, with some children having DLD, while others have *Language Disorder associated with* (another disability, e.g. *Autism Spectrum Disorder*), and
4. The term *Language, Literacy and Learning Disorder* (LLLD does not conflict with, and can incorporate, other terms and categories, e.g., Dyslexia, *Developmental Language Disorder* (DLD) and other disorders?

Q.19 What are the current numbers of Speech Language Pathologists (SLPs) per capita in Australia, and, with reference to Finland and USA, to what extent are the levels sufficient for meeting children's needs?
1. To what extent should our SLP services be expanded?

Q.20 To what extent would Australia be advantaged by the education system being in charge of funding for all in-school and out-of-school services for all children, 0 to 18 years, as is done in other nations, given that this reduces current inefficiencies created by overlaps and gaps between services, which often disadvantage children?
1. To what extent are SLP clients accepted for, vs rejected for, or not eligible for, NDIS funding, similar and different?
2. To what extent are children without NDIS funding and their families being disadvantaged in our current NDIS-funding environment, with SLP fees having risen and very high demand for service from clients with NDIS funding?
3. Given the wording of our Education Act and disability documents in terms of the supports which are to be provided for Australian children, to what extent does it seem stated and implied that families should not have to pay for needed services?

Q.21 As discussed in Tour 6, for school-aged children, is the dichotomy of Expressive Language skills vs Receptive Language skills useful and practical, given that these skills overlap and integrate in many ways in the written and spoken communication of school-aged children?
1. How do the criteria used for children to achieve government funding, both in-school Special Education funding, and out-of-school NDIS funding, compare to criteria used in the USA, where laws stringently require that the rights of children with disabilities are met effectively?
2. Using the USA requirements and criteria, and Australia's Education Act and disability documents, to what extent does Australia adequately support children with communication disabilities, including literacy and learning disabilities?
3. How do Australian services compare with those of USA and Finland, as regards meeting children's rights for services?

Research Questions Section 5:
Literacy Components and Quadrants:
Our Balance of Word-Reading and Language Skills

Q.22 Using appropriate measures of word-reading, word-writing, and language skills, and the *Literacy Component Model*'s equations of *Reading Comprehension = Word-Reading x Language Skills*, and *Written Expression = Word-Writing x Language Skills*,

1. What is the relationship between the print-accuracy skills (word-reading, spelling) and language skills, in reading comprehension and written expression, for Australian children in different year-levels, with reference to thirds, tenths, and the lowest and highest 5% and 2% of achievers?
2. Does the role of print-accuracy skills decline as proficiency builds, with language skills' role becoming more dominant?
3. Is the *Fourth Grade Slump* (late-emerging difficulties) evident in Australian children?
4. What are the proportions of children with weak language skills and weak print-accuracy skills (word-reading, spelling) in children with weak reading comprehension and written expression, in primary and high school?
5. To what extent do these children have early-emerging vs late-emerging difficulties in print-accuracy and language skills?
6. What value is added to PIRLS and PISA reporting, when participating Australian children complete tests of word-reading and language skills after PIRLS and PISA testing?
7. What information is gained when NAPLAN testing includes tests of word-reading and language skills, perhaps initially for a 10% sample of children across Years 3, 5, 7, 9?
8. To what extent is there evidence of late-emerging difficulties across literacy areas, in Australia's numbers of NAPLAN low achievers (children in the lowest two bands) rising from Year 3 to Year 9 (Tour 8, Figure 15, Table 3)?
   a. To what extent does this suggest needs for higher levels of support services in Australian schools?

Q.23 Using school data, to what extent do Australian percentages of children with early-emerging vs late-emerging difficulties, and language-skills vs word-reading weakness compare with those found in Leach et al.'s (2003) component study?

1. To what extent do schools find the Simple View and Literacy Component models and use of quadrants, as explored in Tour 7, beneficial for considering children's strengths, weaknesses and specific instructional needs?

2. What measures and cut-point criteria are found useful by schools for testing word-reading and language skills?
3. Towards exploring written-expression subskills, is word-writing sufficiently represented by spelling-test results, or by assessing spelling efficiency in text writing, including accuracy and fluency of spelling approximations used?

Research Questions Section 6: The Crosslinguistic Gap: Major Differences Between Anglophone Nations and Regular-Orthography Nations

Q.24 What crosslinguistic differences are present between Australian children and children in regular-orthography nations, both sole-orthography nations (e.g., Finland, Estonia) and Taiwan, Japan and China (nations that moved last century to 2-Stage early literacy), as regards ease of development and progress rates for
1. Functional literacy skills, including accuracy and fluency of word-reading, spelling, vocabulary and language skills used in literacy, and independent reading and writing?
2. The range of language skills used in literacy, listed above in Research Questions Section 4?
3. Key literacy subskills including orthographic skills and knowledge, phonological and phonemic awareness, and diverse executive-function skills, including inhibition control, cognitive processing, working-memory efficiency, statistical-learning efficiency, and skills for working independently, to action and complete tasks?

Q.25 With reference to thirds, tenths, and the lowest and highest 5% and 2% of achievers,
1. To what extent are crosslinguistic differences heightened in lower-achieving readers and writers?
2. In crosslinguistic differences evident in lower achievers, what is the role of weakness in phonological and phonemic awareness, letter-sound and orthographic awareness, and executive-function skills?
3. How does the word-reading, spelling, and independent reading and writing of regular-orthography children with intellectual disability compare with that of Anglophone children, both those with intellectual disability, and those of healthy ability?

Q.26 What differences exist in the number of risk factors, and their extent of influence in impeding early-literacy development in regular-orthography vs Standard-English at-risk children?
1. What roles do high cognitive load, complex learning, and the

impeded statistical learning that Standard-English readers experience across learning to read, play in
a. Increasing the number of risk factors for Anglophone children?
b. Increasing the likelihood that risk factors will be activated for Anglophone children, resulting in reading and writing difficulties?

Research Questions Section 7: Orthographic Advantage and Disadvantage

Q.27 In what ways do Anglophone and regular-orthography nations experience aspects of orthographic advantage and disadvantage, respectively, as defined and used in Knight et al.'s (2019) *Orthographic Advantage Theory*, such as

1. Early-education advantage, through easy, rapid, homogenous early-literacy development, strong self-teaching and low cognitive load?
2. Later-education advantage through children being confident, proficient word-readers and spellers, and independent readers and writers?
3. Optimising education advantage, through it being easier to optimise education when literacy learning difficulties are few and less severe?
4. Generational advantage through elevated high-school graduation rates, and high adult literacy levels enabling parents to support their children's language and literacy development?
5. Adult-life advantage through adults with proficient literacy and academic skills having access to education, career, income, and social-emotional benefits associated with effective literacy?
6. Workplace and economic advantage, through adults having higher workplace literacy levels?

Q.28 To what extent are orthographic impacts equal to, or greater than, the impacts of other factors including multilingualism, older age when learning to read, and highly effective instruction?

Q.29 To what extent have Taiwan, Japan, China and South Korea experienced orthographic advantage, and in which dimensions, since changing last century to 2-Stage early literacy, with schools using a beginners' orthography for earliest reading and writing, thus ending the severe orthographic disadvantage they'd experienced until then, when using 1-Stage early literacy with their highly complex orthographies?

Q.30 In what ways can orthographic advantage and disadvantage be observed, and measured, using different research designs, e.g.,
1. Classroom observation and interview?
2. Document analysis?
3. OECD and PIRLS data?
4. World Bank education and economic data?
5. Research studies comparing aspects of school functioning including child and teacher workload, school and learning efficiency, and literacy and academic achievement levels?

Research Questions Section 8: Beginners' Orthographies and 2-Stage Early Literacy

Q.31 What advantages and benefits do children experience in Taiwan, Japan and China doing 2-Stage early-literacy development, and using a fully-regular beginners' orthography, as regards
1. Ease and speed of learning to read and write, and becoming confident, self-teaching, independent readers and writers?
2. Building phonemic, orthographic, executive-function, statistical-learning and self-teaching skills?
3. Empowering self-teaching and independence in reading, writing and learning?
4. Reducing the likelihood of word-reading and spelling difficulties, and the extent of such difficulties?
5. Achieving Success Inoculation and reducing likelihood of developing Acquired Helplessness?
6. Readying children for learning to read and write their complex orthography?
7. Reducing the cognitive load of that learning, through children already being confident and skilled in many aspects of reading and writing?
8. Supporting children's transitioning to reading and writing their complex orthography, e.g., through new or difficult words being written in both scripts?
9. Achieving success in subject-area learning?

Q.32 What advantages might Australian children experience, if, in addition to 2-Stage handwriting development (first printing, then cursive script), Australia actioned 2-Stage early literacy for reading and writing, as per Change 8 of the 10 Changes, with children first reading and writing a fully-regular beginners' orthography?

Q.33 To what extent would this reduce word-reading, spelling and independent reading and writing difficulties, and their severity?
1. In what ways does the effectiveness of instruction and

intervention programs such as GraphoLearn, Comprehension Game, Multilit and Minilit vary for 1-Stage (Standard-English) vs 2-Stage (beginners' orthography) early-literacy cohorts?

Q.34 To what extent would using an English beginners' orthography accommodate, support and enhance language and learning skills:
1. Accommodate weak language skills through weak verbal language skills and cognitive-processing skills being far less likely to result in word-reading and writing difficulties?
2. Support language development through children soon being independent readers and writers who then build language skills through reading and writing?
3. Remove the high cognitive load that stresses Standard-English beginning readers' language and literacy skills, replacing it with more manageable levels of cognitive load?
4. Provide a tool for transitioning to reading and writing the complex orthography?
5. Provide a tool for learning new words and language through text being easily read?

Q.35 What knowledge can be built from (a) survey, interview, and discussion research conducted with researchers and academics in Taiwan, Japan, China and South Korea, and (b) document analysis of research literature written in Taiwanese, Japanese, Chinese, and South Korean research journals, on
1. Children's levels of achievement for accuracy and fluency of word-reading, spelling, written-expression, reading-comprehension, self-teaching and independent reading, writing and learning?
2. The language and literacy skills used in writing samples, e.g., writing for 10 minutes on *Things I like about school*?
3. The extent to which at-risk children experience difficulties with word-reading, spelling and independent reading and writing, in both the initial and complex orthography?
4. The extent to which intervention is successful in overcoming those difficulties?
5. The advantages and disadvantages of those nations having moved from 1-Stage early literacy, using a sole, highly-complex orthography, to all schools first using a highly-regular orthography which was then used to support the children's transitioning to reading and writing their complex orthography?
6. The extent to which advantaging effects are evidenced in the full range of achievers, with reference to thirds, tenths, and the lowest and highest 5% and 2% of achievers?
7. The impacts of age and maturity at start of school?

8. Efficiency and effectiveness of subject-area learning across primary and high-school years?
9. The impacts of numbers of years of instruction, and the effectiveness of each year of instruction?
10. The impacts of other factors that expedite executive-function development, e.g., multilingualism?

Q.36 What knowledge on the above factors, and the effectiveness of English beginners' orthographies and 2-Stage early literacy, can be built, through document analysis of the many research studies on the Initial Teaching Alphabet in the 1960s, still available, some of which we explored in Tour 5 (see Figure 10)?

Q.37 Which beginners' orthography might Australia choose to trial?
1. What can be learned from exploring the features and effectiveness of the Initial Teaching Alphabet (ITA), and Fleksispel with its multiple transitioning stages (Galletly, 2005b, 2023a, In press), as well as the ITA research on effectiveness of different types of beginners' orthographies?

Q.38 In what ways does the effectiveness of intervention for word-reading and writing difficulties vary for
1. Anglophone children doing 1-Stage early literacy, and using solely Standard English, and
2. Anglophone children doing 2-Stage early literacy, and using a fully-regular beginners' orthography, prior to Standard English?

Research Questions Section 9:
The Roles of Word-Reading and Spelling in Crosslinguistic Differences

Q.39 With reference to thirds, tenths, and the lowest and highest 5% and 2% of achievers, what are the progress rates of word-reading and spelling development, and how long does it take to reach the accuracy level of Galletly's 2035 goal (see below), for
1. Anglophone children reading and writing solely Standard English in 1-Stage early literacy?
2. Anglophone children doing 2-Stage early literacy, and reading and writing a beginners' orthography prior to reading and writing Standard English?
3. Children in regular-orthography nations using a sole orthography, e.g., Finland?
4. Children doing 2-Stage early-literacy in Taiwan, Japan and China, using a regular then complex orthography?

The 2035 Goal: By 2035, Australian education will be routinely, efficiently, gently and easily achieving highly effective, rapid development of children's word-reading, spelling, writing and early-literacy skills, in GENTLE manner, in every early-years classroom, in all schools across our nation, as efficiently as is achieved routinely across schools in regular-orthography nations such as Taiwan, Japan and China, with at least 98% of Australian school children being confident, independent readers and writers, able to read 90% of the 10,000 most-frequent words, by age 8.5 years, or within 18 months of starting formal word-reading instruction.

Q.40 In longitudinal crosslinguistic studies of early-literacy development in Standard-English and regular-orthography children, to what extent are crosslinguistic differences more marked for word-reading, spelling, and their underlying cognitive-processing skills, than for other skills?
1. With reference to thirds, tenths, and the lowest and highest 5% and 2% of achievers, are these crosslinguistic differences more marked in weaker readers than advanced readers?

Q.41 What is the value of, and usefulness in, crosslinguistic research of Galletly's model of two levels of automisation and automisation weakness, proposed in Tour 2, with (a) Level 1 Automisation being mastery of accuracy to a proficient level such that skills do not get forgotten, and (b) Level 2 Automisation being mastery of fluency (speed and efficiency) given that
1. Children forgetting word-reading accuracy skills, with progress lost (Level 1 Automisation weakness) is a serious issue in Anglophone nations, in low-progress word readers and spellers, creating workload issues for children and teachers, as skills need to be retaught and relearned.
2. It is likely there are multiple levels within Level 1 Automisation, including (a) the level where children no longer forget a skill, with it then staying accurate, and (b) the level where children are confidently accurate about many aspects of word-reading and spelling, with Level 2 Automisation then able to develop.
3. Difficulties mastering fluency (Level 2 Automisation weakness) is a serious issue for a small number of regular-orthography children with weakness in Rapid Automisation Naming (RAN), creating fluency difficulties which are difficult to overcome.

Q.42 What are the ways forward towards optimising Level 1 and Level 2 Automisation?
1. What are the ways forward towards supporting Standard-

English struggling word-readers to achieve Level 1 Automisation with skills no longer being forgotten?
2. To what extent does Level 1 Automisation weakness occur in Standard-English and regular-orthography children, as regards mastering letter-sounds, word-reading, maths facts, and other learned skills?
3. What are the ways forward towards supporting regular-orthography dysfluent word-readers to achieve Level 2 Automisation with fluent, well-paced reading and writing?
4. To what extent does Level 2 Automisation weakness occur in Standard-English and regular-orthography children, as regards mastering word-reading, counting up and down, and other skills?
5. What extent of Level 1 and Level 2 Automisation do regular-orthography children with intellectual disability who mastered word-reading have (e.g., Cossu et al., 1993)?
6. In what ways do automisation factors differ in the weakest 10% of word-readers in regular-orthography and Anglophone nations?
7. In what ways do automisation factors differ in regular-orthography children with intellectual disability who have mastered word-reading accuracy, and Standard-English word-readers of healthy ability in the weakest 10% of word-readers (See Tours 4 and 14)?
8. In what ways is Level 1 automisation and weakness impacted by
   a. Working-memory capacity?
   b. Efficiency in managing cognitive load?
   c. The high cognitive load that Standard-English developing and struggling readers experience across early literacy?
   d. Interactions between these factors?

Q.43 Does word-reading play a stronger role than spelling in crosslinguistic differences, or are the skills equally important (Weak spelling doesn't often completely impede writing as children usually write spelling approximations, but word-reading difficulties can severely impede reading: blocking reading, discouraging readers, and disrupting comprehension)?

Q.44 Using school data, in what ways are word-reading, spelling and cognitive-processing skill levels similar and different for older *struggling readers* and younger *developing readers*, matched on word-reading or spelling age?

Q.45 What knowledge is built through individuals, schools and districts replicating earlier studies (that compared word-reading levels of Standard-English readers and regular-orthography readers) with Australian children, using the word lists included in research articles,

or obtained by contacting the researchers, to compare results obtained with the results obtained in the original studies, e.g.,
1. Frith et al.'s (1998) and Landerl et al.'s (1997) range of German vs English comparisons?
2. Seymour, Aro & Erskine's (2003) Grade 1 and 2 comparison of children of 14 European nations, including Grade 1 and Grade 2 English readers?
3. Caravolas' (2018) Grade 1 and 2 Slovak vs Czech vs English comparison?
4. Spencer and Hanley's (2003, 2004) Grade 1 and 2, and Hanley et al.'s (2004) Grade 5 Welsh vs English comparison?
5. Oney and Goldman's (1984) Grade 1 to 3 Turkish vs English comparison?

Q.46 What additional knowledge is built when these studies are extended by e.g.,
1. Also using the two subtests of Test of Word Reading Efficiency 2 (TOWRE-2), to include objective measures of word-reading?
2. Also testing spelling and written expression?
3. Also testing cognitive-processing skills, including phonemic awareness, and Rapid Automised Naming (RAN)?
4. Doing collaborative research with schools in relevant regular-orthography nations, to achieve contrasts of Standard-English and regular-orthography readers?
5. Including in this collaborative research a spelling test and writing task, e.g., 10-minutes writing on *Things I like about school*.

Q.47 To what extent is reading unfamiliar words a major Standard-English challenge, for both *developing* and *struggling readers*?

Q.48 With difficulties reading unfamiliar words, particularly multisyllabic words being present in both Hanley et al.'s (2004) Grade 5 English readers, and Frith et al.'s (1998) English 12-year-olds, with weakness also evident in those who seemed readers in other ways, what evidence is found in Australian children in upper-primary and high-school year-levels of difficulties reading and writing unfamiliar words, using the TOWRE-2's two subtests, a spelling test and writing samples?

Q.49 To what extent is reading and writing of unfamiliar words less of an issue for Australian children doing 2-Stage early literacy, and reading and writing a beginners' orthography before transitioning to Standard English?

Q.50 To what extent do Standard-English readers pause more than regular-orthography readers, during reading and writing, working to

resolve unfamiliar words?
1. To what extent does this pausing create high cognitive load, and interrupted thinking and comprehension?

Q.51 What insights are gained by replicating and extending studies of statistical learning investigating word-reading development, including Apfelbaum et al., (2013) and Kyle et al.'s (2013) GraphoLearn study, with Australian children?
1. What insights are gained when these programs, or modified forms thereof, are used with two groups of Australian children: 1-Stage (Standard-English) vs 2-Stage (beginners' orthography) early-literacy cohorts?

Research Questions Section 10: Our Teachers' High Workload

Q.52 What are the impacts on teacher workload and schools, of Australia having severe orthographic disadvantage, e.g., of
1. Impeding of ease and efficiency of early-literacy development?
2. High numbers of struggling readers, many with severe weakness?
3. The challenges of overcoming reading and writing difficulties?
4. The major difficulties with subject-area learning that these children experience?
5. Major difficulties supporting weak learners to successfully complete high school due to their academic struggles?
6. Generational disadvantage, caused by so many children leaving school with poor literacy skills, who then become parents with weak literacy skills who have difficulties readying and supporting their children for school learning?
7. Major difficulties improving education and outcomes due to the above challenges?

Q.53 How does Australian child and teacher workload compare with that of regular-orthography nations with orthographic advantage in these areas?

Q.54 In what ways is teacher workload reduced vs expanded in regular-orthography and Anglophone nations, respectively, by
1. Rapid vs impeded word-reading and spelling development?
2. Rapid vs impeded development of self-teaching, and independence in reading, writing and learning?
3. Low vs high cognitive load across learning to read and write, and when actioning literacy tasks in subject-area learning?
4. Low vs high needs for adult support, due to cognitive load, self-teaching, and independence?

5. Homogeneity vs heterogeneity of word-reading and spelling development (regular-orthography children master word-reading and spelling to a proficient level largely simultaneously, in quite a short period of time, whereas Standard-English word-reading and spelling have highly variable rates of development, and differing skill levels impact teaching in all school years)?

Q.55 When considering the weakest 10% of regular-orthography and Standard-English word-readers and spellers, in what ways, and to what extent, do the more severe reading and writing difficulties of Standard-English readers result in heightened teacher workload, beyond the workload of teachers of regular-orthography readers?

Q.56 In what ways does teacher workload differ for subject-area teaching, in regular-orthography vs Anglophone nations, given that most regular-orthography children are highly accurate, independent readers and writers by Grade 2, while Anglophone teachers have to accommodate and support a wide range of word-reading and writing skills, while working to achieve effectiveness in subject-area teaching and learning, for children who have appreciably weak reading and writing skills across many school years?

Q.57 To what extent, and in which ways, is Australia's high teacher workload relative to regular-orthography nations exacerbated by Australia's much higher numbers of teaching hours, e.g., 200 more hours than Finland, Estonia and Japan (OECD, 2015, 2022)?

Q.58 What knowledge can be built by partner teachers in regular-orthography and Anglophone nations, who record and share data on their daily workload and student learning for a specific unit of subject-area learning taught in all nations?

Q.59 When partner teachers and schools in Anglophone and regular orthography nations measure the word-reading and spelling skills of children in their classes, what additional knowledge is gained on teacher workload, with regard to the extent of workload (a) actually used and (b) which they'd like to have used, had time permitted, for children at different levels of reading and writing ability.

Q.60 What is the cost-benefit ratio that class teachers experience with regard to Australia's *"Nationally Consistent Collection of Data"* (NCCD):
1. The workload time and effort costs of work expended in providing information for the NCCD on children with difficulties and disabilities in their classes, vs
2. The benefits they receive that compensate for the above workload, and provide supports for those children, and

resourcing that enables more effective teaching of these and other children in their classes?

Q.61 What is the level of effectiveness of the many teaching-improvement initiatives that schools implement in response to pressure to increase outcomes, and in what ways do they appreciably support our teachers and their teaching?
1. Given our teachers are already very busy, to what extent does the law of diminishing returns apply, with teaching-improvement initiatives adding to teacher busyness, but not being able to achieve improved teaching and learning?

Q.62 In what ways would Changes 8 and 9 of the 10 Changes reduce teacher workload?
1. In what ways would moving to 2-Stage early literacy reduce teacher workload through heightened early-literacy development, independence and self-teaching?
2. In what ways would adding in 2.5 years of language and learning enrichment at the start of school, and commencing literacy and numeracy instruction in mid-Year 2 reduce teacher workload?
3. What ways would actioning both these changes result in further reductions in teacher workload?

Q.63 To what extent would Australian teachers' workload become more manageable if Australia implemented
1. A reduction of 200 hours of classroom teaching each year, so our teachers taught approximately the same number of hours as teachers in, e.g., Finland?
2. Each classroom teacher having a full-time teacher aide, to provide support in administrative duties, and teaching?
3. More effective national-curriculum resourcing that reduces the amount of work currently done at individual school and teacher level, e.g. of curriculum units, and curriculum-unit supports for weaker learners, and subject-area textbooks and workbooks, incorporating curriculum units?
4. All three of these changes?

Research Questions Section 11: Our Children's High Workload

Q.64 To what extent do children who learn to read and write Standard English as a sole orthography have heightened workload relative to regular-orthography children, because of
1. The additional workload of learning to read and write, which

takes many years?
2. Many children developing word-reading and writing difficulties, thus having additional intervention workload?

Q.65 Using the *Transition from Early to Sophisticated Literacy* (TESL) model (Galletly & Knight, 2011b, see Tour 1, Figure 6), to what extent do Anglophone children using solely Standard English have higher workload than regular-orthography children, whilst trying to do the subject-area learning that all nations do, due to
1. Core Literacy (learning to read and write) taking many years?
2. The high cognitive load of learning to read and write and doing literacy tasks, during Early Literacy and transitioning?
3. Transitioning not being actioned early and homogenously, as happens for regular-orthography children?

Q.66 What are the impacts on child workload of Australia having severe orthographic disadvantage, with its many facets?
1. How does Australian child workload compare with that of children in regular-orthography nations that have orthographic advantage in these areas?

Q.67 To what extent is Australian children's high workload relative to regular-orthography nations exacerbated by having many more hours of schooling each year, e.g., 300 more hours than Finland, Estonia and Japan (OECD, 2015, 2022)?
1. What are the costs and benefits of that 300 extra hours?
2. Does our lack of improvement in PISA, PIRLS and NAPLAN suggest that costs outweigh benefits, and that change is needed?
3. To what extent do regular-orthography nations need less teaching and learning time because of the efficiency of their children's early-literacy development?

Q.68 To what extent would Australian struggling readers be better supported by tailored national-curriculum strands that enable flexible learning, reducing literacy and time demands in learning and assessment tasks, to enable time to build needed earlier skills?

Q.69 In what ways would Changes 8 and 9 of the 10 Changes reduce Australian children's workload?
1. In what ways would moving to 2-Stage early-literacy reduce children's workload through rapid, easy, *Early Literacy*, reduced likelihood of word-reading and spelling difficulties, homogenous *Transitioning from Early to Sophisticated Literacy* (TESL), and more successful subject-area learning due to healthy literacy skills?
2. In what ways would adding in 2.5 years of language and learning enrichment at the start of school, and then

commencing literacy and numeracy instruction in mid-Year 2 reduce our children's workload?
3. In what ways would actioning both changes result in further reductions in children's workload?

Q.70 In what ways would at-risk and struggling readers be more effectively supported, by Australia using a resourcing model whereby, for every 500 enrolled children, schools were resourced with
1. One highly skilled learning-support teacher and four learning-support teacher aides,
2. One speech language pathologist with education training, and four communication aides,
3. One occupational therapist with education training, with four occupational therapy aides,
4. One social worker with education training, and
5. One educational psychologist with education training?

Research Questions Section 12: Differential Disadvantaging of Our At-Risk Learners

Q.71 Using Galletly and Knight's *Differential Disadvantage Theory* (Galletly & Knight, 2011a; see Figure 17a and 17b in Tour 10),
1. To what extent do Anglophone children who learn to read Standard English as a sole orthography experience disadvantage of various types due to lacking the advantages built from initially using a fully-regular beginners' orthography, e.g.,
   a. Ease of learning to self-teach, read and write, and be independent readers and writers,
   b. Cognitive-processing weakness and low intellectual skills not preventing mastery of word-reading and word-writing,
   c. Having strong word-reading and spelling from the first school years,
   d. Having low likelihood of word-reading and writing difficulties,
   e. Word-reading remediation being of short duration and highly successful, and
   f. Strong *Early Literacy* skills expediting independent reading, writing and learning; language development; and *Sophisticated Literacy* learning?
2. To what extent do Anglophone children who start school with weak cognitive-processing skills, and other weak language skills, experience more severe disadvantage, relative to both regular-orthography and Standard-English readers, as per the factors detailed in *Differential Disadvantage Theory*?

The Research Tours: Impacts of Orthographic Disadvantage

Q.72 With reference to thirds, tenths, and the lowest and highest 5% and 2% of achievers, to what extent is differential disadvantage experienced relative to regular-orthography and Standard-English peers, by higher and lower achievers as regards word-reading, spelling, language skills, independent reading and writing, subject-area learning and effectiveness in completing tests and assignments?
1. What factors heighten differential disadvantage?
2. To what extent did Taiwan, Japan, China and South Korea reduce differential disadvantage by moving to 2-Stage early literacy, using a beginners' orthography for earliest literacy?
3. To what extent would Anglophone nations reduce differential disadvantage by moving to 2-stage early literacy, with a beginners' orthography?
4. Would differential disadvantage be reduced further, and more effectively by the inclusion of other changes such as Change 9: language and learning enrichment for the first 2.5 school years, which also enables time for needed remediation and heightening of needed pre-skills?
5. What research methods can be used to explore differential disadvantage e.g., analysis of the skill levels and extent of disadvantage experienced by individual children, class and school cohorts, and cohorts in isolated aboriginal communities?

Research Questions Section 13: Motivation, Engagement, Persistence, and Resilience

Q.73 Using Maier and Seligman's revised form of Learned Helplessness (Maier & Seligman, 2015), and with reference to thirds, tenths, and the lowest and highest 5% and 2% of achievers, to what extent are *Acquired Helplessness* and *Success Inoculation* (Knight & Galletly, 2017b) present in higher and lower-achieving regular-orthography and Standard-English readers for skills such as word-reading, spelling, language skills, and skills used in independent reading and writing, subject-area learning and effectiveness in assessment situations, including school tests and assignments?

Q.74 What are the characteristics of Acquired Helplessness and Success Inoculation for word-reading development in Standard-English and regular-orthography readers, with reference to thirds, tenths, and the lowest and highest 5% and 2% of achievers?
1. What are the characteristics as regards other literacy and language skills and academic learning?

The 100 Research Questions

Research Questions Section 14: Young Vs Older Starting Age When Learning to Read

Q.75 What differences, in the impact of age when starting school, and of years of schooling, are found in comparing children in Australian and Anglophone nations with children in regular-orthography nations e.g., when 8-year-old, Year-3, Australian children, in fourth year of formal literacy and numeracy education, are compared with 8-year-old, Grade-2, Finnish children in second year of formal learning?
1. To what extent does young age at start of school interact with other factors, e.g., low Literate Cultural Capital, and weak language skills?

Q.76 What evidence of advantage and disadvantage as regards impacts of young vs older age when children start school is found in teacher knowledge-building in cooperative exchange visits and ongoing partnerships?

Q.77 What can be learned through crosslinguistic studies that match both age-level and year-level, using general observations, record-keeping, teaching of an identical unit of work, and analysis of children's work samples, with, e.g., Australian Year 4 teachers working in partnership, with both Grade 2 (age-matching) and Grade 5 (year-level matching) teachers in Finland or Estonia?

Q.78 What impacts are noted with regard to the numbers of years of instruction children have received, and the effectiveness of each year of instruction, in crosslinguistic studies of various types that Australia conducts with regular-orthography nations?
1. What impacts are noted for other factors that expedite executive-function development, e.g., being proficiently multilingual prior to starting school?

Q.79 How might teaching and learning in 1-Stage and 2-Stage early literacy be enhanced by children being older when learning to read?

Research Questions Section 15: Models for Guiding Research and Practice

Q.80 For at-risk and struggling readers, both at start of school and across the school years, through its inclusion of the three areas of weakness experienced, (weakness in language skills, literacy skills, and school learning), in what ways is the term *Language, Literacy and Learning Disorder* (LLLD) a useful overarching term for use by Australian school systems?

Q.81 What is the potential of the two models, (a) Pennington's

Multiple Deficits Model, and (b) Knight, Galletly & April's *Literacy Component Model,* and, for our weaker learners, (c) the term *Language, Literacy and Learning Disorder* (LLLD), for use, separately and in integrated fashion, as a framework for research and practice in Australian education and research focused on improving early-literacy, literacy, and learning, as Australia works to optimise early-literacy development in healthy-progress *developing readers,* at-risk readers, and *struggling readers?*

Q.82 How effectively do the term and models work as overarching models, with regard to other pertinent models that are useful and relevant in research and practice, such as

1. *Orthographic Advantage Theory?*
2. *Cognitive Load Theory?*
3. The *Literacy Component Model,* with
   a. Its equations for both reading and writing, which support quadrant use,
   b. Its focus on factors underlying and supporting reading and writing, and
   c. It being a flexible model with schools and researchers encouraged to modify it, to highlight emphases they prioritise (Knight et al., 2021).
4. The term *Language, Literacy and Learning Disorder* (LLLD), explored in Tour 6?
5. The *Transition from Early to Sophisticated Literacy* (TESL) model, discussed in Tour 1?
6. The model of automisation levels, discussed in Tour 2: Level 1 being proficient accuracy, and Level 2 being proficient fluency?

Q.83 In what ways do schools find these models useful?

Q.84 In what ways might Galletly's 10 Changes, ABCs, 2035 Goal, Mantra, and 20-item list for Australian education positioning word-reading appropriately within literacy instruction, be useful tools and checkpoints for use in Australia's education-improvement journey (Galletly, 2022a, 2022b)?

Research Questions Section 16: School Instruction and Assessment Practices

Q.85 Are there certain types of reading instruction which accelerate Standard-English word-reading and writing development, such that Australian and regular-orthography word-reading and writing development occur at similar rates, and Australia might achieve Galletly's 2035 goal, whilst using solely Standard English, without

The 100 Research Questions

a fully-regular beginners' orthography?

Q.86 What levels of resourcing would be needed to achieve this effectiveness of instruction routinely across Australian schools?
1. Is it possible for Australia to achieve the 2035 goal using Standard-English in 1-Stage early literacy, with 98% of children having efficient word-reading, or will Changes 8 and 9 need to be actioned, for this to be achieved?
2. With reference to thirds, tenths and the lowest 5% and 2% of achievers, what factors are involved in Standard-English weak word-readers making quite minimal progress from intervention relative to the gains made by regular-orthography weaker readers, as discussed in Tour 14?

Q.87 To what extent do parents in Anglophone and regular-orthography nations differ on literacy levels, and ability to support and encourage their children's early language and pre-school literacy development, and support their children's school progress?
1. To what extent do Anglophone nations perpetuate a cycle of generational disadvantage through their inability to resolve the word-reading and writing difficulties of many children, who consequently leave school with weak literacy and academic skills, then later, as parents, are insufficiently able to build their children's phonological and language skills and Literate Cultural Capital?
2. In what ways do the school achievement paths differ for regular-orthography and Anglophone children who commence school with low levels of language skills, phonological awareness skills, or Literate Cultural Capital?

Q.88 To what extent do regular-orthography and Anglophone nations differ in the importance of reading instruction being rigorous and research based; and the impact of beyond-classroom factors, e.g., teacher planning time, levels of teacher-aide resourcing, word-reading development taking many years, and thus being impacted by multiple teachers with possibly differing expertise levels, and children possibly having year-to-year inconsistency of reading-instruction methods?
1. How do these factors differ for
   a. Children of higher and lower achievement levels, with reference to thirds, tenths, and the lowest and highest 5% and 2% of achievers?
   b. Use of 1-Stage vs 2-Stage early-literacy development?
   c. Orthographies of different types, including fully-regular and highly-regular orthographies, fully-regular beginners' and transitional orthographies, and Standard English?

Research Questions Section 17: Executive-Function Skills and Learning

Q.89 What executive-function skills are involved in the many early-literacy crosslinguistic differences between Anglophone and regular-orthography nations, including
1. The slowed, impeded nature of Standard-English word-reading and spelling development?
2. The impeded statistical-learning our Standard-English readers experience due to our overlapping GPCs?
3. Our children's young age perhaps exacerbating our impeded development of word-reading and writing, through insufficiently mature executive-function skills?
4. Reading and writing of unfamiliar words being a challenge for both developing and struggling Standard-English word-readers, even in upper-primary and high-school years?
5. The likelihood of developing Success Inoculation and Acquired Helplessness?
6. Impacts of Success Inoculation and Acquired Helplessness?
7. Low vs high cognitive load and learning complexity?
8. Needs for effective cognitive-processing and executive-function skills to manage cognitive load and learning complexity?
9. Environmental and genetic factors in reading difficulties, e.g., Australian children seem to have higher rates of inherited weakness when family history is considered, but this may be a consequence of our having very high rates of literacy difficulties, more than genetic predisposition?

Q.90 What executive-function interventions and tests are likely to become routinely used in Australian schools in the next few decades?
1. What easy-to-use tests of different executive-function skills are relevant and practical for use in schools?
2. What programs of prevention and intervention are useful for building executive-function skills for literacy learning?

Q.91 What executive-function skills are useful to focus on and explore, in school instruction, skill monitoring, and research?
1. Are working memory, cognitive flexibility, and inhibition control, which are often considered the three key executive-function skills, necessary and sufficient as skills beneficial for schools to test and monitor or should others be considered?
2. Given that working memory is often considered more as cognitive-processing capacity than as an actioning skill, might *Efficiency in Managing Cognitive Load* be a better executive-function skill, with working memory then positioned as a

subskill of that efficiency?
   a. Alternatively, if working memory is retained, should *Efficiency in Managing Cognitive Load* be included as an additional executive-function skill?
3. To what extent might there be value in also including executive-function skills such as self-regulation, actioning and completing tasks effectively, and listening for, and following instructions?

Research Questions Section 18: The Ethics of Our Status Quo

Q.92 Is it ethically appropriate for Australia's most disadvantaged children, including children with intellectual disability and children with many, major risk factors, to be quite possibly experiencing greatest disadvantage, as regards likelihood of mastering reading and writing, through being born in Australia, rather than in a regular-orthography nation, given that their likelihood of success there is high, but at present low in Australia, because we use a highly complex orthography as a sole orthography, without a beginners' orthography?
1. Is it ethically appropriate that our adults and children with significant word-reading and spelling difficulties are similarly disadvantaged, given that regular-orthography intervention is highly successful, with children catching up to age level then continuing with healthy progress?
2. Is it ethically appropriate for Australia to continue using Standard-English orthography as a sole orthography if using Standard English as a sole orthography impedes early-literacy development, and increases the likelihood of word-reading and writing difficulties, and the likelihood that remediation will not be highly effective?
3. With orthographies, and orthographic changes such as the introduction of a beginners' orthography, being sociocultural choices that nations make, are there issues of responsibility for the severe disadvantage that is currently experienced by at-risk and struggling Australian word-readers and spellers?

Q.93 Given that Australian teachers have high workload relative to regular-orthography nations, what ethical issues are involved in our teachers being required to teach approximately 200 more classroom hours per year than teachers in many leading nations?
1. What extent of off-class time is required for administrative and other duties per teaching hour, in the range of teaching contexts?

Q.94 What ethical issues are involved in Australian states and territories using *cognitive referencing* (discussed in Tour 6): highly

restrictive criteria for children's eligibility for Special Education funding for their schools; and extremely low eligibility cut-points, at first and second percentile for e.g. language disorder; with little allowance for multiple disabilities with scores just outside those cut-points?
1. When our Education Act and disability documents do not set requirements that disability categories must be used?
2. When our Education Act and disability documents imply that schools should be effectively resourced, so children aren't disadvantaged by the education they receive?
3. When other nations that use disability categories, in particular, USA, use considerably more disability categories, and far less restrictive criteria, such that much higher proportions of children receive disability supports,
4. When *diagnostic labelling* (the requirement that children must obtain a disability diagnosis to be eligible for Special Education) can be disadvantaging for children,
5. When many children aren't found eligible due to their families having difficulty pursuing the appointments and challenges involved in obtaining a diagnosis,
6. When it's likely children's needs can be more effectively met by schools being resourced on a needs basis rather than families having to pursue *diagnostic labelling*, and
7. When schools need far more resourcing than is currently provided to meet the needs of children with disabilities?

Q.95 What discrepancies are found present between
1. The teaching and supports that class teachers are able to achieve in current teaching circumstances,
2. The teaching and supports teachers feel are needed, and
3. The instructional and support needs of at-risk and struggling Australian learners, including
   a. Children starting school with *established* vs *emerging* needs, and
   b. Children receiving Special Education disability funding vs children with similarly severe needs who've not been found eligible for funding?

Research Questions Section 19:
The Impacts of Beliefs on Change

Q.96 To what extent are inaccurate, inherited beliefs, from dominant thinking of previous decades, present in Australian academics, teachers, professionals working with school-aged children, and families, e.g.,
1. That the impacts that orthographies and orthographic

complexity have on literacy development and education are minor, and relatively inconsequential?
2. That assessing word-reading and monitoring word-reading development is inappropriate, and even harmful?
3. That effective teaching of Standard-English word-reading is all that is needed to achieve proficient word-reading in the vast majority of at-risk and struggling word-readers, including the weakest 10% of word-readers?
4. That the much stronger early-literacy development and high levels of word-reading and spelling achievement of regular-orthography nations are irrelevant to Anglophone nations?
5. That average levels of word-reading and spelling by Standard-English norms represent effective achievement, and should be the goal that education in Anglophone nations should aspire to?

Q.97 How might such beliefs be reconsidered, if discussions were focused on facts and data, e.g., through Australia assessing the word-reading and language skills (including cognitive-processing and executive-function skills), of a 10% sample of Years 3, 5, 7 and 9 children in one NAPLAN round, providing detailed analysis of this data and data on the other skills tested each year in NAPLAN?

Research Questions Section 20: Our Education Future

Q.98 What potential does Australian education have for achieving marked improvement, if it actively focuses on optimising early-literacy development, with awareness of current crosslinguistic differences, and the value of exploring both optimising of current instruction, and strategic changes?

Q.99 What knowledge will be built through Australia actively exploring four strategic strands, to carefully investigate both the separate and combined benefits of actioning Changes 8 and 9 of the 10 Changes:
1. Working to achieve optimal Standard-English word-reading instruction that starts in Prep (Foundation), with all needed resourcing provided,
2. Holding back formal Standard-English instruction until mid-Year 2, with the first 2.5 school years being language and learning enrichment (with options of an earlier start for advanced learners using play-based learning),
3. Using a fully-regular beginners' orthography, and starting word-reading instruction in Prep, and
4. Holding back both the beginners' orthography and formal word-

reading instruction until mid-Year 2, with the first 2.5 school years being language and learning enrichment (with earlier start options for advanced learners using play-based learning)?

Q.100 Which of the three *roads* explored in Tour 6 will Australia find most helpful in its improvement journey:
1. The *Effective Education Road*: using 2-Stage early literacy and a beginners' orthography (Change 8),
2. The *Pre-School Child Road*: the Heckman equation road, a more expensive path, with intensive work with our children from earliest childhood used to increase the odds of achieving well at school, or
3. The *Enhanced Effective Education Road*, a middle road combining the above two roads, actioning both Changes 8 and 9, with pre-school supports provided as needed, but with these likely to be far less in demand, because our children would begin school with 2.5 years of language and learning enrichment, with ample opportunities for intervention where it's needed?

About thirty per cent of Australian children who are leaving the school system in Australia are functionally illiterate.
Brendan Nelson, Federal Minister for Education, 2005

Australian schooling will place the highest priority on
a) identifying and addressing the needs of school students, including barriers to learning and wellbeing; and
b) providing additional support to school students who require it.
Australian Government, 2013 *Australian Education Act*

Our goal is to create educational contexts
that enhance the learning of all students.
For those students with special needs,
we must ensure that the most effective means
are used to achieve this goal.
Christa van Kraayenoord, 2006

It always seems impossible until it's done.
Nelson Mandela

Thanks

Many thanks to everyone involved in the contents of this book and its preparation. I am enormously grateful for, and forever humbled by, your generous contributions.

Particular thanks go to Emeritus Professor Bruce Knight, for his guidance, support and leadership across the decades; to Emeritus Professor Heikki Lyytinen, for his input and writing the foreword to this book; and to Bev Lenton, Glenys Goodingham, Mark and Marion Gibbs, and Judy Morris, for their wonderful, exhausting, time-consuming work, in reading, critiquing, editing and advising, for this book and its partners.

Thank you so much!

Reference Resources

The resources in this section are provided to support readers in locating and searching out reference information discussed in this book. The resources include

1. A List of Tables included in the book.
2. A List of Figures included in the book.
3. A list of all references cited in the book.
4. A detailed Table of Contents that includes subsection headings.
5. An Index of key topics, with associated page numbers.

A reader's reflection guide is also available on the book's website: www.susangalletly.com.au.

List of Tables

Table 1. Word-reading and child age in nations ordered by extent of orthographic complexity (Knight & Galletly, 2017, using data from Seymour et al., 2003) 34

Table 2. 2021 NAPLAN Year 3 low achievers (≤NMS) 244

Table 3. 2021 NAPLAN Year 3, 5, 7 and 9 low achievers for spelling (% of cohort ≤NMS) 247

Table 4. Double Deficit features of Standard-English and regular-orthography weak readers (from Galletly, 2005b) 293

Table 5. States and territories' entry dates for Foundation year-level 325

List of Figures

Figure 1. Our needs for the 10 Changes (Galletly 2022a, In press) 9

Figure 2a. Text using Stage-1 Fleksispel (Galletly, 2005b, 2023a, In press) 22

Figure 2b. Fleksispel: Stage-1 GPCs (Galletly, 2022a, 2023a) 23

Figure 3. Phonemic recoding (Alphabetic Principle), showing the skills and single-stage learning of regular-orthography word-reading and spelling (Knight et al., 2017b, 2019) 31

Figure 4. Phonological recoding: the multiple stages of learning to read and write Standard English (Galletly, 2008, adapted) 32

Figure 5. Queensland word-reading age-levels in Years 1, 3, 5 and 7 (Knight & Galletly, 2006; Knight et al., 2017a) 40

Figure 6. Transition from Early to Sophisticated Literacy (TESL) for Standard-English and regular-orthography readers (Galletly & Knight, 2011b, Knight et al., 2017a, 2019) 57

Figure 7. Number of words read correctly by Grade 1 and 2 Welsh and English readers (Spencer & Hanley, 2003) 68

Figure 8. Standard Deviation (SD) groups (% of population) with percentile cut-points for a Normal Distribution (Bell Curve) 72

Figure 9a. Word-reading levels of Standard Deviation (SD) groups for Hanley et al.'s (2004) Grade 5 weaker 50% of Welsh and English readers, in table form 73

Figure 9b. Word-reading levels of Standard Deviation (SD) groups in bar graph form for Hanley et al.'s (2004) Grade 5 weaker 50% of Welsh and English readers, ... 74

Figure 9c. Unfamiliar-word word-reading levels of Standard Deviation (SD) groups in Hanley et al.'s (2004) Grade 5 Welsh and English readers 75

Figure 10. The Initial Teaching Alphabet (ITA) 119

Figure 11. The Literacy Component Model (Knight et al., 2021) .. 212

Figure 12a. Quadrants for reading-comprehension subskills: word-reading and language skills (Knight et al., 2021)....................... 219

Figure 12b. Quadrants for written-expression subskills: word-writing (spelling) and language skills (Knight et al., 2021)..................... 219

Figure 13a. Quadrant distributions of Leach et al.'s (2003) Grade 4-5 readers 227

Figure 13b. Quadrant distributions of Leach et al.'s (2003) children with early vs late-emerging reading difficulties......................... 229

Figure 14. Mean reading scores of Anglophone nations, PISA 2000 to 2018.. 241

Figure 15. 2021 NAPLAN Year 3, 5, 7, 9 low achievers (% of cohort ≤NMS) for reading, written expression and spelling................... 245

Figure 16. Orthographic Advantage Theory (Galletly & Knight, 2004; Knight et al., 2017a, 2017b, 2019) 264

Figure 17a. Model of Differential Disadvantage of Anglophone children: Part 1: Disadvantage against regular-orthography weak readers (Galletly & Knight, 2011a, adapted).............................. 290

Figure 17b. Model of Differential Disadvantage of Anglophone children, Part 2: Disadvantage relative to Standard-English peers (Galletly & Knight, 2011a, adapted)... 291

Figure 18a. Double-deficit quadrants for Skills 1 and 2................. 295

Figure 18b. Standard-English double-deficit quadrants for phonological awareness and Rapid Automised Naming (RAN).. 297

Figure 19 a. & b. Word-reading levels of Standard Deviation (SD) groups for Caravolas' (2018) Grade 2 Slovak and English readers, in (a) table, and (b) line-graph form 354

Figure 20a. Word-reading levels of Standard Deviation (SD) groups for Frith et al.'s (1998) weaker 50% German and English 7-year-old readers, in table form 360

Figure 20b. Word-reading levels of Standard Deviation (SD) groups for Frith et al.'s (1998) weaker 50% of German and English 7-year-old readers, in line-graph form 361

Reference list

1. Abu-Rabia, S. (2001). The role of vowels in reading Semitic scripts: Data from Arabic and Hebrew. *An Interdisciplinary Journal*, 14(1), 39-59.
2. Adams, M. J. (1990). *Beginning to read: Thinking and learning about print.* Cambridge, Mass: MIT Press.
3. Adlof, S. M., Catts, H. W., & Little, T. D. (2006). Should the Simple View of Reading include a fluency component? *Reading and Writing*, *19*, 933–958.
4. Adlof, S. M., & Hogan, T. P. (2018). Understanding dyslexia in the context of developmental language disorders. *Language, Speech, and Hearing Services in Schools*, 49(4), 762-773.
5. Ahmed, H., Wilson, A., Mead, N., Noble, H., Richardson, U., Wolpert, M. A., & Goswami, U. (2020). An evaluation of the efficacy of GraphoGame Rime for promoting English phonics knowledge in poor readers. *Frontiers in Education* (Lausanne), 5, 132.
6. Al Otaiba, S., & Fuchs, D. (2002). Characteristics of children who are unresponsive to early literacy intervention: A review of the literature. *Remedial and Special Education*, 23(5), 300-316.
7. Al Otaiba, S., & Fuchs, D. (2006). Who are the young children for whom best practices in reading are ineffective?: An experimental and longitudinal study. *Journal of Learning Disabilities*, 39(5), 414-431.
8. Alloway, T. P., Tewolde, F., Skipper, D., & Hijar, D. (2017). Can you spell dyslexia without SLI? Comparing the cognitive profiles of dyslexia and specific language impairment and their roles in learning. *Research in Developmental Disabilities*, 65, 97-102.
9. American Psychiatric Association (APA). (2013). *Diagnostic and Statistical Manual of Mental Disorders* (DSM-5), Fifth edition. American Psychiatic Association.
10. Anderson, J. F. (2021). *My research journey with the Initial Teaching Alphabet* (ITA). www.itafoundation.org.
11. Anderson, P. J., Lee, K. J., Roberts, G., Spencer-Smith, M. M., Thompson, D. K., Seal, M. L., … Pascoe, L. (2018). Long-term academic functioning following Cogmed working memory

training for children born extremely preterm: A randomized controlled trial. *The Journal of Pediatrics*, 202, 92-97.e94.

12. Anderson, S. A., Hawes, D. J., & Snow, P. C. (2016). Language impairments among youth offenders: A systematic review. *Children and Youth Services Review*, 65, 195-203.

13. Angus, M., Olney, H., & Ainley, J. (2007). *In the balance: The future of Australia's primary schools*. Canberra: Australian Primary Principals Association (APPA).

14. Angus, M., Olney, H., Selleck, R., Ainley, J., Burke, G., Caldwell, B. & Spinks, J. (2004). *The sufficiency of resources for Australian primary schools*. Canberra: Department of Education, Science and Training.

15. Apfelbaum, K. S., Hazeltine, E., & McMurray, B. (2013). Statistical learning in reading: Variability in irrelevant letters helps children learn phonics skills. *Developmental Psychology*, *49*(7), 1348-1365.

16. Arciuli, J. (2018). Reading as statistical learning. *Language, Speech and Hearing Services in Schools (Online)*, *49*(3S), 634-643.

17. Arciuli, J., & Simpson, I. C. (2012). Statistical learning is related to reading ability in children and adults. *Cognitive Science*, *36*(2), 286-304.

18. Aro, M. (2004). *Learning to read: The effect of orthography*. Thesis: University of Jyvaskyla.

19. Aro, M. (2017a). Learning to read Finnish. In L. T. W. Verhoeven & C. A. Perfetti (Eds.), *Learning to read across languages and writing systems* (pp. 416-436). Cambridge University Press.

20. Aro, M. (2017b). *What is special about Special Education in Finland?* Keynote presentation at the opening conference of The Center for Justice in Education, Pontificial University of Santiago de Chile, Santiago de Chile, Chile, 8.11.2017.

21. Aro, T., Eklund, K., Eloranta, A.-K., Ahonen, T., & Rescorla, L. (2022). Learning disabilities elevate children's risk for behavioral-emotional problems: Differences between LD types, genders, and contexts. *Journal of Learning Disabilities*, 55(6), 465-481.

22. Aro, T., Poikkeus, A.-M., Laakso, M.-L., Tolvanen, A., & Ahonen, T. (2015). Associations between private speech, behavioral self-regulation, and cognitive abilities. *International Journal of Behavioral Development*, 39(6), 508-518.

23. Aram, D., Abiri, S., & Elad, L. (2014). Predicting early spelling: The contribution of children's early literacy, private speech during spelling, behavioral regulation, and parental spelling support. *Reading and Writing, 27*(4), 685-707.
24. Ashkenazi, S., Black, J. M., Abrams, D. A., Hoeft, F., & Menon, V. (2013). Neurobiological underpinnings of math and reading learning disabilities. *Journal of Learning Disabilities, 46*(6), 549-569.
25. AUSPELD. (2019). *Understanding learning difficulties: a practical guide for teachers, Revised ed.* www.auspeld.org.au.
26. Austin, C. R., Vaughn, S., & McClelland, A. M. (2017). Intensive Reading interventions for inadequate responders in Grades K–3: A synthesis. *Learning Disability Quarterly, 40*(4), 191-210.
27. Australian Bureau of Statistics. (2013). 2011-2012 Programme for the International Assessment of Adult Competencies (PIAAC): Preliminary findings. www.abs.gov.au.
28. Australian Curriculum Assessment and Reporting Authority (ACARA). (2021). *National Assessment Program Literacy and Numeracy (NAPLAN): Achievement in reading, writing, language conventions and numeracy: National report for 2021.* www.nap.edu.au.
29. Australian Education Research Organisation (AERO, 2022), *Writing development:What does a decade of NAPLAN data reveal?* edresearch.edu.au.
30. Australian Government (2015). Australian Education Act 2013, including amendments. www.legislation.gov.au.
31. Australian Government. (2005a). Disability Discrimination Act 1992, including amendments. www.legislation.gov.au.
32. Australian Government. (2005b). Disability Standards for Education 2005. www.legislation.gov.au.
33. Australian Institute for Health & Welfare (AIHW), (2020). *Australia's children.* www.aihw.gov.au
34. Australian Primary Principals Association (APPA). (2008a). *Delivering better educational outcomes in Australian primary schools: Submission to the Commonwealth Minister for Education regarding quadrennial funding for 2009-2012.* www.appa.asn.au.
35. Australian Primary Principals Association (APPA). (2008b). *Position paper: Australian Primary Principals Association.* www.appa.asn.au.

36. Australian Primary Principals Association (APPA). (2020). *The impact of childhood anxiety on primary schooling.* www.appa.asn.au.
37. Babayigit, S. (2022). Does a truly symmetrically transparent orthography exist? Spelling is more difficult than reading even in an orthography considered highly transparent for both reading and spelling. *Reading and Writing, 35*(10), 2453-2472.
38. Bach, S., Richardson, U., Brandeis, D., Martin, E., & Brem, S. (2013). Print-specific multimodal brain activation in kindergarten improves prediction of reading skills in second grade. *NeuroImage, 82*, 605-615.
39. Bailey, L., & Challen, A. (2012). The UK Penn resilience programme: A summary of research and implementation. *The Psychology of Education Review, 36*(2), 32-39.
40. Baker, S., Berninger, V. W., Bruck, M., et al. (2002). Evidence-based research on Reading Recovery: Reading Recovery is not successful with its targeted student population, the lowest performing students. *Education News (EducationNews.org)*, www.wrightslaw.com.
41. Barac, R., Bialystok, E., Castro, D. C., & Sanchez, M. (2014). The cognitive development of young dual language learners: A critical review. *Early Childhood Research Quarterly, 29*(4), 699-714.
42. Barac, R., Moreno, S., & Bialystok, E. (2016). Behavioral and electrophysiological differences in executive control between monolingual and bilingual children. *Child Dev, 87*(4), 1277-1290.
43. Bar-Kochva, I., & Breznitz, Z. (2012). Does the reading of different orthographies produce distinct brain activity patterns? An ERP study. *PLoS ONE, 7*(5).
44. Bedard, K., & Dhuey, E. (2006). The persistence of early childhood maturity: International evidence of long-run age effects. *The Quarterly Journal of Economics, 121*(4), 1437-1472.
45. Bedard, K., & Dhuey, E. (2012). School-entry policies and skill accumulation across directly and indirectly affected individuals. *The Journal of Human Resources, 47*(3), 643-683.
46. Berent, I., & Perfetti, C. A. (1995). A rose is a REEZ: The two-cycles model of phonology assembly in reading English. *Psychological Review, 102*(1), 146-184.
47. Bialystok, E. (2015). Bilingualism and the development of executive function: The role of attention. *Child Development*

Perspectives, 9(2), 117-121.

48. Biemiller, A. (2003). Vocabulary: Needed if more children are to read well. *Reading Psychology, 24*, 323-335.
49. Bishop, D. V. M., Snowling, M. J., Thompson, P. A., & Greenhalgh, T. (2016). CATALISE: A multinational and multidisciplinary Delphi consensus study. Identifying language impairments in children. *PLoS ONE, 11*(7).
50. Bishop, D. V. M., Snowling, M. J., Thompson, P. A., Greenhalgh, T., Adams, C., et al. (2017). Phase 2 of CATALISE: a multinational and multidisciplinary Delphi consensus study of problems with language development: Terminology. *Journal of Child Psychology and Psychiatry, 58*(10), 1068-1080.
51. Block, J. R. (1966). A critique of research with the initial teaching alphabet and some recommendations. i.t.a. Foundation Report. https://eric.ed.gov.
52. Block, J. R. (1968). *i.t.a as a language arts medium.* Proceedings of the Fourth International i.t.a Conference, August 1967, McGill University, Montreal. https://eric.ed.gov.
53. Block, J. R. (1971). I.T.A A status report - 1971: The beginning of a second decade. https://eric.ed.gov.
54. Boivin, M. J., Kakooza, A. M., Warf, B. C., Davidson, L. L., & Grigorenko, E. L. (2015). Reducing neurodevelopmental disorders and disability through research and interventions. *Nature, 527*(7578), S155-S160.
55. Borleffs, E., Maassen, B. A. M., Lyytinen, H., & Zwarts, F. (2017). Measuring orthographic transparency and morphological-syllabic complexity in alphabetic orthographies: a narrative review. *Reading and Writing, 30*(8), 1617-1638.
56. Borleffs, E., Maassen, B. A. M., Lyytinen, H., & Zwarts, F. (2019). Cracking the code: The impact of orthographic transparency and morphological-syllabic complexity on reading and developmental dyslexia. *Frontiers in Psychology, 9*(1), 2534-2534.
57. Bowen, C. (2018). Developmental Language Disorder: #DevLangDis. *Journal of Clinical Practice in Speech-Language Pathology, 20*(1), 35-40.
58. Bower, A., & Hayes, A. (1994). Short-term memory deficits and Down Syndrome: A comparative study. *Down Syndrome Research and Practice, 2*(2), 47-50.
59. Boyle, S. A., McNaughton, D., & Chapin, S. E. (2019). Effects of

shared reading on the early language and literacy skills of children with Autism Spectrum Disorders: A systematic review. *Focus on Autism and Other Developmental Disabilities.*

60. Bruno, J. L., Manis, F. R., Keating, P., Sperling, A. J., Nakamoto, J., & Seidenberg, M. S. (2007). Auditory word identification in dyslexic and normally achieving readers. *Journal of Experimental Child Psychology, 97*(3), 183-204.

61. Buckingham, J., Beaman-Wheldall, R., & Wheldall, K. (2014). Evaluation of a two-phase experimental study of a small group (MultiLit) reading intervention for older low-progress readers. *Cogent education, 1*(1).

62. Buckingham, J., Wheldall, K., & Beaman, R. (2012). A randomised control trial of a Tier-2 small-group intervention ('MiniLit') for young struggling readers1. *Australian Journal of Learning Difficulties, 17*(2), 79-99.

63. Burgoyne, K., Duff, F. J., Clarke, P. J., Buckley, S., Snowling, M. J., & Hulme, C. (2012). Efficacy of a reading and language intervention for children with Down syndrome: a randomized controlled trial. *J. Child Psychology and Psychiatry, 53*(10), 1044-1053.

64. Bushnell, M. (1971). *I/t/a/ news.* https://eric.ed.gov.

65. Byrne, B. (1998). *The foundation of literacy: The child's acquisition of the alphabetic principle.* Hove: Psychology Press.

66. Cadime, I., Rodrigues, B., Santos, S., Viana, F. L., Chaves-Sousa, S., do Céu Cosme, M., & Ribeiro, I. (2017). The role of word recognition, oral reading fluency and listening comprehension in the Simple View of Reading: a study in an intermediate depth orthography. *Reading and Writing, 30*(3), 591-611.

67. Cain, K., & Oakhill, J. (2006). Assessment matters: issues in the measurement of reading comprehension. *The British Journal of Educational Psychology, 76*(4), 697.

68. Caldwell, B. J. (2016). Professional autonomy, school innovation and student achievement in the 21st century. *Australian Educational Leader, 38*(4), 9-13.

69. Caldwell, B. J., & Spinks, J. M. (2008). *Raising the stakes: From improvement to transformation in the reform of schools.* London: Routledge.

70. Campbell, F. A., Pungello, E. P., Kainz, K., Burchinal, M., Pan, Y., Wasik, B. H., Barbarin, O., Sparling, J. J., & Ramey, C. T. (2012). Adult outcomes as a function of an early childhood

educational program: An abecedarian project follow-up. *Developmental Psychology, 48*(4), 1033-1043.

71. Campbell, F. A., Conti, G., Heckman, J. J., Moon, S. H., Pinto, R., Pungello, E. P., & Pan, Y. (2014). Early childhood investments substantially boost adult health. *Science, 343*(6178), 1478–1485.

72. Caravolas, M. (2004). Spelling development in alphabetic writing systems: A cross-linguistic perspective. *European Psychologist, 9*(1), 3-14.

73. Caravolas, M. (2018). Growth of word and pseudoword reading efficiency in alphabetic orthographies: Impact of consistency. *Journal of Learning Disabilities, 51*(5), 422-433.

74. Caravolas, M., Lervåg, A., Defior, S., Seidlová Málková, G., & Hulme, C. (2013). Different patterns, but equivalent predictors, of growth in reading in consistent and inconsistent orthographies. *Psychological Science, 24*(8), 1398-1407.

75. Caravolas, M., Kessler, B., Hulme, C., & Snowling, M. (2005). Effects of orthographic consistency, frequency, and letter knowledge on children's vowel spelling development. *Journal of Experimental Child Psychology, 92*(4), 307-321.

76. Carroll, J. B., Davies, P., & Richman, B. (1971). *The American heritage word frequency book.* Boston: Houghton Mifflin.

77. Carroll, J. M., Solity, J., & Shapiro, L. R. (2016). Predicting dyslexia using prereading skills: The role of sensorimotor and cognitive abilities. *J. of Child Psychology and Psychiatry, 57*(6), 750-758.

78. Carson, K. L. (2020). Can an app a day keep illiteracy away? Piloting the efficacy of Reading Doctor apps for preschoolers with developmental language disorder. *International Journal of Speech-Language Pathology, 22*(4), 454-465.

79. Catts, H. W. (2018). The Simple View of Reading: Advancements and false impressions. *Remedial and Special Education, 39*(5), 317-323.

80. Catts, H. W., & Hogan, T. P. (2003). Language basis of reading disabilities and implications for early identification and remediation. *Reading Psychology, 24*, 223-246.

81. Catts, H. W., Adlof, S. M., Hogan, T. P., & Weismer., S. E. (2005). Are specific language impairment and dyslexia distinct disorders? *J. of Speech, Language, and Hearing Research, 48*(6), 1378-1397.

82. Catts, H. W., Adlof, S. M., & Ellis Weismer, S. (2006).

Language deficits in poor comprehenders: A case for the Simple View of Reading. *Journal of Speech, Language, and Hearing Research, 49*(2), 278-293.

83. Catts, H. W., Bridges, M., Little, T., & Tomblin, J. (2008). Reading achievement growth in children with language impairments. *Journal of Speech, Language, and Hearing Research, 51*(6), 1569.

84. Catts, H. W., Compton, D., Tomblin, J. B., & Bridges, M. S. (2012). Prevalence and nature of late-emerging poor readers. *Journal of Educational Psychology, 104*(1), 166-181.

85. Catts, H. W., Nielsen, D. C., Bridges, M. S., Liu, Y. S., & Bontempo, D. E. (2015). Early identification of reading disabilities within an RTI framework. *Journal of Learning Disabilities, 48*(3), 281-297.

86. Catts, H. W., & Petscher, Y. (2022). A cumulative risk and resilience model of dyslexia. *J. of Learning Disabilities, 55*(3), 171-184.

87. Centre for Education Statistics and Evaluation. (2017). *Cognitive load theory: Research that teachers really need to understand.* NSW Government. www.cese.nsw.gov.au.

88. Chall, J. S. (1967). *Learning to read: The great debate: An inquiry into the science, art and ideology of old and new methods of teaching children to read,* 1910-1965. New York; Maidenhead: McGraw-Hill.

89. Chall, J. S. (1999). Some thoughts on reading research: Revisiting the first-grade studies. *Reading Research Quarterly, 34*(1), 8.

90. Chall, J. S., & Jacobs, V. A. (2003). Poor children's fourth-grade slump. *American Educator, 27*(1).

91. Chan, S. W. Y., & Rao, N. (2022). Relation between executive function and early language and literacy development in Bengali, Chinese, and Hindi. *Reading and Writing, 35*(10), 2341-2364.

92. Chard, D. J., Vaughn, S., Tyler, B.-J., & Sloan, K. (2000). Building a school-wide model for preventing reading difficulties. *Australasian J. of Special Education, 24*(1), 32-46.

93. Chen, S.-L., Shih-Jay, T., & Chu, S.-Y. (2015). Evaluating effectiveness of two types of Chinese remedial materials for low-achieving and disadvantaged second graders. *The Asia-Pacific Education Researcher, 24*(1), 111-123.

94. Chen, S.-L., & Tzeng, S.-J. (2019). The effect of a long-term

Chinese reading intervention program on primary grade students' reading growth. *Jiao Yu Yan Jiu Yu Fa Zhan Gi Kan, 15*(2), 57-88.

95. Chien, S.-J. (2010). The effects of 3 early reading programs on social-economically disadvantaged kindergartners. *NTTU Educational Research Journal, 21*(1), 93-123.

96. Chirkina, G. V., & Grigorenko, E. L. (2014). Tracking citations: A science detective story. *J. of Learning Disabilities, 47*(4), 366-373.

97. Chow, J. C., Chow, J. C., Wehby, J. H., & Wehby, J. H. (2018). Associations between language and problem behavior: A systematic review and correlational meta-analysis. *Educational Psychology Review, 30*(1), 61-82.

98. Christoforou, M., Jones, E. J. H., White, P., & Charman, T. (2023). Executive function profiles of preschool children with autism spectrum disorder and attention-deficit/hyperactivity disorder: A systematic review. *JCPP advances*.

99. Christopher, M. E., Hulslander, J., Byrne, B., Samuelsson, S., Keenan, J. M., Pennington, B., ... Olson, R. K. (2015). Genetic and environmental etiologies of the longitudinal relations between prereading skills and reading. *Child Development, 86*(2), 342-361.

100. Cirino, P. T., Romain, M. A., Barth, A. E., Tolar, T. D., Fletcher, J. M., & Vaughn, S. (2013). Reading skill components and impairments in middle school struggling readers. *Reading and Writing, 26*(7), 1059-1086.

101. Cirrin, F. M., Schooling, T. L., Nelson, N. W., Diehl, S. F., Flynn, P. F., Staskowski, M., ... Adamczyk, D. (2010). Evidence-based systematic review: Effects of different service delivery models on communication outcomes for elementary school-age children. *Language Speech and Hearing Services in School Journal, 41*(3), 233-264.

102. Claessen, M., Tucker, M., Dawes, E., & Leitao, S. (2020). The information score as a measure of oral discourse comprehension in the early school years. *International Journal of Speech-Language Pathology, 22*(3), 338-346.

103. Clay, M. M. (1993). *Reading Recovery: A guidebook for teachers in training*. Heinemann.

104. Clayton, F. J., West, G., Sears, C., Hulme, C., & Lervåg, A. (2020). A longitudinal study of early reading development: Letter-sound knowledge, phoneme awareness and RAN, but not letter-sound integration, predict variations in reading

development. *Scientific Studies of Reading, 24*(2), 91-107.
105. Colenbrander, D., Kohnen, S., Beyersmann, E., Robidoux, S., Wegener, S., Arrow, T., ... Castles, A. (2022). Teaching children to read irregular words: A comparison of three instructional methods. *Scientific Studies of Reading, 26*(6), 545-564.
106. Commonwealth of Australia. (2016). Australian Early Development Census (AEDC) national report 2015. www.aedc.gov.au.
107. Commonwealth of Australia. (2019). Australian Early Development Census (AEDC) national report 2018. www.aedc.gov.au.
108. Compton, D. L., Gilbert, J. K., Jenkins, J. R., Fuchs, D., Fuchs, L. S., Cho, E., Barquero, L. A., & Bouton, B. (2012). Accelerating chronically unresponsive children to Tier 3 instruction: What level of data is necessary to ensure selection accuracy? *Journal of Learning Disabilities, 45*(3), 204-216.
109. Compton, D. L., Miller, A. C., Elleman, A. M., & Steacy, L. M. (2014). Have we forsaken reading theory in the name of "quick fix" interventions for children with reading disability? *Scientific Studies of Reading, 18*(1), 55-73.
110. Connor, C. M., Adams, A., Zargar, E., Wood, T. S., Hernandez, B. E., & Vandell, D. L. (2020). Observing individual children in early childhood classrooms using Optimizing Learning Opportunities for Students (OLOS): A feasibility study. *Early Childhood Research Quarterly, 52*, 74-89.
111. Connor, C. M., Jakobsons, L. J., Crowe, E. C., & Meadows, J. G. (2009). Instruction, student engagement, and reading skill growth in reading first classrooms. *Elementary School J., 109*(3), 221-250.
112. Connor, C. M., Kelcey, B., Sparapani, N., Petscher, Y., Siegal, S. W., Adams, A., Hwang, J. K., & Carlisle, J. F. (2020). Predicting second and third graders' reading comprehension gains: Observing students' and classmates talk during literacy instruction using COLT. *Scientific Studies of Reading, 24*(5), 411-433.
113. Connor, C. M., & Morrison, F. J. (2016). Individualizing student instruction in reading: Implications for policy and practice. *Policy Insights from the Behavioral and Brain Sciences, 3*(1), 54-61.
114. Connor, C. M., Morrison, F. J., Fishman, B., Crowe, E. C., Otaiba, S. A., & Schatschneider, C. (2013). A longitudinal cluster-randomized controlled study on the accumulating

effects of individualized literacy instruction on students' reading from first through third grade. *Psychological Science, 24*(8), 1408-1419.

115. Connor, C. M., Morrison, F. J., Schatschneider, C., Toste, J. R., Lundblom, E., Crowe, E. C., & Fishman, B. (2011). Effective classroom instruction: Implications of child characteristics by reading instruction interactions on first graders' word reading achievement. *J. of Research on Educational Effectiveness, 4,* 173-207.

116. Connor, C. M., Morrison, F. J., & Slominski, L. (2006). Preschool instruction and children's emergent literacy growth. *Journal of Educational Psychology. Vol., 98*(4), 665-689.

117. Connor, C. M., Phillips, B. M., Kim, Y. S. G., Lonigan, C. J., Kaschak, M. P., Crowe, E., Dombek, J., & Al Otaiba, S. (2018). Examining the efficacy of targeted component interventions on language and literacy for third and fourth graders who are at risk of comprehension difficulties. *Scientific Studies of Reading, 22*(6), 462-484.

118. Connor, C. M., Spencer, M., Day, S. L., Giuliani, S., Ingebrand, S. W., McLean, L., & Morrison, F. J. (2014). Capturing the complexity: Content, type, and amount of instruction and quality of the classroom learning environment synergistically predict third graders' vocabulary and reading comprehension outcomes. *Journal of Educational Psychology, 106*(3), 762-778.

119. Conti-Ramsden, G., Mok, P., Durkin, K., Pickles, A., Toseeb, U., & Botting, N. (2018). Do emotional difficulties and peer problems occur together from childhood to adolescence? The case of children with a history of developmental language disorder (DLD). *European Child and Adolescent Psychiatry, 28*(7), 993-1004.

120. Conti-Ramsden, G., St Clair, M. C., Pickles, A., & Durkin, K. (2012). Developmental trajectories of verbal and nonverbal skills in individuals with a history of Specific Language Impairment: From childhood to adolescence. *Journal of Speech Language and Hearing Research, 55*(6), 1716-1735.

121. Cooper, H. (2003). Summer learning loss: The problem and some solutions. *ERIC Digest, May 2003.*

122. Cossu, G. (1999). The acquisition of Italian orthography. In M. Harris & G. Hatano (Eds.), *Learning to reading and write: A cross-linguistic perspective* (pp.10-34). Cambridge Uni. Press.

123. Cossu, G., Gugliotta, M., & Marshall, J. (1995). Acquisition of reading and written spelling in a transparent orthography:

Two non-parallel processes? *Reading and Writing, 7*(9-22).
124. Cossu, G., Rossini, F., & Marshall, J. C. (1993). When reading is acquired but phonemic awareness is not: A study of literacy in Down's Syndrome. *Cognition, 46*(2), 129-138.
125. Cragg, L., & Nation, K. (2006). Exploring written narrative in children with poor reading comprehension. *Educational Psychology, 26*(1), 55-72.
126. Craig, F., Margari, F., Legrottaglie, A. R., Palumbi, R., de Giambattista, C., & Margari, L. (2016). A review of executive function deficits in Autism Spectrum Disorder and Attention-Deficit/Hyperactivity Disorder. *Neuropsychiatric disease and treatment, 12,* 1191-1202.
127. Crippa, A., Marzocchi, G. M., Piroddi, C., Besana, D., Giribone, S., Vio, C., ... Sora, M. L. (2015). An integrated model of executive functioning is helpful for understanding ADHD and associated disorders. *J. of Attention Disorders, 19*(6), 455-467.
128. Crowe, E. C., Connor, C. M., & Petscher, Y. (2009). Examining the core: Relations among reading curricula, poverty, and first through third grade reading achievement. *Journal of School Psychology, 47*(3), 187.
129. Crowther, F. (2011). *From school improvement to sustained capacity: The parallel leadership pathway.* Thousand Oaks, CA., USA: Corwin (Sage).
130. Crowther, F. with Boyce, K. (2017). *Energising teaching: The power of your unique pedagogical gift.* Australian Council Educational Research (ACER).
131. Council of Australian Governments Education. (2019). *The Alice Springs (Mparntwe) Education Declaration.* Retrieved from https://docs.education.gov.au/documents/alice-springs-mparntwe-education-declaration
132. Cowan, N. (2016). Working memory maturation: can we get at the essence of cognitive growth? *Perspectives in Psychological Science, 11*(2), 239-264.
133. Cunningham, A. E., & Stanovich, K. E. (1997). Early reading acquisition and its relation to reading experience and ability 10 years later. *Developmental Psychology, 33*(6), 934-945.
134. Daniels, P. T., & Share, D. L. (2018). Writing system variation and its consequences for reading and dyslexia. *Scientific Studies of Reading, 22*(1), 101-116.
135. d'Apice, K., & von Stumm, S. (2020). The role of spoken language and literacy exposure for cognitive and language

outcomes in children. *Scientific Studies of Reading, 24*(2), 108-122.

136. Daraganova, G., & Joss, N. (Eds.). (2019). *Growing Up In Australia – The Longitudinal Study of Australian Children (LSAC), Annual Statistical Report 2018*. Melbourne: Australian Institute of Family Studies.

137. Das, J. P., Hayward, V., Georgiou, G. K., Janzen, T., & Boora, N. (2008). Comparing the effectiveness of two reading intervention programs for children with reading disabilities. *Journal of Cognitive Education and Psychology, 7*(2), 199-222.

138. Daucourt, M. C., Erbeli, F., Little, C. W., Haughbrook, R., & Hart, S. A. (2020). A meta-analytical review of the genetic and environmental correlations between reading and Attention-Deficit/Hyperactivity Disorder symptoms and reading and math. *Scientific Studies of Reading, 24*(1), 23-56.

139. Day, S. L., Connor, C. M., & McClelland, M. M. (2015). Children's behavioral regulation and literacy: The impact of the first grade classroom environment. *Journal of School Psychology, 53*(5), 409-428.

140. Debner, B., & Anderson, J. (2017). *Correction of phonological deficits in students with dyslexia through the use of a phonemic alphabet, the initial teaching alphabet (i.t.a.)*. Proceedings of the EDULEARN17 Conference. Barcelona, Spain.

141. Dehaene, S. (2009). *Reading in the brain: The new science of how we read*. UK: Penguin Books.

142. Dehaene, S. (2011). *The number sense: How the mind creates mathematics* (Revised ed.). New York: Oxford University Press.

143. Dehaene, S. (2014). Reading in the Brain, revised and extended: Response to comments. *Mind & Language, 29*(3), 320-335.

144. Dehaene, S. (2021). *How we learn: The new science of education and the brain*. UK: Penguin Books.

145. Denckla, M. B., & Rudel, R. (1974). Rapid "automatized" naming of pictured objects, colors, letters and numbers by normal children. *Cortex, 10*(2), 186-202.

146. Denton, C. A., Fletcher, J. M., Taylor, W. P., Barth, A. E., & Vaughn, S. (2014). An experimental evaluation of guided reading and explicit interventions for primary-grade students at-risk for reading difficulties. *Journal of Research on Educational Effectiveness, 7*(3), 268-293.

147. Denton, C. A., Tamm, L., Schatschneider, C., & Epstein, J. N.

(2020). The effects of ADHD treatment and reading intervention on the fluency and comprehension of children with ADHD and word reading difficulties: A randomized clinical trial. *Scientific Studies of Reading, 24*(1), 72-89.

148. Denton, C. A., Tolar, T. D., Fletcher, J. M., Barth, A. E., Vaughn, S., & Francis, D. J. (2013). Effects of Tier 3 Intervention for students with persistent reading difficulties and characteristics of inadequate responders. *Journal of Educational Psychology, 105*(3), 633-648.

149. Department of Education and Science. (1975). *The Bullock Report: A language for life: Report of the Committee of Enquiry.* www.educationengland.org.uk.

150. Department of Social Services (DSS, 2014). *Footprints in Time: the Longitudinal Study of Indigenous Children: Report from Wave 5.* National Centre for Longitudinal Data, Canberra.

151. Depew, B., & Eren, O. (2016). Born on the wrong day? School entry age and juvenile crime. *J. of Urban Economics, 96,* 73-90.

152. Desiree, G., Alicia, D., Natalia, S., & Juan, E. J. (2014). Development of phonological and orthographic processing in teenagers with and without reading disabilities. *INFAD, 3*(1), 137-146.

153. Dewey, G. (1970). *Relative frequency of English spellings.* Columbia University: Teachers College Press.

154. Dewey, G. (1971). *English spelling: Roadblock to reading.* Columbia University: Teachers College.

155. Dewey, G. (1978). *Relative frequency of occurrence as a factor in the phonemic and graphemic problems of English.* Spelling Progress Bulletin, 18(4), 11-17.

156. Diamanti, V., Goulandris, N., Stuart, M., Campbell, R., & Protopapas, A. (2018). Tracking the effects of dyslexia in reading and spelling development: A longitudinal study of Greek readers. *Dyslexia, 24*(2), 170-189.

157. Diamond, A. (2013). Executive functions. *Annual Review of Psychology, 64,* 135-168.

158. Dickinson, D. K. (2011). Teachers' language practices and academic outcomes of preschool children. *Science, 333*(6045), 964-967.

159. Didion, L., & Toste, J. R. (2022). Data Mountain: Self-monitoring, goal setting, and positive attributions to enhance the oral reading fluency of elementary students with or at risk for reading disabilities. *J. of Learning Disabilities, 55*(5), 375-392.

160. Ding, M., Li, Y., Li, X., & Kulm, G. (2008). Chinese teachers' perceptions of students' classroom misbehaviour. *Educational psychology (Dorchester-on-Thames), 28*(3), 305-324.
161. Dion, E., Brodeur, M., Gosselin, C., Campeau, M.-È., & Fuchs, D. (2010). Implementing research-based instruction to prevent reading problems among low-income students: Is earlier better? *Learning Disabilities Research & Practice, 25*(2), 87-96.
162. Dolean, D. D., Lervåg, A., Visu-Petra, L., & Melby-Lervåg, M. (2021). Language skills, and not executive functions, predict the development of reading comprehension of early readers: evidence from an orthographically transparent language. *Reading and Writing, 34*(6), 1491-1512.
163. Downing, J. (1965). *The initial teaching alphabet.* Macmillan.
164. Downing, J. (1967a). The effects of the initial teaching alphabet (i.T.A.) on young children's written composition. *Educational Research Review, 9*(2), 137-144.
165. Downing, J. (1967b). *Evaluating the initial teaching alphabet.* Littlehampton Book Services Ltd.
166. Downing, J. (1967c). *Recent developments in i.T.A.* https://eric.ed.gov.
167. Downing, J. (1969a). *The effectiveness of i.T.A. (initial teaching alphabet) in the prevention and treatment of dyslexia and dysgraphia.* World Mental Health Assembly (Washington, D.C., November 17-21, 1969), https://eric.ed.gov.
168. Downing, J. (1969b). Initial teaching alphabet: Results after six years. *The Elementary School Jou*rnal, 242-249.
169. Downing, J. (1972a). The orthography factor in literacy acquisition in different languages. *Literacy Discussion, 3*(3-4), 409-427.
170. Downing, J. (Ed.). (1972b). *Comparative reading.* Macmillan.
171. Downing, J., & et al. (1967). The effects of the initial teaching alphabet (i.t.a.) on young children's written composition. *Educational Research. 9*(2), 137-44.
172. Downing, J., & Halliwell, S. (1964). *The i.t.a reading experiment in Britain.* London University Institute of Education. https://eric.ed.gov.
173. Doyle, O., Harmon, C. P., Heckman, J. J., & Tremblay, R. E. (2009). Investing in early human development: Timing and economic efficiency. *Economics and Human Biology, 7,* 1-6.
174. Drucker, P. (1994). *The age of social transformation.* Atlantic Monthly, 274(November), 53-80.

175. Duesund, L., & Ødegård, M. (2018). Students' perception of reactions towards disruptive behaviour in Norwegian and American schools. *Emotional and behavioural difficulties, 23*(4), 410-423.
176. Duffy, C. (2020). *Closing Australia's education divide will take a generation, landmark study finds.* abc.net.au/news/2020-10-28.
177. Dykstra, R. (1968). *Classroom implications of the First-Grade Reading Studies.* Paper presented at College Reading Association Conference, Knoxville, Tenn., April 1968. 1-12.
178. Dyslexia Foundation of New Zealand. (2008). *4D is for Dyslexia: A guide for New Zealand schools Version 2.1.* www.4d.org.nz.
179. Dyson, H., Best, W., Solity, J., & Hulme, C. (2017). Training mispronunciation correction and word meanings improves children's ability to learn to read words. *Scientific Studies of Reading, 21*(5), 392-407.
180. Ebbels, S. H., McCartney, E., Slonims, V., Dockrell, J. E., & Norbury, C. F. (2019). Evidence-based pathways to intervention for children with language disorders. *Int J. of Language & Communication Disorders, 54*(1), 3-19.
181. Ebert, K. D., & Scott, C. M. (2016). Bringing the Simple View of Reading to the clinic: Relationships between oral and written language skills in a clinical sample. *Journal of Communication Disorders, 62*, 147-160.
182. Education Queensland. (2000). *Literate futures: Report of the literacy review for Queensland state schools.* Brisbane: State of Queensland (Department of Education).
183. Eklund, K., Torppa, M., Aro, M., Leppänen, P. H. T., & Lyytinen, H. (2015). Literacy skill development of children with familial risk for dyslexia through Grades 2, 3, and 8. *Journal of Educational Psychology, 107*(1), 126-140.
184. Eklund, K. M., Torppa, M., & Lyytinen, H. (2013). Predicting reading disability: Early cognitive risk and protective factors. *Dyslexia, 19*(1), 1-10.
185. Ellis, N. C., & Hooper, A. M. (2001). Why learning to read is easier in Welsh than in English: Orthographic transparency effects evinced with frequency-matched tests. *Applied Psycholinguistics, 22*(4), 571-599.
186. Engel de Abreu, P. M. J., Abreu, N., Nikaedo, C. C., Puglisi, M. L., Tourinho, C. J., Miranda, M. C., ... Martin, R. (2014). Executive functioning and reading achievement in school: A study of Brazilian children assessed by their teachers as "poor

readers". *Frontiers in Psychology, 5*, 550-550.
187. Espy, K. A., Molfese, D. L., Molfese, V. J., & Modgline, A. (2004). Development of auditory event-related potentials in young children and relations to word-level reading abilities at age 8 years. *Annals of Dyslexia, 54*, 9-38.
188. Etmanskie, J. M., Partanen, M., & Siegel, L. S. (2016). A longitudinal examination of the persistence of late emerging reading disabilities. *J. of Learning Disabilities, 49*(1), 21-35.
189. Fachinetti, A. (2015). A short personal and political history of NAPLAN. *Education Today, Term 4*, 20-22.
190. Fawcett, A. J., & Jones, N. (2020). Evaluating a screening and support system for early intervention in Wales. *Journal of Research in Special Educational Needs, 20*(3), 231-245.
191. Filderman, M. J., & Toste, J. R. (2022). Effects of varying levels of data use to intensify a multisyllabic word reading intervention for upper elementary students with or at risk for reading disabilities. *J. of Learning Disabilities, 55*(5), 393-407.
192. Florit, E., & Cain, K. (2011). The Simple View of Reading: Is it valid for different types of alphabetic orthographies? *Educational Psychology Review, 23*(4), 553.
193. Flynn, J. M. (2000). *Synthesis of research on the use of the Initial Teaching Alphabet for remediation of dyslexia*. The Initial Teaching Alphabet Foundation. New York, NY.
194. Foley, G. M. (2017). Play as regulation promoting self-regulation through play. *Topics in Language Disorders, 37*(3), 241-258.
195. Francis, D., Hudson, J. L., Kohnen, S., Mobach, L., & McArthur, G. M. (2021). The effect of an integrated reading and anxiety intervention for poor readers with anxiety. *PeerJ*, 9:e10987.
196. Freire, P. (1974). *Education: The practice of freedom*. Writers and Readers Publishing Cooperative
197. Frith, U., Wimmer, H., & Landerl, K. (1998). Differences in phonological recoding in German- and English-speaking children. *Scientific Studies of Reading, 2*(1), 31-54.
198. Frost, R. (2012). Towards a universal model of reading. *Behavioral and Brain Sciences, 35*(5), 263-279.
199. Fry, E. B. (2004). Phonics: A large phoneme–grapheme frequency count revised. *Journal of Literacy Research, 36*(1), 85-98.
200. Fry, E. B., Kress, J. E., & Fountoudidis, D. L. (2004). *The*

reading teacher's book of lists. Paramus: NJ: Prentice Hall.
201. Fuchs, D., Fuchs, L. S., Thompson, A., Otaiba, S. A., Yen, L., Yang, N. J., Braun, M., & O'Connor, R. E. (2002). Exploring the importance of reading programs for Kindergartners with disabilities in mainstream classrooms. *Exceptional Children, 68*(3), 295-311.
202. Furnes, B., Elwér, Å., Samuelsson, S., Olson, R. K., & Byrne, B. (2019). Investigating the Double-Deficit hypothesis in more and less transparent orthographies: A longitudinal Study from Preschool to Grade 2. *Scientific Studies of Reading, 23*(6), 478-493.
203. Gabay, Y., Schiff, R., & Vakil, E. (2012a). Attentional requirements during acquisition and consolidation of a skill in normal readers and developmental dyslexics. *Neuropsychology, 26*(6), 744-757.
204. Gabay, Y., Schiff, R., & Vakil, E. (2012b). Dissociation between the procedural learning of letter names and motor sequences in developmental dyslexia. *Neuropsychologia, 50*(10), 2435-2441.
205. Gabay, Y., Thiessen, E. D., & Holt, L. L. (2015). Impaired statistical learning in developmental dyslexia. *Journal of Speech, Language, and Hearing Research, 58*(3), 934-945.
206. Gabay, Y., Vakil, E., Schiff, R., & Holt, L. L. (2015). Probabilistic category learning in developmental dyslexia: Evidence from feedback and paired-associate weather prediction tasks. *Neuropsychology,* 29(6), 844–854.
207. Galletly, S. A. (1999a). Analogies for explaining information processing. In S. McLeod & L. McAllister (Eds.), *Towards 2000: Embracing change, challenge and choice: Proceedings of the 1999 Speech Pathology Australia National Conference.* Melbourne: Speech Pathology Australia.
208. Galletly, S. A. (1999b). *Sounds & vowels: Keys to literacy progress.* Mackay, Qld, Australia: Literacy Plus.
209. Galletly, S. A. (2000). *Phonological fun.* Mackay, Qld, Australia: Literacy Plus.
210. Galletly, S. A. (2001). *Two vowels talking: Keys to literacy progress.* Mackay, Australia: Literacy Plus.
211. Galletly, S. A. (2002). The challenge: Improving core literacy outcomes in Education Queensland schools. In B. Knight (Ed.), *Reconceptualising knowledge in the knowledge society* (pp. 1-16). Flaxton, QLD: Post Pressed.
212. Galletly, S. A. (2003). *The Literacy Plus CD.* Mackay,

Australia: Literacy Plus.
213. Galletly, S. A. (2004a). Reading accuracy and phonological recoding: Poor relations no longer. In B. Knight & W. Scott (Eds.), *Learning disabilities: Multiple perspectives*. Melbourne: Pearson Education Australia, www.literacyplus.com.au.
214. Galletly, S. A. (2004b). *The role of working memory in literacy and language processing*. (Unpublished doctoral paper). Mackay: Central Queensland University, www.literacyplus.com.au.
215. Galletly, S. A. (2005a). *Galletly Most-Frequent Words 50-Word Probes*. www.literacyplus.com.au.
216. Galletly, S. A. (2005b). *The Galletly Report: Reading-accuracy development, difficulties and instruction in Australia: Report submitted to the Australian National Inquiry into the Teaching of Literacy*. www.literacyplus.com.au.
217. Galletly, S. A. (2008). *An exploration of rapid-use reading-accuracy tests in an Australian context (Doctoral Thesis, PhD)*. Central Queensland University, www.literacyplus.com.au.
218. Galletly, S. A. (2013). *Holborn Reading Scale: Adapted version*. www.literacyplus.com.au.
219. Galletly, S. A. (2014a). 'Echo reading' empowers text reading. *Literacy Plus Newsletter 1*, www.literacyplus.com.au.
220. Galletly, S. A. (2014b). *Galletly Language and Early Literacy Tests* (GLERT). www.literacyplus.com.au.
221. Galletly, S. A. (2014c). *Galletly Phonological Awareness Tests*. www.literacyplus.com.au.
222. Galletly, S. A. (2014d). *Galletly Rapid Automised Naming (RAN) Pictures Test*. www.literacyplus.com.au.
223. Galletly, S. A. (2014e). *Literacy Plus Newsletter 1: Word-Reading*, www.literacyplus.com.au.
224. Galletly, S. A. (2014f). *Three categories & seven 'types' of weak readers: Common patterns of strength and weaknesses in children with reading difficulties*. www.literacyplus.com.au.
225. Galletly, S. A. (2015a). Galletly Diagnostic Vowel Word-Reading Tests. *Literacy Plus Newsletter 2*. www.literacyplus.com.au.
226. Galletly, S. A. (2015b). *Literacy Plus Newsletter 2: Reading Fun with Common Vowel Graphemes*. www.literacyplus.com.au.
227. Galletly, S. A. (2015c). Maximise statistical learning: Reduce confusion then give lots of practice. *Literacy Plus Newsletter 2*,

www.literacyplus.com.au.
228. Galletly, S. A. (2015d). Reading fun with common vowel graphemes. *Literacy Plus Newsletter 2,* www.literacyplus.com.au.
229. Galletly, S. A. (2017a). *Optimising spelling development in children with word-reading and spelling weakness.* www.literacyplus.com.au.
230. Galletly, S. A. (2017b). *The power of crosslinguistic research for elucidating factors impeding optimising of anglophone education (Roundtable presentation).* Paper presented, 2017 International Academy for Research in Learning Disabilities Conference, U of Qld, Brisbane. www.literacyplus.com.au.
231. Galletly, S. A. (2018). *Honing research directions into the future: Under-explored research issues & their potential for future knowledge building.* Paper presented at the Speaking Tour presentation at six Taiwan Universities, January 2018. www.literacyplus.com.au.au
232. Galletly, S. A. (2022a) Bunyips in the Classroom: The 10 Changes. Vol. 1. *Aussie Reading Woes.* Mackay, Qld, Australia: Literacy Plus.
233. Galletly, S. A. (2022b). *Key Concepts of 'Bunyips in the Classroom: The 10 Changes and the Aussie Reading Woes trilogy.* www.literacyplus.com.au.
234. Galletly, S. A. (2022c). *Rosner's Test of Auditory Analysis: Adapted version.* www.literacyplus.com.au.
235. Galletly, S. A. (2023a). *Fleksispel: A fully regular English orthography with transitioning stages for free flexible use by educators and researchers.* www.literacyplus.com.au.
236. Galletly, S. A. (2023b). *Pattern Word word-reading unit.* www.literacyplus.com.au.
237. Galletly, S. A. (2023c). *Rapid Reads: Sets of reading words grouped by orthographic form.* www.literacyplus.com.au.
238. Galletly, S. A. (2023d). *Sample client assessment report.* www.literacyplus.com.au.
239. Galletly, S. A. (2023e). *Sets of 10: Frequent Words word-reading units.* www.literacyplus.com.au.
240. Galletly, S. A. (2023f). *Sets of 10: Regular Words word-reading units.* www.literacyplus.com.au.
241. Galletly, S. A. (2023g). *Spelling Games word-reading unit.* www.literacyplus.com.au.

242. Galletly, S. A. (In press) The 10 Changes: The Nitty Gritty. Vol. 3. *Aussie Reading Woes.* www.susangalletly.com.au.

243. Galletly, S. A., & Knight, B. A. (2004). The high cost of orthographic disadvantage. *Australian Journal of Learning Disabilities, 9*(4), 4-11.

244. Galletly, S. A., & Knight, B. A. (2006). The Dynamic Indicators of Basic Early Literacy Skills' (DIBELS) use in an Australian context. *Australian J. of Learning Disabilities, 11*(3), 147-154.

245. Galletly, S. A., & Knight, B. A. (2010). *CQUniversity Accelerated Metacognitive Literacy Intensive Tuition (CAMLIT): Program for middle school students experiencing literacy difficulties.* CQUniversity. Mackay: Qld.

246. Galletly, S. A., & Knight, B. A. (2011a). Differential disadvantage of Anglophone weak readers due to English orthographic complexity and cognitive processing weakness. *Australasian Journal of Special Education, 35*(1), 72-96.

247. Galletly, S. A., & Knight, B. A. (2011b). Transition from Early to Sophisticated Literacy (TESL) as a factor in cross-national achievement differences. *Australian Educational Researcher, 38*(3), 329-354.

248. Galletly, S. A., & Knight, B. A. (2013). Because trucks aren't bicycles: Orthographic complexity as an important variable in reading research. *Australian Educational Researcher, 40*(2), 173-194.

249. Galletly, S. A., Knight, B. A., Dekkers, J., & Galletly, T. A. (2009). Indicators of late emerging reading-accuracy difficulties in Australian schools. *The Australian Journal of Teacher Education, 34*(5), 54-64.

250. Galletly, S. A., Knight, B. A., & Dekkers, J. (2010). When tests frame children: The challenges of providing appropriate education for children with special needs. *Australasian Journal of Special Education, 34*(2), 133-154.

251. Gallop, G., Kavanagh, T., & Lee, P. (2021). *Valuing the teaching profession: An independent inquiry.* New South Wales Teachers Federation. www.nswtf.org.au.

252. Gandolfi, E., Traverso, L., Zanobini, M., Usai, M. C., & Viterbori, P. (2021). The longitudinal relationship between early inhibitory control skills and emergent literacy in preschool children. *Reading & Writing, 34*(8), 1985-2009.

253. García, J. R., & Kate, C. (2014). Decoding and Reading Comprehension: A meta-analysis to identify which reader and

assessment characteristics influence the strength of the relationship in English. *Review of Ed. Research, 84*(1), 74-111.
254. Garvey, W., O'Connor, M., Quach, J., & Goldfeld, S. (2020). Better support for children with additional health and developmental needs in school settings: Perspectives of education experts. *Child Care and Health Development, 46*(4), 522-529.
255. Gathercole, S. E., & Alloway, T. P. (2008). *Working memory and learning: A practical guide for teachers.* London: Sage Publications.
256. Gathercole, S. E., Alloway, T. P., Kirkwood, H. J., Elliott, J. G., Holmes, J., & Hilton, K. A. (2008). Attentional and executive function behaviours in children with poor working memory. *Learning and Individual Differences, 18*(2), 214-223.
257. Gathercole, S. E., Dunning, D. L., & Holmes, J. (2012). Cogmed training: Let's be realistic about intervention research. *Journal of Applied Research in Memory and Cognition, 1*(3), 201-203.
258. Gathercole, S. E., & Pickering, S. J. (2000a). Assessment of working memory in six- and seven-year-old children. *Journal of Educational Psychology, 92*(2), 377-390.
259. Gathercole, S. E., & Pickering, S. J. (2000b). Working memory deficits in children with low achievements in the national curriculum at 7 years of age. *The British Journal of Educational Psychology, 70*(2), 177-194.
260. Gathercole, S. E., & Pickering, S. J. (2001). Working memory deficits in children with special educational needs. *British Journal of Special Education, 28*(2), 89 - 97.
261. Gathercole, S. E., Pickering, S. J., Ambridge, B., & Wearing, H. (2004). The structure of working memory from 4 to 15 years of age. *Developmental psychology, 40*(2), 177-190.
262. Georgiou, G. K., Guo, K., Naveenkumar, N., Vieira, A. P. A., & Das, J. P. (2020). PASS theory of intelligence and academic achievement: A meta-analytic review. *Intelligence, 79,* 101431.
263. Georgiou, G. K., Papadopoulos, T. C., Fella, A., & Parrila, R. (2012). Rapid naming speed components and reading development in a consistent orthography. *Journal of Experimental Child Psychology, 112*(1), 1-17.
264. Georgiou, G. K., Parrila, R., Cui, Y., & Papadopoulos, T. C. (2013). Why is Rapid Automatized Naming (RAN) related to reading? *J. of Experimental Child Psychology, 115*(1), 218-225.
265. Georgiou, G. K., Parrila, R., & Papadopoulos, T. C. (2008).

Predictors of word decoding and reading fluency across languages varying in orthographic consistency. *Journal of Educational Psychology, 100*(3), 566-580.

266. Georgiou, G. K, Parrila, R., & Papadopoulos, T. C. (2016). The anatomy of the RAN-reading relationship. *An Interdisciplinary Journal, 29*(9), 1793-1815.

267. Georgiou, G. K., Torppa, M., Manolitsis, G., Lyytinen, H., & Parrila, R. (2012). Longitudinal predictors of reading and spelling across languages varying in orthographic consistency. *Reading and Writing, 25*(2), 321-346.

268. Geva, E., & Siegel, L. (2000). Orthographic and cognitive factors in the concurrent development of basic reading skills in two languages. *An Interdisciplinary Journal, 12*(1), 1-30.

269. Gill, J. (2004). Having our work cut out!: reflections on the Australian Association for Research in Education and the current state of Australian educational research *Australian Educational Researcher, 31*(1), 1-14.

270. Gladwell, M. (2005). *Blink: The power of thinking without thinking.* New York: New York: Penguin Group.

271. Gladwell, M. (2008). *Outliers: The story of success.* Camberwell, Vic: Allen Lane.

272. Goldfeld, S., Beatson, R., Watts, A., Snow, P., Gold, L., Le, H. N. D., ... Eadie, P. (2022). Tier 2 oral language and early reading interventions for preschool to grade 2 children: a restricted systematic review. *Australian Journal of Learning Difficulties, 27*(1), 65-113.

273. Goldfeld, S., Snow, P., Eadie, P., Munro, J., Gold, L.,... Watts, A. (2017). Classroom Promotion of Oral Language (CPOL): protocol for a cluster randomised controlled trial of a school-based intervention to improve children's literacy outcomes at Grade 3, oral language and mental health. *BMJ Open, 7*(11), e016574.

274. Gonski, D., Arcus, T., Boston, K., Gould, V., Johnon, W., O'Brien, L., ... Roberts, M. (2018). *Through growth to achievement: Report of the Review to Achieve Educational Excellence in Australian Schools.* Canberra. www.education.gov.au.

275. Gonski, D., Boston, K., Greiner, K., Lawrence, C., Scales, B., & Tannock, P. (2011). *Review of Funding for Schooling: Final Report.* Canberra. www.education.gov.au.

276. Gooch, D., Hulme, C., Nash, H. M., & Snowling, M. J. (2014).

Comorbidities in preschool children at family risk of dyslexia. *Journal of Child Psychology and Psychiatry, 55*(3), 237-246.
277. Gooch, D., Thompson, P., Nash, H., Snowling, M., & Hulme, C. (2016). The development of executive function and language skills in the early school years. *Journal of Child Psychology & Psychiatry, 57*(2), 180-187.
278. Good, R. H., & Kaminski, R. A. (Eds.). (2002). *Dynamic indicators of basic early literacy skills (dibels)* (6th ed.). University of Oregon: Institute for the Development of Educational Achievement.
279. Good, R. H., Wallin, J. U., Simmons, D. C., Kame'enui, E. J., & Kaminski, R. A. (2002). *System-wide percentile ranks for DIBELS benchmark assessment (Technical Report No. 9)*.
280. Goswami, U. C (2002). Phonology, reading development, and dyslexia: A cross-linguistic perspective. *Annals of Dyslexia, 52*, 141-163.
281. Gough, P. B., Juel, C., & Griffith, P. L. (1992). Reading, spelling, and the orthographic cipher. In Gough, Ehri, & Treiman (Eds.), *Reading Acquisition*. NY: Lawerence Erlbaum Associates.
282. Gough, P. B., & Tunmer, W. E. (1986). Decoding, reading and reading disability. *Remedial and Special Education, 7*(1), 6-10.
283. Gray, P. (2017). What exactly is play, and why is it such a powerful vehicle for learning? *Topics in Language Disorders, 37*(3), 217-228.
284. Groen, M. A., Laws, G., Nation, K., & Bishop, D. V. M. (2006). A case of exceptional reading accuracy in a child with Down Syndrome: Underlying skills and the relation to reading comprehension. *Cognitive Neuropsychology, 23*(8), 1190-1214.
285. Guo, Y., Sun, S., Breit-Smith, A., Morrison, F. J., & Connor, C. M. (2015). Behavioral engagement and reading achievement in elementary-school-age children: a longitudinal cross-lagged analysis. *Journal of Educational Psychology, 107*(2), 332-347.
286. Gutiérrez, N., Rigobon, V. M., Marencin, N. C., Edwards, A. A., Steacy, L. M., & Compton, D. L. (2023). Early prediction of reading risk in Fourth Grade: A combined latent class analysis and classification tree approach. *Scientific Studies of Reading, 27*(1), 21-38.
287. Hahn, H. T. (1965). Study of the relative effectiveness of three methods of teaching reading in Grade One. https://eric.ed.gov.
288. Hämäläinen, J. A., Leppänen, P. H. T., Eklund, K., Thomson,

J., Richardson, U., Guttorm, T. K., ... Lyytinen, H. (2009). Common variance in amplitude envelope perception tasks and their impact on phoneme duration perception and reading and spelling in Finnish children with reading disabilities. *Applied Psycholinguistics, 30*(3), 511-530.

289. Hamre, B. K., & Pianta, R. C. (2005). Can instructional and emotional support in the first-grade classroom make a difference for children at risk of school failure? *Child Development, 76*(5), 949-967.

290. Hanley, J. R., Masterson, J., Spencer, L. H., & Evans, D. (2004). How long do the advantages of learning to read a transparent orthography last? An investigation of the reading skills and reading impairment of Welsh children at 10 years of age. *Quarterly Journal of Experimental Psychology: Part A: Human Experimental Psychology, 57*(8), 1393.

291. Hanna, P. R., Hanna, J. S., Hodges, R. E., & Rudorf, E. H. (1996). *Phoneme-grapheme correspondences as cues to spelling improvement.* Washington DC: U.S. Govt Printing Office

292. Hargreaves, A. (1994). *Changing teachers, changing times.* London: Cassell.

293. Hargreaves, A. (1997). Going deeper and wider in the quest for success. In J. Houtz (Ed.), *Rethinking educational change with heart and mind 1997 ASCD Yearbook.* Alexandria: Association for Supervison and Curriculum Development.

294. Hargreaves, A. (2021). What's next for schools after coronavirus? Here are 5 big issues and opportunities. *The Conversation,* April 17, 2020.

295. Harm, M. W., & Seidenberg, M. S. (2004). Computing the meanings of words in reading: Cooperative division of labor between visual and phonological processes. *Psychological Review, 111*(3), 662–720.

296. Harrison, L. J., & McLeod, S. (2010). Risk and protective factors associated with speech and language impairment in a nationally representative sample of 4- to 5-year-old children. *J. of Speech, Language, and Hearing Research, 53*(2), 508-529.

297. Harrison, L. J., McLeod, S., Berthelsen, D., & Walker, S. (2009). Literacy, numeracy, and learning in school-aged children identified as having speech and language impairment in early childhood. *International Journal of Speech-Language Pathology, 11*(5), 392-403.

298. Hart, B., & Risley, T. R. (1995). Meaningful differences in the everyday experience of young American children. USA:

Brookes.
299. Hart, B., & Risley, T. R. (2003). The early catastrophe: The 30 million word gap by age 3. *American Educator 27*(1), 4-9.
300. Hattie, J. (2005). The paradox of reducing class size and improving learning outcomes. *International Journal of Educational Research, 43*(6), 387-425.
301. Hattie, J. (2008). Visible teaching, visible learning: A synthesis of over 800 meta-analyses relating to achievement. Routledge, UK.
302. Hayiou-Thomas, M. E., Bishop, D. V. M., & Plunkett, K. (2004). Simulating SLI: General cognitive processing stressors can produce a specific linguistic profile. *Journal of Speech, Language, and Hearing Research, 47*(6), 1347-1456.
303. Hayiou-Thomas, M. E., Oliver, B., & Plomin, R. (2016). Genetic influences on specific versus nonspecific language impairment in 4-year-old twins. *J. of Learning Disabilities, 38*(3), 222-232.
304. Hayiou-Thomas, M. E., Carroll, J. M., Leavett, R., Hulme, C., & Snowling, M. J. (2017). When does speech sound disorder matter for literacy? The role of disordered speech errors, co-occurring language impairment and family risk of dyslexia. *Journal of Child Psychology and Psychiatry, 58*(2), 197-205.
305. Heckman, J. J. (2020a) *The Heckman Equation: Invest in early childhood development: Reduce deficits, strengthen the economy*, 1-2. www.heckmanequation.org.
306. Heckman, J. J. (2020b) *James Heckman changes the equation for American prosperity*. 1-8. www.heckmanequation.org.
307. Heikkilä, R., Aro, M., Närhi, V., Westerholm, J., & Ahonen, T. (2013). Does training in syllable recognition improve reading speed? A computer-based trial with poor readers from second and third grade. *Scientific Studies of Reading, 17*(6), 398-414.
308. Hempenstall, K. (2016). *Read about it: Scientific evidence for effective teaching of reading.* www.cis.org.au.
309. Hendren, R. L., Haft, S. L., Black, J. M., White, N. C., & Hoeft, F. (2018). Recognizing psychiatric comorbidity with reading disorders. *Front Psychiatry, 9*, 101-101.
310. Hersh, C. A., Stone, B. J., & Ford, L. (1996). Learning disabilities and learned helplessness: A heuristic approach. *International Journal of Neuroscience, 84*(1-4), 103-113.
311. Hill, P. W., & Crevola, C. A. (1999). Key features of a whole-school design approach to literacy teaching in schools. *Australian Journal of Learning Disabilities, 4*(3), 5-12.
312. Hindson, B., Byrne, B., Fielding-Barnsley, R., Newman, C.,

Hine, D. W., & Shankweiler, D. (2005). Assessment and early instruction of preschool children at risk for reading disability. *Journal of Educational Psychology.* 97(4), 687-704

313. Hintikka, S., Landerl, K., Aro, M., & Lyytinen, H. (2008). Training reading fluency: Is it important to practice reading aloud and is generalization possible? *Annals of Dyslexia, 58*(1), 59-79.

314. Hirsch, E. D. (2003). Reading comprehension requires knowledge – of words and the world. *American Educator, 27,* 10-48. https://eric.ed.gov.

315. Ho, W. C. (1972). *An interim report on the Youngstown i.t.a Study: Third year results (Grade 2).* Educational Research Council of America. https://eric.ed.gov.

316. Ho, W. C., & Eiszler, C. F. (1970). *Interaction effects of socio-economic status, intelligence and reading program on beginning reading achievement* American Educational Research Association, Minneapolis, Minn. https://eric.ed.gov.

317. Ho, W. C., Eiszler, C. F., & Stroh, V. (1970). *Longitudinal effects of i.T.A. on pupils' reading achievement through Grade Three.* Educational Research Council of America. https://eric.ed.gov.

318. Ho, W. C. et al. (1972). *Effects of teaching i.t.a to inner-city black children in Kindergarten and First Grade* Annual Meeting of the American Ed. Research Assn., Chicago. https://eric.ed.gov.

319. Hogan, T. P., Adlof, S. M., & Alonzo, C. N. (2014). On the importance of listening comprehension. *International Journal of Speech-Language Pathology, 16*(3), 199-207.

320. Holdaway, D. (1979). *Foundations of literacy.* Ashton-Scholastic.

321. Holopainen, L., Ahonen, T., & Lyytinen, H. (2001). Predicting delay in reading achievement in a highly transparent language. *Journal of Learning Disabilities, 34*(5), 401-413.

322. Hoover, W. A., & Gough, P. B. (1990). The Simple View of Reading. *Reading and Writing, 23*(2), 127-160.

323. Horbach, J., Mayer, A., Scharke, W., Heim, S., & Günther, T. (2020). Development of behavior problems in children with and without specific learning disorders in reading and spelling from Kindergarten to fifth grade. *Scientific Studies of Reading, 24*(1), 57-71.

324. Hoxhallari, L., van Daal, V. H. P., & Ellis, N. C. (2004).

Learning to read words in Albanian: A skill easily acquired. *Scientific Studies of Reading, 8*(2), 153-166.

325. Huang, H. S., & Hanley, J. R. (1994). Phonological awareness and visual skills in learning to read Chinese and English. *Cognition, 54,* 73-98.

326. Huang, H. S., & Hanley, J. R. (1997). A longitudinal study of phonological awareness, visual skills, and Chinese reading acquisition among first-graders in Taiwan. *International Journal of Behavioural Development, 20*(2), 249-268.

327. Hubert-Dibon, G., Bru, M., Le Guen, C. G., Launay, E., & Roy, A. (2016). Health-related quality of life for children and adolescents with Specific Language Impairment: A cohort study by a Learning Disabilities Reference Center. *PLoS ONE, 11*(11), e0166541-e0166541.

328. Huemer, S., Aro, M., Landerl, K., & Lyytinen, H. (2010). Repeated reading of syllables among Finnish-speaking children with poor reading skills. *Scientific Studies of Reading,* 14(4), 317-340.

329. Huemer, S., Landerl, K., Aro, M., & Lyytinen, H. (2008). Training reading fluency among poor readers of German: Many ways to the goal. *Annals of Dyslexia, 58*(2), 115-137.

330. Hulme, C., Nash, H. M., Gooch, D., Lervåg, A., & Snowling, M. J. (2015). The foundations of literacy development in children at familial risk of dyslexia. *Psychological Science, 26*(12), 1877-1886.

331. Hunter, J., Sonnemann, J., & Joiner, R. (2022). *Making time for great teaching: How better government policy can help* (Vol. No. 2022-1, Jan 2022): Grattan Institute.

332. Initial Teaching Alphabet (ITA) Foundation. (1971). i.t.a. research abstracts: forty-two studies of the effectiveness of i.t.a. abstracted in systematic form. Special issue of the i.t.a. Foundation Report. https://eric.ed.gov.

333. Isabel , L. B., & Margaret , G. M. (2007). Increasing young low-income children's oral vocabulary repertoires through rich and focused instruction. *Elementary School J., 107*(3), 251-271.

334. Isoaho, P., Kauppila, T., & Launonen, K. (2016). Specific language impairment (SLI) and reading development in early school years. *Child Language Teaching & Therapy, 32*(2), 147-157.

335. Jacob, R., & Parkinson, J. (2015). The potential for school-based interventions that target executive function to improve academic achievement: A review. *Review of Educational*

Research, 85(4), 512-552.

336. Jesson, R., McNaughton, S., Rosedale, N., Zhu, T., & Cockle, V. (2018). A mixed-methods study to identify effective practices in the teaching of writing in a digital learning environment in low income schools. *Computers & Education, 119*, 14-30.

337. Jesson, R., McNaughton, S., & Wilson, A. (2015). Raising literacy levels using digital learning: a design-based approach in New Zealand. *Curriculum Journal, 26*(2), 1-26.

338. Jessup, B., Ward, E., Cahill, L., & Keating, D. (2008a). Prevalence of speech and or language impairment in preparatory students in northern Tasmania. *International Journal of Speech-Language Pathology, 10*(5), 364-377.

339. Jessup, B., Ward, E., Cahill, L., & Keating, D. (2008b). Teacher identification of speech and language impairment in kindergarten students using the kindergarten developmental check. *Advances in Speech-Language Pathology, 10*(6):449-59.

340. Jimenez, J. E., Siegel, L. S., & Lopez, M. R. (2003). The relationship between IQ and reading disabilities in English-speaking Canadian and Spanish children. *Journal of Learning Disabilities, 36*(1), 15-23.

341. Jones, M. W., Snowling, M. J., & Moll, K. (2016). What automaticity deficit? Activation of lexical information by readers with dyslexia in a rapid automatized naming stroop-switch task. *Journal of Experimental Psychology: Learning, Memory, and Cognition, 42*(3), 465-474.

342. Joshi, R. M., & Aaron, P. G. (2000). The Component Model of Reading: Simple View of Reading made a little more complex. *Reading Psychology, 21*(2), 85 - 97.

343. Joshi, R. M., Ji, X. R., Breznitz, Z., Amiel, M., & Yulia, A. (2015). Validation of the Simple View of Reading in Hebrew: A Semitic language. *Scientific Studies of Reading, 19*(3), 243-252.

344. Joyner, R. E., & Wagner, R. K. (2020). Co-occurrence of reading disabilities and math disabilities: A meta-analysis. *Scientific Studies of Reading, 24*(1), 14-22.

345. Juel, C. (1988). Learning to read and write: A longitudinal study of 54 children from first through fourth grades. *Journal of Educational Psychology, 80*, 437-447.

346. Juma, N. (2022). *Thomas Edison quotes on greatness and innovation.* (August 10, 2022). www.everydaypower.com.

347. Kadar, N. (2021). Vindicating a traduced genius: Ignaz Philipp Semmelweis (1818–1865). *American journal of obstetrics and*

gynecology, 225(3), 310-324. doi:10.1016/j.ajog.2021.06.054

348. Kahneman, D. (2013). *Thinking, fast and slow*. New York, NY: Farrar, Straus and Giroux.
349. Kamil, M. L., & Hiebert, E. H. (2010). The teaching and learning of vocabulary: Perspectives and persistent issues. In M. L. Kamil & E. H. Hiebert (Eds.), *Teaching and learning vocabulary: Bringing research to practice* (pp. 1-23). New York: Routledge.
350. Karr, C., & et al. (1974). *A six-year experiment in the use of the initial teaching alphabet (i.T.A.) in the teaching of reading*. https://eric.ed.gov.
351. Kasperski, R., Shany, M., & Katzir, T. (2016). The role of RAN and reading rate in predicting reading self-concept. *Reading and Writing: An Interdisciplinary Journal, 29*(1), 117-136.
352. Kendeou, P., Papadopoulos, T. C., & Kotzapoulou, M. (2013). Evidence for the early emergence of the Simple View of Reading in a transparent orthography. *Reading and Writing, 26*(2), 189-204.
353. Kennedy, M. M. (2005). *Inside teaching: How classroom life undermines reform*. Harvard University Press.
354. Kennedy, M. M. (2010). Attribution error and the quest for teacher quality. *Educational Researcher, 39*(8), 591-598.
355. Kessler, B., Pollo, T. C., Treiman, R., & Cardoso-Martins, C. (2013). Frequency analyses of prephonological spellings as predictors of success in conventional spelling. *Journal of Learning Disabilities, 46*(3), 252-259.
356. Kikkawa, D. (2014). Multiple Disadvantage. In D. o. S. Services (Ed.), *Footprints in Time: the Longitudinal Study of Indigenous Children – Report from Wave 5* (pp. 84.89). Canberra: National Centre for Longitudinal Data, Department of Social Services.
357. Kim, Y. G. (2017). Why the Simple View of Reading is not simplistic: Unpacking component skills of reading using a direct and indirect effect model of reading (DIER). *Scientific Studies of Reading, 21*(4), 310-333.
358. Kim, Y. G. (2022). Co-occurrence of reading and writing difficulties: The application of the Interactive Dynamic Literacy Model. *J. of Learning Disabilities, 55*(6), 447-464.
359. Kirby, J. R., & Savage, R. S. (2008). Can the Simple View deal with the complexities of reading? *Literacy, 42*(2), 75-82.
360. Kisely, S., Mills, R., Strathearn, L., & Najman, J. M. (2020). Does child maltreatment predict alcohol use disorders in young

adulthood? A cohort study of linked notifications and survey data. *Addiction, 115*(1), 61-68.

361. Knight, B. A., & Galletly, S. A. (2005). The role of metacognition in reading-accuracy learning and instruction. *Australian Journal of Learning Disabilities, 10*(2), 63-70.

362. Knight, B. A., & Galletly, S. A. (2006). The Test of Word Reading Efficiencey (TOWRE) used in an Australian context. *Australian Journal of Learning Disabilities, 11*(3), 139-145.

363. Knight, B. A., & Galletly, S. A. (2011). Developing an informed and integrated teaching approach for students with reading-accuracy difficulties in the primary school. In D. Lynch & B. A. Knight (Eds.), *Issues in contemporary teaching* (Vol. 2, pp. 65-89). Brisbane: Australia: AACLM Press.

364. Knight, B. A., & Galletly, S. A. (2016). The effects of an intervention program on middle school students' literacy skills. *Special Education Perspectives, 25*(1), 7-17.

365. Knight, B. A., & Galletly, S. A. (2017). Effective literacy instruction for all students: A time for change. *International Journal of Innovation, Creativity and Change., 3*(1), 65-86.

366. Knight, B. A., & Galletly, S. A. (2020). Practical school-level implications of cognitive processing and cognitive load. In A. M. Columbus (Ed.), *Advances in psychology research* (Vol. 140, pp. 1-90). New York: Nova Science Publishers.

367. Knight, B. A., Galletly, S. A., & Aprile, K. T. (2021). The Literacy Component Model: A pragmatic universal paradigm. *International J. of Innovation, Creativity and Change, 15*(7).

368. Knight, B. A., Galletly, S. A., & Gargett, P. S. (2017a). Managing cognitive load as the key to literacy development: Research directions suggested by crosslinguistic research and research on Initial Teaching Alphabet (i.t.a.). In R. Nata (Ed.), *Progress in education* (Vol. 45, pp. 61-150). NY: Nova Science.

369. Knight, B. A., Galletly, S. A., & Gargett, P. S. (2017b). *Principles of reading instruction towards optimising reading instruction for at-risk readers in Prep to Year 3: Principles developed through teacher reflection on research and practice in the ARC project 'Bridging the gap for at-risk readers: Reading theory into classroom practice'*. Townsville: Qld: CQUniversity.

370. Knight, B. A., Galletly, S. A., & Gargett, P. S. (2019). Orthographic Advantage Theory: National advantage and disadvantage due to orthographic differences. *Asia Pacific Journal of Developmental Differences, 6*(1, January), 5-29. *(Appendix of tables: Key features of Orthographic Advantage*

Theory: National advantage and disadvantage due to orthographic differences. www.literacyplus.com.au).
371. Knight, B. A., Galletly, S. A., & Gargett, P. S. (2020). Bridging the gap between reading theory and teacher practice. *International J. of Innovation, Creativity, & Change, 13*(8), 1-19.
372. Knight, B. A., Galletly, S. A., Morris, J., & Gargett, P. S. (2018). Reading instruction strategies to reduce cognitive load. *Practical Literacy: The Early and Primary Years, 23*(2), 8-10.
373. Konold, T. R., Juel, C., McKinnon, M., & Deffes, R. (2003). A multivariate model of early reading acquisition. *Applied Psycholinguistics, 24*(1), 89-112.
374. Koponen, T., Salmi, P., Eklund, K., & Aro, T. (2013). Counting and RAN: Predictors of arithmetic calculation and reading fluency. *Journal of Educational Psychology, 105*(1), 162-175.
375. Kornilov, S. A., & Grigorenko, E. L. (2018). What reading disability? Evidence for multiple latent profiles of struggling readers in a large Russian sibpair sample with at least one sibling at risk for reading difficulties. *Journal of Learning Disabilities, 51*(5), 434-443.
376. Kuo, L., & Anderson, R. C. (2010). Beyond cross-language transfer: Reconceptualizing the impact of early bilingualism on phonological awareness. *Scientific Studies of Reading, 14*(4), 365-385.
377. Kuo, W. F. (1978). *A preliminary study of reading disability in the Republic of China*. National Taiwan Normal University, Taiwan (1978). 57–78 Collected papers.
378. Kwok, E. Y. L., Joanisse, M. F., Archibald, L. M. D., Stothers, M. E., Brown, H. M., & Oram Cardy, J. (2018). Maturation in auditory event-related potentials explains variation in language ability in children. *European Journal of Neuroscience, 47*(1), 69-76.
379. Kyle, F., Kujala, J., Richardson, U., Lyytinen, H., & Goswami, U. (2013). Assessing the effectiveness of two theoretically motivated computer-assisted reading interventions in the United Kingdom: GraphoGame Rime and GraphoGame Phoneme. *Reading Research Quarterly, 48*(1), 61-76.
380. Lado, R. (Ed.). (1957). Linguistics across cultures: Applied linguistics for language teachers. University of Michigan Press.
381. Lamb, S., Huo, S., Walstab, A., Wade, A., Maire, Q., Doecke, E ... Endekov, Z. (2020). *Educational opportunity in Australia 2020: who succeeds and who misses out*. Melbourne: Centre for

International Research on Education Systems, Victoria University, for the Mitchell Institute.
382. Landerl, K. (2000). Influences of orthographic consistency and reading instruction on the development of nonword reading skills. *European J. of Psychology of Education, 15*, 239-257.
383. Landerl, K., Castles, A., & Parrila, R. (2022). Cognitive precursors of reading: A cross-linguistic perspective. *Scientific Studies of Reading, 26*(2), 111-124.
384. Landerl, K., Freudenthaler, H. H., Heene, M., De Jong, P. F., Desrochers, A., Manolitsis, G., ... Georgiou, G. K. (2019). Phonological awareness and Rapid Automatized Naming as longitudinal predictors of reading in five alphabetic orthographies with varying degrees of consistency. *Scientific Studies of Reading, 23*(3), 220-234.
385. Landerl, K., Ramus, F., Moll, K., Lyytinen, H., Leppänen, P. H. T., Lohvansuu, K., ... Schulte-Körne, G. (2013). Predictors of developmental dyslexia in European orthographies with varying complexity. *Journal of Child Psychology and Psychiatry and Allied Disciplines, 54*(6), 686-694.
386. Landerl, K., & Wimmer, H. (2008). Development of word reading fluency and spelling in a consistent orthography: An 8-year follow-up. *J. of Educational Psychology, 100*(1), 150-161.
387. Landerl, K., Wimmer, H. C. A., & Frith, U. (1997). The impact of orthographic consistency on dyslexia: A German-English comparison. *Cognition, 63*, 315-334.
388. Lara-Martínez, P., Obregón-Quintana, B., Reyes-Manzano, C. F., López-Rodríguez, I., & Guzmán-Vargas, L. (2022). A multiplex analysis of phonological and orthographic networks. *PLoS ONE, 17*(9).
389. Law, J., Levickis, P., McKean, C., Goldfeld, S., Snow, P. C., & Reilly, S. (2017). *Child language in a public health context.* www.mcri.edu.au.
390. Law, J., Mensah, F., Westrupp, E., & Reilly, S. (2015). *Social disadvantage and early language delay.* www.mcri.edu.au.
391. Law, J., Rush, R., Schoon, I., & Parsons, S. (2010). Modeling developmental language difficulties from school entry into adulthood: Literacy, mental health, and employment outcomes. *J. of Speech Language and Hearing Research, 52*(6), 1401-1416.
392. Leach, J. M., Scarborough, H. S., & Rescorla, L. (2003). Late-emerging reading disabilities. *Journal of Educational Psychology, 95*(2), 211-224.

393. Lee, J. J. (2013). Six women scientists who were snubbed due to sexism. *National Geographic*. May 20, 2013.
394. Lervåg, A., Bråten, I., & Hulme, C. (2009). The cognitive and linguistic foundations of early reading development: A Norwegian latent variable longitudinal study. *Developmental Psychology, 45*(3), 764-781.
395. Lewis, B. A., Freebairn, L. A., & Taylor, H. G. (2000). Follow-up of children with early expressive phonology disorders. *Journal of Learning Disabilities, 33*(5), 433-444.
396. Liberman, I. Y., Shankweiler, D. P., & Liberman, A. M. (1989). The Alphabetic Principle and learning to read. In D. P. Shankweiler & I. Y. Liberman (Eds.), *Phonology and reading disability: Solving the reading puzzle* (pp. 1-33). University of Michigan Press. https://eric.ed.gov.
397. Lim, L., Arciuli, J., & Munro, N. (2018). Shared book reading behaviours of children with Down Syndrome before and after participation in the MultiLit reading tutor program: an exploratory study. *Australian Journal of Learning Difficulties*, 23(1), 31-51.
398. Lim, L., Arciuli, J., Munro, N., & Cupples, L. (2019). Using the MultiLit literacy instruction program with children who have Down Syndrome. *Reading and Writing, 32*(9), 2179-2200.
399. Limbrick, L., Wheldall, K., & Madelaine, A. (2011). Why do more boys than girls have a reading disability? A review of the evidence. *Australasian J. of Special Education, 35*(1), 1-24.
400. Limbrick, L., Wheldall, K., & Madelaine, A. (2012). Do boys need different remedial reading instruction from girls? *Australian Journal of Learning Difficulties, 17*(1), 1.
401. Livingston, E. M., Siegel, L. S., & Ribary, U. (2018). Developmental dyslexia: Emotional impact and consequences. *Australian Journal of Learning Difficulties, 23*(2), 107-135.
402. Llamas, R. P. (2017) Public health in action – Anchored upstream. https://flipaswitchblog.wordpress.com/tag/river-metaphor/.
403. Logan, G. D. (1997). Automaticity and Reading: Perspectives from the Instance Theory of Automisation. *Reading and Writing Quarterly, 13*(2), 123-146.
404. Logan, G. D., Taylor, S. E., & Etherton, J. L. (1999). Attention and automaticity: Toward a theoretical integration. *An International Journal of Perception, Attention, Memory and Action, 62*(2-3), 165-181.

405. Lohvansuu, K., Torppa, M., Ahonen, T., Eklund, K., Hämäläinen, J. A., Leppänen, P. H. T., & Lyytinen, H. (2021). Unveiling the mysteries of dyslexia: Lessons learned from the prospective Jyväskylä Longitudinal Study of Dyslexia. *Brain Science, 11*(4), 427.
406. Lonigan, C. J., Burgess, S. R., & Schatschneider, C. (2018). Examining the Simple View of Reading with elementary school children: Still simple after all these years. *Remedial and Special Education, 39*(5), 260-273.
407. Lonigan, C. J., & Phillips, B. M. (2016). Response to Instruction in Preschool: Results of two randomized studies with children at significant risk of reading difficulties. *Journal of Educational Psychology, 108*(1), 114-129.
408. Louden, W., Chan, L. K. S., Elkins, J., Greaves, D., House, H., Milton, M., ... van Kraayenoord, C. E. (2000). *Mapping the territory: Primary school students with learning difficulties in literacy & numeracy (Vol 1-3)*. Canberra: Department Education, Training and Youth Affairs (DETYA).
409. Louden, W., Rohl, M., Barratt-Pugh, C., Brown, C., Cairney, T., Elderfield, J., House, H., Meiers, M., Rivalland, J., & Rowe, K. (2006). *In teachers' hands: Effective literacy teaching practices in the early years of schooling*. www.research-repository.uwa.edu.au.
410. Lubotsky, D., & Kaestner, R. (2016). Do `skills beget skills'? Evidence on the effect of Kindergarten entrance age on the evolution of cognitive and non-cognitive skill gaps in childhood. *Economics of Education Review, 53*, 194-206.
411. Lyytinen, H. (2014). Children at risk of reading problems – from identification to prevention: William Cruickshank Lecture 2014. *International Journal for Research in Learning Disabilities, 2*(1), 2-17.
412. Lyytinen, H., Aro, M., Eklund, K., Erskine, J. M., Guttorm, T., Laakso, M.-L., et al. (2004). The development of children at familial risk for dyslexia: Birth to early school age. *Annals of Dyslexia, 54*(2), 184–220.
413. Lyytinen, H., Aro, M., Holopainen, L., Leiwo, M., Lyytinen, P., & Tolvanen, A. (2006). Children's language development and reading acquisition in a highly transparent language. In R. M. Joshi & P. G. Aaron (Eds.), *Handbook of orthography and literacy*. New York: Routledge. pp. 46-62.
414. Lyytinen, H., Erskine, J., Hämäläinen, J., Torppa, M., & Ronimus, M. (2015). Dyslexia – Early identification and

prevention: Highlights from the Jyväskylä Longitudinal Study of Dyslexia. *Current Developmental Disorders Reports, 2*(4), 330-338.

415. Lyytinen, H., Erskine, J., Tolvanen, A., Torppa, M., & et al. (2006). Trajectories of reading development: A follow-up from birth to school age of children with and without risk for dyslexia. *Merrill-Palmer Quarterly, 52*(3), 514.

416. Lyytinen, H., Semrud-Clikeman, M., Li, H., Pugh, K., & Richardson, U. (2021). Supporting acquisition of spelling skills in different orthographies using an empirically validated digital learning environment. *Frontiers in Psychology, 12*, 556120, 1-11.

417. Ma, E. P. M., Threats, T. T., & Worrall, L. E. (2008). An introduction to the International Classification of Functioning, Disability and Health (ICF) for Speech-Language Pathology: Its past, present and future. *International Journal of Speech-Language Pathology, 10*(1-2), 2-9.

418. Macklin, S., & Pilcher, S. (2020). One quarter of Australian 11-12 year olds don't have the literacy and numeracy skills they need. *The Conversation*. 27 Oct, 2020.

419. Maddox, G. B., Pyc, M. A., Kauffman, Z. S., Gatewood, J. D., & Schonhoff, A. M. (2018). Examining the contributions of desirable difficulty and reminding to the spacing effect. *Memory and Cognition, 46*(8), 1376-1388.

420. Mahapatra, S. (2016). Reading disabilities and PASS reading enhancement programme. *Journal of Education and Practice, 7*(5), 145-149. https://eric.ed.gov.

421. Maier, S. F., & Seligman, M. E. (1976). Learned helplessness: Theory and evidence. *Journal of Experimental Psychology: General, 105*(1), 3-46.

422. Maier, S. F., & Seligman, M. E. P. (2016). Learned Helplessness at fifty: Insights from neuroscience. *Psychological Review, 123*(4), 349-367.

423. Mailend, M.-L., Plante, E., Anderson, M. A., Applegate, E. B., & Nelson, N. W. (2016). Reliability of the Test of Integrated Language and Literacy Skills (TILLS). *International Journal of Language & Communication Disorders, 51*(4), 447-459.

424. Majerus, S., & Cowan, N. (2016). The nature of verbal short-term impairment in dyslexia: The importance of serial order. *Frontiers in Psychology, 7*, 1522-1522.

425. Makita, K. (1968). The rarity of reading disability in Japanese

children. *American Journal of Orthopsychiatry, 38*(4), 599-614.
426. Makita, K. (1974). Reading disability and the writing system. In J. E. Merritt (Ed.), *New horizons in reading*. IRA Press.
427. Marinelli, C. V., Romani, C., Burani, C., & Zoccolotti, P. (2015). Spelling acquisition in English and Italian: A cross-linguistic study. *Frontiers in Psychology, 6*, 1843-1843.
428. Marinelli, C. V., Zoccolotti, P., & Romani, C. (2020). The ability to learn new written words is modulated by language orthographic consistency. *PLoS ONE, 15*(2), e0228129.
429. Martin, A. J. (2004). School motivation of boys and girls: Differences of degree, differences of kind, or both? *Australian Journal of Psychology, 56*(3), 133-146.
430. Martin, A. J. (2010). *Building classroom success: Eliminating academic fear and failure*. Continuum International Publishing.
431. Mascheretti, S., Marino, C., Simone, D., Quadrelli, E., Riva, V., Cellino, M. R., Maziade, M., Brombin, C., & Battaglia, M. (2015). Putative risk factors in developmental dyslexia: A case-control study of Italian children. *Journal of Learning Disabilities, 48*(2), 120-129.
432. Mashburn, A. J., & Myers, S. S. (2010). Advancing research on children with Speech-Language Impairment: An introduction to the Early Childhood Longitudinal Study-Kindergarten Cohort. *Language Speech and Hearing Services in Schools, 41*(1), 61-69.
433. Masters, G. N. (2016). Five challenges in Australian school education. *Policy Insights, May,* 1-32. www.research.acer.edu.au.
434. Mathis, W. (2017). The effectiveness of class size reduction. *Psychosociological Issues in Human Resource Management, 5*(1), 176-183.
435. Mazurkiewicz, A. J. (1965). The initial teaching alphabet for reading? Yes! *Educational Leadership, 22*(6), 390-438.
436. Mazurkiewicz, A. J. (1967). *The initial teaching alphabet in reading instruction: Leighton-Bethlehem evaluation-demonstration project on the use of i.t.a.* Fund for the Advancement of Education. https://eric.ed.gov.
437. Mazurkiewicz, A. J. (1971). *The Early to Read i.t.a Program: Effects and aftermath. A six year longitudinal study.* https://eric.ed.gov.
438. Mazurkiewicz, A. J. (1973a). *i.t.a revisited* Annual Meeting of

the College Reading Assn. (17th, Silver Springs, Md., November 1-3, 1973). https://eric.ed.gov.
439. Mazurkiewicz, A. J. (1973b). *A rationale for using i.t.a* 18th Annual Meeting of the International Reading Association, Denver, Colorado. https://eric.ed.gov.
440. McArthur, G. (2022). Poor reading and anxiety (PRAX): building a theory and practice. *Australian Journal of Learning Difficulties, 27*(1), 169-180.
441. McCormack, J., Harrison, L. J., McLeod, S., & McAllister, L. (2011). A nationally representative study of the association between communication impairment at 4-5 years and children's life activities at 7-9 years. *Journal of speech, language, and hearing research, 54*(5), 1328-1348.
442. McGaw, B., Louden, W., & Wyatt-Smith, C. (2020). *NAPLAN Review Final Report*. www.naplanreview.com.au.
443. McGill, N., Crowe, K., & McLeod, S. (2020). "Many wasted months": Stakeholders' perspectives about waiting for speech-language pathology services. *International Journal of Speech-Language Pathology, 22*(3), 313-326.
444. McGrath, L. M., Peterson, R. L., & Pennington, B. F. (2020). The Multiple Deficit Model: Progress, problems, and prospects. *Scientific Studies of Reading, 24*(1), 7-13.
445. McLean, L., Sparapani, N., Toste, J. R., & Connor, C. M. (2016). Classroom quality as a predictor of first graders' time in non-instructional activities and literacy achievement. *Journal of School Psychology, 56*(C), 45-58.
446. McLeod, S. (2018). Communication rights: Fundamental human rights for all. *International Journal of Speech-Language Pathology, 20*(1), 3-11.
447. McLeod, S., Davis, E., Rohr, K., McGill, N., Miller, K., Roberts, A., Thornton, S., Ahio, N., & Ivory, N. (2020). Waiting for speech-language pathology services: A randomised controlled trial comparing therapy, advice and device. *International Journal of Speech-Language Pathology, 22*(3), 372-386.
448. McTigue, E. M., Solheim, O. J., Zimmer, W. K., & Uppstad, P. H. (2020). Critically reviewing GraphoGame across the world: Recommendations and cautions for research and implementation of computer-assisted instruction for word-reading acquisition. *Reading Research Quarterly, 55*, 45-73.
449. Merga, M. K., & Mason, S. (2021a). Perspectives on institutional valuing and support for academic and

translational outputs in Japan and Australia. *Learned Publishing. 34*(3), 305-314.
450. Merga, M. K., & Mason, S. (2021b). Unis want research shared widely. So why don't they properly back academics to do it? The Conversation,11 Jan 2020. www.theconversation.com.
451. Miciak, J., & Fletcher, J. M. (2020). The critical role of instructional response for identifying dyslexia and other learning disabilities. *J. of Learning Disabilities, 53*(5), 343-353.
452. Middleton, A. E., Farris, E. A., Ring, J. J., & Odegard, T. N. (2022). Predicting and evaluating treatment response: Evidence toward protracted response patterns for severely impacted students with dyslexia. *J. of Learning Disabilities, 55*(4), 272-291.
453. Mills, R., Scott, J., Alati, R., O'Callaghan, M., Najman, J. M., & Strathearn, L. (2012). Child maltreatment and adolescent mental health problems in a large birth cohort. *Child Abuse and Neglect, 37*(5), 292-302.
454. Molfese, V. J., Molfese, D. L., & Modglin, A. A. (2001). Newborn and preschool predictors of second-grade reading scores: An evaluation of categorical and continuous scores. *Journal of Learning Disabilities, 34*(6), 545-554.
455. Moll, K., Gangl, M., Banfi, C., Schulte-Körne, G., & Landerl, K. (2020). Stability of deficits in reading fluency and/or spelling. *Scientific Studies of Reading, 24*(3), 241-251.
456. Moll, K., Ramus, F., Bartling, J., et al. (2014). Cognitive mechanisms underlying reading and spelling development in five European orthographies. *Learning and Instruction, 29*, 65-77.
457. Monster, I., Tellings, A., Burk, W. J., Keuning, J., Segers, E., & Verhoeven, L. (2022). Word properties predicting children's word recognition. *Scientific Studies of Reading, 26*(5), 373-389.
458. Moore, D. (2018). Uniform orthographies and phonetics in Central Australia 1890-1910. *Language & History, 61*(3), 95-115.
459. Moore, T.G. and McDonald, M. (2013). *Acting Early, Changing Lives: How prevention and early action saves money and improves wellbeing.* Prepared for The Benevolent Society. Parkville, Vic: Centre for Community Child Health at Murdoch Childrens Research Institute and Royal Children's Hospital.
460. Morais, J., Cary, L., Alegria, J., & Bertelson, P. (1979). Does awareness of speech as a sequence of phones arise spontaneously? *Cognition, 7*(4), 323-331.
461. Morgan, P. L., Farkas, G., Wang, Y., Hillemeier, M. M., Oh, Y.,

& Maczuga, S. (2019). Executive function deficits in Kindergarten predict repeated academic difficulties across elementary school. *Early Childhood Research Quarterly, 46*, 20-32.

462. Morken, F., Helland, T., Hugdahl, K., & Specht, K. (2014). Children with dyslexia show cortical hyperactivation in response to increasing literacy processing demands. *Frontiers of Psychology, 5*, 1491-1491.

463. Munro, J. (2017). Who benefits from which reading intervention in the primary years? Match the intervention with the reading profile. *Australian Journal of Learning Difficulties, 22*(2), 133-151.

464. Najman, J. M., Aird, R., Bor, W., O'Callaghan, M., Williams, G. M., & Shuttlewood, G. J. (2004). The generational transmission of socioeconomic inequalities in child cognitive development and emotional health. *Social Science & Medicine, 58*, 1147-1158.

465. Najman, J. M., Hayatbakhsh, M. R., Heron, M. A., Bor, W., O'Callaghan, M. J., & Williams, G. M. (2009). The impact of episodic and chronic poverty on child cognitive development. *Journal of Pediatrics, 154*, 284-289.

466. Najman, J. M., Alati, R., Bor, W., Clavarino, A., Mamun, A., McGrath, J. J., ... Wray, N. (2015). Cohort Profile Update: The Mater-University of Queensland Study of Pregnancy (MUSP). *International Journal of Epidemiology, 44*(1), 78-109.

467. Nation, K. (1999). Reading skills in hyperlexia: A developmental perspective. *Psychological Bulletin, 125*(3), 338-355.

468. Nation, K. (2008a). Developmental language disorders. *Psychiatry, 7*(6), 266-269.

469. Nation, K. (2008b). Learning to read words. *Quarterly Journal of Experimental Psychology, 61*(8), 1121-1133.

470. Nation, K., & Norbury, C. F. (2005). Why reading comprehension fails: Insights from developmental disorders. *Topics in Language Disorders, 25*(1), 21-32.

471. Nation, K., Angell, P., & Castles, A. (2007). Orthographic learning via self-teaching in children learning to read English: Effects of exposure, durability, and context. *Journal of Experimental Child Psychology, 96*, 71-84.

472. Nation, K., Cocksey, J., Taylor, J. S. H., & Bishop, D. V. M. (2010). A longitudinal investigation of early reading and language skills in children with poor reading comprehension. *Journal of Child Psychology and Psychiatry and Allied*

Disciplines, 51(9), 1031-1039.
473. Neale, M. D. (1999). *Neale Analysis Of Reading Ability* (Third Ed). Melbourne: Australian Council for Educational Research.
474. Nelson, N. W. (2016). Language XX: What shall it be called and why does it matter? *International Journal of Speech Language Pathology, 18*(3), 229-240.
475. Nelson, N. W., Plante, E., Helm-Estabrooks, N., & Hotz, G. (2016). *The Test of Integrated Language and Literacy Skills (TILLS)*. Brookes Publishing, USA.
476. Nevo, E., & Breznitz, Z. (2013). The development of working memory from kindergarten to first grade in children with different decoding skills. *Journal of Experimental Child Psychology, 114*(2), 217-228.
477. Nevo, E., Vaknin-Nusbaum, V., Brande, S., & Gambrell, L. (2020). Oral reading fluency, reading motivation and reading comprehension among second graders. *Reading & Writing, 33*(8), 1945-1970.
478. New Zealand Government. (2008). *About Dyslexia*. Ministry of Education, NZ.
479. Nguyen, T. Q., Del Tufo, S. N., & Cutting, L. E. (2020). Readers recruit executive functions to self-correct miscues during oral reading fluency. *Scientific Studies of Reading, 24*(6), 462-483.
480. Nguyen, T. Q., Pickren, S. E., Saha, N. M., & Cutting, L. E. (2020). Executive functions and components of oral reading fluency through the lens of text complexity. *Reading and Writing, 33*(4), 1037-1073.
481. Nicolson, R. I., & Fawcett, A. J. (2008). *Dyslexia, learning and the brain*. MIT Press, Cambridge, Ma.
482. Nicolson, R. I., & Fawcett, A. J. (2011). Dyslexia, dysgraphia, procedural learning and the cerebellum. *Cortex, 47*(1), 117-127.
483. Nicolson, R. I., & Fawcett, A. J. (2019). Development of dyslexia: The Delayed Neural Commitment framework. *Frontiers in Behavioral Neuroscience, 13*, 112-112.
484. Nicholson, T., & Dymock, S. (2015). *The New Zealand Dyslexia Handbook*. NZCER Press.
485. Norbury, C. F., & Nation, K. (2011). Understanding variability in reading comprehension in adolescents with Autism Spectrum Disorders: Interactions with language status and decoding skill. *Scientific Studies of Reading, 15*(3), 191-210.
486. Norbury, C. F., McCartney, E., Slonims, V., Dockrell, J. E., & Ebbels, S. H. (2019). Public health approaches still have room

for individualized services: Response to commentaries on 'Evidence-based pathways to intervention for children with language disorders'. *International Journal of Language and Communication Disorders, 54*(1), 28-29.

487. Norton, E. S., & Wolf, M. (2012). Rapid Automatized Naming (RAN) and reading fluency: Implications for understanding and treatment of reading disabilities. *Annual Review of Psychology, 63*(1), 427-452.

488. Norton, E. S., Beach, S. D., & Gabrieli, J. D. E. (2014). Neurobiology of dyslexia. *Current Opinion in Neurobiology, 30*, 73-78.

489. Notarnicola, A., Angelelli, P., Judica, A., & Zoccolotti, P. (2012). Development of spelling skills in a shallow orthography: the case of Italian language. *An Interdisciplinary Journal, 25*(5), 1171-1194.

490. Ober, T., Brooks, P., Homer, B., & Rindskopf, D. (2020). Executive Functions and Decoding in Children and Adolescents: a Meta-analytic Investigation. *Educational Psychology Review, 32*(3), 735-763.

491. O'Connor, M., Chong, S., Quach, J., & Goldfeld, S. (2020). Learning outcomes of children with teacher-identified emerging health and developmental needs. *Child Care and Health Development, 46*(2), 223-231.

492. O'Connor, M., O'Connor, E., Quach, J., Vashishtha, R., & Goldfeld, S. (2019). Trends in the prevalence and distribution of teacher-identified special health-care needs across three successive population cohorts. *Journal of Paediatric Child Health, 55*(3), 312-319.

493. O'Connor, R. E. (2000). Increasing the intensity of intervention in Kindergarten and First Grade. *Learning Disabilities Research & Practice, 15*(1), 43-54.

494. O'Connor, R. E., Bocian, K., Beebe-Frankenberger, M., & Linklater, D. L. (2010). Responsiveness of students with language difficulties to early intervention in reading. *The Journal of Special Education, 43*(4), 220-235.

495. O'Connor, R. E., Jenkins, J. R., Leicester, N., & Slocum, T. A. (1993). Teaching phonological awareness to young children with learning disabilities. *Exceptional Children, 59*(6), 532 - 547.

496. Organisation for Economic Co-operation and Development (OECD, 2015). *Education at a glance 2015: OECD indicators.* OECD Publishing.

497. Organisation for Economic Co-operation and Development (OECD, 2022). *Education at a glance 2015: OECD indicators*. OECD Publishing.
498. Organisation for Economic Co-operation and Development (OECD, 2019). *PISA 2018: Reporting Australia's results: Vol 3: What school life means for students' lives*. OECD Publishing.
499. Ojanen, E., Ronimus, M., Ahonen, T., Chansa-Kabali, T., February, P., Jere-Folotiya, J., … Lyytinen, H. (2015). GraphoGame: A catalyst for multi-level promotion of literacy in diverse contexts. *Frontiers in Psychology, 6,* 671-671.
500. Okrent, A. (2014). The schwa is the laziest sound in all of human speech. *Slate, June 4, 2014.* https://slate.com.
501. Oliver, P. R., Nelson, J. M., & Downing, J. (1972). Differentiation of grapheme-phoneme units as a function of orthography. *J. of Educational Psychology, 63*(5), 487-492.
502. Olofsson, A. (1993). The relevance of phonological awareness in learning to read: Scandinavian longitudinal and quasi-experimental studies. In R. M. Joshi & C. K. Leong (Eds.), *Reading disabilities: Diagnosis and component processes* (pp. 199-212). Kluwer Academic Publishers.
503. Olofsson, A., & Niedersoe, J. (1999). Early language development and kindergarten phonological awareness as predictors of reading problems: From 3 to 11 years of age. *Journal of Learning Disabilities, 32*(5), 464.
504. Oney, B., & Goldman, S. R. (1984). Decoding and comprehension skills in Turkish and English: Effects of the regularity of grapheme-phoneme correspondences. *Journal of Educational Psychology, 76*(4), 557-568.
505. Papadopoulos, T. C. (2001). Phonological and cognitive correlates of word-reading acquisition under two different instructional approaches in Greek. *Journal of Education and Development, 16*(4), 549-568.
506. Papadopoulos, T. C. (2022). *William Cruickshank Memorial Lecture: New directions in the study of neurodevelopmental disorders*. Paper presented at the 44th Annual IARLD Conference (International Academy for Research in Learning Disabilities), University of Oviedo, Spain.
507. Papadopoulos, T. C., Charalambous, A., Kanari, A., & Loizou, M. (2004). Kindergarten cognitive intervention for reading difficulties: The PREP remediation in Greek. *European Journal of Psychology of Education, 19*(1), 79-105.

508. Papadopoulos, T. C., Csépe, V., Aro, M., Caravolas, M., Diakidoy, I.-A., & Olive, T. (2021). Methodological issues in literacy research across languages: Evidence from alphabetic orthographies. *Reading Research Quarterly, 56(S1), S351–S370.*
509. Papadopoulos, T. C., Das, J. P., Parrila, R. K., & Kirby, J. R. (2003). Children at risk for developing reading difficulties: A remediation study. *School Psychology International, 24*(3), 340-366.
510. Papadopoulos, T. C., Georgiou, G. K., Deng, C., & Das, J. P. (2018). The structure of speed of processing across cultures. *Advances in cognitive psychology, 14*(3), 112.
511. Papadopoulos, T. C., Georgiou, G. K., & Kendeou, P. (2009). Investigating the Double-Deficit hypothesis in Greek: Findings from a longitudinal study. *Journal of Learning Disabilities, 42*(6), 528-547.
512. Papadopoulos, T. C., Kendeou, P., & Spanoudis, G. (2012). Investigating the factor structure and measurement invariance of phonological abilities in a sufficiently transparent language. *Journal of Educational Psychology, 104*(2), 321-336.
513. Papadopoulos, T. C., Spanoudis, G. C., & Georgiou, G. K. (2016). How is RAN related to reading fluency? A comprehensive examination of the prominent theoretical accounts. *Frontiers in Psychology, 7,* 1-15.
514. Papadopoulos, T. C., Spanoudis, G., Ktisti, C., & Fella, A. (2021). Precocious readers: A cognitive or a linguistic advantage? *European Journal of Psychology of Education, 36,* 73-90.
515. Parrila, R., Aunola, K., Leskinen, E., Nurmi, J.-E., & Kirby, J. R. (2005). Development of individual differences in reading: Results from longitudinal studies in English and Finnish. *Journal of Educational Psychology, 97*(3), 299-319.
516. Organisation for Economic Co-operation and Development (OECD, 2022). *Education at a glance 2015: OECD indicators.* OECD Publishing.
517. Pascoe, L., Roberts, G., Doyle, L. W., Lee, K. J., Thompson, D. K., Seal, M. L., ... Anderson, P. J. (2013). Preventing academic difficulties in preterm children: A randomised controlled trial of an adaptive working memory training intervention - imprint study. *BMC Pediatrics, 13*(1).
518. Paulesu, E., McCrory, E., Fazio, F., Menoncello, L., Brunswick, N., Cappa, S. F., ... Frith, U. (2000). A cultural effect on brain function. *Nature Neuroscience, 3*(1), 91-96.

519. Peng, P., Barnes, M., Wang, C., Wang, W., Li, S., Swanson, H. L., ... Tao, S. (2018). A meta-analysis on the relation between reading and working memory. *Psychological Bulletin, 144*(1), 48-76.

520. Peng, P., Zhang, Z., Wang, W., Lee, K., Wang, T., Wang, C., ... Lin, J. (2022). A meta-analytic review of cognition and reading difficulties: Individual differences, moderation, and language mediation mechanisms. *Psychological Bulletin, 148*(3-4), 227-272.

521. Pennington, B. F. (2006). From single to multiple deficit models of developmental disorders. Cognition, 101(2), 385-413.

522. Pennington, B. F., Santerre-Lemmon, L., Rosenberg, J., MacDonald, B., Boada, R., Friend, A., ... Olson, R. K. (2012). Individual prediction of dyslexia by single versus multiple deficit models. *J. of Abnormal Psychology, 121*(1), 212-224.

523. Perfetti, C. (2007). Reading ability: Lexical quality to comprehension. *Scientific Studies of Reading, 11*(4), 357-383.

524. Perfetti, C., Beck, I., Bell, L., & Hughes, C. (1987). Phonemic knowledge and learning to read are reciprocal: A longitudinal study of first grade children. *Merrill-Palmer Quarterly, 33*(3), 283-319.

525. Piasta, S. B., Connor, C. M., Fishman, B. J., & Morrison, F. J. (2009). Teachers' knowledge of literacy concepts, classroom practices, and student reading growth. *Journal of Poverty, 13*(3), 224-248.

526. Pimperton, H., & Nation, K. (2014). Poor comprehenders in the classroom: Teacher ratings of behavior in children with poor reading comprehension and its relationship with individual differences in working memory. *Journal of Learning Disabilities, 47*(3), 199-207.

527. Pitman, J. (1973). *Evidence submitted to the Bullock Committee of Inquiry into Reading and the Use of English.* https://eric.ed.gov.

528. Plante, E., & Gómez, R. L. (2018). Learning without trying: The clinical relevance of statistical learning. *Language, Speech & Hearing Services in Schools (Online), 49*(3S), 710-722.

529. Pollo, T. C., Treiman, R., & Kessler, B. (2008). Three perspectives on spelling development. In E. L. Grigorenko & A. J. Naples (Eds.), *Single-word reading: Cognitive, behavioural and biological perspectives*, pp. 175-189. Mahwah, NJ: Lawrence Erlbaum Associates.

530. Poskiparta, E., Niemi, P., Lepola, J., Ahtola, A., & Laine, P.

(2003). Motivational-emotional vulnerability and difficulties in learning to read and spell. *British Journal of Educational Psychology, 73*, 187.

531. Poskiparta, E., Neimi, P., & Vauras, M. (1999). Who benefits from training in linguistic awareness in the first grade, and what components show training effects? *Journal of Learning Disabilities, 32*(5), 437-447.

532. Pressley, M. (2006). *Reading instruction that works: The case for balanced teaching* (Third ed.). New York: Guilford Press.

533. Pressley, M., Allington, R. L., Wharton-McDonald, R., Collins Block, C., & Mandel Morrow, L. (2001). *Learning to read: Lessons from exemplary first grade classrooms.* New York: Guildford Press.

534. Pressley, M., Graham, S., & Harris, K. (2006). The state of educational intervention research as viewed through the lens of literacy intervention. *British Journal of Educational Psychology, 76*(1), 1-19.

535. Pressley, M., Wharton-McDonald, Allington, R., Block, R., Collins, C., & Morrow, L. (1998). *The nature of effective first-grade literacy instruction.* https://eric.ed.gov.

536. Prince, D. M., Rocha, A., & Nurius, P. S. (2018). Multiple disadvantage and discrimination: Implications for adolescent health and education. *Social Work Research, 42*(3), 169-179.

537. Prochnow, J. E., Tunmer, W. E., & Chapman, J. W. (2013). A longitudinal investigation of the influence of literacy-related skills, reading self-perceptions, and inattentive behaviours on the development of literacy learning difficulties. *International J. of Disability, Development and Education, 60*(3), 185-207.

538. Productivity Commission 2022, *Review of the National School Reform Agreement, Study Report*, Canberra.

539. Protopapas, A., Fakou, A., Drakopoulou, S., Skaloumbakas, C., & Mouzaki, A. (2013). What do spelling errors tell us? Classification and analysis of errors made by Greek schoolchildren with and without dyslexia. *Reading and Writing, 26*(5), 615-646.

540. Protopapas, A., Mouzaki, A., Sideridis, G. D., Kotsolakou, A., & Simos, P. G. (2013). The role of vocabulary in the context of the Simple View of Reading. *Reading and Writing Quarterly, 29*(2), 168-202.

541. Protopapas, A., & Vlahou, E. L. (2009). A comparative quantitative analysis of Greek orthographic transparency.

Behavior research methods, 41(4), 991-1008.
542. Quach, J. P., & Barnett, T. M. (2015). Impact of chronic illness timing and persistence at school entry on child and parent outcomes: Australian Longitudinal Study. *Academic Pediatrics, 15*(1), 89-95.
543. Quach, J. P., Clinton, J., Dawson, G., Smith, L., Serry, T., & Goldfeld, S. (2018). Testing of a synthetic phonics-based targeted reading intervention for students with reading difficulties in Year 1: Protocol for an efficacy randomised controlled trial. *BMJ Paediatrics Open, 2*(1), e000301-e000301.
544. Quach, J. P., Nguyen, C. P., O'Connor, M. P., & Wake, M. M. D. (2017). The cumulative effect of health adversities on children's later academic achievement. *Academic Pediatrics, 17*(7), 706-714.
545. Quick, J. (2020a). Re-mapping the territory: An analysis of literacy intervention provision for primary students in five Australian states. *Australian Journal of Learning Difficulties, 25*(2), 183-213.
546. Quick, J. (2020b). Re-mapping the territory: An overview of learning and literacy intervention provision in Australian primary education. *Australian Journal of Learning Difficulties, 25*(2), 109-133.
547. Quinn, J. M., & Wagner, R. K. (2015). Gender differences in reading impairment and in the identification of impaired readers: Results from a large-scale study of at-risk readers. *Journal of Learning Disabilities, 48*(4), 433-445.
548. Rakhlin, N., Cardoso-Martins, C., Kornilov, S., & Grigorenko, E. (2013). Spelling well despite Developmental Language Disorder: what makes it possible? *An Interdisciplinary Journal of The International Dyslexia Association, 63*(3-4), 253-273.
549. Rapoport, S., Rubinsten, O., & Katzir, T. (2016). Teachers' beliefs and practices regarding the role of executive functions in reading and arithmetic. *Frontiers in Psychology, 7*. Article 1567.
550. Rau, A. K., Moll, K., Moeller, K., Huber, S., Snowling, M. J., & Landerl, K. (2016). Same same, but different: Word and sentence reading in German and English. *Scientific Studies of Reading, 20*(3), 203-219.
551. Read, C., Zhang, Y.-F., Nie, H.-Y., & Ding, B.-Q. (1986). The ability to manipulate speech sounds depends on knowing alphabetic writing. *Cognition, 24*(1), 31-44.

552. Reed, D. K., & Vaughn, S. (2012). Comprehension instruction for students with reading disabilities in grades 4 through 12. *Learning Disabilities - A Contemporary Journal, 10*(1), 17-33.
553. Reilly, S., Tomblin, B., Law, J., McKean, C., Mensah, F. K., Morgan, A., Goldfeld, S., Nicholson, J. M., & Wake, M. (2014). Specific language impairment: A convenient label for whom?: The SLI debate: diagnostic criteria and terminology. *International Journal of Language & Communication Disorders, 49*(4), 416-451.
554. Ren, J., & Wang, M. (2023). Development of statistical learning ability across modalities, domains, and languages. *Journal of Experimental Child Psychology, 226,* 105570-105570.
555. Reynolds, M., Buckingham, J., Madelaine, A., Arakelian, S., Bell, N., Pogorzelski, S., ... Wheldall, K. (2021). What we have learned: implementing MiniLit as an intervention with young struggling readers. *Australian Journal of Learning Difficulties, 26*(2), 113-125.
556. Richardson, U., Leppänen, P. H. T., Leiwo, M., & Lyytinen, H. (2003). Speech perception of infants with high familial risk for dyslexia differ at the age of 6 months. *Developmental Neuropsychology, 23*(3), 385-397.
557. Ricketts, J., Bishop, D. V. M., & Nation, K. (2008). Investigating orthographic and semantic aspects of word learning in poor comprehenders. *Journal of Research in Reading, 31*(1), 117-135.
558. Ricketts, J., Lervåg, A., Dawson, N., Taylor, L. A., & Hulme, C. (2020). Reading and oral vocabulary development in early adolescence. *Scientific Studies of Reading, 24*(5), 380-396.
559. Ripoll Salceda, J. C., Alonso, G. A., & Castilla-Earls, A. P. (2014). The Simple View of Reading in elementary school: A systematic review. *Speech Therapy, Phoniatrics and Audiology Journal, 34*(1), 17–31.
560. Ritchie, S. J., Bates, T. C., & Plomin, R. (2015). Does learning to read improve intelligence? A longitudinal multivariate analysis in identical twins from age 7 to 16. *Child Development, 86*(1), 23-36.
561. Roark, M. (no date). Candidate for a Pullet Surprise. In S. Society (Ed.), *Poems showing the absurdities of English spelling.* spellingsociety.org. www.spellingsociety.org.
562. Roberts, G., Torgesen, J. K., Boardman, A., & Scammacca, N. (2008). Evidence-based strategies for reading instruction of older students with learning disabilities. *Learning Disabilities*

Research & Practice, 23(2), 63-69.

563. Roberts, G., Quach, J., Spencer-Smith, M., Anderson, P. J., Gathercole, S., Gold, L., ... Wake, M. (2016). Academic outcomes 2 years after working memory training for children with low working memory: A randomized clinical trial. *JAMA Pediatrics, 170*(5), e154568-e154568.

564. Rocha, R. S., Castro, S. L., & Limpo, T. (2022). The role of transcription and executive functions in writing: a longitudinal study in the transition from primary to intermediate Grades. *Reading and Writing, 35*(8), 1911-1932.

565. Rohrer, D., & Hartwig, M. K. (2020). Unanswered questions about spaced interleaved mathematics practice. *Journal of Applied Research in Memory and Cognition, 9*(4), 433-438.

566. Ronimus, M., Eklund, K., Pesu, L., & Lyytinen, H. (2019). Supporting struggling readers with digital game-based learning (GraphoLearn). *A bi-monthly publication of the Association for Educational Communications & Technology, 67*(3), 639-663.

567. Rose, J. (2009). *Identifying and teaching children and young people with dyslexia and literacy difficulties: An independent report from Sir Jim Rose to the Secretary of State for children, schools and families.* UK Department for Education. www.education.gov.uk.

568. Rosling, H., Rosling, O., & Rosling Ronnlund, A. (2018). *Factfulness: Ten reasons we're wrong about the world - and why things are better than you think.* New York, NY: Flatiron Books.

569. Rosner, J. (1993). *Helping children overcome learning difficulties* (Third edition ed.). New York: Walker and Company.

570. Rothe, J., Cornell, S., Ise, E., & Schulte-Körne, G. (2015). A comparison of orthographic processing in children with and without reading and spelling disorder in a regular orthography. *Reading and Writing, 28*(9), 1307-1332.

571. Rowe, K. J., & Rowe, K. S. (2002). *What matters most: Evidence-based findings of key factors affecting the educational experiences and outcomes for girls and boys throughout their primary and secondary schooling.* www.research.acer.edu.au.

572. Rowe, K. S., & Rowe, K. J. (2004). Literacy, behaviour and auditory processing: Building 'fences' at the top of the 'cliff' in preference to 'ambulance services at the bottom'. *ACER Supporting Student Wellbeing Conference,* October, 2004,

Adelaide. www.research.acer.edu.au.

573. Rueckl, J. G., Paz-Alonso, P. M., Molfese, P. J., Kuo, W.-J., Bick, A., Frost, S. J., ... Frost, R. (2015). Universal brain signature of proficient reading: Evidence from four contrasting languages. *Proceedings of the National Academy of Sciences of the United States of America, 112*(50), 15510.

574. Ruotsalainen, J., Pakarinen, E., Poikkeus, A. M., & Lerkkanen, M. K. (2022). Literacy instruction in first grade: classroom-level associations between reading skills and literacy instruction activities. *Journal of Research in Reading, 45*(1), 83-99.

575. Sabatini, J. P., O'Reilly, T., Halderman, L. K., & Bruce, K. (2014). Integrating scenario-based and component reading skill measures to understand the reading behavior of struggling readers: Assessing comprehension. *Learning Disabilities Research and Practice, 29*(1), 36-43.

576. Saine, N. L., Lerkkanen, M.-K., Ahonen, T., Tolvanen, A., & Lyytinen, H. (2010). Predicting word-level reading fluency outcomes in three contrastive groups: Remedial and computer-assisted remedial reading intervention, and mainstream instruction. *Learning and Individual Differences, 20*(5), 402-414.

577. Saine, N.L., Lerkkanen, M.-K., Ahonen, T., Tolvanen, A., & Lyytinen, H. (2013). Long-term intervention effects of spelling development for children with compromised preliteracy skills. *Reading & Writing Quarterly, 29*(4), 333-357.

578. Samuels, S. J. (1997). Introduction to automaticity: Theory and practice. *Reading & Writing Quarterly, 13*(2), 103-105.

579. Samuels, S. J., & Flor, R. F. (1997). The importance of automaticity for developing expertise in reading. *Reading & Writing Quarterly, 13*(2), 107-121.

580. Sarris, M. (2022). Learning to read in a shallow orthography: The effect of letter knowledge acquisition. *International Journal of Early Years Education, 30*(4), 661-678.

581. Savage, R. S., Burgos, G., Wood, E., & Piquette, N. (2015). The Simple View of Reading as a framework for national literacy initiatives: A hierarchical model of pupil-level and classroom-level factors. *British Educational Research Journal, 41*(5), 820-844.

582. Savage, R., Georgiou, G., Parrila, R., & Maiorino, K. (2018). Preventative reading interventions teaching direct mapping of graphemes in texts and set-for-variability aid at-risk learners. *Scientific Studies of Reading, 22*(3), 225-247.

583. Savage, R., Georgiou, G., Parrila, R., Maiorino, K., Dunn, K., & Burgos, G. (2020). The effects of teaching complex grapheme-phoneme correspondences: Evidence from a dual site cluster trial with at-risk Grade 2 students. *Scientific Studies of Reading, 24*(4), 321-337.

584. Sawi, O. M., & Rueckl, J. (2018). Reading and the neurocognitive bases of statistical learning. *Scientific Studies of Reading*, 1-16.

585. Scammacca, N. K., Roberts, G. J., Cho, E., Williams, K. J., Roberts, G., Vaughn, S. R., & Carroll, M. (2016). A century of progress: reading interventions for students in Grades 4–12, 1914–2014. *Review of Educational Research, 86*(3), 756-800.

586. Scammacca, N. K., Roberts, G., Vaughn, S., & Stuebing, K. K. (2015). A meta-analysis of interventions for struggling readers in Grades 4-12: 1980-2011. *Journal of Learning Disabilities, 48*(4), 369-390.

587. Scammacca, N. K., Vaughn, S., Roberts, G., Wanzek, J., & Torgesen, J. K. (2007). *Extensive reading interventions in Grades K-3: From research to practice*. Portsmouth, NH: RMC Research Corporation, Center on Instruction.

588. Scarborough, H. S. (2001). Connecting early language and literacy to later reading (dis)abilities: Evidence, theory, and practice. In S. N. D. Dickinson (Ed.), *Handbook for research in early literacy* (pp. pp. 97–110). New York, NY: Guilford Press.

589. Schiff, R., & Ravid, D. (2013). Morphological processing in Hebrew-speaking students with reading disabilities. *Journal of Learning Disabilities, 46*(3), 220-229.

590. Schneider, W., Ennemoser, M., Roth, E., & Kuspert, P. (1999). Kindergarten prevention of dyslexia: Does training in phonological awareness work for everybody? *Journal of Learning Disabilities, 32*(5), 429-442.

591. Schneider, W., Kuspert, P., Roth, E., & Vise, M. (1997). Short- and long-term effects of training phonological awareness in kindergarten: Evidence from two German studies. *Journal of Experimental Child Psychology, 66*, 311-340.

592. Schoon, I., Parsons, S., Rush, R., & Law, J. (2010). Childhood language skills and adult literacy: A 29-year follow-up study. *Pediatrics, 125*(3), 459-466.

593. Scragg, D. (1974). *A history of English spelling*. Manchester University Press.

594. Seabrook, R., Brown, G. D. A., & Solity, J. E. (2005).

Distributed and massed practice: From laboratory to classroom. *Applied Cognitive Psychology, 19*(1), 107-122.
595. Segura-Pujol, H., & Briones-Rojas, C. (2021). Treatment intensity for Developmental Language and Disorder: A systematic review. *International Journal of Speech Language Pathology, 23*(5), 465-474.
596. Seidenberg, M. S. (2005). Connectionist models of word reading. *Current Directions in Psychological Science, 14*(5), 238-242.
597. Seidenberg, M. S. (2013). The science of reading and its educational implications. *Language Learning and Development, 9*(4), 331-360.
598. Seidenberg, M. S., & McClelland, J. L. (1989). A distributed, developmental model of word recognition and naming. *Psychological Review, 96*(4), 523-568.
599. Seligman, M. E. (2007). *The optimistic child* (13 ed.). Boston, Mass: Houghton Mifflin.
600. Seligman, M. E., & Maier, S. F. (1967). Failure to escape traumatic shock. *J. of Experimental Psychology, 74*(1), 1-9.
601. Senate Standing Committee on Education and Employment. (2016). *Access to real learning: The impact of policy, funding and culture on students with disability.* www.aph.gov.au.
602. Senge, P. M., Cambron-McCabe, N., Lucas, T., Smith, B., Dutton, J., & Kleiner, A. (2000). *Schools that learn.* Doubleday.
603. Senge, P. M., Lucas, T., Nelda, C.-M., Lucas, T., Smith, B., Dutton, J., & Kleiner, A. (2000). A primer to the five disciplines. In P. Senge, T. Lucas, C.-M. Nelda, T. Lucas, B. Smith, J. Dutton, & A. Kleiner (Eds.), *Schools that learn* (pp. 59-98). New York: Currency Books.
604. Serry, T. A., & Hammond, L. (2015). What's in a word? Australian experts' knowledge, views and experiences using the term dyslexia. *Australian Journal of Learning Difficulties, 20*(2), 143-161.
605. Serry, T. A., Rose, M. L., & Liamputtong, P. (2014). Reading Recovery teachers discuss Reading Recovery: A qualitative investigation. *Australian Journal of Learning Difficulties, 19*(1), 61-73.
606. Seymour, P. H. K., Aro, M., & Erskine, J. M. (2003). Foundation literacy acquisition in European orthographies. *British Journal of Psychology, 94*(2), 143-174.
607. Shahar-Yames, D., & Share, D. L. (2008). Spelling as a self-

teaching mechanism in orthographic learning. *Journal of Research in Reading, 31*(1), 22-39.

608. Shany, M., & Share, D. (2011). Subtypes of reading disability in a shallow orthography: a double dissociation between accuracy-disabled and rate-disabled readers of Hebrew. *An Interdisciplinary Journal of The International Dyslexia Association, 61*(1), 64-84.

609. Shapiro, L. R., & Solity, J. (2008). Delivering phonological and phonics training within whole-class teaching. *British Journal of Educational Psychology, 78*(4), 597-620.

610. Shapiro, L. R., & Solity, J. (2016). Differing effects of two synthetic phonics programmes on early reading development. *British Journal of Educational Psychology, 86*(2), 182-203.

611. Share, D. L. (1995). Phonological recoding and self teaching. *Cognition, 55*, 151-218.

612. Share, D. L. (1999). Phonological recoding and orthographic learning: A direct test of the self-teaching hypothesis. *Journal of Experimental Child Psychology, 72*(2), 95-129.

613. Share, D. L. (2008). On the Anglocentricities of current reading research and practice: The perils of overreliance on an 'outlier' orthography. *Psychological Bulletin, 134*(4), 584-615.

614. Share, D. L., & Bar-On, A. (2017). Learning to read a Semitic abjad: The triplex model of Hebrew reading development. *Journal of Experimental Child Psychology, 0*(0), 1-10.

615. Share, D. L., & Shalev, C. (2004). Self-teaching in normal and disabled readers. *Reading and Writing, 17*(7), 769-800.

616. Share, D. L., & Stanovich, K. E. (1995). Cognitive processes in early reading development: Accommodating individual differences into a model of acquisition. Issues in Ed, 1(1), 1-57.

617. Shaywitz, S. E., Shaywitz, B. A., Fletcher, J. M., & Escobar, M. D. (1990). *Prevalence of reading disability in boys and girls: Results of the Connecticut longitudinal study*. Journal of the American Medical Association, 264, 998-1002.

618. Shen, T., & Konstantopoulos, S. (2017). Class size effects on reading achievement in Europe: Evidence from PIRLS. *Studies in Educational Evaluation, 53*, 98-114.

619. Sherrington, T. (2019). *Rosenshine's principles in action*. Saxmundham, Suffolk: John Catt Educational, Limited.

620. Siddaiah, A., & Padakannaya, P. (2015). Rapid Automatized Naming and reading: A review. *Psychological Studies, 60*(1), 70-76.

621. Sideridis, G. D., Simos, P., Mouzaki, A., Stamovlasis, D., & Georgiou, G. K. (2019). Can the relationship between Rapid Automatized Naming and word reading be explained by a catastrophe? Empirical evidence from students with and without reading difficulties. *Journal of Learning Disabilities, 52*(1), 59-70.

622. Silven, M., Poskiparta, E., & Niemi, P. (2004). The odds of becoming a precocious reader of Finnish. *Journal of Educational Psychology, 96*(1), 152-164.

623. Silverman, R. D., Speece, D. L., Harring, J. R., & Ritchey, K. D. (2013). Fluency has a role in the Simple View of Reading. *Scientific Studies of Reading, 17*(2), 108-133.

624. Smith, R., Snow, P., Serry, T., & Hammond, L. (2021). The role of background knowledge in reading comprehension: A critical review. *Reading Psychology, 42*(3), 214-240.

625. Snow, C. E., Burns, M. S., & Griffin, P. (Eds.). (1998a). *Preventing reading difficulties in young children.* National Academy Press.

626. Snow, C. E., Burns, M. S., & Griffin, P. (Eds.). (1998b). *Starting out right: A guide to promoting children's reading success.* National Academy Press.

627. Snow, P. C. (2016). Elizabeth Usher Memorial Lecture: Language is literacy is language – Positioning speech-language pathology in education policy, practice, paradigms and polemics. *International Journal of Speech-Language Pathology, 18*(3), 216-228.

628. Snow, P. C., Graham, L. J., McLean, E. J., & Serry, T. A. (2020). The oral language and reading comprehension skills of adolescents in flexible learning programmes. *International Journal of Speech-Language Pathology, 22*(4), 425-434.

629. Snowling, M. J., Duff, F. J., Nash, H. M., & Hulme, C. (2015). Language profiles and literacy outcomes of children with resolving, emerging, or persisting language impairments. *Journal of Child Psychology and Psychiatry.*

630. Snowling, M. J., Hayiou-Thomas, M. E., Nash, H. M., & Hulme, C. (2019). Dyslexia and Developmental Language Disorder: Comorbid disorders with distinct effects on reading comprehension. *Journal of Child Psychology and Psychiatry, 61*(6), 672-680.

631. Snowling, M. J., & Melby-Lervåg, M. (2016). Oral language deficits in familial dyslexia: A meta-analysis and review. *Psychological Bulletin, 142*(5), 498-545.

632. Solari, E. J., Grimm, R. P., & Henry, A. R. (2022). An exploration of the heterogeneous nature of reading comprehension development in first grade: The impact of word and meaning skills. *J. of Learning Disabilities, 55*(4), 292-305.
633. Solis, M., Kulesz, P., & Williams, K. (2022). Response to intervention for high school students: examining baseline word reading skills and reading comprehension outcomes. *Annals of Dyslexia, 72*(2), 324-340.
634. Solity, J. (2015). *The rhetoric and reality of evidence-based practice and teaching reading: How to bridge the curriculum gap.*www.cse.edu.au
635. Sonnemann, J., & Joiner, R. (2022). Teachers don't have enough time to prepare well for class: We have a solution. *The Conversation,* January 30, 2022.
636. Spanoudis, G. C., Papadopoulos, T. C., & Spyrou, S. (2019). Specific Language Impairment and Reading Disability: Categorical distinction or continuum? *Journal of Learning Disabilities, 52*(1), 3-14.
637. Sparapani, N., Connor, C. M., Day, S., Wood, T., Ingebrand, S., McLean, L., & Phillips, B. (2019). Profiles of foundational learning skills among first graders. *Learning and Individual Differences, 70,* 216-227.
638. Sparapani, N., Connor, C. M., McLean, L., Wood, T., Toste, J., & Day, S. (2018). Direct and reciprocal effects among social skills, vocabulary, and reading comprehension in first grade. *Contemporary Educational Psychology, 53,* 159-167.
639. Sparks, R. L., Patton, J., & Murdoch, A. (2013). Early reading success and its relationship to reading achievement and reading volume: Replication of '10 years later'. *Reading and Writing,* 1-23.
640. Speech Pathology Australia (SPA). (2018). *Developmental Language Disorder: Policy brief.* www.speechpathologyaustralia.org.au.
641. Spencer, L. H., & Hanley, J. R. (2003). Effects of orthographic transparency on reading and phoneme awareness in children learning to read in Wales. *British J. of Psychology, 94*(1), 1-28.
642. Spencer, L. H., & Hanley, J. R. (2004). Learning a transparent orthography at five years old: reading development of children during their first year of formal reading instruction in Wales. *Journal of Research in Reading, 27*(1), 1-14.
643. Spencer, M., Quinn, J. M., & Wagner, R. K. (2014). Specific

reading comprehension disability: Major problem, myth, or misnomer? *Learning Disabilities Research & Practice, 29*(1), 3-9.
644. Stanback, M. L. (1992). Syllable and rime patterns for teaching reading: Analysis of a frequency-based vocabulary of 17,602 Words. *Annals of Dyslexia, 42,* 196-221.
645. Stanovich, K. E., & Stanovich, P. J. (1995). How research might inform the debate about early reading instruction. *Journal of Research in Reading, 18*(2), 87-105.
646. Steacy, L. M., Kirby, J. R., Parrila, R., & Compton, D. L. (2014). Classification of double deficit groups across time: An analysis of group stability from kindergarten to second grade. *Scientific Studies of Reading, 18*(4), 255-273.
647. Stein, J., Talcott, J., & Witton, C. (2001). The sensorimotor basis of developmental dyslexia. In A. J. Fawcett (Ed.), *Dyslexia: Theory and good practice*: Whurr Publishers.
648. Stevenson, H. W. (1998). A study of three cultures: Germany, Japan and the United States – An overview of the TIMSS Case Study Project. *Phi Delta Kappan, 79*(7), 524-529.
649. Stevenson, H. W., James, W. S., Lucker, G. W., Shin-ying, L., Chen-chin, H., & Seiro, K. (1982). Reading disabilities: The case of Chinese, Japanese, and English. *Child Development, 53*(5), 1164-1181.
650. Stevenson, H. W., Lee, S.-Y., Chen, C., Stigler, J. W., Hsu, C.-C., Kitamura, S., & Hatano, G. (1990). Contexts of achievement: A study of American, Chinese, and Japanese children. *Monographs of the Society for Research in Child Development, 55*(1-2), 1-119.
651. Stevenson, H. W., & Nerison-Low, R. (2002). *To sum it up: Case studies of education in Germany, Japan, and the United States.* https://eric.ed.gov.
652. Stothard, S. E., Snowling, M. J., Bishop, D. V. M., Chipchase, B. B., & Kaplan, C. A. (1998). Language-impaired preschoolers: A follow-up into adolescence. *J Speech Lang Hear Res, 41*(2), 407-418.
653. Stuart, M., & Stainthorp, R. (2015). *Reading development and teaching*. London:Sage.
654. Suggate, S., Reese, E., Lenhard, W., & Schneider, W. (2014). The relative contributions of vocabulary, decoding, and phonemic awareness to word reading in English versus German. *Reading and Writing: An Interdisciplinary Journal, 27*(8), 1395-1412.

655. Swanson, H. L., Hoskyn, M., & Lee, C. (1999). *Interventions for students with learning disabilities: A meta-analysis of treatment outcomes.* The Guilford Press.
656. Swanson, H. L., & Howell, M. (2001). Working memory, short-term memory, and speech rate as predictors of children's reading performance at different ages. *Journal of Educational Psychology, 93*(4), 720-734.
657. Sweller, J., van Merriënboer, J., & Paas, F. (1998). Cognitive architecture and instructional design. *Educational Psychology Review, 10*(3), 251-296.
658. Sweller, J., van Merriënboer, J., & Paas, F. (2019). Cognitive architecture and instructional design: 20 years later. *Educational Psychology Review, 31*(2), 261-292.
659. Taylor, I., & Taylor, M. M. (2014). *Writing and literacy in Chinese, Korean and Japanese* (Revised ed., Vol. 14). John Benjamins Publishing Company. Philadelphia:US.
660. Thaler, V., Ebner, E. M., Wimmer, H., & Landerl, K. (2004). Training reading fluency in dysfluent readers with high reading accuracy: Word specific effects but low transfer to untrained words. *Annals of Dyslexia, 54,* 89-113.
661. Thomas, S., Meissel, K., & McNaughton, S. (2019). *What developmental resources do our pre-schoolers have approaching the transition to school?* He Whakaaro, Education Insights, 19 April, 2019. New Zealand.
662. Thompson, G. B., McKay, M. F., Fletcher-Flinn, C. M., Connelly, V., Kaa, R. T., & Ewing, J. (2008). Do children who acquire word reading without explicit phonics employ compensatory learning? Issues of phonological recoding, lexical orthography, and fluency. *Reading and Writing, 21,* 505-537.
663. Thompson, P. A., Hulme, C., Nash, H. M., Gooch, D., Hayiou-Thomas, E., & Snowling, M. J. (2015). Developmental dyslexia: Predicting individual risk. *Journal of Child Psychology & Psychiatry, 56*(9), 976-987.
664. Thomson, S., De Bortoli, L., Underwood, C., & Schmid, M. (2019). *PISA 2018: Reporting Australia's Results: Volume 1: Student Performance.* ACER, www.acer.edu.au.
665. Thomson, S., & Hillman, K. (2019). *The Teaching and Learning International Survey (TALIS) 2018. Australian Report, Volume 1: Teachers and school leaders as lifelong learners.* Australian Council for Educational Research. www.acer.edu.au.

666. Thomson, S., Hillman, K., Schmid, M., Rodrigues, S., & Fullarton, J. (2017). *Highlights from PIRLS 2016: Australia's perspective.* ACER. www.acer.edu.au.
667. Thordardottir, E., Topbaş, S., & Working Group 3 of COST Action ISI406. (2021). How aware is the public of the existence, characteristics and causes of language impairment in childhood and where have they heard about it? A European survey. *Journal of Communication Disorders, 89,* 106057-106057.
668. Thorstad, G. (1991). The effect of orthography on the acquisition of literacy skills. *British Journal of Psychology, 82,* 527-537.
669. Tobia, V., & Bonifacci, P. (2015). The Simple View of Reading in a transparent orthography: The stronger role of oral comprehension. *Reading and Writing, 28*(7), 939-957.
670. Tomas, E., & Vissers, C. (2019). Behind the scenes of Developmental Language Disorder: Time to call neuropsychology back on stage. *Frontiers in Human Neuroscience, 12*:517.
671. Tomblin, J. B., & Zhang, X. (2006). The dimensionality of language ability in school-age children. *Journal of Speech, Language, and Hearing Research, 49*(6), 1193.
672. Tops, W., Callens, M., Lammertyn, J., Hees, V. V., & Brysbaert, M. (2012). Identifying students with dyslexia in higher education. *Annals of Dyslexia, 62*(3), 186-203.
673. Tops, W., Callens, M., van Cauwenberghe, E., Adriaens, J., & Brysbaert, M. (2013). Beyond spelling: The writing skills of students with dyslexia in higher education. *Reading and Writing, 26*(5), 705-720.
674. Torgesen, J. K. (1998). Catch them before they fall: Identification and assessment to prevent reading failure in young children. *LD Online, Spring/Summer,* www.ldonline.org.
675. Torgesen, J. K. (2000). Individual differences in response to early interventions in reading: The lingering problem of treatment resisters. *Learning Disabilities Research & Practice (Lawrence Erlbaum), 15*(1), 55.
676. Torgesen, J. K. (2009). The Response To Intervention instructional model: Some outcomes from a large-scale implementation in Reading First schools. *Child Development Perspectives, 3*(1), 38-40.

677. Torgesen, J. K., Wagner, R. K., & Rashotte, C. A. (1997). Approaches to the prevention and remediation of phonologically based reading disabilities. In B. A. Blachman (Ed.), *Foundations of reading acquisition and dyslexia: Implications for early intervention* (pp. pp. 287-304). Hillsdale, NJ: Lawrence Erlbaum Associates.

678. Torgesen, J. K., Wagner, R. K., & Rashotte, C. A. (1999). *Test of Word Reading Efficiency (TOWRE)*. Austin, Texas: Pro-Ed, Inc.

679. Torgesen, J. K., Wagner, R. K., & Rashotte, C. A. (2012). *Test of Word Reading Efficiency 2 (TOWRE-2)*. Austin, Texas: Pro-Ed.

680. Torgesen, J. K., Wagner, R. K., Rashotte, C. A., Herron, J., & Lindamood, P. (2010). Computer-assisted instruction to prevent early reading difficulties in students at risk for dyslexia: Outcomes from two instructional approaches. *Annals of Dyslexia, 60*(1), 40-56.

681. Torppa, M., Eklund, K., van Bergen, E., & Lyytinen, H. (2015). Late-emerging and resolving dyslexia: A follow-up study from age 3 to 14. *J. of Abnormal Child Psychology, 43*(7), 1389-1401.

682. Torppa, M., Georgiou, G. K., Lerkkanen, M. K., Niemi, P., Poikkeus, A. M., & Nurmi, J. E. (2016a). Examining the Simple View of Reading in a transparent orthography: A longitudinal study from Kindergarten to Grade 3. *Merrill-Palmer Quarterly, 62*(2), 179-206.

683. Torppa, M., Georgiou, G. K., Niemi, P., Lerkkanen, M.-K., & Poikkeus, A.-M. (2016b). The precursors of double dissociation between reading and spelling in a transparent orthography. *Annals of Dyslexia, 67*(1), 42-62.

684. Torppa, M., Lyytinen, P., Erskine, J., Eklund, K., & Lyytinen, H. (2010). Language development, literacy skills, and predictive connections to reading in Finnish children with and without familial risk for dyslexia. *Journal of Learning Disabilities, 43*(4), 308-321.

685. Torppa, M., Parrila, R., Niemi, P., Lerkkanen, M. K., Poikkeus, A. M., & Nurmi, J. E. (2013). The double deficit hypothesis in the transparent Finnish orthography: A longitudinal study from Kindergarten to Grade 2. *Reading and Writing, 26*(8), 1353-1380.

686. Torppa, M., Soodla, P., Lerkkanen, M. K., & Kikas, E. (2019). Early prediction of reading trajectories of children with and without reading instruction in kindergarten: a comparison study of Estonia and Finland. *Journal of Research in Reading, 42*(2), 389-410.

687. Tosh, R., Arnott, W., & Scarinci, N. (2017). Parent-implemented home therapy programmes for speech and language: A systematic review. *International Journal of Language & Communication Disorders, 52*(3), 253-269.
688. Toste, J. R., Heath, N. L., Connor, C. M., & Peng, P. (2015). Reconceptualizing teacher-student relationships: Applicability of the working alliance within classroom contexts. *Elementary School Journal, 116*(1), 3-48.
689. Traverso, L., Viterbori, P., & Usai, M. C. (2015). Improving executive function in childhood: Evaluation of a training intervention for 5-year-old children. *Frontiers in Psychology, 6*, 1-14.
690. Treiman, R., Mullennix, J., Bijeljac-Babic, R., & Richmond-Welty, E. D. (1995). The special role of rimes in the description, use and acquisition of English orthography. *Journal of Experimental Child Psychology, 124*(2), 107-136.
691. Tunmer, W. E., Chapman, J. W., & Prochnow, J. E. (2006). Literate cultural capital at school entry predicts later reading achievement: A seven year longitudinal study. *New Zealand Journal of Educational Studies, 41*(2), 183-204.
692. Tunmer, W. E., & Chapman, J. W. (2012). The Simple View of Reading redux: Vocabulary knowledge and the independent components hypothesis. *Journal of Learning Disabilities, 45*(5), 453-466.
693. Tunmer, W. E., Chapman, J. W., Greaney, K. T., Prochnow, J. E., & Arrow, A. W. (2013). Why the New Zealand National Literacy Strategy Has failed and what can be done about it: Evidence from the Progress in International Reading Literacy study (PIRLS) 2011 and Reading Recovery monitoring reports. *Australian Journal of Learning Difficulties, 18*(2), 139-180.
694. Tunmer, W. E., & Greaney, K. T. (2010). Defining Dyslexia. *Journal of Learning Disabilities, 43*(3), 229-243.
695. Tunmer, W. E., & Hoover, W. (1992). Cognitive and linguistic factors in learning to read. In P. B. Gough, L. C. Ehri, & R. Treiman (Eds.), *Reading acquisition*. Hillsdale NJ: Laurence Ehlbaum Associates.
696. Tunmer, W. E., & Hoover, W. A. (2019). The cognitive foundations of learning to read: A framework for preventing and remediating reading difficulties. *Australian Journal of Learning Difficulties, 24*(1), 75-93.
697. Tzeng, S.-J. (2007). Learning disabilities in Taiwan: A case of cultural constraints on the education of students with

disabilities. *Learning Disabilities Research & Practice, 22*(3), 170-175.
698. United Nations. (1989). *Convention on the rights of the child.* www.un.org.
699. United Nations. (2006). *Convention on the rights of persons with disabilities.* www.un.org.
700. United States Government. (2004a). *Individuals with Disabilities Education Improvement Act (IDEA).* Washington: US.
701. United States Government. (2004b). *The facts about Reading First.* https://eric.ed.gov.
702. Uno, A., Wydell, T. N., Haruhara, N., Kaneko, M., & Shinya, N. (2009). Relationship between reading/writing skills and cognitive abilities among Japanese primary-school children: Normal readers versus poor readers (Dyslexics). *Reading and Writing, 22*(7), 755-789.
703. Unsworth, N., & Engle, R. W. (2007). On the division of short-term and working memory: An examination of simple and complex span and their relation to higher order abilities. *Psychologial Bulletin, 133*(6), 1038-1066.
704. van Daal, V. H. P., & Wass, M. (2017). First- and second-language learnability explained by orthographic depth and orthographic learning: A "natural" Scandinavian experiment. *Scientific Studies of Reading, 21*(1), 46-59.
705. Vakil, E., Blachstein, H., Wertman-Elad, R., & Greenstein, Y. (2012). Verbal learning and memory as measured by the Rey-Auditory Verbal Learning Test: ADHD with and without learning disabilities. *Child Neuropsychology, 18*(5), 449-466.
706. Vakil, E., & Heled, E. (2016). The effect of constant versus varied training on transfer in a cognitive skill learning task: The case of the Tower of Hanoi Puzzle. *Learning and Individual Differences, 47*, 207-214.
707. Vakil, E., Lowe, M., & Goldfus, C. (2015). Performance of children with developmental dyslexia on two skill learning tasks - Serial Reaction Time and Tower of Hanoi Puzzle. *Journal of Learning Disabilities, 48*(5), 471-481.
708. Valås, H. (1999). Students with learning disabilities and low-achieving students: Peer acceptance, loneliness, self-esteem, and depression. *Social Psychology of Education, 3*(3), 173-192.
709. Valås, H. (2001a). Learned helplessness and psychological adjustment 1: Effects of age, gender and academic achievement. *Scandinavian Journal of Educational Research,*

45(1), 71-90.
710. Valås, H. (2001b). Learned helplessness and psychological adjustment 2: Effects of learning disabilities and low achievement. *Scandinavian Journal of Educational Research, 45*(2), 101-114.
711. van Kraayenoord, C. E. (1999). Literacy and numeracy: Action for and with students with learning difficulties. In P. Westwood & W. Scott (Eds.), *Learning disabilities: Advocacy and action*. Melbourne: Australian Resource Educators Association Inc.
712. van Kraayenoord, C. E. (2006). Des English Memorial Lecture - Special education, evidence-based practices and policies: Re-think? Re-butt? Re-make? Re-value? Respond. *Australasian Journal of Special Education, 30*(1), 4-20.
713. van Kraayenoord, C. E. (2007). School and classroom practices in inclusive education in Australia. *Childhood Education, 83*(6), 390-394.
714. van Kraayenoord, C. E., Elkins, J., Palmer, C., & Rickards, F. W. (2001). *Literacy, numeracy and students with disabilities* Canberra: DETYA.
715. Vaughn, S., Grills, A. E., Capin, P., Roberts, G., Fall, A.-M., & Daniel, J. (2022). Examining the effects of integrating anxiety management instruction within a reading intervention for upper elementary students with reading difficulties. *Journal of Learning Disabilities, 55*(5), 408-426.
716. Vaughn, S., Roberts, G. J., Miciak, J., Taylor, P., & Fletcher, J. M. (2019). Efficacy of a word- and text-based intervention for students with significant reading difficulties. *Journal of Learning Disabilities, 52*(1), 31-44.
717. Vaughn, S., Wanzek, J., Murray, C. S., Scammacca, N., Linan-Thompson, S., & Woodruff, A. L. (2009). Response to early reading intervention examining higher and lower responders. *Exceptional Children, 75*(2), 165-183.
718. Vellutino, F. R. (2000). Differentiating between difficult-to-remediate and readily remediated poor readers: More evidence against the IQ-achievement discrepancy definition of reading disability. *Journal of Learning Disabilities, 33*(3), 223.
719. Vellutino, F. R., Scanlon, D. M., Sipay, E. R., Small, S. G., Pratt, A., Chen, R., & Denckla, M. B. (1996). Cognitive profiles of difficult-to-remediate and readily remediated poor readers: Early intervention as a vehicle for distinguishing between cognitive and experiential deficits as basic causes of specific

reading disability. *J. of Educational Psychology, 88*(4), 601-638.
720. Venezky, R. L. (1967). English orthography: Its graphic structure and its relation to sound. *Reading Research Quarterly, 2,* 75-106.
721. Verhoeven, L., & Perfetti, C. (2022). Universals in learning to read across languages and writing systems. *Scientific Studies of Reading, 26*(2), 150-164.
722. Vibulpatanavong, K., & Evans, D. (2019). Phonological awareness and reading in Thai children. *Reading and Writing, 32*(2), 467-491.
723. Vousden, J. I. (2008). Units of English spelling-to-sound mapping: a rational approach to reading instruction. *Applied Cognitive Psychology, 22*(2), 247-272.
724. Vousden, J.I., Ellefson, M., Solity, J., & Chater, N. (2011). Simplifying reading: Applying the simplicity principle to reading. *Cognitive Science, 35*(1), 34.
725. Wagner, R. K., Edwards, A. A., Malkowski, A., Schatschneider, C., Joyner, R. E., Wood, S., & Zirps, F. A. (2019). Combining old and new for better understanding and predicting dyslexia. *New Directions in Child & Adolescent Development, 2019*(165), 11-23.
726. Wagner, R. K., Herrera, S. K., Spencer, M., & Quinn, J. M. (2015). Reconsidering the Simple View of Reading in an intriguing case of equivalent models: Commentary on Tunmer and Chapman (2012). *J. of Learning Disabilities, 48*(2), 115-119.
727. Wagner, R. K., & Ridgewell, C. (2009). A large-scale study of specific reading comprehension disability. *Perspectives on Language and Literacy, 35*(5), 27-31.
728. Wagner, R. K., & Torgesen, J. K. (1987). The nature of phonological processing and its causal role in the acquisition of reading skills. *Psychological Bulletin, 101*(2), 192-212.
729. Walberg, H. J., & Wang, M. C. (1987). *Learner characteristics and adaptive education.* Great Britain: Pergamon Press.
730. Walker, C., & Haddock, R. (2020). *Developmental Language Disorder: A disability, health and education challenge.* (Deeble Institute Evidence Brief, Issue. www.ahha.asn.au.
731. Wang, M. C. (1987). Toward achieving educational excellence for students: Program design and instructional outcomes. *Remedial and Special Education, 8*(3), 25-34.
732. Wang, M. C., & Walberg, H. J. (1983). Adaptive instruction and classroom time. *American Educational Research Journal., 20*(4), 601-626.

733. Wang, Z., Sabatini, J., & O'Reilly, T. (2020). When slower is faster: Time spent decoding novel words predicts better decoding and faster growth. *Scientific Studies of Reading, 24*(5), 397-410.

734. Wanzek, J., Stevens, E. A., Williams, K. J., Scammacca, N., Vaughn, S., & Sargent, K. (2018). Current evidence on the effects of intensive early reading interventions. *Journal of Learning Disabilities, 51*(6), 612-624.

735. Wanzek, J., Vaughn, S., Scammacca, N., Gatlin, B., Walker, M. A., & Capin, P. (2016). Meta-Analyses of the Effects of Tier 2 Type Reading Interventions in Grades K-3. *Educational Psychology Review, 28*(3), 551-576.

736. Wanzek, J., Vaughn, S., Scammacca, N. K., Metz, K., Murray, C. S., Roberts, G., & Danielson, L. (2013). Extensive reading interventions for students with reading difficulties after Grade 3. *Review of Educational Research, 83*(2), 163-195.

737. Warburton, F., & Southgate, V. (1969). *I.T.A: An independent evaluation*. London. Murray, Chambers for the Schools Council.

738. Washington, K. N. (2007). Using the ICF within speech-language pathology: Application to developmental language impairment. *International Journal of Speech-Language Pathology, 9*(3), 242-255.

739. Watt, T. S. (1954). Brush up on your English with hints on pronunciation for visiting foreigners. *Manchester Guardian.* www.spellingsociety.org.

740. Watts, A. F. (1948). *The Holborn Reading Scale*. London: Harrap & Co.

741. Wehmeyer, M. L. (2013). Disability, disorder, and identity. *Intellectual and Developmental Disabilities, 51*(2), 122-126.

742. Weinstein, Y., Sumeracki, M., & Caviglioli, O. (2018). *Understanding how we learn: A visual guide*. Taylor & Francis.

743. Weiss, Y., Katzir, T., & Bitan, T. (2015). Many ways to read your vowels: Neural processing of diacritics and vowel letters in Hebrew. *NeuroImage, 121*, 10-19.

744. Weiss, Y., Katzir, T., & Bitan, T. (2016). When transparency is opaque: Effects of diacritic marks and vowel letters on dyslexic Hebrew readers. *Cortex, 83*, 145-159.

745. Westby, C., & Washington, K. N. (2017). Using the International Classification of Functioning, Disability and Health in assessment and intervention of school-aged children

with language impairments. *Language Speech and Hearing Services in Schools, 48*(3), 137-152.
746. Wheldall, K., & Limbrick, L. (2010). Do more boys than girls have reading problems? *J. of Learning Disabilities, 43*(5), 418-429.
747. Wheldall, K., Wheldall, R., Madelaine, A., Reynolds, M., & Arakelian, S. (2017). Further evidence for the efficacy of an evidence-based, small group, literacy intervention program for young struggling readers. *Australian Journal of Learning Difficulties, 22*(1), 3-13.
748. Wheldall, K., Wheldall, R., Madelaine, A., Reynolds, M., Arakelian, S., & Kohnen, S. (2019). 'Just teach our kids to read': Efficacy of intensive reading interventions for both younger and older low progress readers in schools serving mainly remote Indigenous communities. In J. Rennie, and H. Harper (Eds.), *Literacy education and indigenous Australians*. Singapore: Springer 221–246.
749. Wheldall, R., Glenn, K., Arakelian, S., Madelaine, A., Reynolds, M., & Wheldall, K. (2016). Efficacy of an evidence-based literacy preparation program for young children beginning school. *Australian J. of Learning Difficulties, 21*(1), 21-39.
750. Wiig, E. H., Semel, E., & Secord, W. A. (2013). *Clinical Evaluation of Language Fundamentals-5 (CELF-5)*. Pearson.
751. Wimmer, H., & Goswami, U. (1994). The influence of orthographic consistency on reading development: word recognition in English and German children. *Cognition, 51*(1), 91-103.
752. Wimmer, H., & Landerl, K. (1997). How learning to spell German differs from learning to spell English. In C. A. Perfetti, L. Rieben, & M. Fayol (Eds.), Learning to spell: Research, theory, and practice across languages (pp. 81–96): Lawrence Erlbaum Associates Publishers.
753. Wimmer, H., Landerl, K., Linortner, R., & Hummer, P. (1991). The relationship of phonemic awareness to reading acquisition: More consequence than precondition but still important. *Cognition, 40*(3), 219-249.
754. Wimmer, H., & Mayringer, H. (2002). Dysfluent reading in the absence of spelling difficulties: A specific disability in regular orthographies. *Journal of Educational Psychology, 94*(2), 272-277.
755. Wimmer, H., Mayringer, H., & Landerl, K. (1998). Poor reading: A deficit in skill-automatization or a phonological deficit? *Scientific Studies of Reading, 2*(4), 321-340.

756. Wimmer, H., Mayringer, H., & Landerl, K. (2000). The double-deficit hypothesis and difficulties in learning to read a regular orthography. *J. of Educational Psychology, 92*(4), 668-680.
757. Wimmer, H., Mayringer, H., & Raberger, T. (1999). Reading and dual-task balancing: Evidence against the automatization deficit explanation of developmental dyslexia. *Journal of Learning Disabilities, 32*(5), 473-478.
758. Wimmer, H., & Schurz, M. (2010). Dyslexia in regular orthographies: manifestation and causation. *Dyslexia, 16*(4), 283-299.
759. Winskel, H., & Iemwanthong, K. (2010). Reading and spelling acquisition in Thai children. *Reading and Writing, 23*(9), 1021-1053.
760. Wolf, M. (2007). *Proust and the squid: The story and science of the reading brain.* New York: NY: Harper Collins.
761. Wolf, M. (2016). *Tales of literacy for the 21st century: The literacy agenda.* UK: Oxford University Press.
762. Wolf, M., & Bowers, P. G. (1999). The double-deficit hypothesis for the developmental dyslexias. *Journal of Educational Psychology, 91*(3), 415-438.
763. Wolf, M., Bowers, P. G., & Biddle, K. (2000). Naming-speed processes, timing, and reading: A conceptual review. *Journal of Learning Disabilities, 33*(4), 387-407.
764. Wolf, M., Pfeil, C., Lotz, R., & Biddle, K. (1994). Towards a more universal understanding of the developmental dyslexias: The contribution of orthographic factors. In V. W. Berninger (Ed.), *The varieties of orthographic knowledge I: Theoretical and developmental issues* (pp. 137-171). Kluwer.
765. Wolf, S., & McCoy, D. C. (2019). The role of executive function and social-emotional skills in the development of literacy and numeracy during preschool: a cross-lagged longitudinal study. *Developmental Science, 22*(4), e12800-n/a.
766. Woods, A. F., Wyatt-Smith, C., & Elkins, J. (2005). Learning difficulties in the Australian context: Policy, research and practice. *Curriculum Perspectives, 25*(3), 1-14.
767. World Health Organisation (WHO, 2007). *International Classification of Functioning, Disability and Health* (ICF). www.who.int.
768. Wren, S. (2001). *Cognitive foundations of learning to read: A framework.* Southwestern Educational Development Laboratory, www.sedl.org.

769. Yael, W., Tami, K., & Tali, B. (2015). The effects of orthographic transparency and familiarity on reading Hebrew words in adults with and without dyslexia. *Annals of Dyslexia, 65*(2), 84-102.

770. Yagon, M. A., & Margalit, M. (2016). Specific learning disabilities: The Israeli perspective. *Learning Disabilities: A Contemporary Journal, 14*(1), 39.

771. Younger, R., & Meisinger, E. B. (2022). Group stability and reading profiles of students with dyslexia: A double-deficit perspective. *Learning Disability Quarterly, 45*(4), 239-251.

772. Yovanoff, P., Duesbery, L., Alonzo, J., & Tindal, G. (2005). Grade-level invariance of a theoretical causal structure predicting reading comprehension with vocabulary and oral reading fluency. *Educational Measurement, Issues and Practice, 24*(3), 4-13.

773. Ziegler, J. C., Bertrand, D., Tóth, D., Csépe, V., Reis, A., Faísca, L., Saine, N., Lyytinen, H., Vaessen, A., & Blomert, L. (2010). Orthographic depth and its impact on universal predictors of reading: A cross-language investigation. *Psychological Science, 21*(4), 551-559.

774. Ziegler, J. C., & Goswami, U. C. (2005). Reading acquisition, developmental dyslexia and skilled reading across languages: A psycholinguistic grain size theory. *Psychological Bulletin, 131*(1), 3-29.

775. Ziegler, J. C., Perry, C., & Zorzi, M. (2014). Modelling reading development through phonological decoding and self-teaching: Implications for dyslexia. *Philosophical Transactions of the Royal Society of London. Series B, Biological Sciences,* 369(1634), 20120397.

776. Zuk, J., Dunstan, J., Norton, E., Yu, X., Ozernov-Palchik, O., Wang, Y., Hogan, T. P., Gabrieli, J. D. E., & Gaab, N. (2020). Multifactorial pathways facilitate resilience among kindergarteners at risk for dyslexia: A longitudinal behavioral and neuroimaging study. *Developmental Science,* e12983.

777. Zyngier, D. (2014). Class size and academic results, with a focus on children from culturally, linguistically and economically disenfranchised communities. *Evidence Base, 2014*(1), 1-24

Detailed Table of Contents

Foreword vii
    The Challenge of Reading Difficulties viii
    The JLD Study and Its Findings viii
    GraphoLearn and GraphoGame xi
    The Importance of Strong Motivation and Engagement xii
    Finnish Letter Sounds and Basic Literacy xiii
    Readers Need Both Full and Basic Literacy xiv
    ComprehensionGame and Building of Full Literacy xv
    GraphoLearn's Expanding International Use xvi
    Using GraphoGame with English Readers xviii
    Integrating, Not Sequencing, GraphoGame and ComprehensionGame xx
    The Power of Learning Together in Research xxii

A Brief Pre-Read Glossary xxvi

Welcome 1

The 10 Changes 6
    The Thesis Statement 6
    The 10 Changes 7
    The ABCs of Improving Education 7
    Our Mantra 8
    The 2035 Goal 8
    Our Education Bunyips 10

We've Swiss-Cheese Research Gaps 11
    The Ivory-Towering Vs Swiss-Cheese Contrast 13
        The Non-Cambridge "Cambridge Email" 13
        Key Word-Reading Subskills 14
    Let's Build from Available Studies 16

Analogy Time: Pot-Bound Tomatoes 19
    Lessons from Pot-bound Tomatoes 20
    Solving Seidenberg's Puzzle 23

A Caveat 26

The Research Tours: Impacts of Orthographic Disadvantage

The Research Tours Begin 28
Research Tour 1. Too Slow Word-Reading and Spelling
Development 30
    The COST-A8 14-Nation Word-Reading Study 33
        English Readers' Very Young Age 36
        Standard-English Test Norms 37
    Aro's Finnish Study 38
        The Regular-Orthography "Aha!" Moment 38
        Our Teachers' Higher Workload 39
    Huang and Hanley's Taiwanese Study 41
    The Developmental Trio: Phonemic Awareness, Word-Reading &
    Spelling 45
        Exploring Phonemic Awareness in Cognitive Processing 48
    Slow Vs Rapid Spelling Development 48
        Differing Phonological-Awareness and RAN Impacts 50
    Regular-Orthography Struggles With Learning to Spell Irregular
    Words 51
        Irregular Spellings Are Hard to Learn 51
        Our Children's Strength for Learning Irregular Spellings 52
    Confirmatory Supporting Evidence 53
    Transition from Early to Sophisticated Literacy (TESL) 56
    Our Research Needs 59
    Key Findings from Tour 1 60
Research Tour 2. Orthography Is the Key Factor 63
    Studies in Bilingual Schools 63
    An Additional COST-A8 Study's Findings 65
    Role Model Welsh-English Studies 66
    Standard-English Unfamiliar Words: A Major Challenge 69
    Struggles of Weaker English Word-Readers 71
    Higher English Reading Comprehension 76
    Watching Our Long Sad Tail Develop 78
    Weak Phonemic Awareness in Grade 5 79
    Statistical Learning and Automisation Weakness 79
    Level 1 Automisation Weakness: Accuracy 82
        Letter-Sound Weakness as Universal Level 1 Weakness 83
        Level 1 Automisation Weakness as Forgetting of Skills 84
        When Standard-English Struggles Are Entrenched 86

Reference Resources

Level 2 Automisation Weakness: Fluency 87
The Struggles of Overcoming Level 2 Automisation Weakness
.... 88
Our Children Forget, Regular-Orthography Children Don't 89
Key Findings from Tour 2 90

Research Tour 3. Success Inoculation Vs Acquired Helplessness 92
English Readers Need Success Inoculation 97
Needs for Strong Emotional Supports 98
Inadequate Education As Possible Neglect 99
Motivational-Emotional Struggles of Regular-Orthography
Children 100
Setting Children Up for Success 103
The GraphoLearn Success Inoculation Story 103
Key Findings from Tour 3 106

Research Tour 4. Regular Orthographies and Intellectual
Disability 108
Key Findings from Tour 4 111

Research Tour 5. The Power of Beginners' Orthographies 113
Early Literacy in Taiwan, Japan and China 115
Maximising Learning of a Second Orthography 117
The Initial Teaching Alphabet (ITA) 119
ITA Research Findings 122
Areas ITA Research Did Not Explore 131
ITA Spelling Development 132
Preventing and Overcoming Standard-English Struggles 134
ITA Readers Showed Strong Success Inoculation 135
Regular-Orthography Citizenship Impacts 136
Lack of Research of ITA's Impacts on Later Development 138
ITA Strongly Achieved Its Primary Goals 142
Whole Language Minus ITA Couldn't Win 144
Let's Ensure Success 146
Setting Our Beginners' Orthography Goals 150
ITA Research Suggests Cognitive-Processing Growth 152
More Recent ITA Research 153
Key Findings from Tour 5 155

Research Tour 6. Our Epidemic of Language Weakness 160
We've Widespread Language Weakness 161

Needs for Strong School Services and Supports 166
We've Widespread Insufficient Services 168
Australian Research Is Insufficiently Resourced 172
    The Jyvaskyla Longitudinal Study of Dyslexia (JLD) 173
    The "Early Childhood Longitudinal - Kindergarten Cohort" Study 175
Dyslexia Is Language Disorder! 175
Language Weakness and Reading 179
They Go Together and Grow Together 182
Language, Literacy & Learning Disorder (LLLD) 185
Let's Build Awareness of Language Disorder 187
School Usefulness of the Term *Developmental Language Disorder* 188
    Let's End Cognitive Referencing 190
Receptive Vs Expressive Weakness? Perhaps Not! 191
How Intensive Should Intervention Be? 194
Value in Education Department Oversight of Services 198
Language Disorder as Executive-Function Disorder 199
Improvement: Hugely Expensive Vs Far Less So 201
    The Effective Education Road 201
    The Pre-School Child Road 202
    The Middle Path: The Enhanced Effective Education Road .. 204
    Key Findings from Tour 6 206

Research Tour 7. Literacy Components and Quadrants 209
    The Simple View Model 209
    The Literacy Component Model 211
    Components' Impacts Start Early 215
    Quadrants Show Children's Instructional Needs 218
    Studies Using the Simple View Model 222
        Study 1. Juel's 1988 Study 222
        Study 2. Hoover and Gough's 1990 Study 223
        Study 3. Lonigan et al.'s 2018 Study 224
        Study 4. Torppa et al.'s Finnish Study 224
        Study 5. Gutiérrez et al.'s Prediction Study 225
    Quadrants of Early and Late-Emerging Difficulties 226
        Proportions of Early and Late-Emerging Reading Difficulties 228

Reference Resources

Evidence from Other Anglophone Studies 230
Let's Conduct Component and Quadrant Research 232
Key Findings from Tour 7 234

Research Tour 8. Our Too Many Low Literacy Achievers 237
   PISA and PIRLS Anglosphere Struggles 238
      Australia's PIRLS Performance 238
      Australia's PISA Performance 239
   Major NAPLAN Struggles 243
   Large Standard Deviations Show Many Struggling Learners ... 246
   Our Increasing Numbers of Weak Learners 249
   Of Word-Reading and Language Skill Struggles 249
   Let's Reset our National Minimum Standard (NMS) 250
   Key Findings from Tour 8 251

Research Tour 9. Needs for Workload Research 255
   Workload: A Key Factor Towards Improving Education 257
   Research We Could Work From 259
   Let's Research Workload Impacts of Word-Reading and Spelling Development 262
   Let's Research the Impacts of Orthographic Advantage and Disadvantage 263
   Let's Take Account of Hurdles Nations Have Overcome 265
   Let's Research the Impacts of GENTLE 267
   Let's Research the Impacts of Low School Resourcing 269
   Let's Research Allied-Health Supports 271
   Let's Research Impacts of Automisation Weakness 271
      Our Children Forget Word-Reading Skills 273
      Our Children Forget Maths Facts Too 273
   Let's Research National Curriculum Impacts 275
   Let's Research the Impacts of Class Size 276
   Let's Research Impacts of Teaching Classes for 2-3 Years 277
   Let's Research Excessive Testing and Report Cards 278
   Let's Research the Impacts of Our Young Starting Age 278
   Let's Research the Impacts of Behaviour Issues 278
   Let's Go Well Beyond PIRLS and PISA 280
   Key Findings from Tour 9 283

Research Tour 10. A Multiple Deficits Vs Phonological Basis? ... 286
   A Multiple Deficits or Phonological Basis 287

The Research Tours: Impacts of Orthographic Disadvantage

Our Children Experience Differential Disadvantage 290
Single and Double Deficits.. 292
The Power of Displaying Instructional Needs........................... 295
    Quadrants for Early Identification of At-Risk Children......... 296
Let's Explore Other Double Deficits 298
Key Findings from Tour 10.. 302

Research Tour 11. Executive-Function Skills Empower Word-Reading 304
Cognitive-Processing and Executive-Function Skills 306
Three Key Executive-Function Skills 308
Executive-Function Skills Develop Across Childhood 310
Our Children Need Strong Executive-Function Skills 312
    Working Memory Is Important 313
    Inhibitory Control Is Important.. 313
    Cognitive Flexibility Is Important 314
The Impacts of High Cognitive Load 314
    High Cognitive Load Induces Language Weakness............... 315
    The High Cognitive Load of Our Number Wording................ 315
High Cognitive Load Activates Risk Factors............................. 317
    The Reading Skills of Children with ASD and AD/HD 318
Word-Reading Instruction Methods Change Executive-Function and Language Skills... 320
Building Executive-Function Skills Can Build Word-Reading Readiness... 322
Powerful Byproducts of Effective Cognitive Processing 323
Starting Age Cut-Offs Can Be Punitive...................................... 324
Key Findings from Tour 11.. 327

Research Tour 12. Impeded Statistical Learning 330
A Study of Implicit Statistical Learning..................................... 332
Different Findings in a Similar Study 337
Boys Are More Vulnerable... 339
Regular-Orthography At-Risk Children and Impeded Statistical Learning... 341
When Regular Orthographies Include Complexities 341
    Israel: Unpointed and Pointed Hebrew 342
    South Korea: Hanguel Using Syllable Block Units 344
Key Findings from Tour 12.. 345

Reference Resources

Research Tour 13. Unfamiliar Words: Our Standard-English Nemesis 348
   Needs to Research Reading of Unfamiliar Words 351
   English-Czech-Slovak Word-Reading Differences 352
   English-German Word-Reading Differences 356
      Study 1 Word-Reading Development 357
   Our Major English Vowel Troubles 362
   Study 2 Healthy-Progress Readers' Errors 363
      The Major Errors of English 8-Year-Olds 364
      The Major Errors of English 12-Year-Olds 364
      Vowel-Error Rates and Whole Word Substitutions 365
   Study 3: German Vs English Dyslexic Readers 368
   Developing and Struggling Readers Show Similar Skills 369
   English-Turkish Word-Reading Differences 371
   Australian Needs for Strong Word-Reading Instruction 373
   Needs for Crosslinguistic Research 374
   Australia's Big-20 List for Positioning Word-Reading 376
   Key Findings from Tour 13 377

Reflections As The Tours End 385
      Change 1. Understand how orthographies matter: English spelling is dragging us down. 389
      Change 2. Own our struggling reader woes: End hypocrisy and pretence. 390
      Change 3. Weigh workload: Our children and teachers are working far too hard. 390
      Change 4. One-size education does not fit all: Teach to the decidedly different instructional needs of upper-third and lower-third readers. 391
      Change 5. End our data deficiency: Build strong knowledge on word-reading levels. 392
      Change 6. Enrich every child: Ensure effective supportive tailored education. 392
      Change 7. Insist on easy literacy development: Reach regular-orthography nations' achievement levels. 392
      Change 8. Investigate the potential of fully-regular beginners' orthographies: They're winners. 393
      Change 9. Play to learn first: Start Standard-English word-reading instruction from mid-Year 2 394

Change 10. Build needed research knowledge as quickly as possible: Use collaborative school-based research. 395

Research Tour 14. Our Insufficiently Effective Word-Reading Intervention 396

The Challenge of Achieving Then Maintaining Healthy Word-Reading 398
The Regular-Orthography Intervention Success Story 400
  Successful Intervention with Taiwanese At-Risk Readers 401
    Study 1. Remedial Reading Materials 401
    Study 2. Long-Term Intervention 402
    Study 3. Differing Intervention Foci 402
  Successful Intervention with German Weakest Readers 403
  Successful Intervention with Danish Weakest Readers 404
  Successful Intervention with Italian Weakest Readers 404
  Successful Intervention with Finnish Weakest Readers 404
The Anglophone Insufficient-Success Story 406
Let's Research Intervention Effectiveness 408
Let's Reflect on Workload and Resourcing Implications 408
Let's Include Children with Other Disabilities 409
Let's Research Intervention Responsiveness 410
Let's Talk about "Nonresponders" 411
Let's Reflect on Insufficiently Effective Intervention 412
Let's Compare Apples with Apples 413
Our Intervention Resourcing Needs Are Huge 415
  Reduced Class Sizes 415
  Effective Intervention-Resourcing Levels 416
Let's Amply Resource Intervention 417
Let's Amply Resource Our Class Teachers 420
  1. Fewer Teaching Hours 421
  2. A Full-Time Teacher Aide 421
  3. Effectively Resourced Learning Support 421
  4. A Strong National Curriculum and Resourcing 421
Let's Research Upstream and Downstream 422
It's Time to Rethink Cut-Off Criteria 423
Key Findings from Tour 14 426

Let's Research Together 430
Let's Resource Research Impressively 430

Reference Resources

Let's Prioritise Factful Thinking 433
    Let's be Possibilists and Factfulists, not Ideologists 435
    Crucial for Heightened Clear Thinking: Facts and Data 436
    Let's Avoid Ideological Thinking 438
    Let's Keep the Discussion Going 439

The 100 Research Questions 441
    Research Questions Section 1: The Generic Research Questions 443
    Research Questions Section 2: Our Research Drought, Needs, and Future Directions 446
    Research Questions Section 3: Our Status Quo: Current Levels of Literacy Skills 448
    Research Questions Section 4: Language Skills for Literacy 449
    Research Questions Section 5: Literacy Components and Quadrants: Our Balance of Word-Reading and Language Skills 452
    Research Questions Section 6: The Crosslinguistic Gap: Major Differences Between Anglophone Nations and Regular-Orthography Nations 453
    Research Questions Section 7: Orthographic Advantage and Disadvantage 454
    Research Questions Section 8: Beginners' Orthographies and 2-Stage Early Literacy 455
    Research Questions Section 9: The Roles of Word-Reading and Spelling in Crosslinguistic Differences 457
    Research Questions Section 10: Our Teachers' High Workload . 461
    Research Questions Section 11: Our Children's High Workload 463
    Research Questions Section 12: Differential Disadvantaging of Our At-Risk Learners 465
    Research Questions Section 13: Motivation, Engagement, Persistence, and Resilience 466
    Research Questions Section 14: Young Vs Older Starting Age When Learning to Read 467
    Research Questions Section 15: Models for Guiding Research and Practice 467
    Research Questions Section 16: School Instruction and Assessment Practices 468
    Research Questions Section 17: Executive-Function Skills and Learning 470
    Research Questions Section 18: The Ethics of Our Status Quo.. 471
    Research Questions Section 19: The Impacts of Beliefs on Change 472

Research Questions Section 20: Our Education Future 473
Thanks 475
Reference Resources 475
List of Tables... 476
List of Figures... 476
Reference list 478
Detailed Table of Contents... 545
Index... 555

Index

10 Changes, 2, 3, 4, 6, 7, 8, 9, 10, 18, 23, 27, 28, 59, 65, 76, 114, 144, 146, 147, 167, 181, 199, 201, 204, 205, 208, 249, 250, 255, 256, 257, 265, 266, 282, 319, 327, 375, 377, 389, 394, 396, 414, 419, 422, 430, 431, 432, 434, 437, 438, 439, 443, 444, 445, 455, 463, 464, 468, 473
100 research questions, 441
1-Stage early-literacy, 76, 79, 114, 115, 217, 256, 263, 351, 356, 377, 386, 393, 397, 408, 429, 447, 454, 456, 457, 461, 467, 469
2035 goal, v, 6, 8, 233, 271, 284, 285, 392, 429, 431, 439, 443, 445, 457, 468, 469
2-Stage early-literacy, 41, 42, 43, 48, 52, 59, 62, 97, 100, 114, 115, 117, 139, 155, 156, 158, 204, 205, 226, 256, 259, 263, 266, 297, 319, 321, 323, 342, 343, 344, 351, 356, 362, 375, 376, 377, 386, 387, 388, 389, 392, 393, 394, 408, 428, 442, 447, 453, 454, 455, 456, 457, 460, 461, 463, 464, 466, 467, 469, 474
4D for Dyslexia, 187
ABCs, 6, 7, 8, 115, 147, 201, 257, 389, 390, 391, 439, 443, 445, 468
Acquired Helplessness, 21, 24, 79, 86, 92, 93, 94, 95, 96, 97, 98, 99, 102, 104, 106, 107, 113, 135, 136, 156, 195, 223, 256, 272, 296, 304, 317, 326, 339, 341, 375, 376, 385, 403, 455, 466, 470
African studies, vii, xv, xvi
age
  age effects, 326
  age-advantage effects, 326, 327
  age-disadvantage effects, 325
  starting, 7
  starting age, xviii, 6, 21, 24, 36, 63, 65, 67, 69, 100, 127, 162, 181, 272, 278, 284, 324, 356, 442, 467, 470
Albanian studies, 53
Alice Springs (Mparntwe) Education Declaration, 164, 253, 257, 420
allied-health support, 3, 7, 162, 169, 172, 185, 194, 195, 197, 198, 199, 204, 205, 206, 207, 208, 221, 258, 266, 267, 268, 270, 271, 283, 284, 418, 419, 420, 421, 445
Alphabetic Principle, 31, 32, 108, 144
assessment
  assignments, 176, 215, 275, 276, 466
  in-class testing, 278, 284
  report cards, 278
  tasks, 276, 464
Attention-Deficit/Hyperactivity Disorder (ADHD), 101, 175, 318, 319
auditory processing, 161, 175, 278, 340, 406

Australian Early Development Census (AEDC), 165, 166, 167, 270
Australian Education Research Organisation, 250
Australian Institute of Health and Welfare (AIHW), 251
Austrian studies, 49, 54
autism, 176, 188, 189, 200, 286, 288, 302, 306, 307, 318, 319, 340, 451
Autism Spectrum Disorder (ASD), 176, 200, 299, 307, 318, 319, 451
automaticity, 14, 81, 88, 155, 177, 272, 286, 337, 358, 364, 365, 371, 374, 377, 403
automisation
  Level 1, 82, 83, 84, 86, 87, 88, 89, 91, 155, 196, 240, 263, 271, 272, 273, 284, 292, 303, 337, 358, 364, 365, 371, 374, 377, 399, 401, 402, 403, 411, 412, 458, 459, 468
  Level 2, 87, 88, 89, 91, 155, 240, 242, 243, 271, 292, 303, 358, 364, 371, 374, 458, 459, 468
  weakness, 15, 78, 79, 80, 81, 82, 83, 84, 86, 87, 88, 89, 90, 91, 177, 271, 272, 273, 274, 275, 284, 288, 290, 292, 317, 338, 399, 411, 412, 458, 459
Bangladesh studies, 311
Basic Literacy, ix, xii, xiii, xiv, xv, xvi, xvii, xix, xx, 545
behaviour issues, 94, 101, 102, 116, 129, 141, 176, 185, 206, 207, 208, 225, 271, 278, 279, 281, 284, 288, 299, 304, 306, 307, 312, 340, 409, 411, 526
Big-20 List for Positioning Word-Reading, 376, 377, 443, 445, 468

bilingual schools, 63, 64, 67, 153
biliteracy, 154
BoPoMoPho, 42
Bridging the Gap project, 98, 211, 215, 221, 231, 234, 296, 444
bunyips, 10, 440
Canadian studies, 63, 231, 239, 240, 241, 242
CCVCC words, 85, 273
Change 1, 7, 114, 146, 256, 349, 389, 395
Change 10, 7, 18, 60, 114, 257, 395
Change 2, 7, 114, 250, 251, 256, 390
Change 3, 7, 114, 256, 257, 390
Change 4, 7, 114, 256, 391
Change 5, 7, 114, 256, 392
Change 6, 7, 114, 146, 256, 392
Change 7, 7, 105, 114, 146, 256, 392
Change 8, 7, 48, 79, 105, 114, 146, 199, 202, 204, 205, 208, 226, 257, 297, 319, 320, 362, 387, 393, 455, 463, 464, 469, 473, 474
Change 9, 7, 48, 105, 114, 146, 199, 204, 205, 208, 226, 257, 297, 319, 320, 327, 387, 394, 450, 463, 464, 466, 469, 473, 474
Chinese studies, xvii, xxvi, 2, 8, 22, 41, 42, 43, 46, 55, 59, 62, 64, 106, 113, 115, 116, 117, 118, 128, 138, 139, 147, 152, 153, 155, 156, 190, 201, 202, 205, 208, 240, 242, 259, 276, 281, 284, 301, 311, 316, 344, 375, 379, 386, 392, 393, 401, 422, 423, 425, 428, 429, 439, 447, 453, 454, 455, 456, 457, 458, 466
class size, 99, 255, 260, 261, 266, 276, 277, 284, 415, 416

Clinical Evaluation of Language Fundamentals-5, 192
cognitive flexibility, 207, 299, 311, 312, 314, 316, 318, 319, 327, 364, 366, 470
Cognitive Foundations Framework, 211
cognitive load, xv, xxvii, 10, 14, 15, 16, 21, 24, 25, 43, 52, 55, 58, 59, 80, 86, 87, 97, 100, 102, 109, 112, 120, 121, 123, 125, 177, 178, 184, 190, 199, 213, 236, 259, 261, 262, 265, 268, 278, 288, 290, 300, 303, 308, 309, 310, 314, 315, 316, 317, 318, 320, 328, 329,335, 340, 343, 345, 350, 351, 372, 384, 386, 388, 440, 441, 449, 453, 454, 455, 456, 459, 461, 464, 468, 470, 471
Cognitive Load Theory, 261, 468
cognitive referencing, 189, 190, 191, 206, 298, 471
cognitive-processing skills, 14, 21, 24, 29, 41, 44, 45, 48, 50, 53, 55, 59, 61, 62, 64, 65, 66, 67, 78, 80, 81, 86, 87, 90, 91, 96, 106, 110, 111, 112, 117, 132, 152, 153, 160, 161, 179, 182, 184, 193, 195, 199, 207, 213, 215, 238, 246, 265, 278, 288, 289, 290, 291, 292, 300, 301, 302, 304, 305, 306, 307, 308, 310, 311, 315, 317, 320, 321, 322, 323, 324, 329, 340, 345, 351, 375, 386, 388, 411, 423, 428, 435, 437, 441, 445, 446, 447, 448, 449, 450, 453, 456, 458, 459, 460, 465, 470, 473, 498, 503, 508
comorbidities, 288, 290, 299, 302
ComprehensionGame, xiv, xv, xvi, xxii, 175, 447, 456

Consonant-Vowel-Consonant (CVC) words, 82, 85, 145, 273, 332, 333, 334, 335, 339, 346
Continuing Literacy, 56, 57, 58
Convention on the Rights of Persons with Disabilities, 257
Convention on the Rights of the Child, 257
Core Literacy, 56, 57, 58, 59, 60, 62, 464
COST studies, vi, 33, 59, 65, 69, 187, 395
Creating Opportunities to Learn from Text (COLT), 262
critical readers, xiv, xv
crosslinguistic differences, vi, xvii, 48, 55, 56, 62, 102, 120, 121, 190, 263, 274, 387, 389, 391, 425, 442, 453, 458, 459, 470, 473
curriculum pressure, 40, 97
CVCe words, 82, 85, 273
CVCVCV words, 363, 364, 365
Cyprian studies, 320, 328, 331, 337, 341, 367
Czech studies, 49, 53, 54, 352, 353, 355, 356, 358, 360, 407, 408, 445, 460
Danish studies, 34, 35, 64, 240, 404
Deeble Institute, 171
Default Helplessness, 95
Delayed Neural Commitment framework, 289
developing vs struggling readers, 48, 366, 369, 370, 377, 378, 442, 459, 468
differential disadvantage, 56, 184, 290, 291, 465, 466
double deficits, 50, 292, 293, 298, 299, 300, 303

double-deficit model, 292, 293, 294, 295, 296, 297, 298, 299, 300
Down Syndrome, 89, 109, 110, 111, 404, 406
DSM-5, 186, 299
Dutch studies, 33, 82, 88, 242, 292, 357, 400
dynamic assessment, x, xi, xiii, xx
Dynamic Indicators of Basic Early Literacy Skills (DIBELS), 85, 248
NonWord Reading, 85
Oral Reading Fluency, 85
dyscalculia, 178, 274
dysfluent readers, 87, 88, 89, 91
dysgraphia, 178
dyslexia, viii, xxix, 16, 54, 83, 88, 93, 95, 104, 109, 161, 173, 174, 175, 176, 178, 179, 180, 182, 184, 185, 186, 187, 188, 199, 201, 210, 220, 221, 274, 286, 287, 289, 294, 307, 368, 378, 400, 426, 451, 524
Early Childhood Longitudinal Study (ECLS), 173, 175, 326
Early Literacy Inservice Course (ELIC), 145
Early Years Factory, xxviii, 2, 24, 87, 97, 105, 113, 147, 167, 185, 205, 243
Educational Opportunity report, 163, 164, 202
Effective Education Road, 201, 202, 203, 204, 205, 208, 387, 393, 474
Estonian studies, xxvi, 8, 58, 59, 60, 120, 240, 242, 255, 259, 266, 267, 268, 270, 277, 278, 282, 284, 285, 395, 418, 422, 432, 433, 447, 453, 462, 464, 467
executive-function skills, 44, 45, 50, 59, 62, 64, 66, 80, 81, 86, 90, 92, 94, 96, 97, 98, 106, 129, 152, 153, 160, 161, 177, 182, 195, 199, 200, 207, 215, 238, 239, 261, 278, 288, 289, 299, 300, 303, 304, 305, 306, 307, 308, 309, 311, 312, 317, 318, 319, 320, 321, 322, 323, 324, 325, 326, 328, 329, 330, 335, 336, 339, 340, 341, 345, 375, 386, 388, 404, 441, 446, 448, 449, 450, 453, 455, 457, 467, 470, 471, 473
explicit learning, 334, 335, 338, 341
explicit teaching, 330, 331, 333, 337, 338, 341, 347, 367
expressive language, xxix, 176, 184, 192, 193, 220, 300, 303, 400
Finnish studies, vii, ix, xi, xii, xv, xxii, xxvi, 8, 31, 33, 35, 36, 38, 39, 41, 45, 48, 49, 54, 55, 58, 59, 61, 65, 66, 84, 88, 89, 96, 101, 102, 103, 105, 106, 110, 120, 144, 161, 164, 173, 176, 187, 190, 224, 225, 242, 255, 258, 259, 267, 268, 269, 270, 278, 281, 282, 284, 293, 295, 301, 305, 333, 338, 340, 344, 374, 395, 397, 404, 405, 406, 407, 408, 409, 417, 418, 421, 422, 424, 427, 431, 446, 447, 451, 453, 457, 462, 463, 464, 467
Fleksispel, 22, 23, 52, 127, 149, 457
Fourth Grade Slump, 226, 227, 228, 230, 235, 236, 250, 452
French studies, 34, 35, 64, 187, 239, 242, 292, 431
Full Literacy, xiii, xiv, xv, xvi, xix, xx, xxi, 545
gender, xiv, xxii, 151, 243, 244, 245, 279, 312, 318, 334, 335, 336, 338, 339, 340, 341, 347, 368

generational disadvantage, xxviii, xxix, 163, 167, 181, 184, 201, 203, 207, 243, 256, 461, 469
GENTLE, xxviii, 8, 100, 144, 205, 267, 268, 273, 284, 390, 393, 395, 429, 439, 458
German studies, 33, 36, 49, 50, 51, 53, 54, 64, 88, 89, 240, 292, 300, 356, 357, 358, 359, 360, 361, 362, 363, 364, 365, 366, 367, 368, 369, 370, 378, 397, 403, 404, 407, 408, 424, 445, 460
Grapheme-Phoneme Correspondences (GPCs), xxvi, 1, 23, 25, 31, 32, 119, 348, 349, 366, 369, 470
graphemes, ix, xxii, xxvi, xxix, 36, 49, 51, 52, 117, 119, 126, 127, 179
GraphoGame, vi, ix, x, xv, xvi, xvii, xix, xxii, 84, 103, 104, 337, 346
  Phoneme, xviii, xxii, 337
  Rime, xviii, xxii, 337, 346
GraphoLearn, vii, x, xvi, xxii, 84, 102, 103, 106, 174, 175, 323, 337, 338, 341, 405, 447, 456, 461
Grattan Institute, 259
Greek studies, xxvi, 33, 50, 53, 64, 101, 292, 294, 320, 321, 322, 323, 324, 328, 331, 332, 337, 341, 357, 367
HEARTSH, xxviii, 8, 100, 144, 205, 267, 268, 273, 390, 395
Home Literacy, 56
Hong Kong studies, 116, 240, 242
hyperlexia, 210, 220, 221
Icelandic studies, 33, 65, 66, 190
ideological thinking, 438

implicit learning, 322, 330, 331, 333, 334, 335, 336, 338, 341, 344, 345, 346, 347, 368
independent learning, 148, 202
India studies, 311
indigenous children, 243, 245, 246, 247, 248, 250, 252, 253, 280
indigenous languages, 64, 65, 154
inhibition control, 207, 299, 312, 318, 319, 327, 448, 453, 470
inhibitory control, 307, 308, 311, 312, 313, 314, 362
Initial Teaching Alphabet (ITA), xxvi, 21, 38, 55, 59, 97, 113, 119, 120, 121, 122, 123, 124, 125, 126, 127, 128, 129, 130, 131, 132, 133, 134, 135, 136, 137, 138, 139, 140, 141, 142, 143, 144, 145, 146, 147, 148, 149, 150, 151, 152, 153, 154, 155, 156, 157, 158, 159, 351, 375, 392, 407, 414, 437, 439, 441, 457
ITA Foundation, 122, 154
instructional needs, 6, 7, 40, 76, 114, 167, 191, 193, 196, 212, 218, 220, 221, 231, 232, 235, 255, 256, 295, 296, 377, 387, 391, 392, 426, 440, 452
intellectual disabilities, 83, 108, 109, 110, 111, 112, 113, 256, 385, 386, 390, 404, 409, 453, 459, 471
International Classification of Functioning, Disability and Health, 186
International Longitudinal Twin Study (ILTS), 293
interventions
  effectiveness, 197, 401, 408, 457
  resourcing, 416, 421

Response to Intervention
(RTI), 191, 195, 296, 410,
419, 427
responses, 195
Tier 1, 195, 196, 419, 427
Tier 2, 195, 196, 296, 297,
405, 419, 427
Tier 3, 195, 196, 197, 198,
204, 298, 419, 420, 427
Irish studies, 239, 240, 241,
242
irregular words, 32, 51, 52, 53,
61, 69, 70, 77, 78, 82, 109,
145, 148, 152, 272, 308, 349,
351, 352, 379
Israeli studies, 63, 64, 342,
343, 344
Italian studies, xxvi, 33, 35,
36, 49, 51, 52, 53, 64, 77,
109, 110, 111, 153, 239, 358,
404
ivory-towered research, 12, 13,
16, 20, 232
Japanese studies, xxvi, 2, 8,
22, 41, 59, 62, 64, 106, 110,
113, 115, 116, 117, 118, 128,
139, 147, 152, 153, 155, 156,
190, 201, 202, 205, 208, 259,
266, 277, 281, 282, 284, 285,
316, 344, 375, 379, 386, 392,
393, 401, 422, 423, 425, 428,
429, 432, 433, 439, 447, 453,
454, 455, 456, 457, 458, 462,
464, 466
Hiragana, 115, 117, 139
Kanji, 115, 117, 118, 156
Katakana, 115
*Jyvaskyla Longitudinal Study
of Dyslexia* (JLD), vi, vii, x,
xxii, 103, 161, 173, 174, 175,
176, 344, 447
Kahneman, Daniel, 434, 435
language disorder, 162, 168,
175, 176, 177, 178, 180, 185,
187, 188, 189, 190, 192, 195,
199, 201, 206, 221, 231, 233,
298, 307, 315, 409, 420, 422,
450, 451, 472
Developmental Language
Disorder (DLD), 162, 171,
178, 179, 187, 188, 189,
190, 200, 450
Language Experience, 145,
149, 154
language skills, viii, ix, x, 59,
62, 64, 112, 116, 134, 138,
150, 156, 157, 160, 161, 162,
172, 173, 174, 175, 178, 179,
180, 182, 183, 184, 186, 187,
189, 192, 193, 196, 206, 209,
210, 211, 214, 215, 216, 218,
220, 221, 222, 223, 224, 225,
228, 230, 231, 232, 234,
235,237, 238, 246, 249, 252,
271, 296, 312, 315, 320, 328,
336, 343, 376, 380, 386, 387,
402, 406, 411, 432, 436, 437,
442, 445, 446, 448, 450, 452,
453, 456, 465, 466, 469, 473
expressive, viii, 179, 191,
193, 298, 299, 449, 451
Language Skills for
Literacy, xxix, 180, 193,
212, 213, 215, 234, 295,
449
receptive, viii, 191, 193, 298,
451
weakness, vii, xxviii, xxix,
80, 148, 161, 162, 171,
172, 176, 177, 178, 179,
180, 181, 183, 184, 188,
189, 199, 206, 217, 218,
220, 226, 227, 228, 230,
235, 250, 253, 284, 291,
295, 299, 304, 307, 395,
452, 467
language weakness, 2, 10, 80,
160, 161, 162, 163, 165, 166,
168, 169, 175, 176, 179, 181,
182, 183, 184, 185, 186, 187,
188, 189, 190, 194, 198, 199,
201, 206, 207, 208, 222, 227,

230, 252, 256, 258, 271, 283, 291, 303, 315, 329, 376, 386, 394, 440
Language, Literacy and Learning Disorder (LLLD), xxix, 16, 185, 187, 188, 189, 195, 198, 201, 206, 271, 288, 294, 315, 386, 450, 451, 467, 468
Learned Helplessness, 25, 92, 93, 94, 95, 98, 152, 213, 466
Learned Resilience, 95
Learning Disabilities Reference Centers, 187
learning disabilties, 167, 176, 191
letter-sounds, ix, x, xiv, xvii, xviii, 26, 30, 31, 32, 53, 87, 149, 217, 308, 321, 333, 335, 345, 366, 402, 403, 404, 410, 453, 459
skills, x, 22, 39, 84, 293, 322, 448
weakness, 83, 295, 449
Lexicality Effect, 366
Literacy Component Model, 55, 56, 193, 209, 211, 212, 213, 214, 215, 221, 222, 234, 236, 296, 300, 302, 303, 388, 452, 468
Literate Cultural Capital, 180, 216, 217, 223, 449, 467, 469
Longitudinal Study of Australian Children (LSAC), 162, 169, 172, 173, 175, 183
Mantra, 6, 8, 391, 439, 443, 445, 468
Masters, Geoff, 165, 418
Mater-University of Queensland Study of Pregnancy (MUSP), 305
MiniLit studies, 398
motivation and engagement, xx, 86, 95, 98, 215, 351, 442, 466

MultiLit studies, 398, 399
multiple deficits, 199, 200, 288, 290
Multiple Deficits Basis model, 288, 289, 302, 303
multiple-year teaching, 277
Murdoch Children's Research Institute, 171
NAPLAN, xxx, 2, 163, 167, 173, 207, 223, 230, 232, 235, 238, 243, 244, 245, 246, 247, 248, 249, 250, 251, 252, 253, 254, 262, 270, 273, 280, 336, 339, 382, 383, 387, 396, 414, 432, 445, 452, 464, 473
National Assessment of Educational Progress (NAEP) (US), 225, 237
national curriculum, 97, 118, 269, 273, 274, 275, 276, 280, 284, 313, 384, 418, 421, 422, 427
National Minimum Standards (NMS), 163, 164, 243, 244, 245, 247, 248, 249, 250, 251, 254
Nationally Consistent Collection of Data (NCCD), 270, 462
NDIS, 169, 170, 172, 197, 198, 270, 420, 451
New South Wales Teachers Federation, 260
New Zealand studies, 2, 187, 216, 239, 241, 242, 415, 417
Northern Irish studies, 239
Norwegian studies, 33, 36, 54, 240, 293
Optimizing Learning Opportunities for Students (OLOS), 262
orthographic advantage, 56, 59, 114, 138, 157, 205, 263, 265, 284, 355, 384, 386, 389, 390, 454, 455, 461, 464

Orthographic Advantage Theory,
55, 56, 263, 264, 265, 454,
468
orthographic awareness, 44,
62, 152, 153, 306, 322, 453
orthographic disadvantage,
xxi, xxviii, 1, 3, 4, 8, 55, 59,
111, 113, 114, 138, 139, 146,
184, 185, 205, 265, 277, 283,
284, 375, 376, 387, 389, 390,
395, 454, 461, 464
orthographic grainsize, xxii,
32, 333, 335, 346
orthographic impacts, 3, 4, 25,
67, 357, 395, 454
orthographies, vi, ix, xxii, xxvi,
xxvii, xxix, 1, 2, 4, 5, 7, 21,
22, 23, 24, 27, 31, 33, 34, 35,
36, 37, 38, 39, 41, 42, 43, 44,
47, 48, 49, 50, 51, 52, 53, 54,
55, 56, 57, 58, 60, 61, 63, 64,
65, 66, 67, 69, 70, 76, 77, 78,
79, 82, 83, 84, 86, 87, 88, 89,
90, 91, 92, 93, 94, 96, 97,
101, 102, 103, 105, 107, 108,
109, 110, 111, 114, 115, 117,
118, 119, 120, 121, 122, 123,
124, 125, 126, 127, 131, 133,
134, 138, 139, 140, 141, 144,
146, 147, 148, 149, 150, 151,
152, 153, 155, 156, 157, 158,
161, 163, 175, 184, 189, 190,
196, 201, 202, 203, 217, 226,
238, 256, 257, 258, 259, 262,
263, 264, 266, 267, 268, 281,
282, 283, 284, 285, 287, 288,
290, 292, 293, 297, 300, 301,
314, 317, 319, 320, 323, 324,
325, 328, 338, 341, 342, 346,
348, 349, 350, 351, 352, 356,
357, 358, 359, 362, 363, 366,
367, 369, 370, 372, 374, 375,
377, 379, 384, 385, 386, 387,
388, 389, 390, 393, 397, 399,
400, 401, 402, 403, 404, 407,
408, 409, 410, 411, 412, 413,
414, 420, 422, 423, 424, 425,
426, 428, 429, 439, 440, 441,
442, 447, 453, 454, 455, 456,
457, 459, 460, 461, 462, 463,
465, 466, 468, 469, 471, 472,
473, 474
alphabetic, 45, 118, 292
complex, xvii, xxii, xxvi,
xxvii, 1, 3, 6, 14, 21, 22,
23, 24, 28, 30, 34, 36, 37,
41, 42, 44, 45, 50, 55, 59,
62, 63, 64, 66, 68, 69, 78,
81, 86, 90, 100, 112, 113,
117, 118, 120, 121, 128,
138, 145, 152, 155, 156,
157, 181, 190, 195, 226,
252, 255, 258, 259, 263,
265, 267, 278, 283, 284,
292, 308, 311, 315, 318,
328, 333, 340, 342, 343,
345, 348, 349, 351, 368,
371, 373, 379, 384, 385,
386, 389, 394, 400, 401,
404, 423, 428, 454, 455,
456, 457, 471, 473
fully-regular beginners',
xxvi, 2, 6, 22, 23, 42, 44,
45, 48, 52, 59, 61, 62, 91,
97, 99, 112, 113, 114, 125,
137, 143, 146, 181, 204,
208, 256, 329, 356, 362,
376, 394, 408, 419, 420,
425, 426, 428, 438, 455,
457, 465, 469, 473
highly-regular, xxvi, 34, 39,
47, 59, 61, 63, 64, 65, 66,
86, 122, 137, 225, 281,
301, 320, 321, 357, 456,
469
morpho-logographic, 41,
122, 401
regular, x, xxii, xxvi, xxvii,
xxviii, 7, 8, 21, 22, 26, 27,
28, 30, 32, 33, 35, 37, 39,
41, 42, 45, 46, 48, 50, 54,
55, 56, 58, 60, 61, 62, 63,

64, 65, 69, 74, 76, 77, 79, 80, 83, 84, 86, 87, 88, 90, 91, 93, 96, 97, 100, 101, 105, 107, 108, 109, 110, 111, 113, 114, 117, 118, 121, 123, 128, 130, 138, 139, 140, 144, 146, 150, 151, 152, 153, 161, 174, 180, 181, 184, 185, 189, 190, 202, 204, 225, 238, 242, 253, 256, 257, 258, 259, 262, 263, 265, 266, 267, 268, 272, 273, 276, 277, 283, 284, 285, 288, 292, 293, 302, 303, 308, 311, 314, 315, 317, 319, 320, 321, 322, 328, 329, 331, 333, 338, 341, 342, 344, 345, 350, 351, 352, 355, 356, 368, 369, 373, 374, 375, 376, 378, 384, 386, 388, 390, 391, 392, 393, 395, 396, 397, 400, 401, 405, 406, 407, 409, 412, 414, 419, 422, 423, 424, 425, 426, 428, 429, 433, 438, 439, 440, 442, 447, 448, 453, 454, 457, 458, 459, 460, 461, 462, 463, 464, 467, 469, 470, 471, 473
  traditional, 120, 122, 124, 125, 127, 130, 131, 134, 136, 139, 140, 141, 142, 143, 144
  transitional, 126, 143
  transparent, vi, ix, xvii, xviii, xxii, 30
PASS Reading Enhancement Program (PREP), 322, 323
Pattern Words, 32, 314, 333, 334, 335, 337, 338, 339, 346
Peabody Picture Vocabulary Test-3, 172
phoneme grainsize, xvii, 32, 333, 379
phonemes, viii, xxvi, xxix, 36, 49, 51, 367
phonemic awareness, xxix, 33, 43, 44, 45, 46, 47, 48, 59, 61, 62, 79, 156, 160, 207, 223, 226, 265, 286, 287, 305, 306, 403, 411, 432, 448, 449, 453, 460
phonemic recoding, 31, 32, 331, 332, 333, 335, 345, 346, 363, 372
phonemic-awareness skills, 33, 38, 43, 44, 45, 46, 47, 48, 50, 61, 67, 79, 90, 91, 109, 177, 182, 286, 289, 294, 301, 305, 328
phonological awareness, xxix, 16, 50, 53, 132, 161, 217, 224, 225, 287, 288, 289, 292, 293, 294, 296, 297, 302, 303, 322, 324, 337, 400, 403, 404, 449, 469
phonological recoding, 32, 289, 335, 356, 359, 366, 367
phonological-verbal information-processing, 14, 177, 199, 201
PIRLS, xxx, 2, 42, 58, 77, 100, 117, 120, 150, 157, 231, 238, 239, 243, 246, 251, 254, 260, 270, 273, 279, 280, 281, 336, 339, 383, 387, 396, 414, 452, 455, 464
PISA, xiv, xxx, 2, 42, 55, 58, 77, 100, 117, 120, 150, 157, 231, 238, 239, 240, 241, 242, 243, 246, 251, 254, 255, 260, 266, 270, 273, 279, 280, 281, 336, 339, 383, 387, 396, 414, 452, 464
Planning, Attention, Simultaneous and Successive Processing (PASS), 322, 323, 328

Reading Enhancement Program (PREP), 322, 323
play-based learning, xii, 7, 130, 204, 205, 419, 428, 438, 473, 474
Polish studies, xxvi, 240, 242
Portuguese studies, 34, 46, 137, 159
Pre-School Child Road, 201, 202, 203, 204, 205, 208, 387, 474
print exposure, 216, 222
processing efficiency, 14, 15
pseudowords, 33, 53, 54, 69, 109, 314, 352, 353, 357, 358, 359, 360, 363, 364, 366, 368, 369, 371, 372, 374, 378, 379, 380, 381, 383, 397
Puerto Rican studies, 154
Ojibwe, 154, 155
Rapid Automised Naming (RAN), viii, x, 14, 15, 16, 22, 50, 59, 62, 83, 88, 89, 91, 132, 156, 174, 177, 225, 289, 292, 293, 294, 295, 296, 297, 298, 299, 303, 305, 306, 324, 432, 448, 449, 458, 460, 477, 486, 496, 499, 500, 507, 509, 519, 521, 546
reading comprehension, vii, xiv, xv, xxix, 42, 59, 62, 76, 77, 78, 116, 117, 148, 156, 160, 163, 173, 174, 175, 180, 183, 209, 210, 211, 212, 213, 214, 215, 216, 217, 218, 220, 221, 222, 223, 224, 225, 226, 227, 228, 230, 231, 232, 234, 235, 236, 237, 238, 239, 249, 250, 252, 295, 300, 301, 313, 322, 339, 343, 372, 374, 380, 382, 383, 386, 402, 403, 446, 452
Reading Recovery, 416, 417
Reading Wars, 126, 149, 210, 383, 392, 435, 437

receptive language, 192, 218
Regular Words, 32, 314, 331, 333, 334, 346
remediation
 reading materials, 401
 studies, 400
Renfrew Word Finding Test, 176
research
 applied, 16, 18, 20, 444
 bricolage, 431, 432, 446
 case-study, 242, 280, 281, 282
 Consensus, 431, 433
 crosslinguistic, 21, 41, 48, 55, 59, 62, 101, 109, 116, 120, 156, 184, 185, 215, 225, 230, 287, 305, 317, 318, 319, 320, 324, 352, 375, 377, 388, 393, 400, 441, 458, 467
 educational, 12, 13, 20, 233, 305, 430
 funding, x, 13, 26, 139, 172, 173, 175, 395, 431, 446
 Initial Teaching Alphabet, 21, 59, 120, 121, 122, 123, 126, 131, 132, 135, 138, 140, 141, 142, 147, 148, 150, 151, 152, 156, 157, 158, 437, 439, 457
 quadrants, 209, 218, 219, 220, 221, 226, 227, 230, 231, 235, 256, 295, 296, 297, 298, 299, 387, 442, 452
 workload, 259, 262, 276, 283
Response to Intervention (RTI). *See* interventions
Review of the National School Reform Agreement, 259
risk factors, 2, 21, 22, 25, 65, 80, 81, 83, 97, 108, 150, 162, 163, 181, 182, 201, 202, 204, 226, 254, 256, 265, 278, 284,

288, 317, 318, 320, 388, 409,
  422, 428, 453, 454, 471
Rosling, Hans, 435, 438
Russian studies, 239, 266
school resourcing, xxviii, 149,
  181, 258, 259, 269, 271, 284,
  382, 384, 394, 408, 412, 415,
  416, 417, 418, 421, 425, 427,
  437, 469, 472
self-teaching, 31, 39, 43, 44,
  62, 70, 96, 118, 136, 153,
  346, 350, 373, 403, 441, 454,
  455, 456, 461, 463
Semmelweis reflex, 438
short-term memory, 14, 15, 53,
  300, 306, 308, 309, 321, 328
Simple View of Reading model
  (SVR), 180, 209, 210, 211,
  212, 213, 214, 218, 220, 221,
  222, 223, 224, 225, 232, 234,
  237, 249, 295, 300, 452
Singapore studies, 239, 240,
  242
Slovakian studies, 53, 352,
  353, 354, 355, 356, 358, 360,
  407, 408, 445, 460
Socio-Economic Status (SES),
  xxviii, 24, 127, 162, 164,
  165, 167, 180, 183, 243, 244,
  245, 246, 248, 250, 253, 265,
  280, 305, 312, 326, 340, 402,
  403, 405, 406, 449
  high, 24, 243
  low, 128, 164, 167, 181, 203,
    204, 207, 216, 222, 245,
    246, 247, 248, 250, 252,
    253, 299, 305, 402, 403
Sophisticated Literacy, 56, 58,
  59, 62, 343, 464, 465
South Korean studies, 59, 201,
  202, 240, 242, 259, 266, 282,
  284, 285, 344, 345, 392, 393,
  447, 454, 456, 466
  Hanguel, 344
Spanish studies, xxvi, 33, 155,
  223

Special Education, 167, 176,
  233, 269, 409, 411, 412, 417,
  419, 447, 451, 472, 485
Specific Learning Disability,
  186
speech language pathologists,
  2, 162, 170, 171, 176, 178,
  183, 186, 187, 188, 191, 193,
  195, 197, 199, 220, 268, 281,
  282, 345, 418, 421, 427, 465
speech language pathology,
  162, 168, 169, 170, 171, 172,
  182, 194, 195, 197, 206, 220
speech perception, viii, ix, 161,
  173, 179, 182
spelling, 30, 45, 48, 50, 51, 52,
  132, 262
Spelling Generations, 1, 47,
  138, 147, 167, 205, 243, 323
statistical learning, xviii, xix,
  xxvii, 23, 25, 43, 51, 60, 78,
  80, 86, 118, 136, 177, 199,
  261, 304, 317, 330, 332, 333,
  334, 335, 336, 337, 339, 341,
  342, 343, 345, 346, 349, 350,
  364, 367, 373, 376, 441, 448,
  454, 455, 461, 470
Success Inoculation, 92, 93, 94,
  95, 96, 97, 99, 103, 106, 107,
  113, 129, 135, 136, 148, 150,
  152, 156, 223, 256, 281, 317,
  341, 366, 385, 455, 466, 470
*Sustainable Development
  Goals*, 240
Swedish studies, 33, 54, 240,
  293
Swiss-cheese research, 12, 13,
  15, 16, 17, 25, 176, 232, 259,
  370, 431
Taiwanese studies, xxvi, 2, 8,
  22, 33, 41, 42, 43, 45, 59, 61,
  62, 64, 66, 113, 115, 116,
  117, 118, 128, 139, 147, 152,
  153, 155, 156, 190, 201, 202,
  205, 208, 240, 259, 266, 282,
  284, 285, 305, 316, 321, 333,

344, 375, 379, 386, 392, 393,
401, 402, 403, 405, 422, 423,
425, 428, 429, 432, 433, 439,
447, 453, 454, 455, 456, 457,
458, 466
Hanzi, 42, 43, 44, 156
ZhuYin FuHao, 42, 43, 44,
  139, 402, 403
task avoidance, 96, 99, 102,
  135, 174
Test of Integrated Language
  and Literacy Skills (TILLS),
  192, 193, 194, 298
  Digit Span Backwards, 177
  Digit Span Forward, 177
  Following Directions, 177
  Vocabulary Awareness, 176
Test of Word-Reading
  Efficiency (TOWRE,
  TOWRE-2), 37, 40, 54, 232,
  248, 249, 351, 378, 380, 381,
  382, 383, 424, 425, 426, 448,
  460
   Phonemic Decoding
    Efficiency subtest, 248,
    352, 378, 380
   Sight Word Efficiency
    subtest, 54, 352, 378, 380
Thai studies, 45, 59, 156
Thesis Statement, 6, 443, 445
Thumbprint Experiment, 330,
  346
TIMMS (Trends in
  International Mathematics
  and Science Study), 251
Transition from Early to
  Sophisticated Literacy (TESL),
  xix, 55, 56, 57, 58, 59, 60,
  62, 263, 343, 464, 468
Tricky Words, 152, 313, 331,
  350
Triple Whammy disadvantage,
  184
Turkish studies, 33, 49, 77,
  357, 371, 372, 392, 460
Ugandan studies, 60

UK studies, 2, 19, 65, 121, 123,
  124, 135, 136, 140, 148, 149,
  150, 167, 217, 218, 240, 241,
  270, 311, 313, 315, 337, 338
unfamiliar words, xxvii, 35, 43,
  52, 53, 69, 70, 71, 76, 82, 86,
  89, 91, 109, 153, 248, 253,
  262, 287, 308, 321, 328, 331,
  333, 334, 336, 338, 339, 341,
  343, 349, 350, 351, 352, 353,
  354, 355, 356, 357, 358, 359,
  362, 365, 367, 368, 369, 370,
  371, 372, 373, 374, 375,
  377, 378, 379, 380, 388, 396,
  397, 448, 449, 460, 461, 470
USA studies, 2, 11, 47, 85, 98,
  116, 121, 123, 127, 128, 130,
  137, 154, 167, 173, 175, 176,
  178, 186, 190, 192, 196, 220,
  222, 223, 225, 226, 230, 231,
  237, 239, 240, 241, 249, 250,
  258, 287, 293, 294, 312, 326,
  332, 333, 336, 349, 352, 371,
  372, 376, 399, 406, 407, 408,
  410, 412, 418, 432, 433, 445,
  446, 451, 472
Verbal Efficiency Theory, 321
vocabulary, xxix, 52, 59, 60,
  70, 96, 118, 126, 143, 156,
  161, 173, 180, 181, 182, 183,
  192, 215, 216, 223, 224, 225,
  227, 301, 310, 362, 378, 379,
  406, 411, 448, 453, 488, 505,
  507, 523, 525, 532, 533, 544
  expressive, 62, 160, 176,
    178, 192, 207, 226, 231,
    232, 300, 449
  receptive, 62, 160, 176, 178,
    192, 207, 231, 300, 399,
    449
vowel errors, 362, 365, 366,
  367, 369, 378
Welsh-English studies, 19, 47,
  53, 66, 67, 68, 69, 70, 71, 73,
  74, 75, 76, 77, 78, 79, 80, 83,
  86, 94, 128, 170, 260, 305,

327, 339, 352, 355, 358, 360,
371, 372, 407, 408, 432, 433,
445, 460
Whole Language, 120, 140,
144, 145, 146, 147, 149, 158,
320, 344, 345
word-reading, vi, xiii, xviii, 14,
30, 33, 38, 41, 45, 48, 60, 63,
65, 66, 68, 71, 78, 82, 84, 90,
109, 110, 111, 113, 115, 134,
155, 182, 201, 209, 211, 218,
222, 226, 230, 234, 252, 304,
320, 330, 332, 337, 339, 341,
344, 345, 352, 362, 363, 368,
377, 396, 398, 400, 401, 403,
404, 406, 411, 426
word-reading remediation,
397, 416
word-substitution errors, 362
working memory, xiv, xvii,
xxvii, 14, 15, 16, 98, 109,
110, 111, 112, 160, 177, 178,
207, 215, 275, 289, 298, 299,
300, 301, 304, 306, 307, 308,
309, 310, 311, 312, 313, 314,
315, 316, 318, 319, 321, 327,
328, 405, 449, 470, 471
workload
child, 262, 284, 464
impacts, 90, 257, 258, 259,
262, 265, 267, 268, 269,
271, 278, 279, 283, 284,
415
pressure, 36, 59
teacher, 2, 6, 7, 99, 118, 129,
147, 157, 166, 205, 207,
257, 258, 259, 265, 267,
268, 270, 271, 272, 280,
283, 284, 387, 391, 394,
415, 418, 420, 421, 427,
433, 437, 446, 455, 461,
462, 463
written expression, vii, 59, 60,
123, 126, 148, 156, 173, 183,
184, 209, 211, 212, 213, 214,
218, 222, 231, 234, 237, 245,
249, 250, 252, 253, 296, 300,
301, 320, 321, 343, 382, 386,
450, 452, 460
WYSYAIN, xxviii, 147, 434,
435, 436, 438

www.ingramcontent.com/pod-product-compliance
Lightning Source LLC
Chambersburg PA
CBHW070713020526
44107CB00078B/2356